Additional Praise for
Performing Arts Management: A Handbook of Professional Practices

"This book presents clear, succinct explanations of key topics necessary for performing arts leaders to understand, all delivered firsthand from some of this country's most knowledgeable experts in the field."

—Todd Haimes, Artistic Director, Roundabout Theatre Company

"This is a very comprehensive and clear presentation of the many aspects of performing arts management and best practices. It will provide an extremely useful tool for professionals in the field at all levels."

—Katherine E. Brown, Chief Operating Officer, WNYC Radio

"*Performing Arts Management: A Handbook of Professional Practices* delivers exactly what the title suggests and more. The interviews and resources utilized throughout capitalize on the authors' own connections to the arts management field, and provide real-world models that both current and future arts managers will no doubt find invaluable. Specifically, Chapter Eight: Performing Arts Education, clearly outlines the relationship possible between arts organizations and schools, and underlines the immense rewards both will experience when a well planned and executed Arts Education program is put in place. Performing Arts Education is an important component of many organizations' missions, and the practices discussed in this book provide more than a jumping off point for any manager charged with either creating or refining his or her organization's education programs."

—Sarah Stevens, Manager of Education Programs, The Chamber Music Society of Lincoln Center

"Chapter Two: Mission, Vision, and Strategy, is a terrific resource for the budding arts manager as well as for those of us with many years in the field. There are many golden nuggets of advice scattered through the text, and the case studies add immeasurable value. The authors' presentation is savvy, well-organized, and clear, with a dual perspective that reflects their estimable track record of both running arts organizations and teaching and mentoring hundreds of arts managers-in-the-making."

—Jonathan Hollander, Artistic Director, Battery Dance Company

"*Performing Arts Management: A Handbook of Professional Practices* offers a comprehensive and wide-ranging overview of our industry. A great resource not only for students, young professionals, and artists wanting to establish their own company, but an invaluable refresher course for the experienced manager. In Chapter Two: Mission, Vision, and Strategy, the authors provide specific examples from leading performing arts institutions in this country about how to create and maintain a mission and vision for an organization, along with the strategy and planning needed to implement it. The discussion questions at the end of each section are ideal to ignite conversation amongst colleagues, whether it be in a classroom or boardroom setting."

—Margo Saulnier, Assistant Director of Artistic Planning for the Boston Pops, Boston Symphony Orchestra, Inc.

Performing Arts Management

A Handbook of Professional Practices

TOBIE S. STEIN
and
JESSICA BATHURST

ALLWORTH PRESS
NEW YORK

12   11   10   09   08   5   4   3   2   1

Published by Allworth Press
An imprint of Allworth Communications, Inc.
10 East 23rd Street, New York, NY 10010

Cover design by Derek Bacchus
Interior design by Kristina Critchlow
Page composition/typography by Susan Ramundo

ISBN-13: 978-1-58115-650-8
ISBN-10: 1-58115-650-2

Library of Congress Cataloging-in-Publication Data:
   Stein, Tobie S.
   Performing arts management : a handbook of professional practices / Tobie S. Stein and Jessica Bathurst.
      p.   cm.
   Includes bibliographical references and index.
   ISBN-13: 978-1-58115-650-8
   ISBN-10: 1-58115-650-2
   1. Performing arts—Management I. Bathurst, Jessica. II. Title.

PN1584.S74   2008
791.068—dc22

                                                          2008015408

Printed in Canada

CONTENTS

ACKNOWLEDGEMENTS

It is with great pleasure and gratitude that we recognize those who have contributed to the success of this three-year project. Writing this book required a great deal of support from our colleagues and loved ones. We devote this first section to them: Richard Frankel, Marc Routh, Richard Grossberg, James Bathurst, Christoph M. Kimmich, Steve G. Little, Roberta Matthews, Nicole Potter-Talling, Kate Ellison, Melanie Tortoroli, Tad Crawford, Robert Porter, Amy Hughes, Benito Ortolani, Samuel L. Leiter, Rose Bonczek, Tom Bullard, the Brooklyn College Theater Department, and the Brooklyn College MFA Theater classes of 2006 and 2007.

In addition, we received contributions, research support, and guidance from a phenomenal number of professionals and graduate students in the field of performing arts management. We present a list of those individuals who touched this book in some way:[1]

Richard Akins, Dorothy Allen, Michael Aman, Rada Angelova, Nick Armstrong, James Ashford, Sophia Athié, Darrell Ayers, Cary Baker, Steve Baruch, Cecelia Beam, Kurt Beattie, Shira Beckerman, Alice Bernstein, Judith Binney, Dev Bondarin, Sarah Bordy, Neal Brilliant, Christopher Brockmeyer, Laurie Brown, Adrian Bryan-Brown, Chris Burney, Dale Byam, Terry Byrne, Cora Cahan, Catherine Cahill, Tania Camargo, Eugene Carr, Megan Carter, Peter B. Carzasty, Carolyn Casselman, Elizabeth Coen, Robert Cohen, Kevin Condardo, Joy Cooper, Marion Cotrone, Tom D'Ambrosio, Sandra D'Amelio, Ken Davenport, Tiki Davies, Aimee Davis, Rob de la Fuente, Dr. Edie Demas, Lisa Dennett, Bill Dennison, Debra Cardona-DePeahul, Patrick Dewane, Maria Di Dia, Amy Duma, Dale Edwards, Alan Eisenberg, Barrack Evans, Gillian Fallon, John Federico, Richard Feiner, Rebecca Feldman, Susan Feldman, Bob Fennell, Dave Fishelson, Sean Patrick Flahaven, Michael Flanagan, Andrew Flatt, Richard Frankel, Don Frantz, Alexander Fraser, Robert Freedman, Cecilia Friederichs, Robert Friend, Boo Froebel, Tom Gabbard, Vallejo Gantner, Peter Gee, Shelley Gilbride, Patrick Glynn, Holly Golden, Alan Gordon, Laura Green, Jennie Greer, Mary Grisalano, Richard Grossberg, Ron Gubin, Denis Guerin, Rebecca Habel, Jonathan Hadley, Claire Hallereau, Pat Halloran, Emma Halpern, Nur-ul-Haq, James Harding, Amy Harris, Barbara Hauptman, Nancy Hereford, Linda Herring, Gaynor Hills, Jane Hirshberg, Edythe Holbrook, John Holden, Elena Holy, Karen Brooks Hopkins, Timothy Hsu, Lynn Hyde, Mike Isaacson, Damian Jackson, Dionne Carty-Jackson, Jessica R. Jenen, Nikki Johnson, Jessica Johnston, Arlene Jordan, Ilene Karmel, Susan Keappock, Eric Keith, Dona Lee Kelly, Cristin Kelly, Paul King, Woodie King, Jr., David Kissel, David Kitto, Christina Klapper, Adam Knight, Kati Koerner, Kim Peter Kovac, Hoong Yee Lee Krakauer, Ben Krywosz, Fred Lake, Mario LaMothe, Renee Lasher, Emily Lawson, Jennifer Leeson, Sharon Lehner, Veronique Le Melle, Jeff Levine, Marjorie Damashek Levine, Simma Levine, Mary Rose Lloyd, Debra Sue Lorenzen, Robert Lynch, Kristin Madden, Kate Maguire, Cyndy A. Marion, Danny Martin, Lorraine Martin, Rhett Martinez, Laura Matalon, Maria Mazza, Katie McAllister, Jen McArdle, Gary McAvay, Margaret Salvante-McCann, Greg McCaslin, Timothy J. McClimon, Sean McGlynn, Carter Anne McGowan, Kent McIngvale, Joseph V. Melillo, Ann Meschery, Ross Meyerson, Kristen Miles, Bill Miller, Laura Miller, Susan Miller, Erin Moeller, Monty Moeller, Jessica Morgan, Dr. David Morris, John Munger, Will Nedved, Andrea Nellis, Amanda Nelson, Rachel Neuburger, William Ngai, James Nicola, Kate Nordstrum, Harold Norris, Valencia Ojeda, Terri Osborne, James Patrick, Amanda Pekoe, Karen Pinzolo, Greg Pierson, John Pinckard, Jon B. Platt, Jonathan Pollard, Mim Pollock, Seth Popper, Lisa

Lawer Post, Jonathan Post, Gary Powers, Michael Presser, Thomas Proehl, Dara Prushansky, Jimena Duca Ramon, Mark Ramont, Nigel Redden, Michael Redman, Alisa E. Regas, Geoffrey Rich, Philip Rinaldi, Dana Rodriguez, Lana Rogachevskaya, Ilana B. Rose, Todd Rosen, Johnmichael Rossi, Janette Roush, Marc Routh, Joel Ruark, Mary Six Rupert, Michael Sag, Rachel Salzman, Melissa Sanders, Sandy Sawotka, Amy Schwartzman, Marc Scorca, Patrick Scully, Nicole Novy Schneider, Ralph Sevush, Andrey Shenin, Kyle Shepherd, Josh Sherman, Arlene Shuler, Jean Sidden, Alan Siege, Valerie Simmons, Harriet Slaughter, Anne Rhea Smith, Michael Scolamiero, Seth Soloway, Jaime Sommella, Sarah Sosa, Alison Spiriti, Julie Stabiner, John Starr, Sarah Stevens, Megan Stevenson, Lynn M. Stirrup, Andrea Stover, Jonathan Summey, Diana Swartz, Carl Sylvestre, Ken Tabachnick, Julie Tatum, Karen Tecott, Steven Tennen, Paul Tetreault, Walter Thinnes, Christopher Thomasson, Ladan Hamidi-Toosi, Susan Trapnell, Nancy Umanoff, Hank Unger, Gina Vernaci, Tom Viertel, Shorey Walker, Donna Walker-Kuhne, Cheri Walsh, Alanna Weifenbach (CPA), Will Maitland Weiss, Ella Weiss, Bruce Whitacre, Robert Widman, Mark Wier, Cathryn Williams, Robyn Williams, Nadeisha Williams, Jan Wilson, Jamie Winnick, Sarah Wiseman, Harold Wolpert, Amy Wratchford, Kumiko Yoshii, Suzanne Youngerman, Dana Zell, and Meredith Zolty.

NOTE

1. The names listed include the names of individuals who provided the authors and MFA Brooklyn College graduate students with taped, telephone, or e-mail interviews. While we were not able to present and publish all of the research collected, we do appreciate the participants' information and time. If we inadvertently omitted your name, we apologize.

PREFACE

Performing Arts Management: A Handbook of Professional Practices presents the wisdom and expertise of over 150 performing arts management professionals. Practicing managers and students alike will find hundreds of examples of practical ways to approach and solve problems within the workplace. Through in-depth interviews with leaders in producing and presenting organizations throughout the United States, we explore, ask, and answer many of the questions that are facing managers in nonprofit and commercial organizations, including:

- How do mission, vision, and strategy merge?
- What is the difference between management and leadership?
- What is the IRS two-part test for determining whether a nonprofit organization is meeting the operational test?
- How does a commercial producer get investors for a Broadway production?
- How is a budget created?
- What are the major components of a fundraising plan?
- How do you approach a major donor for a gift?
- What is marketing? How does marketing the arts differ from conventional product marketing?
- How can assessment of student learning shape the performing arts education program structure and delivery?
- What is the process for negotiating a collectively bargained agreement?
- How can the road market for a potential tour be determined?
- How do facility managers protect against theft?
- What are the "unspoken rules" of an organization, and how do you go about learning them?

This book contains twelve chapters. Within each chapter, professionals provide working examples of successful business and communications processes, as well as model documents. At the end of each chapter, you will find resource lists of Web sites, books, and articles that pertain to the particular subject matter being discussed.

In chapter 1, "Organizational Structures and Managerial Positions," we explore the nonprofit and commercial performing arts management sectors, focusing on the differences and similarities between the sectors, as well as their organizational types, structures, and managerial positions.

Chapter 2, "Mission, Vision, and Strategy," investigates the roles of the board, management, artists, and artistic managerial team in executing the mission and vision of the organization; the distinction between management and leadership; and the process of strategic planning in achieving vision through the setting of mission-oriented goals.

In chapter 3, "Nonprofit Formation and Legal Considerations," we examine the process of nonprofit formation and tax-exempt status. We also study other important legal considerations, such as the fiduciary and legal duties of the board of directors, insurance policies, nonprofit corporate tax obligations, excessive salaries and benefits, the extent to which nonprofit organizations can form joint ventures and partnerships, the degree to which they can lobby, and the federal laws concerning fundraising activities.

Chapter 4, "Commercial Producing," details the specific types of commercial productions (Broadway, Off-Broadway, and touring productions) as well as outlining the process of producing a commercial production.

Chapter 5, "Financial Management," explores basic accounting terms and procedures, budget types, the creation of budgets by estimating revenue and expenses, and the management of the budget creation process in commercial and nonprofit organizations. We will also address other administrative responsibilities of the financial manager, such as the creation and management of information systems; the purchase of insurance; the administration of payroll and taxes; the production of accurate financial reports; the management of financial audits; and the ensuring of accountability to make sure that the company acts in a financially responsible way.

Chapters 6 and 7 discuss contributed income and revenue from ticket sales. Chapter 6, "Developing a Funding Base," reveals the ways in which nonprofit performing arts organizations raise contributions from individuals and institutions (corporations, foundations, and the government). In chapter 7, "Strategies for Selling Tickets," we focus on marketing and publicity, outlining the strategies and processes used to sell tickets.

Chapter 8, "Performing Arts Education," focuses on presenting and producing organizations that use both the performance itself and performance-related education programs to make curricular connections with public schools—from prekindergarten through the twelfth grade.

In chapter 9, "Labor Relations," we explore contract creation, labor law, unions, multi-employer collective bargaining groups, the process of collective bargaining, and human resources in the workplace.

Chapter 10, "Touring Productions," examines the creation, booking, and presentation of touring productions, as well as different types of touring productions.

Chapter 11, "Facility Management," discusses the role of the facility manager and examines the various operational duties in producing, presenting, and rental facilities that comprise this vital position.

And finally, chapter 12, "Career Development Strategies: The Role of the Internship," explores the role of the internship from two significant points of view: the employer's and the student's. Managers in the field, as well as students, discuss utilizing the internship as a career development strategy; finding the right internship; and structuring a successful internship—as well as creating and maintaining the status and value of the internship through ongoing recognition, training, evaluation, and mentorship.

CHAPTER ONE

Organizational Structures and Managerial Positions

Performing arts managers lead and manage theaters, symphony orchestras, performing arts centers, opera companies, dance and ballet companies, festivals, and everything in between. Some managers produce or present performing arts events as nonprofit organizations, while others have selected the for-profit model. A nonprofit organization is defined by its public purpose; if an organization is created to serve the public, that organization is eligible for nonprofit tax-exempt status from the federal government, exempting it from the bulk of taxes.[1] The for-profit, or commercial, model does not need to serve a public purpose (although it may), but focuses on earning profit (income exceeding expenses) as its main goal. The nonprofit organization cannot have a profit-making purpose and must put all money earned over expenses back into the organization to serve its public purpose.

In this chapter, we will explore the nonprofit and commercial performing arts management sectors, focusing on the differences and similarities between the sectors, as well as their organizational types, organizational structures, and managerial positions. Managers from both sectors comment on the ways in which the differences are becoming less evident, and the extent to which the sectors, as well as organizations within the sectors, are working together.[2]

In the next section, we will discuss the differences and similarities between the nonprofit and commercial performing arts sectors concerning goals, artistic process, legal structures and governance, and budgeting methods.

GOALS

Nonprofit organizational goals are defined by the mission, which is the public purpose of the organization.[3] The mission is the guiding principle of the organization. A goal is the desired result that an organization strives to attain. The mission of the organization can encompass a number of goals, including: producing or programming performances or series of performances as an ongoing concern; creating educational activities, ranging from professional training to exploration of the arts; creating programs for local schools, seniors, and patrons; and raising money to support the renovation of existing facilities, construction of a new facility, and ongoing operational support. Each of these goals serves the mission of the nonprofit organization.

As part of their mission, nonprofit theater organizations, such as Ford's Theatre in Washington, D.C., and the Guthrie Theater in Minneapolis, Minnesota, produce plays to serve the community. Nonprofit dance and ballet companies, such as the Bill T. Jones/Arnie Zane Dance Company and the San Francisco Ballet serve their respective missions through activities such as producing New York premieres for the Lincoln Center Festival (a festival presented by the Lincoln Center for the Performing Arts). All of these organizations are nonprofit organizations.

Additionally, the Guthrie Theater, Ford's Theatre, the Bill T. Jones/Arnie Zane Dance Company, and the San Francisco Ballet are producing organizations. They create or produce their own productions from scratch; they select the piece to be performed, as well as the performers (dancers, actors, musicians, singers), designers, composers, directors, choreographers, and so forth. They create and rehearse the physical production. A producing organization will then perform the play, dance, or opera in one of its venues or in a venue it rents for that particular show for a specified run.[4]

In contrast, the Lincoln Center for the Performing Arts is a nonprofit presenting organization. "Presenting organizations purchase a series of pre-packaged [preproduced] events (both commercial and nonprofit) to appear before their local communities for a specified run. Events are 'purchased' directly or indirectly through a booking agent; the booking agent sells an attraction to a presenter and negotiates the terms of the engagement. Presenters pay the costs needed to present the show, including performance fees, transportation, freight, hotel, etc. Presenters typically do not directly pay any costs associated with the creation of the production (e.g., design fees, scenery construction, rehearsal costs)."[5] The Brooklyn Academy of Music in Brooklyn, New York; Playhouse Square Center in Cleveland, Ohio; and Ruth Eckerd Hall in Clearwater, Florida, are examples of nonprofit presenting organizations. Some nonprofit presenting organizations also produce work, and some nonprofit producing organizations may present performances.

Commercial producers organize the project (known as the "property"), find investors who put up the money for it, and either manage the project or, most frequently, hire a general manager to manage it. Commercial productions have very different goals from nonprofit organizations. "A commercial production's primary intent is to return a profit to its investors [individuals who invest money into a production, who expect to have their investment returned]," states Harold Wolpert, managing director of the Roundabout Theatre Company, a nonprofit producing theater. "It's not just to put a show on that people will like. It's to put a show on that actually will make money back for the people who put money in."[6] Tom Proehl, executive director of the Minnesota State Arts Board and former managing director of the Guthrie Theater, elaborates, "The commercial theater's main purpose is to make money through the exploitation of a single property (play or musical). The production is supported and funded by investors, and investors are generally looking for a return on their investment. For instance, if a play gets awful reviews on Broadway, and tickets are not selling, the investors will generally close the show to cut their losses. However, if it is a hit, the show will run for as long as possible in order to return the highest profit to the investors." Proehl notes that investors in the long-running commercial productions of *Cats*, *Wicked*, and *The Phantom of the Opera* have received a huge return on their original investment.[7] Sean Patrick Flahaven, managing director of the Melting Pot Theatre, a small Off-Broadway nonprofit producing theater, adds: "The goals of the commercial venture are to first pay back its investors, then make a profit, and then make something with artistic integrity."[8]

Commercial producer Tom Viertel (*Hairspray*, *The Producers*) illustrates the difference between nonprofit and commercial theater: "Commercial theater requires productions to make a profit, to actually have the shows work out economically so that the show standing by itself is a successful, profitable entity, rather than the theater as a whole being a profitable entity. I work on both sides of the fence, because I'm the chairman of the board at the Eugene O'Neill Theater, which is a nonprofit theater in Connecticut. At the O'Neill, the theater's budget encompasses a lot of different activities, including production workshops and the school that we run. Every budget for a nonprofit theater has a lot of elements to it; income from ticket sales is one element of the budget, but it's only one part of how a nonprofit theater stays alive. It's also funded to a significant extent by contributions from individuals, foundations, and the government. In commercial theater, ticket income for a show has to stand on its own. As a commercial producer, each of the shows that I do represents a significant set of potential income streams for me, and so as an economic matter, I need to make sure that each of those shows is successful in terms of ticket sales. From a nonprofit theater's point of view, it expects to put on a season, and it knows that the shows in that season will come to an end. (The shows have to come to an end, or the theater won't have a place to put the next show in.) The purpose of a nonprofit theater is to produce a range of shows in order to satisfy a subscription audience that is expecting anywhere from five to eleven or twelve productions in the course of a year. In those circumstances, you approach each production with a great deal less desperation about the individual production. You're more concerned with making sure that it moves along through the production process, so that it can have its time in the theater, and then the next show can take its place. That's a completely different mindset from a commercial producer, who tends to approach individual shows as if they were life-and-death matters, because if these projects don't work, the shows are quickly out of business. If the production isn't successful, it represents no opportunity for a continuing sustained income at all, and the commercial producer has to start over with a new show."[9]

So when Richard Frankel Productions, a commercial producer, produces a successful show and makes money from one of its properties—such as *The Producers* or *Hairspray*—it will distribute this money to its investors, first as repayment of their investment, and then as profit. The producers will receive part of the profit once the investors are paid back. In contrast, while nonprofit organizations can earn a profit (called a "surplus"), they must reinvest the surplus into the organization to support their nonprofit activities, such as producing opera or presenting performances. No individual in a nonprofit organization may benefit directly from the profits of the organization.

Another way for a producer to earn a profit is to tour a production. (A tour is a production that moves from one location to another.) If a producer chooses to tour a commercial attraction, he will engage a for-profit booking and touring company, such as On the Road, to create a profitable tour for the play or event. The booking and touring organization will book the event in theaters throughout the country by working with presenting organizations to present the tour. As both the commercial producer and for-profit booking and touring company are organized to make a profit, their participating principals (e.g., producers and investors) are allowed to benefit. Also, some presenters operate as for-profit entities; these commercial presenters program or book a series of events or a season to make a profit. If a commercial presenter, such as the Fox Theatre in St. Louis, Missouri, makes a profit, the presenter will keep that profit. However, as noted previously, if a nonprofit presenter makes money on the touring event, the profits must be redistributed within the organization to fund presenting activities.

CLASSROOM DISCUSSION

How are nonprofit goals defined? What are some examples of nonprofit goals?

What is a nonprofit presenting organization? Give some examples.

What is a nonprofit producing organization? Give some examples.

If a nonprofit organization earns a profit, what must it do?

What is the goal of a for-profit performing arts organization?

What are investors?

What is the role of a commercial producer?

What is the role of a commercial booking and touring organization?

How does a commercial presenter differ from a nonprofit presenter?

THE ARTISTIC PROCESS

Nonprofit producing and presenting organizations have an artistic process that corresponds to the

mission or purpose of their organizations. As an example, let's examine Playhouse Square Center's mission to "present and produce a wide variety of quality performing arts, advance the arts in education, and create a theatre district that is a superior location for entertainment, business, and housing, thereby strengthening the economic vitality of the region."[10] In executing this mission, the organization "seeks [to program] the highest quality of offerings available."[11] According to Gina Vernaci, vice president of theatricals for Playhouse Square Center, "The programming process begins with figuring out what the needs of the resident companies are. Resident companies (for us, the Great Lakes Theater Festival, DANCECleveland, Cuyahoga Community College, and Opera Cleveland) have a permanent performing status with the presenter and appear at the venue every year." Once the resident companies have selected their performance dates, Vernaci books the rest of the season by speaking to various booking agents within the industry. "We have an obligation to our community to bring in the very best. Booking the very best artists sends a message of how you value the patron and how your organization is viewed in the industry."[12] As we discussed earlier, the mission or the goal of the nonprofit organization must have a public purpose. In the case of nonprofit presenters and producers, the artistic process must engage the public or the community. For Vernaci, servicing the resident companies and booking artists of the highest quality is the method by which she serves and values her community.

Another example of a nonprofit presenting organization with a strong mission and artistic process is the Brooklyn Academy of Music (BAM). BAM's mission is "to be the globally acknowledged, preeminent progressive performing and cinema arts center of the 21st century."[13] Joseph V. Melillo, executive producer, states, "The programming process at BAM serves its public purpose by animating its venues with an artistic menu of local and global performances that advances our understanding of the performing arts within a contemporary context."[14] General manager Patrick Scully reports that "our programming office puts together a season that has the different disciplines represented. We have a mix of new artists, as well as artists that we've presented over the years."[15]

A nonprofit producing organization's artistic season of plays must also reflect the mission of the organization. Harold Wolpert emphasizes that "each season typically starts from reflecting on the theater's mission and working within the mission. 'The mission of Roundabout Theatre Company is to team great theatrical works with the industry's finest artists in an effort to reenergize classic plays and musicals. Develop and produce new works by today's great writers and composers. Provide educational programs that will enrich the lives of children and adults. Retain a loyal audience through a commitment to the subscription model.'[16] You start there first. As an example, our view of 'classic plays' means that we produce post-Shakespearean plays, typically those written in the last two hundred years or so."[17]

Wolpert continues, "When you select your season of plays, you must have a balance. There's often a balancing act between what an artistic director wants to do and what a theater can afford to do. Sometimes a theater can get special funding to do a play that the artistic director really wants to do and feels passionate about, and sometimes we have to say, 'We really can't do this play.' At that point, we need to go back to the drawing board."[18] Scully makes a similar point: "My area is constantly making budgets based on the executive producer's selection of programs. We occasionally lose programs that we're all really excited about because we are just not able to come up with a deficit that we can support in the context of the season."[19] The artistic process in a nonprofit organization must support the mission of the organization, but also fit within the budget.

Although commercial producers and presenters do not have a mission to support, they must also keep the balancing act between artistic process and budget in mind. As mentioned previously, commercial producers and presenters find products that will make money for their investors. (Specifically, commercial producers generally produce one event for the purposes of making a profit; commercial presenters program or book a series of events or a season to make a profit.) Alison Spiriti, vice president of programming at Live Nation, describes the process of presenting commercially in Live Nation's venues: "We construct a season that makes sense aesthetically, as well as financially. Our goal is to increase our subscription base and advance ticket sales, thus mitigating our risk on any deal. There needs to be a balance of expensive blockbuster musicals, such as *Wicked* and *The Phantom of the Opera*; midsize musicals, such as *Hairspray*; less expensive musicals, such as *STOMP*; and plays, like *Doubt*. I also try to program based on what the market dictates, as well as the current economic climate."[20]

As commercial presenters and producers have a goal of recouping (earning back) their investment on a show and earning a profit, taking artistic risks is not a likely option. Nonprofit organizations, on the other hand, are more likely to take artistic risks, such as producing or presenting a premiere of a new work. However, nonprofit organizations and commercial producers or presenters commonly work together to develop new projects. For example, Alexander Fraser, a freelance executive producer, notes that "new work is almost exclusively developed in the nonprofit sector, but the norm today is a partnership between commercial and nonprofit producing organizations. Nonprofit organizations have funded play and musical development programs, encouraging new work with commissions, readings, and workshops.[21] The producer tops off the budget with enhancement funds, which have become a major part of the nonprofit theater's bottom line [income]. In return, the artists get a full production with plenty of audience reaction."[22]

CLASSROOM DISCUSSION
Why must the nonprofit organization's artistic programming support its mission?
When programming or presenting a season, what must the nonprofit programmer or artistic director keep in mind?
When booking a season, what must the commercial presenter keep in mind?

LEGAL STRUCTURES AND GOVERNANCE
Nonprofit organizations are structured as corporations. The corporate status is granted by the state government, and the tax-exempt status is a federal designation, which is approved in turn by the state. (See chapter 3 for a more detailed discussion.)

As part of their incorporation, nonprofit organizations are governed by a board of directors (or trustees), who are usually volunteers and don't receive compensation (although they may). The board's main role is to make sure that the mission of the organization is carried out and that the finances and resources of the organization are used for their originally stated public purpose. According to Tom Proehl, "Board members are responsible for the general oversight of the management of the institution. They also raise money to support the institution and its programs, and serve as a representative or ambassador of the organization in the community."[23] James Patrick, executive director of the Warner Theatre, explains that the board is responsible for hiring the executive director or chief executive officer of the institution, for creating the committee structure (smaller groups of board members with a specific focus, e.g., nominating committee, fundraising committee, marketing committee, finance committee, audit committee), and for establishing the executive committee, which is usually comprised of all of the chairs of the subcommittees.[24] Board members may be appointed by a nominating or governance committee of the board.[25]

Although the board of directors is responsible for the general oversight of the organization, it should not have an active role in the day-to-day operations.[26] Sean Patrick Flahaven agrees, emphasizing that, although the board has a legal duty to make sure that the organization has a budget and stays on course, it "should not be picking your season or be involved with the day-to-day running of the organization."[27]

For-profit ventures may be structured as corporations, limited partnerships, or limited liability companies. (For a more detailed discussion of for-profit legal structures, see chapter 4.) As in nonprofit corporations, a board of directors also governs commercial corporations, which is the structure used by a few large producing organizations. For example, Disney Theatrical Productions, a division of the Walt Disney Company, produces and books its own productions and licenses its shows to third-party producing partners around the globe. The Walt Disney Company has a board of directors that governs the corporation. Governance may include hiring and firing the chief executive officer, as well as other officers of the corporation, and reviewing the corporation's financial reports. Corporate directors of large corporations are generally paid for their time and expertise.

Most commercially produced shows are organized as limited partnerships and limited liability companies (LLC). A limited partnership consists of general partners and limited partners. In the customary theatrical model for a limited partnership, the limited partners are investors who usually put up 100 percent of the capital and receive some percentage of the profits after recoupment (when the investment has been paid back). Additionally, they are only liable (responsible) for the amount of money they invest, and they have no say in the management of the partnership. The general partners manage the partnership, are personally liable or responsible for all losses over and above the amount of the capital investment of the limited partners, and also receive a percentage of the profits after recoupment. To avoid unlimited personal liability, the general partners or producers may incorporate, so that their corporate status protects them.

Like limited partnerships, limited liability companies consist of two parties: managing members and investing members. In comparison to the exposure faced by the general partners of a limited partnership, limited liability companies have the advantage of giving the managing members (who are usually the producers) limited liability from losses. Like limited partners, investing members are only responsible for the amount of money they put into a production. Unlike a corporation, which is usually formed for broad business purposes that may include multiple projects or productions, limited liability companies are often formed for a specific project or production, and are frequently dissolved when the project ends.

CLASSROOM DISCUSSION

What is the legal structure of a nonprofit performing arts organization?

What is the primary role of a nonprofit board of directors?

Name and define the various legal structures under which a for-profit performing arts organization may be formed.

BUDGETING METHODS

Nonprofit organizations generally budget for a calendar year, but the majority of income and expenses falls within a season (a series of arts events), which traditionally lasts from September or October through June. The budgeting process should "lay out the guidelines for decision-making for a given show, project, or year."[28] Both producing and presenting organizations have a budgeting process, accounting for expenses (costs incurred by the business activity) and income (money generated from ticket sales and other fee-for-service activity, as well as contributed income or grants). Tom Proehl states that "organizational budgets are prepared on an annual basis and are generally divided into the four major components of the organization: administration or overhead (general operating expenses, such as salaries, lighting, heat, and air conditioning); production-related (expenses related to preproduction and production); fundraising, marketing, and public relations (created to sell tickets and increase visibility for the institution and its productions); and performance projects (educational workshops, relationships with educational institutions)."[29]

Sean Patrick Flahaven describes the components of his budget: "We have a budget for the year that has to be approved by the board of directors. The budget covers general operating expenses, such as administrative costs like rent, salaries, insurance, taxes, and office supplies. Then we have a budget for each production that runs between $150,000 and $250,000 for our small Off-Broadway theater. We have mainstage, developmental [new] work, and educational work—each production or activity is broken down with the same line items, such as artist fees, design fees, costumes, sets, etc. This is the expense side of the budget. Then you have the income side, which lists your projected earned income or income earned through ticket sales, fees, and concessions, as well as contributed income or donations from foundations, government, corporations, and individuals."[30]

Gina Vernaci adds: "In a nonprofit presenting organization, like Playhouse Square Center, the process begins with the calendar. We program seven theaters year-round, although the primary season runs from October through June. With the calendar for various spaces, we first lay out the dates for the resident companies. After we finalize the dates with our resident companies, we look at the rest of the calendar, including the Jewish and Christian holidays, our series projections, and the single-night attractions we have booked and projected."[31]

For each show that Vernaci books into her theaters, she first evaluates the expense side of the equation. "After speaking with the booking agent, I know what the quoted fee is for an artist for a specific event. It is important to note that the fees quoted by agents are often negotiable. The agent will send me a contract.[32] Always ask for a technical rider early in your conversations with an agent; this spells out the technical needs for the show, providing a guideline for labor costs, equipment rental, catering, etc. I can then estimate my expenses, which may include artist fees, production rentals (sound and lights), royalties, marketing, labor, venue costs, credit card fees, insurance, catering, transportation, and housing." After she projects or estimates the expenses, she then scales the house (seating area of the venue) to determine her gross income potential. "*Scaling the house* is the term that refers to going through each section of the house and assigning ticket prices. During this step we may refer to past history of the act or show, or look for similar productions to guide us with the decision of pricing. Also helpful is the touring history of the particular type of show. We research that data and apply local market conditions [economic and social data on the local population]. We take all of this information into account when scaling the house. Once the ticket prices are established, you calculate the breakeven point, which is the amount of money you need to earn to cover your expenses on the show. I then translate that into the number of tickets I need to sell for the engagement. So, if the breakeven is $50,000 and your average ticket price is $45, you need to sell 1,111 tickets to make the nut (break even). Finding the breakeven point is a good reality check. If the house seats 2,500 people, 1,111 tickets equals 44 percent of the house. On the other hand, if you need 1,111 seats to break even, and you are in an 850-seat house, there is a potential problem. The artist fee is too high, the ticket prices are too low or you need underwriting (fundraising income) of some type. Also, it is important to be realistic. If the math says you need to sell 1,111 tickets to make the nut, but the sales history for that type of event or artist is less than that, there is a reason to pause. Common sense would tell you that you are not likely to break the mold if the history tells you to be cautious."[33]

Since it is unlikely that a nonprofit will break even with ticket sales alone, the nonprofit organization must plan ahead to make sure there is money available from other earned income sources (fees earned from services such as concession income and parking income) and philanthropic support (also known as contributed income) to fill the gap. Philanthropic support, raised by the board and staff, includes contributions from individuals, corporations, foundations, and the government; these contributions are tax-deductible for the contributor (donor).

If all income, both earned and contributed, does not meet expenses, the budget won't balance, leading to a deficit. Since most nonprofit organizations don't have the resources to absorb a deficit, they must have a strategy in place to balance the budget.

In the end, nonprofit organizations are looking to break even, where income will equal expenses, or to have a surplus, where income will exceed expenses. For example, James Patrick has a $2.6 million operating budget, and when he presents his budget to the board, "they want to see a budget that shows a surplus."[34] Vernaci reminds us that "nonprofit status stipulates that the revenues are applied toward the mission portion of the goals. For instance, a nonprofit presenter may present a Broadway touring show or a concert that generates a profit for the engagement. Those dollars may then be applied toward an operational item, such as new carpeting or updating a computer system."[35]

In the commercial world, there are no tax-deductible contributions to fill the gap. If a show isn't earning a profit, then the show should close. If the show closes without recouping (making back its initial investment), the producer and her investors will lose their initial investments.

Entities that produce commercially also plan for income and expenses. Budgets are built for the capitalization and weekly running costs. Tom Proehl explains: "The major expenses are specifically related to the single production (rather than a series of productions) and include the initial capitalization budget (e.g., preproduction costs or the costs of the production through the official opening), which is funded by a group of investors. Weekly running costs [the cost of operating the production for a week] are funded first through ticket sales. Additional income is generated from the sale of products developed in connection with the show (e.g., T-shirts, recordings), as well as subsidiary rights for future exploitation of the property (e.g., film and television rights). Shortfalls in the budget are funded with reserves from the initial capitalization or additional investments. Any overages (surplus) are captured and applied to the recoupment of the initial production costs."[36]

CLASSROOM DISCUSSION

How do Tom Proehl and Sean Flahaven structure their budgets?

What are the major components of Gina Vernaci's budgeting process?

Define these terms: "breakeven point" and "deficit."

How do nonprofit organizations balance income with expenses?

What is philanthropic support? Give some examples.

How do commercial producers fill the gap between income and expenses?

Define these terms: "recoupment," "capitalization," "preproduction costs," and "weekly running costs." How are weekly running costs funded in a commercial theatrical production?

NONPROFIT ORGANIZATIONS: ORGANIZATIONAL TYPES

In a continuation of our study of nonprofit and commercial organizations, we will examine some of the nonprofit and commercial organizational types, organizational structures, and managerial positions. In this section, we will explore the following types of nonprofit producing organizations: dance companies, symphony orchestras, opera companies, and theater companies. We will examine nonprofit presenting organizations as well.

Dance Companies

According to Dance/USA, the national service organization for professional dance companies, there are approximately 2,500 ballet, modern, ethnic, jazz, tap, and assorted other dance companies in the United States. Of these, approximately 400 are fully institutionalized, with paid staff, salaried dancers, and a track record of regular productions over time.[37] The annual budgets of these dance companies range from $54 million to less than $25,000. According to John Munger, director of research of Dance/USA, "Ballet companies have larger budgets than modern dance companies because ballet companies are generally larger organizations due to their historic and structural roots."[38] However, small dance companies of all kinds, which have a budget of under $500,000, account for 65 to 70 percent of Dance/USA's membership, and over 90 percent of dance companies in America.[39]

Institutionalized dance companies generally have an executive or managing director who manages the administrative part of the organization, as well as an artistic director (most often a choreographer) who manages the artistic and production aspects of the organization. The majority of dance companies earn revenue by performing one or more seasons of productions to local audiences, and many companies, especially modern companies, also tour. Some companies own their own facilities; others either rent facilities or are presented and paid a fee by a presenting organization. The Paul Taylor Dance Company, the Pennsylvania Ballet, the New York City Ballet, the American Ballet Theatre, and the Alvin Ailey American Dance Theater are all examples of large dance companies that have a season of local productions and also tour.

Symphony Orchestras

The League of American Orchestras (formerly the American Symphony Orchestra League) reports that there are 1,800 symphony, chamber, collegiate, and youth orchestras in the United States.[40] More than 950 member orchestras belong to the League of American Orchestras. Member organizational budgets range from over $14 million to less than $130,000.[41] Orchestras often have a music director or conductor who is responsible for the artistic direction in the organization, and an executive director, chief executive officer, or president responsible for the administrative end of the organization. Orchestras, like dance companies, perform locally and may also tour to earn additional revenue. The New York Philharmonic and the Boston Symphony Orchestra are examples of orchestras that present a season locally and tour as well. Orchestras may own or rent a facility for their performances, or they may be paid a fee and presented as part of a season by a presenting organization.

Opera Companies

According to OPERA America, there are 114 professional opera companies operating in forty-three states, with collective budgets of $735 million.[42] The vast majority of these companies are led by a general director (chief executive officer) who reports to the board of directors. While the general director may also oversee artistic planning, this responsibility may fall to an artistic director and/or music director.[43] Like many dance companies and symphony orchestras, opera companies either rent or own their facilities and earn revenue from their seasons. The Metropolitan Opera, the New York City Opera, the Seattle Opera, and the Minnesota Opera are examples of opera companies that produce their work within a season.

Theater Companies

Theatre Communications Group, a national service organization serving nonprofit American theater companies, conducts an annual fiscal survey that examines 1,893 professional theaters, ranging in budget size from less than $50,000 to more than $10 million.[44] Many nonprofit theaters may employ both artistic and managing directors to codirect the organization. In some organizations, a producing director is at the helm, responsible for selecting the season and administering the organization. Non-profit theaters generally produce a season of plays and/or musicals and either own or rent their facilities. Some also tour their productions. Professional non-profit theaters include: American Conservatory Theater (San Francisco, California); Arena Stage and Ford's Theatre (both in Washington, D.C.); the Alley Theatre (Houston, Texas); Manhattan Theatre Club; and the Roundabout Theatre Company (New York).

Presenting Organizations

According to Thomas Wolf, one-third of professional nonprofit presenters are educational institutions (e.g., colleges and universities), and one-third are facilities that present the performing arts as a core activity. The remaining presenters are festivals, local arts agencies, and cultural series. Budgets range from less than $100,000 to tens of millions of dollars.[45] In a nonprofit presenting organization, the executive director, director of programming, or executive pro-

ducer is responsible for artistic programming; managerial responsibilities fall to the executive director, president, or chief executive officer. Nonprofit presenters rent or own their facilities. The John F. Kennedy Center for the Performing Arts in Washington, D.C. and the Krannert Center for the Performing Arts in Urbana, Illinois are examples of nonprofit presenters.

Nonprofit presenting organizations are likely to be members of the Association of Performing Arts Presenters (APAP). APAP has approximately 1,900 members.[46] APAP serves its members by conducting an annual conference where presenters meet with artists, performing arts companies, and their agents. APAP also conducts research on the field and engages in advocacy by "informing legislators and policy makers about the vital role of the performing arts in American life."[47] Additionally, both profit and nonprofit presenting organizations may be members of the Independent Presenters Network (IPN). All of the organizations in the IPN (fifty-six members representing seventy facilities) come together to collectively invest in and book Broadway shows throughout North America and Japan.[48]

CLASSROOM DISCUSSION

List the significant producing organizations in each producing category.

Who are the artistic and managerial leaders of nonprofit producing organizations?

What are the different types of presenting organizations?

Who are the artistic and managerial leaders of presenting organizations?

NONPROFIT ORGANIZATIONS: ORGANIZATIONAL STRUCTURES AND MANAGERIAL POSITIONS

In the following sections, we will examine the organizational structures of various nonprofit producing and presenting organizations, as well as their board of directors, and primary managerial and artistic positions. In examining the responsibilities of the artistic and managerial staff, we will discuss, for the most part, the senior-level managers, or the managers who appear on the organizational chart directly beneath the board of directors or executive management of the organization. Organizational structures are represented visually by the use of organizational charts, which illustrate the reporting relationship of one position to another. Job descriptions are used to define the roles and responsibilities of managerial and artistic positions within the organization.

Organizational Structures

In all nonprofit organizations, the board of directors has the ultimate authority for the organization; the board of directors is always at the top of the organizational chart. The executive leadership of the organization reports to the board, and this relationship is noted by a direct line from the board to the president, or from the board to the artistic director and managing director. Senior-level managers have junior-level managers reporting to them; this relationship is noted in the chart by placing senior managers above the junior managers. If the managers are on the same level, they have equal authority in the organization and don't report to each other.

Not all nonprofit organizations within each producing and presenting category have the same organizational structures. This section will give you an understanding of how these organizations may be structured, and the types of managers who play a part in producing and presenting organizations.

We will first take a look at some examples of large and small producing organizations. Since large organizations are defined by the size of their annual budget, they can afford to hire more managers and artists than smaller organizations. The following producing organizations (shown on pages 10–12) are classified as large organizations: the Pennsylvania Ballet ($9.7 million), Seattle Opera ($20 million), and Roundabout Theatre Company ($44 million).[49]

Now let's look at some smaller producing organizational structures (shown on pages 12–14): the Liz Lerman Dance Exchange ($1.4 million), Brooklyn Symphony Orchestra ($38,000), Opera Company of Brooklyn ($75,000), and Melting Pot Theatre ($398,000).[50]

Finally, let's look at the organizational charts for presenting organizations (see pages 15–25). The Brooklyn Academy of Music ($25 million) and Ruth Eckerd Hall ($18.5 million) are considered large presenting organizations. We will also examine a small presenter, Tribeca Performing Arts Center ($600,000).[51]

CLASSROOM DISCUSSION

Take a look at the producing and presenting organizational charts. What do they all have in common? What are some of the differences?

Who reports to the board in each of the organizations?

In addition to the top executive staff, who report to the board, who are the other senior managers in each producing organization? Which junior managers report to them?

Which senior managers are present in every organization?

What managers are present in the large organizations, but are missing in the smaller organizations?

The Board of Directors and Managerial Positions

In our next section, we will examine the board of directors, as well as the primary artistic and managerial staff positions of nonprofit producing and presenting organizations. The following job descriptions serve simply as a guide to some of the best practices utilized in the industry. As we define the responsibilities of the board of directors and the management staff of producing and presenting organizations, take a look at the organizational charts.

The Board of Directors

At the top of every nonprofit organizational chart is the board of directors. The board of directors has the ultimate responsibility for establishing and overseeing policies (best practices) and providing guidance to the staff, so that the staff may implement those policies. In carrying out these obligations, the board members act as fiduciaries to the nonprofit. In other words, they are in a position of trust and confidence, and hence are subject to a heightened duty to act in the best interests of the corporation. It is a greater duty than a simple legal duty, which can be imposed by law or contract, but imposes no obligation to act in the best interests of the organization. (For a detailed discussion of the board's fiduciary and legal responsibilities, please see chapter 3.) Sean McGlynn, director of finance and strategic initiatives for the Department of Cultural Affairs in New York City, adds, "In addition to these oversight responsibilities, the board hires and fires the executive managers of the organization; raises money for the organization; and makes sure that the organization is meeting its goals and, of course, living up to its mission."[52] The executive leadership of the board consists of its officers: the chairman, president, vice president, treasurer, and secretary.[53] In many nonprofit theaters, the artistic director and managing director also serve on the board, though without voting privileges (to avoid conflict of interest, since those positions report directly to the board).

As part of its fiduciary responsibility, the board has a legal responsibility to make sure that systems are in place to properly manage the finances of the organization. Wolpert states, "Donors are giving money to the organization, and they expect the organization will be run well, and that the money will

Fig. 1.1. Pennsylvania Ballet Organizational Chart

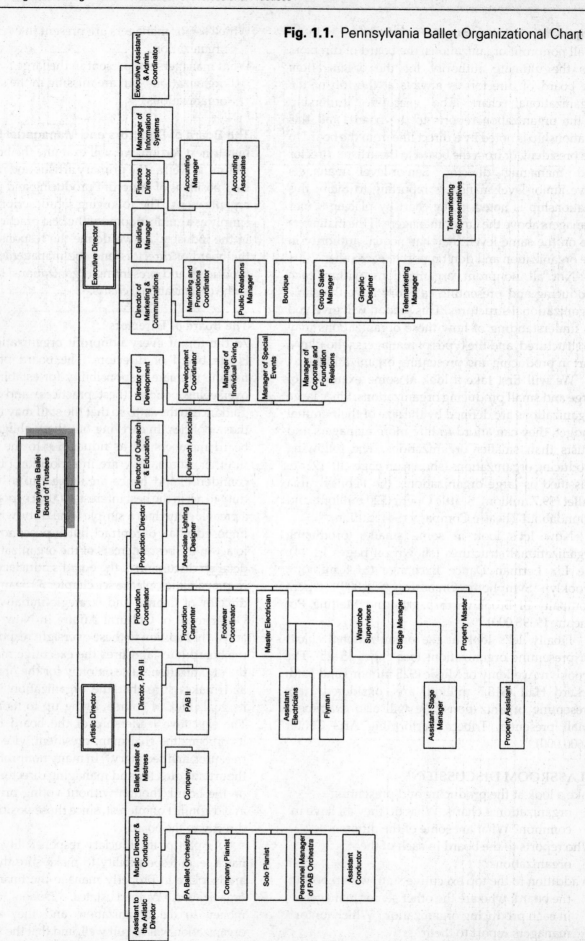

Fig. 1.2. Seattle Opera Organizational Chart

BOARD OF TRUSTEES

Guest Artists, Directors, Designers, Conductors

General Director

Administrative Director

Company Manager

Community and Artists Relations Mgr.

Executive Asst. to Speight Jenkins

Executive Assistant to AD and Co. Mgr.

Dir. of Human Resources
- Payroll Administrator
- Payroll Processor

Chief Financial Officer
- Accounting Supervisor
- Accounting AP
- Accounting Assistant
- Finance Consultant

Director of Development
- Development Assistant
- Research Associate
- Associate Director
- Major Gifts/Planned Giving Officer
- Major Gifts Coordinator
- Indivd. Giving/Info. Services Officer
- Dev. Database Coor.
- Development Assistant
- Corp./Found. Rel. Manager
- Grant Writer
- Special Events Manager
- Special Events Assistant
- Financial Services Coordinator

Director of Marketing & Communications
- Associate Marketing Dir.
- Web Producer
- PT Marketing Asst.
- Advertising & Prom. Mgr.
- Creative Services Manager
- Direct Sales Manager
- Direct Sales Supervisor
- Direct Sales Supervisor
- Direct Sales Assistant
- Direct Sales Reps.
- Director of Public Relations
- Communications Editor
- Public Relations Assoc.
- Public Relations Coor.
- Financial Services Coord.
- Associate Director of Sales
- Ticket Office Manager
- Ticket Office Supervisor
- Ticket Agents
- Grp Sales/Aud. Dev. Mgr.
- Receptionist

Director of Education
- Associate Director
- Events Manager
- Education Programs Coor.
- Education Associate

Production Director
- Production Supervisor
- Dancers & Supers
- Production Administrator
- Costume Shop Manager
- Show Manager
- Assistant Manager
- Costume Shop Assistant
- Rental/Stock Coordinator
- Costume Crews
- Wardrobe Master
- Wardrobe Crews
- Hair and Make-up Designer
- Hair and Make-up Manager
- Hair and Make-up Crews
- Assistant Conductor
- Head of Coach/Accompanists
- Coach/Accompanists
- Music Administrator
- Music Librarian
- Chorusmaster
- Orchestra & Chorus
- Resident Stage Manager
- Stage management staff

Technical Director
- Associate Tech. Director
- Assistant Tech. Director
- Master Electrician
- Electrics Crews
- Properties Coordinator
- Properties Master
- Prop Crews
- Master Stage Carpenter
- Stage Crews
- Scenic Studios Manager
- Scenic Carpenters
- Master Scenic Artist
- Scenic Artists
- Financial Services Admin.
- Financial Services Coor.
- Operations Manager
- IS Manager
- Network Sys. Admin.
- Database Admin.
- Facilities Assistant

Seattle Opera
Organizational Chart
Last update 02/28/2006

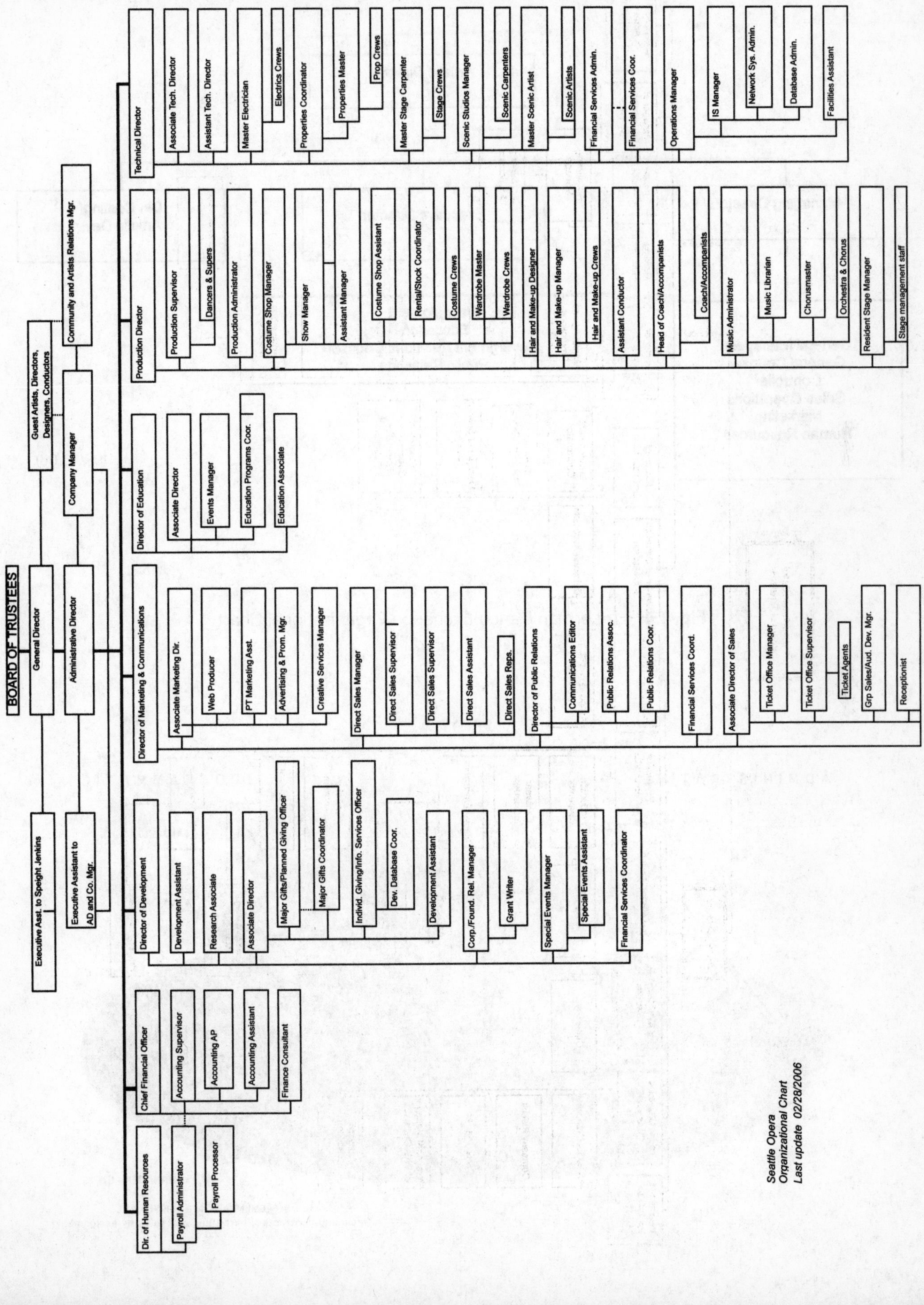

Fig. 1.3. Roundabout Theatre Company Organizational Chart

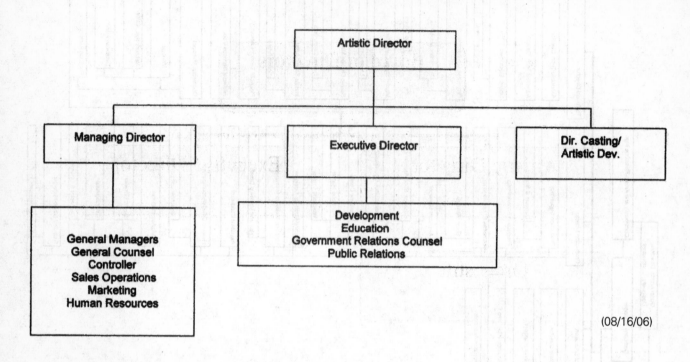

Fig. 1.4. Liz Lerman Dance Exchange Organizational Chart

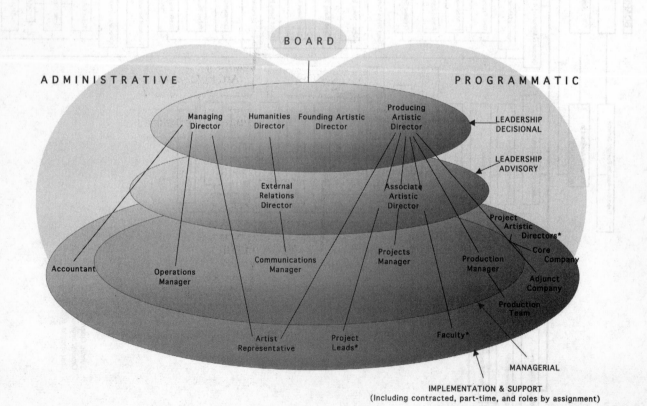

Fig. 1.5. Brooklyn Symphony Orchestra Organizational Chart

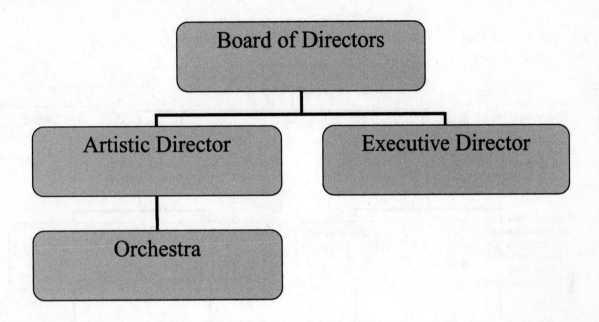

Fig. 1.6. Opera Company of Brooklyn Organizational Chart

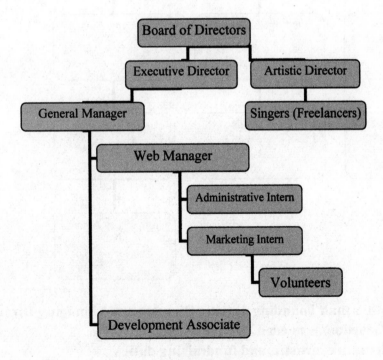

MELTING POT THEATRE COMPANY
Small Off-Broadway Nonprofit Theatre in New York City
Organizational Chart 2005

Fig. 1.7. Melting Pot Theatre
Organizational Chart

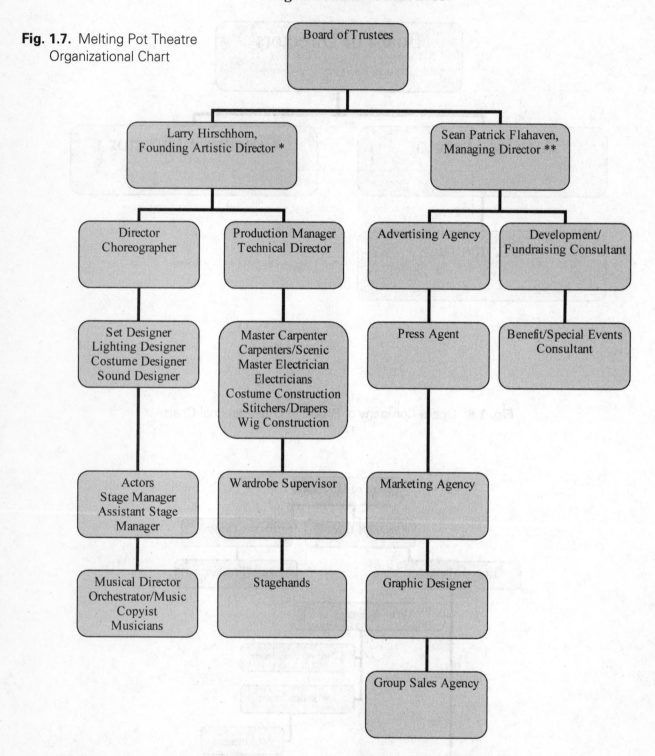

NOTE: All positions other than Founding Artistic Director and Managing Director are part-
time/temporary/per production/as needed
*   Includes administrative, artistic, and fundraising duties
**   Includes administrative, artistic, general management, company management, accounting,
marketing, and fundraising duties

Fig. 1.8. Brooklyn Academy of Music Organizational Charts

Brooklyn Academy of Music
President & Executive Producer

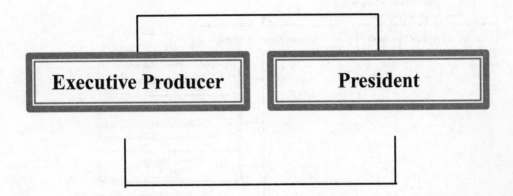

Brooklyn Academy of Music
Executive Team

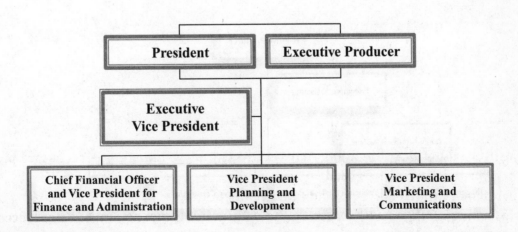

Fig. 1.8. (continued)

Brooklyn Academy of Music
President's Office

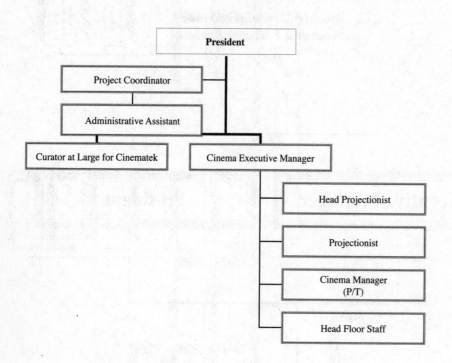

Brooklyn Academy of Music
Executive Producer's Office

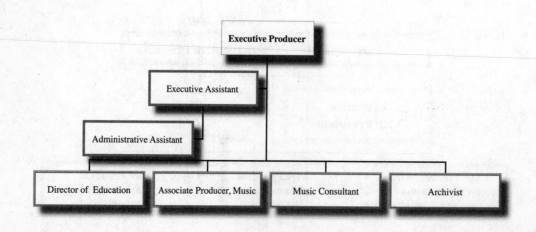

Brooklyn Academy of Music
General Management

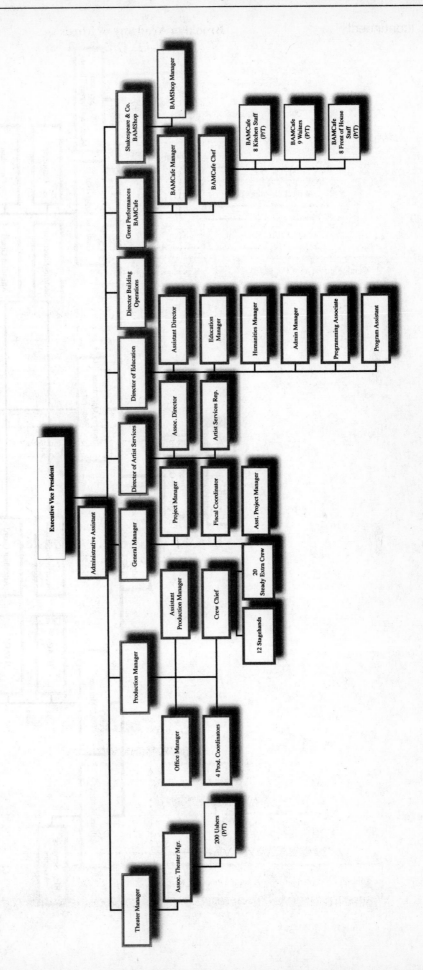

Fig. 1.8. (continued)

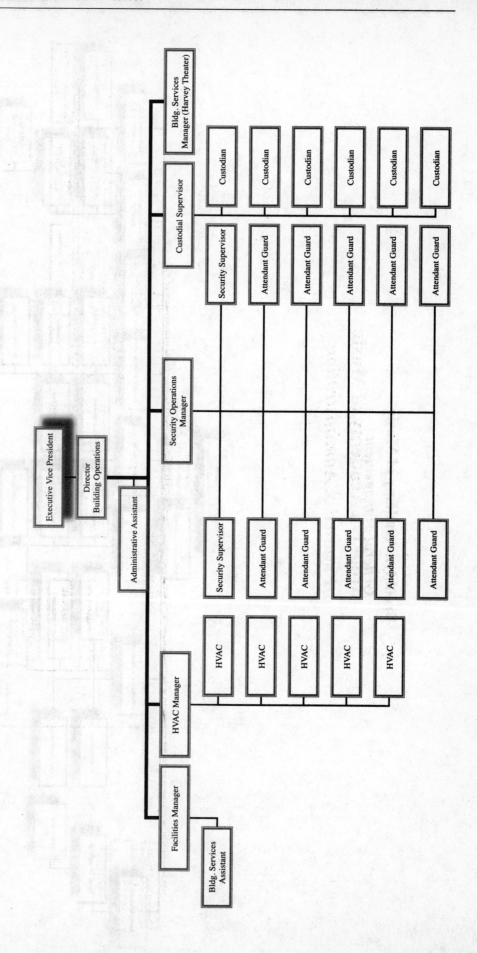

Brooklyn Academy of Music
Building Operations

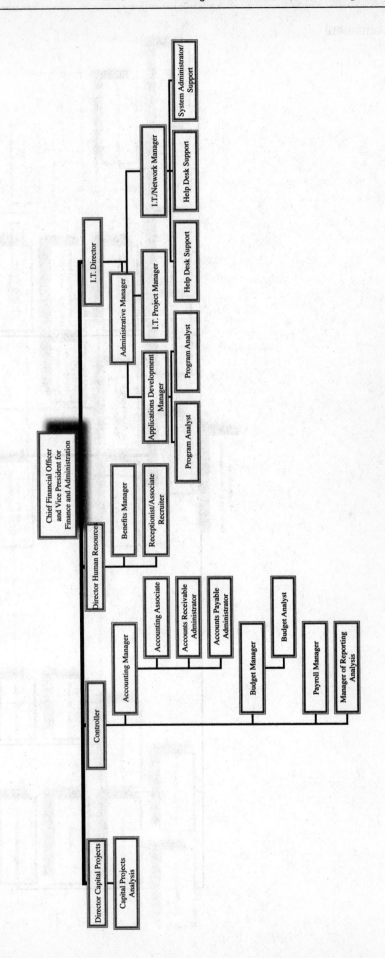

Brooklyn Academy of Music
Finance & Administration

Fig. 1.8. (continued)

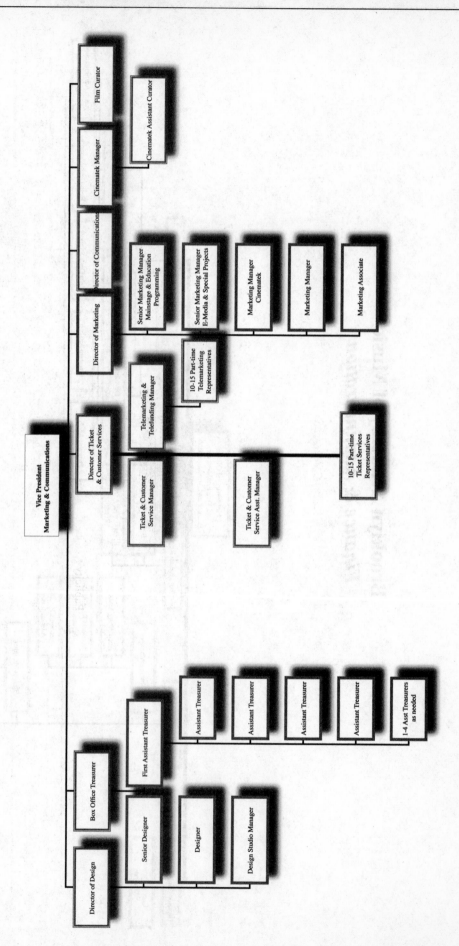

Brooklyn Academy of Music
Marketing & Communications

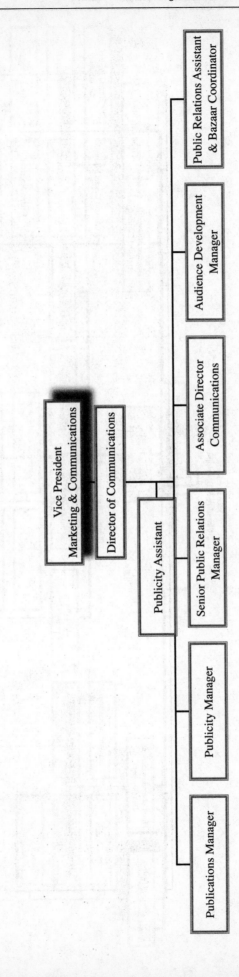

Brooklyn Academy of Music
Communications

Fig. 1.8. (continued)

Brooklyn Academy of Music
Planning & Development

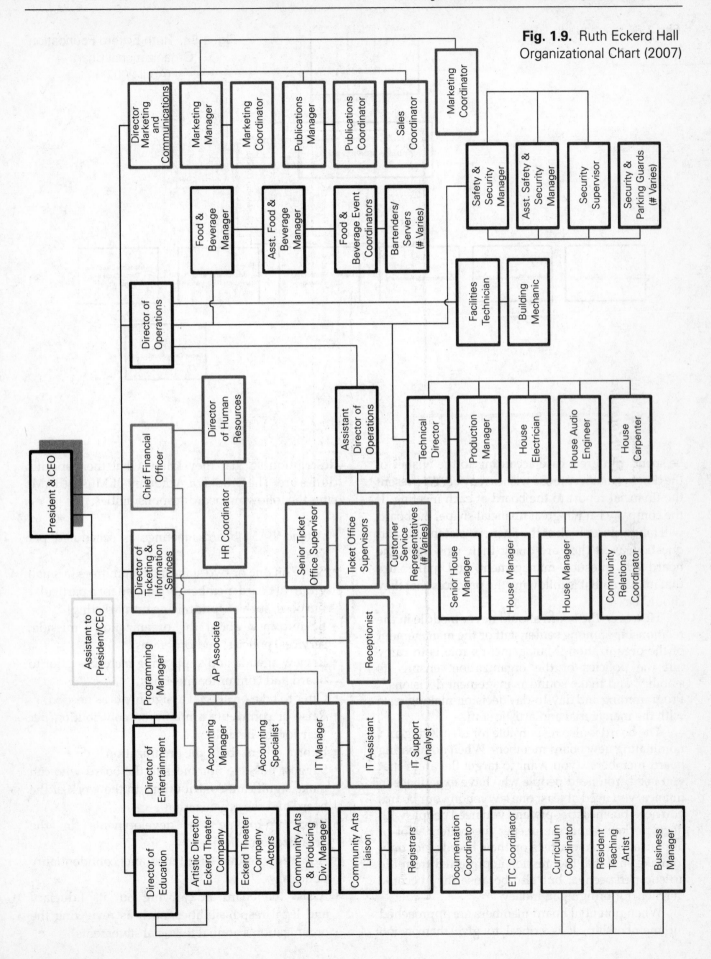

Fig. 1.9. Ruth Eckerd Hall Organizational Chart (2007)

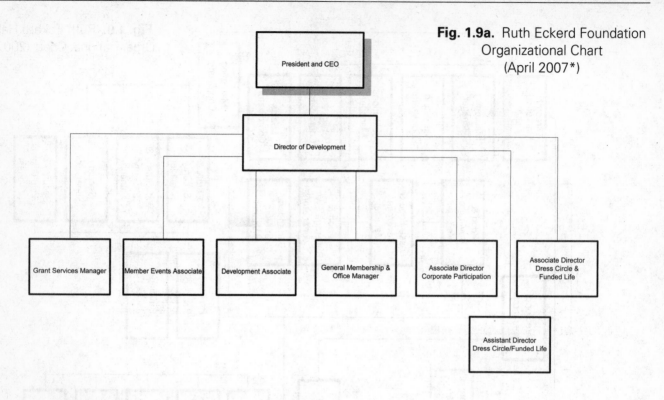

Fig. 1.9a. Ruth Eckerd Foundation Organizational Chart (April 2007*)

*The Ruth Eckerd Hall Development Department is organized as a separate foundation.

be spent with great care according to the wishes of the donor, whatever those wishes may be. We present the financial report to the board at each meeting. If the company isn't in great financial shape, the board will take a closer look at the financial statements and question us. If they are doing their jobs right, the board will question management, and make sure that management is following the practices that they should be."[54]

However, the board should never meddle in the relationships among senior staff or the management of the organization. Management's role is to carry out the policies of the organization, ensure its stability, and make sound management decisions.[55] Programming and day-to-day decision-making rests with the managerial and artistic staff.

The board is also responsible for identifying and nominating new board members. When nominating board members, "you want to target the areas that you need. You need people who have experience in finance, you need at least one lawyer on your board, you need business people, and you need people with deep pockets—and the deeper the better. A lot of organizations have artists on their boards, not only to make sure that the mission is protected from the artistic perspective, but also because they become magnets for bringing in money."[56]

When potential board members are approached for membership, it is critical to give them a job description so that they know what their specific duties are. The Brooklyn Academy of Music (BAM) cites the following board responsibilities:

- Attend BAM board meetings as scheduled per year
- Serve on one or two standing committees [a small group of board members organized for a particular purpose, such as fundraising or marketing]
- Be informed about the organization's mission, services, policies, and programs
- Review agenda and supporting materials prior to board and committee meetings
- Offer to take on special assignments as needed
- Raise or contribute a minimum contribution per year for the institution
- Inform others about the organization
- Suggest possible nominees to the board who can make significant contributions to the work of the board and the organization
- Keep up-to-date on developments in the organization's field
- Adhere to conflict-of-interest and confidentiality policies
- Assist the board in carrying out its fiduciary and legal responsibilities, such as reviewing the organization's annual financial statements[57]

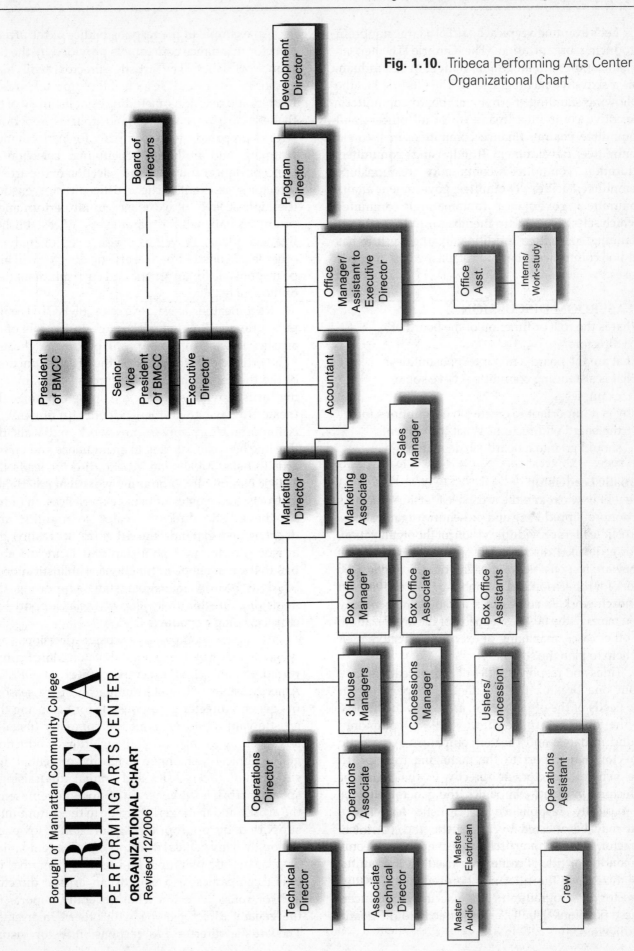

Fig. 1.10. Tribeca Performing Arts Center Organizational Chart

Borough of Manhattan Community College

TRIBECA
PERFORMING ARTS CENTER
ORGANIZATIONAL CHART
Revised 12/2006

Board of Directors

President of BMCC

Senior Vice President Of BMCC

Executive Director

Development Director

Program Director

Office Manager/ Assistant to Executive Director

Office Asst.

Interns/ Work-study

Accountant

Marketing Director

Sales Manager

Marketing Associate

Box Office Manager

Box Office Associate

Box Office Assistants

3 House Managers

Concessions Manager

Ushers/ Concession

Operations Director

Operations Associate

Operations Assistant

Technical Director

Associate Technical Director

Master Electrician

Master Audio

Crew

Let's examine a typical board of a large nonprofit producing organization. The Guthrie Theater, an organization with an annual budget of $20 million, has a sixty-five member board. The Guthrie has the following standing (permanent) board committees: executive committee (made up of all officers and committee chairs); finance committee; investment committee; development (fundraising) committee; education committee; community relationships committee; facilities committee; government affairs committee; governance (nominating) committee (which selects new board members); and long-range planning committee. Additionally, the Guthrie has ad hoc committees that are established as the need arises.[58]

CLASSROOM DISCUSSION

What is the role or function of the board of directors?

What are the board's major responsibilities?

What is a standing committee? Give some examples.

Why is it important to create job descriptions for the board of directors? What components should go into a board job description?

Artistic Leadership

We will now explore the artistic leadership positions in nonprofit producing and presenting organizations. Artistic leaders provide the vision for the organization. (For a detailed discussion of vision, see chapter 2.) They are responsible for creating or selecting artistic work for the season and assembling the creative team for each work. In some cases, artistic managers may also manage the business aspects of the organization; in other cases, managing or executive directors plan or help to plan the season.

Titles and responsibilities of artistic leaders vary from one organization to another depending on the needs of the organization, as well as the history of the job. The artistic director title is commonly found in dance and theater companies. An artistic director may report to the managing director, to the general director, or directly to the board of directors. In opera companies, the general director is typically responsible for artistic leadership, but may be assisted by an artistic and/or music director. In symphony orchestras, the music director or conductor title is commonly used. In presenting organizations, the title may be executive director, director of programming, or executive producer. These positions usually report directly to the board of directors.

An example of the responsibilities of the artistic director in a dance company is provided by the San Francisco Ballet: The artistic director "will have authority over and responsibility for all artistic matters and decisions, including establishment of the [ballet's] artistic standards and policies; repertoire [works prepared by the company for performance] planning and building; scheduling; selection of dancers; dancer training; and selection of the artistic director's assistants. The artistic director ensures the highest level of excellence in all performances produced, all within parameters of established financial plans, as well as existing contractual and other legal constraints. The artistic director will also be responsible for all artistic and curriculum matters of the school."[59]

Kurt Beattie, artistic director of ACT Theatre in Seattle, Washington, elaborates on the role of an artistic director in a nonprofit producing theater: "The artistic director controls the artistic functions of the theater—primarily selecting seasons, matching artists with scripts, and programming the theater to have an aesthetic identity. In our case, it is important to promote new work and walk the fine line between catering to an audience and taking artistic risks. Ideally, an artistic director leads the artistic community, promoting work that entertains, instructs, and creates unusual experiences. In doing so, the artistic director creates community, and deepens and expands the art form. In reality, the artistic director is a politician and is inextricably tied to the management functions of an institution—building boards, managing staff, supporting the managing director to develop financial support—in essence, being a producer."[60]

At opera companies, artistic decisions are typically made by the general director. Marc Scorca, president and chief executive officer of OPERA America, states: "In determining an opera season, the general director is responsible for balancing the artistic values and goals of the company (usually advanced by the artistic staff, including production and technical personnel) with the potential for subscription/ticket sales and annual fundraising/sponsorship. It is the general director who represents the artistic and managerial profile to the community, supported by appropriate senior staff. However, although many general directors of opera companies oversee artistic planning, an increasing number of opera companies also employ an artistic director and/or music director who, generally, reports to the general director along with other senior staff. The artistic director has responsibility for visual and theatrical elements (sets, costumes, direction), while the music director only has responsibility for the musical aspects of the production (orchestra, chorus, coaches, soloists)."[61] For example, Julie Tatum, director of human resources for the Seattle Opera, notes, "Seattle Opera has a general director who is also the artistic director. In many U.S. opera companies, the structure is a bit different, with the artistic director reporting to the general director."[62]

Another example is provided by the Opera Company of Brooklyn, whose artistic director "sets the creative direction for the company, and selects all repertoire, develops new programs, casts each production, conducts all performances, selects the orchestra personnel, and prepares all singers for each production."[63] The artistic director "reports to the board and works alongside the executive director in managing the long-term and day-to-day affairs of the organization. In consultation with the executive director, the artistic director is responsible for the selection of the repertoire to be performed by the company, submitting the list each year for approval [by the board]. The artistic director will have final say in cast selection."[64] The formal written job description also notes, "In the event that the executive director and the artistic director should disagree about any issue, it is the duty of each one to report the disagreement to the board chair (and only to the chair), and in consultation with the chair, a final decision will be made."[65]

In an orchestra, a music director typically serves as the main conductor. At the Brooklyn Philharmonic Orchestra, the music director also "supervises all artistic and educational planning for future seasons in consultation with the Brooklyn Philharmonic Orchestra chief executive officer, selects orchestra advisors and/or specialized staff and appropriate board committees, helps to build and improve the quality of the orchestra, holds auditions as deemed necessary for soloists and future members of the Brooklyn Philharmonic Orchestra, and advises on and supervises orchestra personnel matters."[66] As music directors often travel to conduct other orchestras, the Brooklyn Philharmonic Orchestra specifies the amount of time the music director must spend with the orchestra, "in order to plan these visits, which will be used to facilitate his/her role as mentor to special composer projects; make fundraising appearances/solicitations; attend donor events, board meetings and donor/board dinners; press/media and promotional activities; and any other special projects as mutually agreed."[67]

In a nonprofit presenting organization, the staff member in charge of programming selects the season by working directly with artists or managers, or with their booking agents. James Patrick states, "I am the executive director, and I oversee the day-to-day operations of the organization, including the artistic decisions. I have a lot to say in the programming and the artistic side of the organization. I decide which shows get presented and produced."[68] Gina Vernaci also plays this important role in her organization. Let's take a look at her job description on page 28.[69]

Another important member of the artistic leadership is the dramaturg. "Dramaturgs generally have training in dramatic theory, theater practice, and history, equipping them to serve in a number of artistic capacities. Production dramaturgs may serve as partner to the director, acting as a sounding board for ideas, as an extra set of eyes in the rehearsal room, and as a researcher. In a nonprofit theater, a dramaturg may also be a literary manager, responsible for the upkeep and assessment of new play submissions, as well as creating and maintaining relationships with artists. An on-staff dramaturg or literary manager may also aid in season selection and curatorial duties, host readings, and serve as moderator for pre- or post-performance discussions. Additionally, dramaturgs often work within a theater's education department, creating study guides and supplemental materials that will enrich the audience's understanding of the play. In opera as well as the theater, dramaturgs may serve as the translator of texts or the author of subtitles, in addition to their other duties. Finally, a number of dance companies and choreographers use dramaturgs for work that encompasses textual elements and dance-theater."[70]

CLASSROOM DISCUSSION

Discuss the importance of creating and reviewing managerial titles, job descriptions, and organizational charts.

Define and describe the responsibilities of the artistic leader of each type of nonprofit organization.

What is a dramaturg?

Managerial Leadership

We will now examine managerial leadership positions within nonprofit producing and presenting organizations, beginning with the managing director. The title of managing director is often interchangeable with the titles of executive director, chief executive officer (CEO), and president, depending

Fig. 1.11. Vice President of Theatricals Job Description, Playhouse Square Center

JOB TITLE: Vice President of Theatricals

RELATIONSHIP: Reports to the President

**GENERAL
DESCRIPTION:**   Full-time, Salaried, Exempt Position

RESPONSIBILITIES:

1.   Develop long-range strategic programming and artistic goals for the Center.

2.   Develop and maintain relationships with performers, producers, agents, general managers, and other presenters throughout all facets of the industry.

3.   Work in coordination with the Education Director to program events supportive of the goals of that department and the Foundation's mission.

4.   Develop and manage annual department budget; oversee budgets for all productions.

5.   Oversee and advise activities of Programming, Marketing, and Sales Departments.

6.   Responsible for contract negotiations with musicians, actors, directors, and designers' unions.

7.   Function as Executive Producer for Playhouse Square productions, galas, and other special events.

8.   Seek and develop programming partnerships in the community.

QUALIFICATIONS:

1.   Minimum of ten years of theatrical programming experience.

2.   Bachelor's degree.

3.   Outgoing, people-oriented person, with outstanding interpersonal skills.

4.   Self-motivated, with strong organizational skills.

5.   Excellent communication skills, both verbal and written.

EMPLOYEE'S
SIGNATURE:_____DATE:_____
APPROVED BY:_____ DATE:_____
UPDATED: June 6, 2006

on the structure of the producing and presenting organization. The title of producing director may also be used, and typically implies a combination of both the artistic and managerial functions. As mentioned previously, the chief managerial executive in an opera company is usually called the general director.[71] Most managing directors report directly to the board of directors. The managing director's primary function is to implement the artistic leader's vision. He is responsible for the administrative side of the organization, working with the board and staff to create a strategic plan for the organization, as well as supervising the financial management, marketing, development, education, and general management positions. In smaller organizations, the managing director will not only manage these positions, but will actually perform them. Thus, a managing director may also act as a general manager. The Brooklyn Philharmonic Orchestra has a job description that describes the chief executive's responsibilities in great detail (see pages 30–31).[72]

The next section provides a brief description of major positions in the finance, marketing, development, education, and general management departments. (In future chapters, we will examine these positions in more detail.) Please note that the majority of these positions are found in both presenting and producing organizations.

Financial Management

The head of the financial management department is also called the chief financial officer, the business manager, the finance director, or the vice president for finance and administration. This position should report to the executive or managing director of the organization. The Playhouse Square Center's job description provides a thorough description of the major responsibilities of the job (see page 32).[73]

Depending on the organization, the human resources manager, the information technology (IT) manager, the controller, the operations manager, and the box office treasurer may report to the chief financial officer. The human resources manager "oversees the hiring practices of the organization; administers the health insurance and benefit programs; interacts with employees and their supervisors on all personnel matters, including performance evaluations, disciplinary actions, and terminations; and administers employee orientation programs, training programs, and employee recognition programs."[74] The information technology manager "manages and coordinates all data processing, planning, and production activities.

He meets with managers to determine functional information requirements, discusses proposed computer equipment acquisitions, and establishes necessary user-department cooperation in the development and operation of computer systems."[75] The controller is responsible for implementing accounting, payroll, and budgeting functions for the organization.

The operations manager or facilities manager is responsible for all activities related to the maintenance and operation of the building, including: booking the rentals for the theater, scheduling and event management, managing the front-of-house and technical staff, providing security, and operating and maintaining the heat and air-conditioning systems.[76] (Please see chapter 11 for more information on facility management.) In a presenting or producing organization, depending on the size, the general manager and the director of theater operations may be the same person. In a larger presenting or producing organization, the manager of theater operations may also report to the general manager.

The box office treasurer handles the ticket income for the organization, and for this reason, may report to the financial manager. In some organizations, the box office treasurer will report to the marketing director, because the marketing director must keep a close eye on ticket-purchasing trends in order to create a successful marketing strategy. The box office treasurer is responsible for training box office staff and for the management of season ticket and single-ticket sales.

Marketing and Communications

The marketing manager reports to the managing or executive director and is responsible for all earned revenue or income earned from ticket sales and fees for service, such as concessions. In addition, in many organizations, the director of marketing is responsible for supervising the public relations manager and the box office treasurer. The public relations or communications manager is responsible for creating the institutional image and generating publicity for each of the shows and events. The Seattle Opera provides a marketing and communications job description, in which the final responsibility of marketing and public relations falls to the director of marketing and communications (see pages 33–36).[77]

Development

The director of development is responsible for raising the contributed income for the organization. Contributed income takes the form of donations

Fig. 1.12. Chief Executive Officer Job Description, Brooklyn Philharmonic Orchestra

BROOKLYN philharmonic
MUSIC DIRECTOR michael christie

JOB TITLE: Chief Executive Officer

REPORTS TO: Chairman of the Board of Directors. Works as peer with the Music Director in coordinating and implementing artistic plans.

SUPERVISES: Senior Staff

JOB SUMMARY: The Executive Director serves as the Chief Executive Officer of the Brooklyn Philharmonic Orchestra and is charged with leading the institution, guided by the orchestra's mission and values. The Executive Director will provide organizational leadership that supports and encourages fulfillment of the artistic mission. The scope of responsibilities include facilitating and direction planning and board development, financial and administrative management, directing labor relations with musicians, assuring effective communication, external and community relations, coordinating production of concerts and promoting the mission of the organization. As regards the Board of Directors, it is understood that it is the Board's responsibility to raise funds and set policy; it is the Executive Director's responsibility to run the institution and assist and support the Board in all development efforts.

JOB DUTIES AND RESPONSIBILITIES:

ADMINISTRATIVE MANAGEMENT AND LEADERSHIP
- Supervises and directs all activities of staff of the orchestra.
- Has complete hiring and termination authority for staff as well as the responsibility for training and reviewing staff.
- Creates an empowered workforce and a teamwork environment using a leadership style that encourages fulfillment of the artistic mission.
- Structures and directs concert production, artistic administration, development, education, finance, marketing, public relations, and general administration.
- Acts as a facilitator and counselor to the institution, including musicians and volunteers, so that issues are raised, discussed, and resolved in the most productive and professional manner.

ARTISTIC POLICIES AND ACTIVITIES
- Supervises and directs all activities of the musicians of the orchestra except those activities supervised and directed by the Music Director.
- Negotiates and fulfills all contracts for the institution, including musicians' master agreement with AFM Local 802, which governs musicians employed by the orchestra.
- Establishes an environment of trust and cooperation with musicians and other contractual partners.
- Provides Music Director with financial constraints, artist and hall availability, and related circumstances necessary for the artistic planning process.
- Collaborates with the Music Director on matters of overall philosophy and programming and works in partnership to determine performance schedules, repertoire, and artists.

FUNDRAISING AND GENERATION OF FINANCIAL SUPPORT
- Exercises overall managerial responsibilities for achieving the fundraising goals of the orchestra.
- Directly participates in raising contributed income.
- Supervises staff in implementing all fundraising effort.
- Supports board in enlisting board and volunteer participation in campaign leadership, planning, and solicitation.
- Makes personal solicitations alone, and with trustees and volunteers, to individuals, corporation, foundations, government agencies and community leaders.
- In partnership with the Board, initiates planning and execution of endowment and planned giving campaigns.

BOARD, GOVERNMENT, AND COMMUNITY RELATIONS
- Serves as primary spokesperson, representing the institution to its many constituencies, both internal and external.
- Builds constructive ongoing relationships with board members, government officials, and community leaders.
- Develops opportunities to further diversify the board.
- Works with the Board Chairman and committees on issues pertaining to Board structure and development, organization, bylaws, governance, and the nomination process.
- Fosters healthy and positive working relationships and partnerships with other community political, educational, and cultural constituents.
- Identifies and implements new partnerships and relationship as appropriate.

COMMUNICATION
- Establishes and maintains timely, direct, and clear communication among the components of the orchestra family – Board, Music Director, musicians, staff, conductors, volunteers, donors, members of the arts community, and media.

PLANNING
- Provides leadership in the strategic and long-range planning processes necessary to fulfill and advance the mission of the institution.

FINANCIAL PLANNING AND CONTROL
- Has direct and principal responsibility for ongoing business and financial management of the organization.
- Works with the Finance Committee and the board to develop annual and long-term operating budgets for board approval.
- Works with the Finance Committee to ensure accurate tracking and monitoring of all income, expense, and investment items to ensure effective cost controls, sufficient cash flow, and timely and accurate reporting of financial information in order to support the Board of Trustees in upholding their fiduciary responsibility to the community.
- Works with the Finance Committee to develop strategies for development of financial resources.

MARKETING AND PROMOTION
- In tandem with the Marketing Committee, promotes the orchestra locally, regionally, and nationally through well-conceived marketing and public relations strategies.
- Maximizes visibility and revenue while maintaining artistic integrity.
- Develops programs to increase concert attendance through promotion of subscriptions and greater sales of single tickets.
- Develops new opportunities for earned revenue.
- Ensures that excellent customer service is provided to patrons.
- Lends a visible and consistent presence at performances and activities.

Fig. 1.13. Vice President of Finance/Administration and
General Counsel Job Description, Playhouse Square Center

JOB TITLE: Vice President of Finance/Administration and General Counsel

RELATIONSHIP: Reports to the President

**GENERAL
DESCRIPTION:**   Full-time, Salaried, Exempt Position.

RESPONSIBILITIES:

1. Direct all financial functions for the Foundation and its related entities including monthly financial reports, financial analysis, financing of new projects, annual budgets, strategic plans, and taxes.

2. Act as liaison to the President, Finance Committee, and the Board on all financial issues.

3. Oversee and advise Human Resources regarding administration and implementation of organizational policy.

4. Direct the activities of the Accounting department, the Human Resources Department, OHvations, and the MIS department.

5. Serve as in-house counsel. Responsible for overseeing all legal issues, and for reviewing/drafting legal documents for all PSF entities.

QUALIFICATIONS:

1. Minimum of ten years experience in financial management.

2. BS in Accounting with a CPA; J.D. degree.

3. Minimum of three years corporate legal experience.

4. Outgoing, people-oriented person, with outstanding interpersonal skills.

5. Self-motivated with strong organizational skills.

6. Excellent communication skills, both verbal and written.

EMPLOYEE'S SIGNATURE: _____ DATE:_____
APPROVED BY:_____ DATE:_____
UPDATED: August 10, 2001

Fig. 1.14. Director, Marketing and Communications
Job Description, Seattle Opera

Seattle Opera

Job Description

Job Title:	**Director, Marketing and Communications**
Group:	Marketing and Communications
Department:	N/A
Basic Function:	Coordinates all Company marketing and advertising efforts to obtain maximum effectiveness in creating demand for Company's offerings. Individual is responsible to the Administrative Director for recommendations with respect to marketing and advertising policies, strategy, budgets, and media, for the Company's marketing and public relations programs.
	Responsible for the identity of the Company, working with the General Director, Administrative Director, and all groups and departments as necessary for the development of printed materials as they relate to the total Company image.
Scope:	Directs all departments within the Marketing and Communications Group so as to provide an effective service organization to other groups within the Company, with priority given to marketing and public relations activities.
	In collaboration with the General Director, Administrative Director, and Group Directors, establishes Company operating goals, predicated upon the successful performance of the Marketing and Communications Group. The Director of the Group develops the overall marketing plans for the Company to meet these goals. Upon implementation of the plans, the individual must direct the overall marketing performance, continually evaluating results and revising strategy.
	Accountable for earned-income objectives of the Company as they pertain to ticket sales.
	Major functions operating under the leadership of the Director, Marketing and Communications, are:
	Marketing Advertising & Promotions Public Relations/Communications Creative Services Ticket Sales Telemarketing Audience Development

Fig. 1.14. (continued)

Principal Accountabilities:

- Represents the Marketing and Communications Group's needs in the development of Company policy.

- Formulates earned-income goals as they pertain to ticket sales. Develops marketing plans and strategy, and directs the execution of same for the achievement of corporate marketing objectives.

- Directs the development of special marketing plans pertinent to other Company groups, including providing support services such as promotional literature and advertising.

- Develops, recommends, and implements the Company's advertising strategy.

- Conducts continual market research and relays pertinent findings to General Director and Administrative Director, predicting their impact on Company decisions.

- Effectively controls area costs through the establishment of budgets, followed by strict conformance to them.

- Continually seeks new and creative ways to manage the group efficiently and effectively, always with an eye to the bottom line.

- Ensures that marketing and communications activities are complemented by effective customer service.

- Selects, develops, and motivates necessary managerial and support talent to maintain an organization with breadth and depth sufficient to attain established Company objectives and to address current and future needs.

Supervision Exercised:

a) Full-Time Positions Directly Supervised:
Director, Public Relations/Communications
Associate Director, Marketing
Associate Director, Sales
Manager, Creative Services
Manager, Advertising and Sales Promotion
Manager, Direct Sales (Telemarketing)
Total Department Directors and Managers: 6

Assistant to the Departments (1)
Financial Allocator (1)
Total Support Staff: 2

Total Directly Supervised: **8**

b) Full-Time Positions Indirectly Supervised:
Publications Coordinator (1)

Public Relations Associate (1)
Web Producer (1)
Receptionist (1)
Ticketing Operations (2)
Telemarketing Supervisor (1)

Total Indirectly Supervised: **7**

Also indirectly supervises part-time, temporary, work-study, and intern personnel as required to meet the objectives of the group and in accordance with established budget.

Supervision Received: Reports to Administrative Director. Works toward Company objectives, requiring independent judgment and decision-making. Refers to supervisor for clarification of policies and procedures.

Responsibility and Authority: *Employee Relations:*
Makes recommendations regarding hires, terminations, promotions, demotions, and transfers, reviews merit increases, and administers personnel procedures within company policies. Makes major recommendations for actions affecting subordinates.

Materials:
Responsible for ordering, purchase, and inventory of supplies and materials as required for marketing/merchandising operations.

Equipment:
Responsible for proper utilization of office equipment assigned to Marketing and Development Services Group. Makes recommendation for software purchases intended to increase the effectiveness of the group.

Money:
Responsible for the administration of the Marketing and Development Services Group's budget. Has goal of achieving ticket revenue of $8M for the 2004-2005 season and $4.7M for 2005 *Ring* Cycle. Ensures that the Group's departments stay within the budgets presented by other groups/departments within the Company requesting services.

Internal Relationships:
Work involves extensive internal contacts with General Director, Administrative Director, staff Directors, and the Board of Trustee's Vice President, Marketing. Serves as the staff liaison with the Marketing Committee of the Board of Trustees.

External Relationships:
Requires membership in various civic and business organizations to project an appropriate company image and develop business contacts. High-level contact with service providers.

Fig. 1.14. (continued)

Minimum Requirements:

Equivalent Education Level Required:
Bachelor's Degree in Business/Marketing

Experience Required:
5 years of experience as Director of Marketing or comparable position with comparable scope and budget in relevant industry. Some experience in not-for-profit institution preferred. Bachelor of Arts in relevant business field. Portfolio of fully executed and implemented marketing programs with measurable results. Demonstration of ability to create, design, implement, and direct successful marketing campaigns with quantifiable results.

Knowledge Required:
Knowledge of latest marketing techniques and trends. Computer literate, with strong analytical capabilities.

Skills Required:
Initiative. Strong strategic planning and organizational skills. Excellent communication skills, both oral and written, with the ability to skillfully interact with senior management, board members, and major donors. Ability to supervise a broad variety of talented professionals and to motivate, guide, and inspire professional growth.

Special Requirements:
Ability to work evenings and weekends for Company-sponsored events.

Salary Range: $_____

Exempt_____Non-exempt_____

from individuals, corporations, foundations, and the government. The director of development reports to the managing or executive director of the organization. Let's take a look at the Brooklyn Philharmonic's director of development's job description (see pages 38–39).[78]

Education

The director of education is responsible for all areas of education for both adults and children. In many producing and presenting organizations, the director of education will report to the general director, managing director, or executive director of the organization. In other organizations, one or both of these areas will report to the artistic director.

General Management

As we indicated earlier, there is no one organization chart or job description that will fit every producing or presenting organization. This statement is especially true for the general manager. The general manager is responsible for the day-to-day operations of the organization, which may include budget and contract creation, contract management, company management, facility management, and house management, as well as management of the production and technical operations of the stage. The general manager reports to the managing or executive director of the organization. We will now examine the general management position at the Brooklyn Academy of Music (see page 40).[79]

CLASSROOM DISCUSSION

What is the managing or executive director responsible for implementing?

Define and describe the responsibilities of the following managers: chief financial officer, director of marketing, director of development, director of education, and general manager.

COMMERCIAL ORGANIZATIONS: ORGANIZATIONAL TYPES

Following our discussion of nonprofit organizations, we will now examine the organizational structures and managerial positions in commercial organizations. (More detailed information about commercial organizations may be found in chapter 4.) We will begin by examining the types of commercial organizations commonly encountered in the performing arts: Broadway, Off-Broadway, and touring productions.

Broadway

Broadway productions are those produced within a specific area in New York City, known as the "Broadway box," defined as theaters located "in an area bounded by Fifth and Ninth Avenues from 34th Street to 56th Street and by Fifth Avenue and the Hudson River from 56th Street to 72nd Street."[80] To be considered a Broadway theater, the theater must seat more than 499 people. There are thirty-nine Broadway theaters in New York, including the Al Hirschfeld Theatre, the Gershwin Theatre, the New Amsterdam Theatre, the Shubert Theatre and many more.[81] (Four of the theaters in the Broadway box are owned by nonprofit organizations: Manhattan Theatre Club's Biltmore Theatre, Roundabout Theatre's American Airlines Theatre and Studio 54, and Lincoln Center Theater's Vivian Beaumont Theater; these theaters will be discussed in chapter 4.) All Broadway productions are eligible to receive Tony Awards, the highest recognition one can receive for producing a Broadway show; the Tony Awards are broadcast on national television each year. Broadway productions are produced by a producer or group of producers, who license (rent) a Broadway theater from its owner.

Off-Broadway

Off-Broadway productions are those produced within theaters that seat between 100 and 499 people and are located in Manhattan. Off-Broadway productions are eligible to receive Lucille Lortel Awards, recognizing achievement for excellence in Off-Broadway productions.[82] Off-Broadway productions are also produced by a producer or group of producers, who license (rent) an Off-Broadway theater from its owner. (As with Broadway, some Off-Broadway productions may be produced by nonprofit theaters, such as Playwrights Horizons, the Public Theater, Second Stage, and the New York Theatre Workshop.[83])

Touring

Finally, commercial productions may tour. Commercial touring productions are referred to as being "on the road," and "the road" may also refer to the presenters in the touring market. (Nonprofit productions may also tour; the touring process is described in more detail in chapter 10.) The world of touring productions consists of commercial producers and general managers who produce and manage Broadway and Off-Broadway productions on tour; commercial and nonprofit presenters who present these tours; and booking agents who work for the producers of touring shows.

Fig. 1.15. Director of Development Job Description, Brooklyn Philharmonic Orchestra

REPORTS TO: CEO

SUPERVISES: Manager of Institutional Giving, Manager of Special Events, Development Associate, Development Assistant, Development Interns, and external consultants, including government lobbyists

JOB SUMMARY: The Development Director is responsible for the development, management, implementation, and evaluation of an overall fund-raising program consistent with the Brooklyn Philharmonic's needs and goals. To that end, the Development Director manages staff and volunteers in planning and executing all annual, sponsorship, capital, and planned giving programs, as well as fund-raising events and benefits. The Development Director is also responsible for making grant applications to federal, state, and local government agencies that provide arts funding; and researching and applying to private foundations and corporations that provide arts grants. The Development Director will recommend fund-raising policies and procedures to the Executive Director and Board with the goal of building a year-round development program that demonstrates the highest standards of professionalism and ethical conduct.

JOB DUTIES AND RESPONSIBILITIES:

Fund-raising

• Plan, manage, and implement all phases of the Annual Fund campaign; oversee the solicitation and acknowledgment process, maintenance of records, and establishment and disclosure within IRS guidelines of donor benefits; monitor progress and make adjustments as needed.

• Develop a comprehensive case statement for support of the Brooklyn Philharmonic, based on long-range plan; update annually. Work with Board to develop and direct year-round program to cultivate new prospects and seek out new funding opportunities.

• Develop and implement a corporate sponsorship program; research and identify potential sponsors; prepare proposals and work with Board to identify matches between Brooklyn Philharmonic's program and each company's interests.

• Prepare grant applications with the Manager of Institutional Giving for corporations, foundations, and government agencies that provide arts funding; research all grant possibilities and write reports and back-up materials to support each application; follow up on each proposal.

• Work with volunteers to plan all special fund-raising events and benefits; participate in establishing the budget and oversee the execution of each event.

• Oversee the development and production of all materials used to support the Brooklyn Philharmonic's fund-raising events and campaigns.

• Develop an ongoing planned giving program; work with Board to identify, cultivate, and solicit prospects.

Budgeting and Planning

• Assist the Chief Executive Officer and Board in establishing appropriate goals for the Annual Fund and all other fund-raising campaigns deemed necessary (endowment, capital, planned giving, etc.) each year.

• Develop a plan for achieving those goals and establish a master calendar that outlines all fundraising events and campaigns; coordinate all activities with the Brooklyn Philharmonic's master calendar.

• Develop budgets for each event and campaign; monitor the progress of each, and adjust plans when necessary.

• Work closely with the Chief Executive Officer and other designated staff in long-range planning for the Brooklyn Philharmonic; prepare budget projections as needed.

Board of Directors

• Staff the Development Committee of the Board and other volunteers enlisted to participate in the development program.

• Report to the Board and Executive Committee on progress of all fund-raising events and campaigns; provide other reports and statements as requested.

• Develop Board and volunteer leadership through participation in Board committee meetings and ongoing donor cultivation efforts; participate in identifying and recruiting new leadership.

• Recommend fund-raising policies and procedures to the Chief Executive Officer and Board with the goal of building a year-round development program that demonstrates the highest standards of professionalism and ethical conduct.

Administrative

• Organize staff and volunteers to carry out all fund-raising campaigns and events; evaluate effectiveness of each campaign.

• Oversee the maintenance of all donor files and records; develop and administer all donor benefits programs in accordance with IRS guidelines.

• Provide periodic progress reports on all campaigns; prepare listings and financial statements as needed by the Board and staff.

• Serve as part of the senior management team to assist the Chief Executive Officer in setting and implementing administrative and artistic policies established by the Board.

• Hire, train, manage, and evaluate the performance of all development staff, including interns and volunteers.

Other

• Develop and maintain internal and external contacts to optimize fund-raising efforts.

• Maintain ongoing contact with contributors, corporate sponsors, and business and community leaders.

• Support Board and staff efforts to solicit in-kind contributions.

• Keep abreast of recent research on fund-raising; maintain a collection of current fund-raising resource materials.

• Attend other civic and cultural events in the community; represent the Brooklyn Philharmonic by speaking at public events as requested.

• Perform other duties as assigned by the Chief Executive Officer.

Fig. 1.16. General Manager Job Description, Brooklyn Academy of Music

GENERAL MANAGEMENT DEPARTMENT

Brooklyn Academy of Music (BAM), an internationally recognized presenter of contemporary performing arts and cinema, seeks a General Manager to oversee the General Management department. The individual in this position will report to the Executive Vice President.

Specific responsibilities include:

- Administer all mainstage contracts; negotiate specific contracts as assigned.
- Monitor budgets for all mainstage programs and any other programs managed by the GM department.
- Oversee the institutional calendar; manage content of BAM's Internet and event management software.
- Supervise the day-to-day operations of the institution; facilitate and coordinate interdepartmental communication and coordination as it relates to BAM's programming.
- Supervise the Assistant GM, Fiscal Coordinator, Project Coordinator, and the GM's Administrative Assistant.

Requirements: Bachelor's degree or M.F.A. and seven years of theatre management experience required; nonprofit environment preferred. Creative abilities as well as project management, leadership, facilitation and consensus-building skills. Must be highly organized and creative, with the ability to coordinate projects and create and meet budgets.

Apply by resume and cover letter to:

Director of Human Resources
Brooklyn Academy of Music
30 Lafayette Ave.
Brooklyn, NY 11217
Fax: (718) 636-4179
E-mail: hrresumes@bam.org

EOE: 10/16/2003

COMMERCIAL ORGANIZATIONS: ORGANIZATIONAL STRUCTURES AND MANAGERIAL POSITIONS

In the following section, we will look at some of the commercial organizational structures, as well as the managerial positions of commercial producing organizations, booking agents, presenters, and theater owners. Within each category, the organizational structure may vary, so these examples are not blueprints for all types of organizations within each category.

Commercial Producing Organizations

Producers are responsible for locating the product and finding the investors to finance it. This is quite an undertaking, since large-scale Broadway musicals can cost somewhere between $11 and 16 million to produce, and Broadway plays run between $2 and 2.5 million to produce.[84] Producing organizations such as Richard Frankel Productions, Marc Routh Productions, and Scorpio Entertainment produce Broadway and Off-Broadway productions, as well as touring Broadway and Off-Broadway shows. These organizations general manage their shows; other producing organizations may hire outside general managers to perform this function. Richard Frankel Productions also operates a subsidiary company, a booking agency to book both their own touring shows and the touring shows of other producers. A subsidiary is a company that is controlled by another corporation or company. Let's take a look at Richard Frankel's organizational chart on page 42.[85]

We will now define the positions found in a producing office: producer, associate producer, general manager, company manager, attorneys, accountants, and the production team. We will also examine areas of responsibility that may not be found in the producing office itself, including marketing and advertising, group sales, and publicity.

Producer

Laura Green, general manager of Richard Frankel Productions, states that a producer's "key function is acquiring the author's rights to the material, and putting together the creative team: director, choreographer, and design teams. The producer makes decisions about when to move forward, how to move forward, and where the production should first appear: out of town, Broadway, or Off-Broadway. The producer also finds the investors."[86]

Investors "contribute money to the capitalization of the production. There are often several producers and associate producers involved in the production. Each one is required to bring in a predetermined amount of money to be raised from his group of investors. Producers have decision-making power, while investors do not. Each producer solicits his investors on an individual basis. Investors have no say in the operation of the company, but are entitled to financial updates, and hopefully a check toward the recoupment of their investment if the show is successful.

"To attract investors, first-time producers will often approach friends and family; more experienced producers often have a circle of friends and professional contacts who regularly invest with them. Producers may invite potential investors to a backers' audition. A backers' audition is typically held during the workshop phase of the production. The producers set aside a day for potential investors to attend the workshop, with the understanding that it is a 'rough draft' of the production, allowing them to see a piece of the product they would be buying into, as well as have a better understanding of the budget and design documentation they have been given."[87] Recently, motion picture companies such as Miramax, Universal Pictures, and Fox Searchlight are investing in commercial theatrical productions.[88]

Associate Producer

The associate producer "isn't as involved as the producer and may come into the game after many of the production decisions are made. It's sometimes someone who has found a big piece of the capitalization and will then receive an associate producer credit. [This person does] sit at the table with the producers and help in making some decisions."[89]

General Manager

The general manager and assistant general manager "compile budgets; negotiate contracts for designers, creative staff, and actors; work with producers to secure the proper ad agency and press agent; and oversee hiring of the production office and management positions."[90] Laura Green "gets involved in the early development process of Richard Frankel's productions." She creates multiple budgets to "make sure that the project is commercially viable." She helps the producers answer the following questions: "How much money are we going to raise? What will our weekly operating expenses be? What theater will we use? What is our gross potential (the total amount of money we can earn in a week)? What is our recoupment schedule? (How long will it take to pay back our investors, so that we may begin to make a profit?)" Green also negotiates and executes

Fig. 1.17. Richard Frankel Productions
Organizational Chart

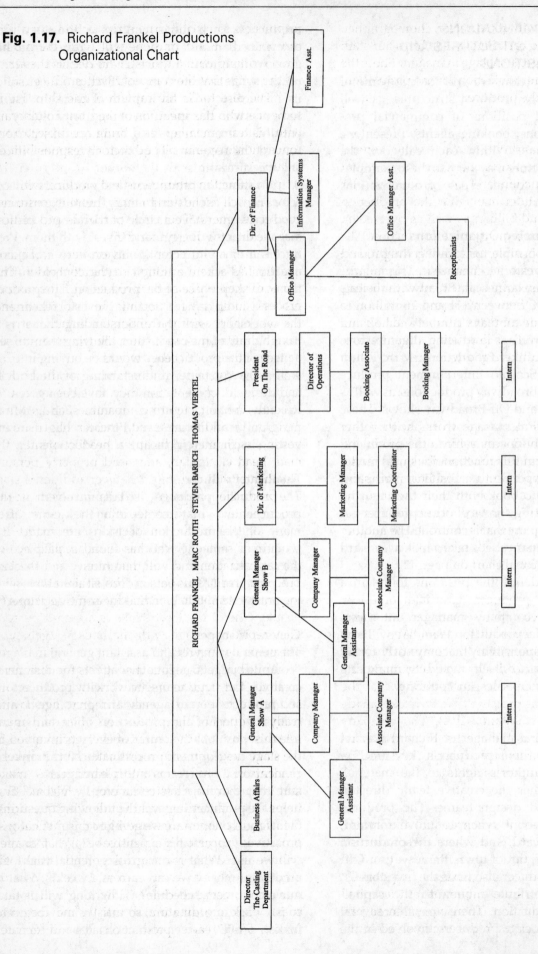

all of the contracts with the director, choreographer, designers, crew, and cast. Finally, she hires her staff: the company manager and stage managers. She is the central figure of communication for the production, and she reports to the producer.[91]

Company Manager

"The company manager reports to the general manager, and is the liaison between the cast and crew of the production and the producers. Her responsibilities include: managing the production budgets, payroll, and billing, as well as overseeing the day-to-day management of the production. The company manager is in the theater every night, and at the box office for each performance, signing off on (certifying) the box office statement with the box office treasurer."[92] On tour, the company manager also "takes care of the company's travel and housing arrangements, as well as providing the company with an overview of the city where the production will tour."[93]

Attorneys

"Richard Frankel Productions works with a law firm that gets involved very early in the producing process and helps us to structure our business model (which is usually a joint venture, limited partnership, or limited liability company) and creates the author's contract.[94] The author's contracts can get complicated, in that there may be multiple authors and they all have their own attorneys. This law firm also represents the entire show."[95]

Accountants

"Our finance director oversees the entire office, including our accountants. We have show accountants who understand the complexity of our financial models. For each show, the accountant sets up the accounts and looks at the budget that the general manager has prepared. We have an outside certified public accountant (CPA). The company manager writes all of the checks, but the internal accountant is responsible for the books, and the CPA is responsible for our external audit."[96]

Production Team

The production team is comprised of the author, composer, and lyricist (if a musical), director, music director, music department arrangers, technical supervisor (or production manager), stagehands, and technicians. The company manager (described above) and stage manager are also considered part of the team. "The author, if he's the book writer, is responsible for writing the script or the story. The composer, if it is a musical, will write the music, often working with a lyricist, who creates the lyrics for the songs that the composer writes."[97]

"The director is the captain of the ship. He is someone who has great vision and can collaborate with his team members and bring the project from conception to opening. The director's responsibilities include: working with the author to interpret the script, casting the production, and working with the actors as well as the design team (lighting, costume, and set designers). There is no part of the production that the director doesn't touch.[98]

"The music director comes on very early and usually has a connection with the composer. The music director will also be involved with the casting process: auditioning, selecting the cast, rehearsing the cast and the orchestra. Some productions may have an arranger, who creates the transition music between changes of scenes or sets.[99]

For the physical production, a producer will employ a technical supervisor to coordinate and manage the set, lighting, costume, and sound designs. In addition, "every theater has its own house stagehands, including a head carpenter, fly man, head electrician, and head property person. The theater will then hire whatever additional staff the production requires. If the production needs ten carpenters, the theater will hire ten carpenters. These stagehands are considered to be part of the production's crew. These employees are paid by the theater, and the producer reimburses the theater. The producer has no say in who is hired. We have four carpenters, two electricians, and two property people. One of the electricians is a sound person. They work backstage with the house stagehands, but are on our payroll."[100]

And finally, "the stage manager is the director's copilot." The stage manager works with the actors and production team to make sure that the show is ready for opening night.[101] Robert Cohen defines his role this way: "At the center of every production is the stage manager, who coordinates all the diverse elements of a production into a harmonious whole that is true to the director's vision, while meeting union rules, remaining within budget, and ensuring the safety of everyone on stage. The calm, meticulous, proactive, perpetually positive stage manager creates and dispenses schedules, [and] tracks all production elements (e.g., actors' blocking, scenic movement, costume changes, lighting and sound cues), while coordinating all artistic and technical needs. Since each production has differences regarding its script and design—not to mention its unique mix of personalities—the most accomplished stage managers are able to provide solutions before problems arise, all the while displaying diplomacy, efficiency, and a sense of humor throughout the life of any production. On performance night, the stage manager is a 'field general' who is literally in command of the show from a half-hour before the show to final curtain, leading all personnel through the intricacies of a performance with precise execution of all cues and patient understanding."[102]

Marketing and Advertising

In order to make the public aware of the production and to sell tickets, advertising and marketing companies create and manage a marketing campaign. Marketing campaigns contain print and media advertising, as well as special promotions that may be created for the production.[103] Two major advertising companies in New York are Serino/Coyne and SpotCo. "Their role is creating the logo and writing the copy for our [Richard Frankel Production's] television commercials, radio spots, print ads, and outdoor advertising (billboards, bus signs, and taxi tops)."[104] Marketing companies, such as HHC Marketing or TMG—The Marketing Group—manage the marketing campaign for a production, including the creation of special promotions; these promotions often ally the Broadway production with a corporation like Apple Computer or QVC Television, for the marketing benefit of both companies. Producers may work with independent marketing and advertising companies or form their own department. Richard Frankel Productions has established its own marketing department, but works with an outside advertising agency.

Group Sales

Most producers contract a group sales organization, such as Broadway.com, to sell large blocks of tickets to groups at a discount. Group sales organizations work with national and international tour operators (travel organizations that organize tours for groups), as well as other large parties, such as charities.

Publicity

The publicity campaign for a commercial production is headed by a press agent. Press agents are hired by the producer to be "the spokesperson for the show."[105] The job of the press agent is to generate publicity (positive public perception), including editorial coverage or "press" for the show; this press may consist of reviews, feature stories, and guest appearances on television and radio shows. Publicity differs from advertising in that publicity is not paid for; the editorial coverage originates from the media outlet itself. Press agents working on Broadway and Off-Broadway include The Publicity Office, Barlow/Hartman, and Boneau/Bryan-Brown.

CLASSROOM DISCUSSION

Define these terms: "Broadway," "Off-Broadway," and "touring productions."

Define the role of the investor.

Define the responsibilities of the following people in a commercial production: producer, associate producer, attorney, accountant, general manager, company manager, group sales manager (or company), press agent.

Who are the key members of the production team for a Broadway musical?

What are the roles of the advertising and marketing companies for a commercial production?

Booking Agencies

Alison Spiriti, a commercial presenter, asserts, "The Broadway booking agencies I generally work with have a president, under which is a director of Equity tours and a director of non-Equity tours.[106] Several booking agents work under the directors. Each agent has a territory in which she 'sells' the shows to presenters."[107] Simma Levine, president of On the Road, a theatrical booking agency owned by Richard Frankel Productions, Scorpio Entertainment, and Marc Routh Productions, shares her organizational chart on page 45.[108]

On the Road has a president, director of booking, director of operations, and booking agents. Levine stresses that the "president of a booking agency is responsible for overseeing all aspects of booking multiple tours; project development and acquisition; and long-range planning. Included in these duties is supervising the negotiations of all booking agreements between producers and presenters. She is also ultimately responsible for the budget of her company. The director of booking oversees the booking and management of all non-Equity productions, Equity tours, and other attractions. Together with the president, the director of booking also oversees and attends regional booking conferences and maintains the presenter database. The director of operations, along with the contract manager, contracts all tour engagements, which involves managing the flow of ticket sales and expenses, updating contract status reports, providing daily tour reconciliations (how much money is generated at the box

Fig. 1.18. On the Road Organizational Chart

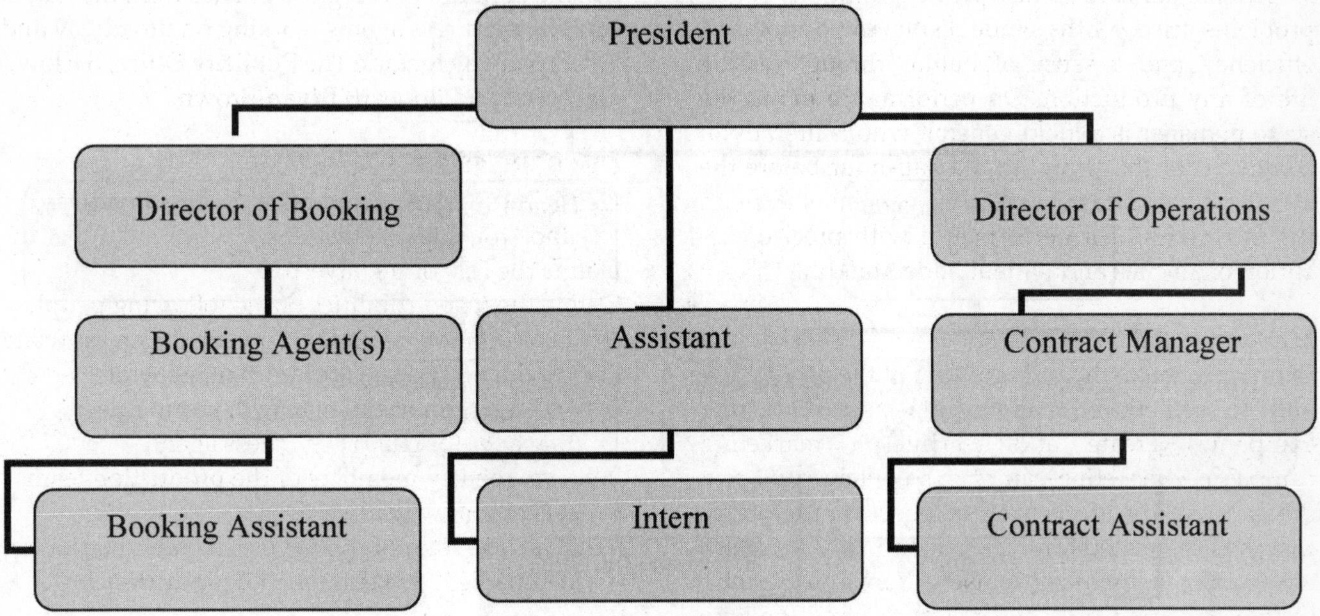

office), and issuing as well as managing contracts between the producer and presenter. The managerial assistant oversees the Web site and the brochure production and distribution process for each season, and is also entirely responsible for managing all of the regional booking conferences. Finally, under the supervision and guidance of the booking director, the booking agent sells and services presenters with a roster of attractions, gains an understanding of the specific geographic region in order to appropriately book and route the shows, negotiates engagement expenses, and attends regional booking conferences."[109]

Commercial Presenting Organizations

Live Nation is one of the most prominent commercial presenting organizations on the road.[110] Its theatrical division is based in New York, with regional offices across the United States and in Toronto, Canada. The New York office oversees and manages the programming, booking, budgeting, and overall management of its Broadway Across America series in fifty markets. The regional offices are responsible for the day-to-day operations in running the Broadway series, selling the tickets, managing the load-in and load-out of the shows, settlements, and partner relations (please see chapters 9 and 11 for a detailed description of the load-in and load-out and settlement processes). Live Nation's

partners are nonprofit and commercial presenting organizations that participate in all decisions that are made (programming, marketing, and financial). Commercial presenters differ from nonprofit presenters in that their major goal is to make a profit; however, commercial and nonprofit presenters are structured in much the same way.[111]

Theater Owners

Terry Byrne provides us with an organizational chart of a commercial Off-Broadway theater on page 46.[112] The key three staff members of the Westside Theatre are the general manager, the operations manager, and the box office treasurer. "The general manager is the supervisor for all of the theater staff. It is the general manager who has the chief responsibility for staffing the theater; hiring the support staff (including the attorney and accountant); reviewing and executing contracts; administering health plans, retirement plans, tax matters, and payroll matters; making decisions relating to insurance; and, in consultation with the operations and building managers, hiring contractors and vendors to maintain, improve, and service the building and systems.

"The theater's operations manager is responsible for maintaining the theater's schedule, including rehearsals, technical maintenance calls, and performances. The operations manager also

Fig. 1.19. Westside Theatre Organizational Chart

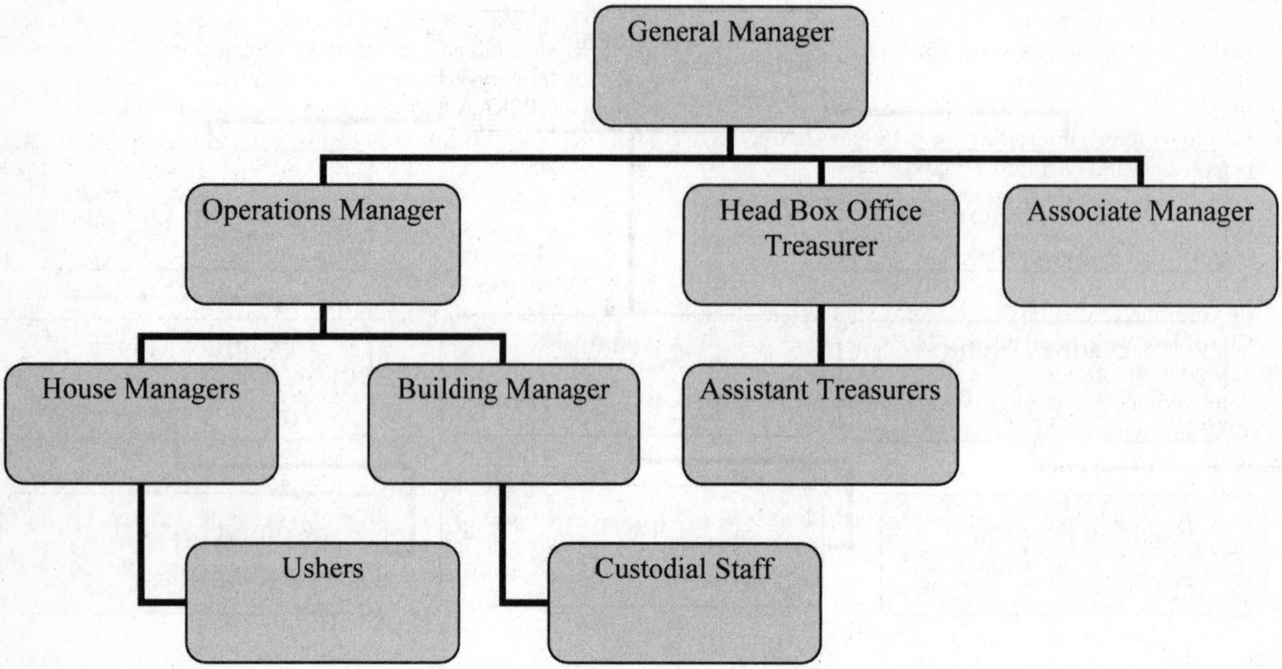

schedules other uses of the theater and lounge spaces, including readings, auditions, college showcases, and rentals. Finally, the operations manager schedules all repairs, replacements, and maintenance projects for the physical plant. In addition to maintaining the schedule, the operations manager has the responsibility of maintaining all licenses and permits for the theater; serves as the information technology expert; supervises the building manager and house manager; and assists the general manager with producer settlements, box office reconciliation, payroll, and paying bills.

"The box office treasurer is responsible for the oversight and reconciliation of all ticket sales and box office accounts, as well as the the supervision and scheduling of assistant box office treasurers and ticket sellers. The treasurer at the Westside Theatre oversees two shows' accounts and acts as the bookkeeper on both. He is the liaison with the ticket servicing center (in our case, Telecharge) and handles all communication with respect to setup and configuration of each theater; performance scheduling; ticket pricing; discounts; and customer service information that appears on the Telecharge Web site and is disseminated to ticket sales personnel. The treasurer creates a weekly 'boss' report that summarizes sales, deposits, and payables for each sales account (Telecharge, group sales, brokers,

discounts, company charges, etc.) within the system, and produces a separate report that details the group sales activity from week to week. The box office treasurer supervises his staff in the creation of credit card activity reports and reconciliation of daily sales activity and daily deposits. He is also responsible, along with his staff, for the approval of performance reports [box office statements]."[113]

CLASSROOM DISCUSSION

Define the various positions found within a
   booking agency.
Name the staff members found in a commercial
   Off-Broadway theater and describe their
   responsibilities.

NOTES

1. Public purpose as it applies to incorporation as a nonprofit is defined in chapter 3.
2. The authors would like to thank the following individuals for their contributions to this chapter: Nick Armstrong, Cecelia Beam, Kurt Beattie, Judith Binney, Terry Byrne, Catherine Cahill, Elizabeth Coen, Robert Cohen, Sandra D'Amelio, Sean Patrick Flahaven, Richard Frankel, Alexander Fraser, Robert Freedman, Laura Green, Pat Haltabloran, Nur-ul-Haq, Linda Herring, Jane Hirshberg, Simma Levine, Maria Mazza, Sean McGlynn, Carter Anne McGowan, Joseph V. Melillo, John Munger, Andrea Nellis, Valencia Ojeda, James Patrick, Greg Pier-

son, Thomas Proehl, Ilana B. Rose, Michael Sag, Michael Scolamiero, Marc Scorca, Patrick Scully, Alison Spiriti, Julie Tatum, Gina Vernaci, Jan Wilson, and Harold Wolpert.

3. Please see chapters 2 and 3.

4. Patrick Scully, interview by Jen McArdle, October 24, 2005.

5. Ibid.

6. Harold Wolpert, interviews by Jonathan Hadley, October 17, 2005 and November 22, 2005.

7. Tom Proehl, e-mail interview to author, November 6, 2005.

8. Sean Patrick Flahaven, Maria Mazza, and James Patrick, "Organizational Structures and Managerial Positions" (lecture moderated by Tobie Stein, Manhattan Theatre Club, New York, September 6, 2005).

9. Tom Viertel, interview by author, February 17, 2006.

10. Gina Vernaci, e-mail interviews to author, November 1, 2005, February 16, 2006, and February 20, 2006.

11. Ibid.

12. Ibid.

13. Brooklyn Academy of Music, *Brooklyn Academy of Music Strategic Plan: Executive Summary* (Brooklyn, N.Y.: Brooklyn Academy of Music, 2000), 7.

14. Joseph V. Melillo, e-mail to author, February 26, 2007.

15. Scully, "Interview."

16. Roundabout Theatre Company, *2004–2005 Annual Report* (Roundabout Theatre Company, New York, 2005), 1.

17. Wolpert, "Interview."

18. Ibid.

19. Scully.

20. Alison Spiriti, e-mail interviews to author, November 8, 2005 and May 31, 2006. In January 2008, Live Nation's theatrical division, including most of its presenting business (Broadway Across America), was bought by Key Brand Entertainment.

21. When an organization commissions new work, an artist is given the financial resources to develop the project. Depending on the contract, either the producing/presenting organization or the artist may own the new work.

22. Alexander Fraser, e-mail interview to author, November 30, 2005.

23. Proehl, "E-mail interview."

24. Flahaven, Mazza, and Patrick, "Lecture."

25. Vernaci, "E-mail interview."

26. Proehl, "E-mail interview."

27. Flahaven, Mazza, and Patrick.

28. Vernaci.

29. Proehl.

30. Flahaven, Mazza, and Patrick.

31. Vernaci.

32. A contract is a legally binding agreement between two or more parties.

33. Vernaci.

34. Flahaven, Mazza, and Patrick.

35. Vernaci.

36. Proehl.

37. Dance/USA Web site, *www.danceusa.org*; John Munger, e-mail message to author, February 5, 2007.

38. John Munger, e-mail message to author, August 16, 2006.

39. Dance/USA Web site.

40. Jan Wilson, e-mail message to author, August 29, 2006; American Symphony Orchestra League, "Music Matters," 2005, *www.americanorchestras.org*.

41. Jan Wilson, "E-mail message"; American Symphony Orchestra League, "Member Orchestras 2006," *Symphony*, January–February 2006, 74–123.

42. OPERA America Web site, *www.operaamerica.org*.

43. Marc Scorca, e-mail message to author, February 21, 2007.

44. Zannie Giraud Voss, Glenn B. Voss, Christopher Shuff, and Ilana B. Rose, *Theatre Facts 2006* (New York: Theatre Communications Group, 2006), 1.

45. Thomas Wolf, *Presenting Performances* (Washington, D.C.: Association of Performing Arts Presenters, 2000), 48.

46. Association of Performing Arts Presenters Web site, *www. artspresenters.org*.

47. Ibid.

48. Robert Freedman, e-mail message; Pat Halloran, telephone conversation, February 27, 2007.

49. GuideStar.org, "Internal Revenue Service Form 990, 2003." The authors would like to thank the Pennsylvania Ballet, Seattle Opera, and Roundabout Theatre Company for granting us permission to reproduce these organizational charts.

50. GuideStar.org, "IRS Form 990, 2004" (Melting Pot Theatre). The authors would like to thank Liz Lerman Dance Exchange, Brooklyn Symphony Orchestra, Opera Company of Brooklyn, and Melting Pot Theatre for providing financial information, as well as granting us permission to reproduce their organizational charts.

51. GuideStar.org, "IRS Form 990, 2003." The authors would like to thank the Brooklyn Academy of Music, Ruth Eckerd Hall, and Tribeca Performing Arts Center for granting permission to reproduce their organizational charts.

52. Sean McGlynn, "Artistic Mission and Organizational Structure" (lecture moderated by Tobie Stein, Brooklyn College, Brooklyn, N.Y., September 6, 2004).

53. The duties of each officer are defined in the organization's bylaws (rules for governing the organization) as created by the organization.

54. Wolpert.

55. Ibid.

56. McGlynn.

57. Scully.

58. Proehl.

59. "Artistic Director (Job Description)" (San Francisco Ballet, San Francisco, Calif., 2005).

60. Kurt Beattie, "Artistic Director's Job Description" (cited in Megan Carter and Erin Moeller's final project for "Principles of Performing Arts Management," Brooklyn College, Brooklyn, N.Y., 2004).

61. Marc Scorca, e-mail message to author, February 21, 2007. The music director works with soloists in conjunction with the artistic director.

62. Julie Tatum, "Job Descriptions for Seattle Opera, 2006," e-mail to author.

63. "Artistic Director (Job Description)" (Opera Company of Brooklyn, Brooklyn, N.Y., 2000).

64. Ibid.

65. Ibid.

66. "Music Director Job Description" (Brooklyn Philharmonic Orchestra, Brooklyn, N.Y., June 27, 2007).

67. Ibid.
68. Flahaven, Mazza, and Patrick.
69. The authors would like to thank the Playhouse Square Center for allowing us to reproduce this job description.
70. Elizabeth Coen, e-mail to author, January 8, 2007.
71. Marc Scorca, "E-mail."
72. The authors would like to thank the Brooklyn Philharmonic Orchestra for granting us permission to reproduce this job description.
73. The authors would like to thank Playhouse Square Center for granting us permission to reproduce this job description.
74. "Director of Human Resources (Job Description)" (Playhouse Square Foundation, Cleveland, Ohio, September 10, 2004).
75. "Information Systems Manager (Job Description)" (Seattle Opera, Seattle, Wash., 2006).
76. The front-of-house refers to the areas of the venue that are accessible to the public, including the seating area, the lobby, and the restrooms. Front-of-house staff are directly supervised by a house manager.
77. The authors would like to thank the Seattle Opera for granting us permission to reproduce this job description.
78. The authors would like to thank the Brooklyn Philharmonic Orchestra for granting us permission to reproduce this job description.
79. The authors would like to thank the Brooklyn Academy of Music for granting us permission to reproduce this job description.
80. Actors' Equity Association, *Agreement and Rules Governing Employment Under the Off Broadway Agreement (October 24, 2005–October 25, 2009)* (New York: Actors' Equity Association, 2005), *www.actorsequity.org/docs/rulebooks/OB_Rulebook_05-09.pdf.*
81. The Broadway League, *www.broadwayleague.com.*
82. Terry Byrne, e-mail interview to author, November 9, 2005.
83. The distinction between Off-Broadway and Off-Off-Broadway (performances created as an alternative to Off-Broadway) is becoming more blurred in recent years; although Off-Broadway theaters are defined by theatrical unions by their seating capacities, more and more theaters are designating themselves as Off-Broadway theaters in marketing materials and press releases.
84. Marc Routh, interview by Michael Flanagan, November 28, 2005.
85. The authors thank Richard Frankel Productions for granting us permission to reproduce their organizational chart.
86. Laura Green, interview by Radoslava Angelova, February 24, 2006.
87. Maria Mazza, e-mail interview to author, October 17, 2005.
88. Spiriti.
89. Green, "Interview."
90. Ibid.
91. Ibid.
92. Mazza. The box office statement is the record of ticket sales for a particular performance.
93. Green.
94. Joint ventures will be described in chapter 4.
95. Green, "Interview."
96. Ibid. An audit is a review of an organization's financial accounts.
97. Ibid.
98. Ibid.
99. Ibid.
100. Ibid.
101. Ibid.
102. Robert Cohen, e-mail message to author, September 12, 2006. A cue is the indicator of an action that takes place on stage (e.g., change in sound and light levels, an actor's entrance).
103. Advertising is paid promotional placement in various media (e.g., newspaper, magazine, radio, television, Internet). A promotion is a marketing effort designed to draw attention to the show in an unconventional manner.
104. Green, "Interview."
105. Ibid.
106. Actors' Equity Association (AEA) is the union representing actors and stage managers. A union negotiates salaries, benefits (health insurance, pension, etc.), and working conditions on behalf of its members. A more detailed discussion will take place in chapter 9.
107. Spiriti.
108. The authors wish to thank On the Road for granting us permission to reprint their organizational chart.
109. Simma Levine, e-mail interview to author, February 14, 2006.
110. As mentioned previously, the presenting assets of Live Nation were bought by Key Brand Entertainment in January 2008.
111. Spiriti.
112. The authors wish to thank the Westside Theatre for granting us permission to reproduce their organizational chart.
113. Byrne.

BIBLIOGRAPHY

Actors' Equity Association. *Agreement and Rules Governing Employment in Resident Theatres (28 February 2005–24 February 2008).* New York: Actors' Equity Association, 2005. *www.actorsequity.orgdocs/rulebooks/LORT_Rulebook_05-08.pdf.*

———. *Agreement and Rules Governing Employment under the Off-Broadway Agreement (24 October 2005–25 October 2009).* New York: Actors' Equity Association, 2005. *www.actorsequity.org/docs/rulebooks/OB_Rulebook_05-09.pdf.*

———. "Document Library/Agreements." Actors' Equity Association. *www.actorsequity.org/library/library.asp?cat=3.*

Americans for the Arts. *Arts & Economic Prosperity III Full Report.* Washington, D.C.: Americans for the Arts, 2007.

American Symphony Orchestra League. "Member Orchestras 2006." *Symphony,* January–February 2006, 74–123.

———. "Music Matters." Paper presented at the American Symphony Orchestra League 60th National Conference. Washington D.C., July 2005. *www.americanorchestras.org.*

Association of Performing Arts Presenters. *www.artspresenters.org.*

Beattie, Kurt. "Artistic Director's Job Description." In *Final Project for Principles of Performing Arts Management*, by Megan Carter and Erin Moeller. Brooklyn College, 2004.

Behrens, Web. "What the Heck's a Dramaturg?" *Chicago Tribune*, 19 February 2006.

The Broadway League. *www.broadwayleague.com*.

Brooklyn Academy of Music. "Brooklyn Academy of Music Organizational Chart." Brooklyn, N.Y., 2007. Photocopy.

———. "General Manager Job Description." Brooklyn, N.Y., 2003.

Brooklyn Philharmonic Orchestra. "Chief Executive Officer Job Description." Brooklyn, 2004.

———. "Director of Development Job Description." Brooklyn, N.Y., 2004.

———. "Music Director Job Description." Brooklyn, 2007.

Brooklyn Symphony Orchestra. "Brooklyn Symphony Orchestra Organizational Chart." Brooklyn, N.Y., 2006. Photocopy.

Broward Center for the Performing Arts. "Director of Production Services." Fort Lauderdale, Fla., 2006.

Byrne, Terry. "Organizational Structures and Managerial Positions." Interview by Tobie Stein. E-mail to author, 9 November 2005.

Coen, Elizabeth. "Paragraph on Dramaturgy." E-mail to author, 6 January 2007.

Cohen, Robert. "Stage Management." E-mail to author, 12 September 2006.

Cox, Gordon. "Live Nation Sells Off Theater Division." *Variety*, 24 January 2008.

Dance/USA. *www.danceusa.org*.

Dobrin, Peter. "Critic's Notebook: NY Philharmonic in Tune with Times." *Philadelphia Inquirer*, 18 July 2007.

Dreeszen, Craig, ed. *Fundamentals of Arts Management*. 4th ed. Amherst, Mass.: Arts Extension Service, 2003.

Flahaven, Sean Patrick. "Organizational Structures and Managerial Positions." Interview by Tobie Stein. E-mail to author, 18 October 2005.

Flahaven, Sean Patrick, Maria Mazza, and James Patrick. "Organizational Structures and Managerial Positions Lecture," 6 September 2005. Manhattan Theatre Club, New York.

Fraser, Alexander. "Organizational Structures and Managerial Positions." Interview by Tobie Stein. E-mail to author, 30 November 2005.

Freedman, Robert. "IPN." E-mail to author, 27 February 2007.

Green, Laura. "Organizational Structures and Managerial Positions." Interview by Radoslava Angelova. Tape recording, 24 February 2006. Richard Frankel Productions, New York.

GuideStar.org. Philanthropic Research, Inc. *www.guidestar.org*.

Halloran, Pat. "IPN." Phone call with author, 27 February 2007.

Jones, Chris. "Can They Spell Hit?" *Chicago Tribune*, 19 March 2006.

The League of Off-Broadway Theatres & Producers. *www.offbroadway.org*.

The League of Resident Theatres. "Member Theatres." The League of Resident Theatres. *www.lort.org/members.htm*.

———. "Membership Requirements." The League of Resident Theatres. *www.lort.org/newmembership.htm*.

———. "The By-Laws of the League of Resident Theatres." The League of Resident Theatres. *www.lort.org/by-laws.htm*.

Levine, Simma. "Organizational Structures and Managerial Positions." Interview by Tobie Stein. E-mails to author, 17 November 2005 and 14 February 2006.

Liz Lerman Dance Exchange. "Liz Lerman Dance Exchange Organizational Chart." Takoma Park, Md., 2006. Photocopy.

Lortel Archives: The Internet Off-Broadway Database. "About the Lortel Archives." Lucille Lortel Foundation. *www.lortel.org/LLA_archive/index.cfm*.

Mazza, Maria. "Organizational Structures and Managerial Positions." Interview by Tobie Stein. E-mail to author, 17 October 2005.

McGlynn, Sean. "Artistic Mission and Organizational Structures Lecture." 6 September 2004. Brooklyn College, Brooklyn, NY.

McKinley, Jesse. "Far from the Spotlight, the True Powers of Broadway." *New York Times*, 16 February 2006.

———. "The High Cost of Breaking Even," *New York Times*, 26 February 2006.

McNulty, Timothy. "While Some Cities Take Do-It-Yourself Approach, Pittsburgh Books Broadway Tours." *Pittsburgh Post Gazette*, 6 May 2007.

Melillo, Joseph V. "Programming." E-mail to author, 26 February 2007.

Melting Pot Theatre. "Melting Pot Theatre Organizational Chart." New York, 2006. Photocopy.

Mulcahy, Lisa. *Building the Successful Theater Company*. New York: Allworth Press, 2002.

Munger, John. "Dance/USA." E-mail to author, 16 August 2006.

O'Hare, Patrick K. "Organizing a Nonprofit." In *The Nonprofit Legal Landscape*, edited by Thomas K. Hyatt. Washington, D.C.: BoardSource, 2005.

On the Road. "On the Road Organizational Chart." New York, 2006. Photocopy.

OPERA America. *www.operaamerica.org*.

———. Annual Field Report 2004. Washington, D.C.: OPERA America, 2004.

Opera Company of Brooklyn. "Artistic Director Job Description." Brooklyn, 2000.

———. "Opera Company of Brooklyn Organizational Chart." Brooklyn, 2000. Photocopy.

Pandolfi, Keith. "Get Your Fest On." *Stage Directions*, April 2005, 60–61.

Patrick, James. "Organizational Structures and Managerial Positions." Interview by Tobie Stein. E-mails to author, 22 October 2005 and 20 February 2006.

Pennsylvania Ballet. "Pennsylvania Ballet Organizational Chart." Philadelphia, 2006. Photocopy.

Playbill.com. "Independent Presenters Network."

Playhouse Square Foundation. "Director of Human Resources Job Description." Cleveland, OH, 2004.

———. "Vice President of Finance/Administration and General Counsel Job Description." Cleveland, Ohio, 2001.

———. "Vice President of Theatricals Job Description." Cleveland, Ohio, 2006.

Proehl, Thomas. "Organizational Structures and Managerial Positions." Interview by Tobie Stein. E-mail to author, 6 November 2005.

Richard Frankel Productions. "Richard Frankel Productions Organizational Chart." New York, 2007. Photocopy.

Roundabout Theatre Company. "Roundabout Theatre Company Organizational Chart." New York, 2006. Photocopy.

Routh, Marc. "Commercial Producing." Interview by Michael Flanagan. Tape recording, 28 November 2005. Richard Frankel Productions, New York.

Ruth Eckerd Hall. "Ruth Eckerd Hall Organizational Chart." Clearwater, Fla., 2006. Photocopy.

———. "Ruth Eckerd Hall Foundation Organizational Chart." Clearwater, Fla., 2006. Photocopy.

Sag, Michael. "Off-Broadway." E-mail to author, 19 April 2006.

San Francisco Ballet. "Artistic Director Job Description." San Francisco, Calif., 2005.

Scorca, Marc. "Opera Management." E-mail to author, 21 February 2007.

Scully, Patrick. "Organizational Structures and Managerial Positions." Interview by Jen McArdle. Tape recording, 24 October 2005. Brooklyn Academy of Music, Brooklyn, N.Y.

Seattle Opera. "Director of Marketing and Communications Job Description." Seattle, Wash., 2006.

———. "Information Systems Manager Job Description." Seattle, Wash., 2006.

———. "Seattle Opera Organizational Chart." Seattle, Wash., 2007. Photocopy.

Society of Stage Directors and Choreographers. *League of Resident Theatres and the Society of Stage Directors and Choreographers Collective Bargaining Agreement, 15 April 2005–14 April 2009.* New York: Society of Stage Directors and Choreographers, 2005. *www.ssdc.org/LORT_05-09.pdf.*

Spiriti, Alison. "Organizational Structures and Managerial Positions." Interview by Tobie Stein. E-mails to author, 8 November 2005 and 31 May 2006.

Tatum, Julie. "Job Descriptions: Seattle Opera." E-mail to Kevin Condardo, 23 August 2006.

Tribeca Performing Arts Center. "Tribeca Performing Arts Center Organizational Chart." New York, 2006. Photocopy.

Vernaci, Gina. "Organizational Structures and Managerial Positions." Interview by Tobie Stein. E-mails to author, 1 November 2005, 16 February 2006, and 20 February 2006.

Viertel, Tom. "Commercial Producing." Interview by Jessica Bathurst. Tape recording, 17 February 2006. Richard Frankel Productions, New York.

Volz, Jim. *How to Run a Theater.* New York: Backstage Books, 2004.

Voss, Zannie Giraud, Glenn B. Voss, Christopher Shuff, and Ilana B. Rose. *Theatre Facts 2006.* New York: Theatre Communications Group, 2006.

Westside Theatre. "Westside Theatre Organizational Chart." New York, 2006. Photocopy.

William Collins and the World Publishing Company. *Webster's New World Dictionary.* New York: William Collins and the World Publishing Company, 1975.

Wilson, Jan. "American Symphony Orchestra League." E-mails to author, 29–30 August 2006.

Wolf, Thomas. *Presenting Performances: A Basic Handbook for the Twenty-first Century.* Washington, D.C.: Association of Performing Arts Presenters, 2000.

Wolpert, Harold. "Organizational Structures and Managerial Positions." Interview by Jonathan Hadley. Tape recordings, 17 October 2005 and 22 November 2005. Roundabout Theatre Company, New York.

CHAPTER TWO

Mission, Vision, and Strategy

In this chapter, we discuss nonprofit mission, vision, and strategy. We will define these terms in the first section. Next, we will examine the importance of understanding an organization's core values in the development of good mission statements. We will study the process of establishing mission and vision statements, setting mission-oriented and visionary goals, and evaluating the mission and vision statements for effectiveness. We will also explore the roles of the board, management, artists, and the artistic-managerial leadership in executing the mission and vision of the organization; the distinction between management and leadership; and the process of strategic planning in achieving vision through the setting of mission-oriented goals.[1]

DEFINITIONS: MISSION, VISION, AND STRATEGY

Robert Lynch, president and chief executive officer of Americans for the Arts, defines mission, vision, and strategy in the following manner: "The mission or purpose of an organization should state why the organization should exist, say for whom it exists, and suggest the goals or end results it will try to achieve. The mission is used to carry out the vision of the organization. The vision is the leadership's picture of how things will be or can be in the future. It is a hope for something great, but may not be realized. And finally, a strategy is the overall approach or method for the use of resources."[2]

Nancy Umanoff, executive director of the Mark Morris Dance Group, defines these terms for her organization: "The mission is the stated purpose of the organization, the reason for its existence. Our mission is: 'To develop, realize, promote, and sustain dance, music, and opera productions by Mark Morris, and to serve as a cultural resource that both engages and enriches the community.' Vision flows from an individual—the artistic director or the founder of the organization. The artistic director's vision describes his future for his art form. Morris's vision is to continually work with brilliant artists to create new works of great acclaim, to attain eminence within the fields of dance and music, and to sustain a physical plant [building] where people from all walks of life can come together to experience art. Strategy is the method or plan by which we connect this vision to mission and realize it. In our organization, we ask these strategic planning questions: How does the artistic vision translate to reality? How do you apply it throughout the organization to achieve your goals?"[3]

Another example comes from the New Federal Theatre and its visionary leader and founder, Woodie King, Jr. New Federal Theatre's mission is to "integrate African-Americans and women into the mainstream of American theater." King contends, "Vision is a reflection of the theater's leadership. The organization may have the same mission, but the vision will change, depending on the leader. The strategy is a plan; having a strategy has allowed us to produce continually for thirty-five years. Our strategy consists of the things we do and the decisions we make in selecting the right kind of plays written by African-Americans and women. We then negotiate the theatrical terrain to make sure the plays and the artists are integrated into the mainstream of American theater."[4]

Kate Maguire, executive director of the Berkshire Theatre Festival (BTF) in Stockbridge, Massachusetts, defines her organization's mission and her role as a visionary leader: "The Berkshire Theatre Festival's mission is to sustain, promote, and produce theater through performance and educational activities. The mission of the BTF was established seventy-eight years ago by founding members Alexander Kirkland and Eva LaGallienne and their board of trustees. Just as it was with my predecessors, it is also my role to create a vision that will sustain, promote, and produce theater through performance and educational activities—all for the public good. Three years ago, I wrote a vision plan for the organization. I spoke of several components and ways to make manifest our mission. In order to sustain and promote our mission, I spoke of creating plays on our stages that would not only recognize our venerable past, but that would provide a home for the next generation of creative artists as well. I spoke of developing our programs for students in order to sustain our educational component. By envisioning a future filled with performance and educational mission-oriented goals or outcomes, the organization was then able to strategize or plan how to accomplish them."[5]

Nigel Redden, director of both the Lincoln Center Festival (New York) and the Spoleto Festival USA (Charleston, South Carolina), has a different view regarding vision. "I would hope that a vision is not made by one person. I think that the performing arts are essentially a communal activity; that's the wonderful thing about them. You can be a visionary painter and be off by yourself; you can be a visionary writer and sitting in a cab. It's very difficult to sit by yourself if you're running a performing arts organization. You're inevitably working with other people, which I think is sort of the charm of it all. The leader of the organization obviously has more opportunity to change the organization in one way or another, and obviously, in a startup organization, the leader forms the vision. If there isn't a shared vision within the organization, then it is very difficult for the leader to get his point of view to work. Because if you can't get the people you are paying to agree with you, then how can you get the people who are paying you to agree with you?"[6]

Maguire describes the process of merging of mission, vision, and strategy: "We have a mission of producing theater. One of the ways in which we accomplish this is by creating new work (this is a mission-oriented goal or outcome). I want to create an environment where we can develop new work—this is my ongoing vision. In order to carry out this vision, we need a strategy or plan. For example, during our recent planning process, we determined that we needed to provide workshop time and space for a new production during our off-season. We would then have the option to move the play to full production in the summer. (The active season of the BTF is from May to June, when we produce ten plays on our two stages.) We already own property that includes performance facilities, as well as housing and rehearsal studios. However, in order to workshop

new plays in the winter, we realized we would need to provide heat in our buildings. We also realized that, if we were going to operate the buildings on a year-round basis, we would need to expand maintenance staff. Furthermore, we determined that, with the support of a new marketing director, we could develop a marketing plan to publicize our new ability to develop workshops and performance in the off-season. These needs set in motion a budgeting process and a fundraising plan to heat two rehearsal studios, renovate two housing units, and create a salary for a new marketing director. From beginning to end, the project took two years to strategize, reach our fundraising goals, and ultimately complete the first workshop."[7]

CLASSROOM DISCUSSION

Define and give examples of these terms: "mission," "vision," and "strategy." How do mission, vision, and strategy merge?

UNDERSTANDING CORE VALUES

Kate Maguire's strategy for implementing her vision of creating an environment to develop new work allows her to fulfill her purpose or stated mission. Before an organization can undergo the process of creating a mission, vision, and strategy for implementation, the organization must understand its core values. Core values encompass the belief system of the organizational stakeholders: the board, staff, audience, donors, etc. These values are guiding principles that do not need to be justified; they are widely held beliefs and are at the center of every mission and vision statement. Mission and vision statements are articulations of the organization's mission and vision. The core values of an organization must be reflected in the mission and vision statements.

Core values influence every decision and goal concerning art form and presentation, community served and educational outreach, and even the degree to which the organization utilizes cultural and racial diversity in its casting and hiring practices. In the following section, five visionary leaders—Paul Tetreault (Ford's Theatre), Kate Maguire (Berkshire Theatre Festival), Mary Rose Lloyd (The New Victory Theater), and Joseph V. Melillo (Brooklyn Academy of Music)—discuss core values and their relationship to art form and presentation, community served and educational outreach, and diversity.

Art Form and Presentation

Ford's Theatre's mission is "To celebrate the legacy of President Abraham Lincoln and explore the American experience through theatre and education."[8] Core values at Ford's Theatre clearly embrace the need to honor President Lincoln's legacy through theater and education. A specific type of programming is valued by the stakeholders at Ford's Theatre and guides every programming decision. Ford's Theatre's producing director, Paul Tetreault, provides an example: "We at Ford's Theatre want to speak to the American experience. In the spring [of 2006], we are producing a revival of *Shenandoah*, a musical that first appeared on Broadway in 1975. *Shenandoah* has not had a major revival in nearly twenty years, and it is a quintessentially American play. It is set during the Civil War when Abraham Lincoln was president of the United States, and it touches on imperative issues, speaking with an American voice created through and by American artists. This musical, written as a response to the Vietnam War, is the story of a Virginian farmer who does not want to fight in the Civil War, a war in which he does not believe. And, essentially, the musical asks, 'What is worth fighting for?' and 'What is worth losing your family for?' Ultimately, *Shenandoah* is so poignant because its themes transcend the boundaries of a certain time period. More than three decades after the show was originally produced, we find ourselves in a similar situation, asking all-too-familiar questions."[9]

The Berkshire Theatre Festival also recognizes a specific type of programming as a core value and central to its mission. Maguire explains, "On our stages, we present the classics as well as new work and readings throughout the year. The BTF has presented premiere work by some of the country's most celebrated playwrights: Thornton Wilder, Terrence McNally, Robert Sheridan, Craig Lucas, Beth Henley, Eugene Ionesco, and William Gibson. Actors Al Pacino, Anne Bancroft, Dustin Hoffman, Jamey Sheridan, Katherine Hepburn, Holly Hunter, Louis Gossett, and Frank Langella represent some of the talent that performed at the BTF before they became 'stars.' Directors John Rando, Michael Greif, John Tillinger, Arthur Penn, Scott Schwartz, Josephine Abady, and Gordon Edelstein were considered 'young directors' when they first worked at the BTF. Eight years ago, the board and staff recognized the need to support and provide a home for emerging ideas and artists and built what is our current Unicorn Theatre.[10]

"We also embrace the word 'festival' and understand it to mean that the selection of plays and work is eclectic; our seasons vary in terms of style and content of production. Audiences may expect to see work as varied as August Strindberg, Stephen Sondheim, Lillian Hellman, and Charles Ludlam. Styles employed by directors and actors vary, with some directors basing their work on traditional forms, others using techniques from schools of the avant-garde."[11]

The New Victory Theater provides another example of core values in artistic programming. "We program the best professional, illuminating, noncondescending work for young audiences that we can find worldwide," states Mary Rose Lloyd, director of programming. "The New Victory Theater is a multifaceted presenting theater. We curate seasons of national and international theater, dance, music, puppetry, and circus arts for young audiences and families. Typically, we include eleven or twelve shows per season, and we must have seen each piece before we can consider it for presentation. Overall the work must have strong production values and be thought-provoking, surprising, sophisticated, humorous, or all of the above, and relate to both the child and the adult/parent on various levels. Many adults actually come to the New Victory on their own, without kids. Over the years since we've opened, our programming has received eighteen Drama Desk nominations in categories for both Broadway and Off-Broadway shows.[12]

"Some young audience programmers feel they must look for 'plays about math,' for example, so that they can link the work to the public-school curriculum. This isn't our first consideration. It's our job to help teachers make a curricular connection to the work. [For more information about performing arts education, please see chapter 8.] We don't 'just' have an education program, nor can we be classified as 'just' a kids' theater. We are a theater presenting wonderful performing arts for young audiences, and we have a fantastic education program that supports that work. The two are completely integrated."[13]

Community Served and Educational Outreach

The relationship between the organization and the community is also a core value that should resonate in the mission. Paul Tetreault talks about the audience of Ford's Theatre: "We serve two communities: the community of the Greater Washington area and the public that comes from around the country. One-third of our audience is made up of people from out of town. One of our core values is to understand the role that Ford's Theatre plays as a national institution. If you respect the position of Ford's Theatre and its history, you must recognize the necessity of producing quality work on the stage. We have a responsibility to produce something significant for all who come to see a production, hoping that our audience members will take the Ford's experience back to their respective communities and ultimately embrace theater as an art form in those communities."[14] The stakeholders at Ford's Theatre believe that creating exceptional work for a national audience will ultimately affect the quality of theater nationwide. In other words, producing quality theater will help to educate the audience.

More and more, performing arts organizations recognize the importance of educational outreach as a core value. Educational outreach involves designing educational programs for children and adults. Kate Maguire discusses the ways in which creative expression and its manifestation through educational outreach is central to her mission: "We understand the value creative expression brings to the spiritual life of our community. We know the theater can provide a doorway to growth for young people, and so the BTF provides an extensive program for young students. Annually, we teach and work with five thousand local schoolchildren through a curriculum-based playwriting program and tour component."[15]

Diversity

Diversity practices in the performing arts accept the contributions of all individuals, regardless of race, gender, sexual orientation, or cultural background. These practices influence casting, programming, selecting board members, hiring staff, and generating audiences. As a "preeminent progressive performing arts center" (according to its mission), the Brooklyn Academy of Music (BAM) embraces diversity as a core value.[16] When Joseph V. Melillo programs for the Brooklyn Academy of Music, he recognizes that "Brooklyn has the one of the largest African-American populations of any county in the United States of America." He states, "In a global context, I'm always looking for work that would communicate specifically to our African-American communities. We presented *Tall Horse*, an intra-African collaboration between Handspring Puppet Company, based in Cape Town, South Africa, and the Sogolon Puppet Company from Mali. The company was composed of white and black performers from Africa."[17]

Paul Tetreault comments on the ways in which diversity practices are used in casting performances at Ford's Theatre: "Ford's Theatre is based in Washington, D.C., where a significant portion of the population is African-American. As such, my predecessor produced programming that would speak to this community. For example, *Your Arms Too Short to Box with God* and *Don't Bother Me, I Can't Cope* originated here. When I took over as producing director, I decided to employ color-blind casting for our production of *A Christmas Carol*, ensuring that race was not used as a criterion for selection. (Our *Christmas Carol* had been done with an all-white cast for nearly twenty years.) For example, each of the three ghosts was of a different race. Audience members wrote to me, expressing their disapproval of the casting without explicitly stating their apparent belief that this was—and should remain—a white show. From the letters, it became obvious that some of our audience members did not understand our reasoning for the use of color-blind casting in this classic production. In realizing our core values in terms of diversity, we needed to reach out to the African-American community in which we reside and be more representative of our community."[18]

CLASSROOM DISCUSSION

What are core values?

What are organizational stakeholders?

What are some of the key core values found in Ford's Theatre, the Berkshire Theatre Festival, The New Victory Theater, and the Brooklyn Academy of Music? How do these core values affect art form and presentation, community served and educational outreach, and diversity?

ESTABLISHING A MISSION STATEMENT AND SETTING GOALS

We have examined the core values of some of the leading performing arts institutions, as well as the way in which core values influence the mission and help establish goals for artistic form and presentation, community served and educational outreach, and diversity. Once an organization has determined its core values, it is ready to create its mission statement.

All nonprofit organizations must have a mission statement in order to become a nonprofit corporation. (Please see chapter 3 for more information on becoming a nonprofit corporation.) A mission statement is an articulation of an organization's purpose. Kate Maguire asserts, "The mission is the reason behind all activity. A good mission statement is one that is defined and supported by the organization's leaders. It is easily understood and is specific to the institution. It is most imperative that all board members and then ultimately staff members understand and fully stand behind the organization's mission."[19]

Arlene Shuler, president and chief executive officer of New York City Center, a nonprofit performing arts organization, states, "The mission statement needs to be broad enough to have flexibility and narrow enough to define what you are all about. You don't want to have a mission statement that is so narrow that as times change, you have to change your mission statement. You also want to make sure that you don't have a mission statement that is relevant to every type of organization."[20] Sean McGlynn, director of finance and strategic initiatives for the New York City Department of Cultural Affairs, maintains that "a good mission statement should set boundaries; motivate your stakeholders to support you (e.g., organizational members, funders, board members, artists, audience members); and serve as an evaluation tool (e.g., how well are we doing?)."[21]

Why is it important to have a strong mission statement? Robert Lynch states, "It's a confusing, complex, and fast-changing world. A mission statement is a signpost, both internally and externally, that gives a clear indication of organizational direction. If clear, it then protects staff at times when a new board or board members, in their enthusiasm, want something different. And it protects the board, because they have benchmarks (standards) toward which the organization should be working."[22]

Let's take a look at Ford's Theatre's mission statement, as it pertains to McGlynn's criteria. The mission statement reads: "To celebrate the legacy of President Abraham Lincoln and explore the American experience through theater and education."[23] The boundaries are clear. Tetreault can't produce work that doesn't celebrate the American experience in some way. Tetreault will know if he is motivating his stakeholders and meeting his goals if leading American artists want to work with Ford's Theatre, if audiences come and see the work, and so forth.

When Paul Tetreault took over as producing director of Ford's Theatre, he was charged with something all new leaders are faced with—creating a set of mission-oriented goals, or long-term desired results that support the mission of the organization. Based on the core values and the mission statement of the organization, here are the mission-oriented goals he created for his theater and education programming:[24]

THEATER
- To revitalize classic American plays and musicals, including those that have been neglected or forgotten

- To select works that emphasize the optimism and hopefulness that distinguishes the American character
- To produce new American plays and musicals that reflect the American experience
- To serve as a national theater by producing the work of this country's foremost writers as envisioned by our leading directors, designers, and performers
- To produce work that reflects the tremendous diversity of race and culture that is unique to American society
- To contribute to the artistic development of the Greater Washington community by investing in local artists of the highest caliber or potential
- To build our national sense of community by producing plays and musicals that explore and stimulate intelligent debate over the important issues of our time
- To cultivate the audience of tomorrow by reaching out to new, young, and underrepresented constituencies

EDUCATION
- To educate young audiences about the history, culture, and life of Abraham Lincoln as it relates to the American society today
- To incorporate the history of President Lincoln and the Civil War era into our programming on stage, in the classroom, and at the museum
- To use theater as a tool to educate students of all ages about American history and the presidency of Abraham Lincoln
- To incorporate technology, especially the Internet, to educate students across the country and around the world about President Lincoln and the Civil War era
- To serve the needs-based communities and at-risk youth in the D.C. Metro area by providing in-school programming that explores the legacy of the Lincoln presidency through the art of theater
- In partnership with the National Park Service, to maintain Ford's Theatre as an exciting and dynamic place where all Americans can come to learn about the inspiring life and tragic death of our sixteenth president
- In partnership with the National Parks Service, to upgrade, expand, maintain, and fully utilize the museum as a major component of the new education efforts
- In partnership with the National Parks Service, to provide interpretive programming, including

ranger talks, theatrical presentations, museum exhibits, and other worthwhile projects to expand and improve the visitor experience

CLASSROOM DISCUSSION

What are the characteristics of a good mission statement?

Why is it important to have a strong mission statement?

Discuss the mission-oriented goals of Ford's Theatre and the ways in which they support the mission.

CREATING THE VISION STATEMENT

Once the organizational stakeholders can articulate why the organization exists, for whom it exists, and what it wants to achieve, the artistic and managerial leaders of the organization can begin to dream, creating a vision for the future. Paul Tetreault shares his visionary statement on pages 57–60.[25]

CLASSROOM DISCUSSION

According to Paul Tetreault, why is it difficult to articulate the vision for an organization?

In developing a vision statement, why is it important to gain input from organizational stakeholders?

Discuss and define the critical components of Tetreault's vision for Ford's Theatre.

EVALUATING THE EFFECTIVENESS OF THE MISSION AND VISION STATEMENTS

How does an organization evaluate the effectiveness of mission and vision statements? Paul Tetreault maintains, "People will tell you how effective you've been. And it is not just in words—they'll tell you with their donations and their ticket-buying practices. You may also know through your media coverage (e.g., Are you being reviewed? What is the media saying about your institution?). Individual donors as well as foundation giving officers will tell you, and they usually articulate their opinions very well. They will tell you whether they like what you're doing or not."[26]

CLASSROOM DISCUSSION

Let's examine the mission statements of two organizations. The mission of the Brooklyn Academy of Music (BAM) is "to be the globally acknowledged, preeminent progressive performing and cinema arts center of the 21st century." New Federal Theatre's mission is "to integrate African-Americans and women

into the mainstream of American theater." To what degree do these mission statements meet McGlynn's criteria? What are the boundaries? Who is being motivated to join, give, belong, or participate? How would you evaluate whether or not the organization is meeting its intended purpose?

EXECUTING THE MISSION AND VISION

The board of directors, managerial staff, and artists each play a role in executing the mission and vision statements of the organization. In addition, healthy organizations have an artistic-managerial team that collaborates to support the artistic process. "Across the board, you are looking for a collective embracing of the mission by artists, the management, the board, and ultimately, the audience. Actually, these four groups are joining together to create a lifecycle. They are the machinery that makes an institution thrive. If you're lacking any one of these—artists that are good, management that knows what they're doing, a board that provides leadership, and an audience that is supportive—then you struggle. You must have these four units working together in order to get the best results."[27] The next section is a discussion of these roles.

Board of Directors

Karen Brooks Hopkins, the president of the Brooklyn Academy of Music, and Ken Tabachnick, general manager of the New York City Ballet, provide insights into the role of the board in supporting the mission and vision of their organizations. Hopkins begins: "The board provides oversight, leadership, guidance, and support for an arts institution. You want the board to be your representative and the face of the institution, so to speak, in the community. So, however you wish to portray the organization, the board becomes a vehicle for projecting an image or a persona for the institution. The board also provides fiduciary [acting in the public's trust] responsibility for the institution's existence, and therefore the board also represents the ethical backbone of the organization."[28]

However, the board does not work in a vacuum. Hopkins continues, "It is important to have board members who are interested in the mission of the institution and also are willing to support it. And it is important for the organization to delineate how they expect that support to be delivered, whether it's through attending X number of board meetings, X number of performances, giving a certain amount of money, or serving on a certain

Fig. 2.1. Ford's Theatre Vision Statement

A Vision for Ford's Theatre

Vision is essential to the health and vitality of every nonprofit organization. Without it, an organization languishes in a directionless malaise that saps energy from everyone involved. With it, an organization gains purpose, energy, drive, and passion. While vision is generally defined as being a thought or concept that is imagined and immaterial, I also think of it as foresight, as a view of what an organization has the potential to be in five years, ten years—and beyond.

The mission of Ford's Theatre is to celebrate the legacy of President Lincoln and explore the American experience through theatre and education. This statement, adopted by the Board of Trustees in 2006, is an expansion of the organization's traditional mission. With its equal emphasis on theatre *and* education, the statement mandates a new vision for Ford's. The mission statement articulates what we will do and why we will do it. Vision determines *how* we do it and what it looks like along the way. As the Producing Director of Ford's Theatre responsible for both its management and programming, the most important aspect of my job is to create, articulate, promote, guide, and expedite a vision for Ford's Theatre.

Articulating a vision is never an easy thing. It is, by its nature, elusive, consisting of the imaginative and the concrete, the tangible and the ephemeral, the practical and the idealistic, and the very specific and wildly general. It is the goal of this statement to describe my vision for Ford's Theatre as it has developed over the past three years with significant input from the Board, artists, staff, consultants, and colleagues.

To aid in the presentation of my vision, this document has been divided into four parts: artistic, education, management, and governance. These four areas overlap and all work toward the fulfillment of the mission.

Artistic

Theatre has always been at the core of Ford's Theatre Society's reason for being, and, although this core is expanding to include educational programming of equal weight and stature, theatre is, and will always remain, a central component to the fulfillment of our mission. Space and time limit our ability to grow theatre-based revenues and audience, but the pursuit of excellence is an ongoing challenge. Artistic excellence on our stage is at the heart of my vision for Ford's Theatre. It begins with programming—the selection of the plays and musicals that we produce—and, therefore, programming *must* be the most important and essential focus of my vision for theatre at Ford's.

Ford's should always produce work that is uniquely American in its expression. These can be American classics, musicals, or new work, but they must all share in common a deep understanding of, and appreciation for, what it means to be an American. This theatre has the potential to contribute to the body of dramatic literature significantly by presenting new works, such as *Meet John Doe*, and commissioning new works, as in the case of playwright James Still, who will write a new play about Abraham Lincoln for the 2008–2009 Lincoln Bicentennial Season.

Central to my vision for programming at Ford's is the principle of diversity in the broadest sense of the word. Lincoln embraced all life as having worth, regardless of race, sex, social status, or education. This inclusiveness was, I believe, a key to his success as a leader and the reason that he is openly embraced by so many varied groups as this nation's greatest leader. It seems fitting that Ford's Theatre should champion this principle. Ford's seeks to attract the most diverse audience possible through programming that reflects a wide range of cultural, social, racial, political, and humanitarian concerns. I am also committed to hiring a diverse company of artists, craftspeople, technicians, and support staff, as we bring this vision of humanity to life in every aspect of our work.

While *what* we produce is key, *how* we produce it is equally important to our success. I envision Ford's as a theatre that attracts leading directors, actors, designers, and craftsmen from across the country. In order to attract top-level talent, we need to provide artists with the ability and resources to realize *their own* visions. We must offer competitive wages, an outstanding support staff, a com-

Fig. 2.1. (continued)

fortable working environment, high-quality materials, and state-of-the-art facilities in order to create a home that is welcoming and supportive.

I envision Ford's as, essentially, a *national* theatre. With our unique position in American history, our extraordinary ties to the federal government, and the historic nature of our producing venue, we have unmatched potential to become a cultural destination for all Americans. With productions of plays and musicals such as *State of the Union* and *Shenandoah*, we have the ability to contribute to the national debate regarding the great issues of our time, in ways both constructive and healing.

Ford's also has the distinct responsibility to nurture and develop the talent of those artists who live and work in Washington, as we have done with this season's completely "homegrown" production of August Wilson's *Jitney*. Artists nurtured by Ford's can go on to take their place in the national theatre community, returning to Ford's time and time again as the place that gave them support.

Finally, Ford's can set the artistic standard and provide leadership to the Washington theatre community. I envision our staff establishing productive, collegial relationships with their counterparts at other local theatres, believing that a healthy and thriving theatre community helps us all.

Education

While growth in the theatre is limited, educational programming provides Ford's with an extraordinary and relatively open-ended opportunity for expansion. Until recently, education at Ford's had not been pursued as a separate venture. We do not have a Director of Education or a Department of Education, but all of that is about to change in exciting and profound new ways.

An education department at Ford's will provide unprecedented educational opportunities in American history, specifically using Abraham Lincoln, his presidency, and the Civil War as a point of departure. By tapping into our theatrical talents and master storytelling skills, Ford's will present history and the social sciences to students of all ages in ways that are compelling, entertaining, and unforgettable.

I envision an education program that is based at our Tenth Street "campus"—including the Theatre, Petersen House, and the new education center to be located directly across from the Theatre—and which, through the Web and off-site programming, also reaches into classrooms across the nation.

I embrace the concept of a Ford's Theatre Web site that is the "go-to" Web site for students who wish to learn about Lincoln, his presidency, the Civil War, and Lincoln's legacy. This imaginatively designed Web site will provide access to an inexhaustible amount of information for students and will include teaching curriculums and programs for educators. It will provide an exciting and interactive way to engage students in the pursuit of the values of this country's most important President and his unparalleled examples of leadership and moral vision.

Theatre is also an extraordinary teaching tool, and I envision the creation of a number of original theatrical presentations that present directly relevant historical information through theatrical storytelling, along the lines of the highly successful *One Destiny*. Creative dramatics and work with visiting artists will also serve as the foundation for on- and off-site classroom experiences designed to give students an experiential understanding of the challenges that President Lincoln faced during his presidency. These plays would supplement those which we already produce, which often indirectly explore aspects of the presidency and the social concerns confronted by Lincoln—and by Americans still today.

As part of the new Department of Education, I envision a reimagined museum. Visitors would begin their journey in the newly redesigned museum in Ford's Theatre, which will provide them with a context for their visit to Ford's by telling the story of Washington, D.C., as it was during Lincoln's presidency. Visitors would then move into the theatre for a presentation that focuses on the tragic events of April 14, 1865. They would continue their journey across the street at the Petersen House, where they would learn more about Lincoln's final hours. Visitors would end their journey in the education center with changing exhibitions that explore Lincoln's legacy and the lasting effect his presidency—and its untimely ending—has had on our country. New classrooms will offer additional opportunities for families to explore Lincoln's legacy through a variety of theatre and creative dramatics-based opportunities.

Finally, I envision an education program that reaches deep into the underserved and underprivileged communities of the greater Washington, D.C., area. By providing after-school programming, artist residencies, and creative competitions, Ford's Theatre will be able to impact positively the lives of many young students who might otherwise be defeated by the barriers of poverty, crime, and a lack of educational opportunities.

In the future, Ford's will become a place where scholars and future leaders of America can come to study the great lessons in leadership that Lincoln's presidency offers. It is my hope that this "Leadership Institute" will ultimately become a place that will train future leaders to be the most effective and inspiring leaders possible.

Management

The best programming cannot exist without great management. It is management's job to provide the resources for the programming: to develop, prepare, produce, maintain, and promote the work that Ford's presents on its stage, on the Internet, in the museums, and in the classrooms.

First and foremost, I am committed to economic sustainability and fiscal responsibility. Management will always work with a balanced budget, which is the foundation of fiscal responsibility. I also plan to increase the reserves substantially, which is a necessary component of economic security and sustainability.

Great management begins with a great staff, and I want to assemble a staff that will be the envy of the American theatre. The senior staff will be the leaders of the theatrical and educational communities, bringing to Ford's unique abilities and experience in finance, marketing, development, press relations, general management, audience services, education, and artistic management. In the coming years, I see us significantly increasing the size of our staff to reflect the expansion of our mission. Within the next several years, I anticipate hiring a Director of Education, as well as Associate Directors of Education in Theatre and Museums. We will also need to expand our Development and Communications Departments to provide our programming with maximum funding and earned income. The expansion of staff will require the expansion of space and support materials, all of which are covered in our plan to purchase the property at 514 Tenth Street.

Ford's has a unique relationship with the National Park Service. My vision for Ford's is to create a better-integrated institution that works more collaboratively with the NPS in order to create a fully seamless sense for the public as to where the "historic site" ends and the "theatre" begins. I see Ford's working with the NPS to design more effective presentations and exhibits, as well as a more polished and welcoming historic site.

Governance

As a not-for-profit organization, Ford's relies on governance by the Board of Trustees. No vision of this organization can be considered complete without addressing the place of the Board in that vision.

I see the Board as an active, *essential* partner in maintaining, nurturing, and developing a healthy organization. By working with senior management to plan for the future, establish broad managerial policies, and raise the funds needed to sustain the mission of Ford's Theatre Society, the Board fulfills a critical leadership role without which the organization cannot survive.

In no area is the Board's involvement more critical than in that of fundraising. This is particularly true as we prepare to launch a $40 million campaign—a campaign that has no chance of success without 100 percent participation and commitment from the Board. And success is essential if we are to fulfill our newly revised and expanded mission. The additional space, renovated facilities, improved audience services, and increased endowment envisioned in the plans for the capital campaign are all foundational to the healthy growth of this institution. Without the successful completion of the campaign, I see only a period of stagnancy as Ford's struggles to maintain the status quo.

Fig. 2.1. (continued)

No institution has a better opportunity than Ford's to tap into a unique place in the national psyche in order to attract funding from an almost unlimited number of sources. We have already expanded our Board to include prominent members of the corporate and funding communities. We have planned multiple cultivation events designed to position us for a successful campaign. There is, of course, much more to be done. With the Board's help, I want to create "Friends of Ford's" chapters from Seattle to Orlando. I look to create a National Advisory Board of high-level supporters from all over the country. This group would be called the National Advisory Council of the Friends of Ford's, and members would contribute $5,000 annually, in addition to attending a yearly meeting in Washington. With the active participation of the Board and the support of an effective and experienced development team, I see us increasing our contributed dollars, placing us well on our way to providing the resources necessary to make our vision of Ford's Theatre a reality.

In Conclusion

The vision articulated in this document is only a starting place. A vision is a living, changing thing, and this vision will adapt to the challenges and opportunities that come our way.

It is also incomplete—and will remain so until action turns this vision into reality. The support, time, energy, passion, and commitment needed to realize this vision is not insignificant. It will take extraordinary effort on the part of all involved, but it will also reap extraordinary rewards for all who participate.

---

number of committees. Whatever the expectations of the institution are, they should be worked out with the board member in advance of his or her election to the board."[29]

The board members of the New York City Ballet are well acquainted with its mission and vision, featured prominently in the organization's annual report:

George Balanchine and Lincoln Kirstein formed New York City Ballet with the goal of producing and performing a new ballet repertory that would reimagine the principles of classical dance. Under the leadership of Ballet Master in Chief Peter Martins, the Company remains dedicated to their vision as it pursues two primary objectives: 1) to preserve the ballets, dance aesthetic, and standards of excellence created and established by its founders, and 2) to develop new work that draws on the creative talents of contemporary choreographers and composers, and speaks to the time in which it is made. This mission is accompanied by a commitment to expand the Company's audience and make ballet accessible to the widest possible public through touring, education programs, the creative use of media, and other outreach efforts.[30]

Tabachnick states, "One of the primary roles of the board is to help support the organization financially through personal giving or through encouragement and solicitation of other donors. One of the goals contained in our mission statement is to develop new work that draws on the creative talents of contemporary choreographers. Board members have specifically taken on obligations to help foster this goal. For example, they have instituted the New Combinations Fund (NCF), which is a group of donors who contribute money solely devoted to the creation of new choreography. There are specific events we hold for the NCF; there are specific programs that are funded by the money that they give. There are also a number of board members who contribute to the creation of new repertory by specific choreographers. There are other board members who give directly or help solicit contributions for maintenance of repertory; this maintenance is also included in our mission. Board members can be very intimately involved, either through personal giving or through active participation, in helping to raise money to support our mission.

"In addition to making contributions, board members meet to discuss the core mission: what we are trying to do and whether we should continue to be doing it. They ask the important questions: What is our vision for the future? Are we trying to effectively execute the mission in the right way?"[31]

Management's Role

Hopkins maintains, "First of all, it's management's role to recruit and work with the board because both the senior management and the board form the collective leadership that will provide the governance, structure, and lifeline for the institution's work. Therefore, you want management that is invested in and understands the mission of the institution. Clearly, you wouldn't hire someone who only knew classical music to run an institution that was all about pop music unless you had a reason for specifically wanting to do that. Mainly, though, you want managers who have good management skills and are also in tune with and sensitive to the product.

"Management supports the mission [and vision] on a day-to-day basis by raising the money, doing the marketing and press, and running the finances. Senior management exists to support the mission and vision of an organization. So, for example, the job of the director of education and humanities is to run and support a program in education and humanities. That is her focus. The job of the fundraising department is to raise money for all of the productions, for the institution, and for everything that the institution is doing. Everybody, from top to bottom, is working in service to the overall mission. At the senior management level, staff is working at setting policy and strategy; at every other organizational level, staff is executing that policy and strategy."[32]

Tabachnick concurs. "Management's role—in terms of the mission—is really one of execution in that we are responsible for the operation of the company. We have to ensure that the activities are furthering the mission and leading toward the vision of the company. That doesn't mean we're not involved in advice about whether the mission should change or not; we do that also. But on a day-to-day basis, my job is to get choreography up on the stage, or to get ballet performances up on the stage. As a senior manager, my job is to ensure that, in the most cost-effective way, the existing choreography gets on stage in the fashion in which it was originally done. I ensure that it is maintained and preserved. I have to check and make sure that there is enough money allocated to all elements of the performance, including costume maintenance, orchestra rehearsals, and crew time to set up scenery and rehearse ballets. I have to hire artists who are appropriate for the preserved repertory that we're doing. One of my colleagues, the director of external affairs, has to market the existing ballets, as well as market the new ballets that we're doing. So management has a direct responsibility for achieving the mission or following through on the mission that has been approved."[33]

The Artist's Role

Hopkins explains, "The artist is the personification of the mission. I mean, without the artist, there is no reason for arts organizations to be in business. Therefore, whatever the artistic mission is, there are groups of artists or individual artists involved who reflect that mission. For example, if you have an opera company and are producing operas, the artists who are in the operas and the technical staff that run the productions are what the organization is about."[34]

Tabachnick discusses the artist's role at the ballet: "The dancers are the tools, the actual vessels of the artistic product that we produce. Their part of fulfilling the mission is to maintain themselves in peak form to be the best tools possible for the company to do its work. In the case of the existing repertory, they need to learn the repertory to the best of their ability, to try to preserve the repertory, and to help pass it on to the next generation of dancers, who may not have been around when the original choreographers taught the piece. With regard to the second mission, the new choreography, they need to be open to whatever new ideas, new techniques, and new things are being brought in by the new choreographer who is coming to work with the company."[35]

The Artistic-Managerial Team

Artists and managers rely on each other to support the mission and vision of the organization. Hopkins elaborates, "I think that the organization has to be thoughtful about the work that they put on the stage or put on the walls in an exhibition. Management needs to understand the work of their artists, and the artists need to work within the rules and context of the institution. If an institution, for example, has labor unions, the artists who are working in the institutions need to understand that there are rules and limitations, and that they have to work within these rules. If an institution is working with a certain artist, and that artist is going to need trapdoors to pop in and out of, and that's essential to the production, then the institution has to be able to provide those materials for the artist to do his work in an effective way. And, again, when there are unrealistic expectations on either side, when there's not a clear path for working together, problems arise."[36]

CLASSROOM DISCUSSION

What are some of the ways in which the board of directors, managers, artists, and artistic-managerial team support the mission and vision of an organization?

MANAGEMENT VERSUS LEADERSHIP

Throughout this chapter, you have heard from executive managers who are considered leaders in the field. Is there a difference between management and leadership? What are the characteristics of an exemplary manager and leader? Karen Brooks Hopkins believes that there is a relationship between the two: "Leadership is a creative process that is directed at enhancing the institution's reputation, reinforcing its stability, and creating a path for its future. Management is involved in executing those things that leadership has articulated. Many times, the most effective managers are leaders, and the most effective leaders are managers. The point is that you have to have a vision for where you want to be and where you want to go as an institution, and then you have to get there. You need leadership not only to create that direction, but also to motivate others to follow in that direction, and to follow it in a dedicated way. In every case, the best institutions are those where managers and leaders intermix.

"Exemplary managers are dedicated to the mission and have the ability to get things done. A successful person in any profession must have passion, dedication, common sense, and the ability to close the deal. Leaders don't panic in a crisis, but try to stay calm and evaluate how to move ahead. They tend to get good advice from experts before making their own decisions. Leaders create communication channels that allow input. Leaders recognize that input from all relevant organizational members and stakeholders will help in the creation of a strategic plan for the future."[37]

CLASSROOM DISCUSSION

What is the difference between management and leadership? What is the connection between the two?

What are the characteristics of an exemplary manager?

What are the characteristics of an exemplary leader?

STRATEGIC PLANNING PROCESS

The process of strategic planning allows the organization to create mission-oriented goals that support its mission and vision. Paul Tetreault is well acquainted with the strategic planning process,

having created plans for the Alley Theatre in Houston, Texas, as well as Ford's Theatre. According to Paul Tetreault, "Strategic planning is a tool to help an organization focus its energy and ensure that members of the organization are working toward the same goals. Strategic planning might be the single most important process that any organization, for-profit or nonprofit, will ever go through.

"Tactically, strategic planning is a disciplined effort needed to assess and adjust the organization's direction and to make decisions that shape and guide what an organization is, what it does, and why it does it—all with a focus on the future. The goal of the process is a 'road map' providing a clear description of the intended 'destination,' with signposts that will tell team members if they are on track, and a timetable identifying progress milestones. A strategic plan, when developed and implemented thoughtfully, becomes a tool that can be used to manage the organization.

"The strategic planning process itself can be as important as the strategic plan document. While it can be an overwhelming and daunting task, the activities involved often empower nonprofit staff and boards to be more effective in understanding their roles. The very practical results of strategic planning are better decision-making, enhanced organizational capabilities, improved communications and public relations, and increased public support."[38]

Who Should the Planning Process Include?

Tetreault advises, "Every organization must individually decide the necessary players in the planning process. In addition to the organization's leadership, a planning process should include all key stakeholders at appropriate points during the process. An inclusive process helps to build enthusiasm and commitment to the organization and its strategies, as well as to develop foundations for productive working relationships. In short, being part of the process ensures buy-in on the outcomes.[39] Key stakeholders may include:

- Board of Directors: The role of the full board is one of governance and oversight. Its focus should remain on the overall goals and strategies necessary to achieve organizational success.
- Staff: Staff is a critical link between the visions and the everyday activities of an organization. The staff's involvement will ensure the realism of the plan, encourage ownership of organizational vision and goals, and unite individual visions into a single collective vision for the organization.

• Clients/Audiences/Visitors: It is critical to ask and answer the question, "How well are we meeting the needs of our clients/audiences/members?"[40]

Ideally, the process will leverage a combination of individuals who see what the organization can be and those who ensure that the planned goals and tasks are realistic. ('Tasks are the individual activities that serve as the building blocks to carry out a strategy.'[41])

"The planning process should be managed by a formal planning team or committee. The planning committee has responsibility for directing the overall work, rather than doing all of the work. By creating initial drafts of planning documents, identifying stakeholders for input, and prioritizing or narrowing information for consideration in the process, the committee can help ensure the efficiency of the process. The planning committee should not be too large—no fewer than four, no more than ten. If you feel that more than ten members are needed, consider employing a facilitator to ensure effective use of valuable time and energy. The committee should be comprised of a combination of board and staff members, including the executive director or chief executive officer, and the individual who will write the final plan."[42]

Strategic Planning Process: Ten Steps

Tetreault maintains, "Organizations should look at strategic planning as a ten-step process that will take six to eight months. The timeline and steps will vary depending on the organization and the strength of both board and staff leadership."[43]

The ten-step process is as follows:
- ✓ Initial Agreement and Preparation
- ✓ Set the Foundation: Mission and Vision
- ✓ Clarify Mandates
- ✓ Assess the Environment
- ✓ Identify Strategic Issues
- ✓ Develop Goals, Objectives, and Strategies[44]
- ✓ Prepare a Written Plan
- ✓ Board Review and Approval
- ✓ Implementation
- ✓ Ongoing Evaluation[45]

Please see figure 2.2 on page 64 for a sample timeline of this planning process.[46]

Initial Agreement and Preparation

"An organization must first assess whether conditions are right for moving forward with a planning process. Most organizations will require an updated or first-time strategic plan prior to or immediately following a major organizational change. Some examples of such a change include: senior leadership change; plans for a major capital campaign; need for a facility change; or receipt of a major grant or bequest (e.g., Joan Kroc's $1.5 billion gift to the Salvation Army).

"If this is an update or a second plan, this step might be rather brief, such as a meeting of the board of directors, or a series of focused conversations with the board leadership. If this is a first-ever plan or a plan after a lengthy hiatus from a planning process, this step could take a couple of months. However, once the decision is reached to move forward, the key is to gain consensus from the relevant participants (board, staff, and external resources) as to the substance and scope of the planning process. One will want to ensure that everyone is aligned on the following points: purpose of the effort; stakeholder buy-in; agreement on the steps; agreement on the schedule, role, function, and makeup of the committee empowered to oversee the process; and commitment of necessary resources to proceed."[47]

Set the Foundation: Mission and Vision

"A good strategic plan is based on understanding your mission and vision:

Mission: Who and what are we, what do we do now, and why?

Vision: What do we want to be and do in the future?

The plan will explain how you get from where you are to where you want to be."[48]

"An organization's mission should be defined or reaffirmed early on in the planning process. An organization's mission is its purpose or reason for existing. It should be defined in relation to the organization's stakeholders. It is what you do every day. Figure 2.3 shows the fundamental components that comprise Ford's Theatre's new mission, including 'Lincoln,' 'American Experience,' and 'Education.'"[49]

"The vision should be defined for success, describing what the organization should look like as it successfully implements its strategies and achieves its full potential (see figure 2.4)."[50]

"As you can see from figure 2.4, there are many elements which constitute a robust vision, such as: 'Expectations about the Future Environment' and 'Core Values and Beliefs.'"[51]

Clarify Mandates

"Both formal and informal mandates should be clarified, which will help inform the implications for the organization. Mandates will describe what should and must be done. Examples of mandates

Fig. 2.2. Ford's Theatre Ten-Step Strategic Planning Process and Timeline

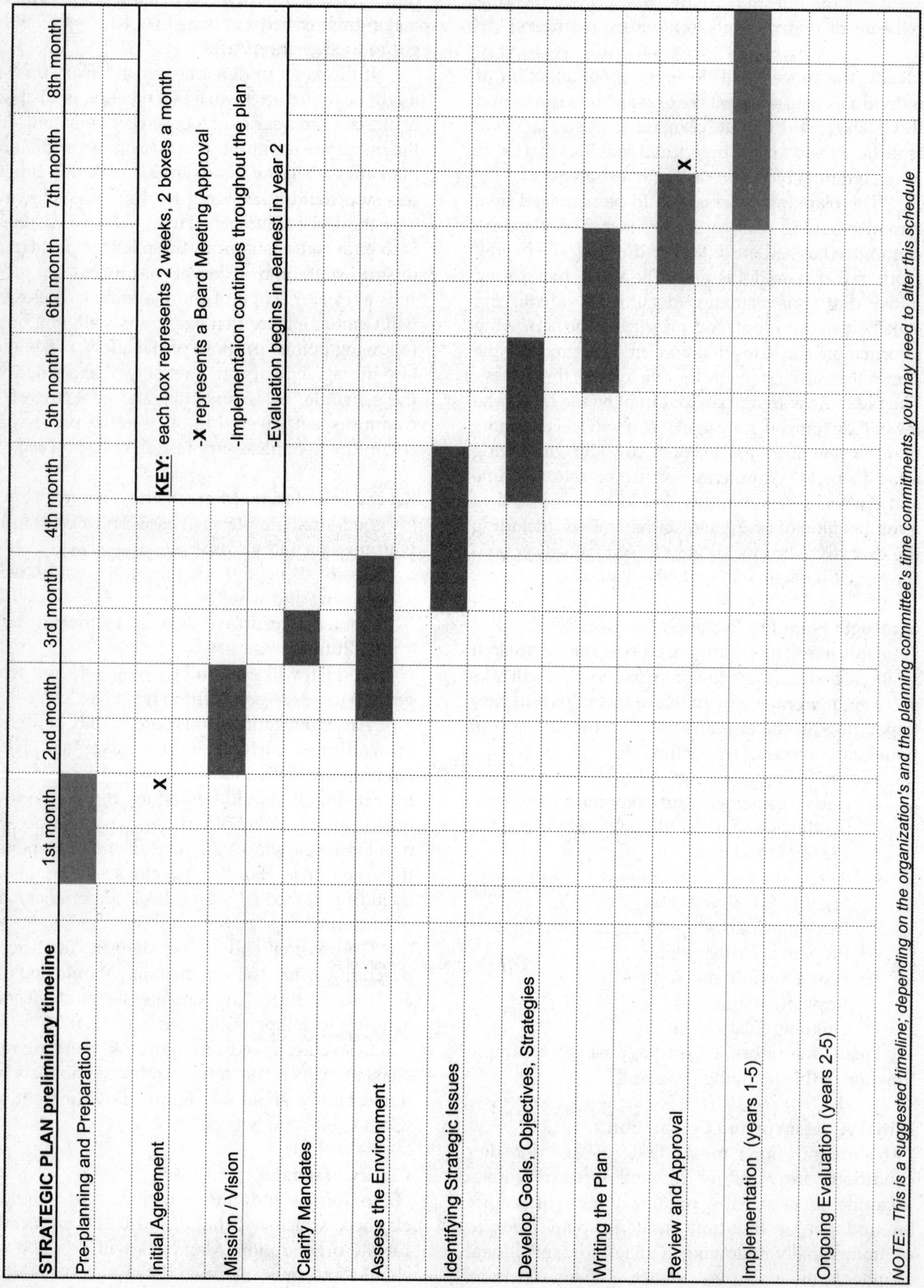

STRATEGIC PLAN preliminary timeline	1st month	2nd month	3rd month	4th month	5th month	6th month	7th month	8th month
Pre-planning and Preparation	▓							
Initial Agreement	X							
Mission / Vision		▓						
Clarify Mandates			▓					
Assess the Environment		▓						
Identifying Strategic Issues				▓				
Develop Goals, Objectives, Strategies					▓			
Writing the Plan						▓		
Review and Approval							X	
Implementation (years 1-5)								▓
Ongoing Evaluation (years 2-5)								

KEY: each box represents 2 weeks, 2 boxes a month
- X represents a Board Meeting Approval
- Implementaion continues throughout the plan
- Evaluation begins in earnest in year 2

NOTE: This is a suggested timeline; depending on the organization's and the planning committee's time commitments, you may need to alter this schedule

Fig. 2.3. Ford's Theatre's Strategic Plan, 2006, Attachment A

Building on those lessons and incorporating the off-site results led to a new, balanced mission statement

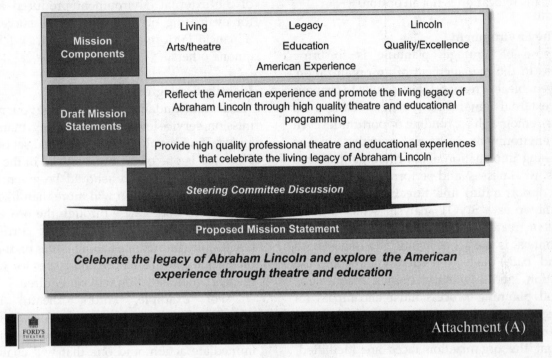

Fig. 2.4. Ford's Theatre's Strategic Plan, 2006, Attachment B

There are many elements that constitute a robust Vision that can drive strategy

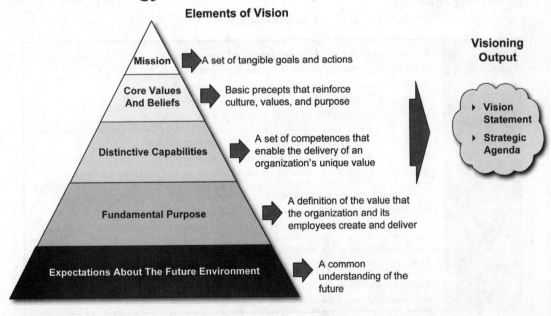

might be that the organization operates within (or in association with) a university; that 50 percent of its audiences must be students; or that the physical plant is a historic structure and cannot be altered, which means relocation is not an option."[52]

Assess the Environment

"A purpose of strategic planning is to bring awareness to the management of an organization. This will enable it to respond successfully to changes in the external environment (e.g., changes in audience demographics, funding opportunities). An external environment assessment provides a means for obtaining information about the organization's strengths, weaknesses, and performance, as well as external opportunities and threats. [This analysis is also known as a SWOT analysis, which will be described in greater detail in chapter 7.] Assessment, in this context, is the act of identifying issues, both good and bad, that are currently affecting the organization, and making decisions accordingly. Any good planning process must encompass an honest assessment of the challenges one faces and the opportunities one has to ensure that critical issues that the organization faces are identified.

Successful strategic planning builds on strengths, takes advantage of opportunities, and overcomes or minimizes weaknesses and threats."

"One can see in figure 2.5 that our assessment of the external environment produced a baseline for evaluating or determining the success of our 'Financial Performance,' 'Education,' and 'Facilities,' among others."[54]

Identify Strategic Issues

"Issues that fundamentally challenge your mandates, mission, service level, costs, financing, management, and staffing should be identified and set out clearly. This step is one of the most crucial in the planning process and, therefore, should be given sufficient time. The organization will more than likely repeat this step as issues arise through the process. Three main categories of issues include: current issues that require immediate action; issues on the horizon that require future action; and issues for which it is unclear whether action will be required.

"For example, Ford's Theatre identified education as a strategic issue. As stated in our mission, education is a current issue that needs immediate action, and one that will challenge the

Fig. 2.5. Ford's Theatre's Strategic Plan, 2006, Attachment C.[53]

The baseline analysis over the past two months produced the following findings

Baseline Findings

Financial Performance	▸ Average compared to national peers, but not its DC peers ▸ There is limited upside to increasing Theatre-based income ▸ Merchandising and concession sales are essentially non-existent ▸ Ford's needs a better mix of contributed income ▸ Endowment is relatively low for size of current operations
Theatre	▸ Widely recognized as having improved the quality of the productions ▸ Strong name recognition based on historical prominence ▸ Gala is primary source of contributed income and reinforces Ford's national significance
Education	▸ Ford's current program, including NPS, is small today ▸ Most prominent theatres have significant education programs ▸ Not currently utilizing the web to drive/deliver education programming
Tourist Attraction	▸ 850,000 people visit Ford's annually – the most popular destination off the Mall ▸ Ranks 9th among Washington DC national historic sites and monuments
Facilities	▸ Theatre facilities are in dire need of renovation ▸ Most other prominent DC theatres have completed renovations

FORD'S THEATRE   Attachment (C)

mandate of the organization. Furthermore, you will note from figure 2.6 that we have reviewed 'Education' against the education programs of our peers, and deemed education to be critical to Ford's Theatre's future."[55]

Develop Goals, Objectives, and Strategies

"Even though the two terms are often used interchangeably, a goal and an objective differ greatly because of the intangible nature of the former and the tangible nature of the latter. An objective is a definite endpoint toward which efforts are aimed. A goal, on the other hand, tends to be more theoretical, an idea achieved through a set of actions, yet immeasurable on its own. For example, an objective may be to increase the amount of artistic programming produced within an institution. A goal would be to heighten the quality of artistic programming.

"Strategies are needed in order to meet the outlined objectives, and thereby fulfill certain goals. Strategy formulation is the creation of a set of methods to address each issue that has been identified so that the organization can better fulfill its mission, meet its mandates, and achieve its goals. Strategies vary by level of importance, function, and time frame.

"Strategies are defined by purpose, key elements, manner in which they address a specific goal, and requirements for successful implementation. In figures 2.7 and 2.8, one can follow the key elements in Ford's plan, such as 'Theatrical Product' or 'Education Product,' that will need to be addressed in the detailed version of the written strategic plan."[57]

Prepare a Written Plan

"Once the vision and mission have been affirmed, critical issues identified, and strategies developed, it is crucial to put ink to paper. Usually one member of the planning committee, the executive director or planning consultant, will draft a final planning document and submit it for review to all key decision makers (usually the board and senior staff). This is also the time to consult with senior staff to determine whether the document can be translated into day-to-day operating plans (the subsequent detailed action plans for accomplishing the goals proposed by the strategic plan) and to ensure that the plan answers key questions about priorities and directions in sufficient detail to serve as a guide. Revisions should not be dragged out for months, but action should

Fig. 2.6. Ford's Theatre's Strategic Plan, 2006, Attachment D[56]

Most prominent theatres have significant education programs

▸ Conducted extensive interviews with world-class theatres and education institutions (Guthrie Theater, Goodman Theatre, Folger Shakespeare Library, Shakespeare's Globe Theatre, Carrie Nath, Abraham Lincoln Presidential Library and Museum

▸ Education fully integrated into the theatre and viewed as an integral part of its mission

▸ Spending on education represents 10-15% of total operating budget

▸ Educational mission provides a compelling story for raising contributed income

▸ Education programs are another source of earned income

▸ Programs are multi-faceted:
  – School-based programs
  – On-site programs targeted at students and adults
  – Teacher-specific programs
  – Internet programming
  – Varied Content (e.g., Lincoln-related and theatre-related)

Attachment (D)

Fig. 2.7. Ford's Theatre's Strategic Plan, Attachment E

The business model emphasizes the tie to Lincoln and balances the importance of the professional theatre and education

Ford's Theatre Business Model – At a Glance

Theatrical Product	▸ High quality professional theatre that mainly produces own productions ▸ Artistically significant works that promote the living legacy of Lincoln
Education Product	▸ Programming variety (i.e., workshops, classes, camp, video) to serve patrons of all ages ▸ Extensive online programming to stand alone and/or enhance on-site programming, video production ▸ Themed around Lincoln and the theatre
Show Structure	▸ Add summer show ▸ More student-centered matinee performances ▸ Video productions for use as teaching tools
Operations	▸ Develop fully-staffed education department and increase marketing and development staffs ▸ Fully invest in additional facilities (i.e., classrooms, offices, exhibition space and/or interactive learning space) ▸ Develop website with materials and educational kits ▸ Invest in museum
Promotion	▸ Leverage existing tourist market for short-term ▸ Emphasis the quality of the theatre and opportunities for theatre-goers to experience theatre in new ways ▸ Build national market of school children and teachers through tie-ins with curriculum requirements and continuing education credits ▸ Advertise in tri-state school systems for school-related audience and in tourist outlets for tourist audience

Attachment (E)

be taken to answer any important questions that are raised at this step. It would certainly be a mistake to bury conflict at this step just to wrap up the process more quickly, because the conflict, if serious, will inevitably undermine the potency of the strategic directions chosen by the planning committee.

"A good strategic plan will include step-by-step actions, along with corresponding financial models. A full strategic plan might also be called a long-range plan. Figure 2.9 shows the 'Summary of Initiatives' for Alley Theatre's Long-Range Plan (2000–2005), along with a detail of 'Initiative 5,' with accompanying timeline and financials."[58,59]

"Once the plan is devised and written, you will need to begin to create performance measures that will evaluate the success of the plan. Performance measures might include: acceptability by key internal stakeholders; acceptability by the general public; user impact; relevance to issue; consistency with mission; coordination/integration with other strategies; technical feasibility; cost and financing; cost effectiveness; and long-term impact."[60]

Board Review and Approval

"The board of directors must officially adopt the strategic plan, including its implementation. A board review and approval process will take on the following steps:

1. Determine who needs to participate
2. Assess who will support or oppose the plan
3. Determine what can be done to gain greater support
4. Communicate with all stakeholders"[61]

Implementation

"The chosen strategies must be adopted throughout the entire organization. Developing an effective action plan and implementation is essential. This process must be set up by both the board and management, then executed by the staff. Without the proper collaboration from both the board and management, the plan will not work. The implementation process should include:

Fig. 2.8. Ford's Theatre's Strategic Plan, Attachment E-1

The business model emphasizes the tie to Lincoln and balances the importance of the professional theatre and education (continued)

Ford's Theatre Business Model – At a Glance

Target Market	▸ School children and teachers for online learning and workshops when visiting ▸ Local, regional patrons and tourists ▸ All interested in exploring the values of Lincoln ▸ Adults interested in continuing education of the theatre and civics/leadership
Development	▸ Expand current capital campaign and grow annual contributed income target areas ▸ Focus on educational programming to attract new donors ▸ Focus on emphasizing the historical significance of the landmark and maintaining the legacy of Lincoln
Market Opportunities	▸ Built-in tourist and school-related markets ▸ General consensus believes there is room in the DC market for another high-end professional theatre
Value Proposition	▸ Opportunity to celebrate the spirit of Lincoln and learn in an authentic theatrical and historical setting
Competition Distinctiveness	▸ Only educational institution offering extensive programming wrapped around a unique historic site and a theatre ▸ Lincoln-centered programming offered in a site directly associated with Lincoln
Competitors	▸ Other historic sites in DC metro area, other Lincoln-focused history centers nationwide ▸ Other DC Theatres
Key Functional Skills	▸ Educational professionals to develop and manage programs ▸ Technology professionals to develop and maintain website ▸ Curatorial staff for museum ▸ Additional theatre staff to continue to improve production excellence

 FORD'S THEATRE

Attachment (E-1)

- Understanding and agreement of what needs to be done, by whom, and when
- Introduction of strategies throughout the organization
- Use of a "debugging" process to fix problems that may not have been thought of when the plan or action items were first introduced
- Formal evaluation
- A formal review process to ensure that strategies remain appropriate, set up by the management with approval by the board
- Measurement of impact and outcome, both internally and externally
- Timely updating of plan and implementation process"[62]

Ongoing Evaluation

"To what degree is the strategic planning process working? Management, along with the board of directors, must evaluate whether or not strategic planning goals are being achieved. Reevaluation needs to be ongoing, especially if an organization has not been engaged in the planning process for a while. The staff and board must be in agreement as to the structure of the evaluation process. As a prelude to a new round of strategic planning, review implemented strategies and the planning process. This may take place as part of the ongoing implementation stage and may take many different forms."[63]

CLASSROOM DISCUSSION

When do organizations need to implement a strategic planning process?

Name and discuss the ten-step planning process.

Why is it important to gain consensus from participants in the planning process? Name the areas of the process in which consensus from the group are essential.

Why should an organization's management evaluate its strengths, weaknesses, opportunities, and threats (conduct a SWOT analysis)?

Fig. 2.9. Alley Theatre's Long-Range Plan (2000–2005)

V. SUMMARY OF INITIATIVES

ARTISTIC INITIATIVES

INITIATIVE 1: Expand and strengthen the resident acting community

The Alley Theatre is one of the few resident theatres in the country that maintains a resident acting company. The Alley's investment in its resident company significantly enhances the quality of its productions and the development of its actors. Over the next five years, the Alley will take the following steps to expand and strengthen its company:

♦ Increase the size of the resident acting company from eight members to twenty-four.
♦ Initiate an active recruiting process
♦ Begin acting apprenticeships.
♦ Offer actors more opportunities for professional growth.
♦ Develop company-centered projects that capitalize on the unique talents and capabilities of the Alley's resident company actors.

INITIATIVE 2: Develop and produce more plays

While the Alley is applauded for the quality of its programming, the Theatre produces fewer new plays than the leadership believes is appropriate for a theatre of its caliber. It is important to present new plays, as well as to produce the best contemporary work created elsewhere and to create revitalized productions of "classic" plays from all periods. Over the next five years, the Alley will take the following steps to foster the development and production of new plays:

♦ Commission new plays.
♦ Develop a "pipeline" for new work.
♦ Create a Literary Department.
♦ Research and evaluate creating a flexible slot within the subscription series, specifically for new works.

INITIATIVE 3: Increase collaborations with other theatre groups & professionals

Over the past several years, the Alley has developed projects with many theatres. Collaborations between the Alley and local, national and international theatres and theatre professionals will benefit each by cultivating the public's enthusiasm for live theatre, enhancing Houston's reputation as a center for world-class performing arts and augmenting the Theatre's creative resources. This plan calls for the Alley to increase collaborative work in the following ways:

♦ Expand and build upon existing collaborations.
♦ Pursue new relationships with other collaborative partners.
♦ Take the lead in developing local theatre initiatives.
♦ Develop an exchange program with peer theatres.
♦ Explicitly define and formalize the position of Associate Artist.
♦ Initiate an artistic residency program.

AUDIENCE INITIATIVES

INITIATIVE 4: Strengthen outreach, marketing and developing

Over the next five years, the Alley will take the following steps to develop a strong
outreach/marketing/development program designed to build the Alley's audiences, raise the Theatre's
profile in Houston and in the national and international theatre community and increase its revenues:

- ◆ Craft the Alley's identity for the future.
- ◆ Use focus groups and surveys to develop qualitative information about audience
  attitudes about the Alley.
- ◆ Restructure the Alley's outreach, marketing and development departments to enhance
  communications.
- ◆ Expand outreach and programs that bring in new audiences.
- ◆ Develop a marketing plan to bring in new audiences.
- ◆ Establish a comprehensive development plan that expands the Alley's audience while
  addressing capital and operating needs.

INITIATIVE 5: Expand the Alley's educational programs

Through its educational programs the Alley seeks to introduce the art form of theatre to new
audiences and enhance the experiences of those already attending theatre at the Alley. Over the
next five years, the Alley will take the following steps to engage current and future audiences:

- ◆ Expand successful programs.
- ◆ Strengthen ties with Houston's academic community.
- ◆ Establish programs targeting high school students.
- ◆ Create a competitive, productive and respected internship program.
- ◆ Expand adult education programming.

INITIATIVE 6: Position the Alley as a destination

In order to capitalize on the opportunities created by downtown redevelopment and to support the
Theatre's efforts in building its audience and meeting the needs of contemporary Houstonians, the Alley
must undertake the necessary renovations to position itself as a primary downtown destination:

- ◆ Study the Alley's existing and potential audiences' needs and interests, considering
  also the offerings of other cultural and entertainment organizations in the marketplace.
- ◆ Create amenities to suit the needs of 21st century audiences, possibly including a
  bookstore and/or gift shop, a restaurant and/or coffee bar, short programs at lunchtime or
  after work, poetry readings, cabaret space, cocktails before performances, etc.
- ◆ Add staff positions to manage the facility and programming.

Fig. 2.9. (continued)

INFRASTRUCTURE INITIATIVES

INITIATIVE 7: Upgrade the facility

The Alley's 30-year-old building has been strategically maintained through the years, however, several areas now require significant renovation. The Alley staff and the Board of Directors' Facilities Committee has developed a facilities master plan that provides a comprehensive plan for renovation of the Theatre's stage areas, audience areas, production support spaces and administrative support spaces. The following capital improvements are included in the plan:

- ♦ Renovate key areas of the building and undertake deferred maintenance projects to restore the building to the high standard expected by patrons and needed by staff.
- ♦ Improve, reconfigure and/or renovate carefully identified spaces in the building.

INITIATIVE 8: Attract, energize and retain a strong and unique staff

The Alley's greatest resource is its people. The Theatre must strengthen its staff resources to ensure its ongoing creative excellence and financial health. Over the next five years, the Alley will take the following steps to improve staff efficiency and to attract and retain the best possible staff:

- ♦ Evaluate the staff's organizational structure.
- ♦ Strengthen recruiting efforts.
- ♦ Create a comprehensive benefits package.
- ♦ Encourage and enable continuing professional development.

INITIATIVE 9: Strengthen the Theatre's governance

The Long-Range Planning Committee has identified several areas that require re-evaluation, improvement, or change to strengthen the overall governance of the Theatre. The following steps will address these issues and ensure that the Alley's governance structure best meets the needs of the Board and the Theatre:

- ♦ Refine and clarify expectations and responsibilities for Board members.
- ♦ Implement a process for Board self-evaluation.
- ♦ Establish meaningful giving levels.
- ♦ Reduce the size of the Board to improve its efficiency and effectiveness.
- ♦ Establish Life Trustees of the Alley Theatre.
- ♦ Establish a Corporate Council to enhance corporate support of the Theatre.

INITIATIVE 5: Expand the Alley's educational programs

Background and Rationale

Through its educational programs the Alley seeks to introduce the art form of theatre to new audiences and enhance the experiences of those already attending theatre at the Alley. An engaged and educated audience expects and demands better and better work; thus the Alley serves its goal of constantly improving the quality of its productions by cultivating a theatre-literate public.

This cultivation of an audience must start as early as possible in the life of a theatergoer. To that end, the Alley offers touring productions for school-age children as well as programs that bring young people to the theatre, such as backstage tours, student matinees and career days. Expanding these already successful programs would enable us to attract more people to Alley performances and adding a teacher-training component would ensure a deeper impact on school-age audiences.

In order to accomplish its mission of promoting the art of theatre, the Alley must encourage talented young people to engage in that art. Building upon the success of Houston Young Playwrights Exchange (HYPE), the Alley needs to be more deeply involved with the community's high-school age population. Finally, a high-caliber professional internship program would serve not only to further the art of the theatre, but also to help raise the Alley's art to new levels with the help of input from some of the nation's most talented young artists and staff members.

Strategies

a. *Expand successful programs.*

1. Expand the Living History Series to six productions, touring throughout the year.
2. Expand the number of student matinees available by building more weekday matinees into the schedule.
3. Expand *Between the Lines* to 400 teachers per installment.
4. Expand programs similar to the Leisure Learning course.

b. *Strengthen ties with Houston's academic community.*

1. Establish an advisory committee composed of Houston area educators.
2. Develop and present teacher-training programs.
3. Create an artistic residency program in local high schools.
4. Capitalize on the Alley's existing relationships with local colleges and universities.

Fig. 2.9. (continued)

c. *Establish programs targeting high school students.*

1. Create a program or programs that will tap into the vast resource of Houston teenagers and engage these young people in the life of the Alley through exposure to its work.
2. Expand HYPE and create new opportunities for young people to become involved in the art of theatre.

d. *Create a competitive, productive and respected internship program.*

1. Establish the position of intern coordinator.
2. Launch a program to promote the program and recruit qualified candidates nationwide.
3. Pay interns a competitive stipend.

e. *Expand adult education programming.*

1. Offer at least six informances and talk-backs per production.
2. Create a "town-hall" discussion series with one installment per production.
3. Institute "Lunch with the Director" or similar weekday education program.
4. Create portable performance program for corporate setting.

INITIATIVE 5.A: Expand the Alley's educational programs

STRATEGY

	Additional Personnel	Base Year 1999-2000	Year 1 2000-2001	Year 2 2001-2002	Year 3 2002-2003	Year 4 2003-2004	Year 5 2004-2005
A Expand successful programs							
Expand "Living History" programs			1	1	1		
Increase student matinees				5	5	10	15
Expand "Between the Lines" teacher program per installment			200 teachers	400 teachers	X		
Expand backstage tour opportunities			X	X			
Expand programs like the Leisure Learning course			X	X			
B Strengthen ties with Houston's academic community							
Establish advisory committee			X	X			
Offer teacher training sessions			X	X			
Create a residency program				X			
Capitalize on the relationships with local colleges and universities							
C Establish programs targeting high school students							
Create a high school theatre program			X				
Expand HYPE and create new opportunities			X				
D Create internship program – program length to be in 3, 6, 9 month increments							
Number of interns	15		5	10	15		
Create position of Intern Director with consultant to market program	1		X				
E Expand adult education programming							
Offer at least six informances & talk-backs per production			X	X	X	X	X
Create "town hall" discussion series			X	X	X	X	X
Institute "lunch with the director" or weekday program			X	X	X	X	X
Create portable performance program for adults			X	X	X	X	X

Fig. 2.9. (continued)

INITIATIVE 5.B: Expand the Alley 's educational programs

COST	Add'l Number/ Personnel	Base Year 1999-2000	Year 1 2000-2001	Year 2 2001-2002	Year 3 2002-2003	Year 4 2003-2004	Year 5 2004-2005	Grand Total
A Expand successful programs								
Expand "Living History" programs	3 programs		$4,000	$6,000	$10,000	$12,000	$12,000	$44,000
Increase student matinees				12,000	12,000	18,000	18,000	60,000
Expand "Between the Lines" teacher program per installment	400 teachers		12,000	12,000	18,000	24,000	30,000	96,000
Expand backstage tour opportunities			1,000	500	500	500	500	3,000
Expand programs like the Leisure Learning course			1,000	1,000	1,500	1,500	1,500	6,500
B Strengthen ties with Houston's academic community								
Establish advisory committee								
Offer teacher training sessions				5,000	5,000	6,000	6,000	22,000
Create a residency program				2,000	2,000	3,000	4,000	11,000
Capitalize on the relationships with local colleges and universities								
C Establish programs targeting high school students								
Create a high school theatre program			1,500	2,000	2,000	2,000	2,000	9,500
Expand HYPE and create new opportunities								
D Create internship program - program length to be in 3, 6, 9 month increments								
Number of interns	15		30,000	60,000	60,000	60,000	60,000	270,000
Create position of Intern Director with consultant to market program	1		28,000	29,400	30,870	32,414	34,034	154,718
E Expand adult education programming								
Offer at least six informances & talk-backs per production			1,000	100	2,000	2,000	2,000	7,100
Create "town hall" discussion series			800	800	800	800	800	4,000
Institute "lunch with the director" or weekday program								
Create portable performance program for adults			2,000	4,000	6,000	8,000	8,000	28,000
TOTAL COST FOR STRATEGIES		$0	$81,300	$134,800	$150,670	$170,214	$178,834	$715,818

What are strategic issues, and how should they be categorized?

What is strategic formulation?

How do you go about evaluating whether your strategies are working?

NOTES

1. The authors would like to thank the following individuals for their contributions to this chapter: Karen Brooks Hopkins, Woodie King, Jr., Mary Rose Lloyd, Robert Lynch, Kate Maguire, Sean McGlynn, Joseph V. Melillo, Nigel Redden, Arlene Shuler, Ken Tabachnick, Paul Tetreault, and Nancy Umanoff. In addition, the authors would like to thank McKinsey & Company (Alley Theatre's Long-Range Plan) and Booz Allen Hamilton, Albert Hall & Associates, Paula Gant, and Mark Ramont (Ford's Theatre's Strategic Plan).
2. Robert Lynch, e-mail interview to author, January 30, 2006. Americans for the Arts is a national organization promoting the arts for all Americans.
3. Nancy Umanoff, interview by Kristen Miles, April 24, 2006.
4. Woodie King, Jr., interview by Rhett Martinez, November 11, 2005.
5. Kate Maguire, e-mail interview to author, October 31, 2005.
6. Nigel Redden, interview by Ladan Hamidi-Toosi, March 3, 2006.
7. Maguire.
8. Paul Tetreault, "Ford's Theatre Mission Statement and Goals" (draft, Ford's Theatre, Washington, D.C., 2006).
9. Joseph V. Melillo and Paul Tetreault, "Mission, Vision, and Strategy" (lecture moderated by Tobie Stein, Roundabout Theatre, New York, September 13, 2005).
10. The Berkshire Theatre Festival has two theaters: the Mainstage, which is a 415-seat proscenium stage, and the Unicorn Theatre, which seats 120 and is a thrust stage. For more information on proscenium and thrust stages, please see Eldon Elder's *Will It Make a Theatre?* as listed in the bibliography.
11. Maguire, "E-mail interview."
12. The Drama Desk Awards are given by a group of theater critics, reporters, and editors for excellence in Broadway, Off-Broadway, Off-Off-Broadway, and nonprofit theaters in New York City.
13. Edie Demas, Mary Rose Lloyd, and Lisa Lawer Post, interview by Tobie Stein, May 22, 2006.
14. Melillo and Tetreault, "Mission, Vision, and Strategy."
15. Maguire.
16. Brooklyn Academy of Music, *Brooklyn Academy of Music Strategic Plan: Executive Summary* (Brooklyn, N.Y.: Brooklyn Academy of Music, 2000), 7.
17. Melillo and Tetreault.
18. Ibid.
19. Maguire.
20. Arlene Shuler, interview by Cristin Kelly, May 24, 2006.
21. Sean McGlynn, "Artistic Mission and Organizational Structure" (lecture moderated by Tobie Stein, Brooklyn College, Brooklyn, N.Y., September 6, 2004).
22. Lynch, "E-mail interview."
23. Tetreault, "Mission Statement."
24. Ibid.
25. Paul Tetreault, "A Vision for Ford's Theatre" (Ford's Theatre, Washington, D.C., 2006). The authors would like to thank Ford's Theatre for granting us permission to publish this document.
26. Melillo and Tetreault.
27. Karen Brooks Hopkins, interview by Jennifer McArdle, May 31, 2006.
28. Ibid.
29. Ibid.
30. New York City Ballet, *Annual Report* (New York: New York City Ballet, 2005), 1. In this context, a repertory is a collection of works that the company is prepared to perform.
31. Ken Tabachnick, interview by Kristen Miles, May 8, 2006.
32. Hopkins, "Interview."
33. Tabachnick, "Interview."
34. Hopkins.
35. Tabachnick.
36. Hopkins.
37. Ibid.
38. Paul Tetreault, "Strategic Planning for Nonprofit Organizations," December 1, 2006.
39. Ibid.
40. Ibid.
41. Lynch.
42. Tetreault, "Strategic Planning."
43. Ibid.
44. Robert Lynch makes the distinction between goals and objectives. "A goal is a broad long-term outcome. An objective is the measured result that the organization hopes to achieve in fulfillment of the goals, which is less measurable."
45. Tetreault.
46. Tetreault, "Strategic Planning." The authors would like to thank Ford's Theatre for granting us permission to publish this chart.
47. Ibid.
48. Ibid.
49. Ford's Theatre, *Developing a Vision and Strategy for Ford's Theatre Society* (Ford's Theatre, Washington, D.C., 2006). The authors would like to thank Ford's Theatre for granting us permission to publish this document.
50. Tetreault. The authors would like to thank Ford's Theatre for granting us permission to publish this document.
51. Ibid.
52. Ibid.
53. Ibid. The authors would like to thank Ford's Theatre for granting us permission to publish this document.
54. Ibid.
55. Ibid.
56. Ibid. The authors would like to thank Ford's Theatre for granting us permission to publish this document.
57. Ibid. The authors would like to thank Ford's Theatre for granting us permission to publish this document.
58. Ibid.
59. Alley Theatre, *Alley Theatre's Long-Range Plan (2000–2005)* (Alley Theatre, Houston, Tex., 2005). The authors would like to thank Alley Theatre for granting us permission to publish this document.
60. Tetreault.

61. Ibid.
62. Ibid.
63. Ibid.

BIBLIOGRAPHY

Águila, Justino. "Calling Outlets for Their Work." *Santa Ana (California) Orange County Register*, 28 August 2005.

Alley Theatre. *Alley Theatre's Long-Range Plan (2000–2005)*. Houston: Alley Theatre, 2005.

Allison, Michael, and Jude Kaye. *Strategic Planning for Nonprofit Organizations: A Practical Guide and Workbook*. 2nd ed. Hoboken, N.J.: Wiley, 2005.

Armbrust, Roger. "Nonprofit Theatre's Challenges, Threats, and Needs Are Real." *Backstage*, 17 November 2005.

Arts Journal. *www.artsjournal.com*.

Axelrod, Nancy R. *Advisory Councils*. Washington, D.C.: BoardSource, 2004.

———. *Chief Executive Succession Planning: The Board's Role in Securing Your Organization's Future*. Washington, D.C.: BoardSource, 2002.

Backstage. "Three New TCG Leaders Discuss State of Theatre." *Backstage.com* (3 September 2004).

Beattie, Kurt. Interview by Megan Carter, and Erin Moeller. 9 December 2004. "Questions and Answers Final Project." Principles of Performing Arts Management, Brooklyn College, 2004.

Bebea, Inés. "Tribeca Performing Arts Center: An Alternative to Lincoln Center?" *The Network Journal* (June 2005): 52.

Bent, Eliza, and Covey Crolius. "Around the World in 180 Days." *American Theatre*, May/June 2007, 44–49.

Berkshire, Jennifer C. "Charity CEO's Tales of Woe." *Chronicle of Philanthropy*, 9 March 2006.

Berson, Misha. "What's the Rep's Future under New Leadership?" *Seattle Times*, 6 February 2005.

Brinckerhoff, Peter C. *Nonprofit Stewardship: A Better Way to Lead Your Mission-Based Organization*. St. Paul, Minn.: Amherst H. Wilder Foundation, 2004.

Brooklyn Academy of Music. *BAM's Strategic Plan: Executive Summary*. Brooklyn: Brooklyn Academy of Music, 30 June 2000.

Burstein, Joann Morgan. *BoardSteps: The Framework for Effective Nonprofit Governance*. Philadelphia: Nonprofit Board Advisors, 2004.

Byrnes, William J. *Management and the Arts*. Boston: Focal Press, 2003.

Cameron, Ben. "Creative Abrasion." *American Theatre*, October 2004, 8.

———. "Compounding Diversity." *American Theatre*, March 2004, 4.

Carver, John. *John Carver on Board Leadership*. San Francisco: Jossey-Bass, 2002.

Chait, Richard P. *How to Help Your Board Govern More and Manage Less*. Revised ed. Washington, D.C.: BoardSource, 2003.

Chait, Richard, William P. Ryan, and Barbara E. Taylor. *Governance as Leadership: Reframing the Work of Nonprofit Boards*. Hoboken, N.J.: Wiley, 2004.

Chang, Daniel. "Director Struggles to Keep Post at Theater." *Miami Herald*, 30 April 2006.

Channick, Joan. "Turn Around at the Roundabout: An Artistic Director Explains How He Led a Theatre from Bankruptcy to Broadway." *American Theatre*, March 2003, 30–54.

Connolly, Paul M. *Navigating the Organizational Lifecycle: A Capacity-Building Guide for Nonprofit Leaders*. Washington, D.C.: BoardSource, 2005.

Dambach, Charles F. *Structures and Practices of Nonprofit Boards*. Washington, D.C.: BoardSource, 2003.

Demas, Edie, Mary Rose Lloyd, and Lisa Lawer Post. "Performing Arts Education." Interview by Tobie Stein. Tape recording, 22 May 2006. The New Victory Theater, New York.

Dezell, Maureen. "Facing Debt, Wang to Produce Its Own Shows." *Boston Globe*, 27 April 2005.

Dobrin, Peter. "Orchestra Hires Conservatory Dean as Leader." *Philadelphia Inquirer*, 20 April 2006.

Elder, Eldon. *Will It Make a Theatre?: Find, Renovate, & Finance the Non-Traditional Performance Space*. Washington, D.C.: Americans for the Arts, 1993.

Feingold, Michael. "Even Bad is Better 'Off.'" *Village Voice*, 15 May 2006.

———. "Stage Beauty: Downtown Theater and the 'Voice' Grow Up Together." *Village Voice*, 28 October 2005.

Feldman, Susan. "Mission, Vision, and Strategy." Interview by Tobie Stein. E-mail to author, 16 February 2006.

Fishelson, David. "Mission, Vision, and Strategy." Interview by Jen Leeson. Tape recording, 31 October 2005. Manhattan Ensemble Theater, New York.

Fishelson, David, James C. Nicola, and Meredith Zolty. "Creating a Creative Team." Discussion moderated by India Branch and Halina Ujda, 15 March 2005. Richard Frankel Productions, New York.

Flynn, Outi. *A Guide to Better Nonprofit Board Meetings*. Washington, D.C.: BoardSource, 2006.

Ford's Theatre. *Developing a Vision and Strategy for Ford's Theatre Society*. Washington, D.C.: Ford's Theatre, 2006.

———. "Ford's Theatre Ten-Step Strategic Planning Process and Timeline," 2006.

Fry, Robert P., Jr. *Minding the Money: An Investment Guide for Nonprofit Board Members*. Washington, D.C.: BoardSource, 2004.

Gale, Robert L. *Leadership Roles in Nonprofit Governance*. Washington, D.C.: BoardSource, 2003.

Goldstein, Ezra. "Keeping the Faith: The Theatre of Woodie King, Jr." *Dramatics* (May 2003): 16–21.

Grace, Kay Sprinkel. *The Nonprofit Board's Role in Setting and Advancing the Mission*. Washington, D.C.: BoardSource, 2003.

Grady, Jamie. "Understanding the Roles of Management and Leadership in Nonprofit Arts Organizations." *Arts Reach*, April 2004, 1, 13–14.

Greene, Richard. "Muting Some Notable Work." *Philadelphia Inquirer*, 2 May 2007.

Hall, Holly. "Getting Over Growing Pains." *Chronicle of Philanthropy*, 6 April 2006.

Hall, Holly, and Suzanne Perry. "Turning Fund Raisers Into CEOs." *Chronicle of Philanthropy*, 6 April 2006.

Hancock, Jay. "Finance Woes at Symphony Likely to Keep It Out of Tune." *Baltimore Sun*, 23 April 2006.

Hart, Sarah. "An American Revolution: The 75-Year-Old Berkshire Theatre Festival Looks to Its Star-Spangled Past to Inspire a Still-Fermenting Future." *American Theatre*, November 2003, 32–112.

Herring, Linda. "Artistic Managerial Relationship Lecture." 14 September 2004. Tribeca Performing Arts Center, New York.

———. "Mission, Vision, and Strategy." Interview by Jimena Duca. Tape recording, 28 October 2005. Tribeca Performing Arts Center, New York.

Hoban, Phoebe. "For Manhattan Theatre Club, Up Year After a Down." *New York Times*, 8 June 2005.

Holl, John. "Montclair State Opens Theater That Has a Mission, and Ambition." *New York Times*, 3 October 2004, late edition.

Hopkins, Karen Brooks. "Mission, Vision, and Strategy." Interview by Jennifer McArdle. Tape recording, 31 May 2006. Brooklyn Academy of Music, Brooklyn, N.Y.

Hurwitt, Robert. "San Jose Rep Moves from Red to Black." *San Francisco Chronicle*, 14 February 2006.

Hurwitz, Robert. "A Raspberry for BlackBerrys." *New York Times*, 16 April 2006.

Hutton, Mary Ellyn. "What's Next for the Symphony?" *Cincinnati Post*, 10 March 2006.

Illinois Arts Alliance Foundation. *Succession: Arts Leadership for the 21st Century*. Chicago: Illinois Arts Alliance, 2003.

Isherwood, Charles. "The Light in the Lincoln Center Plaza." *New York Times*, 5 March 2006.

Jackson, Charlissa, Veronique Le Melle, Sunny Oh, and Paul Tetreault. "Diversity in Performing Arts Management Seminar." Discussion moderated by Jane Delgado, 12 December 2002. Lincoln Center Theater, New York.

Jefferson, Margo. "Will Theater in Los Angeles Fade to White?" *New York Times*, 7 August 2005.

Jensen, Brennen. "640,000 New Senior Managers Will Be Needed to Run Nonprofit Groups in Next Decade." *Chronicle of Philanthropy*, 6 April 2006.

Jepson, Barbara. "Classical, Now without the 300-Year Delay." *New York Times*, 26 March 2006.

Jones, Vanessa E. "Latino Playwrights and Their Diverse Works Are Taking Center Stage in Boston and Beyond." *Boston Globe*, 18 November 2004.

Kelly, Fred, and Dánica Coto. "Charlotte Rep Announces Fight to Survive Is Lost." *The Charlotte Observer*, 20 February 2005.

King, Jr., Woodie. "Come by Bullins." *Black Literary Quarterly* 7 (1994): 17.

———. "Mission, Vision, and Strategy." Interview by Rhett Martinez. Tape recording, 11 November 2005. New Federal Theatre, New York.

———. "Supporting the Black Arts." *Inside the Minds: The Performing Arts Business—Industry Leaders on Business and Financial Strategies for Lasting Success in Music in Theatre*. Edited by Kari Russ and Matt Wickenheiser. Boston: Aspatore, 2004.

Kocsis, Deborah L., and Susan A. Waechter. *Driving Strategic Planning: A Nonprofit Executive's Guide*. Washington, D.C.: BoardSource, 2003.

Kosman, Joshua. "Opera Summer Season to Start with Outside Simulcast." *San Francisco*, 29 March 2006.

Kourlas, Gia. "Teetering in Modernism's Temple, Minus a Goddess." *New York Times*, 16 April 2006.

LaBute, Neil. "Casting for the Stage Should Be Color-Blind." *Los Angeles Times*, 6 May 2007.

Lacher, Irene. "Theater Chief in Los Angeles Looks Forward From Past." *New York Times*, 6 April 2005.

Lakey, Berit M., Sandra R. Hughes, and Outi Flynn. *Governance Committee*. Washington, D.C.: BoardSource, 2004.

Lewis, Nicole. "A Leading Performance: Head of Kennedy Center Aims to Improve Skills of Arts Leaders." *Chronicle of Philanthropy*, 26 May 2005.

———. "Second Fiddle to None." *Chronicle of Philanthropy*, 27 October 2005.

———. "Writing a New Script." *Chronicle of Philanthropy*, 12 June 2003.

Light, Mark. *Executive Committee*. Washington, D.C.: BoardSource, 2004.

Liteman, Merianne. *Planning for Succession: A Toolkit for Board Members and Staff of Nonprofit Arts Organizations*. Chicago: Illinois Arts Alliance, 2003.

Lockwood, Marianne. "This Orchestra Is Conducting Business." *BusinessWeek*, 24 March 2006. *www.businessweek.com/bwdaily/dnflash/mar2006/nf20060324_8135.htm?chan=search*.

Lynch, Robert "Mission, Vision, and Strategy." Interview by Tobie Stein. E-mail to author, 30 January 2006.

Maguire, Kate. "Mission, Vision, and Strategy." Interview by Tobie Stein. E-mail to author, 31 October 2005.

Management Consultants for the Arts. *Leadership: The Key to the Future*. Management Consultants for the Arts. *www.mcaonline.com/MCApage11.html*.

Masaoka, Jan. *The Best of the Board Café: Hands on Solutions for Nonprofit Boards*. St. Paul, Minn.: Wilder, 2003.

McGlynn, Sean. "Artistic Mission and Organizational Structure." 6 September 2004. Brooklyn College, Brooklyn, N.Y.

McKinley, Jesse. "Exiting the Public Stage." *New York Times*, 29 May 2005.

———. "For Public's New Director, Big Shoes Loom." *New York Times*, 18 November 2004.

———. "Public Is Set to Appoint Providence Director." *New York Times*, 17 November 2004.

McLaughlin, Thomas A. *Nonprofit Strategic Positioning: Decide Where to Be, Plan What to Do*. Hoboken, N.J.: Wiley, 2006.

McNulty, Charles. "Succeeding at the Public." *Village Voice*, 25 February–2 March 2004.

Melillo, Joseph V. "Mission, Vision, and Strategy." Interview by Tobie Stein. E-mail to author, 21 September 2005.

Melillo, Joseph V., and Paul Tetreault. "Mission, Vision, and Strategy Lecture."13 September 2005. Roundabout Theatre, New York.

Midgette, Anne. "In Search of the Next Great American Opera." *New York Times*, 19 March 2006.

Murray, Matthew. "Hungry Like a Wolfe." *Stage Directions*, July 2005, 37–39

New York City Ballet. *Annual Report*. New York: New York City Ballet, 2005.

Niven, Paul. R. *Balanced Scorecard Step-by-Step for Government and Nonprofit Agencies*. Hoboken, N.J.: John Wiley & Sons, 2003.

Page, Tim. "Chicago Symphony Names Haitink and Boulez to Conducting Posts." *Washington Post*, 28 April 2006.

———. "A Leading Question for the NSO." *Washington Post*, 16 April 2006.

Pandolfi, Keith. "Get Your Fest On." *Stage Directions*, April 2005, 60–61.

Panepento, Peter. "Crafting a New Role." *Chronicle of Philanthropy*, 13 October 2005.

Papatola, Dominic P. "Guthrie Ticket Holders Seethe Over New Seating." *Minnesota's Pioneer Press*, 8 April 2006.

Patterson, Sally. *Generating Buzz: Strategic Communication for Nonprofit Boards*. Washington, D.C.: BoardSource, 2006.

Perrone, Michela M., and Janis Johnston. *Presenting Strategic Planning: Choosing the Right Method for Your Nonprofit Organization*. Washington, D.C.: BoardSource, 2005.

Phills, James A. "The Sound of No Music." *Stanford Social Innovation*, 2 (Fall 2004): 45-53.

Pogrebin, Robin. "Baryshnikov Center Gets Resident Theater." *New York Times*, 12 September 2007.

———. "Saratoga Center Cited for Mismanagement." *New York Times*, 23 November 2004.

Post, Paul. "Audit: SPAC Now On the Right Track." *Saratogian*, 16 March 2006.

———. "SPAC Panel Picks 10 Proposed New Members." *Saratogian*, 12 May 2005.

Pressley, Nelson. "Ford's Star General." *Washington Post*, 26 September 2004.

Preston, Caroline. "It Takes a Village." *Chronicle of Philanthropy*, 13 October 2005.

Proscio, Tony, and Clara Miller. "Steppenwolf's New Stage." *Stanford Social Innovation*, 1 (Winter 2003): 66-73.

Redden, Nigel. "Mission, Vision, and Strategy." Interview by Ladan Hamidi-Toosi. Tape recording, 3 March 2006. Lincoln Center, New York.

Renz, David O. "Exploring the Puzzle of Board Design: What's Your Type?" *The Nonprofit Quarterly* 11, no. 4 (Winter 2004).

Rizzo, Frank. "Managing Director Decides to Quit Job at Long Wharf." *Hartford Courant*, 4 August 2005.

Robertson, Campbell. "A Black 'Cat,' Catching an Elusive Audience." *New York Times*, 20 March 2008.

———. "La Jolla Playhouse Gets New Artistic Director," *New York Times*, 10 April 2007.

Roche, Nancy, and Jaan Whitehead, eds. *The Art of Governance*. New York: Theatre Communications Group, 2005.

Rockwell, John. "Kevin McKenzie Keeps American Ballet Theater in a State of Permanent Renewal." *New York Times*, 21 May 2006.

———. "The Martha Graham Troupe Looks Back on 80 Years of Milestones." *New York Times*, 20 April 2006.

Royce, Graydon. "Guthrie Theater Ends Year in the Black Even Though Spending Rose Nearly 30%." *Star Tribune*, 17 July 2007.

S.D., Trav. "Return of the Repressed." *Village Voice*, 4 January 2005.

Seiffert, Alan F. "Producing Minority Art: A Conversation with Woodie King." *The Newsletter of the Arts Administration Program at New York University*, Winter/Spring 1987.

Shuler, Arlene. "Mission, Vision, and Strategy." Interview by Christina Klapper. Tape recording, 3 March 2006. New York City Center, New York.

———. "Mission, Vision, and Strategy." Interview by Cristin Kelly. Tape recording, 24 May 2006. New York City Center, New York.

Smith, Tim. "Black Tenors Fight Prejudice in Quest for Opera's Leading Roles." *Baltimore Sun*, 28 March 2006.

Stevens, Susan Kenny. *Nonprofit Lifecycles: Stage-Based Wisdom for Nonprofit Capacity*. Long Lake, Minn.: Stagewise Enterprises, 2002.

Stoudt, Charlotte, ed. *Stages of Transformation: Collaborations of the National Theatre Artist Residency Program*. New York: Theatre Communications Group, 2005.

Stryker, Mark. "10 Years & Counting." *Detroit Free Press*, 16 April 2006.

Summey, Jonathan. "Final Project." Principles of Performing Arts Management, Brooklyn College, 2003.

Tabachnick, Ken. "Mission, Vision, and Strategy." Interview by Kristen Miles. Tape recording, 8 May 2006. New York City Ballet, New York.

Tetreault, Paul. "Alley Theatre Lecture." 21 September 2004. Manhattan Theatre Club, New York.

———. "Ford's Theatre Mission Statement and Goals (Draft)." Washington, D.C., 2006. Photocopy.

———. "Mission, Vision, and Strategy." Interview by Tobie Stein. E-mail to author, 29 October 2005.

———. "Strategic Planning for Nonprofit Organizations." E-mail to author, 1 December 2006.

———. "A Vision for Ford's Theatre." Washington, D.C., 2006. Photocopy.

Theatre Communications Group. "For Institutions, Is Art the Bottom Line?" *American Theatre*, May/June 2003, 32.

Trescott, Jacqueline. "Ford's Upgrade Puts Lincoln at Center Stage." *Washington Post*, 26 October 2007.

Tribeca Performing Arts Center. "BMCCPAC Business Plan." New York, 2005. Photocopy.

Tweeten, Byron. *Transformational Boards: A Practical Guide to Engaging Your Board and Embracing Change*. San Francisco: Jossey-Bass, 2002.

Umanoff, Nancy. "Mission, Vision, and Strategy." Interview by Kristen Miles. Tape recording, 24 April 2006. Mark Morris Dance Group, Brooklyn, N.Y.

Wakin, Daniel J. "New Boss at Opera, Emphasis on the New." *New York Times*, 7 May 2007.

———. "Joseph Volpe Bids the Met a Most Operatic Adieu." *New York Times*, 30 April 2006.

Warshawski, Morrie, ed. "Organizational Self-Assessment Checklist." National Endowment for the Arts—Lessons Learned: Essays. *http://arts.endow.gov/resources/Lessons/ WARSHAWSKI.html*.

Weiss, Ella. "Mission, Vision, and Strategy." Interview by Tobie Stein. E-mail to author, 15 November 2005.

Weiss, Hedy. "Steppenwolf's 30th Is Risky Business." *Chicago Sun-Times*, 10 February 2005.

West, Martha Ullman. "Making Dance Sing: Mark Morris's Choreography for Opera," *Chronicle of Higher Education*, 20 April 2007.

Whitehead, Jaan. "Art Will Out." *American Theatre*, October 2002, 30.

Wisdom, Barry. "To Premiere or Not to Premiere." *Backstage*, 20 January 2006.

Yankey, John A., and Amy McClellan. *The Nonprofit Board's Role in Planning and Evaluation*. Washington, D.C.: BoardSource, 2003.

CHAPTER THREE

Nonprofit Formation and Legal Considerations

In this chapter, we will discuss the decision to incorporate as a nonprofit organization. We will then explore the process of forming a nonprofit corporation, creating a mission statement and adopting bylaws, and securing and maintaining tax-exempt status. We will also examine the fiduciary and legal duties of the board of directors. The authors stress that the information contained in this chapter is to be used purely for educational purposes and is not meant to replace the need for legal counsel. In solving a legal problem, we suggest consulting an attorney specializing in nonprofit corporate law.[1]

TO INCORPORATE OR NOT TO INCORPORATE?

Performing arts managers and artists may want to create their own nonprofit corporation for the purpose of effectuating a mission and vision that will benefit the community. In this section, we will define "incorporation" and the characteristics of nonprofit corporations. We will discuss the decision to incorporate and explore alternatives to incorporation as a nonprofit.

A corporation, whether for-profit or nonprofit, is a legal entity with its own identity separate from the owners, directors, and officers of the business.[2] A corporation can own property, enter into contracts, incur debt, and conduct business under its own name. In addition, corporations are regarded as having perpetual life, unless stated otherwise in their organizing papers; a corporation's existence is not dependent on the continued participation of its original directors and officers.

It is important to distinguish the difference between for-profit and nonprofit corporations. A for-profit corporation exists to make a profit or to make money. For-profit corporations have investors or shareholders who own the corporation and can earn income based on its earnings or profits. The primary purpose of a nonprofit is to serve a public,

nonprofit purpose. In fact, it must be clearly stated in the articles of incorporation (the state-required document for forming a corporation, also known as the certificate of incorporation) that the primary purpose of the corporation is nonpecuniary—that it is not in the business of making money. In fact, if there is a surplus in any given year, it must be allocated to support the nonprofit corporation and its mission, not distributed among its employees, directors, or officers. However, if a nonprofit organization is doing well and can reasonably afford to raise salaries without compromising its programs, a well-deserving manager can certainly be given a raise, as long as it is considered to be reasonable and customary for industry standards in the given geographic area. (It should be noted that the managers, directors, and officers of a nonprofit corporation manage it for the benefit of the public. They do not own it.)

Along with having a public purpose, the nonprofit corporation must meet annual local, state, and federal filing and reporting requirements for the rest of its existence until it dissolves. (Remember, corporations—unless their creators choose otherwise—are created with perpetual life.). For the most part, nonprofit performing arts organizations are incorporated in the state where they do business, though they have the option of incorporating elsewhere and registering to do business in the state in which they reside. Corporate formation is governed by state law and, since laws vary from state to state (though the general principles are the same), it's necessary to contact the attorney general, secretary of state, or other state government office responsible for forming corporations to determine the requirements for formation.

A nonprofit corporation must also have a board of directors or trustees (the minimum number varies by state), which has the responsibility of governing the organization in the public interest and has the ability to hire and fire its executive manager(s). Board members and officers of a corporation have limited liability. They are not held personally responsible for the company's fiscal obligations, except in specific circumstances that will be discussed later.

Many nonprofit organizations incorporate because they want to be eligible for exemption from federal, state, and local taxes. A nonprofit organization must apply to the federal government for tax-exempt status. This tax-exempt status makes it easier for nonprofit organizations to apply for and receive grant monies from individuals, corporations, foundations, and government agencies. Nonprofit incorporation gives its officers and directors limited liability (as mentioned previously) and a formal structure for operating, always placing the purpose above the personal interests of the individuals associated with it.

In making the decision to form a nonprofit corporation, a performing arts organization needs to determine if such incorporation is necessary. According to Amy Schwartzman, an attorney specializing in nonprofit corporate law, "If your desires are to produce on a regular and ongoing basis; your main goal is not to make money, but to produce the work; and you are prepared to take on the taxation and corporate filing obligations that go along with incorporating, then you may be ready to incorporate."[3]

However, if an organization's only purpose is to advance a director's own artistic ambitions, and it is not otherwise interested in educating or serving the public through the presentation of theater, dance, opera, workshops, and classes, then it is not operating in the public interest. Finally, an organization shouldn't incorporate as a nonprofit if at some point it wants to become a for-profit corporation, since the assets of a nonprofit corporation can't be transferred to a for-profit corporation or private individual. (In fact, as discussed later in this chapter, the certificate of incorporation should provide that, in the event the corporation is dissolved, the assets of a nonprofit corporation be distributed for a tax-exempt purpose, usually to an organization whose purpose is close to that corporation's purpose.)

Thus, incorporating as a nonprofit isn't right or necessary for everyone, or it may be premature for an organization or artist to create a nonprofit corporation at a particular time. In these cases, there are two other options to consider: forming an unincorporated association and/or finding a fiscal sponsor. An unincorporated association is a group of people who have come together for a similar purpose. Distinct from a corporation, it does not have an identity separate from its members, nor is it a legal entity. An association does not need to file paperwork with the state or federal governments to create the association. However, it may have a more difficult time getting tax-exempt status, making it harder to raise money since most donors want to be able to make a tax-deductible contribution. Also, unlike a corporation, an unincorporated association is not a legal entity, and thus the association (being separate from its members) cannot own property or have contracts signed on its behalf; any contracts signed on its behalf will expose its members to personal liability. Indeed, any member could potentially hold herself as having authority, or be regarded as having such authority, to bind (place under legal obligation by contract or oath) the association.[4]

For those not yet sure they want to take on the obligation of a separate corporate existence, or those with nonprofit projects that have a short-term duration, a good alternative to incorporation is working with a fiscal sponsor. A fiscal sponsor must be a nonprofit charitable corporation that has been given tax-exempt status under section 501(c)(3) of the Internal Revenue Code (IRC), one consequence of which is that it can accept charitable contributions from individuals, corporations, and foundations.

A fiscal sponsor serves as an umbrella organization for individuals, as well as incorporated and unincorporated organizations (both for-profit and nonprofit), who are seeking monies for public, nonprofit purposes that align with the mission of the fiscal sponsor. Most fiscal sponsors have an application or other approval process for accepting the projects they sponsor. One thing they must determine is whether the proposed project aligns with the sponsor's mission; if the project does not, the fiscal sponsor cannot sponsor that project.

Grants made to a fiscal sponsor are made to support the fiscal sponsor's public purpose. The fiscal sponsor then makes the determination to regrant the funds to the sponsored project. A fiscal sponsor may create a preapproved grant program for a project, in which case it simply accepts and disburses the money received for that program. If it does not, and the sponsor receives a contribution from a donor for a particular project, the sponsor takes it under advisement to disburse the funds to the project, but has no legal obligation to do so (though in most cases it will). In either case, the check is still made out to the sponsor to support the sponsor's public purpose.[5]

The fiscal sponsor usually takes a percentage of the donation as payment for managing the donation. Many fiscal sponsors maintain the books of their sponsored projects and/or provide grant-writing assistance and advice. In all instances, if a sponsor learns that the monies have not been used toward the purpose for which the applicant indicated they would be used, the sponsor is legally obligated to seek a return of the funds. The sponsor will then redisburse the funds according to the purposes for which they were made or return the funds to the donors.

The obvious advantage to finding a fiscal sponsor is that the sponsor already has an organizational system in place, making it easier to raise funds. Problems may arise, however, if the fiscal sponsor and the sponsored project are competing for the same types of funds, or if the arrangement or project isn't preapproved. When an organization or individual is a project of a fiscal sponsor, it really doesn't have complete control over the money it raises. If an organization or individual chooses to have a relationship with a fiscal sponsor, it's crucial to have a written letter of agreement outlining the duties and liabilities of each party.[6]

CLASSROOM DISCUSSION

What are the characteristics of a corporation? What distinguishes a nonprofit corporation from a for-profit corporation?

What are the advantages and disadvantages to incorporating as a nonprofit corporation?

What does "limited liability" mean?

If an organization chooses not to incorporate, what are its alternatives?

What is fiscal sponsorship? What are the advantages and disadvantages of finding a fiscal sponsor? Discuss these points as they relate to your own career objectives.

THE PROCESS OF NONPROFIT INCORPORATION

Incorporation, as previously mentioned, is a state process. A nonprofit organization may incorporate in the state in which it resides, or it may choose to select another state where the laws tend to be more favorable (e.g., the fees are lower, or there is less regulation). If a nonprofit organization incorporates in a state other than the state in which it resides, it will still have to register to do business or apply for authority to do business in the state where the organization has its primary office.[7]

The following section describes the process for incorporation in New York State: articulating a nonprofit public purpose; reserving a corporate name; creating the articles of incorporation; and selecting nonprofit incorporators. The New York State attorney general has created a document called *Procedures for Forming and Changing Not-for-Profit Corporations in New York*.[8] This document specifies the procedures for incorporating in New York. Though there are similarities from state to state regarding the process of incorporating, it's best to speak to a lawyer about the requirements in a specific state.

Determining a Nonprofit Public Purpose

When filing for incorporation, the organization will be asked to state clearly and succinctly what it plans to do to advance its public purpose. It will need to prove that it has a charitable, cultural, and/or educational purpose that will benefit the public. The organization's public purpose must demonstrate that it will offer services that differ from those of a commercial enterprise. For example, an organization may offer a season of performances to educate the public. It must verify that it doesn't exclude any segment of the population through its work, and that no individual will profit from the services rendered. In New York State, if an organization plans to engage in educational activities, it must write a letter to the Department of Education at the time of incorporation, asking them for a waiver (see appendix A for an example of a waiver request).

The public purpose clause should always be wide enough to embrace a large array of organizational activities. If the public purpose is broad enough, the organization won't need to change it if the organization decides to move in a new, but similar, direction.

If the public purpose is too narrow, and the organization needs to change that purpose, it must either create a new nonprofit corporation or amend/expand the public purpose in the articles of incorporation. Changing or amending the public purpose requires a meeting—and the notice of a meeting—with the board of directors, in which they will vote on changing the public purpose of the organization. The policies and procedures for voting on this type of change are found in the organization's bylaws (rules for governing the organization) and should adhere to state nonprofit laws.[9] Most importantly, if an organization changes its public purpose, it must inform the Internal Revenue Service (IRS) in its next informational return, which may affect its tax exemption.

Let's look at an example of a public purpose. Queens Council on the Arts has the following charitable purpose:

The purpose of this corporation shall be to act as a coordinating, educational, and service organization to promote and encourage the knowledge, appreciation, and practice of the arts through cultural activities in Queens. The corporation shall operate without profit so that no part of its net earnings or assets shall ever be distributed as a dividend to the benefit of any private shareholder or individual. The Council may sponsor cooperative planning, research, fundraising, public education programs, training programs for arts organizations, and individual artists, and undertake such other services and programs deemed necessary to encourage participation in and appreciation of the arts by all citizens of Queens County.[10]

It is evident that this organization has a public purpose, is inclusive of all segments of society, and exists to provide the public with cultural and educational services.

Choosing a Corporate Name

Nonprofit organizations must choose a name. In selecting a name for your organization, you must first make sure that the name is available. In New York State, organizations begin this process by filling out an Application for Reservation Form, available from the secretary of state's Web site (*www.dos.state.ny.us*). An organization files a Reservation Form for each name choice and includes a letter to the secretary of state, ranking its name preferences in order. The organization will receive the first available choice. Organizations may also begin this process online by searching the Corporation and Business Entity Database at *http://appsext8.dos.state.ny.us/corp_public/corpsearch.entity_search_entry*. This database contains the names of both nonprofit and for-profit corporations doing business in New York State. After the organization receives approval of an eligible name or determines that the name is not in use, it can reserve a name for sixty days and can renew if necessary.

When choosing a corporate name, the organization must take several factors into consideration. Some words are not permitted to be used in corporate names. The *Procedures for Forming and Changing Not-for-Profit Corporations in New York* guide has a list of over twenty words that can't appear in the name of a corporation. For example, the name of the organization cannot contain "lawyer" or "doctor."[11] An organization also can't use the word "school"

or "museum" unless that organization falls into either category.[12] In addition, it's not the best idea to name an organization after an individual, since it may raise concerns with the IRS about whether the organization is being created for private or public interests. Finally, the organization must add the word "incorporated" (Inc.) or "limited" (Ltd.) after the name.[13]

Creating the Articles of Incorporation and Selecting Incorporators

After choosing a corporate name, an organization must create articles of incorporation. In New York State, a performing arts organization must file the certificate of incorporation (also known as the articles of incorporation) with the secretary of state for a Type B corporation. A Type B corporation "is formed for one or more of the following non-business purposes: charitable, educational, religious, scientific, literary, cultural, or for the prevention of cruelty to children or animals."[14] The organization must state the name of its corporation and its charitable purposes within the certificate. The certificate should also contain language regarding the nonprofit corporation's intent to engage in exempt business activities; to provide reasonable compensation to its employees; to limit political actions by limiting its lobbying activities and not interfering in political campaigns; and in the case of dissolution, to distribute any remaining assets after satisfying its debts to a similar nonprofit tax-exempt institution.[15]

In New York State, the organization must also list the names and addresses of at least three directors/incorporators over the age of eighteen years who are willing to take fiduciary and legal responsibility for the corporation being formed.[16] It should be noted that most organizations list three individuals who do not necessarily become actual board members, since board members must be elected or appointed at the first organizational meeting.

If one proceeds diligently, the entire process of incorporation should take about a month. The organization sends the certificate of incorporation to the secretary of state, along with the filing fee and any necessary approvals or waivers. "When a Certificate of Incorporation is accepted for filing by the secretary of state, the organization's corporate existence begins. The secretary of state's office will send the organization confirmation that the certificate has been filed. The confirmation will contain the filing date, which is also the date of incorporation."[17]

CLASSROOM DISCUSSION

Why is it necessary to consult a lawyer when seeking to incorporate a nonprofit organization?

What government office is responsible for designating nonprofit corporate status in your state?

Where do you obtain filing instructions for your certificate (or articles) of incorporation?

What information do you need to provide on the form?

How do you go about obtaining a name for your organization?

How many incorporators must you have in your state?

Do you need to provide any waiver letters with your application? Write a waiver request letter.

Define the term "public purpose."

Call your favorite nonprofit performing arts organization and find out what its nonprofit public purpose is and how it relates to its nonprofit mission. Review the organization's public purpose. Is it broad enough to encompass a range of activities? If the organization wants to change it, what are its options?

NEW NONPROFIT CORPORATE RESPONSIBILITIES: ESTABLISHING THE MISSION STATEMENT AND BYLAWS

At the point at which an organization is incorporated, it becomes responsible for paying federal and state income taxes (which will be refunded in the event that it qualifies for tax exemption). In addition, if an organization plans on raising money, it must check the state charities registration requirements. Currently, thirty-two states require nonprofit organizations to register before seeking donations. Registration allows both the state and the public to research the activities of the charity. Some states require that nonprofit organizations file their federal informational tax returns with the state before raising contributions; others require audited annual statements.[18] Further legislation in some states mandates that the names of the solicitors be disclosed and that an "organization's treasurer and another officer at a high level sign the charity's registration form, stating that they understand what they have signed and that there are consequences for them and the organization if the information is found not to be true."[19]

Also, after an organization is incorporated, it must hold its first official organizational meeting to create the organizational mission statement and craft the bylaws. The mission statement provides an articulation of the organization's core values, as described in the previous chapter. For legal purposes, the mission statement of the organization should be in line with the public purpose stated within the articles or certificate of incorporation.

Nonprofit bylaws are the internal governing documents of an organization and define how an organization will be managed and run within parameters established by the nonprofit law in its state. The bylaws will also provide a method for electing a board of directors and officers and establishing board committees. Bylaws state which staff, board members, and officers have authority and decision-making responsibilities, and how these responsibilities should be executed. They create a framework for the organization, ensuring that income will be properly distributed. They also aid in resolving internal disputes.

A nonprofit organization must have a governing organizational document in order to secure tax-exempt status;[20] when applying for tax-exempt status from the federal government, the organization will submit bylaws and its certificate of incorporation as part of the application process.

In preparing bylaws, it is advisable to seek legal counsel familiar with state law to draft them. The founding board members, as well as the founding artistic and managing directors, should have input.[21] Here are the primary elements that should appear in the bylaws. Please note that these are the parameters for creating bylaws in New York State:

1. Powers and Numbers: In New York State, a nonprofit organization must have a minimum of three directors; there is no maximum number required by law. However, bylaws can place limits on the number of board members elected or appointed to serve. Board members must be eighteen years of age to serve. Board members are required to exercise their powers commensurate with the laws of the state. They are legally empowered to make decisions related to the governing of the nonprofit organization, including the hiring and firing of the artistic and managing directors. The artistic and/or managing director may also be a voting member of the board. However, if the artistic director or managing director is on the board, the board will exercise its hiring and firing power over such individuals subject to a conflict-of-interest policy, as explained later in this chapter.

2. Election and Term of Office: The nonprofit organization must elect or appoint board members.

It should specify its procedure for election or appointment. Elections should take place once a year. It should also set the term limit and process for resignation. Board members should have staggered terms so that no more than one-third of the board is changing at any given time.

3. Removal: The organization must specify whether a board member can be removed with and/or without cause.

4. Notice of Meetings: When and where will meetings be held? How often will meetings be held? In order to give latitude to the board, it is often best to state that meetings shall be held at least once a year at location(s) to be determined by the board of directors.

5. Quorum and Voting: A quorum is the number of people that must be present at a meeting in order for the board to conduct business and vote. In New York State, under section 707 of the Nonprofit Corporation Law (unless stated otherwise in an organization's bylaws or its certificate of incorporation), a majority of the entire board constitutes a quorum. A corporation can require a higher number for a quorum (though this would not be recommended). An organization can also specify that a quorum shall be as little as one-third in an organization with fifteen or fewer board members; in an organization that has greater than fifteen board members, a quorum must consist of at least five board members, plus one additional member for every ten members (or fraction thereof).[22]

6. Action: Action describes the process of taking action or voting. For example, the bylaws can state that the board can operate via "telephonic or other comparable means." In other words, every other person voting must be able to hear any members joining the meeting by phone, and the person on the telephone must be able to hear everyone else who will be voting in the meeting. There is also the option of "unanimous written consent in lieu of a meeting." This means that the action can be taken only if everyone consents; action can't be taken unless everyone agrees. In this instance, each person must sign her agreement to the resolution. The written evidence must be kept with the organization's minutes.

7. Officers: In New York State (section 713 of the New York Nonprofit Law), the organization's board may elect a president, vice presidents (as desired), a secretary, and a treasurer (or other corresponding offices); the organization should have at least a president, secretary, and treasurer. Any two offices, other than president and secretary,

may be held by the same person. The duties and powers of each of the officers should be specified, as well as their election or appointment, term of office, and procedures for removal.

8. Compensation: If the organization plans on compensating its board members or officers, it should state this compensation plan in the bylaws. Since the federal government has regulations regarding executive compensation, these regulations should be consulted before the bylaws are finalized.

9. Committees: Committees may be elected or appointed in the same manner as the officers of the corporation. In addition to the executive committee (usually comprised of the heads of all the other committees; it acts on behalf of the board between board meetings), which other committees will the board want to create? Important committees to consider are: the nominating committee, responsible for nominating potential board members; the finance committee, responsible for monitoring the organization's finances; the audit committee, responsible for working with the external auditor (more on the audit committee in chapter 5); and the development committee, responsible for working with the development director to raise money. Their duties should be spelled out in the bylaws. It is important to recognize that state law may prohibit the delegation of certain matters to the executive committee or any other committee; these prohibitions may include, but are not limited to: matters that involve the approval of the entire board of directors; the filling of vacancies on the board or any other committee; the fixing of compensation of the board or any other committee; and the amendment or repeal of any resolution of the board (section 712, New York State Law).

10. Office: This clause specifies the place where all accounts, contracts, the certificate of incorporation, and board minutes shall be available for viewing by all board members and the general public. The board will also select the board member(s) authorized to open a bank account, as well as sign checks and contracts.

11. Fiscal Year (Dates of Operation): It is advisable to leave the dates of operation open and to simply state that the dates of operation will be determined by the board of directors.

12. Indemnification: An indemnification clause states that the corporation will protect its board members and officers from liability for the corporation's debts and financial obligations. We previously affirmed that board members and officers have limited liability under corporate law.

However, protection from liability under the law doesn't prevent a board member or an officer from being sued. If this happens, the nonprofit corporation guarantees the board member protection under the law and will reimburse her for legal expenses incurred, providing the board member has acted in good faith or in the best interests of the corporation. For further discussion, please see the insurance policies section of this chapter.

13. Conflict-of-Interest Policy: This section specifies that the board of directors will not personally benefit as a result of their board involvement. Please see the section of this chapter that defines this policy in greater detail.

14. Amendments: Amendment clauses stipulate the ways in which your bylaws can be amended and under what conditions. For example, the organization may need a two-thirds vote in favor of amending the bylaws.[23]

After drafting the bylaws, the organization should elect a board of directors and officers, as well as form committees. Those authorized should also open a bank account, designating the officers that have the authority to sign checks.

CLASSROOM DISCUSSION

Once you receive your certificate of incorporation from the state, do you have to pay income taxes? Why?

Why do most states require nonprofit organizations to register?

What should you do at your first organizational meeting?

What are bylaws, and why do nonprofit organizations need to create them?

TAX EXEMPTION

Once the corporation is formed, its bylaws adopted, and its board members and officers elected or appointed, the corporation must apply to the Internal Revenue Service for 501(c)(3) status if it wants to be tax-exempt. Tax-exempt status means that the organization does not have to pay the bulk of federal taxes. Nonprofit corporations are required to pay taxes up to the point that they are given tax-exempt status by the Internal Revenue Service.

An organization can apply for exemption from federal income tax under section 501(c)(3) of the Internal Revenue Code only if it meets both an organizational and an operational test. In order to meet the organizational test, the organization's articles of incorporation must demonstrate that it is organized for one or more of the following purposes: "charitable, religious, educational, scientific, literary, testing for public safety, fostering national or international amateur sports competition, and the prevention of cruelty to children or animals." In addition, the organization must state that its assets will be dedicated and distributed for tax-exempt purposes (public purposes), and that private individuals will not incur anything more than an incidental benefit (and if an individual has control over the organization, that individual should not benefit in any way, incidental or otherwise). Finally, the articles of incorporation must state that upon dissolution, the organization's assets will be distributed to a beneficiary with a similar tax-exempt purpose.[24]

To qualify for tax exemption under section 501(c)(3), the organization must also pass an operational test. In other words, it must actually operate on behalf of one of the listed tax-exempt purposes (as opposed to merely being organized for that purpose as stated in the organizing papers), and no private individuals can receive anything more than incidental financial benefits. The IRS states:

It must not be organized or operated for the benefit of private interests, such as the creator or the creator's family, shareholders of the organization, other designated individuals, or persons controlled directly or indirectly by such private interests. No part of the net earnings of an IRC Section 501(c)(3) organization may inure to the benefit of [financially benefit] any private shareholder or individual. A private shareholder or individual is a person having a personal and private interest in the activities of the organization. If the organization engages in an excess benefit transaction [for a detailed discussion, see below] with a person having substantial influence over the organization, an excise tax may be imposed on the person and any managers agreeing to the transaction.[25]

Prior to or contemporaneous with seeking tax-exempt status from the Internal Revenue Service, the nonprofit corporation must have obtained an employer identification number (EIN) by submitting an SS-4 Application for Employer Identification Number. A nonprofit corporation must have this number, even if it doesn't have any employees. This form and all other forms mentioned in this section can be found online at *www.irs.gov*.

Nonprofit corporations should file their applications for tax exemption (Form 1023) within twenty-seven months of the time that they are incorporated. To avoid having to amend the certificate of incorporation and bylaws when submitting the federal application, they should review the instructions for Form 1023 when submitting the state incorporation papers. The filing process generally takes anywhere from three to nine months, and the organization should use the services of an attorney or nonprofit accountant to complete this process.[26]

If tax exemption is granted, the status will be retroactive to the date of incorporation. This allows nonprofit corporations to be exempt from paying taxes and to raise tax-deductible contributions from donors, from the date of incorporation. Of course, if tax-exempt status is denied, the donor will have to file an amended tax return, and the organization will have to pay taxes.

The nonprofit corporation must also file for tax exemption from the state and local governments. Ordinarily, nonprofit organizations are exempt from paying state and local taxes, including sales tax, property tax, and income tax. There may be exceptions that vary from state to state.

The next sections describe Form 1023 in detail, as well as distinguishing between two types of 501(c)(3) nonprofit organizations.

Form 1023

Form 1023 includes the employer identification number; a "conformed copy" of the articles of incorporation and the certificate issued by the state; the organization's bylaws; a description of the purposes and activities of the organization; financial statements "showing the receipts and expenditures for the current year and three preceding years (or for the number of years the organization was in existence, if less than four years);" and a balance sheet. (Balance sheets and other financial statements will be discussed in chapter 5.) If the organization has not yet begun operations, or has operated for less than one year, it must submit a proposed budget for two full accounting periods and a current statement of assets and liabilities. The nonprofit organization submits a fee with the application.[27]

A conformed copy of the articles of incorporation is a "copy that agrees with the original and all amendments to it. The officer [of the organization] must certify that the document is a complete and accurate copy of the original. A certificate of incorporation should be approved and dated by an appropriate state official."[28] With regard to the "description of activities," the IRS requires that the corporation include the "standards, criteria, procedures, or other means that [the] organization will use to carry out those activities." The IRS, in this case, is looking for a written strategic and fundraising plan. Additionally, for each accounting period in which the organization has been in existence, the IRS wants to see "the sources of receipts and the nature of the organization's expenditures."[29] An audited financial statement (a financial statement reviewed by an independent certified public accountant) will satisfy these requirements.

Given the increased scrutiny placed on nonprofits to pass the organizational and operational tests, in 2005 the IRS added a new section to the 1023 form requesting information on the compensation of employees, board members, and officers; data concerning nonprofit payments to third parties that may have helped create these payments; and nonprofit corporate connections to family businesses. These additional questions are used to flag excessive compensation practices, uncover illegal business practices by which a person may personally benefit from the creation of a charity, and locate potential conflict-of-interest practices.[30]

Public Charity versus Private Foundation

On Form 1023, the IRS asks the nonprofit organization if it will be operating as a public charity or a private foundation. A private foundation, while still a 501(c)(3) organization, must distribute part of its net investment income (investment income before allowable deductions), pay an annual tax on its net investment income, and accept restrictions on the use of the funds.[31] Private foundations are primarily created by individuals for the purpose of distributing money. The IRS distinguishes private foundations from public charities in that private foundations don't receive public support. Public charities, as defined by the IRS, are publicly supported organizations, meaning a "substantial part of [their] financial support, in the form of contributions, comes from publicly supported organizations, from a government unit, or from the general public."[32] To become a public charity, a nonprofit organization must pass a public support test when it files for tax-exempt status. In order to maintain its status, it must continue to pass this test. If all financial support comes from a single individual or a private foundation, the public support test will not be met. The public support test requires that at least one-third of the organization's income come from public sources, such as ticket sales and contributions from individuals, corporations, foundations, and the government. The IRS is willing to allow an organization initially to have 10 percent of its income deriving from public sources, as long as there is a fundraising plan in place to show the IRS that the organization is working on meeting the one-third public support test requirement.[33]

Every year, when the nonprofit fills out its Form 990, also known as "Return of Organization Exempt From Income Tax," the nonprofit organization will have to prove to the IRS that it is meeting its public support test. In any year that the organization doesn't meet this test, it may be classified as a private foundation. A private foundation is still a nonprofit organization, but it receives less favorable tax treatment, and the organization itself may be subject to certain excise taxes in connection with investment income. The nonprofit charity will also have to continue to meet the organizational and operational tests, proving that the organization is organized and operated for charitable and public purposes.

CLASSROOM DISCUSSION

Define "tax-exempt."
What does Form 1023 include?
What is a conformed copy of the articles of incorporation?
Define "organizational tests" and "operational tests."
What is the difference between a public charity and a private foundation?
What is the public support test?
What is Form 990?

MAINTAINING TAX-EXEMPT STATUS

Once the IRS issues the nonprofit corporation a determination letter, the organization is officially tax-exempt. In maintaining tax-exempt status, the organization has operational requirements, including public disclosure of financial documents, paying certain taxes (including unrelated business income tax), preventing private benefit, limiting lobbying efforts, and complying with fundraising regulations. The next section will discuss each area.

Financial Disclosure and Paying Taxes

Nonprofit organizations are legally required to file information returns to the IRS. The information return is known as Form 990. Organizations may file either the full Form 990, Form 990-EZ (a simplified version for smaller organizations), or Form 990-N (the e-Postcard, stating the contact information

for the organization); financial thresholds for each type of form are described in chapter 5. The 990-N, 990-EZ, or 990 must be filed "by the 15th day of the 5th month after the end of [the] organization's accounting period."[34] Most states also require that the filer attach Form 990 to the state charities registration form. Nonprofit organizations are expected to make "their last three annual information returns (Forms 990), and their approved application for recognition of exemption with all supporting documents, available for public inspection without charge (other than a reasonable fee for reproduction and copying costs)."[35]

Nonprofit organizations are legally required to withhold and deposit employment taxes based on wages and fringe benefits; these taxes include federal and state income tax, Social Security, and Medicare.[36] Employers are also mandated to pay unemployment taxes that are not withheld from the employee's paycheck. Not all fringe benefits are taxed, but all fringe benefits must be disclosed by the employer. Fringe benefits that an employee would normally deduct as a business expense, such as a car utilized for work, a subscription to a work-related magazine, or health benefits, are not taxed.[37] Failing to pay payroll taxes will result in IRS penalties and potential lawsuits, and will jeopardize nonprofit status. In addition, board members can be personally liable for this debt, as can executive directors.

In maintaining nonprofit status, the nonprofit corporation must also be aware of its legal responsibility to pay unrelated business income tax (UBIT) to the federal and state governments on all income not related to the organization's stated purposes. If the income-producing activity is deemed not to be "substantially related" to the public purpose of the nonprofit organization, the organization must fill out IRS Form 990-T and pay the tax on the gross earnings of income (less deductions directly connected with producing that income) over $1,000. This form is filed on the fifteenth day, four months after the end of the nonprofit organization's fiscal year.[38] Nonprofit organizations must make Form 990-T available for public inspection.[39]

The next section focuses on the types of income that constitute unrelated business income.

Unrelated Business Income

Unrelated business income is "the income from a trade or business that is regularly carried on by an exempt organization and that is not substantially related to the performance by the organization of its exempt purpose or function, except that the organization uses the profits derived from the activity."[40] A "trade or business," as defined by the IRS, is "any activity carried on for the production of income from selling goods or services." A trade or business that is "regularly carried on" is conducted on a frequent and continued basis in "a similar manner comparable to commercial activities of nonexempt organizations." Unrelated business taxable income is the "gross income derived from any unrelated trade or business regularly carried on by the exempt organization, less the deductions directly connected with carrying on the trade or business."[41] For example, a performing arts center with a year-round parking lot will pay unrelated business income tax on its gross income derived from parking, less deductions directly connected with producing that income.

What activities are considered "substantially related" to the public purpose of a nonprofit organization? In the IRS publication *Tax on Unrelated Income of Exempt Organizations*, there are many examples of trade and business activities that are, in fact, substantially related to the nonprofit organization's tax-exempt purpose. Other activities, of course, are not and must be taxed. Let's examine both types of activities.

If a theater presents an educational film related to its tax-exempt purpose, the admission fee won't be taxed. However, if the theater charges admission for an ongoing series of commercial feature films, the theater will be taxed. In this case, the theater is presenting a continuous series of commercial films that not only is competing on a regular basis with the local commercial movie house, but also is not substantially related to its tax-exempt purpose of presenting plays.

If a symphony orchestra exchanges or rents its subscriber or donor list to another nonprofit organization, it won't be taxed on any income derived from this business transaction. This activity supports the tax-exempt purposes of all of those involved in the transaction. However, if the orchestra sells its list to a commercial real estate company, it will be taxed at the corporate rate.

If a presenting organization owns real estate and rents apartments to artists, the presenter will pay tax on the net income. This type of real estate transaction is not linked to the tax-exempt purpose of the presenting organization.

Sponsorship income is tax-exempt if the nonprofit organization "provides no substantial benefit other than the use or acknowledgement

of the business name, logo, and product lines in connection with the organization's activities. Use or acknowledgement does not include advertising the sponsor's products and services. The organization's activities include all activities, whether or not related to its [the organization's] exempt purposes."[42]

If an organization has a restaurant that may be used by its employees, and will "encourage more people to come" to the organization, the income will not be taxed. The IRS believes that the organization is creating an atmosphere in which the patron will not have to leave the building to have a meal, therefore adding to the "enhancement of public awareness."[43] Concession income on food sold during the performance falls under this category as well and is not taxed by the federal government, although the organization collects sales tax on behalf of the city and state governments.

If a nonprofit theater company receives enhancement money from a commercial producer for developing and improving the production value of a show, this money will not be taxed because the business activity is not regularly carried on, and the production of the play is substantially related to the mission of the nonprofit organization. If the commercial producer, who enhanced the show, decides to produce the show on Broadway, the producer will form a for-profit commercial venture, such as a limited liability company, where the gross earnings will be taxed (less the deductions directly connected with producing that income).

When a nonprofit theater company receives royalty payments (payments for the rights to use or produce the work) from a production that has a commercial run on Broadway, it will not pay tax on the royalties received. Royalty payments made to the organization are considered to be substantially related to the nonprofit's public purpose. However, if a nonprofit theater company has a for-profit subsidiary (a for-profit company controlled by the nonprofit theater, created to produce commercially), the for-profit subsidiary will pay tax on any profit it generates from its commercial productions, including royalties and fees. Nonprofit theaters that create for-profit subsidiaries are doing so to avoid running afoul of meeting the operational test of the organization.[44]

CLASSROOM DISCUSSION

What types of documents must a nonprofit organization share with the public?

What taxes are nonprofit organizations legally responsible for paying?

What is UBIT? What is unrelated business income? Name three types of activities that produce unrelated business income.

Define the following terms: "trade or business," "regularly carried on," and "substantially related."

Preventing Private Inurement: Excessive Benefits and Joint Ventures

Although nonprofit tax-exempt organizations are organized and operated to serve public purposes, they daily confer private benefits: e.g., employees are paid, members of the public are the beneficiaries of services, and vendors who provide goods and services receive fees. As long as the private benefit is purely incidental—qualitatively and quantitatively—to the exempt activity from which it flows, no problem exists. If the private benefit is not incidental to the exempt activity, however, it can present a conflict. The IRS will assess all cases based on their facts and, in the worst-case scenario, an organization can lose its tax-exempt status or not be granted one at all.[45]

Private inurement (personal financial gain) is a subset of private benefit, but, as opposed to private benefit, which is not prohibited outright, private inurement is prohibited. It can result where there is excessive compensation, particularly to an insider (e.g., employee), and in other circumstances. Nonprofit organizations have a legal responsibility to monitor their activities, preventing private inurement. In the following section, we discuss two areas of concern for nonprofit organizations: excessive benefits and compensation, and forming joint ventures with commercial for-profit partners.[46]

In May 2006, two IRS employees, Karen Fitch and David Fish, discussed the August 2004 new enforcement effort designed to "identify and halt abuses by public charities and private foundations that pay excessive compensation and benefits to their officers and other insiders."[47] The IRS is primarily interested in making sure that disqualified persons, or "persons in a position to exercise substantial influence over the affairs of an applicable tax-exempt organization," are not receiving excessive benefits or compensation.[48] Disqualified individuals include board members and high-level managers, such as the chief executive or chief financial officers. On Form 990, nonprofit organizations are required to list "transactions between related individuals or leases of property to officers and directors; receivables from trustees, officers, directors, and key employees with an explanation; and compensation for directors, officers, and employees."[49]

Nonprofit organizations must also answer as to whether they entered into an excessive benefit transaction. Excessive benefits include: personal use of an automobile, reimbursement for personal expenses, and personal use of employer-owned property, loans, and club memberships. These benefits are considered excessive by the IRS because the insider is personally benefiting at the expense of the nonprofit organization. Insiders are responsible for paying income tax on these items.

While executive benefits are easy to identify, recognizing excessive executive compensation becomes a bit more difficult. According to Fitch, "reasonable compensation is not an exact science. Reasonable compensation is the amount that would ordinarily be paid for like services by like enterprises, whether taxable or tax-exempt, under like circumstances."[50] When comparing "like enterprises," the IRS requires that the organization compare the duties, responsibilities, size of the organization, number of hours devoted to the job, geographic area, industry, and actual compensation package.

Failure to list all benefits, even if they are considered reasonable by the organization, may be treated as excessive compensation by the IRS. In the event that benefits and compensation are deemed to be unreasonable, the insider is subject to tax, and, in egregious cases, the nonprofit may lose its tax-exempt status. Fitch maintains, "Exempt organizations are not likely to get in trouble with the IRS if they develop and follow procedures for setting compensation and if they make an honest, reasonable effort, commensurate with their size and revenues, to determine what the appropriate level of compensation is for their size, revenues, organizational structure, and mission."[51]

Nonprofit organizations that engage in joint ventures with for-profit corporations must also scrutinize the degree to which private inurement or anything other than incidental private benefit results from this arrangement. "A joint venture is a relationship in which two or more persons or business entities combine their efforts or property for a single transaction or a series of transactions or projects. Unless otherwise agreed, joint ventures share profits and losses equally."[52] The joint venture need not have a separate venture entity distinct from the identity of the venture partners, though it frequently may be organized as a separate corporation or partnership, and its gross income is taxed. When a nonprofit engages in a joint venture, it must determine if its board, officers, and employees are personally benefiting (other than incidentally) from the joint venture, or if a third party is obtaining more than an incidental benefit by virtue of this joint venture relationship.

For example, if a nonprofit theater accepts enhancement money from a commercial producer with the express purpose of being a legal partner in the commercial transfer of the play to Broadway, the nonprofit is entering into a joint venture with the commercial producer. According to entertainment attorney Carolyn Casselman, "The IRS has a two-part test for 'careful scrutiny' of joint ventures between for-profit and nonprofit entities. The first part considers whether the joint venture furthers an organization's charitable purpose. The second part requires that the nonprofit have the ability to act exclusively in furtherance of its exempt purpose, not for anything more than incidental benefit to private partners."[53] In other words, the nonprofit must pass the operational test and stay clear of nonincidental private benefits.

Casselman's article, "Waltzing with the Muse or Dancing with the Devil: Enhancement Deals between Nonprofit Theaters and Commercial Producers," provides an exceptional analysis of the risks involved with accepting enhancement money from a commercial producer. If a nonprofit organization accepts enhancement money from a commercial producer, the board must make sure that the project to which the money is dedicated will advance the charitable purpose of the organization. If the play is deemed suitable for a commercial transfer, the board must make sure that the nonprofit theater—regardless of what role it plays in the transfer—will be able to carry out its mission without interference from its private partners. In doing so, the board is executing its fiduciary and legal duties. To avoid the breaching of their duties, board members should make sure that the artistic director has not accepted enhancement money or entered into any type of joint venture without the offer being fully disclosed to the board. In addition, if the enhancement deal and its eventual commercial transfer interfere with the ability of the organization to fulfill its mission, the organization should decline the offer.[54]

CLASSROOM DISCUSSION
Define "private inurement."
What is a disqualified person?
Define "excessive compensation and benefit transactions."
Define "joint venture."

What is the IRS two-part test for determining whether a joint venture meets the operational test?
What can the board do to protect the nonprofit organization against bad enhancement or joint venture deals?

Lobbying Limitations and Political Campaigns
Nonprofit organizations are allowed to lobby for a specific cause, as long as the activity is insubstantial in relation to the overall work of the organization. When an organization lobbies for a specific cause, it attempts to work with elected officials to influence legislation, such as the appropriation of more money for the National Endowment for the Arts.

According the IRS, "attempting to influence legislation" includes the following:

1. Any attempt to influence any legislation through an effort to affect the opinions of the general public or any segment thereof (grassroots lobbying), and
2. Any attempt to influence any legislation through communication with any member or employee of a legislative body or with any government official or employee who may participate in the formulation of legislation (direct lobbying).

However, the term "attempting to influence legislation" *does not* include the following activities:

1. Making available the results of nonpartisan analysis, study, or research.
2. Examining and discussing broad social, economic, and similar problems.
3. Providing technical advice or assistance (where the advice would otherwise constitute the influencing of legislation) to a governmental body or to a committee or other subdivision thereof in response to a written request by that body or subdivision.
4. Appearing before, or communicating with, any legislative body about a possible decision of that body that might affect the existence of the organization, its powers and duties, its tax-exempt status, or the deduction of contributions to the organization.
5. Communicating with a government official or employee, other than:

a. A communication with a member or employee of a legislative body (when the communication would otherwise constitute the influencing of legislation), or

b. A communication with the principal purpose of influencing legislation.

Also excluded are communications between an organization and its bona fide members about legislation or proposed legislation of direct interest to the organization and the members, unless these communications directly encourage the members to attempt to influence legislation or directly encourage the members to urge nonmembers to attempt to influence legislation, as explained earlier.[55]

If a nonprofit chooses to engage in lobbying activity, it may elect to submit itself to a limit on its lobbying expenditures imposed by the IRS. (This limit allows the nonprofit organization to conduct as much lobbying activity as it wishes as long as the lobbying expenses remain under the limit.) Nonprofit organizations must report all lobbying expenditures to the IRS.[56] Lobbying expenditures are restricted to a certain percentage of the organization's expenses and cannot exceed $1 million.[57] According to Robert Lynch, president and chief executive officer of Americans for the Arts, a national organization promoting the arts for all Americans, "the extent to which a 501(c)(3) can lobby is limited to a small portion of the organization's expenditures, unofficially estimated at 5 percent, but this cap can be raised to as much as 20 percent, depending on the organization's operating budget."[58]

While nonprofit organizations are permitted to lobby legislators for the purpose of influencing public policy, they are unequivocally "prohibited from participating in partisan political campaigns in support of, or in opposition to, candidates for public office."[59] If their advocacy in favor of or against a political issue is seen as an obvious cover for advocacy for or against a candidate, this will raise a red flag for the IRS and may lead to the revocation of nonprofit status.[60] Nonprofit organizations are allowed to rent their facility to politicians running for office, as long as they offer the use of the facility to all political parties and candidates involved. Nonprofit organizations can't show preferential treatment of a particular candidate. They should also prohibit their employees from using any organizational resources, even their office computers, to send personal e-mails advocating for or against candidates, as this can also jeopardize the organization.[61]

CLASSROOM DISCUSSION

Under what conditions can a nonprofit lobby?
What percentage of a nonprofit organization's budget may be allocated to lobbying?
What are the consequences of endorsing a public official for office?

Fundraising Regulations

The federal government requires that donors obtain a written acknowledgement from the nonprofit organization stating the amount of the donation.[62] The acknowledgement, according to Amy Schwartzman, should read as follows: "Thank you for your contribution of [amount]. Since you did not receive goods or services in return for the contribution, the full amount is tax-deductible to the extent permitted by law."[63]

However, if the donor receives goods or services in return for the donation, the IRS considers this a "quid pro quo" or *something for something* contribution. In this case, the organization must send the donor a written disclosure statement recognizing the gift amount if it is greater than $75, stating the value of the goods and services received for the gift and the amount that is tax-deductible. The donor is only allowed to take a tax-deductible contribution to the extent the contribution exceeds the fair market value of the goods or services. The disclosure statement should read something like this: "Thank you for your contribution of $100. Since the value of your dinner was $50, your tax-deductible contribution is $50 to the extent permitted by law."[64]

What if the food for the dinner was donated to the organization? Schwartzman asserts, "It's irrelevant that the food was donated; you still have to deduct the 'fair market value' of the food to determine the actual tax-deductible donation." In fact, with regard to donated goods (also known as in-kind contributions), the donor can only deduct the "fair market value," or the usual and customary price, of the item from his taxes.[65]

CLASSROOM DISCUSSION

Who is responsible for obtaining an acknowledgement letter?
What is a quid pro quo contribution?
Write a sample disclosure statement.

BOARD OF DIRECTORS: FIDUCIARY AND LEGAL RESPONSIBILITIES

As mentioned earlier in this chapter, the board of directors is responsible for "ensuring that the organization meets legal requirements and that it is operating in accordance with the purpose for which it was granted tax exemption."[66] Every board member has specific fiduciary and legal responsibilities. By acting as fiduciaries, board members are in a position of trust and confidence, and hence are subject to a heightened duty to act in the best interests of the corporation. It is a greater duty than a simple legal duty, which can be imposed by law or contract but imposes no obligation to act in the best interests of the other party.

The primary fiduciary and legal duties include care, loyalty, and obedience. New York State's attorney general has defined the duties in the following sections.[67] Along with the definitions of the duties, we will provide examples of the ways in which the duties may be executed. Also, we will examine the purchase of insurance policies to protect the assets of the organization and the board of directors.

Finally, we will discuss the breaching of fiduciary and legal duties by members of the board of directors and the remedies that must be taken if breach occurs.

Duty of Care

"The duty of care requires a director (e.g., board member) to be familiar with the organization's finances and activities and to participate regularly in its governance. In carrying out this duty, directors must act in 'good faith' using the 'degree of diligence, care, and skill' that prudent people would use in similar positions and under similar circumstances. In exercising the duty of care, responsible board members should, among other things, do the following:

- Attend all board and committee meetings and actively participate in discussions and decision-making, such as setting of policies. Carefully read the material prepared for board and committee meetings prior to the meetings and note any questions they raise. Allow time to meet without senior management present.
- Read the minutes of prior meetings and all reports provided, including financial statements and reports by employees. Make sure votes against a particular proposal are completely and accurately recorded. Do not hesitate to suggest corrections,

clarification, and additions to the minutes or formal documents.
- Make sure to get copies of the minutes of any missed committee or board meeting and read them in a timely manner, suggesting any changes that may be appropriate.
- Make sure there is a clear process for approval of major obligations such as fundraising, professional fees (including auditors), compensation arrangements, and construction contracts.
- Make sure that board minutes reflect any dissenting votes in action taken by the board or that any dissenting vote is expressed in writing by letter to the board. Such records are necessary in order to allow a board member to disclaim responsibility for any particular decision. Absent board members must do this promptly in writing.
- Read any literature produced as part of the organization's programs.
- Make sure that monthly financial charts of accounts and financial reports prepared for management are available to the board or finance and audit committees, and that they are clear and communicate proper information for stewardship. Make sure there is an ongoing actual-costs-to-budget comparison, with discrepancies explained. [More information on reporting financial information to the board may be found in chapter 5.]
- Participate in risk assessment and strategic planning discussions for the future of the organization.
- Ensure that the organization has addressed the sufficiency of its written internal financial controls [discussed in detail in chapter 5] and written policies that safeguard, promote and protect the organization's assets, and that these controls and policies are updated regularly. Obtain employees', officers', and directors' fidelity bond to protect the organization from embezzlement.[68] Have a policy regarding disclosure and identification of fraud (whether or not material). Make sure a policy for records retention and whistle-blower protection is in place.[69] Create a background check policy for prospective employees.
- Determine whether or not the organization indemnifies its officers and directors from liability and has directors' and officers' liability insurance. If it does, find out what is covered and what is not. If it does not, find out why.
- Encourage diversity among board members. Diversity will help ensure a board committed to serve the organization's mission with a range of appropriate skills and interests.

- Be involved in the selection and periodic review of the performance of the organization's chief executive officer, chief financial officer, and other key employees responsible for the day-to-day activities of the organization. The board is responsible for ascertaining whether these individuals have the appropriate education, skills, and experience to assume a key position and then evaluating their performance."[70]

Duty of Loyalty

"Directors and officers are charged with the duty to act in the interest of the corporation. This duty of loyalty requires that any conflict of interest, real or possible, always be disclosed in advance of joining a board, as well as when such conflicts arise. Board members should avoid transactions in which they or their family members benefit personally. If such transactions are unavoidable, [they should] disclose them fully and completely to the board.[71]

"The board should have a written conflict-of-interest policy so that all members are aware of the type of transactions that may prohibit them from joining the board. Some such policies prohibit board members from engaging in any transaction that may result in even the appearance of a conflict of interest. They should provide for written disclosure of anticipated or actual conflicts.[72]

"In order to exercise this duty of loyalty, directors must be careful to examine transactions that involve board members or officers. The board must not approve any transaction that is not fair and reasonable, and a conflicted board member may not participate in the board vote. There should be an established code of ethics in place that is updated annually as well.

"Transactions involving conflicts should be fully documented in the board's minutes, and conflicts policies and disclosure statements should be discussed with the organization's auditors and attorneys."[73]

Duty of Obedience

"A board has a duty of obedience to ensure that the organization complies with applicable laws and regulations and its internal governance documents and policies, including:

- Dedicating the organization's resources to its mission.
- Ensuring that the organization carries out its purposes and does not engage in unauthorized activities.

- Complying with all appropriate laws, including registering with the attorney general's Charities Bureau in New York State; complying with registration and reporting laws and other applicable laws of all states in which it conducts activities and/or solicits contributions; filing required financial reports with the attorney general, the State Workers' Compensation Board, the State Department of Taxation and Finance, and the Internal Revenue Service; and paying all taxes, such as Social Security, income tax withholding (federal, state, and local), and any unrelated business income tax. Board members may be personally liable for failing to pay employees' wages and benefits and withholding taxes on employees' wages.
- Providing copies of its applications for tax-exempt status (IRS Form 1023), federal reports (IRS Forms 990, 990-EZ, 990-N), and its financial reports filed with the attorney general's Charities Bureau to members of the public who request them."[74]

CLASSROOM DISCUSSION

Discuss the terms "good faith" and the "degree of diligence, care, and skill," as they pertain to the duty of care. In other words, what would a board need to do to act in good faith or in the best interests of the organization?

Why must a board member exercise a "degree of diligence" when working for a nonprofit organization?

Why should a board member familiarize herself with prior minutes?

What is the purpose of having a clear process for approval of major obligations such as fundraising, professional fees, compensation arrangements, and construction contracts?

Define the duties of loyalty and obedience.

Insurance Policies

The fiduciary and legal duties of the board of directors also include protecting the assets of the corporation. The acquisition of the right insurance policies to protect these assets is an essential part of good governance. Robert Freedman, president and chief executive officer of Ruth Eckerd Hall in Clearwater, Florida, stresses, "The purpose of insurance is to protect the organization from financial loss that could happen from a variety of reasons: lawsuits from patrons concerning trips and falls in the auditorium; wrongful termination or harassment of employees; and disaster recovery from hurricanes, tornados, or other natural disasters."[75]

Therefore, it is necessary to purchase several types of insurance. The nonprofit corporation is mandated by the state government to pay workers' compensation to employees injured on the job, or who become ill as a result of the job. In addition, Freedman advises purchasing the following types of insurance: real and personal property (covers damages to real estate and personal property), general liability (covers bodily injury and property damage), automobile (protects vehicles against theft and damages), sign coverage (protects all signage leading to and in the building), crime (protects against theft), fiduciary (protects for employee claims made against welfare and pension benefit plans), and umbrella (purchased in excess of general liability).[76] It is also recommended that nonprofit organizations purchase errors and omissions insurance, which will, depending on the scope of coverage, generally allow the organization to recover losses arising out of allegations that a production produced by the organization has infringed on a copyright, contains defamatory material, or has violated an individual's legal rights to privacy or publicity.[77]

According to Amy Schwartzman, "People sue for all types of reasons, so be sure to purchase insurance policies to protect the board of directors and its officers from lawsuits, even if these lawsuits prove to be unsuccessful. A basic directors' and officers' liability insurance (D&O) policy will cover the legal costs of your directors and officers for defending against lawsuits. Note, however, that D&O insurance won't cover the cost of a lawsuit if it can be proven that there is gross negligence or fraud caused to the injured parties."[78]

Nonprofit organizations, depending on their size, hire risk management specialists to assess the potential risk to the organization, and to determine the types of insurance needed to cover these risks, including potential lawsuits involving the board, its officers, and the corporation itself.

CLASSROOM DISCUSSION

What other types of insurance should a nonprofit organization carry to protect its assets?

What type of insurance should a nonprofit organization purchase for its board of directors and officers?

Breaching Fiduciary and Legal Duties

As mentioned earlier, the fiduciary and legal duties are the duty of care (acting as a reasonably prudent person in similar circumstances would act), the duty of loyalty (acting in the corporation's interest, not self-interest), and the duty of obedience (to the corporation, as well as state and federal laws). If board members and officers breach (fail to observe) their fiduciary and legal duties, they can be held personally liable. What does this mean? Board members are responsible for the financial oversight of the organization, and the duty of care requires that they exercise the level of care that an ordinarily prudent person would in a similar circumstance. But what if a board invests some of its endowment funds in the stock market, and the nonprofit loses its investment? (An endowment is an investment account used to provide revenue to the organization; a more detailed discussion of endowment revenue can be found in chapter 5.) As long as the board consulted with a reputable financial advisor, did the appropriate research, and considered the long- and short-term needs of the corporation in carrying out its purposes, then the board did what the ordinary prudent person would do; even though the investment went bad, the board has not breached its duty of care.[79] If, however, there was gross negligence in regard to a transaction (e.g., the board knew the organization was in failing health and would not be able to pay back a debt after taking out a loan), the board would be breaching its duty of care. A board member who breaches his fiduciary and legal duties should be dismissed from the board.

Also, if a board member or officer funnels money through the nonprofit organization, this is considered fraudulent behavior, not just a breach of the duty of care.[80] A board member or officer who steals money from the organization is obviously committing a crime and is violating not only his duty of care, but his duty of loyalty. Neither board member would be indemnified by the nonprofit organization if these criminal acts were proven to be true.

The duty of loyalty requires that the board of directors act in the interest of the corporation. The board should have a conflict-of-interest policy, and any conflicts, actual or potential, should be disclosed. Whenever a member of the board has a personal interest in the outcome of a matter, she must disclose her personal interest in the matter even if the transaction will benefit the nonprofit organization. The board must also set up procedures to ensure that, if the nonprofit organization goes forward with transactions in which board members have personal interests, it is because those transactions are in the nonprofit organization's best interest from a price and quality perspective. If the board of directors continually acts in its self-interest, rather than in the organization's interest, particularly on an ongoing basis, there may be consequences, ranging from fines or dismissal by outside authorities to the loss of tax-exempt status. If a board member breaches his duty of loyalty, the nonprofit organization's board should dismiss that board member.

For example, assume that a board member is an owner of a construction company that is interested in securing a contract with the nonprofit organization to build its new performing arts center. In order to do business with the company without running afoul of the duty of loyalty and the law regarding conflicts of interest, several things must happen. The board member must disclose her involvement with the company. The nonprofit organization should undertake a competitive bidding process. Findings of fact that the board member's company is as good as (if not better than) all the others and that its costs and services are equal to (if not better than) its competitors should be made. At a meeting of the board of directors with a quorum present, these findings of fact should be reported and incorporated into the minutes. The board should then vote upon the contract. The conflicted board member should not participate in the vote. The minutes should reflect who voted and what the vote was. Finally, the interested director must abide by the decision without any type of coercive behavior.

Finally, the duty of obedience requires that the corporation pays its payroll taxes and the employees' salaries. Failure to do so is considered gross negligence, for which board members and officers will be held accountable.[81]

CLASSROOM DISCUSSION

Under what conditions can a board of directors be held personally liable?

Give an example of a fraudulent act.

NOTES

1. The authors wish to thank the following contributors to this chapter: Carolyn Casselman, Robert Freedman, the Internal Revenue Service, Hoong Yee Lee Krakauer, Fred Lake, Robert Lynch, Timothy J. McClimon, Carter Anne McGowan, Erin Moeller, New York State Department of Law Charities Bureau, James Patrick, Marc Routh, Amy Schwartzman, Diana Swartz, Paul Tetreault, and Robert Widman.
2. Unlike a corporation, which is owned by shareholders, a nonprofit organization is not owned by anyone.
3. Amy Schwartzman, "Nonprofit Law" (lecture moderated by Tobie Stein, Richard Frankel Productions, New York, October 25, 2005).
4. Ibid.
5. Ibid.
6. Ibid.
7. Ibid.

8. A copy of this document may be found at *www.oag.state. ny.us/business/not_for_profit.pdf*.
9. Schwartzman, "Lecture."
10. Queens Council on the Arts, Inc., "Bylaws" (draft, Queens Council on the Arts, Inc., Woodhaven, N.Y., 2004). The authors would like to thank the Queens Council on the Arts for allowing us to reproduce this section of a draft of their bylaws.
11. These professions are licensed and regulated by the Board of Regents.
12. Schools and museums must go through a special chartering process with the Board of Regents.
13. Schwartzman, "Lecture."
14. New York State Attorney General's Charities Bureau. *Procedures for Forming and Changing Not-for-Profit Corporations in New York* (New York: New York State Attorney General, 2002), 4, *www.oag.state.ny.us/business/not_for_ profit.pdf*.
15. Schwartzman, "Lecture."
16. As stated in chapter 1, fiduciary responsibilities are duties to act in the best interests of the corporation.
17. New York State Charities Bureau, 8.
18. Grant Williams, "Two Reports Track State Fees and Requirements and Their Advisors," *Chronicle of Philanthropy*, June 9, 2005, 22.
19. Amy Schwartzman, e-mail interview to author, April 22, 2005.
20. Amy Schwartzman, "Nonprofit Law" (cited in Jonathan Summey's "Questions and Answers: Final Project," for Principles of Performing Arts Management, Brooklyn College, Brooklyn, N.Y., 2003).
21. Schwartzman, "Lecture."
22. As an example, for a board consisting of 25 members, 6 members would constitute a quorum. For a board of 23, 6 would also constitute a quorum. For a board of 35, 7 would be a quorum.
23. Schwartzman, "Lecture on Nonprofit Law," 2005. Please see Article 7 of New York's Not-for-Profit Corporation law, found at *http://public.leginfo.state.ny.us*.
24. Internal Revenue Service, "Exemption Requirements," *www.irs.gov/charities/charitable/article/0,,id=96099,00.html*.
25. Ibid.
26. Schwartzman, "Lecture," 2005.
27. Internal Revenue Service, *Publication 557: Tax-Exempt Status for Your Organization* (Washington, D.C.: Internal Revenue Service, March 2005), 3, *www.irs.gov/pub/irs-pdf/ p557.pdf*.
28. Ibid.
29. Ibid.
30. Brad Wolverton, "IRS Asks Organizations Seeking Charity Status to Supply More Details," *Chronicle of Philanthropy*, January 6, 2005, 27.
31 Thomas K. Hyatt, "Tax Considerations for Nonprofits," in *The Nonprofit Legal Landscape*, Thomas K. Hyatt, ed. (Washington, D.C.: BoardSource, 2005), 22.
32. Internal Revenue Service, *Publication 557*, 31.
33. Ibid.
34. Internal Revenue Service, "Frequently Asked Questions: New Annual Electronic Notice—e-Postcard (Form 990-N)." April 3, 2007. *www.irs.gov/pub/irs-tege/epostcard_ faqs_final.pdf*; Internal Revenue Service. "Filing Requirements," *www.irs.gov/charities/article/0,,id=96103,00.html*.

35. Internal Revenue Service, "Application for Recognition of Exemption," *www.irs.gov/charities/article/0,,id=96122,00.html*.

36. Fringe benefits are benefits offered to the employee in addition to his salary; they include such items as health insurance, pension contributions, and vacation pay. The employer is responsible for "depositing payroll taxes imposed by the federal government, and by many state and municipal governments." The employer must pay her share of Social Security and Medicare taxes, as well as Federal Unemployment Taxes. Charles Grippo, *The Stage Producer's Business and Legal Guide* (New York: Allworth Press, 2002), 202–3.

37. Internal Revenue Service, *Publication 15: Employer's Tax Guide* (Washington, D.C.: Internal Revenue Service), 11, *www.irs.gov/pub/irs-pdf/p15.pdf*.

38. Ibid., 2.

39. Internal Revenue Service, "Notice 2007-45," *www.irs.gov/pub/irs-drop/n-07-45.pdf*.

40. Internal Revenue Service, *Publication 598: Tax on Unrelated Business Income of Exempt Organizations* (Washington, D.C.: Internal Revenue Service, November 2007), 3, *www.irs.gov/pub/irs-pdf/p598.pdf*.

41. Ibid.

42. Internal Revenue Service, *Publication 598*, 7.

43. Ibid., 5.

44. The authors wish to thank Marc Routh and Erin Moeller for providing information concerning the taxation of royalty payments.

45. For more information, please view the IRS Web site.

46. Schwartzman, "Lecture."

47. Internal Revenue Service, "May 17-18 2006 Executive Compensation Phone Forum," 1, *www.irs.gov/pub/irs-tege/may_17_final_script_exec_comp_phone_forum.pdf*.

48. Ibid, 3.

49. Ibid., 2.

50. Ibid., 8.

51. Ibid., 15.

52. Kenneth W. Clarkson, et al., *West's Business Law* (Mason, Ohio: South-Western College/West, 2004), 724.

53. Carolyn Casselman, "Waltzing with the Muse or Dancing with the Devil: Enhancement Deals between Nonprofit Theaters and Commercial Producers," *Columbia Journal of Law and the Arts*, 27 (Spring 2004): 333.

54. Ibid.

55. Internal Revenue Service, *Publication 557*.

56. BoardSource, "Can Nonprofits Lobby?" *www.boardsource.org/Knowledge.asp?ID=3.157*.

57. Internal Revenue Service, *Publication 557*.

58. Robert Lynch, e-mail interview to author, January 30, 2006.

59. Elizabeth Schwinn, "59 Groups Violated Rules on Electioneering in 2004, IRS Says," *Chronicle on Philanthropy*, March 9, 2005, 35.

60. Schwartzman, "E-mail interview."

61. Internal Revenue Service, "Election Year Activities and the Prohibition on Political Campaign Intervention for Section 501(c)(3) Organizations," *www.irs.gov/newsroom/article/0,,id=154712,00.html*.

62. The IRS states that all donations require that the donor keep either a canceled check or a written acknowledgement from the organization on file as substantiation for a tax deduction. In addition, if the donor is claiming a donation of $250 or more (to one organization in one sum), the donor must obtain an acknowledgement letter from the organization to keep on file.

63. Amy Schwartzman, interview by Jessica Johnston; Internal Revenue Service, *Publication 1771: Charitable Contributions—Substantiation and Disclosure Requirements* (Washington, D.C., Internal Revenue Service), May 2007, *www.irs.gov/pub/irs-pdf/p1771.pdf*.

64. Ibid.

65. Ibid.

66. BoardSource, "Why Do Nonprofits Have Boards, and What Do Boards Do?" *www.boardsource.org/Knowledge.asp?ID=3.383*.

67. New York State Attorney General's Charities Bureau. *Right From the Start: Responsibilities of Directors and Officers of Not-for-Profit Corporations* (New York: New York State Attorney General, January 2005), 5-8, *www.oag.state.ny.us/charities/not_for_profit_booklet.pdf*.

68. The fidelity bond will reimburse the organization from dishonest acts.

69. Nonprofit organizations are required by the Sarbanes-Oxley Act to establish procedures for communicating complaints and the observation of illegal actions. Employees must be assured that they will not be punished for reporting actions deemed inappropriate or worse. In addition, nonprofit organizations must establish procedures for archiving documents, including e-mail and voice mail, that may later be used to support evidence that a crime occurred. BoardSource and Independent Sector, *The Sarbanes-Oxley Act and Implications for Nonprofit Organizations* (Washington, D.C.: BoardSource and Independent Sector, 2006, 2003), 9–10.

70. *Right From the Start*, 5.

71. Ibid., 7.

72. Ibid.

73. Ibid.

74. Ibid., 8.

75. Robert Freedman, e-mail message to author, February 26, 2007.

76. Ibid.

77. Carter Anne McGowan, e-mail message to author, February 19, 2007.

78. Amy Schwartzman, interview by Jessica Johnston, November 13, 2005.

79. As stated in section 717 of the New York State nonprofit corporation law, other considerations would include the organization's "present and anticipated financial requirements, expected total return on its investments, price level trends, and general economic conditions." New York State, "Section 717," *http://public.leginfo.state.ny.us/menugetf.cgi?commonquery=laws*.

80. Schwartzman, e-mail message to author, February 23, 2007. Fraud is defined as "deliberately deceiving another in order to damage them, usually to obtain property or services unjustly." Ellen S. Podgor, "Criminal Fraud," *American Law Review* 48 (April 1999): 1.

81. Schwartzman, "E-mail." Gross negligence is defined as "reckless disregard for the safety or lives of others." *www.thelawencyclopedia.com*, 2004.

APPENDIX A: State Education Department Waiver Request Letter

Sam Brown
State Education Department
Education Building
Office of Counsel
Room 148
Albany, NY 12234

Dear Mr. Brown:

Enclosed please find the fee and a copy of Blank Inc.'s not-for-profit Certificate of
Incorporation for your review. We request a document indicating that the State
Education Department has no objection to this filing for not-for-profit incorporation.

Thank you very much.

I enclose a self-addressed stamped envelope for your convenience. Please do not hesitate
to call me if there are any questions or problems. I can be reached at (   )-xxx-xxxx.

Very truly yours,

Name (or name of lawyer)
Incorporator
Name of Organization

[This document was reprinted with the permission of Amy Schwartzman.]

BIBLIOGRAPHY

Andrew, Leonard D., and Richard S. Hobish, eds. "Employment Law Guide for Nonprofit Organizations." Pro Bono Partnership, 2003. *www.probonopartnership.org/PBPGuide/frame.htm.*

Anft, Michael, and Grant Williams. "Redefining Good Governance." *Chronicle of Philanthropy*, 19 August 2004.

Association of Fundraising Professionals. "The Charleston Principles Guidelines on Charitable Solicitations using the Internet." The Association for Fundraising Professionals. *www.afpnet.org/tier3_cd.cfm?folder_id=893&content_item_id=2324.*

Berkshire, Jennifer C. "Starting from Scratch: How Charities Cope When Their Boards Need a Makeover." *Chronicle of Philanthropy*, 31 May 2007.

Blazek, Jody. *IRS Form 1023 Tax Preparation Guide.* Hoboken, N.J.: Wiley, 2005.

BoardSource. *www.boardsource.org.*

————. "Can Nonprofits Lobby?" BoardSource Organization. *www.boardsource.org/Knowledge.asp?ID=3.157.*

————. "How Are Nonprofits Monitored, Regulated, and Governed?" BoardSource Organization. *www.boardsource.org/Knowledge.asp?ID=3.384.*

————. "How Do We Become a Nonprofit?" BoardSource Organization. *www.boardsource.org/Knowledge.asp?ID=3.367.*

————. "How Does a Nonprofit Safeguard against Organizational Conflict of Interest?" BoardSource Organization. *www.boardsource.org/Knowledge.asp?ID=3.389.*

————. "How Much Should Be Spent on Overhead or Fundraising?" BoardSource Organization. *www.boardsource.org/Knowledge.asp?ID=3.391.*

————. "How Should the Board Be Structured?" BoardSource Organization. *www.boardsource.org/Knowledge.asp?ID=3.388.*

————. "What Are the Legal Responsibilities of Nonprofit Boards?" BoardSource Organization. *www.boardsource.org/Knowledge.asp?ID=3.364.*

————. "What Should I Know before Joining the Board?" BoardSource Organization. *www.boardsource.org/Knowledge.asp?ID=3.362.*

————. "Why Are Nonprofit Organizations Tax-Exempt?" BoardSource Organization. *www.boardsource.org/Knowledge.asp?ID=3.171.*

————. "Why Do Nonprofits Have Boards, and What Do Boards Do?" BoardSource Organization. *www.boardsource.org/Knowledge.asp?ID=3.383.*

BoardSource and Independent Sector. *The Sarbanes-Oxley Act and Implications for Nonprofit Organizations.* Washington, D.C.: BoardSource and Independent Sector, 2006, 2003.

————. "The Sarbanes-Oxley Act and Implications for Nonprofit Organizations." Philanthropic Research, Inc. *www.guidestar.org/news/features/sarbanes_oxley.jsp.*

Bondarin, Dev, and Seth Soloway. "Questions and Answers Final Project." Principles of Performing Arts Management, Brooklyn College, 2004.

Casselman, Carolyn. "Waltzing with the Muse or Dancing with the Devil: Enhancement Deals between Nonprofit Theaters and Commercial Producers." *Columbia Journal of Law and the Arts* 27 (Spring 2004): 323–347.

Clarkson, Kenneth W., Roger LeRoy Miller, Gaylord A. Jentz, and Frank B. Cross. *West's Business Law.* Mason, Ohio: South-Western College/West, 2004.

Crenshaw, Albert B. "Tax Abuse Rampant in Nonprofits, IRS Says." *Washington Post*, 5 April 2005.

Davis, Deryl. "Going Nonprofit: Everything You Need to Know about Turning Your Theater into a Nonprofit Entity." *Stage Directions*, October 2004, 59–61.

Department of State, Division of Corporations. *Certificate of Incorporation, under Section 402 of the Not-for-Profit Corporation Law.* New York, September 2005.

Eisenberg, Pablo. "The Real Scandal at the Smithsonian Goes Beyond Executive Pay and Perks." *Chronicle of Philanthropy*, 3 May 2007.

Federal Election Commission. "Quick Answers to PAC Questions." Federal Election Commission. *www.fec.gov/ans/answers_pac.shtml.*

Freedman, Robert. 26 February 2007, e-mail.

Garner, Bryan A., ed. *Black's Law Dictionary.* 8th ed. Eagan, Minn.: West Publishing, 2004.

Grippo, Charles. *The Stage Producer's Business and Legal Guide.* New York: Allworth Press, 2002.

Hall, Holly. "Time Short for Using New Tax Breaks to Increase Charitable Gifts." *Chronicle of Philanthropy*, 13 October 2005.

Hopkins, Bruce R. *650 Essential Nonprofit Law Questions Answered.* Hoboken, N.J.: Wiley, 2005.

————. *Legal Responsibilities of Nonprofit Boards.* Washington, D.C.: BoardSource, 2003.

————. *Planning Guide for the Law of Tax-Exempt Organizations: Strategies and Commentaries.* Hoboken, N.J.: Wiley, 2004.

————. *The Tax Law of Charitable Giving.* Hoboken, N.J.: Wiley, 2005.

————. *The Tax Law of Unrelated Business for Nonprofit Organizations.* Hoboken, N.J.: Wiley, 2006.

Hyatt, Thomas K., ed. *The Nonprofit Legal Landscape.* Washington, D.C.: BoardSource, 2005.

Internal Revenue Service. *www.irs.gov.*

————. "Application for Recognition of Exemption, under Section 501(c)(3) of the Internal Revenue Code." *www.irs.gov/charities/article/0,,id=96122,00.html.*

————. "E-File for Charities and Nonprofits." Internal Revenue Service. *www.irs.gov/efile/article/0,,id=108211,00.html.*

————. "Election Year Activities and the Prohibition on Political Campaign Intervention for Section 501(c)(3) Organizations." Internal Revenue Service. *www.irs.gov/newsroom/article/0,,id=154712,00.html.*

————. "Exemption Requirements." Internal Revenue Service. *www.irs.gov/charities/charitable/article/0,,id=96099,00.html.*

————. "Filing Requirements." Internal Revenue Service. *www.irs.gov/charities/article/0,,id=96103,00.html.*

————. "Frequently Asked Questions: New Annual Electronic Notice—e-Postcard (Form 990-N)." April 3, 2007. *www.irs.gov/pub/irs-tege/epostcard_faqs_final.pdf.*

————. *Form 990: Return of Organization Exempt from Income Tax.* Washington, D.C. *www.irs.gov/pub/irs-pdf/f990.pdf.*

————. *Form 990-T: Exempt Organization Business Tax Return.* Washington D.C. *www.irs.gov/pub/irs-pdf/f990t.pdf.*

————. *Form 1023: Application for Recognition of Exemption.* Washington, D.C., June 2006. *www.irs.gov/pub/irs-pdf/f1023.pdf.*

————. *May 17-18, 2006 Executive Compensation Phone Forum.* Washington, D.C., 2006. *www.irs.gov/pub/irs-tege/may_17_final_script_exec_comp_phone_forum.pdf.*

———. "Notice 2007-45." Internal Revenue Service. *www.irs. gov/pub/irs-drop/n-07-45.pdf*.

———. *Publication 15: Employer's Tax Guide*. Washington, D.C. *www.irs.gov/pub/irs-pdf/p15.pdf*.

———. *Publication 15-A: Employer's Supplemental Tax Guide*. Washington, D.C., January 2007. *www.irs.gov/pub/irs-pdf/ p15a.pdf*.

———. *Publication 557: Tax-Exempt Status for Your Organization*. Washington, D.C., March 2005. *www.irs.gov/pub/irs-pdf/ p557.pdf*.

———. *Publication 598, Tax on Unrelated Business Income of Exempt Organizations*. Internal Revenue Service. November 2007. *www.irs.gov/pub/irs-pdf/p598.pdf*.

———. *Publication 1771: Charitable Contributions—Substantiation and Disclosure Requirements*. Washington, D.C., May 2007. *www.irs.gov/pub/irs-pdf/p1771.pdf*.

———. "Tax-Exempt Organizations Tax Kit." Internal Revenue Service. *www.irs.gov/charities/article/0,,id=96774,00.html*.

Jackson, Peggy M. *Sarbanes-Oxley for Nonprofit Boards*. Hoboken, N.J.: Wiley, 2007.

Jackson, Peggy M., and Toni E. Fogarty. *Sarbanes-Oxley and Nonprofit Management: Skills, Techniques, and Methods*. Hoboken, N.J.: Wiley, 2006.

Jarvis, Robert M., and Steven E. Chaikelson, Christine A. Corcos, Edmund P. Edmonds, Jon M. Garon, Shubha Ghosh, William D. Henslee, Mark S. Kende, Charles A. Palmer, Nancy L. Schultz, Marin R. Scordato, and Libby A. White. *Theater Law: Cases and Materials*. Durham, N.C.: Carolina Academic Press, 2004.

———. *Theater Law: Cases and Materials, Teacher's Manual*. Durham, N.C.: Carolina Academic Press, 2004.

Kurtz, Daniel L., and Sarah E. Paul. *Managing Conflicts of Interest*. Washington, D.C.: BoardSource, 2006.

Lawyers Alliance for New York. *Advising Nonprofits*. 4th ed. New York: Lawyers Alliance for New York, 1995.

———. *Fiscal Sponsorship Arrangements*. 3d ed. New York: Lawyers Alliance for New York, 1995.

———. *Getting Organized*. 5th ed. New York: Lawyers Alliance for New York, 1999.

———. *Mergers and Strategic Alliances for New York Not-for-Profit Corporations*. New York: Lawyers Alliance for New York, 2003.

———. *Serving on the Board of a Not-For-Profit Corporation: A Layperson's Guide*. New York: Lawyers Alliance for New York, 1993.

Lynch, Robert. "Lobbying." Interview by Tobie Stein. E-mail to author, 30 January 2006.

Mancuso, Anthony. *How to Form a Nonprofit Corporation*. 7th ed. Berkeley, Calif.: NOLO, 2005.

McGowan, Carter Anne. 19 February 2007 and 20 October 2006, e-mail.

———. "Lecture on Nonprofit Law." 28 September 2004. Richard Frankel Productions, New York.

Minnesota Council of Nonprofits. "Info Central." Minnesota Council of Nonprofits. *www.mncn.org/infocentral.htm*.

Moeller, Erin. "Royalties." E-mail to author, 19 July 2006.

New York Department of State. "Corporation and Business Entity Database." *http://appsext8.dos.state.ny.us/corp_ public/corpsearch.entity_search_entry*.

———. "Not-for-Profit Corporations FAQs." New York Department of State. *www.dos.state.ny.us/corp/nfpfaq. htm#form*.

New York State Attorney General's Charities Bureau. "Charitable and Other Non-Profit Organizations Forms and Filings Frequently Asked Questions." Office of New York State Attorney General, Eliot Spitzer. *www.oag.state. ny.us/charities/forms/forms_faq.html*.

———. *Disclosure Requirement for Solicitation of Contributions Pursuant to New York State Executive Law Section 174-b*. New York, January 2004. *www.oag.state.ny.us/charities/ disclosure.pdf*.

———. *Procedures for Forming and Changing Not-for-Profit Corporations in New York State*. New York, 2002. *www.oag. state.ny.us/business/not_for_profit.pdf*.

———. *Solicitation and Collection of Funds for Charitable Purposes*. New York, October 2006. *www.oag.state.ny.us/ charities/statute_booklet.pdf*.

———. *Summary of Registration and Filing Requirements for Charitable Entities*. New York, 2006. *www.oag.state.ny.us/ charities/forms/char023.pdf*.

New York State. "Section 717." *http://public.leginfo.state.ny.us/ menugetf.cgi?commonquery=laws*.

Nonprofit Coordinating Committee of New York, Inc. "Compliance Checklist." *www.npccny.org/compliance_ checklist.htm*.

Ober/Kaler. *The Nonprofit Legal Landscape*. Washington, D.C.: BoardSource, 2005.

Panepento, Peter, and Grant Williams. "A Question of Calculation." *Chronicle of Philanthropy*, 7 February 2008.

Philanthropic Research, Inc. "Form 990 FAQs." Philanthropic Research, Inc. *www.guidestar.org/help/faq_990.jsp#whatis990*.

Podgor, Ellen S. "Criminal Fraud." *American Law Review* 48 (April 1999): 1.

Price, Hugh B. "The Best Ways for Boards to Operate." *Chronicle of Philanthropy*, 26 January 2006.

Quotah, Eman. "Getting a Head Start: Fiscal Sponsorship Helps Fledgling Charitable Programs Fly," *Chronicle of Philanthropy*, 5 April 2007.

———. "Sponsorships Could Cut Waste in Charity World," *Chronicle of Philanthropy*, 5 April 2007.

Rogachevskaya, Lana, and Karen Tecott. "Questions and Answers: Final Project." Principles of Performing Arts Management, Brooklyn College, 2004.

Queens Council on the Arts, Inc. "Bylaws." 2004.

Routh, Marc. "Enhancement." E-mail to author, 7 November 2005.

Ruppel, Warren. *Not-for-Profit Audit Committee Best Practices*. Hoboken, N.J.: Wiley, 2005.

Russell, Jacob Hall. "Executive Pay Takes the Stage." *Wall Street Journal*, 11 February 2006.

Saidel, Judith R. *Guide to the Literature on Governance: An Annotated Bibliography*. Washington, D.C.: BoardSource, 2002. *www.boardsource.org/UserFiles/File/Research/introtoc. pdf*.

Sanders, Michael I. *Joint Ventures Involving Tax-Exempt Organizations*. 2d ed. Hoboken, N.J.: Wiley, 2005.

Schwartzman, Amy. 23 February 2007 and 12 February 2007, e-mail.

———. "Nonprofit Law." Interview by Jessica Johnston. Tape recording, 13 November 2005. New York.

———. "Nonprofit Law." Interview by Tobie Stein. E-mail to author, 22 April 2005.

———. "Lecture on Nonprofit Law." 25 October 2005. Richard Frankel Productions, New York.

————. "Waiver Letter to New York State Department of Education." New York, 2005. Photocopy.

Schwinn, Elizabeth. "59 Groups Violated Rules on Electioneering in 2004, IRS Says." *Chronicle of Philanthropy*, 9 March 2006.

————. "Tax Watch." *Chronicle of Philanthropy*, 3 March 2005.

Spitzer, Eliot, Attorney General of New York. *Internal Controls and Financial Accountability for Not-for-Profit Boards*. New York, January 2005. *www.oag.state.ny.us/charities/internal_controls.pdf*.

————. *Procedures and Forms for a Simplified Non-Judicial Dissolution Pursuant to Article 10 of the Not-for-profit Corporation Law*. New York, April 2006. *www.oag.state.ny.us/charities/forms/no_assets.pdf*.

————. *Right From the Start: Responsibilities of Directors and Officers of Not-for-Profit Corporations*. New York, January 2005. *www.oag.state.ny.us/charities/not_for_profit_booklet.pdf*.

————. *Tips for Charities Raising Funds in New York State*. New York, December 2004. *www.oag.state.ny.us/charities/charities_raising_funds.pdf*.

"State Registration Requirements for Charities and Fund Raisers." *Chronicle of Philanthropy*, 9 June 2005.

Summey, Jonathan. "Questions and Answers: Final Project." Principles of Performing Arts Management, Brooklyn College, 2003.

Tesdahl, Benson. *The Nonprofit Board's Guide to Bylaws: Creating a Framework for Effective Governance*. Washington, D.C.: BoardSource, 2003.

The Concise Law Encyclopedia. "Definition of Gross Negligence." The Concise Law Encyclopedia Web site. *www.thelawencyclopedia.com*, 2004.

Vogel, Brian H., and Charles W. Quatt. *Dollars and Sense: The Nonprofit Board's Guide to Determining Chief Executive Compensation*. Washington, D.C.: BoardSource, 2005.

Widman, Robert. "Lecture on Sarbanes-Oxley Law," February 21, 2007.

Williams, Grant. "Two Reports Track State Fees and Requirements for Charities and Their Advisors." *Chronicle of Philanthropy*, 9 June 2005.

Winnick, Jamie, and Amy Wratchford. "Questions and Answers: Final Project." Principles of Performing Arts Management, Brooklyn College, 2004.

Wolverton, Brad. "IRS Asks Organizations Seeking Charity Status to Supply More Details." *Chronicle of Philanthropy*, 6 January 2005.

CHAPTER FOUR
Commercial Producing

In this chapter, we will define commercial producing, detailing the specific types of commercial productions: Broadway, Off-Broadway, and touring productions.[1] We will then outline the process of producing a commercial production. This process consists of finding and developing the work to be produced (known as "the property"), obtaining the right to produce the property, forming the business entity to act as a producer, and finding investors for the project. The producer then must rent a theater to house the production, hire artistic and production staff, and manage the creation of contracts and budgets. Finally, the producer will supervise the marketing efforts of the production as tickets begin to be sold, arrange for out-of-town tryouts and previews for the work as necessary, and oversee the maintenance of the show after it opens.

COMMERCIAL PRODUCTIONS

Simply put, commercial productions exist to make money. Unlike nonprofit organizations, which can depend on donations and grants to make up any budget deficits, commercial productions must rely on earned income (such as ticket sales, sponsorship, and merchandising) alone.[2] If a commercial production does not have enough earned income to cover all costs, it cannot make a profit for its producers and investors. If the show cannot make a profit, it must close.

This focus on profit differentiates commercial productions from nonprofit productions. Producer Marc Routh (*The Producers, Swing!*) elaborates on this difference: "The nonprofit theater has a much more complex mission; it might want to support a group of artists, or perform a certain type of work, or make art accessible to a particular community. The mission of the commercial theater producer is simple. It's to make money. Some commercial producers may also want to produce quality art, but art is not the main goal for a commercial producer."[3]

Even though commercial productions must appeal to a large audience in order to sell tickets, not all commercial productions are the same. "Commercial" is a means of production, not an artistic statement; a commercial production can be a big, splashy Broadway musical like *Mamma Mia!* or *The Phantom of the Opera*, or it can be a small, experimental production such as the Off-Broadway production of the English avant-garde theatrical collective Complicite's *Mnemonic*. Successful commercial productions do not simply pander to the audience. If a commercial production does not have anything to offer to the public, it will not succeed. As producer and general manager Richard Frankel (*The Producers, Sweeney Todd* [2005]) states, "I believe that in order to make money you have to move people. You have to engage the audience on an emotional level. People will pay money to be moved, and they will tell their friends to pay money for that experience. Therefore, I believe that the pressures of the marketplace actually produce quality."[4]

Producer Jon B. Platt (*Wicked, Copenhagen*) agrees. "I was a producer on *Angels in America*, which was an extremely challenging show to mount, but one that all of the producers loved and to which they were deeply committed. By any logical estimation, this show should have lost money, but it transcended the expected business model and became financially, as well as artistically, successful. So much love was put into the production that the audience knew they were watching something special. Conversely, I've also done some shows primarily for financial reasons and (with some exceptions) they've failed to make a profit. You have to love the project. Critics can tell instantly if a show is produced simply to make money, and audiences tend to follow the critics' lead and stay away. If, as a producer, you are not emotionally touched by a piece, how can you expect to generate enthusiasm and emotion in your audience?"[5]

Although all commercial theater productions exist to earn a profit, there are many different avenues available to realize the commercial production. The world of commercial producing consists of different types of productions based on theater (venue) size and/or location. A producer must choose the right type for the production at hand, basing her decision on such factors as the projected audience for the project, the costs of mounting the production, and the size of the set and other physical production elements. In the upcoming sections, we will define the following types of commercial productions: Broadway, Off-Broadway, and touring productions.

Broadway

In terms of theater size and location, Broadway is the most specifically defined of the commercial producing types. A Broadway production is any production that plays in a theater that has over 499 seats and is located in the area known as the "Broadway box," which is "bounded by Fifth and Ninth Avenues from 34th Street to 56th Street, and by Fifth Avenue and the Hudson River from 56th Street to 72nd Street."[6] Although the vast majority of Broadway productions are commercially produced, nonprofit theater companies do produce shows as Broadway productions as well.

Most Broadway producers and theater owners (also known as landlords) belong to The Broadway League (formerly the League of American Theatres and Producers). In labor negotiations, The Broadway League serves as a collective bargaining unit.[7] A collective bargaining unit is a group (in this case, of employers) engaged in negotiating labor agreements with unions, who represent the employees. Forming an employer collective bargaining unit allows individual producers and theater owners to negotiate contracts as a group, giving the members of the group more power and leverage than they would have as individual negotiators. Collectively bargained agreements outline the minimum terms that must be met by the producer in order to hire a member of the union; these terms include such items as fees, salaries, royalty rates, and work rules.[8]

Broadway productions are fully unionized, meaning all employees working on the production and in the theater are members of a union and are employed under collectively bargained agreements. These unions include:

• Actors' Equity Association (AEA), representing actors and stage managers

• Society of Stage Directors and Choreographers (SSDC), representing directors and choreographers
• American Federation of Musicians (AFM), Local 802, representing musicians
• Service Employees International Union, Local 32BJ, representing maintenance and cleaning personnel
• International Union of Operating Engineers, Local 30, covering operators of heating, air-conditioning, and ventilation systems
• International Alliance of Theatrical Stage Employees (IATSE), an international union covering the United States and Canada, with local unions representing employees in specific jobs or geographic areas. For Broadway, these locals are:

  o Local 1, representing stagehands in Manhattan
  o United Scenic Artists (USA), Local USA 829, covering scenic, lighting, costume, and sound designers
  o Association of Theatrical Press Agents and Managers (ATPAM), Local 18032, representing company managers, house managers, and press agents
  o Theatrical Wardrobe Union, Local 764, covering all wardrobe personnel
  o Hair and Makeup Union, Local 798, covering all hair and makeup artists
  o Treasurers and Ticket Sellers Union, Local 751, representing all box office personnel
  o Ushers, Ticket Takers, and Doormens' Union, Local 306

• International Brotherhood of Teamsters, representing loaders required on every show to unload trucks for scenery entering the building and to load trucks for scenery exiting the building

In addition to these unions, Broadway commercial producers work with members of the Dramatists Guild of America, a professional organization serving playwrights, composers, and lyricists (collectively known as "authors"). Although the Guild is not a union, it does provide a model contract (the Approved Production Contract) for its members to use in negotiations with producers. Authors produced on Broadway (or in any other arena) have no obligation to become members of the Dramatists Guild. (More information about collectively bargained agreements, unions, and the Dramatists Guild can be found in chapter 9.)

In addition to its responsibilities as a collective bargaining unit, The Broadway League also creates marketing opportunities for Broadway theaters such as "Kids' Night on Broadway," a night in which a child gets a free ticket to a Broadway show with the purchase of one adult ticket. The Broadway League negotiates corporate sponsorships for Broadway productions, partnering with corporations to provide benefits for both ticket buyers and Broadway producers and theater owners. The Broadway League also co-presents the American Theatre Wing's Antoinette Perry Awards (commonly known as the Tony Awards), an award ceremony celebrating excellence on Broadway; the annual Tony Awards ceremony is shown on network television, garnering much exposure for the featured productions.

Given these parameters, what sorts of properties are produced on Broadway? As Broadway theaters must have more than 499 seats (most Broadway theaters have between 1,000 and 1,700 seats), commercial producers must select productions that will play well in larger theaters. In addition, the use of union personnel with set salaries and the high production costs associated with larger physical productions cause Broadway productions to be much more expensive than other types of commercial productions. The capitalization cost of a large-scale Broadway musical is between $11 and 16 million; the capitalization cost of a Broadway play is between $2 and 2.5 million.[9] (The capitalization or "production" cost includes all expenses incurred from the conception of the project through opening night.) High capitalization costs mean that Broadway productions must sell as many tickets as possible to pay back investors and make a profit. It also means that Broadway productions usually need to run a long time in order to sell the tickets needed to make a profit.

Thus, Broadway productions are selected to appeal to a broad audience. As Richard Frankel says, "You have to choose material that you can sell. For a musical, you have to sell $100,000 worth of tickets a day just to keep it afloat. So, you can't pick esoteric material that doesn't appeal to a large number of ticket buyers. Similarly, you can't do playwrights like William Shakespeare, Anton Chekhov, and Henrik Ibsen on Broadway unless you have a star in the cast."[10]

Beyond the challenges of appealing to a mass audience, the tremendous cost of producing a show on Broadway has significantly reduced the chances that a show will recoup its capitalization (pay back the investors). Jon B. Platt remarks, "The modest hit on Broadway has mostly disappeared. It used to be that a Broadway show would run for six months to a year, make its money back (with a modest profit), and be considered a success. Not anymore. Now a show tends to be a smash or a flop. Eighty percent of all Broadway productions fail, in that they don't make back their capitalization costs. A show like *Wicked*, which is arguably the most successful production of the last ten years, is one show in a season of twenty or twenty-five shows. Multiply those shows by ten, and you can see that your odds [of] getting a *Wicked*-type success once in a decade are about one in 250."[11]

Nonprofit Theaters Producing on Broadway

Although nonprofit theaters can produce directly on Broadway simply by renting a theater, as the Public Theater did with its 1998 production of *On the Town*, three nonprofit theaters own or operate venues that are considered Broadway theaters.[12] These nonprofit Broadway venues are: the American Airlines Theatre and Studio 54 (owned by Roundabout Theatre Company), Vivian Beaumont Theatre (Lincoln Center Theater), and the Biltmore Theatre (Manhattan Theatre Club). Although these theaters are often included in Broadway marketing campaigns, and the shows produced in them are eligible for Tony Award nominations, these theaters are still nonprofit organizations and actually are members of the collective bargaining organization for nonprofit resident (producing) theaters, the League of Resident Theatres (LORT).[13] As LORT members, they have collectively bargained agreements with the Actors' Equity Association, the Society of Stage Directors and Choreographers, and United Scenic Artists (although each theater has individual agreements with other unions); because these nonprofit Broadway theaters operate under LORT agreements, their minimum contractual pay rates are reduced from the commercial Broadway minimum rate.[14]

As Harold Wolpert, managing director of the Roundabout Theatre Company, sees it, the nonprofit Broadway theaters should be treated as LORT theaters because "we have much more in common with many LORT theaters around the country than we do with commercial theater. The Roundabout is an institutional theater in the type of work we do and how we do it. The only way that we interact with the commercial world is in the marketplace, selling tickets. Otherwise, we don't formally interact."[15]

Wolpert continues, "Some commercial producers and union representatives might scorn us because we're getting what they consider to be cut-rate deals while competing for the same audience. But the nonprofit theaters are typically producing limited runs in smaller theaters, and we're producing work that commercial producers wouldn't. For example, a commercial producer would not have taken a chance on a show like *The Light in the Piazza* [produced by Lincoln Center Theater]; it was a new musical, and its composer had never been produced on Broadway. Nonprofit theaters also engage in many other activities, besides producing shows, that commercial producers don't have to do. At the Roundabout, we have an extensive educational program that we consider part of our mission to serve the community."[16]

Off-Broadway

As might be inferred by the name, Off-Broadway is defined as an alternative to Broadway. Off-Broadway productions play in theaters with 100 to 499 seats and can be located in any part of Manhattan. (This definition follows the one outlined in the Actors' Equity Off-Broadway Agreement; when used as a marketing term, "Off-Broadway" may encompass smaller shows that are not part of this commercial agreement.[17]) Off-Broadway productions may be produced within the Broadway box, but must follow specific rules: "Shows in theaters with 499 seats or less require special permission from Actors' Equity to operate as Off-Broadway productions within the Broadway box. However, under the current Actors' Equity agreement, productions may operate under the Off-Broadway agreement in theaters up to 350 seats (for Off-Broadway League members; the Off-Broadway League is explained below) and up to 299 seats (for non-League members) without special permission."[18]

Like Broadway producers and theater owners, Off-Broadway producers and theater owners also have a professional association and collective bargaining unit, known as the League of Off-Broadway Theatres and Producers. The League of Off-Broadway Theatres and Producers negotiates collectively bargained agreements with AEA, SSDC, and ATPAM; individual producers and theaters may have separately negotiated contracts as needed. In addition, the League of Off-Broadway Theatres and Producers is active in creating marketing opportunities for its members and coordinating promotional display racks for Off-Broadway productions within its member theaters. Off-Broadway productions produced by League members are eligible for the Lucille Lortel Awards, celebrating excellence in Off-Broadway theater. (Productions that are officially registered as Lortel Awards participants with the League of Off-Broadway Theatres and Producers are also eligible for these awards.)

As Off-Broadway productions play in smaller theaters and do not have as many collectively bargained agreements with theatrical unions, they are much less expensive to produce. The average capitalization cost for an Off-Broadway musical is $1.2 million, nearly $10 million less than for a Broadway musical. Similarly, the average capitalization cost of an Off-Broadway play is approximately $800,000.

Although costs Off-Broadway are significantly less than on Broadway, a commercial producer still faces a significant challenge in creating a successful Off-Broadway production. Producer Jonathan Pollard (*I Love You, You're Perfect, Now Change*) explains: "In the past ten years, capitalization costs Off-Broadway have greatly increased; an Off-Broadway musical production that would have had a capitalization of $500,000 in the mid-nineties will now be capitalized at $1 million. Weekly running costs [the weekly cost of operating the production after it opens] have increased as well. Salaries as dictated by the unions have increased, the theater rental is more expensive, equipment rentals cost more, and media costs are much more than they were ten years ago. However, Off-Broadway theaters, by definition, cannot have more than 499 seats. The costs have gone up, but the capacity of the theater [number of seats] has not increased. The total amount of tickets available to sell for a particular production has not changed. You can only raise prices so high for an Off-Broadway production when the top ticket price for a Broadway production is $120. The producer ends up being squeezed between rising costs and stagnant ticket income; if a show does not make money within its first couple of weeks, it may not be able to stay open for long."[19]

Touring Productions

If a Broadway or Off-Broadway show is successful, then the producers of the show may decide to tour the production; in addition, a tour may begin directly on the road without ever being produced in New York. (Although this section defines a touring production as a type of commercial production, the process of creating and touring a production will be described in chapter 10.) A tour or touring production is a production that moves from one city to another in a set route. Touring productions may play one location for one or two nights, for part of a week (known as a split-week), for an entire week, or for multiple weeks (in large urban markets such as Los Angeles, California; Chicago, Illinois, and San Francisco, California). Commercial productions also tour internationally to such markets as London, England, and Shanghai, China. In many cases, the first tour of a production after that production opens on Broadway is typically an Equity tour; these initial tours play large theaters in major markets such as Chicago, Los Angeles, and Boston for at least one week. Touring productions may also be created using non-Equity actors, or with no union personnel at all.

Companies may also be formed to play only in one market; as these "sit-down productions" require separate capitalization and do not move from place to place, they may also be considered as commercial productions originating outside of New York. A renewed force as a destination for sit-down productions is Las Vegas. Although commercial productions with reduced running times (known as "tabbed" versions and usually about ninety minutes long) played in Las Vegas during the 1960s and 1970s, new hotel owners have created a vogue for commercial theatrical productions as added attractions for tourists coming to gamble in their casinos. Both Broadway and Off-Broadway productions have traveled across the country to Las Vegas. Although *Mamma Mia!* (in 2003) was the first of these new musicals to open in Las Vegas, the current Las Vegas theatrical boom was inaugurated in 2005 by *Avenue Q*; it played as an exclusive engagement at the Wynn Las Vegas resort and chose not to tour in North America.[20] (It has now toured.) Tabbed productions of *Hairspray*, *The Phantom of the Opera*, *The Producers*, *Spamalot*, and *Jersey Boys* soon followed, with mixed success. Both *Hairspray* and *Avenue Q* closed earlier than expected, but *Mamma Mia!*, *The Phantom of the Opera*, *Spamalot*, and *Jersey Boys* are still running as of this writing.

CLASSROOM DISCUSSION

What are the differences between a commercial production and a nonprofit production?

What defines a Broadway production?

What is The Broadway League, and what are the benefits of belonging to it?

What unions have collectively bargained agreements with The Broadway League, and what workers do these unions represent?

What types of work are successful on Broadway?

What are the advantages and disadvantages of owning a Broadway theater as a nonprofit organization?

What defines an Off-Broadway production?

What is the League of Off-Broadway Theatres and Producers, and what are the benefits of belonging to it?

What unions have collectively bargained agreements with the League of Off-Broadway Theatres and Producers?

Define these terms: "tour" and "sit-down production."

Why has Las Vegas experienced an increase in theatrical productions in its hotels?

PRODUCING A COMMERCIAL PRODUCTION: THE PROCESS

The process of producing a commercial production varies from show to show. Marc Routh states, "I think that if you look at the process for producing a show, you'll find that no two shows are alike. Some shows spring fully grown from a creator's head, and all you have to do is start getting financing and selling tickets; to a degree, that's the story of producing *The Producers*. Other shows take a long, slow, painful, laborious process to fruition. In the case of *Smokey Joe's Cafe*, we produced a workshop version of the show, then two more productions, and then we finally entered our rehearsal period for the Broadway production.[21] That process took four or five years. One of the quickest gestation periods we had was for the Broadway musical *Swing!*, which went from a kernel of an idea about turning swing music and dancing into a theatrical experience to a fully produced Broadway musical in about two years. However, in all cases you not only need the work itself to come together, but you also need an available venue, the right creative team, and all of the financing to come together as well. It's not a quick, easy task. I've talked to a lot of people who say they have a show that hasn't been written yet, but they expect it to be on Broadway next season. I usually just say to myself, 'I don't think so.'"[22]

Although every commercial production is different, all begin with the producer. A producer finds and develops the property, acquires the rights to produce the property, forms the producing entity, raises the money for the production, finds an appropriate theater, hires all artistic and production staff, and oversees the contracting and budgeting processes for the production with the general manager. The producer also oversees the marketing campaign and monitors ticket sales; arranges for tryouts and previews; and continues to manage the production once it opens.

Finding and Developing the Property

Some commercial productions are commissioned directly by a producer. A producer has an idea for the show (such as producing swing dancing as a theatrical event, as in *Swing!*). He acquires all necessary rights (legal permissions) to produce this idea in a theater and assembles a creative team to realize the idea. Typically, the first part of the creative team to be brought into the potential production is the writing team, which would include playwrights or librettists, composers, and lyricists. After the script is created, the rest of the creative team is hired, and the financing and production of the show commences. (In some cases, the director may be attached to the production before the script is entirely complete, as Susan Stroman was for *The Producers*.) It can take from two to seven years from the conception of the idea to realize a production in this way.[23]

Other productions begin from an existing script. In this case, a writing team has created a project that is attractive to a commercial producer, who then acquires the rights to produce the project. Generally, such productions require additional time to develop into a finished, commercial piece, even though the major work on the script, libretto, or music has already been done; a production with rights acquired from its original creators usually takes three to five years to open.[24]

An example of this process is Richard Frankel's involvement with *The Producers*, which began when he accepted an invitation to a reading of the musical. "The unusual thing about *The Producers* reading was that no producer was attached to the project. Mel Brooks [the author] and Susan Stroman [the director/choreographer] produced the reading themselves and invited commercial producers to the reading to pick the ones they wanted to produce their show. In effect, the creators were auditioning the producers. Our office was absolutely mad for *The Producers*. We wanted to produce that show. The next day, I sat down and wrote Mel Brooks a letter detailing my enthusiasm for the show, my expertise as a producer, and how much the movie [of *The Producers*] meant to me and to my children. At one point in the letter I wrote, 'I WANT THAT MONEY!,' which is a line from the movie. Mel Brooks called us after he received the letter and interviewed us. He ended up selecting us as one of the producers of the show, because we could also act as the general manager for the production."[25]

The least time-consuming method of producing is transferring a property that has already been produced to a commercial theater. Marc Routh states, "We're always looking for new projects [to transfer]. I pay a lot of attention to regional theaters to see if there are any productions in which I'm interested. Also, if someone calls me and says that there's a show playing in Madrid, Moscow, or Shanghai that I should see, then I jump on a plane and go see it."[26] A production can transfer to a commercial theater in as little as a few months, but many productions wait a year or more to transfer in order to find a suitable theater.[27] Productions are usually transferred from nonprofit theaters or from commercial theaters in other cities (often London).

Transferring a production from a nonprofit theater to a commercial theater can be done in several ways. A producer can see a production at a nonprofit theater and decide to transfer the production as is. In this situation, a producer negotiates an agreement with the theater company for the rights to the production; with the author(s) to obtain the commercial rights for the property; and with the creative team to adapt the work for the commercial production.[28] The producer then determines if the physical production needs to be modified in any way for the new theater, negotiates new contracts with the cast members, and opens the commercial production.[29] The nonprofit theater may be a coproducer of the commercial production, or it may simply receive a royalty (payment for the rights to the production) and/or a share of the net profits (revenue remaining after expenses are deducted) for the transfer without direct participation in the commercial production.

However, a producer can also enter into an agreement with a nonprofit theater to produce a production as part of the nonprofit theater's season. The producer licenses the necessary rights (gives permission) to produce the production to the nonprofit theater and contributes money to enhance the production; these additional funds allow the nonprofit theater to create a more elaborate physical production or hire more actors and musicians as the production requires it.[30] This contribution by the producer is known as enhancement money. When a producer negotiates an enhancement deal with a nonprofit theater, the theater agrees to produce the property with the addition of the enhancement money in exchange for royalties and/or net profits from future commercial productions; the nonprofit theater may also receive the right to invest in or become one of the producers of the commercial production.[31] "Typically, an enhancement deal includes a royalty of 1 to 2 percent of the net adjusted gross receipts, and will also include a percentage of any profits."[32] The percentage of profit received by the nonprofit organization may range from .5 to 10 percent. In addition to mounting the production, the nonprofit theater and the commercial producers may work closely together to manage the marketing and press campaign for the nonprofit production.[33] However, the nonprofit theater is in complete control of the production itself and makes all artistic and production decisions, including decisions about the involvement of the commercial producers in the enhanced production.

Geoff Rich, managing director of The New Group, describes the commercial transfer of *Avenue Q* from the perspective of the nonprofit theater: "*Avenue Q* was originally developed from a series of workshops and readings by Robyn Goodman, a commercial producer. She brought in Jeffrey Seller and Kevin McCollum as producing partners. The three of them felt that, because of the unique nature of the show, it needed the loving care and lower profile that a nonprofit theater could provide. They invited a number of nonprofit theaters to a reading of the show to see which ones would be interested. Our artistic director, Scott Elliott, attended the reading and fell in love with the material, so we indicated that we would be glad to include it as one of our productions. At the time, we also felt that we needed to work on the production with another nonprofit theater that had more experience producing musicals. The Vineyard Theatre was interested in *Avenue Q* as well, so the two theaters acted as coproducers; the production itself was housed at the Vineyard Theatre. The commercial producers gave us one-third of the production expenses (about $150,000) as an enhancement. The nonprofit theaters retained artistic control of the production, but because the commercial producers had brought it to us, it was understood that they had control over the future commercial life of the production. We created the production, and after it transferred to Broadway, we received a royalty from the Broadway production. We will also receive a royalty from any future commercial productions of the show."[34]

Rich believes that it is essential that the nonprofit theater retain artistic control over the enhanced production. "An enhancement deal is not a partnership. When a nonprofit theater produces a work, it is in charge of the show. Since commercial interests are financially involved with the production, we want to keep them informed of critical decisions that are being made during the

course of the production. But once the decision is made to have the nonprofit theater produce the show, the nonprofit theater makes all of the artistic choices for the production, such as casting actors and adding or cutting musical numbers."[35]

Although nonprofit theaters gain financially from enhancement deals, Rich urges nonprofit theaters to enter into such deals with caution. "A nonprofit theater doesn't want to be in a situation where it takes on enhancement deals as a way of paying for the cost of its productions, because then it's no longer being true to its nonprofit mission. If nonprofit theaters come to depend on commercial enhancement money in order to balance their budgets, it would be a dangerous thing for our art form."[36]

In addition to transferring a production from a nonprofit theater, commercial producers may also transfer commercial productions playing in other cities. Richard Frankel describes the process of transferring a commercial production (the 2005 revival of *Sweeney Todd*) from London. "We were asked to see *Sweeney Todd* in London by its London producer, with whom we partnered on the London production of *Smokey Joe's Cafe*. We saw it, we loved it, and we decided to bring it here. We needed to license [obtain the rights to] the production from the U.K. producers who had the U.S. rights. In addition, we also had to get the approval of Stephen Sondheim [the composer and lyricist]."[37]

Beyond these methods of finding a suitable commercial property, some commercial productions develop from other forms of entertainment. Some Off-Broadway productions, such as *Blue Man Group*, developed first as performance pieces in small theaters before transferring to a larger commercial theater. In addition, some commercial productions develop out of cabaret acts or stand-up comedy. For example, *Defending the Caveman* developed from an act by stand-up comic Rob Becker, ran on Broadway for 674 performances, and went on to have several successful national tours.[38]

After the producer chooses a property to produce, the developmental process begins. The developmental process differs from show to show. For a property with an existing script that has been previously produced, the development process might consist of minor script revisions. On the opposite end of the spectrum, a property in development for a Broadway production may have several readings or workshop productions before a full production is mounted. A workshop is a production of the entire show staged in a rehearsal room by a director (and choreographer, if necessary), presented after four or five weeks of rehearsal to an audience of approximately fifty to one hundred people.[39] A workshop may cost up to $400,000, depending on the show.[40]

Even productions that are direct transfers may have some adjustments before going into rehearsals. For *Sweeney Todd*, the London production was recast with American actors. Richard Frankel explains: "We had to make a decision about the use of stars in this production. Obviously, casting stars in your production can make it easier to raise money and to sell tickets to the show. However, in London, there were no stars; *Sweeney Todd* was an ensemble production.[41] The idea of the ensemble was integral to the piece, but we decided that, if we could find stars who would work well in an ensemble, then we would cast them. We eventually chose to cast two particular stars in our production—Michael Cerveris and Patti LuPone—because they are wonderful actors, they have a great history with Stephen Sondheim, and they are true ensemble players."[42]

CLASSROOM DISCUSSION

Describe the ways in which commercial producers find and develop properties.

From where may productions be transferred?

How may a commercial producer transfer a show originating in a nonprofit theater?

Define "enhancement deal." How is enhancement money used? When a production is enhanced at a nonprofit theater, what responsibilities does the commercial producer have? When a production is enhanced at a nonprofit theater, what responsibilities does the nonprofit theater have?

What is a workshop?

Acquiring the Rights

After a commercial producer finds a property, he must acquire the right to produce it. In order to do this, a producer must find the party that holds the copyright to the property and obtain a license to produce the property.

As defined by the United States Copyright Office, a copyright is "a form of protection provided by the laws of the United States to the authors of 'original works of authorship,' including literary, dramatic, musical, artistic, and certain other intellectual works."[43] Copyright protection prohibits the exploitation of the author's work by giving "the owner of the copyright exclusive right to do and to authorize others to do the following:

to reproduce the work in copies or recordings; to prepare derivative works based upon the work; to distribute copies or recordings of the work to the public by sale or other transfer of ownership, or by rental, lease, or lending; to perform the work publicly, in the case of literary, musical, dramatic, and choreographic works, pantomimes, and motion pictures and other audiovisual works; to display the work publicly, in the case of literary, musical, dramatic, and choreographic works, pantomimes, and pictorial, graphic, or sculptural works, including the individual images of a motion picture or other audiovisual work; and in the case of sound recordings, to perform the work publicly by means of a digital audio transmission."[44] A copyright covers only the tangible expression of an idea, not the idea itself. For example, two authors—Andrew Lloyd Webber and the team of Maury Yeston and Arthur Kopit—decided separately to create musical versions of the novel *The Phantom of the Opera*. Both works were copyrighted, and neither would be considered as infringing on the other's copyright unless the work itself (i.e., the libretto or the score) were copied.[45]

Under current copyright law, a work is copyrighted from the moment of creation. As soon as an author puts pen to paper or types into a computer, that work is protected under copyright. A work does not have to be published or registered with the copyright office to be copyrighted. In fact, the work does not even need to have a notice of copyright to be protected, although the United States Copyright Office recommends that the copyrighted materials contain a notice with the copyright symbol (©), the year of publication, and the name of the copyright holder.[46] However, the Copyright Office strongly suggests that all works be registered. Registration confers certain advantages on the copyright holder, including the establishment of a public record of the copyright claim, which allows the copyright holder to provide evidence of the copyright in court and collect additional damages and fees in a lawsuit.[47]

However, if an author creates a work as part of his duties as an employee, or if an author agrees to grant copyright to an employer as part of his contract for producing the work, that work is considered a work made for hire.[48] If a work is made for hire, the employer, not the author, holds the copyright. Most films are created as works made for hire; the studios or producers generally hold the copyright to the film, not the screenwriter or the director.

The duration of copyright depends on the date that the work was created. If a work was created after January 1, 1978, copyright protection is in effect for the duration of the author's life plus seventy years after his death. In the case of a joint work, created by two or more parties, copyright protection lasts seventy years after the death of the last surviving author.[49] For works made for hire, copyright duration is "95 years from publication or 120 years from creation, whichever is shorter."[50] If a work was created and published before January 1, 1978, the duration of copyright protection is ninety-five years from the date a work was published with a copyright notice or the date a work was registered with the United States Copyright Office.[51]

If a work is no longer under copyright protection, it is considered to be "in the public domain" and can be exploited by anyone. The plays of William Shakespeare and the poetry of Emily Dickinson are examples of works in the public domain. Generally, works created before 1923 can be considered to be in the public domain, but a producer should always check on a work's copyright status if there is any doubt about copyright protection.[52]

If a producer wants to acquire the rights to an existing work, or if the producer is commissioning a property based on an existing work, then she must determine if the work is protected under copyright and if so, who owns the copyright. If a copyright notice is on the work itself, then the producer can pursue the copyright holder named in the notice. If no copyright notice exists, the producer must conduct a search at the United States Copyright Office. (More details on how best to conduct this search can be found in the Copyright Office's Circular 22, "How to Investigate the Copyright Status of a Work," *www. copyright.gov/circs/circ22.html*.) A copyright attorney should be consulted if there are any questions as to the copyright status of the work.[53]

After the producer has determined the owner of the copyright, he must acquire a license, or option, to produce the work in a commercial production. An option gives the producer permission to produce the work in a specified manner (the scope) in a specific place (the territory) for a specific period of time (the term).[54] For example, a producer may purchase an option for a Broadway production (scope) in New York City (territory) for one year (term). An option is almost always exclusive, meaning that no other producer will be given the right to produce that show during the period of the option.[55] A producer must produce the work during the specified term or surrender the option.

"In order to make sure that the producer is serious about actually producing the show, she must pay the author an option fee."[56] In most cases, the producer may extend the term of the option by paying an additional fee. For example, in an option for a Broadway play, the producer pays $5,000 for the rights to produce the work in the first six months, $2,500 to renew the option for a second consecutive six-month period, and an additional $5,500 for a period of up to twelve consecutive months after the second option period expires.[57] In order to ensure that the producer is taking steps toward an actual production of the property, the rights holder may impose certain conditions for granting an extension on the option; for example, to obtain a third option period for a play under the Dramatists Guild Approved Production Contract, the option agreement requires that the producer have a director, a star, or a theater attached to the production.[58]

In an option for a Broadway production, a producer typically acquires a package of rights that will go into effect when the option is exercised (the show is produced). She options the Broadway rights themselves, known as the first-class rights, which may also cover a first-class touring production or a production in the United Kingdom (usually London). (Touring and United Kingdom rights may also be negotiated as a separate option.) In addition to first-class rights, other territories may be included in the rights package, including the right to produce the work in other English-speaking countries like Australia and Canada, or countries in Asia or Europe; rights for these territories require separate payments.[59] Off-Broadway rights packages are no different; the rights package covers the Off-Broadway production, as well as the rights to produce the work on tour or in the United Kingdom. A producer may want to option the first-class rights as well if she believes that the production may transfer from an Off-Broadway to a Broadway theater.[60] In all option packages, rights to create a cast album or merchandise (known as "commercial use rights") may also be included.

Options also include subsidiary rights. Subsidiary rights are rights due to the original author of the work for subsequent uses of the work.[61] A producer's share of the subsidiary rights is granted by the author in exchange for the contribution that the producer makes to the work in producing it. If an author licenses a musical, then all subsequent stock and amateur productions for a specific period of time, as well as television or movie versions of the musical, might be included in the subsidiary rights package, giving the producer a financial stake in all of these subsidiary works.

All options are contained in the contract negotiated with the author(s) of the work for the production of the property. For example, the Dramatists Guild's Approved Production Contract includes all of the terms of the option agreement, as well as a schedule for payments to authors. Generally, the first option payment is required upon execution of the contract. An additional payment is required on the first day of rehearsal. All option payments are an advance against royalties, which means that the payment will be subtracted from any royalties owed to the authors after the production recoups.[62] The Approved Production Contract also specifies the royalty due to the author from the Broadway production; because the author's contract is usually the first to be negotiated, it is generally considered the starting point for determining the royalty structure for the entire production.[63]

After the option is exercised, the production may then be licensed for other producers, such as tour producers, schools, and community theaters. Licenses are typically nonexclusive (or exclusive only by region), and the producer who acquires the license receives no participation in future productions of the show.[64] Licenses are typically available for a fee and contain more specific provisions than options; licenses may detail performance dates, location, ticket prices, and number of seats in the theater.[65]

CLASSROOM DISCUSSION

Define the following: "copyright," "work for hire," "public domain," "license," "option," and "advance against royalties."

What rights does copyright protection give to the author(s)?

When is a work copyrighted?

How do copyright provisions differ for works made for hire?

What is the duration of copyright protection for works created after January 1, 1978? For joint works or works made for hire created after January 1, 1978? For works created before January 1, 1978?

What is an option?

What is included in a first-class rights package?

What is included in an Off-Broadway rights package?

Forming the Producing Entity

After a producer acquires the appropriate rights to produce the property, he needs to form an entity to obtain financing and produce the production. (Although large corporations such as Disney Theatrical Productions do produce as commercial entities, this section will focus on the entity formation of individual productions.) The entity that produces the production may take one of the following forms: a sole proprietorship, a joint venture, a limited partnership (LP), or a limited liability company (LLC).

The least complicated type of producing entity is a sole proprietorship. A sole proprietorship is the producer herself, who finances the production with her own money. A sole proprietorship is not a business entity; not only is the sole proprietor responsible for obtaining the funds to capitalize the production, but she is also personally liable (responsible) for all financial losses, debts, and even judgments resulting from lawsuits. Because of this unlimited personal liability, sole proprietorships are quite rare.

Most producers form business entities to produce commercially. When two or more producers agree to produce a property together for profit, they form a joint venture.[66] Each producer has unlimited liability in the joint venture, which means that there is no limit to the amount of losses she can incur as part of the joint venture.[67] Producers can restrict the amount of their liability to the assets of the joint venture by incorporating themselves (creating a separate corporate entity controlled by the producers) and then creating a joint venture between the corporations, thus separating the assets of the joint venture from the rest of the partners' assets.[68]

After forming a joint venture, the producers may decide to form a limited partnership in order to raise the funding needed for the production. In a limited partnership, investors are known as limited partners. The limited partners contribute 100 percent of the money needed for the production but are "passive investors;" limited partners do not have any say in the business operations. The producers are the general partners and are not required to contribute money, but have total control over the activities of the partnership. (General partners, however, may also become limited partners and contribute funds.) The limited partners receive all of the profits from the production until the production has recouped. After recoupment, the profits are split evenly between the limited and general partners.

The advantages of investing as a limited partner are twofold. The limited partner has no liability in the partnership beyond the amount of the initial investment, while the general partners have unlimited liability. Unlimited liability means that if the production goes over budget, the general partners will need to pay for those overages out of their own pockets.[69] However, as in a joint venture, general partners may each incorporate; if the corporations formed serve as the general partners, only the assets of the corporation are at risk, not the general partners' personal assets (except in very rare circumstances).[70] Also, limited partners may use losses incurred from their investments as a tax write-off (credit against taxes paid), which makes investment in a commercial production attractive to some potential investors.[71]

Although an investor is only responsible for the amount of his investment as specified in the partnership documents, a producer may ask an investor for additional money—an overcall or a priority loan—in certain circumstances. If the limited partnership agreement includes an overcall provision, a producer may ask for additional funds up to the level specified in the documents (usually 10 percent of the total investment). The use of the overcall has declined in recent years, as investors generally do not like to give money to a production beyond their initial investment.[72] If the limited partnership agreement does not contain an overcall provision, the general partners may ask for a priority loan if the production requires additional funds in excess of capitalization. (Priority loans are not used to capitalize a production.) A priority loan may be obtained from a general partner, a limited partner, a theater owner, or any person willing to lend money to the production.[73] In return for the loan, the lender may be granted some of the general partners' percentage of the net profits.[74] Priority loans are paid back before the investors begin to receive payments.[75]

The money raised through a limited partnership cannot be spent until a minimum percentage of the capitalization has been raised (usually 75 percent), unless the limited partners sign an agreement authorizing the use of the funds.[76] This minimum amount is known as a "mini-max," because the minimum amount needed to spend the capitalization must be able to fully fund the produced show. For example, if the capitalization required for an Off-Broadway production is $3 million, the mini-max may be set at $2 million, which would be the minimum amount required to produce a production of comparable quality. Because of the mini-max provision, a producer may need to raise front money to cover expenses that are incurred before the limited partnership becomes active. Front money pays for expenses related to acquiring the rights to the property, legal fees, and other initial administrative expenses that need to be paid even if the production does not come to fruition.[77] No more than four investors may contribute funds as front money; if more than four investors are needed, then another limited partnership or LLC must be formed solely to provide front money to launch the production.[78] As compensation for this high-risk investment, investors providing front money are usually given a percentage of the general partners' profits.[79]

Instead of creating a limited partnership, producers may choose to form a limited liability company. A limited liability company (LLC) provides the same limited liability for its investors (called investing members) as a limited partnership, but allows the investing members to materially participate in the business without losing the liability protection. An LLC may have an unlimited number of investing members.

All commercial producing entities are subject to governmental regulations, which vary depending on the specific type of entity. State laws that protect investment in securities also govern theatrical financing and are known as Blue Sky Laws. Blue Sky Laws differ from state to state, but typically require the registration of the investment offering in order to prevent fraud.[80] The federal government also regulates some kinds of theatrical financing; the Securities and Exchange Commission requires specific registration documents for limited partnerships and limited liability companies in order to prevent fraud.[81] Producers should consult with a lawyer when forming any commercial producing entity to ensure that all applicable regulations are followed.

CLASSROOM DISCUSSION

Define the following: "sole proprietorship," "joint venture," "limited partnership," "general partner," "limited partner," "overcall," "priority loan," "front money," and "limited liability company."

How is liability distributed in a joint venture?

In a limited partnership, who controls the partnership and who has all the liability?

What are the advantages of investing as a limited partner?

How are commercial producing entities regulated?

Raising the Money

Once a producer has formed a commercial producing entity, he needs to find investors to fund the production. If a production has more than one producer, each producer will be responsible for raising a portion of the entire capitalization. A producer may choose to contribute his portion of the capitalization from his own pocket. As Jon B. Platt states, "I've always thought that if I believe in the project, then I should absorb the risk involved in the investment. If I don't believe in it and wouldn't invest my own money in it, then I certainly have no right to take investors' money. In fact, I only take on outside investors if the funding required is beyond my capabilities. Because of this philosophy, I've funded shows like *Wicked* that have succeeded beyond all expectations, but I've also put money into shows that have failed and lost some or all of my investment."[82]

However, most producers need to find investors to contribute funds to capitalize the production. A producer generally finds investors among the people she already knows. As Alexander Fraser, a freelance executive producer, states, "Most producers become producers because they have extraordinary access to investment dollars. However, when you're starting out as a commercial producer, you find investors wherever you can, generally among your family and friends. If you are able to get the rights to a desirable production, and you don't have access to large amounts of money, then you can bring on producing partners who can raise that money for you."[83]

Don Frantz, lead producer at Town Square Productions, recommends that producers be creative and act boldly in finding potential investors. "The first step in raising money for a Broadway show is telling people that you're raising money for a Broadway show. I begin with the names in my Rolodex. You can also call people who have invested in past productions and say, 'If you liked investing in that show, let me introduce you to another show with a similar style and aesthetic.' You have to tell potential investors how passionate you are about the project and see if the passion can infect them as well. As a producer, you need to engage the investor in the field of commercial theater: the people, the environment, and the fun. Investors are not involved with a commercial production just to increase the return on their investment; they're in it for the experience as well."[84] In fact, depending on the size of the investment and the personal relationship between the investor and the producers, an investor may be credited in the program as a producer or associate producer.[85] The producer must ensure that all contact with potential investors is in compliance with applicable securities law.

Marc Routh agrees and adds an ethical note: "The best way to convince someone to invest in a production is to tell them about your passion for the project and the reason that this show is a good investment and has a chance of success. Of course, you need to combine this explanation with a reminder that they have to enter into this endeavor knowing that they might lose the entire amount of their investment, and that they need to make sure that they can afford to lose it. [The offering documents must also include this information and state that investors who cannot afford to lose the entirety of their investment should not invest.[86]] Early in my career, I was desperately raising money for a show that was already in rehearsal, and I accepted a contribution from an older woman who was using part of her savings to invest. That show didn't succeed. I've always felt guilty for having accepted the investment, even though I'm sure she's fine, so it's important to me that I take investments from people who can afford to lose this money."[87]

After a producer contacts potential investors about investing in a production, he may invite these potential investors to a staged reading (in which actors read the script on stage) or a workshop of the production. If a producer holds a special meeting for investors, during which pieces of a production are presented solely for the purpose of attracting investors to the project, that meeting is known as a "backers' audition." Marc Routh notes, "Backers' auditions are a bit out of fashion (people do workshops and invited readings, which are really backers' auditions these days), but these auditions are still part of the arsenal of tools used by producers to obtain capital for shows."[88]

In order to formally solicit investors, a producer provides an offering document that details the specifics of the production. This offering document may consist solely of the limited partnership agreement, or it may be a separate prospectus with additional details.[89] In the state of New York, the offering document must be filed with the attorney general, along with an agreement giving the general partners the right to produce the production.[90]

Richard Frankel provides an example of the offering process: "As a general partner, you are only allowed to solicit an investment with an offering paper [offering document]. You're not allowed to say anything significant to the investor outside of the offering papers. It's illegal. I can say to an investor, 'Please invest in *Sweeney Todd*. It has a great cast, including the wonderful Patti LuPone, and it's a new take on the material.' But if I want to discuss facts and money, I have to say, 'If you're interested in *Sweeney Todd*, please look at the offering papers. Everything you need to know about the production is in these papers.' The papers include the budget; the creative team; the cast; the number of productions I've produced, listing those that have made a profit and those that haven't; other specific information particular to the production; and any particular conditions applicable to the production, such as territories for which we have the rights. The offering papers include all the information we have. You can't give people a partial story of the production when you are asking them to invest."[91]

Producer Steve Baruch (*Driving Miss Daisy*, *Company* [2006]) agrees that the producer must "give it to the investors straight." He states, "To me, the most important thing in terms of relating to investors is my credibility. Not only do I never lie to them, but I would go so far as to say that I never even 'puff up' the truth. I'll tell them the details about the director, and if he's someone like Jerry Zaks [*Little Shop of Horrors* (2003), *Guys and Dolls* (1992)], I'll say that he's won four Tony Awards. I'll sell the production as hard as I can, but I'll never spin the truth."[92]

Baruch continues, "The result of acting in this manner is that in twenty years of producing, I've never had a complaint from any of my investors. The Frankel-Routh-Viertel-Baruch Group has a pool of 1,000 investors that we draw from for each production, and not one has felt that I've misled him or done him a disservice. It's to our advantage that we treat our investors well, so that they will continue to invest with us."[93]

Treating investors well does not end when the investor gives the producer her money. Baruch states, "On the financial side, we send unaudited financial statements to our investors every eight weeks. However, I also write to our investors all the time to keep them up to date on the progress of the show. I want to make them feel like part of the process rather than simply passive investors. I send them all of the reviews when the show opens, including the bad ones, because I want them to get the full picture. I also send them press pieces that run outside of the major media outlets, because our investors find those articles interesting. In addition, we send our investors a gift. Every investor receives a framed poster of the show; the money for these posters comes directly from our pockets, not the show's budget. We send them cast albums and souvenir books, if we have them. We also give our investors access to house seats; these seats are a tremendous benefit to the investors, because it makes them into heroes [who] can get good seats to a Broadway show at short notice. Most of this activity

is fairly unusual; often people invest in shows, and they may hear from the producer once a year (and receive a check if they're lucky). We feel that it's important to take good care of our investors."[94]

CLASSROOM DISCUSSION

How do producers find investors?
What is the process for acquiring an investor for a commercial production?
What sorts of things can a producer do to show an investor that he or she is valued?

Finding the Theater

After a producer has acquired a property, formed a business entity, and acquired investors, she must license (rent) a theater in which to produce the work. Finding a suitable theater can be a challenge. Some producers need to wait until a Broadway theater becomes vacant before their production can be produced. Other productions need a specific type or size of theater to best showcase them. When producer Dave Fishelson transferred *Golda's Balcony*, a one-woman show, from a nonprofit theater to Broadway, he needed a theater that would be small enough for the production. He states, "I wanted the Helen Hayes Theatre, because it's the smallest Broadway theater [with 597 seats]. Since *Golda's Balcony* is a challenging drama, I also thought a smaller theater would be easier to fill, giving the play longer life. When we first approached the owner of the Helen Hayes, we were one of seven productions that he was considering. At the time, *Golda* had qualified for many Off-Broadway awards, so I decided to advertise the show's nominations heavily in the *New York Times* and other papers. My strategy had a dual purpose: I not only wanted the award voters to be reminded of *Golda*'s artistic achievements, but the Helen Hayes Theatre's owner as well."[95]

Once the appropriate theater is found, a producer must sign a booking agreement, known as a theater license, with the theater owner. Most Broadway theaters are licensed in a four-wall agreement, in which the producer rents the theater and must provide everything in the space except for the "four walls" of the building. (Occasionally, theater owners may negotiate a "two-wall" deal, in which costs are shared between the producer and the theater owner.[96]) In a four-wall agreement, the theater is rented "as is," and any alterations to the space are paid for by the producer, including any modifications made to restore the theater to its original condition after the show closes. In fact, all expenses incurred by the theater while the production is in its space are paid for by the producer, including all salaries of employees hired by the theater owner for the run of the production.

In addition to setting out the financial terms for the engagement, the theater license includes several other provisions specific to theater rental. For example, as part of the license, the theater owner is permitted to sell food and drink concessions in the theater; all revenue earned from concessions will belong to the theater owner. The producer may sell his own show-related concessions (such as CDs or T-shirts), but must pay the theater owner a commission on all items sold. Another provision grants the theater owner a certain amount of house seats (tickets reserved for the theater owner's use for up to forty-eight hours before the performance) and complimentary (free) tickets.

A vital section of the theater license is the stop clause. The stop clause is a provision that is put into effect if the ticket income drops below a certain negotiated amount for more than two weeks in a row. If the production fails to earn the specified amount of ticket income, the theater landlord has the right to evict the production as negotiated in the license agreement. A producer may negotiate certain weeks to be exempt from the stop clause, such as holiday weeks.

CLASSROOM DISCUSSION
Define "theater license," "four-wall agreement," "two-wall agreement," and "stop clause."
What factors should a producer take into consideration before licensing a theater?
What items are typically included in a theater license?

Hiring Artistic and Production Staff
While a producer is obtaining the rights, arranging the financing, and acquiring a theater for a property, he also is engaged in hiring staff to administer the production. One of the first staff members hired by the producer is the general manager. The general manager is typically hired before or during negotiations with the author, or immediately after the author is contracted.[97] The general manager negotiates all contracts, creates the production and weekly operating budgets, and is responsible for the administration of the entire production. The general manager supervises all of the financial activity of the production on behalf of the producers.[98] Depending on the stage of the production's development and the experience of the producer, the general manager may also refer the producer to potential directors,

designers, attorneys, accountants, and any other personnel needed for the production.[99] A general manager may work on multiple productions (or with multiple companies of the same production); in this case, an associate general manager may also be hired to assist the general manager.[100]

The general manager hires a company manager for each production. As Alexander Fraser defines the position, "The company manager's basic responsibility is to be the producer's representative at every performance. At the theater, he is responsible for all financial matters involving the production, including the box office statement [a statement that details all ticket sales for a given performance; an example may be found in chapter 11 (figure 1.5)], and the weekly settlement between the theater and the producer [reconciling income and expenses; more information on weekly settlements may be found in chapters 10 and 11]. The company manager is also responsible for processing payroll, arranging all house seats, and [with the stage manager] handling all issues that arise backstage with regards to actors, stage crew, and musicians."[101] If a production is on tour, the company manager also arranges travel and housing for all members of the company traveling with the show.[102] Marc Routh adds, "At Richard Frankel Productions, each production has a company manager, an associate or assistant company manager, and an intern to help with company management duties."[103] The company manager is a member of ATPAM.

After the general manager and company manager are in place, the producer must focus on finding the artistic personnel for the production. The major components of the creative team (e.g., directors, choreographers, designers) are selected by the producer, and the general manager then draws up the contracts to formalize the relationship. Producers generally turn to casting agents to cast performers for the production. Casting agents prepare casting breakdowns (showing the requirements for each part), draw up a list of suitable performers for a project, and hold auditions and accept submissions from agents to cast available parts.[104] Casting agents are also used to find replacements for any performers who leave during the run of the production.[105]

Additional personnel must be hired to facilitate the creation of the physical production. Generally, a producer will employ a technical supervisor (or production manager) to coordinate and manage the set, lighting, costume, and sound designs for the production. Alexander Fraser states, "The technical supervisor is in charge of realizing the designs in the most economical way, working with the general manager to create the budget for the technical elements of the show. He works with the shop to realize the design on budget, and he is responsible for loading the physical production into the theater. The technical supervisor supervises the technical rehearsals and maintains the show as it runs. He will also hire and manage the stagehands, wardrobe and hair stylists, and all other technical personnel."[106]

After the production is created, the producer must make the general public aware of the production so that tickets may be sold. To facilitate this process, the producer hires an advertising agency (and sometimes a marketing firm as well) to create a marketing plan for the production. This marketing plan will contain print and media advertising, as well as any corporate sponsorships or special promotions that may be created for the production. As part of the public awareness campaign, the producer will also retain a press agent. The press agent is responsible for persuading various media outlets to run news stories or editorials about the production. These media outlets include newspapers, magazines, television and radio stations, and, increasingly, Web sites. This type of media coverage is not paid for by the production; the press agent cultivates relationships with members of the media and pitches ideas for stories that might be of interest to them. Like the company manager, the press agent is also a member of ATPAM.

Other personnel are hired or retained as needed for a commercial production. The producer retains an attorney to create the business entity for the production and provide any legal advice as required. Many producers also use attorneys to help negotiate the author's contract, because this contract negotiation is a lengthy and complex process that results in a detailed document affecting both subsidiary rights and the royalty structure; a lawyer may also negotiate other contracts as needed.[107] The producer also retains an accountant to monitor the financial aspects of the production, to produce financial reports for the investors, and, together with a lawyer, to ensure all applicable reports are sent to the appropriate governmental agencies.[108] The accountant also files annual taxes for the producing entity and assists in preparing audits. In addition, the producer generally has a relationship with a banker to facilitate any monetary transactions as needed.

CLASSROOM DISCUSSION

What are the job responsibilities of a general manager?

What are the responsibilities of a company manager?

Who are the members of the creative team?

What are the responsibilities of the technical supervisor?

What functions do the advertising agency and press agent perform?

Why does a producer need to have a business relationship with attorneys, accountants, and bankers?

Issuing Contracts

As soon as the general manager is hired, he must begin the process of issuing contracts for all personnel working on the production. A contract is "an agreement between two or more parties creating obligations that are enforceable or otherwise recognizable at law [under the law]."[109] General managers negotiate specific contracts on an individual basis, even when the party being contracted is a member of a union covered by a collective bargaining agreement. In this case, the collectively bargained agreement dictates the minimum terms that the production must grant, such as fees, salaries, royalty rates, and work rules. The producer may always grant more favorable terms if he so desires. For example, if a production is hiring a star, she is probably receiving a higher weekly salary than the minimum dictated by AEA.

General manager Maria Di Dia (*Chicago* [1996], *Zanna Don't!*) describes her process for creating a contract: "Before you start negotiations, you sit down with the producer and discuss the parameters of the deal. For instance, I might say, 'I think the [artist's] agent is going to ask for the minimum salary plus 10 percent for her commission. Is that something you're willing to do?' After I receive these parameters from the producers, I begin the process of creating the deal memo with the agent for the artist. The deal memo is an outline of the contract with all of the major categories, such as fee or salary, royalty agreement, and an advance [against royalties] if applicable. The agent and I discuss the terms of the deal; to keep track of our discussion, I keep a sheet that lists the conversations I've had with the agent and the agreements that we've reached. Deals involving union members are fairly straightforward, as the major points are outlined in the collectively bargained agreement. When the agent and I have finalized the details, I issue a formal deal memo or present a draft contract to the agent for the artist's signature. To create the draft contract, I use some standard language that I've refined over the years, mainly by borrowing paragraphs from other contracts with which I've worked. The draft contract would have all applicable riders attached to it. Riders are addendums to the contract detailing any specific provisions applicable to this particular contract."[110]

When creating deal memos and contracts, Maria Di Dia relies a great deal on her history working with unions and with specific artists to determine appropriate contract parameters. She also consults with colleagues to gather more information if necessary. "The Off-Broadway managerial community likes to share information to try to control costs. When I am working on a deal memo, I often call a colleague who has had more recent negotiations with a particular union than I have to ask for some guidance. For instance, if I were going to deal with Local 802 [the New York branch of AFM], I'd call a colleague who has worked on a recent musical and ask for the details on his deal with 802. Or if I were working with an agent who says, 'My client hasn't worked for minimum in three years,' I might also consult with my colleagues and ask them how much above minimum they paid for the services of that particular artist."[111]

Contract negotiations are slightly more complicated on Broadway productions because of the number of unions involved. Producers and theater owners are bound to different collectively bargained agreements, sometimes with the same union. On a Broadway production, producers directly employ members of the following unions under collectively bargained agreements: AEA; ATPAM (for company managers and press agents); IATSE Local 1 (pink contracts[112]); SSDC; USA, Local 829; Theatrical Wardrobe Union, Local 764; Hair and Makeup Union, Local 798; and the International Brotherhood of Teamsters. Theater owners directly employ members of: AFM, Local 802; IATSE, Local 1 (stagehands employed by the theater; the minimum crew is typically a head carpenter, head electrician, head flyman [works with systems to fly scenery], and properties head); ATPAM (house managers); Treasurers and Ticket Sellers Union, Local 751; Ushers, Ticket Takers, and Doormens' Union, Local 306; SEIU, Local 32BJ (maintenance and cleaning personnel); and the International Union of Operating Engineers, Local 30. Even though theater owners will execute these collectively bargained agreements, the producer, pursuant to his theater license, will be charged for all costs associated with employing the house staff while the production is running.

It is worth noting that musicians needed for a Broadway production are hired by the producer but are under contract with the theater owner, not the producer. As with other union members employed by the theater owner, the producer is responsible for all the costs incurred by the theater owner in employing the musicians. Almost all Broadway theaters are required to hire a minimum number of musicians for each musical produced in their spaces; these minimums are determined by the size of the theater. The producer of a Broadway musical is required to hire the minimum number of musicians, but exceptions may be made to the minimum rule by appealing to AFM, Local 802 on a case-by-case basis.

Off-Broadway producers and theater owners are not bound by as many collective bargained agreements as their Broadway counterparts. Off-Broadway producers directly employ members of the following unions under collectively bargained agreements: AEA, SSDC, and ATPAM (company managers and press agents). Unlike Broadway producers, Off-Broadway producers negotiate individual agreements with AFM, Local 802 for any needed musicians. USA, Local 829 recommends certain rates for designers employed on Off-Broadway productions; the producer observes these suggested rates as he sees fit.[113] Off-Broadway theater owners may employ IATSE, Local 1 stagehands under individually negotiated contracts.

CLASSROOM DISCUSSION
What is a contract?

How is a contract negotiated?

What union members are employed by a Broadway producer?

What union members are employed by a Broadway theater owner?

What union members are employed by an Off-Broadway producer?

What union members are employed by an Off-Broadway theater owner?

Creating Budgets
General managers also begin creating budgets as soon as they are hired. A budget is a planning document that details all income and expenses for a production. Commercial theatrical productions use both a production or capitalization budget (listing expenses from the inception of the idea through opening night) and a weekly operating budget (listing income and expenses incurred in performing the show on a weekly basis after the official opening).[114] Also, general managers determine royalty payments and create payment pools for all royalty participants.

Marc Routh describes the budgeting process for a commercial production. "First, you read the play or musical and make notes about the details mentioned in the script; you note such details as the number of characters, the number of settings, the time of year, and the economic position of each character. By doing this, you know how many actors you need for the show, and you get a sense of what the sets and costumes might cost. You need to be familiar with any applicable union agreements, so that you can accurately account for salaries, fringe benefits, and work rules that might end up costing money if they are violated.[115] You also need to know at what stage your creative team is in their careers, so that you can budget their fees appropriately. (You may have to research the salaries of people performing similar jobs at a similar level to get an accurate fee structure.) Then, after you've done all of the research you can about this particular production, you create your budget line item by line item, noting the assumptions you used to calculate each number so that if anyone asks you about a particular entry, you can explain how you got to that number. You do a draft of your budget and review it with a producer or team of producers. You will then make adjustments to your budget based on that review, submit the revised budget to the producers, and continue this process until the producers approve the budget."[116]

As the manager of the budget, the general manager needs to maintain an objective view of the production. Maria Di Dia states, "The producer may need to fall in love with the show, but the general manager should not. She needs to advise the producer about the budget and help the producer make decisions about the creative elements of the show while staying within the budget. For example, if a designer creates a design that is over the budgeted amount, the general manager must communicate that to the producer so that the producer can tell the designer that his design must be modified in order to comply with the budget."[117]

Although a detailed examination of the budgeting process will be found in chapter 5, it is useful to note certain budget items specific to the production budget. Most productions budget for a cash reserve, which is money reserved to cover the expenses when there are low ticket sales after the production opens. (A general manager will also budget a contingency to cover any unforeseen production expenses before the production opens; the contingency is between 5 and 10 percent of the total production costs.[118]) The producer and general manager determine the total

amount of the reserve. As Alexander Fraser states, "Different people have different ideas about the appropriate size of a cash reserve. Some producers might want two weeks of operating costs in the reserve, so that the production could play two weeks without selling a single ticket. Some producers may want a flat $500,000 in the reserve. You look at the weekly operating costs and the advance sales and decide what you think is reasonable to keep as a reserve; once you open, you decide how much of your reserve that you need to get through hard times, and you distribute the rest to your investors. However, you want to be very careful when making this determination, as your investors don't want to get a call from you asking for some of that distribution back."[119]

As an example, Marc Routh describes his process for determining the reserve for an Off-Broadway production: "Ideally, I budget three or four weeks' worth of running costs as a reserve. For *Cookin'*, a show that I produced Off-Broadway, the actual hard production costs were $600,000, but we budgeted the show at $1.2 million because we wanted to cover losses during our opening weeks and create huge advertising push that would help the show find its audience. For most shows, however, doubling your production costs to create a large reserve is outrageous; it would make a Broadway musical cost $20 million."[120]

A general manager must also budget for load-in (or take-in) costs and closing costs. Load-in costs are all expenses associated with bringing the production into the theater, including crew salaries and the rental of equipment needed to move the physical production into the space.[121] Closing costs are the expenses incurred when the show closes, including loading out the physical production and either storing or destroying it. Closing costs are based on contractual obligations and the general manager's knowledge of the costs of disposing of the set, costumes, and other items used in the production.[122] Contractual obligations would include the salaries and fringe benefits to be paid to members of the various unions when the show posts its closing notice.

As part of the obligations of producing a show, commercial producers are required to provide financial guarantees to various parties that the producer will be able to cover certain costs if the production should close earlier than expected (or when a producer does not live up to his obligations). First, producers must post bonds with various unions. A bond is a specific amount of money designed to cover salaries and fringe benefits for every member of the union employed by the production. For example, on a Broadway production, AEA requires two weeks' salaries and fringe benefits as a bond for every actor and stage manager.[123] A typical bond covers one to two weeks of employment. Similarly, theater owners require a deposit for rent on the theater. Bonds and deposits may be paid in cash or by a letter of credit.[124] A letter of credit is a statement from a bank affirming that the production has enough money to cover the amount of the bond or deposit. The letter of credit freezes the amount of cash in the account to cover the bond, but does not actually remove the cash from the account. The bank charges a negotiated percentage rate as interest to the production upon issuing the letter of credit.[125]

In addition to the production budget, commercial producers also use a weekly operating budget. The weekly operating budget estimates expenses and revenue for the production on a weekly basis after the show opens. Weekly expenses include such items as the rental for the theater, salaries, and maintenance of the physical production. After the weekly expenses are estimated, the general manager can determine the breakeven point. The breakeven point is equal to the total costs of running the show for a week. When the revenue earned from the production is equal to the weekly running costs, then the production is considered to be at the breakeven point, and all revenue earned beyond this point is considered weekly operating profit and can be used to pay back investors.

Revenue estimation for a commercial production begins with a determination of the total potential gross weekly box office receipts (called the "weekly gross potential"). The weekly gross potential is the total amount of money a production could potentially earn per week; the amount is determined by multiplying the total number of seats available by the price per ticket by the number of performances per week. So, if a production plays in a theater with 550 seats at $90 per ticket for eight performances, the weekly gross potential is $396,000. The general manager then subtracts allowable deductions from the weekly gross potential to determine the potential net adjusted gross weekly box office receipts (called, simply, "net adjusted gross," or NAGBOR). These deductions include fees charged by the theater for credit card processing, group sales commissions, and other deductions named in the theater license.[126] On Broadway, deductions also include the amount paid to the unions as part of the Turkus Arbitration Award of 1963, which requires productions to contribute

4.5 percent of the weekly gross to pension funds; this percentage was once an admission tax, but as Broadway productions are now exempt from the tax, the equivalent amount is paid to the pension funds.[127]

After the potential net adjusted gross is determined, then the general manager can create a recoupment schedule. The recoupment schedule displays the amount of time in weeks that a production will need to run in order to recoup its costs. (To give some examples of typical recoupment periods, it can take between nine months and three years for a Broadway musical to recoup, and between six and eighteen months for a Broadway play to recoup.[128]) To determine the rate of recoupment, a general manager first determines the production costs that need to be recouped by subtracting bonds and deposits (known as recoverables, as that money is expected to return to the production) from total production costs. The general manager then determines the net adjusted gross as described above. The rate of recoupment is determined by multiplying the percentage of projected tickets sold by the net adjusted gross, subtracting all weekly running costs (including variable running costs such as royalty payments to the creative team), and then dividing the amount into the production costs to be recouped.

For example, a Broadway production is capitalized at $10 million and has $500,000 worth of bonds and deposits. The total costs to be recouped are:

$$\$10,000,000 \text{ (total production costs)} - \$500,000$$
$$\text{(bonds and deposits)} = \$9,500,000$$

The production will play eight performances per week in a 1,600-seat theater, in which 700 seats are $100 each, 550 seats are $75 each, and 350 seats are $40 each. The gross potential weekly box office receipts are:

$$[(700 \text{ seats} \times \$100) + (550 \text{ seats} \times \$75) + (350 \text{ seats} \times \$40)] \times 8 \text{ performances} = \$1,002,000$$

To determine the potential net adjusted gross weekly box office receipts, the general manager subtracts 8 percent of the gross potential box office receipts for credit card charges and other deductions:

$$\$1,002,000 - \$80,160 \text{ (8 percent of the gross)}$$
$$= \$921,840$$

The weekly running costs for the production are $300,000. Royalties for the various creative personnel are contracted at 15 percent of the net adjusted gross.

The general manager can now determine rates of recoupment for different percentages of projected ticket sales. At 90 percent of capacity, the rate of recoupment is:

[.90 (90 percent represented as a decimal)
× $921,840] − $300,000 (weekly running costs)
− [.15 × (.90 × $921,840)] (royalties) = $405,207.60

$9,500,000 (production costs to be
recouped)/$405,207.60 = 23.44 weeks.

If the production sells 90 percent of its tickets per week, it could recoup in less than six months.

However, if the production sells at 60 percent of capacity, it would take nearly fourteen months to recoup:

[.60 × $921,840] − $300,000 − [.15 × (.60 × $921,840)]
= $170,138.40

$9,500,000 (production costs to be recouped)/
$170,138.40 = 55.84 weeks

Producers and general managers use recoupment schedules to predict the chances of a successful production—one that pays back its investors and makes a profit. If the recoupment schedule does not allow for investors to be paid back in a reasonable period of time, it may not be advisable to go forward with the production in the manner budgeted. Marc Routh describes an example of recoupment analysis: "*Sweeney Todd* [2005] cost $3.5 million to produce and had running costs of approximately $315,000 per week. At those amounts, *Sweeney Todd* seemed like a good work for us to produce on Broadway, because we thought that there was a large enough audience for that style of performance, and that audience would allow us to recoup the costs and make a profit. If that same version of *Sweeney Todd* had cost $12 million, we would not have produced the show, because the audience that we projected would probably not have allowed us to recoup."[129]

CLASSROOM DISCUSSION

Define the following terms: "budget," "cash reserve," "load-in costs," "closing costs," "bond," "deposit," "breakeven point," "weekly gross potential," "net adjusted gross," and "recoupment schedule."

What types of budgets do commercial productions use?
How is a budget created?
How is the breakeven point determined?

We'll Always Have Paris, a jaunty musical about wayward heiresses, has a total production cost of $500,000. $28,000 of that cost consists of bonds and other recoverables. *Paris* will play eight performances a week at Theater 45, which holds 399 people at an average ticket price of $50. Box office deductions are calculated to be 8 percent of the potential gross. The total weekly operating cost is $75,600, with 10 percent of the net adjusted gross going to royalty participants.

Given this information, how many weeks will it take *Paris* to recoup its costs . . .
a) . . . at 100 percent of capacity?
b) . . . at 80 percent of capacity?
c) . . . at 60 percent of capacity?

Royalties and Royalty Pools

In the course of developing the production, the producer agrees to pay royalties to certain artistic personnel, to any originating nonprofit theaters, and to the producer himself. Royalties are payments made by the producer for the use of a specific work; these royalty payments are due to the recipients for each performance of that work. Some royalties are calculated at a fixed rate, meaning that the producer will pay the same amount to the royalty recipient every week; some designers, as well as vocal and dance arrangers, may receive fixed-rate royalties.[130] Other royalties, such as those negotiated for writers, directors, and choreographers, are calculated as a percentage of the net adjusted gross. (Most designers on Broadway take part in these percentage royalties.[131]) After the production opens, these royalty arrangements are put into effect and are considered part of the weekly operating costs.

When a production is selling well, a producer has enough money to pay all royalties with enough left over to distribute payments to investors. However, if a production is not selling many tickets, a situation can develop in which royalty recipients are receiving all the money available after the breakeven point, with the investors receiving nothing. For example, assume an Off-Broadway production has weekly running costs of $90,000, and a royalty arrangement that gives 12 percent of the net adjusted gross to creative personnel and others (6 percent to the author, 2 percent to the director, 2 percent to the originating theater, and 2 percent to the producers). If the net adjusted gross for the production is $100,000 for the week, the royalty payout would be:

$100,000	net adjusted gross
− $90,000	weekly running costs
= $10,000	profit
− $6,000	6 percent of net adjusted gross to author
− $2,000	2 percent of net adjusted gross to director
− $2,000	2 percent of net adjusted gross to originating theater
− $2,000	2 percent of net adjusted gross to producers
= − $2,000	

Not only does the royalty arrangement not allow for investors to be paid back, but it leaves the production with a weekly operating deficit of $2,000, which must be covered by the cash reserve.

In order to address this problem, producers and royalty participants developed the royalty pool, which allows the profit to be split between the royalty participants and investors. This split is determined on a case-by-case basis, typically through negotiation with the author. (Off-Broadway, the agreement with SSDC typically determines the split, allotting 60 percent to the investors and 40 percent to the royalty participants.[132]) After the profit is split, the royalty participants receive a percentage of the amount designated for them in proportion to their percentage of the royalties as a whole. In the example above, the author receives half (6 percent, called six "points") of the total royalty percentage (12 percent), so he would receive half of the amount designated for royalty participants (he has 6/12 of the "participant pool"). The director, originating theater, and producers would split the remaining amount equally because each was entitled to 2 percent (2 points), which would be converted to 2/12 of the participant pool.

Using the previous example, the royalty payout using the royalty pool would be:

$100,000	net adjusted gross
− $90,000	weekly running costs
= $10,000	profit
− $6,000	60 percent of profit to investors
− $2,000	6/12 of profit to author (50 percent of royalty amount)
− $666.66	2/12 of profit to director (16.7 percent of royalty amount)
− $666.67	2/12 of profit to originating theater (16.7 percent of royalty amount)
− $666.67	2/12 of profit to producers (16.7 percent of royalty amount)
= $0	

The production has paid back some of its investment, and the production is no longer running a deficit.

However, when the net adjusted gross of the production rises above a certain level, the royalty pool calculation will actually result in bigger royalties than paying the royalty percentage off of the net adjusted gross. As an example, we can examine the royalty pool payouts for the previous production using a net adjusted gross of $180,000:

$180,000	net adjusted gross
− $90,000	weekly running costs
= $90,000	profit
− $54,000	60 percent of profit to investors
− $18,000	6/12 of profit to author (50 percent of royalty amount)
− $6,000	2/12 of profit to director (16.7 percent of royalty amount)
− $6,000	2/12 of profit to originating theater (16.7 percent of royalty amount)
− $6,000	2/12 of profit to producers (16.7 percent of royalty amount)
= $0	

If the producers made the royalty payments as a percentage of the net adjusted gross, the payout would be:

$180,000	net adjusted gross
− $90,000	weekly running costs
= $90,000	profit
− $10,800	6 percent of net adjusted gross to author
− $3,600	2 percent of net adjusted gross to director
− $3,600	2 percent of net adjusted gross to originating theater
− $3,600	2 percent of net adjusted gross to producers
= $68,400	to distribute to investors

The producer determines if the production will be using the royalty pool formula, based on his calculations of projected royalty payments. If the producer determines that he would be able to pay a lower amount by paying a percentage of the net adjusted gross (as high-grossing productions like *Wicked* do), he would elect not to use the royalty pool. If, however, the production has high operating costs and low ticket sales, the royalty pool may prove to be the most prudent way to distribute royalties.[133] The producer must submit box office statements detailing total ticket sales and the net adjusted gross to royalty participants in order to demonstrate the need for the pool. The royalty pool is usually calculated on a cycle of four weeks. For Broadway productions, once a producer elects to use the royalty pool formula, the pool will generally govern the royalty payments for the life of the production. Off-Broadway, SSDC requires producers to stay in the royalty pool for the rest of the run once the show has recouped; pre-recoupment, the Off-Broadway producer may revert back to full royalties if he chooses.[134]

In addition, most royalty arrangements require that the producer pay a minimum amount to royalty participants. The producer must pay the minimum amount regardless of the amount determined by the royalty pool calculation, and this minimum must be paid every week, whether or not the production breaks even.[135] The minimum is typically calculated by assigning a monetary value to a royalty pool point. For example, if the minimum were determined at $220 per point, the author with six points would receive $1,320 ($220 x 6) as a minimum each week.

CLASSROOM DISCUSSION

Define "royalty" and "royalty pool." Who receives
    a royalty? How does a producer determine
    when a royalty pool should be used?

When Nerds Drink, a sobering Off-Broadway play about the collapse of an Internet company, pays 6 percent of the gross to the author, 2 percent to the director, 2 percent to the originating theater, and 2 percent to the commercial producer. The minimum has been determined at $220 per point. Box office deductions are calculated to be 4 percent of the potential gross. The total weekly operating cost is $145,000.

The first four weeks of box office grosses are:

1) $130,000
2) $155,000
3) $180,000
4) $195,000

For each gross, determine whether you would use the minimum payment, a percentage royalty, or the full royalty pool. Calculate the royalty payments.

Supervising the Marketing Campaign and Monitoring Ticket Sales

After the budgets are approved and all of the contracts are signed, the process continues. Producers are also responsible for approving and supervising the marketing campaign for the production. The marketing campaign contains elements designed to sell tickets for the production. These elements may include ticket discounts offered to selected potential ticket buyers by mail or e-mail; newspaper, television, radio, and Internet advertisements; and special promotions to attract publicity to the production.

To supervise the advertising component of the marketing campaign, the producers hold a weekly advertising meeting at the advertising agency's office. These meetings begin before the production opens and continue for the run of the show. The weekly ad meeting typically includes all producers, and may even include associate producers, making the meeting quite large and a bit unwieldy.

Special promotions for a commercial production are designed to draw attention to the show in an unconventional manner. Gary McAvay, president of Columbia Artists Theatricals, describes a Broadway promotional campaign: "For *Dirty Rotten Scoundrels*, we hired the Margery Singer Company to do marketing and special promotions. The basic plot of the musical involves two con artists who go to the Riviera and steal jewelry from unsuspecting women, so Margery worked with QVC [a television shopping channel] to create a line of jewelry called the Scoundrels Collection. She negotiated a one-hour special on QVC to introduce the jewelry collection. For that whole hour, we played songs from the show and did interviews with the cast, and we sold out the entire Scoundrels Collection. You cannot buy this kind of advertising."[136]

As the marketing campaign commences, tickets are put on sale for the production. The producers carefully monitor all ticket sales and pay special attention to the amount of advance ticket sales, known as the box office advance.[137] The box office advance is the amount of ticket sales that have been purchased for future performances as calculated by the current performance.[138] Before the show opens, all ticket sales are considered part of the advance. As soon as performances commence, the advance consists of all ticket sales less the performances that have already occurred. For example, at 6 P.M. on a Friday night, the advance would include money received from all tickets sold for all performances past that time, including the Friday-night performance. At 8:30 P.M. on that same Friday, when the performance is in progress, the advance would include all ticket sales for performances from Saturday forward. A large advance is desirable, because it can help cushion the production during weeks when ticket sales are not strong.

Arranging Tryouts, Previews, and Opening Night

After all of the artistic and production staff are hired, the performers begin to rehearse and designers begin to create and build the scenic elements. Rehearsals begin between four and eight weeks before opening, depending on the needs of the production. The design elements are created in various shops and transported to the theater during load-in. During this time, the producer and general manager supervise all aspects of the production, handling problems as they arise.

After the rehearsal period ends, and the design process is complete, the production is ready to begin public performances. For a Broadway production, a producer may decide to present the first full commercial production of the show in a city other than New York. (This process differs from enhancing a production at a nonprofit theater because the commercial producers are responsible for mounting the entire out-of-town production and bear all of the costs.) This out-of-town "tryout" allows the producer and the creative team to see the production in front of an audience and make any necessary changes to the work before it opens on Broadway. Marc Routh states, "We would never want to produce a show, especially a new musical, directly on Broadway. A new production needs a lot of work once it is on the stage, and you don't want to be making wholesale changes to a show in front of New York audiences, which are full of people interested in the theater industry. You need to be able to do the creative work without the pressure of friends and colleagues giving advice, and without those New York audiences forming opinions about the show and telling their friends. Even in the current day, when the Internet is everywhere, and people make comments that are posted online by the intermission of the show's dress rehearsal, it's still better to try out the production outside of New York. Also, there's not a lot of time to make changes once the show is on Broadway, and it's very expensive because of all the union costs. It should be noted, however, that an out-of-town tryout is also a cost to the production. The tryout [in Chicago] for *The Producers* had a net cost of $1 million [after ticket sales were accounted for], and that was a very successful out-of-town tryout."[139]

All productions also typically play preview performances, allowing the creative team to make adjustments to the show as necessary before the official opening. Even if a production has an out-of-town tryout or is a transfer, it plays some preview performances before opening. (In this case, these preview performances are generally designed to adjust the technical elements of the show before opening, and also to allow the performers to become comfortable on the new stage.) Musicals require more preview time than plays because of their complexity; a typical preview period for a Broadway play is between two and three weeks, while Broadway musicals play previews for four to five weeks.[140] Critics generally attend the production in the final preview performances before the production opens.

Marc Routh notes, "Previews typically feature tickets sold at a discount [for less than face value] and are generally harder to sell, so you don't want a preview period that's longer than necessary because you don't want to lose revenue. On the other hand, it takes a lot of time to put changes into a show, and if your preview period is too short, you don't have enough time to make those changes. You need the first weekend or week to get the show up on its feet and see how far you've gotten with the show, and you need the final week to finalize all your changes and get the critics in to see the production. You only have the days or weeks between these two periods to make adjustments. This is the reason why most shows, especially musicals, have an out-of-town tryout first; you are able to make some of these adjustments between the time the show closes in the other city and starts performances in New York, and then you continue the preview period in New York."[141]

After the preview period, the production opens. The entire production cast and staff attend the opening-night party, and the producers breathe a sigh of relief. Their relief is short-lived. Reviews for the production usually run the day after opening, but the reviews may be available late on opening night. During the opening-night party, someone acquires the reviews (which are now available online almost immediately after the performance ends); depending on the verdict of the critics, the party will continue or quickly end.

Managing the Production after It Opens

After the opening, the producer must deal with the reviews. If the reviews are good, then the producer may relax a bit; a good review will typically spur tickets sales. However, if a review is bad, it may cost the show ticket sales, and the producer needs to address the potential loss. Marc Routh explains, "As far as the producer is concerned, the function of reviews is to get the initial audience through the door. If you don't get good reviews, you need additional money to spend on advertising and finding other methods to get people into the theater. You draw upon your cash reserve to cover these costs, or you can get a priority loan from your investors. Hopefully, your show has positive word-of-mouth, and your box office will continue to grow to the point where your production becomes profitable. *Smokey Joe's Cafe* is a good example of this process. This show did not get a particularly good review from the *New York Times*, so we needed to spend quite a bit of money on advertising to highlight other good reviews that we got. *Smokey Joe's Cafe* did eventually stabilize; it ran for five years, becoming the longest-running musical revue in Broadway history."[142]

Routh goes on to state that reviews alone do not determine the fate of the production. "Ultimately, every show is dependent on word-of-mouth. People see the show and tell their friends about it. That's the most successful way to make a hit."[143]

Some producers attempt to predict the verdict of the critics in advance and create an appropriate strategy to address potential reviews. Jonathan Pollard states, "We knew *I Love You, You're Perfect, Now Change* was not going to appeal to the typical New York theatergoer, so we decided to aggressively court suburban audiences and tourists by focusing on the male-female relationship aspect of the show. This strategy may have alienated the theater community, but it did attract our target audience. When we opened, we received mixed to negative reviews from the three New York City papers, but extremely good reviews from *Newsday* on Long Island, from both New Jersey papers, and from newspapers in Westchester County and in Connecticut. And although circumstances dictated that we start in the summer, the summer was actually a good period for a broadly popular commercial production like *I Love You, You're Perfect, Now Change*. In the summer, more tourists are going to theater, and potential audiences don't focus on reviews the same way they do in the fall and spring. The show was not an instant success, and we ended up recouping only 5 percent of our capitalization during the first year. Most critics thought that we should close the show, but we were passionate about the production. We wanted to hang in there for a little bit longer. After that first year, we were solidly in the black, and we've never looked back. At this time, I think we've probably returned

fifteen to twenty times more than the investment to our investors. It's gotten to the point that if we don't send a check every four weeks, we get a call."[144]

Unfortunately, sometimes a production cannot overcome bad reviews, or it fails to appeal to potential ticket buyers. A producer must then decide when it is appropriate to close a show. Richard Frankel states, "It's the area where most producers, including us, frequently go wrong. We all think we can turn a show around, but the fact is that, once a show starts going south, it rarely reverses itself. It's possible that a star, a movie adaptation, or other extraordinary events might reverse a show's decline, but usually a show will keep declining. It becomes a matter of how long you can sustain the production. Producers have all sorts of reasons besides money to keep a show open, such as pride, obligation to the creative team, and the fact that you don't want to put people out of work. In my case, I'm also the general manager, so if the show stays open, I'll continue to get my fee. I have to deal with this conflict honestly, and I need to deal with the decline of this production in a responsible way. In addition to all your obligations and conflicts, it's also true that you need to be a real optimist to be in this business. You've got to be accustomed to seeing insurmountable problems and muscling right through them. That kind of optimism and confidence in your own abilities can lead you to run a show longer than you should have."[145]

In addition to determining the fate of the production, the producer has other responsibilities after the show opens. Alexander Fraser states, "After the show opens, the producer is responsible for ensuring that the creative team keeps the production in 'opening-night condition.' The producer also continues to monitor the marketing campaign while pursuing new marketing ideas."[146] Marc Routh adds, "The producer should continue to fully explore all of the rights available for the production that could possibly be licensed in order to maximize the commercial potential of the production."[147]

CLASSROOM DISCUSSION

Define "box office advance," "tryout," and "preview."

What responsibilities does the producer have before opening? Why do productions have out-of-town tryouts?

How does a producer handle bad reviews?

How does a producer decide when to close a show?

What responsibilities does the producer have after the production opens?

NOTES

1. The authors would like to thank the following individuals for their contributions to this chapter: Steve Baruch, Maria Di Dia, Dave Fiselson, Sean Patrick Flahaven, Richard Frankel, Don Frantz, Alexander Fraser, Gary McAvay, Carter Anne McGowan, Jon B. Platt, Jonathan Pollard, Geoff Rich, Marc Routh, and Harold Wolpert.
2. Sponsorship is defined as the mutually beneficial relationship between a production and a corporation, in which the corporation pays the producer a certain amount of money in exchange for mention in the show's marketing materials, etc. Merchandising is defined as the sale of production-related goods, such as T-shirts, mugs, and CDs.
3. Marc Routh, interview by Michael Flanagan, November 28, 2005.
4. Richard Frankel, interview by Ladan Hamidi-Toosi, October 26, 2005.
5. Jon B. Platt, interview by author, January 9, 2007.
6. Actors' Equity Association, *Agreement and Rules Governing Employment Under the Off Broadway Agreement (October 24, 2005–October 25, 2009)* (New York: Actors' Equity Association, 2005), *www.actorsequity.org/docs/rulebooks/OB_Rulebook_05-09.pdf*.
7. A few producers and theater owners, such as Disney Theatricals and Live Nation, do not belong to The Broadway League and conduct their own labor negotiations with applicable unions.
8. Royalty rates are specific percentage rates set for the payment of royalties. Royalties are payments made by the producer for the use of a specific work; creative personnel such as directors, choreographers, and authors (among others) are due royalties for each performance of a work that they created.
9. Routh, "Interview."
10. Frankel, "Interview."
11. Platt, "Interview."
12. Alexander Fraser, interview by Kevin Condardo, October 29, 2005.
13. The League of Resident Theatres (LORT) is a collective bargaining organization comprised of nonprofit resident theaters. Resident theaters are theaters that produce a full season of work and reside physically in a particular community. Most of these theaters are located outside of New York City, and thus are sometimes known as regional theaters as well.
14. Harold Wolpert, phone interview by author, November 22, 2005. Pay rates are the wages paid to a union member for a specific period of time (usually per week or per performance). Minimum pay rates are the lowest pay rates required by the collectively bargained agreement.
15. Wolpert, "Interview."
16. Ibid.
17. Actors' Equity Association, *Agreement and Rules Governing Employment under the Off Broadway Agreement*.
18. Routh.
19. Jonathan Pollard, interview by author, June 5, 2006.
20. Steve Friess, "Broadway puts on a show for Las Vegas," *USA Today*, August 26, 2005.
21. A workshop is a production of the entire show staged in a rehearsal room by a director (and choreographer, if necessary), presented after four or five weeks of rehears-

al to an audience of approximately fifty to one hundred people.
22. Routh.
23. Fraser.
24. Ibid.
25. Frankel.
26. Routh.
27. Fraser.
28. Routh.
29. Ibid.
30. Routh; Carter Anne McGowan, interview by author, August 19, 2007.
31. Routh.
32. Geoff Rich, interview by author, February 7, 2006. Net adjusted gross receipts are ticket sales less any allowable deductions that have been negotiated between the theater owner and the producer.
33. Ibid.
34. Ibid.
35. Ibid.
36. Ibid.
37. Frankel.
38. Gary McAvay, "Commercial Theater" (lecture moderated by Tobie Stein, Brooklyn College, Brooklyn, N.Y., September 27, 2005).
39. Routh.
40. Ibid.
41. Traditionally, an ensemble is a group of performers that support the star. In an ensemble production, all performers work together as a unit; there are no stars.
42. Frankel.
43. United States Copyright Office, "Copyright Office Basics," *www.copyright.gov/circs/circ1.html*.
44. Ibid. A derivative work is a work based upon the original work.
45. Lee Wilson, *The Copyright Guide* (New York: Allworth Press, 2003), 9.
46. United States Copyright Office, "Copyright Office Basics."
47. Ibid.
48. *The Copyright Guide*, 32.
49. United States Copyright Office, "Copyright Office Basics."
50. Ibid.
51. A special note regarding pre-1978 works: Under original United States copyright law, a work was protected for only twenty-eight years, and had to be renewed in its twenty-eighth year to be protected for another twenty-eight years. Although subsequent laws have been passed to lengthen the renewal period and provide for automatic renewal of these works, some works created before 1978 have passed out of copyright protection because of copyright expiration and failure to renew the copyright.
52. *The Copyright Guide*, 17.
53. Ibid.
54. *The Copyright Guide*, 35, 111.
55. Sean Patrick Flahaven, e-mail to author, January 13, 2008.
56. Ibid.
57. Dramatists Guild, *Approved Production Contract for Plays*, (New York: Dramatists Guild, 2007).
58. Fraser; Dramatists Guild, "Approved Production Contract for Plays."

59. Frankel.
60. Fraser.
61. Ibid.
62. Fraser; Dramatists Guild, "Approved Production Contract for Plays."
63. Frankel. In determining the royalty payments for other members of the creative team, the producer generally will use the author's royalty as a reference point in negotiations.
64. Flahaven, "E-mail."
65. Ibid.
66. Marc Routh, *Business Management for the Performing Arts* (New York: Marc Routh, 2006).
67. Ibid.
68. McAvey, "Commercial Theater"; Routh, "Interview."
69. Fraser.
70. McGowan, "Interview."
71. Investments by a limited partner are considered passive activities by the federal government and are subject to IRS regulations on such activities. Passive activities refer to the fact that the limited partner is not involved in the business operations of the partnership on a consistent, substantial basis.
72. Fraser.
73. Routh, *Business Management for the Performing Arts*.
74. Ibid.
75. Ibid.
76. Ibid.
77. Ibid.
78. Fraser.
79. Routh, *Business Management for the Performing Arts*.
80. Ibid.
81. Ibid.
82. Platt.
83. Fraser.
84. Don Frantz, interview by author, February 3, 2006.
85. Fraser.
86. The Securities and Exchange Commission defines such an investor as an "accredited investor" (also known as a "sophisticated investor"). An accredited investor is defined as "a natural person who has individual net worth, or joint net worth with the person's spouse, that exceeds $1 million at the time of the purchase, or a natural person with income exceeding $200,000 in each of the two most recent years or joint income with a spouse exceeding $300,000 for those years and a reasonable expectation of the same income level in the current year." Securities and Exchange Commission, "Accredited Investors," *www.sec.gov/answers/accred.htm*.
87. Routh, "Interview."
88. Ibid.
89. Routh, *Business Management for the Performing Arts*.
90. Ibid.
91. Frankel.
92. Steve Baruch, interview by author, February 27, 2006.
93. Ibid.
94. Ibid. Unaudited financial statements are financial statements that have not been reviewed by an outside accountant. Major media outlets are major newspapers, magazines, and television and radio stations in a particular city; for Broadway productions, these outlets would encompass the most important New York City media.
95. Dave Fishelson, interview by author, November 25, 2005.
96. McAvay.
97. Routh, "Interview."
98. Ibid.
99. Maria Di Dia, interview by author, June 27, 2006.
100. Routh, "Interview."
101. Fraser.
102. Routh, "Interview."
103. Ibid.
104. An agent acts as the performer's representative in business situations, helping that performer to find employment and negotiate contracts.
105. Fraser.
106. Ibid.
107. Ibid.
108. Ibid.
109. Bryan A. Garner, ed., *Black's Law Dictionary*, 8th ed. (Eagan, Minn.: West Publishing, 2004).
110. Di Dia, "Interview."
111. Ibid.
112. Pink contracts cover stagehands who work directly for producers on a production; these stagehands are hired in addition to the "house stagehands" that are employed directly by the theater owner. Pink contracts are known as such because they are, in fact, pink.
113. Routh, *Business Management for the Performing Arts*.
114. Examples of these budgets can be found in chapter 5.
115. Fringe benefits are benefits offered to the employee in addition to his salary; they include such items as health insurance, pension contributions, and vacation pay. These benefits have a cost to the employer.
116. Routh, "Interview."
117. Di Dia.
118. Routh, *Business Management for the Performing Arts*.
119. Fraser.
120. Routh, "Interview."
121. Routh, *Business Management for the Performing Arts*.
122. Routh, "Interview."
123. McAvay.
124. Fraser.
125. McAvay.
126. Group sales commissions are the fees paid to group sales agents, who sell large blocks of tickets to touring groups, school groups, etc.
127. Farber, *Producing Theatre*, 150.
128. Fraser.
129. Routh, "Interview."
130. Routh, *Business Management for the Performing Arts*.
131. McGowan.
132. Ibid.
133. Routh.
134. Ibid.
135. A producer may request that royalty recipients waive royalties for a specific period of time. Royalty waivers must be approved by both the royalty recipient and the union.
136. McAvay.
137. The box office advance differs from the advance against royalties described earlier in this chapter.

House seats are tickets reserved for a particular person's use for up to forty-eight hours before the performance.

138. Fraser.
139. Routh, "Interview."
140. Routh, "Interview"; McGowan.
141. Routh, "Interview."
142. Ibid.
143. Ibid.
144. Pollard, "Interview."
145. Frankel.
146. Fraser.
147. Routh, "Interview."

BIBLIOGRAPHY

Actors' Equity Association. *Agreement and Rules Governing Employment in Resident Theatres (February 28, 2005–Febuary 24, 2008)*. New York: Actors' Equity Association, 2005. *www.actorsequity.org/docs/rulebooks/LORT_Rulebook_05-08.pdf*.

Adler, Steven. *On Broadway: Art and Commerce on the Great White Way*. Carbondale, Ill.: Southern Illinois University Press, 2004.

Associated Press. "Julia Roberts' Show Grosses Nearly $1M." Associated Press, 4 April 2006.

Baruch, Steve. "Investor Relations." Interview by Jessica Bathurst. Phone interview with author, 27 February 2006.

Berliner, Terry. "A Game of Love and Chance." *American Theatre*, April 2006, 26–37.

Berson, Misha. "Why No Review? No Critics Allowed." *Seattle Times*, 17 August 2007.

Boroff, Philip. "'Mary Poppins' Leads Broadway to Season Sales Record." Bloomberg.com, 30 May 2007. *www.bloomberg.com/apps/news?pid=20601088&refer=muse&sid=a5.iODa_Lr5k*.

The Broadway League, *www.broadwayleague.com*.

Campbell, Drew. "Making a Connection." *Stage Directions*, December 2005, 72–76.

Cox, Gordon. "Live Nation Sells Off Theater Division." *Variety*, 24 January 2008.

Daspin, Eileen. "Give My Returns to Broadway." *Condé Nast Portfolio*, May 2007.

David, Cara Joy. "Off Broadway's Frontier Outpost Runs on Dreams." *New York Times*, 2 October 2006.

Di Dia, Maria. "Commercial Producing." Interview by Jessica Bathurst. Tape recording, 27 June 2006. Maria Productions, New York.

Dramatists Guild. *Approved Production Contract for Plays*. New York: Dramatists Guild, 2007.

Farber, Donald C. *From Option to Opening*. Pompton Plains, N.J.: Limelight Editions, 2004.

———. *Producing Theatre*. Pompton Plains, N.J.: Limelight Editions, 2006.

Fishelson, Dave. "Commercial Producing." Interview by Jessica Bathurst. Phone interview with author, 25 November 2005.

Flahaven, Sean Patrick. "Options." Interview by Jessica Bathurst. E-mail to author, 13 January 2008.

Frankel, Richard. "Commercial Producing." Interview by Ladan Hamidi-Toosi. Tape recording, 26 October 2005. Richard Frankel Productions, New York.

Frantz, Don. "Commercial Producing." Interview by Jessica Bathurst. Phone interview with author, 3 February 2006.

Fraser, Alexander. "Commercial Producing." Interview by Kevin Condardo. Tape recording, 29 October 2005. New York.

Friess, Steve. "Broadway on the Strip." *Newsweek*, 13 January 2006, 54.

———. "Broadway Puts on a Show for Las Vegas." *USA Today*, 26 August 2005.

———. "Las Vegas Builds Its Own Great White Way." *Christian Science Monitor*, 11 February 2005.

Garner, Bryan A., ed. *Black's Law Dictionary*. 8th ed. Eagan, Minn.: West Publishing, 2004.

Grant, Adriana. "Farewell Party." *Seattle Weekly*, 7 June 2006.

Green, Jesse. "Live on the Strip: Broadway's Second City." *New York Times*, 2 October 2005.

Grippo, Charles. *Business and Legal Forms for Theater*. New York: Allworth Press, 2004.

———. *The Stage Producer's Business and Legal Guide*. New York: Allworth Press, 2002.

Hughes, Robert J. "Les Biz: Broadway's New Investors." *Wall Street Journal*, 20 January 2006.

Jarvis, Robert M., Steven E. Chaikelson, Christine A. Corcos, Edmund P. Edmonds, Jon M. Garon, Shubha Ghosh, William D. Henslee, Mark S. Kende, Charles A. Palmer, Nancy L. Schultz, Marin R. Scordato, and Libby A. White. *Theater Law: Cases and Materials*. Durham, N.C.: Carolina Academic Press, 2004.

Jones, Chris. "Live Nation to Sell Its Stake in Broadway in Chicago." *Chicago Tribune*, 9 November 2007.

———. "Nederlander is the New Ruler of Theaters in the Loop." *Chicago Tribune*, 18 November 2007.

———. "Non-profit, Commercial Divisions Melt: Broadway Producers Take on Subscription Business." *Chicago Tribune*, 16 December 2007.

———. "Is Vegas the New Broadway?" *Chicago Tribune*, 6 February 2005.

Kachka, Boris. "Long Story Short: How a Perky British Nanny Became a Broadway Superstar." *New York*, 20 November 2006.

Kendt, Rob. "Theater You Can Drop In On." *New York Times*, 23 December 2005.

The League of Off-Broadway Theatres & Producers, *www.offbroadway.org*.

McAvay, Gary. "Lecture on Commercial Theater." 27 September 2005. Brooklyn College, Brooklyn, N.Y.

McGeehan, Patrick. "Theater District Will Get Taller, If Not Richer." *New York Times*, 6 August 2006.

McGowan, Carter Anne. "Commercial Producing." Interview by Jessica Bathurst. E-mail to author, 19 August 2007.

McKinley, Jesse. "Broadway 'Charity' is Now Back On." *New York Times*, 30 March 2005.

———. "Broadway's Havin' a Tropical Heat Wave." *New York Times*, 28 July 2005.

———. "The Call of the Jungle." *New York Times*, 16 April 2006.

———. "Drawn to Broadway From Near and, Mostly, Far." *New York Times*, 13 January 2005.

———. "Executives Must Pay $23.3 Million to Broadway Investors, Judge Says." *New York Times*, 9 February 2005.

———. "An Extinct Species May Walk Broadway Again." *New York Times*, 26 June 2005.

———. "Far from the Spotlight, the True Powers of Broadway." *New York Times*, 26 February 2006.

———. "The High Cost of Breaking Even." *New York Times*, 26 February 2006.

———. "In a Tony Race, Even Winners Often Lose." *New York Times*, 22 May 2005.

———. "Investor Comes to the Rescue of Wilson Play." *New York Times*, 13 November 2004.

———. "Making Good on Broadway, 'Bee' Earns Back Investment." *New York Times*, 12 September 2005.

———. "No Room on Broadway for 2 Off Broadway Hits." *New York Times*, 25 January 2006.

———. "The Odd Ticket." *New York Times*, 3 July 2005.

———. "Off Broadway, Success Grows Costly and Rare." *New York Times*, 1 February 2005.

———. "Ontario Joins Investors in a Musical of the 'Rings'." *New York Times*, 11 October 2005.

———. "Plays Without Music Find Broadway Harsh." *New York Times*, 7 December 2004.

———. "Sales Slow, Las Vegas 'Avenue Q' Will Close." *New York Times*, 16 February 2006.

———. "Starved for Hits, Producer Finds Hard Times on Street of Dreams." *New York Times*, 17 March 2005.

———. "'Wicked' Reaches Financial Nirvana." *New York Times*, 21 December 2004.

Murg, Stephanie. "Broadway, Inc." *Smithsonian Magazine*, August 2007. *www.smithsonianmag.com/arts-culture/10024961.html*.

Nance, Kevin. "Chicago becoming Holy Grail of pre-Broadway tryouts." *Chicago Sun-Times*, 9 January 2005.

Newman, Andy. "Broadway's Numbers for 2005 Are Strong." *New York Times*, 29 December 2005.

Pacheco, Patrick. "'Phantom' Casts a Long Shadow." *Los Angeles Times*, 11 January 2006.

———. "Rescripting the Strip." *Los Angeles Times*, 11 September 2005.

Papatola, Dominic P. "Broadway's Sweet on 'Charity'." *Pioneer Press*, 3 February 2005.

Parsons, Claudia. "Secret of Broadway Musical Hits—Plot or Songs?" Reuters, 21 January 2005.

Platt, Jon B. "Commercial Producing." Interview by Jessica Bathurst. Tape recording, 9 January 2007. New York.

Pollard, Jonathan. "Commercial Producing." Interview by Jessica Bathurst. Tape recording, 5 June 2006. New York.

Riedel, Michael. "Beached Boys." *New York Post*, 19 January 2005.

———. "It's Spama-Not." *New York Post*, 21 December 2005.

———. "Piece of the Pie." *New York Post*, 9 November 2005.

———. "'Rent' Flick's Tix Fix." *New York Post*, 30 November 2005.

Rich, Geoff. "Commercial Transfers." Interview by Jessica Bathurst. Phone interview with author, 7 February 2006.

Rizzo, Frank. "A So-Far Sad, Uninspired Season on Broadway." *Hartford Courant*, 26 December 2004.

Robertson, Campbell. "As 'Hot Feet' Ends Run on Broadway, Transamerica is Content." *New York Times*, 19 July 2006.

———. "As Off Broadway Changes, Some Venerable Theaters Vanish." *New York Times*, 9 August 2007.

———. "Broadway, the Land of the Long-Running Sure Thing." *New York Times*, 10 September 2006.

———. "Broadway's New Math: Top Dollar Tickets Equal Bigger Sales." *New York Times*, 8 May 2006.

———. "The Broadway Strike, Now Starring the Grinch." *New York Times*, 22 November 2007.

———. "'Chorus Line' Returns, As Do Regrets over Life Stories Signed Away." *New York Times*, 1 October 2006.

———. "Great Show! Now Change the Script, Cast and Theater." *New York Times*, 29 October 2006.

———. "'Hairspray' Is to Close in Las Vegas, Following 'Avenue Q,' Another Broadway Offshoot." *New York Times*, 1 June 2006.

———. "How They Did It. The Show, That Is." *New York Times*, 20 July 2007.

———. "Imitation or Flattery in Dueling Shows." *New York Times*, 22 August 2007.

———. "They Get to Put On a Show in the Bronx." *New York Times*, 10 May 2006.

———. "Those First in 'Chorus Line' Gain a Continuing Stake." *New York Times*, 2 February 2008.

———. "Tony Awards Campaigns: Courting Votes (Of Course It's Banned)." *New York Times*, 7 June 2006.

Rosenbloom, Stephanie. "For Rent: Large Theaters, Month-to-Month O.K." *New York Times*, 22 May 2005.

Routh, Marc. *Business Management for the Performing Arts*. New York: Marc Routh, 2006.

———. "Commercial Producing." Interview by Michael Flanagan. Tape recording, 28 November 2005. Richard Frankel Productions, New York.

Salmans, Sandra. "Why Investors in Broadway Hits Are Often Losers." *New York Times*, 22 November 1981.

Salomon, Andrew. "'Hairspray' Won't Stay in Vegas." *Backstage*, 6 June 2006.

Schiller, Gail. "Broadway Slow to Embrace Product Placement." *Hollywood Reporter*. 10 December 2007.

Securities and Exchange Commission, *www.sec.gov*.

———. "Accredited Investors." *www.sec.gov/answers/accred.htm*.

Simonson, Robert. "The Hit Maker of Barrow Street." *New York Times*, 15 July 2007.

Smith, Dinitia. "A New Owner for 5 Theaters on Broadway." *New York Times*, 17 February 2005.

Solway, Diana. "When the Choreographer Is Out of the Picture." *New York Times*, 7 January 2007.

Spindle, Les. "Give Our Regards to Vegas?" *Backstage*, 29 November 2004.

Stimac, Elias. "'Working in the Theatre': Nonprofits Creatively Challenge Broadway." *Backstage*, 12 November 2004.

Theatrical Index. Theatrical Index, published weekly.

United States Copyright Office, *www.copyright.gov*.

———. "Copyright Office Basics." *www.copyright.gov/circs/circ1.html*.

Vogel, Frederic B. and Ben Hodges, eds. *The Commercial Theatre Institute Guide to Producing Plays and Musicals*. New York: Applause Books, 2007.

Wakin, Daniel J. "Control of Dances Is at Issue in Lawsuit." *New York Times*, 4 September 2007.

Weatherford, Mike. "In Depth: Giving Regards to Broadway." *Las Vegas Review-Journal*, 29 January 2006.

Wilson, Lee. *The Copyright Guide*. New York: Allworth Press, 2003.

Wolpert, Harold. "Nonprofit Theaters Producing on Broadway." Interview by Jessica Bathurst. Phone interview with author, 22 November 2005.

Zinoman, Jason. "'Gatz' and 'The Great Gatsby' Vie for Broadway Stages." *New York Times*, 16 July 2006.

CHAPTER FIVE

Financial Management

In this chapter, we will define financial management and explore the many types of financial managers, in both the commercial and nonprofit worlds.[1] We will then examine and illustrate basic accounting terms and procedures.[2] Next, we will examine budget types, creating budgets by estimating revenue and expenses, and managing the budget creation process in commercial and nonprofit organizations. We will address other administrative responsibilities of the financial manager. These include the creation and management of information systems, including bookkeeping procedures; the purchase of insurance; the administration of payroll and taxes; the production of accurate financial reports; and the management of financial audits. Finally, the financial manager must ensure the company's accountability by enacting policies and procedures, as well as safeguarding company assets and ensuring the accuracy of financial reports, to make sure that the company acts in a financially responsible way.

The contents of this chapter should serve as general information only and should not substitute for the advice of an attorney or an accountant. Please consult a professional for further information and your specific needs.

FINANCIAL MANAGERS

Financial management can be defined in a number of different ways. At its most basic, it can "simply be balancing the books, making sure that there's significant revenue to cover expenses—not just on a year-to-year basis, but with a long-term view."[3] Financial management also involves "making a careful plan, ensuring that you clearly communicate the assumptions you've made in your plan to the people who are spending the money, and then ensuring that the plan is carried out. Those responsible for carrying out your plan should keep you informed of changes so that you have the ability

to make other adjustments in order to keep within your financial parameters."[4] In sum, financial management is the "basic oversight of all economic matters that are involved in the operation of a business,"[5] including the finance office, accounting records, and the budgeting and auditing processes.[6]

Financial managers are the fiscal stewards of an arts organization, keeping the budget balanced while ensuring that the organization behaves ethically and responsibly. As Peter Gee, vice president of finance and operations for the Brooklyn Academy of Music (BAM), states, "The finance department does not spend money or create revenue. It is our responsibility to manage the budget. We implement processes that help keep the information flowing into the office so that we can look into all the various divisions of the organization and make sure that the expenditures [expenses] and revenues as budgeted are on track. If there are shortfalls in revenue or overages (larger-than-expected amounts) in expenses, we make sure they are identified as soon as possible, so that remedies can be taken to address and correct them, and the budget is balanced at the end of the year."[7]

Financial managers allocate resources in the most efficient manner and in the manner most consistent with the goal of the organization, whether that goal is making a profit via a commercial enterprise or realizing the primary mission of a nonprofit institution. The financial manager looks at all of the goals of the organization, identifies the cost of achieving those goals, and determines the feasibility of the organization's current plan to realize its goals.[8] Financial managers may also be called upon to help adjust these plans as the financial situation of the organization changes, as Peter Gee explains. "After 9/11, revenue dropped dramatically, but expenses were the same. The executive staff needed to find a way to balance the budget. We discussed layoffs, identifying which areas or which positions could potentially be lost with the least amount of impact, but we also looked at employee furloughs, giving people mandatory time off without pay. We needed to make a choice. Did we want to lose jobs and lay off people, or did we want to have all employees 'share the pain'? The executive staff decided on a weeklong furlough, which we thought was better than letting people go. We hoped the furlough would balance out, and that we could make up the lost salaries to the staff in the future, when revenue improved."[9]

Financial managers may have many titles: general manager and company manager on a commercial production, and general manager, managing director, and director of finance in a nonprofit organization. In the next section, we will examine the job responsibilities of these positions.

In a commercial production, financial management responsibilities fall to the general manager and the company manager. The general manager is hired by the producer early in the producing process, and is responsible for issuing contracts, creating budgets, overseeing the management of the production, and communicating needed financial information to the relevant parties.[10] The company manager is "the representative of the producer at the theater on a daily basis and deals with the financial matters that involve the theater, such as the box office statement [a report detailing ticket sales] and the weekly settlement between the theater and the producer [listing all income and expenses for the engagement]. The company manager is also responsible for communicating and interacting with the acting company, the crew, and the musicians, as well as acting as the eyes and ears of the general manager and producers."[11] The producer also retains an accountant to monitor the financial aspects of the production, to produce financial reports for the investors, and, together with a lawyer, to ensure that all applicable reports are sent to the appropriate governmental agencies.[12] The accountant also files annual taxes for the producing entity and assists in preparing audits. In addition, the producer generally has a relationship with a banker to facilitate any monetary transactions as needed.

Nonprofit organizations also have a general management department. Alice Bernstein, executive vice president at the Brooklyn Academy of Music (BAM), defines the department's responsibilities in a presenting organization as follows: "The general management office facilitates the presentation by creating budgets, creating contracts, and communicating the needs of the presentation to all of the production departments. We administer the contract according to the agreement that we've made and ensure that all of the other departments in the institution, such as marketing, planning [development], and building operations, are in line."[13] The responsibilities of the general manager in a nonprofit producing organization are similar, except that the general manager prepares and administers budgets and contracts for productions produced by the organization. Depending on the size of the organization, the general manager can also be responsible for facility management.[14] In some smaller organizations, the managing director may also act as the general manager.[15]

The financial nuts and bolts of an organization are generally contained in the finance department. Paul Tetreault, producing director of Ford's Theatre in Washington, D.C., describes the responsibilities of the finance department: "The responsibilities of the finance department include complete maintenance of all financial records—cash in and cash out in the most basic sense—as well as budgetary management and budget creation (although some budgeting responsibilities may be handled by the general management office). The audit, payroll, and all tax filings would also come out of the finance office."[16] The finance department may take on additional responsibilities depending on the size of the organization, or may be run by the managing director.[17]

The finance department is typically supervised by a chief financial officer (CFO) or finance director. Reporting to the CFO is the controller, who is responsible for implementing accounting, payroll, and budgeting functions for the organization. Most organizations also have a bookkeeper, who is responsible for recording and reconciling all financial activity into journals and general ledgers (these terms are explained in the next section), as well as managers responsible for accounts receivable (money owed to the organization) and accounts payable (money the organization owes). All performing arts institutions have different organizational structures, but the general management and financial department job duties will be found in every institution, no matter what the specific job title may be.

CLASSROOM DISCUSSION

Define "financial management."

How do financial managers contribute to the realization of an organization's artistic and managerial goals?

Name two types of financial managers found in a commercial arts organization, and define their job responsibilities.

Name two types of financial managers found in a nonprofit arts organization, and define their job responsibilities.

ACCOUNTING BASICS FOR FINANCIAL MANAGERS

The most basic function of the financial manager is the accurate understanding of an organization's financial position. Accounting allows the financial manager to correctly assess the complex financial life of a business with specific, quantifiable terms and concepts. This section will review some basic accounting principles and provide examples illustrating these principles.

The basic accounting equation, which describes an organization's financial position at any point in time, can be expressed as:

Assets = Liabilities + Owner's Equity, or

Assets – Liabilities = Owner's Equity

(In this chapter, we will be using the first equation, solving for assets.)

Assets are "economic resources that are expected to benefit the business in the future."[18] Cash is an asset, as are equipment, buildings, land, and accounts receivable (money owed to the organization which has not been paid). Liabilities (otherwise known as debts) are amounts that the business owes to others, such as accounts payable (money owed by the organization for the purchase of goods and services). Liabilities also include obligations to provide future services for which the organization has already received payment, such as ticket sales for a future performance. Owner's equity is "the owner's claim to the assets of a business. Owner's equity is the residual interest in the assets of a business after deducting liabilities."[19] In other words, after all debts have been paid, owner's equity is what the organization actually owns. Another term for owner's equity is "change in net assets."[20] An organization increases its owner's equity by earning revenue, which is money gained from an organization's business operations.[21] However, these business operations often cost money; these costs are known as expenses and decrease owner's equity.[22] Salaries are an expense, as are rent and utilities (such as electricity or heat). With the addition of revenue and expenses, we can modify the basic accounting equation in this way:

Assets = Liabilities + Owner's Equity
+ Revenues – Expenses

The basic accounting equation allows us to examine an organization's financial position by recording financial transactions. A financial transaction is "any event that affects the financial position of the business and can be measured reliably."[23] Transactions affect accounts, which are "the detailed record of all of the changes that have occurred in a particular asset, liability, or owner's equity during a period."[24] For example, cash is an asset account; all changes (positive or negative) to the amount of cash in the organization would be recorded in that account. The most important point to remember when recording transactions is that the basic accounting equation must always remain balanced. Assets must always equal liabilities plus owner's equity plus revenues minus expenses.

To illustrate some of these concepts, let's examine the Gemwood Dance Company, a hypothetical dance company with assets in cash of $20,000 and liabilities of $8,000; no revenues or expenses have been recorded for this company yet. Thus, its owner's equity is $12,000.

Assets	=	Liabilities	+	Owner's Equity	+	Revenues	–	Expenses
Cash:								
$20,000	=	$8,000	+	$12,000	+	$0	–	$0

If the Gemwood Dance Company wants to hire a lighting designer for a $1,000 fee, which is considered an expense, the financial manager would record the transaction as follows:

Assets	=	Liabilities	+	Owner's Equity	+	Revenues	–	Expenses
Cash:								
$20,000	=	$8,000	+	$12,000	+	$0	–	$0
–$1,000								+$1,000 (salary expense)
$19,000	=	$8,000	+	$12,000	+	$0	–	$1,000

Gemwood Dance Company paid $1,000 in cash to the lighting designer (subtracting it from the cash asset account) and increased the salary expense (adding it to the salary expense account). As expenses are subtracted from owner's equity, the accounting equation remains balanced.

Let's examine another example. After hiring the lighting designer, the Gemwood Dance Company received a $2,000 donation (contributed revenue) from an enthusiastic fan. The financial manager would represent the transaction as follows:

Assets	=	Liabilities	+	Owner's Equity	+	Revenues	−	Expenses
Cash:								
$19,000 =		$8,000	+	$12,000	+	$0	−	$1,000
+$2,000					+	$2,000		
						(contributed revenue)		
$21,000 =		$8,000	+	$12,000	+	$2,000	−	$1,000

The donation increases both the cash asset account and the contributed revenue account.

The basic accounting equation can even show us the effect of financial transactions on different types of assets or liabilities. Remember that an organization's assets encompass more than just cash; assets include land, buildings, equipment, etc. For a performing arts company, assets would also include such items as set pieces and costumes. So if the Gemwood Dance Company purchases costumes for $500 for their next performance, the transaction would be recorded as:

Assets			=	Liabilities	+	Owner's Equity	+	Revenues	−	Expenses
Cash:										
$21,000	+	Costumes: $0	=	$8,000	+	$12,000	+	$2,000	−	$1,000
−$500	+	$500								
Cash:		Costumes:								
$20,500	+	$500								
		$21,000	=	$8,000	+	$12,000	+	$2,000	−	$1,000

In this case, the transaction transferred funds from one class of asset to another. The Gemwood Dance Company owns the costumes and expects to use them to benefit the company, so the costumes are still considered assets. In this transaction, the cash asset account lost $500, but the costume asset account gained $500.

Now let's assume that the Gemwood Dance Company buys some equipment for its office on credit.[25] Buying on credit creates a debt, so the financial transaction would be represented as:

Assets					=	Liabilities	+	Owner's Equity	+	Revenues	−	Expenses
Cash: $20,500	+	Costumes: $500	+	Office Equip.: $0	=	$8,000	+	$12,000	+	$2,000	−	$1,000
			+	$500		+$500 (office equipment liability)						
Cash: $20,500	+	Costumes: $500	+	Office Equip.: $500								
		$21,500			=	$8,500	+	$12,000	+	$2,000	−	$1,000

The purchase of the office equipment on credit created an increase in the office equipment asset account and an increase in the company's liability account. When the office equipment purchase is paid off, the transaction would be represented as:

Assets					=	Liabilities	+	Owner's Equity	+	Revenues	−	Expenses
Cash: $20,500	+	Costumes: $500	+	Office Equip.: $500	=	$8,500	+	$12,000	+	$2,000	−	$1,000
−$500 (cash used to pay liability)						−$500 (liability paid)						
Cash: $20,000	+	Costumes: $500	+	Office Equip.: $500								
		$21,000			=	$8,000	+	$12,000	+	$2,000	−	$1,000

The cash asset account would decrease $500 to pay the liability, while the liability account would decrease $500 because the office equipment liability has been paid.

As you can see, each business transaction has a dual effect, an increase or a decrease in particular accounts. If costumes are purchased, the cash asset account is decreased while the costume asset account is increased. A process called double-entry bookkeeping records the dual effects of these transactions. In this bookkeeping system, transactions are recorded by account in a journal, which is a record of all transactions arranged in chronological order.[26] The data entered into the journal is then copied (or posted) to the organization's book of accounts, known as the general ledger.[27] All accounts are listed together in the organization's chart of accounts; for ease of recording transactions, the accounts are coded with a number that the organization assigns to them.

Since transactions are recorded and posted in chronological order, how does the financial manager determine when a transaction occurs? If an organization buys equipment on credit, is the transaction recorded when the equipment is received, or when it is finally paid for? The transaction may be recorded in one of two ways, depending on whether the organization is using the accrual accounting system or the cash-based accounting system. In accrual accounting, revenue and expenses are recorded when they are earned or incurred, but in cash-based accounting, transactions are recorded as cash is received or paid.[28] For example, a donor promises the Gemwood Dance Company $1,000 in January; she pays $500 in March and $500 in April. Under the accrual accounting system, the donation is recorded as $1,000 in January, but under the cash-based system, $500 would be recorded in March and $500 in April. Most businesses use the accrual accounting system, because it provides a more accurate picture of actual income and expenses; however, this system does not show the actual amount of cash that an organization has available, so financial managers should use cash flow statements (which detail the amount of cash that the organization currently possesses) to ensure that the organization has enough cash available to function.

The process of recording and posting transactions is part of the accounting cycle. The accounting cycle for an organization takes place on a yearly basis, known as a fiscal year. An organization can define any twelve-month period as a fiscal year. Some organizations use the fiscal year as defined by the Internal Revenue Service, which is January 1 to December 31. Other organizations, especially those that have seasons beginning in the fall and ending in the spring, find it more useful to have a fiscal year that runs from July 1 to June 30, which encompasses their whole season.[29]

The accounting cycle begins by recording the starting balances (starting amounts) in each account. All transactions are then recorded to journals and posted to the general ledger in chronological order. As the financial manager prepares to end the accounting cycle, financial statements are prepared to report the organization's current financial status. Financial statements include income statements, cash flow statements, and balance sheets. Income statements show the revenue earned and expenses incurred by the organization during a period of time (usually the fiscal year); income is determined by subtracting expenses from revenue; an example is found is appendix A.[30] Cash flow statements (appendix B) detail the increases and decreases in the cash asset account over a period of time.[31] Balance sheets (appendix C) show the assets, liabilities, and owner's equity of an organization at any given point in time.[32] After the financial statements have been prepared, the financial manager determines the closing balance of all accounts and prepares to begin a new accounting cycle.[33]

The practices of accounting are regulated by the Financial Accounting Standards Board, also known as FASB. FASB is a private organization that monitors accounting practices and procedures and is responsible for updating these practices, known as generally accepted accounting principles (GAAP), on a regular basis.[34] It is the responsibility of the financial manager to be aware of the current FASB regulations and to incorporate any updated practices into the accounting procedures of the organization. In particular, nonprofit organizations should be aware of FASB Statement of Financial Accounting Standards Numbers 116 and 117, which require the following:

- Contributions received by the organization must be recorded as revenue in the period that the contribution was received. (Contributions also include promises to give, as well as actual contributions received.) In addition, contributions must be recorded as permanently restricted net assets (the donor restricts the use of the contribution for a certain purchase or activity), temporarily restricted net assets (the donor restricts the use of the contribution for a certain time period), or unrestricted net assets (the donor places no limitations on the use of the donation). The expiration of donor-imposed restrictions must be recognized in the period in which the restrictions expire.

- If the contribution contains a condition that must be met or the contribution will be refunded, such as a grant for the production of a series of operas in future seasons, then the contribution is not recorded as revenue until the condition is met (e.g., the operas are produced). If the operas are never produced, any portion of the contribution received would be returned.

- The nonprofit organization must prepare three financial statements: the Statement of Financial Position, which provides information about assets, liabilities, and net assets (owner's equity); the Statement of Activities, which reports changes in net assets (revenue and expenses); and the Statement of Cash Flows, which details the increases and decreases in the cash asset account. [35]

CLASSROOM DISCUSSION

Why does a financial manager need to understand basic accounting principles?

What is the basic accounting equation?

What is the difference between cash-based and accrual accounting? What are the advantages of accrual accounting? What are the disadvantages?

What are the stages in the accounting cycle?

Define the following terms: "asset," "liability," "owner's equity," "revenue," "expense," "double-entry bookkeeping," "fiscal year," "FASB," and "GAAP."

What do FASB Statements 116 and 117 require?

The Nolichucky Opera Company (NOC) has the following assets and liabilities at the beginning of the fiscal year:

Assets: $105,000 cash; $55,000 building; $10,000 in office equipment; $5,000 in contributions owed to the organization

Liabilities: $5,000 loan from bank

The following transactions occur during the fiscal year:

a. The NOC gets a $50,000 grant from the city for its next opera.

b. The NOC buys new lighting equipment on credit for $600.

c. The NOC hires a choreographer for a fee of $15,000.

d. The NOC buys $800 worth of advertising.

e. The NOC sells $9,000 worth of tickets.

f. The NOC pays $300 on its purchase of lighting equipment (the equipment purchased in item b).

g. BONUS: The NOC collects $3,000 of the $5,000 owed to it by donors. (Remember that accounts receivable and cash are both assets.)

Record each transaction. After all transactions are recorded, create a balance sheet with the NOC's current balances for assets, liabilities, and owner's equity.

BUDGETS

After learning the current financial position of an organization, the financial manager can begin to plan for the organization's future by creating a budget. Budgets are planning documents that detail how an organization plans to spend money and how it plans to create revenue.[36] In this section, we will examine the types of budgets and the process of creating a budget by estimating budgeted income and expenses. We will then describe the management of the budget creation process, including getting the budget approved by senior management. Finally, we will provide some recommendations for creating the most effective budgets.

Budget Types

Commercial productions and nonprofit organizations use different types of budgets to suit their different needs. Commercial productions generally use two types of budgets for expenses: the production budget and the weekly operating budget. The production budget details all of the costs of a production from conception through opening night; it may also include one-time expenses that continue after the first performance but are not weekly expenses, such as an advertising campaign that begins a month before opening and is scheduled to run for the first two weeks of performances.[37] The production budget also includes the opening and closing costs, the cash reserve, and bonds and deposits, as described in chapter 4. (Please see appendix D for an example of a production budget.[38]) The weekly operating budget projects (estimates) the expenses, also known as running costs, that will occur on a weekly basis once the show has opened.[39] Running costs include weekly salaries, rent for the theater, and ongoing maintenance expenses. (Please see appendix E for an example of a weekly operating budget.[40])

Nonprofit organizations, which typically present a season as opposed to a single show, use two different budgets, the annual operating budget and the capital budget. The annual operating budget lists all of the revenue and expenses for the organization for the entire fiscal year, including both programming and administrative expenses. Revenue may include income from ticket sales, as well as donations from individuals and foundations. Expenses include administrative salaries; production expenses; fundraising, marketing, and publicity expenses; and any additional project expenses, such as educational activities. Some nonprofits may also use an engagement or production budget, which details the expenses and income for a particular show, but these budgets are folded into the annual operating budget for the entire organization.[41] (Please see appendix F for an example of an annual operating budget.[42])

The capital budget lists all expenses that are expected to last for more than one fiscal year; these expenses are amortized over time, meaning that the value of the item is expensed over the fiscal years that the item will last (e.g., a computer system that is expected to last for five years has its cost split over five years, as opposed to being recorded as an expense the year that it was purchased).[43] This budget includes the building (if owned) and any expenses related to the building, as well as computer equipment, theatrical equipment, and furniture. Renovations and additional purchases of real estate are also part of the capital budget. This budget is separate from the annual operating budget. (Please see appendix G for an example of a capital budget.[44])

The next section will examine the process of creating the budget, including the estimation of earned income; the estimation of contributed income; the determination of the ratio between earned and contributed income; the estimation of expenses; and balancing the budget.

Creating the Budget

The financial manager creates a budget by estimating earned income, contributed income (if a nonprofit organization), and expenses. Earned income is "the income earned as the result of specific programs, goods, or services."[45] Contributed income is income donated to a nonprofit organization by individual donors, government agencies, corporations, and foundations. Expenses are costs incurred by the organization as a result of its business activity. Each type of budget contains at least one of these budget categories, if not all; for example, an annual operating budget contains both types of income, as well as expenses, but a capital budget will only contain expenses.

All budget items should be estimated using zero-based budgeting, if possible. Zero-based budgeting requires that the financial manager calculate any estimated figures from scratch, with minimum reliance on prior-year budget entries. Zero-based budgeting can be contrasted with incremental budgeting, which allows the manager to create current-year budget figures by adding a specified percentage to the prior fiscal year's budget (generally about 2 to 3 percent).[46] Zero-based budgeting is preferred because it allows the organization to create the most accurate budgeting picture for each project. Gee explains why incremental budgeting is not effective: "If nothing has changed in your current fiscal year, then you could budget incrementally, just adjusting for inflation. That's not the environment at BAM; BAM is constantly changing. As we're changing and growing, we need to revisit our budget every year to make sure that we've accounted for everything. Incremental budgeting doesn't allow for us to address any new issues; by using this method of budgeting, you can find yourself with only a 3 percent increase, when you really need a 30 percent increase."[47]

However, as a part of the zero-based budgeting process, analysis of prior fiscal years' budgeted and actual figures can be very valuable, especially in attempting to predict ticket sales goals and other figures based on future actions. James Patrick, executive director of the Warner Theatre in Torrington, Connecticut, uses this type of analysis in creating his budgets for the current fiscal year: "This year we did more analysis in advance. We reviewed our entire show history over the last three years, determined each show's genre (such as Broadway-style musical, country music, or stand-up comedy), then calculated the average revenue and expense per genre. For example, the average cost to produce a Broadway-style musical for four performances in our fall slot was X, ticket sales averaged Y, so the profit margin for the run was Y [ticket sales] minus X [costs]. We then used these averages to help project the financial results of our upcoming season."[48]

The following sections will provide a guide to estimating income and expenses, as well as examining the ratio of earned to contributed income and balancing the budget.

Estimating Earned Income

As stated above, earned income includes such items as ticket sales, ticket handling fees, concession and merchandise sales, coat check and parking fees, educational program income, advertising revenue, rental income, and royalties from future productions of a play or musical. Ticket sales may include tickets sold as part of a subscription package, tickets sold as part of a ticket sales to a group, or single (individual) ticket sales.[49] Ticket handling fees are administrative fees added to ticket purchases when tickets are purchased over the phone or on the Internet. Concessions are food or beverages sold by the theater in the lobby before and after the performance, as well as during intermission; merchandise includes souvenir programs, CDs, T-shirts, and other assorted theater- or show-related paraphernalia. An organization that operates a coat check or parking facilities may earn income from these services. Educational program income includes such items as tuition fees for classes or workshops and special performances for students. Advertising revenue is generated from selling advertisements in the program or other publications. An organization may rent its space, set pieces, costumes, or equipment to other parties for additional income. In the context of earned income, royalties are payments made to a nonprofit organization for a commercial transfer. As described in chapter 4, the originating theater might negotiate with the author of the production and with the commercial producers for a royalty (a percentage of the net weekly box office receipts after deducting ticketing and credit card fees, and taxes), as well as a percentage of the net profits of the commercial venture.[50]

For nonprofit organizations, endowment interest income is also earned income. An endowment is an investment account managed by investment consultants. These consultants are hired by the organization and monitored by an investment or endowment committee on the board of directors.[51] The interest earned by the endowment is considered earned revenue, but the principal (the amount of money invested that is generating the interest) is not used as revenue. The principal remains invested and is increased by donations made directly to the organization's endowment and by reinvesting some of the interest earned. For example, if the endowment is earning 10 percent interest for the fiscal year, and the organization only takes 5 percent of the interest as revenue, then the other 5 percent would be added to the endowment principal. Most organizations take 5 to 6 percent of their average endowment interest income over three fiscal years as revenue.[52] Paul Tetreault recommends that all mature organizations think about starting an endowment. "An endowment is the future of the organization.

For every organization that wants to be around for a long time, it's a safety net."[53]

Unlike most contributed income, earned income is unrestricted, which means it can be applied toward any purpose that the organization wishes. (Endowment income may be restricted to specific purposes if the donor so chooses.) Because of the many uses of earned income, organizations try to create as many earned-income streams as possible, including space rentals, concessions, and strategic partnerships, with other organizations. Jessica R. Jenen, executive director of Classic Stage Company (CSC), illustrates: "We have a beautiful theater, which is sought after by many directors and theater companies. When we're not doing our own work, we rent it out to outside groups. We usually make more money from space rentals than we do from our own work. We recently entered into an agreement with Ninth Street Espresso, which has some of the best espresso in the city, to operate a lobby café in our space. This deal has brought in a nice rental income, and it has also helped to make CSC more of a gathering place. It's a great example of synergy, of two companies trying to build each other's businesses. Also, to bring in additional funds, we generally devote one slot in each season to presenting the work of an outside theater group. We work with like-minded theater companies that don't have a home. This is another example of synergy between companies, and really, everyone wins."[54]

Earned income can be estimated in various ways, including basic mathematic equations, observation of the prior financial history of the organization, and informed guesswork. For example, the potential gross amount of ticket sales is determined by multiplying the sales price by the number of seats available at that price. The potential gross does not include any deductions taken from credit card companies, group sales commissions (commission from a block of tickets sold at a discount to a group), etc. The marketing director or general manager then estimates the percentage of tickets that might be sold each night at each price. Many factors enter into the estimation of these percentages, including company history, type of production, time of year, and audience demographics (e.g., average age or income of audience members). If the general manager or marketing director has worked on the same—or a very similar—production recently, then he may look at the actual ticket sales for the prior production and use that figure as the basis for the new ticket sales estimation. However, even when using sales figures for an identical production, any new ticket sales estimation should take into account any variables that may differ from the prior production (such as the time of year or the number of performances). Numbers should never be blindly plugged into a budget.

For example, production #2 in the annual operating budget (appendix F) is expected to bring in $348,750 in single-ticket sales and $3,870 in group-ticket sales. These numbers are determined by first figuring out the potential gross amount of ticket sales. The production runs for five weeks, playing eight performances per week. The theater has 250 seats, which are sold at $45 each; therefore, the potential gross amount of ticket sales is:

$$250 \text{ seats} \times \$45 \times 8 \text{ performances} \times 5 \text{ weeks} = \$450,000$$

As production #2 is a shortened version of a play by Shakespeare, the marketing director takes into account other classical plays produced at the theater, as well as the potential for educational performances to bring in group sales. Based on the history of the organization, plus his knowledge of current factors such as the artistic elements of the production (e.g., star casting) and sales trends, the marketing director determines that approximately 77.5 percent of the tickets will be sold for the run (for a revenue figure of $348,750), and that an additional $3,870 worth of tickets will be sold to school groups.

Other types of earned income can be estimated using similar processes. One example is concessions revenue. Concessions revenue should be estimated based on the history of concessions sales for the organization, in addition to the length of the performance, the number of intermissions, and the likelihood of inclement weather, which would encourage customers to congregate inside the lobby. For example, in the annual operating budget (appendix F), production #1 is budgeted to bring in $1,719 of concessions sales, but production #2 is only budgeted to bring in $250 of concessions revenue. As production #2 has no intermission, the general manager noted that any concession revenue brought in would be negligible (as patrons would be buying refreshments only before the performance, if that), and chose to budget accordingly.

Another example is advertising revenue, which can be estimated based on the history of advertising sales for the organization. The advertising revenue estimation can also be affected by the type of programming planned and any new business relationships that the organization has created since the previous year. As an example, if an organization plans to present a festival of Senegalese dance, the marketing director of the organization may make a concerted effort to draw more advertisers from local African-owned businesses; the projected sales of these advertisements would increase the expected revenue for the organization.

Estimating Contributed Income

For nonprofit organizations, contributed income is estimated by setting a target amount for fundraising based on the productions that are planned and the earned income expected. For example, if the production and organizational expenses total $1 million, but earned income is budgeted at $650,000, then $350,000 must be raised by the fundraising or development department. No estimate of contributed income can be made without the input of the development department. The director of development should be consulted on every aspect of the fundraising budget, and should be a crucial part of any contributed income estimation.

Estimates of contributed income are typically broken into the main components of fundraising: individual giving, government support, and grants from foundations and corporations. Individual giving encompasses all donations made by individuals. Government support includes all grants given by federal, state, and local government agencies. A foundation is a philanthropic institution that gives grants to unrelated nonprofit organizations or individuals who meet the foundation's criteria. Corporate grants are made by corporations to nonprofit organizations that meet the corporation's funding criteria.

The estimation of contributed income should contain all known commitments, such as multiyear grants (money granted for more than one fiscal year) that have already been obtained, or donations that have been promised to the organization. New sources of contributed income should be projected for the new fiscal year; this projection should be based on the prior history of the organization, as well as the current economic climate, new programming initiatives that may allow new sources of funding, and the cultivation of potential new donors.

James Patrick explains his process for estimating contributed income. "We break it down by category. We have an annual appeal, special events, and a membership program [for donations by individuals]. We break those initiatives down individually, and each one we build from the ground up. For example, in estimating corporate support, we calculate how we did the year before, and how we think we can do this year based on our program schedule, and then we build in a modest increase so there's an incentive to reach a higher goal each year."[55]

For example, the organization represented in the annual operating budget (appendix F) has increased its educational programming and wishes to increase its foundation support for this programming. The budget includes an additional $5,000 to be raised for educational production #2 as an increased goal for foundation contributions.

Again, this budget must be created with the substantial input and assistance of the fundraising department in order for it to be most useful.

Determining the Ratio of Earned Income to Contributed Income

At this point in the budgeting process, the organization has determined how much of its budgeted revenue is comprised of earned and contributed sources. The typical ratio of earned to contributed income is 60 percent/40 percent, but this ratio can vary by organization, depending on its programming and its tolerance for risk. For example, BAM's ratio sometimes slips to 70 percent contributed versus 30 percent earned. Bernstein lists the reasons that BAM's earned income is lower than in comparable organizations, including type of programming and available audience: "We're doing important, difficult work, and the reality is that there aren't enough people who want to see that kind of work to enable us to have long engagements, in which we could make back the cost of presenting the performance (which is essentially the flight to New York and the load-in of the production). The fact that 20,000 New Yorkers will come to see a Robert Wilson show is an extraordinary thing, but there aren't 22,000 of them all willing to buy tickets for a specific two-week period; therefore, we can run ten performances of a Robert Wilson work, but we cannot run eleven. Bringing in companies from around the world drives up costs, but does not translate to higher ticket prices. So we have to raise a lot more money to support the work than a performing arts center that might be running extremely popular noninternational shows like *The Phantom of the Opera* and *Wicked*."[56]

On the opposite end of the spectrum, Patrick states, "We're at about 80 percent earned to 20 percent contributed. Even though we're a nonprofit organization, we have a mandate from the board to create show budgets that either break even [expenses and income are equal] or make a profit.

This presents both artistic and financial challenges. That being said, while each individual show might be budgeted to make a profit, some will not meet expectations. In the end, the institution as a whole certainly needs fundraising to offset overhead and to make the overall operating budget balance or reach a surplus [when income exceeds expenses]."[57]

Estimating Expenses

Expenses may be estimated in the same way as income. The more detail that can be included in the budget, the more useful the budget will be.[58] For instance, the budget entry for stagehands while a show is loading into the theater might have this formula:

$$(\text{number of stagehands}) \times (\text{number of hours worked}) \times (\text{number of days worked})$$

However, if overtime (hours worked over the daily minimum as specified by a union) is expected, it should be included in the budget entry, as well as any fringe benefits that the stagehands will accrue.[59] Fringe benefits are nonsalary benefits that have a cost, such as health insurance or pension contributions.

Expenses may be separated into different types, such as fixed, variable, documented, undocumented, and amortized. Fixed expenses, such as weekly salaries, occur at regular intervals and are always the same cost. Variable expenses vary from week to week (like royalties, as described in chapter 4). Most fixed expenses are documented, which means that backup (such as an invoice or a receipt) proves the amount of the expense; some fixed expenses may be undocumented expenses, which are expenses that are negotiated as a fixed amount between two parties and thus do not require documentation or backup. An example of an undocumented expense is the administrative fee that a presenter and producer agree upon for a touring production. Finally, some expenses may also be amortized, which means that the cost may be spread out over several weeks or several productions.

The weekly operating budget (appendix E) contains examples of all of these types of expenses. The salaries are fixed expenses; they are determined on a weekly basis and are the same from week to week. Advertising expenses are variable expenses, as they may change weekly, so the general manager must pay close attention to these expenses to ensure that his budget is accurate. Departmental maintenance expenses (which include expenses to repair/restore production elements during the run of the show) are documented, as the general manager will expect to see backup for these expenses, such as an invoice or a receipt. The general management office charge is an undocumented expense, as it is a fixed amount agreed upon between the producer and the general manager and does not require documentation. Finally, the closing costs are recorded as an amortized expense; the general manager has estimated the total cost of closing and loading out the production and has allocated a portion of that cost over the weeks of the run.

As part of estimating expenses, many financial managers budget a contingency, which is an amount of money, usually 5 to 10 percent of the expense budget, earmarked to cover any unforeseen expenses or costs that cause the organization to go over budget. Producer Marc Routh states, "The contingency is useful because we don't know the actual costs of the expenses we've budgeted. I usually budget a 5 percent contingency, but if I can increase that to 7 or 8 percent, that's even better. I like to have as much leeway as possible."[60]

Balancing the Budget

After the budget has been created, the ratio of income to expenses must be analyzed. If the income exceeds the expenses, then the organization is in the enviable (and rare) position of determining what to do with its surplus income. If, however, expenses exceed income (a far more likely occurrence), then the organization has three basic alternatives to reduce this budget deficit: increase earned income, increase contributed income (if the organization is a nonprofit), or decrease expenses.

The solution an organization chooses depends on the circumstances of the individual organization and the goals it wishes to accomplish. For example, Peter Gee uses a combination of alternatives, decreasing expenses and increasing earned revenue, to reduce the deficit in accordance with programming goals. "Let's say that one of our five-year goals is to have three full operas in BAM's spring season. I create a forecast [a budget estimating future revenue and expenses] based on what we want to do artistically, what our development director believes is realistic fundraising growth, and what our marketing director believes is realistic ticket revenue growth, and then I plug in all the numbers to determine if it's achievable or not. I look over the budget, trying to find potential areas of savings so that, if we want to add something, our savings can help fund that. I'm looking to cut back expenses, but sometimes I also need to look at earned revenue and ask, 'Are we as an organization maximizing our earned revenue

sources? Are there any earned revenue opportunities out there that we should possibly investigate?'"[61]

Financial managers also approach deficits in different ways based on prior experience. For example, before coming to CSC, Jenen worked as a general manager in commercial theater, and she has used her for-profit expertise in her nonprofit position, reducing show expenses to keep them consistent with a production's expected earned income. "When I came here for the first time, they gave me the current draft of the season budget, and every show taken on its own was budgeted to lose money. I didn't understand. How can you budget the show to lose money? But that's the way it is in nonprofit theater, where the art is subsidized, and contributions make up for the individual show deficits. In the commercial world, you have income and expenses; you raise the money, spend the money, and hope to take in more money than you spent. It's cut-and-dried. So right now, we're spending on average approximately $200,000 on a mainstage show. We can't bring in $200,000 in earned revenue unless it's a huge success. So I have been cutting expenses where I can, so that the ratio between income and expenses gets closer, and I reduce the loss for each individual show, making the expenses proportionate to the income expected."[62]

CLASSROOM DISCUSSION

Define the following terms: "budget," "earned income," "endowment," "contributed income," "fixed expense," "variable expense," "documented expense," "undocumented expense," and "amortized expense."

What is the different between zero-based and incremental budgeting? What is the advantage of zero-based budgeting?

Name and define the two commercial and two nonprofit budgets.

Name three types of earned income.

How would you estimate ticket sales for a production?

How does an endowment provide income to an organization?

Name two types of contributed income.

How would you estimate contributed income for an organization or a production?

If your budget doesn't balance, what could you do to balance it?

Select a play or musical and, using the production budget provided as a model, create a budget for your production. Justify each revenue and expense item as fully as you can.

Managing the Budget Creation Process

After exploring the methods of estimating revenue and expenses, we will now examine the budget creation process for a commercial production or within a nonprofit organization. The basic process of creating a budget and getting it approved by senior management will differ depending on the needs of the production or organization, although certain processes are generally the same for commercial productions or nonprofit organizations.

The budgeting process for a commercial production begins with the general manager. After the general manager is hired by the producer, he gathers all available information about the production, including the script, the director's concept for the production, and any preliminary set, lighting, and costume design concepts. For any union personnel that will be hired, the general manager must obtain the current collective bargaining agreement for the applicable union to get the most accurate salary and benefit costs. (Unions and collective bargaining agreements are discussed in detail in chapter 9.) The general manager uses this information to create the production budget, which is then shown to the producers for approval. The producers give feedback on the budget, and the general manager then makes all necessary adjustments and corrections. As contracts are signed and designs are finalized, the general manager incorporates this information into the production budget and revises it. The production budget is generally finalized by the first week of rehearsal, with only minor adjustments after that point.[63]

Routh describes this process. "For a commercial production, the first step is simple. If there's an existing script, you read the script and take notes about the time period in which the show is set, the time of year in which it is set, the number of actors required, the number and type of props needed, and any other information that you can glean from the script. For instance, if the play is set in winter, then most of the characters will need coats, which must be accounted for in the budget. If any of the creative personnel have been hired, then you interview those people about their concepts for the production. However, if the director and the designers have not yet been hired, then you need to make assumptions about the cost of the set, light, and costume designs based on the information contained in the script. You then create the first production budget and see if the numbers are viable. If you budgeted a new Broadway musical at $20 million, and had weekly operating costs of $1 million, then you would need to review your numbers, because those numbers are not reasonable. You wouldn't be able to recoup, to make your money back [because ticket sales will not cover expenses]. After you are satisfied that your numbers are viable, then you present the budget to the producers."[64]

Routh remarks on the importance of keeping track of revisions to the budget as it advances through this process, including noting the date on which the revisions were made. "The production budget is in a constant state of revision as you get closer to production, so it's important to date your budget so that you know with which draft you're working. It's important to keep track of your revisions so that you are aware of the amount of money that every department (set, costumes, etc.) has spent. For example, if you've allocated the money you saved in your costume budget for an extra week of rehearsals, then you know that you can't allocate it for additional set expenses; you cannot spend the same money twice. You'd need to find additional savings elsewhere in your budget. As general manager, you are the only person who sees the whole budget picture."[65]

At the same time that the production budget is created, the general manager for a commercial production begins work on the weekly operating budget. The general manager estimates the costs of such budget items as salaries, sound and lighting rentals, and other weekly expenses based on the current production information, just as he does with the production budget. Other expenses, like advertising, can vary widely from week to week and need to be constantly updated as the numbers change. On the income side, weekly potential gross ticket revenue is estimated by multiplying the number of seats available in the theater by the number of performances per week, then multiplying that number by the average ticket price.

Routh remarks that, as the weekly operating budget changes, it must be closely monitored. "The weekly operating budget is going to change as time goes on, and you need to pay close attention to it. You need to be aware of 'creep,' which is the process of expenses increasing just a little bit from week to week, until you have a significant increase. Creep often happens with salary expense, as salaries can increase incrementally over the life of the show as the cast becomes better known or stays with the show for a long time. That incremental increase can add up over the long run."[66]

Nonprofit organizations have a different budgeting process, because those organizations are typically budgeting for an entire season, not just for one production (although budgets for specific productions may be included in the annual operating budget). The budgeting process for a nonprofit organization begins as soon as the season for the following fiscal year is finalized, or as close to finalized as the organization is able to achieve. The person responsible for preparing the annual operating budget (the general manager, the finance director, or the managing director) creates a preliminary budget, incorporating as much information about the season as is known at the time of the budget's creation. This information would include such projected expenses as the number of productions; the number of people expected to be employed on those productions and their salaries; estimations of set, costume, and light design costs; salary costs for nonproduction-related employees; and office supplies and other miscellaneous items that the organization is expected to need during the fiscal year. Earned and contributed income would also be estimated for inclusion in the annual operating budget.

For example, as a part of creating the next fiscal year's budgets, Peter Gee reviews the current fiscal year's budgets with the heads of all of the departments at BAM. He describes his process for creating the annual operating budget, beginning with an analysis of the current fiscal year: "As department heads are looking at the current year's report detailing actual expenses versus budgeted expenses, we require that they tell us their status within their current budget and explain any discrepancies between the amount they budgeted at the beginning of the fiscal year and their current expenses. We want to understand their planning process. The department heads will then present budgets to the finance department at the beginning of the year, usually February, for the next fiscal year. They have to justify every expense. We start from zero [zero-based budgeting] and ask them, 'What do you need to spend?' The departments don't always get the amount of money that they ask for, but it gives us an opportunity to understand their needs, as well as identify any potential problem areas that could arise in the middle of the year. It gives credence to budget modifications in the middle of the year."[67]

The capital budget is created in much the same way as the annual operating budget, incorporating the costs of any planned equipment purchases, building renovations, and other estimated capital expenses. Tetreault notes that Ford's Theatre now creates a capital budget every year, not just when the organization is conducting a capital campaign (a fundraising campaign designed to fund a significant capital expense, like a building purchase or a major renovation). He describes this process: "To create a capital budget, I first talk to the department heads every year and ask them for their 'wish lists,' equipment that they might like to purchase. The scenery department might ask for a new band saw, or the costume shop might want two new sewing machines. Other departments might need new office equipment or computers. After you receive the wish lists, you meet with your department heads and determine which items are critical and must be purchased this fiscal year. You gather this information and use it to construct your capital budget. Every arts organization should create a capital budget on a yearly basis."[68]

After these annual operating and capital budgets are created, they are given to the board of director's finance committee, a committee within the board of directors responsible for the oversight of the organization's financial activity, for approval. The finance committee should consist of people with a certain level of financial expertise, such as bankers, accountants, and investment professionals, who can provide a high level of fiscal guidance.[69] After the finance committee approves these budgets, they are sent for approval to the board's executive committee, and then the board of directors as a whole must approve them.[70] Some smaller organizations may not have a finance or executive committee, so the approval process may begin with the entire board of directors. This approval process occurs yearly, in time for these budgets to be adopted for the next fiscal year.

For example, at CSC, Jenen begins her annual operating budgeting process in January. She describes her budgeting and board approval process: "At the winter board meeting, I present my [annual operating] budget for the next season, which is really useful for a small theater [CSC's annual budget has generally been about $1 million]; Brian Kulick [CSC's artistic director] and I have worked hard to get to the point where I can put together an initial budget in January, which is a really big accomplishment for us. Now, is this budget a real [final] budget? Not at all. I think my first budget this year was showing a $150,000 deficit. Our board of directors wasn't worried by that deficit, because they knew that it was early on in the process. By presenting the budget early, we're able to start identifying the problem spots, and that's the important thing. For example, the centerpiece of our 2006–2007 season is going to be a high-profile play directed by John Turturro [Yasmina Reza's *A Spanish Play*, which opened in January 2007]. We didn't have enough advertising or marketing money for that project yet, so I indicated that problem in my initial budget in January [2006]. As the year goes on, you try to solve these problems."[71]

During the fiscal year, as adjustments are made, the approved annual operating and capital budgets are updated. This update involves incorporating actual expenses and income, and reforecasting other expenses and income with any new information available. Reforecasting is the reestimation of budget figures based on new or evolving information. For example, if during the fiscal year, an organization decides to add a performance of a particular production, the annual operating budget would need to be updated to include projected income and expenses related to that performance. These updated budgets are then sent to the finance committee to ensure that the board is kept apprised of all changes to the approved budgets. At the end of the fiscal year, the budgeted expenses and income are compared to the actual expenses and income, in order to determine the accuracy of the budgeting process and to highlight any ongoing problem areas.

For example, a nonprofit organization compares actual earned income to budgeted earned income as follows:

INCOME

Earned	Approved Budget	Actual Income
Membership Fees	$29,445	$46,619
Fall Play Ticket Sales	11,500	11,465
Winter Play Ticket Sales	376,029	409,053
Spring Play #1 Box Office (co-presentation)	34,750	6,941
Spring Play #2 Box Office	133,511	133,511
Space Rental	130,746	94,558
Miscellaneous	159,995	157,327
Subtotal	**$1,053,976**	**$1,040,274**

The financial manager examines the actual income numbers and determines that the budget estimation process for ticket sales must be reevaluated, as the winter play exceeded ticket sale expectations, but the spring play #1 sales fell short.

The budget estimation process for membership fees and space rental should also be reexamined, as those estimations either underestimated or exceeded the actual amounts earned.[72]

Recommendations for Creating an Effective Budget

Although creating a budget for a project or an organization can be an intimidating process, remembering some fundamental principles can make the process a bit easier. First of all, know the "philosophy" of the project. Routh describes the importance of determining the philosophy of a production before beginning to create the budget: "We're producing a production of *Porgy and Bess* next year [the production opened in October 2006] in the West End. It's going to be a new version of the show; [director] Trevor Nunn, who's doing the adaptation, has gone to the original source material and the novel, taken out the recitative from the opera, and written dialogue that he's adapted from the source material. There's a real decision to be made about the philosophy of the production. Is it a big, grand piece, or a leaner, meaner theatrical creation? The basic decisions that we make about the size of the physical production, the size of the cast, the number of musicians we need to play the show—these artistic, creative decisions are reflected in the budget."[73]

Next, it is important to remember that, while all budgets are estimates, the more information the financial manager has on which to base her estimates, the more accurate her budget will be. Conversely, a budget is not likely to be of much use if it contains figures that don't have any solid data behind them. For example, the financial manager should interview the director and designers and ask them for as many details as possible on their plans for the show; she should also research the specific expenses of their conceptions if she doesn't know how much those conceptions will cost.[74]

Finally, a financial manager should be as specific as she can when creating a budget. A budget should be broken down into as many discrete categories as possible. By breaking down large categories such as "personnel" into more specific categories like "stagehands" or "box office staff," it becomes possible to see the different pieces of the budget puzzle, and how they fit into the larger whole.

CLASSROOM DISCUSSION

What is the process for creating a production budget?

What is the process for creating a weekly operating
   budget?

What is the budget approval process for a
   commercial production?

What is the process for creating an annual
   operating budget?

What is the process for creating a capital budget?

What is the budget approval process for a nonprofit
   organization?

What is a finance committee?

What types of board members should be on the
   finance committee?

What is reforecasting, and why is it done?

FINANCIAL MANAGER: ADMINISTRATIVE RESPONSIBILITIES

Beyond creating budgets, financial managers
perform many administrative functions crucial to the
financial operations of a commercial production or
a nonprofit organization. Financial managers create
and manage information systems and bookkeeping
procedures to facilitate financial activities; purchase
all required insurance; process payroll; pay taxes;
produce accurate financial reports; and conduct
audits.

Information Systems and Bookkeeping Procedures

In order to properly record financial transactions
according to generally accepted accounting principles (GAAP), financial managers need to create
and manage information systems. These information
systems display the journals and the general ledger
so that account information can be viewed by the
financial management team. Information systems
also facilitate the creation of financial reports, such
as a cash flow statement or a balance sheet. Most
organizations use accounting software programs
like QuickBooks® or Peachtree Accounting® to make
this task easier.

Financial managers also are responsible for
establishing procedures for basic bookkeeping
functions, such as providing cash receipts for
purchases. Proper bookkeeping procedures allow
the organization to keep track of all assets and
liabilities by providing paper or computer backup
for any transactions. Accounting software will also
assist in performing these functions.

As part of good bookkeeping practice, it is vital
to establish a separate bank account for business
expenses. Although this practice seems self-evident
in the case of larger organizations, many smaller
organizations neglect this step, which may result in
confusing personal finances and business finances.
Establishing a separate bank account ensures that the
business manager tracks business-related expenses
accurately.

Insurance

As the fiscal steward of an organization, the financial
manager is responsible for ensuring that the
organization is covered by the appropriate insurance
policies. These policies may include liability
insurance, property insurance, business interruption
insurance, workers' compensation insurance, directors' and officers' liability insurance, as well as other
types of insurance for specific needs.

Both commercial productions and nonprofit organizations should purchase general liability insurance to protect the assets of the organization in case
it is sued for causing personal injury or property
damage. Liability insurance covers the employees
of the organization, as well as the general public.[75]
Typically, insurance companies set a limit on the
amount of money they will pay per damage claim
and also set a limit on the total amount of money
they will pay to the organization over the life of the
policy. Liability insurance may also be purchased to
cover cars driven for business purposes; this insurance, known as non-owned auto and hired car insurance, would be in effect if an accident occurred
and the insurance on the vehicle was inadequate.[76]
For extra protection, the organization may purchase
an umbrella liability policy to protect the organization against claims that exceed the limits of the general liability and non-owned auto and hired car policies.[77] The financial manager should consult with an
insurance broker to determine the amount of coverage most suitable for the organization.

Property insurance is also necessary for both
commercial productions and nonprofit performing
arts companies. Property insurance protects against
monetary loss from damage by fire, theft, or other
disasters. In addition, sign coverage, which protects
all signage leading to and located within the venue,
may also be purchased. Some types of incidents, like
flooding, are not covered by all property insurance
policies; the financial manager should discuss any
additional coverage needed with an insurance broker. In the commercial world, property insurance
covering the building is purchased by the theater
owner, but the property owned by the show (such
as sets and costumes) can also be insured; this type
of property insurance is called a theatrical floater
policy and is purchased by the producer.[78] In addition, Actors' Equity requires the purchase of a float-

er insurance policy specifically to cover the personal property of Equity members working on the production when this property is in the theater space or being shipped by the production company.[79]

Commercial productions and nonprofit organizations may choose to bundle property and liability insurance together into a business owners policy (BOP). BOPs typically include property insurance for building and equipment, liability insurance, and additional insurance known as business interruption insurance. Business interruption insurance covers any revenue loss caused by an incident that interrupts the normal operations of the business, such as the loss of a performance space or set piece.[80] If an organization does not have a comprehensive BOP, it must ensure that it has all of the requisite property and liability insurance.

All employers, both commercial and nonprofit, are required to purchase workers' compensation insurance to protect their employees who are injured on the job, as well as shield the employer from lawsuits pertaining to workplace injuries. When workers' compensation insurance is purchased, the insurance company pays out a claim to any employee injured while at work, based on the severity of the injury and the amount of time the employee will be unable to work. If an employee is injured at work, and the employer has not acquired workers' compensation insurance, the employee can file a lawsuit in civil court against the employer, which can result in significant financial liability.[81] Specific requirements for workers' compensation insurance vary by state. Some states, including New York, require that employers provide disability insurance for employees as well.[82]

Nonprofit organizations should purchase directors' and officers' liability insurance (D&O insurance), which prevents the board of directors and its officers from being personally liable from damages in a lawsuit. D&O insurance covers the cost of attorneys and may also cover any financial penalties levied.[83] However, D&O insurance does not cover all potential liability; each policy has different exclusions, so nonprofit organizations must examine their policies carefully.[84]

Other types of insurance can be purchased as necessary, depending on the requirements of the commercial production or nonprofit organization. For example, an organization may protect against theft, fraud, and forgery in the box office by purchasing 3D crime insurance protection.[85] Fiduciary liability insurance protects the employer against employee claims made against welfare and pension benefit plans. Nonappearance coverage for a star can be purchased to cover any losses incurred by a producer or an organization if a star does not perform.[86] Organizations may also purchase errors and omissions insurance, providing protection against such claims as copyright infringement, plagiarism, or libel.[87] Actors' Equity requires the purchase of accidental death and dismemberment insurance for touring productions utilizing four or more airplane flights or one bus ride; to protect the production in the event of an accident, a producer may purchase catastrophic accident insurance, which would allow him to recast and remount the show in the event of the loss of one-third of the cast due to death or disability.[88] Insurance to cover special events and other one-time events may also be purchased.[89]

Payroll

Although the financial manager may not be involved with the hiring of employees, she is responsible for managing the employee payroll. Ensuring that employees receive their paychecks on time, and with the appropriate taxes withheld, is one of the most important responsibilities of any financial manager. Some organizations habitually pay their employees late or not at all, and those organizations suffer from poor employee morale and an eventual loss of talented personnel. An accurate, timely paycheck helps make a happy, productive employee.

Once the decision has been made to hire an employee, appropriate documentation must be filed with the federal government. Form I-9, the Employment Eligibility Verification Form, must be filled out for all employees and held on file with the employer; this form proves that the employee is eligible to work in the United States.[90] (Additional information on employment eligibility can be found at the U.S. Citizenship and Immigration Services Web site at *www.uscis.gov*.) Also, employers must report all new hires to a designated state agency to help facilitate the collection of child support payments.[91] Each of these state agencies can be found on the Administration for Children & Families Web site at *www.acf.hhs.gov/programs/cse/ newhire/employer/contacts/nh_matrix.htm*. Employers should also keep a copy of the employee's social security number on file, as well as the hire and termination dates.

In addition to calculating the gross amount of wages due to an employee, the financial manager is responsible for calculating the amount of payroll taxes taken out of the employee's wages and depositing those taxes into the correct federal or state account. (For nonprofit organizations, the federal government defines "wages" as remuneration of $100 or more earned by employees during a calendar year.[92]) Payroll taxes withheld from an employee include:

- Federal income tax. Employees fill out an Employee's Withholding Allowance Certificate (also known as a Form W-4), used by the employer to determine the amount of federal income tax to withhold.[93] Employers must file a Wage and Tax Statement (Form W-2) if wages are paid to any employee. All other payments of compensation must also be reported on Form W-2 if the total of these payments and the employee's wages totals $600 or more in a calendar year.[94]
- State and/or city income tax. Since most states base their tax structure on the adjusted gross income determined by the federal government, Form W-4 can usually determine state income tax as well.[95]
- Social Security and Medicare taxes. Also known as the FICA (Federal Insurance Contributions Act) taxes, these taxes provide retirement benefits to the employee and his dependents, as well as benefits to any employee who becomes disabled.[96] The employer is liable for the employee portion of these taxes, whether or not they are withheld from the employee.[97]

Employers are required to pay a matching amount of Social Security and Medicare taxes, as well as the Federal Unemployment Tax (FUTA) and a state unemployment tax, which provide compensation to unemployed workers.[98] (Nonprofit organizations are exempt from FUTA and do not have to pay this tax.[99]) Detailed tax information can be found in Publication 15, Circular E, Employer's Tax Guide (www.irs.gov/pub/irs-pdf/p15.pdf), published by the IRS. Payroll companies such as Paychex, ADP, or Advantage Payroll Systems provide payroll processing services and guarantee accurate tax processing, and many organizations use these services.

The importance of paying payroll taxes accurately and promptly cannot be overemphasized. Occasionally, an organization will try to manage its cash flow by not paying these withholding taxes. If the correct taxes are not paid, the IRS can impose financial penalties on an organization; in extreme cases, these penalties may include the loss of 501(c)(3) status.[100]

While not an employee, any independent contractor hired by your organization must also be paid according to the provisions of his contract. The IRS makes a distinction between an "employee" and an "independent contractor." According to the IRS, "A general rule is that you, the payer, have the right to control or direct only the result of the work done by an independent contractor, and not the means and methods of accomplishing the result."[101] Thus, if you can control how the service will be performed and what actions will be taken, the worker is your employee, not an independent contractor.

An employer is not required to withhold payroll taxes on payments to an independent contractor, nor is the employer required to pay taxes on those payments.[102] (However, if an independent contractor is determined to be an employee by the IRS, then penalties would apply for the unpaid payroll taxes. Thus, the decision to hire someone as an independent contractor must be made carefully, in consultation with an attorney, an accountant, and/or the IRS.) Depending on the amount of the payment, the employer may be required to file an information return (Form 1099-MISC, the Miscellaneous Income Form); details on this information return can be found on the IRS Web site at www.irs.gov/instructions/i1099msc/index.html.

Paying Taxes

Financial managers are also responsible for paying taxes in both commercial and nonprofit organizations. However, both kinds of organizations must have an Employer Identification Number (EIN) in order to pay federal taxes (in addition to city and state taxes), or to apply for an exemption from federal taxes. The IRS also requires an EIN if an employer is "required to report employment taxes or give tax statements to employees."[103] The EIN is a unique nine-digit number issued by the IRS that is used to identify taxpayers.[104] IRS Publication 1635, *Understanding Your EIN*, lists the entities that are required to have EINs and also provides instructions on how to obtain an EIN. (This publication can be found at www.irs.gov/pub/irs-pdf/p1635.pdf.) Some states also issue identification numbers for state tax purposes; the IRS recommends that an organization check with its state to determine if it needs a state number.[105]

For commercial productions, the company manager is responsible for making sure all applicable federal, state, and local taxes are paid, as well as all payroll taxes. Nonprofit organizations are exempt from paying certain federal, state, and local income taxes, but are still responsible for other taxes, such as payroll or real estate taxes. In addition, if a nonprofit organization earns income from a business operation not related to its exempt purpose, that income may be considered unrelated business income by the IRS and may be taxed.[106] For more information on unrelated business income, please see Publication 598, *Tax on Unrelated Business Income of Exempt Organizations* (*www.irs.gov/pub/irs-pdf/p598.pdf*), and chapter 3 of this book.

Financial Reports

Financial managers are responsible for providing accurate, timely reports on the organization's fiscal activities and current financial status. For commercial productions, general managers are responsible for providing reports to producers and investors. Financial managers in nonprofit organizations provide reports to the organization's staff, the board of directors, various governmental bodies, grant-making institutions, and the general public.

General managers on a commercial production will meet weekly with producers to describe the production's current financial position. The producers are presented with a wealth of financial data, including box office summaries (reports on that week's ticket sales), a balance sheet, a report detailing advance sales (ticket sales for performances in the future), and statements showing the status of recoupment (earning back the capitalization costs—the money needed to produce the production) and profit (revenue earned after the capitalization costs are paid back to the investors). This financial data is compiled by a certified public accountant (CPA) hired by the producer and given to the investors on a quarterly basis.[107]

Within a nonprofit organization, the finance department sends out reports to all departments, detailing the variation between budgeted amounts and actual amounts. These reports help the finance department identify budgeting issues within departments, as well as communicate the status of the entire organizational budget to all staff members. Gee describes the benefits of analyzing the reports in order to discover potential problems: "We would like our department heads to review the reports on a monthly basis and balance their budgets. These reports make sure that we're all on the same page, and that people are paying attention to their expenditures. It also helps us avoid surprises. If you find a $1,000 budget problem, tell us. We'll handle it. It's better for every department to deal with unexpected expenses when they occur, rather than waiting for the end of the year and suddenly learning that everybody has a $1,000 budget problem, which is now a $50,000 budget problem. These reports are an in-house early-warning system."[108]

In larger organizations, the finance department needs to disseminate the larger financial picture to other departments so that each department understands the financial challenges of the institution as a whole. For example, the production team may feel that they don't have sufficient funds to put on the production. They may not realize that the development department is having great difficulty raising funds to finance the production, while the development department may be so focused on raising money that they lose sight of the of the mission of the organization: mounting the production.[109] Thus, the financial manager is responsible for ensuring that the organization's financial challenges are communicated to the entire institution.

The finance department also provides reports to the board of directors. BAM provides an institutional budget forecast on a quarterly basis, which contains the prior fiscal year's final budget, the board-adopted budget for the current fiscal year, and the forecast for the current period.[110] The board-adopted budget is used as the base, and any variances are explained through the use of detailed revenue and expense budgets.[111] Most nonprofit organizations also provide balance sheets and income statements to the board.

If the board of directors is big enough, the financial manager may deliver his reports to the finance committee instead of the entire board. Peter Gee describes a typical meeting with the finance committee: "I present the numbers on a quarterly basis to the finance committee. I try to give them a picture of how the organization is doing up to that date, as well as how we're expecting to do at the end of the year. I point out not just the problems we have realized, but also areas of concern, so that there are no surprises later. One of the things the board doesn't want is surprises. For instance, they want to know that we could have a potential sales problem on a particular show because the revenue goal is very high. So, as part of my preparation for the meeting, I would have spoken to the marketing director and asked, 'What is your current sense on how well tickets for this performance are selling, and how many do you think you will sell in total?' I would have asked this question for both best-case and worst-case scenarios, so that I can give that range to the finance committee, and they can see it in the context of the overall budget."[112]

Beyond simply reporting the organization's current financial situation to the board of directors, the financial manager is also expected to arrive at solutions to any financial problems that the organization might face. As Gee explains, "At the end of the day, if there's a problem, if there's a financial issue, the board and leadership would expect that I bring it to them, not only identifying the problem, but also hopefully being able to provide some solutions. Because the finance department has access to all the information across all departments, we're best able to identify potential areas that can help cover budget gaps [deficits]."[113]

Nonprofit organizations are also responsible for reporting financial information to grant-making organizations, various governmental bodies, and the general public. A grant-making organization will specify what sort of financial reports it requires; typically, it will require a detailed report showing exactly how the grant was spent, as well as explanations for any expenditures that went over their budgeted amounts. Nonprofit organizations receiving federal, state, or local government grants will also need to report on the use of the grant according to the specifications of the government agency. Reports for all grant-making organizations are usually due between sixty and ninety days after the end of the fiscal year for which the grant was awarded.

In addition to these reports, nonprofit organizations are required to file Form 990 with the Internal Revenue Service (IRS). Form 990 reports the organization's financial status to the federal government. Nonprofit organizations are also required to make their Forms 990 available to the general public. The following section describes the process of filing Form 990 with the IRS.

Form 990

As a part of their reporting duties to the government, all nonprofit corporations are required to file Form 990 with the IRS.[114] (Exceptions exist to this rule, but they only apply to organizations that are faith-based charities and churches, not performing arts organizations.) Form 990 reports on an organization's mission, programs, and finances.[115] The Form 990 must be filed by the fifteenth day of the fifth month after the organization's fiscal year ends; if the organization needs more time, Form 8868 will grant one automatic extension of three months, and the organization may apply for a second extension.[116] Two version of this form are available: the regular Form 990 and a simplified version for smaller organizations, Form 990-EZ. "For the 2008 tax year (returns filed in 2009), organizations with gross receipts [total income received during the fiscal year before any expenses are deducted] over $1 million or total assets over $2.5 million will be required to

file Form 990. For the 2009 tax year (returns filed in 2010), organizations with gross receipts over $500,000 or total assets over $1.25 million will be required to file Form 990. The filing thresholds will be set permanently at $200,000 gross receipts and $500,000 total assets beginning with the 2010 tax year. Also, starting with the 2010 tax year, the IRS will increase the filing threshold for organizations required to file Form 990-N (the e-Postcard) from $25,000 to $50,000."[117] Form 990-N, the Electronic Notice (e-Postcard) for Tax-Exempt Organizations, must be filed electronically. The e-Postcard certifies to the IRS that the organization's gross receipts are still under the specified amount and ensures that the IRS (as well as potential donors) will have the organization's most current contact information.[118]

In brief, Form 990 consists of eleven parts. (The 990-EZ is a simplified version of the form, but asks for the same information.)

- Part I, Summary, provides the organization's identifying information and a snapshot of key financial, governance, and operating information, including a summary of mission or activities. A two-year comparison of revenues and expenses is reported for the current and prior year.
- Part II, Signature Block [of officer and paid preparer].
- Part III, Statement of Program Service Accomplishments, includes reporting of new, discontinued, or altered program services.
- Part IV, Checklist of Required Schedules, contains the list, in schedule sequence order, of all questions required to determine which schedules must be completed by an organization. [Schedules are additional information required by the IRS for specific organizations; schedules that may be required from nonprofit performing arts organizations include: Schedule A (Public Charity Status and Public Support), which demonstrates the organization's status as a public charity; Schedule B (Schedule of Contributors), which reports all contributions given to the organization over a specified amount; and Schedule C (Political Campaign and Lobbying Activities), which details lobbying and campaign activities and expenses.
- Part V, Statements Regarding Other IRS Filings and Tax Compliance.

- Part VI, Governance, Management, and Disclosure, requires reporting regarding governing body composition, and certain governance and disclosure policies and practices.
- Part VII, Compensation of Officers, Directors, Trustees, Key Employees, Highest Compensated Employees, and Independent Contractors. [A key employee is defined as "any person having responsibilities, powers, or influence similar to those of officers, directors, or trustees" and include executive staff and chief administrators.[119]]
- Part VIII, Statement of Revenues.
- Part IX, Statement of Functional Expenses.
- Part X, Balance Sheet.
- Part XI, Financial Statements and Reporting, requires reporting of certain information regarding financial statement compilations, reviews, or audits.[120]

If a nonprofit organization engages in activity during the fiscal year that is considered to be unrelated business income, and this income totals $1,000 or more, it must also file Form 990-T.[121] This form determines the total amount of unrelated business income earned by the organization and calculates the tax owed on that income. The organization is required to make estimated tax payments if it expects to owe $500 or more in unrelated business taxable income.[122] Form 990-T is due at the same time as Form 990; if Form 990-T is submitted late, the organization may be liable for tax penalties.[123]

All Forms 990 (including Form 990-T) must be made available to any member of the public. Federal law requires that organizations provide their three most recent 990s to anyone who requests them for a small fee, and many 990s are available at no cost on the Internet (at sites such as *GuideStar.org*, a Web site with an electronic database of information on nonprofit organizations).[124] With this in mind, the IRS states:

> Some members of the public rely on Form 990, or Form 990-EZ [and Forms 990-T and 990-N], as the primary or sole source of information about a particular organization. How the public perceives an organization in such cases may be determined by the information presented on its return. Therefore, the return must be complete and accurate, and fully describe the organization's programs and accomplishments.[125]

Audits

Both commercial and nonprofit financial managers must arrange for an annual audit of their companies. An audit is a review of an organization's financial accounts conducted by a CPA not employed by the organization. The financial management team assists the auditor in preparing the audit by providing all necessary financial information.

For commercial productions, an audit is not mandatory. Although commercial productions do file tax returns and prepare financial statements, they are not required to conduct an independent audit. However, Broadway productions do present an annual audit to investors.

Nonprofit organizations present their audits to the audit committee, the committee of the board of directors responsible for reviewing the audit. Much like the finance committee, members of the audit committee must have an understanding of financial statements and be able to guide the organization's practices based on the results of the audit. After the audit committee examines the audit, it is passed on to the entire board of directors for review. If the organization's board of directors is small, it may not have an audit committee, and the audit may be passed to the entire board for review after the audit is completed.

Tetreault suggests that the auditors meet with the audit committee and the board of directors without the presence of the management team. "I always think that an executive session should be held between the board of directors and the auditors to discuss the audit. The board will then be able to ask questions and get unqualified answers directly from the auditors themselves. This fosters transparency in the organization, so there's not a filter between the auditors and the board, which could lead to fraud. I think you always want to have transparency in place to prevent abuse."[126]

CLASSROOM DISCUSSION

Define "independent contractor," "EIN," "unrelated business income," "Form 990," "audit," and "audit committee."

Why are information systems and bookkeeping procedures important to the financial manager?

Name two types of insurance that a commercial production should purchase and describe the reasons for purchasing them.

Name two types of insurance that a nonprofit organization should purchase and describe the reasons for purchasing them.

What payroll taxes must be withheld from an employee's paycheck?

How is an independent contractor different from an employee?

What payroll taxes is an employer required to pay on an independent contractor?

Why is an organization required to obtain an EIN?

What reports are financial managers required to give to producers and investors on a commercial production?

What reports are financial managers required to give to a nonprofit organization's board of directors?

Who is required to file a Form 990?

Name two types of information found on Form 990.

Who is allowed to view an organization's Form 990?

Go to *GuideStar.org* and, using the information provided on its latest Form 990, find out what the budget size is for each nonprofit producing organization listed in the "Organizational Types" section of chapter 1. What do their top managers earn?

Go to *GuideStar.org* and research the budget size of the nonprofit presenting organizations listed in the "Organizational Types" section of chapter 1. Who are the managerial leaders of these nonprofit presenting organizations, and what are their salaries?

What types of board members should be on the audit committee?

ACCOUNTABILITY

The final responsibility of the financial manager is the accountability of the production or the organization. Accountability is the expectation that an organization will act in a financially responsible manner and practice good corporate governance. For nonprofit organizations in New York State, the New York State Attorney General's Office specifies: "Accountability requires that the organization comply with all applicable laws and ethical standards; adhere to the organization's mission; create and adhere to conflict of interest, ethics, personnel and accounting policies; protect the rights of members; prepare and file its annual financial report with the Internal Revenue Service and appropriate state regulatory authorities and make the report available to all members of the board and any member of the public who requests it."[127]

Accountability rests with the board of directors and the executive staff. Gee describes his perception of accountability as the CFO of a nonprofit organization: "I feel that the buck stops here. It's my responsibility to ensure that internal controls are in place, that our liabilities are limited, and that our financial exposure is clear and identified. If a surprise comes up, that's my responsibility. A lot of my policies and procedures are put in place to limit surprises. I need to be proactive, identify risks as soon as possible, and communicate them to the appropriate people. As long I'm asking the questions that need to be asked, I'm doing what I'm supposed to be doing."[128]

Gee goes on to add, "It's critical that the financial manager has a strong ethical compass that can help guide the institution. Sometimes, areas within the organization may want to move forward on certain things, or move too quickly on other things, and could potentially create liability for the institution. The financial manager needs to be willing to take a stand on the issue, stand up, and say, 'What are we doing? We can't just keep spending. We've got to limit ourselves. We've got to watch what we're doing.' You need to take on the president of the organization, if necessary."[129]

The implementation of internal controls and the application of the recommended audit procedures and financial practices of the Sarbanes-Oxley Act strengthen an organization's accountability. The next two sections will detail the specifics of these important tools.

Internal Controls

Internal controls are procedures, policies, and systems that "protect the assets of an organization, create reliable financial reporting, promote compliance with laws and regulations, and achieve effective and efficient operations."[130] Internal controls encompass accounting procedures, financial reporting, communication between the executive staff and the board of directors, and external communication.[131]

The New York State Attorney General's Office recommends the following internal financial controls:

- Preparing an annual income and expense budget and periodic reports—at least quarterly, preferably monthly—comparing actual receipts and expenditures to the budget with timely variance explanations.
- Writing and signing checks or vouchers and receiving, recording, securing, and depositing cash and other receipts. Such procedures should ensure that no single individual is responsible for receiving,

- recording, and depositing funds or writing and signing checks. Checks and balances are essential to make embezzlement more difficult.
- Ensuring that grants and contributions received are properly recorded, accountings required as a condition of any grant are completed and restrictions on the use of such funds, such as contributions given for a restricted purpose (e.g., building fund, scholarships) and prohibitions on the use of the principal of an endowment, are obeyed.
- Requisitioning [requesting payment], authorizing, verifying, recording and monitoring all expenditures, including payment of invoices, petty cash and other expenditures.[132] Such procedures should ensure that no single individual is permitted to request, authorize, verify and record expenditures. For example, the same person should not be responsible for cash disbursements and bank reconciliations [matching recorded deposits and expenditures with bank statements]. These functions should be assigned to different individuals.
- Accessing, inputting and changing electronic data maintained by the organization. Preserving electronic records and ensuring data compatibility when systems change and creating an appropriate records retention policy are part of this process.
- Providing for regular oversight by an audit committee or, if there is no audit committee, by the executive committee or the board of directors itself.
- Reporting to the audit committee or board by employees and volunteers of allegations of fraud or financial improprieties.
- Ensuring that timely and appropriate financial reports are distributed to all directors and officers and reviewed by them, as well as the president, chief executive officer, treasurer, and chief financial officer.
- Providing procedures for approving contracts to which the organization is a party, including securing competitive bids from vendors.
- Making clear the responsibilities of all individuals involved with the organization, including the board of directors and officers, employees, volunteers, and consultants; maintaining an organizational chart; and updating such information as necessary.

- Preparing for the annual audit process in a timely manner.
- Developing a prudent investment strategy and providing proper oversight of the investment assets.
- Complying with governmental and other reporting requirements, including watchdog agencies [such as the Better Business Bureau].
- Complying with obligations to members, employees, and the public, including their right to a copy of the organization's annual financial report.[133]

Sarbanes-Oxley Act

In 2002, Congress passed the American Competitiveness and Corporate Accountability Act (also known as the Sarbanes-Oxley Act), intending to rebuild confidence in American business after the nefarious practices of such organizations as Enron and WorldCom came to light. "The Act requires that the chief executives and chief financial officers of all publicly traded United States companies attest to the accuracy and completeness of their financial statements filed with the Securities and Exchange Commission. It requires that chief executives and chief financial officers swear that the financial statements filed with the Securities and Exchange Commission are accurate and complete to the best of their knowledge. In other words, the chief executive officers and chief financial officers of publicly traded United States companies can no longer say that they were not aware of their legal obligations. Violations can result in criminal penalties. The Act also regulates what corporate boards must do to ensure public auditors' independence from their clients."[134]

More and more states are requiring nonprofit organizations to comply with the Sarbanes-Oxley Act. Two provisions of the Sarbanes-Oxley Act, whistle-blower protection and document destruction, require immediate compliance from nonprofit organizations.[135] Also, according to BoardSource and IndependentSector, service organizations dealing with nonprofit governance issues, the Sarbanes-Oxley law has several provisions that are relevant to nonprofit organizations: the creation of an independent audit committee and auditor responsibilities; certifying financial statements; establishing policies on conflicts of interests; and disclosure.

Protecting the Whistle-Blower and Document Destruction

Nonprofit organizations are required by the Sarbanes-Oxley Act to establish procedures for communicating complaints and the observation of illegal actions. (Employees who report inappropriate or illegal activities are known as whistle-blowers.) Employees must be assured that they will not be punished for reporting actions deemed inappropriate or worse. In addition, nonprofit organizations must establish procedures for archiving documents that may later be used to support evidence that a crime occurred. This includes e-mail and voice mail.[136]

Independent Audit Committee and Auditor Responsibilities

In *Internal Controls and Financial Accountability for Not-for-Profit Boards*, the New York State Attorney General's Office provides advice on the creation of an independent audit committee. The board should set up an audit committee that is independent from the finance committee, as well as independent from the management of the organization. The chief financial officer and executive director should not serve on this committee. The audit committee must have at least one person who understands financial matters and is "comfortable reviewing financial reports and other financial records."[137] Members of the audit committee should not be compensated for their services and should not hold a financial interest in the organization. The audit committee must make sure that the organization has established internal financial controls and auditing systems. In addition to creating internal financial controls, it is necessary to establish internal controls that evaluate staff and programs, inventory real estate holdings, and maintain conflict-of-interest and personnel policies.[138]

The audit committee should hire an independent auditor, who should also be a certified public accountant (CPA), to be responsible for producing a certified financial audit on an annual basis, as well as preparing tax documents for the federal, state, and local governments. The entire board will vote on accepting or rejecting the audit. The auditor should disclose all accounting procedures and recommend the implementation of improved internal control procedures, if warranted. The organization should consider changing auditors every five years.[139]

Certifying Financial Statements

After the audit committee has reviewed the audit and financial statements, the board will vote to approve and certify them. Certifying financial statements is a legal responsibility of the board. Board members who intentionally falsify documents are held liable for their actions. In addition, the CFO or CEO of the organization should review all financial statements, as well as Form 990, for accuracy.[140] BoardSource and Independent Sector recommend that, "just as the financial and audit reports are reviewed and approved by the audit committee and the board, Form 990 . . . should also be reviewed and approved. At a time when Form 990 . . . [is] published on the Internet by third parties, it is more important than ever that directors be familiar with the contents of the organization's 990 each year."[141]

Conflicts of Interest and Disclosure

When there is a conflict of interest, someone has personal interests or self-interest distinct from the interests of the organization. Acting on a conflict of interest means acting out of that self-interest rather than the corporation's interest. Conflict-of-interest policies must include policies on full disclosure. To use the example from chapter 3, assume that a nonprofit board member runs a construction company and wants to do business with the nonprofit organization that he is serving. In order to appropriately manage the conflict of interest that exists, the conflict-of-interest policy should state that the nonprofit organization must research at least two other construction companies to make sure that the rates and service quality are comparable or better. The policy should also require that the minutes of the board meeting reflect this type of conflict-of-interest discussion and findings (full disclosure). Finally, the board member with a financial interest in the construction company should be prohibited from voting on the outcome. Conflict-of-interest policies should appear in the bylaws, or they can be separate. Sample conflict-of-interest policies appear on the application for tax-exempt status, Internal Revenue Service Form 1023, discussed in chapter 3.

CLASSROOM DISCUSSION

What is accountability, and why is it important for financial managers?

What are internal controls? Give three examples.

What is the Sarbanes-Oxley Act and what does it do? Which provisions are legally required for nonprofit organizations?

Why is it important to protect whistle-blowers?

Why is it important to create an independent audit committee? What is the role of the independent auditor?

Who has the ultimate responsibility for certifying financial documents?

What is a conflict of interest? Give an example.

NOTES

1. The authors would like to thank the following contributors to this chapter: Alice Bernstein, Alexander Fraser, Peter Gee, Jessica R. Jenen, James Patrick, Renee Lasher, Marc Routh, Michael Sag, Diana Swartz, Paul Tetreault, Alanna Weifenbach (CPA), Robert Widman, and Meredith Zolty.

2. According to the New York State Society of Certified Public Accountants, accounting is defined as the "recording and reporting of financial transactions." (New York State Society of Certified Public Accountants, "Definition of Accounting," *www.nysscpa.org/prof_library/guide.htm#A*).

3. Peter Gee, interview by author, February 16, 2006.

4. Alice Bernstein, interview by author, November 16, 2005.

5. Marc Routh, interview by author, November 10, 2005.

6. Paul Tetreault, interview by author, February 3, 2006

7. Gee, "Interview."

8. Ibid.

9. Ibid.

10. Routh, "Interview."

11. Ibid.

12. Alexander Fraser, interview by Kevin Condardo, October 29, 2005.

13. Bernstein, "Interview."

14. Ibid.

15. Meredith Zolty, interview by author, February 6, 2006.

16. Tetreault, "Interview." An audit is a review of an organization's financial accounts conducted by a certified public accountant not employed by the organization. Payroll refers to salary payments made to all personnel employed by the organization. A tax filing would cover all taxes paid to federal, state, and local governments.

17. Zolty, "Interview."

18. Charles T. Horngren and Walter T. Harrison, Jr., *Accounting* (Upper Saddle River, N.J.: Pearson Education, Inc., 2007).

19. Ibid.

20. James Patrick, interview by author, November 23, 2005. The term "net" refers to an amount remaining after deductions. (The amount calculated before deductions is known as the gross amount.) Deductions are items subtracted from the gross amount to arrive at the net amount. In this context, net refers to the amount left over after liabilities are subtracted from assets.

21. Ibid.

22. Kermit D. Larson, John J. Wild, and Barbara Chiappetta, *Fundamental Accounting Principles* (Boston: Irwin McGraw-Hill, 1999).

23. Ibid.

24. Ibid.

25. Purchasing an item on credit allows the purchaser to take possession of the item now, but pay for it later.

26. *Fundamental Accounting Principles.*

27. Ibid.

28. Ibid.

29. William J. Byrnes, *Management and the Arts* (London: Focal Press, 2003), 210–11.

30. The authors would like to thank Jessica R. Jenen for allowing us to publish this income statement.

31. The authors would like to thank Jessica R. Jenen for allowing us to publish this cash flow statement.

32. The authors would like to thank Jessica R. Jenen for allowing us to publish this balance sheet.

33. *Management and the Arts.*

34. Ibid.

35. Financial Accounting Standards Board, "Summary of Statement No. 116," *http://72.3.243.42/st/summary/stsum116.shtml*; "Summary of Statement No. 117," *http://72.3.243.42/st/summary/stsum117.shtml.*

36. Gee.

37. Marc Routh, *Business Management for the Performing Arts*, (New York: Marc Routh, 2006).

38. The authors would like to thank Michael Sag for allowing us to publish this budget.

39. Routh, *Business Management for the Performing Arts.*

40. The authors would like to thank Michael Sag for allowing us to publish this budget.

41. Bernstein.

42. The authors would like to thank Jessica R. Jenen for allowing us to publish this budget.

43. Bernstein. If an asset decreases in value over time, as the computer system does in this example, the asset is said to have depreciated in value. If the asset increases in value over time, the asset has appreciated in value.

44. The authors would like to thank Ruth Eckerd Hall for allowing us to publish this budget.

45. Jim Volz. *How to Run a Theater: A Witty, Practical, and Fun Guide to Arts Management* (New York: Backstage Books, 2004), 146.

46. Gee.

47. Ibid.

48. Patrick, "Interview."

49. A subscription is a package of tickets to more than one production purchased in advance at a discount.

50. Routh, "Interview."

51. Tetreault.

52. Ibid.

53. Ibid.

54. Jessica R. Jenen, interview by author, May 24, 2006.

55. Patrick.

56. Bernstein.

57. Patrick.

58. Jenen, "Interview."

59. Ibid.

60. Routh, "Interview."

61. Gee.

62. Jenen.

63. Routh.

64. Ibid.

65. Ibid.

66. Ibid.

67. Gee.

68. Tetreault.

69. Gee.

70. Ibid.

71. Jenen.

72. Membership fees are fees paid to the organization by ticket buyers who wish to buy discounted tickets to each performance.

73. Routh, "Interview."

74. Ibid.

75. Donald C. Farber, *Producing Theatre* (Pompton Plains, N.J.: Limelight Editions, 2006), 146.

76. Routh, *Business Management for the Performing Arts.*

77. Ibid.

78. *Producing Theatre,* 146.

79. Routh, *Business Management for the Performing Arts.*

80. Ibid.

81. New York State Worker's Compensation Board, "Understanding Workers' Compensation Insurance," *www.wcb.state.ny.us/content/main/Small_Business/understandInsurance.jsp.*

82. *Business Management for the Performing Arts.* Disability insurance covers workers who are ill or injured outside of work.

83. GuideStar, "Nonprofit Directors and Officers Insurance: The Good, the Bad, and the Ugly," *www.guidestar.org/news/features/do_insurance.jsp.*

84. Ibid.

85. Routh, *Business Management for the Performing Arts.*

86. *Producing Theatre,* 146.

87. Routh, *Business Management for the Performing Arts.*

88. Ibid.

89. Ibid.

90. United States Citizenship and Immigration Services, "About Form I-9, Employment Eligibility Verification," *www.uscis.gov/portal/site/uscis/menuitem.5af9bb95919f35e66f614176543f6d1a/?vgnextoid=0572194d3e88d010VgnVCM10000048f3d6a1RCRD&vgnextchannel=91919c7755cb9010VgnVCM10000045f3d6a1RCRD.*

91. Administration for Children & Families, "Employer Services—Private Sector Employers—New Hire Reporting," *www.acf.hhs.gov/programs/cse/newhire/employer/private/newhire.htm.*

92. Section 3121(a)(16) of the Internal Revenue Code of 1986, as amended.

93. Internal Revenue Service, "Payroll Taxes and Federal Income Tax Withholding," *www.irs.gov/app/understandingTaxes/jsp/hows/tt/module01/tax_mod1_2.jsp.*

94. Internal Revenue Service, "Title 26, Department of the Treasury, Section 1.6041-2(a)(1)."

95. TaxAdmin.org, "Individual Income Tax Starting Points," *www.taxadmin.org/fta/rate/inc_stp.html.* Touring productions withhold state employment taxes as applicable.

96. Internal Revenue Service, "Payroll Taxes and Federal Income Tax Withholding."

97. United States Department of the Treasury, "Treasury Regulations, Subchapter C, Sec. 31.3202-1."

98. Internal Revenue Service, *Publication 15-A, Employer's Supplemental Tax Guide, www.irs.gov/publications/p15a/index.html.*

99. Ibid.

100. Renee Lasher, interview by Jessica Bathurst, December 2, 2006.

101. Internal Revenue Service, *Publication 15-A, Employer's Supplemental Tax Guide.*

102. Ibid.

103. Internal Revenue Service, *Publication 15, Employer's Tax Guide* (Washington, D.C.: Internal Revenue Service), 8, *www.irs.gov/pub/irs-pdf/p15.pdf.*

104. Internal Revenue Service, *Publication 1635, Understanding Your EIN* (Washington, D.C.: Internal Revenue Service, October 2007), 7, *www.irs.gov/pub/irs-pdf/p1635.pdf.*

105. Internal Revenue Service, "Employer ID Numbers (EINs)," *www.irs.gov/businesses/small/article/0,,id=98350,00.html.*

106. Internal Revenue Service, "Unrelated Business Income Tax," *www.irs.gov/charities/article/0,,id=96106,00.html.*

107. Routh, "Interview."

108. Gee.

109. Ibid.

110. Ibid.

111. Ibid.

112. Ibid.

113. Ibid.

114. Section 6033(a)(2)(A)(ii) of the Internal Revenue Code of 1986, as amended.

115. GuideStar, "Frequently Asked Questions," *www.guidestar.org/help/faq_990.jsp#whatis990.*

116. Internal Revenue Service, *Instructions for Form 990 and Form 990-EZ* (Washington, D.C.: Internal Revenue Service), 8, *www.irs.gov/pub/irs-pdf/i990-ez.pdf.*

117. Internal Revenue Service, "IRS Releases Final 2008 Form 990 for Tax-Exempt Organizations, Adjusts Filing Threshold to Provide Transition Relief," IR-2007-204, December 20, 2007).

118. More information on the E-Postcard may be found at *www.irs.gov/eo.*

119. *Instructions for Form 990 and Form 990-EZ,* 40.

120. Internal Revenue Service, "Form 990 Redesign for Tax Year 2008 Background Paper," December 20, 2007.

121. Internal Revenue Service, *Instructions for Form 990-T, www.irs.gov/instructions/i990t/index.html.*

122. Internal Revenue Service, *Form 990W, Estimated Tax on Unrelated Business Taxable Income for Tax-Exempt Organizations* (Washington, D.C.: Internal Revenue Service), 4, *www.irs.gov/pub/irs-pdf/f990w.pdf.*

123. Internal Revenue Service, *Instructions for Form 990-T.*

124. Internal Revenue Service, "Exempt Organizations—Documents Subject to Public Disclosure," *www.irs.gov/charities/article/0,,id=135008,00.html.*

125. Internal Revenue Service, "Instructions for Form 990 and Form 990-EZ: Political Organizations," *www.irs.gov/instructions/i990-ez/ar02.html#d0e329.*

126. Tetreault.

127. New York State Charities Bureau, *Internal Controls and Financial Accountability for Not-for-Profit Boards* (New York: New York State Attorney General, January 2005), 2, *www.oag.state.ny.us/charities/internal_controls.pdf.*

128. Gee.

129. Ibid.

130. *Internal Controls,* 2.

131. Ibid.

132. Petty cash is a small amount of cash kept on hand for urgent cash purchases.

133. *Internal Controls,* 3-5.

134. Robert Widman, "Sarbanes-Oxley Law" (lecture moderated by Tobie Stein, Brooklyn College, Brooklyn, N.Y., February 21, 2007).

135. BoardSource and Independent Sector, *The Sarbanes-Oxley Act and Implications for Nonprofit Organizations* (Washington, D.C.: BoardSource and Independent Sector, 2006), 1-11. *www.independentsector.org/PDFs/sarbanesoxley.pdf.*

136. Ibid, 9-10.

137. *Internal Controls,* 10.

138. Ibid, 2.

139. BoardSource and Independent Sector, 2-6.

140. Ibid, 7.

141. Ibid.

APPENDIX A: Income Statement

Saracen Players
Income Statement
For the Fiscal Year Ending June 30, 2007

INCOME

Earned

Membership Fees	46,619
Fall Play Ticket Sales	11,465
Winter Play Ticket Sales	376,029
Spring Play #1 Box Office (co-presentation)	34,750
Spring Play #2 Box Office	133,511
Space Rental	130,746
Miscellaneous	157,327
Subtotal	**890,448**

Gala

	178,000

Contributed

Individuals	52,314
Board Contributions	68,858
Corporate	10,640
Foundations	151,500
Government	20,475
Donated Goods/Services	4,548
Other	0
Subtotal	**308,335**

TOTAL INCOME	**1,376,782**

EXPENSE

General

Administrative and Artistic Salaries	263,650
General Production Salaries & fees	2,043
FICA, Unempoyment Ins., Worker's Comp, Disability	36,908
Insurance	16,839
Health Insurance	20,713
Outside Professional Fees	13,673
Pre-Season Production supplies	6,393
Rent	94,661
Postage, copying, mailings, graphic design	38,126
Equipment	9,982
Office Supplies	5,568
Catering, artist events, transportation	5,156
Dues, Subscriptions	3,234
Telephone, Utilities	37,012
Bank, credit card, payroll fees, interest	17,894
Development of future projects	0
Misc.	275
Debt Repayment	99,800
Contingency	
Subtotal	**671,926**

Gala

AEA salaries	0
Crew salaries	0
Production fees	0
Box Office Salaries	0
FICA, Unempoyment Ins., Worker's Comp, Disability	0
AEA Pension & Health	0
SSDC/USA pension/welfare, royalties	0
Artistic Fees	0
Sets, Props, Costumes, Supplies	0
Outside Professional Fees	0
Postage, copying, mailings, graphic design	137
Catering, artist events, transportation	0
Advertising	0
Offsite Rentals	0
Misc.	13,404
Subtotal	**13,541**

Fall Play

AEA salaries	35,509
Crew salaries	42,262
Production fees	3,466
Box Office Salaries	560
FICA, Unempoyment Ins., Worker's Comp, Disability	9,879
AEA Pension & Health	17,652
SSDC/USA pension/welfare, royalties	21,016
Artistic Fees	15,386
Sets, Props, Costumes, Supplies	42,995
Outside Professional Fees	0
Postage, copying, mailings, graphic design	2,418
Catering, artist events, transportation	2,722
Advertising	42,682
Offsite Rentals	4,000
Credit card fees, ticketing fees, Misc.	29,247
Subtotal	**269,793**

Winter Play

AEA salaries	43,450
Crew salaries	25,745
Production fees	3,686
Box Office Salaries	0
FICA, Unempoyment Ins., Worker's Comp, Disability	10,017
AEA Pension & Health	22,729
SSDC/USA pension/welfare, royalties	1,125
Artistic Fees	12,042
Sets, Props, Costumes, Supplies	30,270
Outside Professional Fees	0
Postage, copying, mailings, graphic design	2,530
Catering, artist events, transportation	3,968
Advertising	13,272
Offsite Rentals	3,660
Credit card fees, ticketing fees, Misc.	11,365
Subtotal	**183,859**

Spring Play #1

AEA salaries	0
Crew salaries	0
Production fees	0
Box Office Salaries	35
FICA, Unempoyment Ins., Worker's Comp, Disability	0
AEA Pension & Health	0
SSDC/USA pension/welfare, royalties	0
Artistic Fees	35,000
Sets, Props, Costumes, Supplies	400
Outside Professional Fees	0
Postage, copying, mailings, graphic design	250
Catering, artist events, transportation	108
Advertising	0
Offsite Rentals	0
Credit card fees, ticketing fees, Misc.	725
Subtotal	**36,518**

Spring Play #2

AEA salaries	32,777
Crew salaries	30,000
Production fees	4,500
Box Office Salaries	2,240
FICA, Unempoyment Ins., Worker's Comp, Disability	10,171
AEA Pension & Health	17,145
SSDC/USA pension/welfare, royalties	10,266
Artistic Fees	15,436
Sets, Props, Costumes, Supplies	34,174
Outside Professional Fees	0
Postage, copying, mailings, graphic design	7,050
Catering, artist events, transportation	2,900
Advertising	20,000
Offsite Rentals	3,500
Credit card fees, ticketing fees, Misc.	7,700
Subtotal	**197,859**

TOTAL INCOME	**1,376,782**
TOTAL EXPENSE	**1,373,496**

NET INCOME	**3,286**

APPENDIX B: Cash Flow Statement

	wk of 7/3	wk of 7/10	wk of 7/17	wk of 7/24	wk of 7/31	wk of 8/7	wk of 8/14	wk of 8/21	wk of 8/28	wk of 9/4	wk of 9/11	wk of 9/18	wk of 9/25
Beginning Balance	92,343.12	110,574.46	87,794.72	77,252.03	122,406.62	98,790.25	194,814.90	173,680.74	170,446.43	211,141.31	182,787.21	155,957.67	182,266.02
Beginning Checking Account Balance		110,574.46	37,794.72	27,252.03	72,406.62	48,790.25	144,814.90	123,680.74	120,446.43	161,141.31	132,787.21	105,957.67	132,266.02
Transfer to (-) /from (+) Money Market Account		-50,000.00											
Balance in Money Market Account	50,000.00	50,000.00	50,000.00	50,000.00	50,000.00	50,000.00	50,000.00	50,000.00	50,000.00	50,000.00	50,000.00	50,000.00	50,000.00
EARNED INCOME													
Receipt Date / Contributor													
Theater/Equipment Rental		9,000.00		4,000.00		14,613.75		11,835.00	4,680.00			14,150.00	12,000.00
Ticket Sales				935.00								17,116.56	19,852.36
Events		1,790.00		6,253.00		22,445.13		14,805.00	7,770.00			18,656.01	3,265.00
Memberships				55,000.00		55,000.00			55,000.00				
Other Earned										411.43		411.43	
Loan													
Reimbursed Expenses								761.15				18.80	
Royalties	377.36	34.80		250.00							204.12		
Miscellaneous Income		56.03										10,050.00	1,177.66
Concessions												189.00	213.00
Contingency		70.00		105.00				1,233.00	563.00				
Ticket Handling Fees	377.36						0.00			411.43			
SUBTOTAL	377.36	-6,637.74		66,543.00		37,058.88	0.00	28,634.15	68,013.00	411.43		60,591.80	36,508.02
GALA INCOME	10,000.00	5,600.00		1000		10,000.00							
CONTRIBUTED INCOME													
Receipt Date / Contributor													
Board In-Kind	15,609.60												
Board Contrib.		209.2				250.00			1,500.00	10,000.00	5,061.69		1,500.00
Annual Appeal								3,814.00				1,606.00	225.00
Individual Contributions		138.00		313.00		5,640.00			1,018.00				
Foundation Contributions		1,000.00		7,500.00		55,000.00			15,000.00				
Corporate Contributions				5,000.00									
Government Contributions													
SUBTOTAL	15,609.60	1,347.20		12,813.00		60,890.00	0.00	3,814.00	17,518.00	10,000.00	5,061.69	1,606.00	1,725.00
TOTAL INCOME	25,986.96	309.46		80,356.00		107,948.88	0.00	32,448.15	85,531.00	10,411.43	5,265.81	62,197.80	38,233.02
EXPENSES													
Due Date / Vendor													
every Wed. — Admin Payroll	4,156.91	4,156.91	4,156.91	4,676.48	4,813.40	7,888.41	8,297.96	7,444.49	8,240.80	16,811.98	13,849.32	11,185.65	9,364.55
Equity Payroll													
Crew Payroll													
House Mgmt, Running Crew Payroll		2,030.14	2,030.15	2,250.17	2,284.36	3,402.42	3,556.88	3,189.88	3,499.52	8,336.64	6,000.81	4,905.51	4,140.01
Payroll Taxes		48.85	48.85	55.89	58.15	87.18	66.18	64.94	79.02	101.04	99.80	76.64	67.56
Payroll Fees		357.76	357.76	177.88		357.76			533.64			535.64	177.88
Insurance						0.00	0.00	698.40	338.11	353.25	331.20	331.20	331.20
AEA Pension/Health								4,110.00	1,884.00	1,884.00	1,884.00	1,884.00	1,884.00
AEA Health								473.85	95.09	99.35	93.15	93.15	93.15
AEA Membership													
Loan Repayment										784.04			
Interest on Loan										188.46			
4th — Deduction for Citibank Loan				138.46	801.82	138.46	138.46	138.46	138.46	188.46	138.46	138.46	188.46
1st — Cleaning Service	689.03	690.96		1,927.53	138.46			378.55	1,181.82	784.04			1,181.82
1st — Press Agent					1,181.82								267.46
1st — Press Agent Expenses					241.95								7,871.88
1st — Rent		7,426.30	7,426.30		7,426.30			2,804.49	7,426.30				2,804.49
1st — Health Insurance			425.97	2,804.49		2,804.49	175.00	425.97				75.00	425.97
20th — Garbage Service				425.97		425.97	119.10	3,592.84					
5th — Electric Bill													
Electric Bill Service Charge		4.32			2,893.49	4.32	4.32				4.32		
22nd — Budget Installment													
10th — Telephone Service		355.40		46.00	46.00			378.55	46.00			384.70	
20th — Verizon (pay phone in theater)													
7th — Software Expense													54.57
FedEx		155.00			71.00								
30th — Messenger Service		45.00		360.00		175.00	175.00		335.00		838.64	75.00	272.80
30th — Copying Service		214.40					119.10			335.00	119.10	335.00	
Bookkeeper		119.10	119.10	400.00	400.00	585.05	585.05	400.00		400.00	400.00		400.00
16th — Internet Service Provider													
15th — Hayden (lights in theater)													
6th — Pitney Bowes Credit Corporation (postage)		108.36						707.60		1,834.81	294.42		
6th — Pitney Bowes/Purchase Power (postage)													
14th — Air Conditioning Maintenance												344.89	
Annual- 9/30 — Staples		60.87											
around the 20th — State Insurance Fund		443.17											
25th — Finance Services	165.00	165.00	165.00					165.00					165.00

Appendix B (continued)

5th quarterly

	wk of 7/3	wk of 7/10	wk of 7/17	wk of 7/24	wk of 7/31	wk of 8/7	wk of 8/14	wk of 8/21	wk of 8/28	wk of 9/4	wk of 9/11	wk of 9/18	wk of 9/25
Cleaning Supplies													
Nat'l Benefit Life Insurance		176.00						176.00				176.00	176.00
Sapphire Office Solutions		153.20						52.75					77.59
Ace Hardware Store													
Mutual Hardware Store													
East Hardware Store													
Other Graphic Designer							50.00						
Consultants				1,850.00								200.00	131.75
Actor Fees								216.75	488.75	433.50	616.25	599.25	
Dir/Chor. Fees							400.00		50.00			200.00	400.00
Playwright Royalties								200.00	200.00	200.00		200.00	
Music Royalties													
Costume Designer Fee					750.00		2,000.00	950.00		616.66		616.66	616.66
Costume Expense					200.00								
Dry Cleaning													
Stage Manager Expenses									100.00			42.13	
Production Maintenance									63.00			141.42	
Sets/Props Expenses								423.24		326.75		692.34	299.70
Hauling (transport of sets, etc.)							4,357.50		7,681.38	700.00		85.00	
Prop Master Fee							400.00	850.00				850.00	
Production Manager Fee													
Set Designer Fee			500.00				500.00	950.00		462.50		462.50	
Light Designer Fee										437.50		462.50	
Sound Designer Fee												500.00	
Assistants' Fees								425.00				1,275.00	
Other Tech Fees													
USA Pension/Health													
SSDC Pension/Health					50.00						500.00		
AEA Bond				14,847.00						105.90		1,018.88	
Sound Expense													
Lighting Expense										4,946.40			
Projection Expense													
Program (playbill)								810.00	9,023.34				
Box Office Bank (cash in box office)			800.00		800.00						330.00		
Postage for Mailings													
Lobby Display													
Other Marketing													
Mail House													
TCG Membership													
Photography													
Catering/Food/Gifts									1,918.00		350.00	787.00	
Advertising				5,000.00							4,652.68	1,057.25	4,661.40
Sprinkler System													
Concessions					166.67					219.50	25.56	133.75	
Other Printing Expenses		1,999.12											
Gala Expenses													
Credit Card Fees	0.00	51.96	0.00	0.00	0.00	0.00		757.20	626.24	0.00	0.00		274.72
Other Bank Fees	108.07	61.88						412.30	318.65	25.12	25.12		
Ticketing Service Fees	722.61	551.72						1,645.80					
Miscellaneous Expenses				50.00		50.00		2,497.95				76.00	
Facilities Maintenance			75.83	690.00	75.00				170.00		400	100	76.00
Transportation	83.64								399.00			1,600.00	100
Artist Housing/Per Diem												63.77	63.77
Staff Reimbursements	4,194.30				234.95		483.71				895.83	226.93	1,138.35
Petty Cash								250.00		250.00			200.00
Audit												4,500.00	
Publications													
Member Mailing													
List Purchases													
Outside Rehearsal Space					1,000.00			400.00		320.00		2,160.00	
Annual Appeal Expenses													
Gain/Loss on Investments													
Adjustments to Cash Flow	299.60		2,339.31										
SUBTOTAL	7,755.62	23,089.20	10,542.69	35,201.41	23,616.37	11,924.23	21,134.16	35,682.46	44,836.12	38,765.53	32,095.35	35,889.45	39,722.23
TOTAL CASH	110,574.46	87,794.72	77,252.03	122,406.62	98,790.25	194,814.90	173,680.74	170,446.43	211,141.31	182,787.21	155,957.67	182,266.02	180,776.81
Money in Checking Account	110,574.46	37,794.72	27,252.03	72,406.62	48,790.25	144,814.90	123,680.74	120,446.43	161,141.31	132,787.21	105,957.67	132,266.02	130,776.81
Notes:													

APPENDIX C: Balance Sheet

	March 31, 2007
ASSETS	
Current Assets	
Checking/Savings Accounts	
(Lists different bank accounts maintained by company)	
101 · Cash - Checking Account	159,013.23
102 · Money Market Account	131,110.91
107 · Cash - Savings Account	0.70
112 · Box Office/Concessions Bank	200.00
(Cash held at box office and concessions stand)	
114 · Office Petty Cash	1,466.47
(Cash held in office)	
Total Checking/Savings	291,791.31
Accounts Receivable	
131 · Pledges/Grants Receivable	55,000.00
(Pledges and grants owed to company that have not been paid)	
Total Accounts Receivable	55,000.00
Other Current Assets	
122 · Union Bonds	14,847.00
(Given to unions to cover salaries and benefits for union members)	
120 · Security Deposits	17,437.53
(Given for equipment rentals, etc.)	
162 · Prepaid Insurance (prepaid for the year)	3,470.00
164 · Prepaid Expenses (prepaid for the year)	2,101.63
Total Other Current Assets	37,856.16
Total Current Assets	384,647.47
Fixed Assets	
190 · Fixed Assets (Property Owned by Company)	69,468.61
191 · Theater Improvements	908,787.00
(Improvements made by company to the theater)	
195 · Accumulated Depreciation	
(Decline in Value of Fixed Assets)	-682,681.00
Total Fixed Assets	295,574.61
TOTAL ASSETS	**680,222.08**
LIABILITIES & EQUITY	
Liabilities	
Current Liabilities	
292 · Rent (Future rent payments as per lease)	26,500.00
250 · Loan Payment Due	10,210.87
Total Other Current Liabilities	36,710.87
Total Current Liabilities	36,710.87
Total Liabilities	36,710.87
Equity	
300 · Net Assets	424,142.03
3900 · Retained Earnings	60,042.67
(Earnings retained by company from business in prior season)	
Net Income Earned	159,326.51
(Earnings retained by company from business operations in current season)	
Total Equity	643,511.21
TOTAL LIABILITIES & EQUITY	**680,222.08**

APPENDIX D: Production Budget

Production Budget
Sample Off-Broadway Musical

PHYSICAL PRODUCTION
Scenery	$	25,000.00
Props	$	3,000.00
Costumes, Shoes, Accessories	$	5,000.00
Hair, Make-Up	$	1,000.00
Electrics Prep (in Theater)	$	4,000.00
Electrics Purchases	$	1,000.00
Sound Prep (in Theater)	$	4,000.00
Sound Recordings and Purchases	$	500.00
TOTAL	**$**	**43,500.00**

FEES
Authors	$	-
Director	$	4,500.00
Short-Term Choreographer	$	1,000.00
Set Designer	$	2,000.00
Assistant Set Designer	$	800.00
Costume Designer	$	2,000.00
Assistant Costume Designer	$	750.00
Lighting Designer	$	2,000.00
Assistant Lighting Designer	$	1,000.00
Sound Designer	$	2,000.00
Orchestrator/Copyist	$	15,000.00
Synth Programmer	$	2,000.00
General Manager	$	15,000.00
Casting Director	$	8,000.00
Technical Supervisor	$	5,000.00
Prop Shopper	$	1,000.00
TOTAL	**$**	**62,050.00**

REHEARSAL/TECH SALARIES
Cast	$	14,500.00
Understudies	$	1,500.00
Musical Director	$	3,000.00
Audition Pianist	$	500.00
Orchestra Rehearsal	$	800.00
Stage Manager	$	3,100.00
Asst. Stage Manager	$	2,400.00
Production Assistant	$	-
Crew Prep and Shop Labor	$	3,000.00
Wardrobe	$	500.00
Light Op	$	500.00
Sound Op	$	600.00
General Manager	$	9,000.00
Company Manager	$	3,500.00
Press Agent	$	3,400.00
TOTAL	**$**	**46,300.00**

PRE-PRODUCTION/REHEARSAL EXPENSES
Rehearsal Space	$	3,000.00
Scripts & Blueprints	$	500.00
Casting and Auditions	$	1,000.00
Local Transportation	$	250.00
Musical Instrument Purchase	$	10,000.00
Stage Management Expenses	$	300.00
TOTAL	**$**	**15,050.00**

OPENING/CLOSING EXPENSES
Take-In/Tech (Load-in to Theater)	$	10,000.00
Hauling (of Set)	$	1,000.00
Hardware Purchases	$	1,000.00
Prelim Theater Expenses: Box Office	$	6,000.00
Opening Night Expenses	$	5,000.00
Take-Out/Closing Expenses	$	5,000.00
TOTAL	**$**	**28,000.00**

ADVERTISING AND PUBLICITY
TOTAL	**$**	**225,000.00**

GENERAL AND ADMINISTRATION
Producer's Office Charge	$	1,000.00
General Manager's Office Charge	$	3,500.00
Legal	$	20,000.00
Accounting	$	4,000.00
General Insurance	$	8,000.00
Payroll Taxes	$	7,500.00
Union Benefits	$	12,000.00
Postage/Messenger/Telephone/Xerox	$	500.00
Payroll Service	$	500.00
Miscellaneous	$	1,000.00
TOTAL	**$**	**58,000.00**

TOTAL THEATER EXPENSE	**$**	**5,000.00**
(Front of House, Box Office, Rent, etc.)		
SUB-TOTAL	**$**	**482,900.00**

ADVANCES/OPTION PAYMENTS
Author's Advance	$	3,000.00
Director's Advance	$	3,000.00
Choreographer's Advance	$	600.00
Designers' Advance	$	-
TOTAL	**$**	**6,600.00**

BONDS/DEPOSITS
AEA	$	15,000.00
ATPAM	$	5,000.00
SSDC	$	8,000.00
AFM Local 802	$	10,000.00
Theater Deposit and Advance	$	15,000.00
TOTAL	**$**	**53,000.00**

SUB-TOTAL	**$**	**542,500.00**
CONTINGENCY/RESERVE	**$**	**155,000.00**
TOTAL CAPITALIZATION	**$**	**697,500.00**

APPENDIX E: Weekly Operating Budget

Weekly Operating Budget
Sample Off-Broadway Musical

SALARIES

Cast	$ 3,500.00
Understudies	$ 1,500.00
Musicians	$ 2,300.00
Stage Manager	$ 600.00
Asst. Stage Manager	$ 550.00
Rehearsal Pianist	$ 500.00
Wardrobe/Props	$ 500.00
Light Op	$ 500.00
Sound Op	$ 600.00
General Manager	$ 1,500.00
Company Manager	$ 900.00
Press Agent	$ 850.00
Casting Director	$ 200.00
Tech Supervisor	$ 100.00
TOTAL	**$ 14,100.00**

ADVERTISING/PUBLICITY

Print/Radio	$ 7,500.00
Press Agent Expenses	$ 250.00
Marketing Manager	$ 500.00
TOTAL	**$ 8,250.00**

DEPARTMENTAL/MAINTENANCE (Maintenance includes expenses to repair/restore production elements during the run of the show)

Stg Mgr/Co Mgr Expenses	$ 50.00
Props	$ 300.00
Electrics/Sound	$ 100.00
TOTAL	**$ 450.00**

EQUIPMENT RENTALS

Electrics	$ 1,500.00
Sound	$ 1,500.00
TOTAL	**$ 3,000.00**

GENERAL AND ADMINISTRATION

Producer's Office Charge	$ 250.00
General Manager's Office Charge	$ 250.00
Legal	$ 400.00
Accounting	$ 300.00
General Insurance	$ 500.00
Payroll Taxes	$ 1,860.00
Union Benefits	$ 3,500.00
Postage/Messenger/Telephone/Xerox	$ 100.00
Accrual: Closing Costs	$ 500.00
Miscellaneous	$ 250.00
TOTAL	**$ 7,910.00**

TOTAL THEATER EXPENSE	**$ 7,000.00**
(Front of House, Box Office, Rent, etc.)	

TOTAL OPERATING EXPENSES	**$ 40,710.00**

APPENDIX F: Annual Operating Budget

	Gala	General Development	Education	Theater (Building) Expenses	Marketing	General Administration	Prod. #1	Co-Prod. #1	Prod. #2	General Production	Prod. #3	Prod. #4	Educ. Prod. #1	Educ. Prod. #2	Projected Budget
EARNED INCOME															
Membership Fees										29,445					29,445
BOX OFFICE INCOME							133,511	34,750	348,750		3,000	5,500		14,495	540,150
Group Sales									3,870			200			4,070
Student Matinee Tickets									23,265			2,240			25,505
Member Tickets						1,500									1,500
Subsidiary Rights															
Co-Production Income									250						
Interest and Dividends from Investments						1,500									1,500
Concessions Income						1,401	1,719					22			3,142
Space Rental						130,746									130,746
Other Rental															
Ticket Handling Charges						4,936	1,458		3,212			142		42	9,790
Misc Earned Income			11,000			132,763									143,763
GALA INCOME															
Benefit Tickets	140,000														140,000
Benefit Donation	10,000														10,000
Benefit Auction Income	30,000														30,000
CONTRIBUTED INCOME															
Contributions - Individuals						57,750									57,750
Contributions - Board Dues						116,500									116,500
Contributions - Board															
Contributions - Corporate						12,000									12,000
Contributions - Foundations						332,000			25,000		2,500			5,000	364,500
Contributions - National Endowment for the Arts										11,000					11,000
Contributions - New York State Council on the Arts						20,475									20,475
Contributions - New York City						17,500									17,500
Contributions - Other Govt															
Donated Goods/Services															
Other Contributed Income						500			4,548						5,048
Total Revenues	180,000		11,000			829,571	136,688	34,750	408,895	40,445	5,500	8,104		19,537	1,674,385
EXPENSES															
Administrative Salaries		67,000			28,846	161,645									257,491
Artistic Salaries						82,000									82,000
AEA Salaries							43,450	25,933							69,383
General Prod/Tech Salaries															
Artistic Sal - Programming										1,500					1,500
Crew Salaries							9,356		16,700		250				26,306
Carpenter's Salaries							8,337		7,997						16,334
Electrician's Salaries							4,840		12,477						17,317
Painter's Salaries							3,212		5,088						8,300
Non-Production Salaries															
Box Office Salaries								1,530	868		225			525	3,148
FICA Expense		5,286			2,207	22,854	5,325	234	5,212	115	54			321	41,607
Directors and Officers Insurance						1,503									1,503
NYS Unemployment Insurance		4,824			2,077	17,542	4,692	110	4,618	108	34			38	34,044
Workers Comp/Disability Insurance						6,000									6,000
Health Insurance						23,381									23,381
AEA Pension							22,729		17,652						40,381
AEA Health							1,125		2,067						3,192
SSDC/USA/802 Pension and Health									18,949						18,949
Royalties										5,500					5,500
Commissions/Project Research and Development															
Artistic Fees	750		7,125			500	12,042		15,386		4,525	1,150		3,150	44,628

	Gala	General Development	Education	Theater (Building) Expenses	Marketing	General Administration	Prod. #1	Co-Prod. #1	Prod. #2	General Production	Prod. #3	Prod. #4	Educ. Prod. #1	Educ. Prod. #2	Projected Budget
Production/Tech Fees	1,500				500		3,686		3,466	1,200				60	10,412
Sets	750					50	13,780		7,215	750				300	22,095
Props															4,349
Paints	1,500						1,525		2,074						20,705
Lights	1,750						5,645	700	9,760	3,100					8,159
Projections	1,750								6,409						10,150
Sound/Music							1,918		5,811	625				46	17,551
Costumes							4,597		9,127					3,827	4,244
Production Maintenance	750				25		1,879	500	1,812					53	2,668
Supplies	250						554	300	455					84	2,658
Hauling - Transportation of Set, etc.							1,054		1,354						676
Production - Misc. Expenses							57		244						30,086
Adm Fees/Consultants						27,550		250			125				13,500
Outside Professional Fees	500				2,536		7,438	2,259	17,577		195	375		159	28,003
Computer Ticket Fees					13,000										3,200
Fire Inspection				3,200											7,003
Mail House Fees	2,000	1,781	1,200		1,500		77		446					100	10,750
Design/Graphics Production	1,500	1,250	1,250		6,100		50	500	850		500				3,850
Photography	1,000				750		750								30,035
Printing/Copying	3,000	2,550	2,100		15,778	2,500	1,610	125	1,122		250			1,000	5,146
Office Equipment/Computers		2,100			1,646	3,500									4,600
Office Supplies	250	450			1,450	2,500	189	100	88						8,577
Web Site/Network			450			6,000	44				50				16,604
Postage	800	1,622	200		6,938	6,000	318	750	221						3,114
Delivery/Messenger	150	1,000			350	600	2,098	125	343						4,183
Gifts	250	250			100		350	250	492					292	26,968
Catering/Food/Other - For Special Events	24,750	1,306				1,500									1,500
Conference/Workshop Fees						1,600				500					3,249
Local Transportation	250	100			84	1,000	148	250	317						1,000
Housing/Hotels						3,000	75								3,525
Dues/Subscriptions						400	13,272								59,854
Advertising		450			3,500		3,660		42,682					90	7,750
Offsite Rentals							50		4,000						6,952
Telephone					850	6,000			52						
Administration - Other															
Rent				91,343											91,343
Utilities				46,000		1,000									46,000
Telephone/Computer Repair						22,500									22,500
Liability & Property Insurance				12,500											12,500
Cleaning Services/Supplies				500											500
Lobby Improvement/Decor		995		100											2,845
License Fees, Fines				13,000		1,750									19,000
Building Repairs/Maintenance						3,500				6,000					3,500
Bank Charges						4,300									4,300
Payroll Service Fees	7,200					6,970	3,927	1,390	11,469						31,508
Credit Card Charges		127				6,000					120	222		83	6,000
Interest Expense						1,000									5,200
Miscellaneous Expenses								2,500		1,500	200				99,800
Debt Repayment						99,800									
Contingency						29,000									29,000
Total Expenses	50,650	91,091	12,325	166,643	88,307	554,196	183,858	11,873	260,334	21,398	6,528	1,747	-	10,128	1,459,077
Net Income	129,350	(91,091)	(1,325)	(166,643)	(88,307)	275,376	(47,170)	22,877	148,561	19,047	(1,028)	6,357	-	9,409	215,307

APPENDIX G: Capital Budget

CAPITAL EXPENDITURE LISTS BY DEPARTMENT 06/07

DEPARTMENT NAME	ITEM	COST		DEPT TOTAL	ACTUAL		PO #
EVENT SERVICES							
	Cement Trash Cans for Exterior (x6)	$	3,000.00		$	-	
	Shades for West Lobby	$	6,900.00		$	-	
	Total	$		9,900.00	$	-	
FOOD & BEVERAGE							
	SS Plate Covers (x200)	$	2,600.00		$	-	
	72" Round Tables (x6)	$	1,800.00		$	-	
	8' Tables (x6)	$	1,100.00		$	-	
	60" Round Tables (x12)	$	2,500.00		$	-	
	Table Cart for Rounds	$	600.00		$	-	
	36" Cocktail Tables (x7)	$	1,400.00		$	-	
	Glassware	$	1,900.00		$	-	
	Racks & Dollies for Glassware	$	800.00		$	-	
	Flatware	$	600.00		$	-	
	Recycle Bin for Catering	$	1,500.00		$	-	
	Total	$		14,800.00	$	-	
MIS							
not originally budgeted	Computer for Education	$	-		$	-	
	Headsets for Phones (x12)	$	1,500.00		$	-	
	Server	$	5,100.00		$	-	
	Laptop for IT	$	1,200.00		$	-	
	Computer for Board Room	$	1,000.00		$	-	
	Verizon Equip Upgrade	$	20,000.00		$	-	
	Black Baud Financial System	$	22,500.00		$	-	
	Total	$		51,300.00	$	-	
EDUCATION							
	Worklights for Studio 1	$	1,500.00		$	-	
	Condenser Microphones (x4)	$	1,000.00		$	-	
	Chairs for Institute (x58)	$	3,750.00		$	-	
	Sm Monitor Speakers (x4)	$	1,200.00		$	-	
	Lav Microphones (x5)	$	2,500.00		$	-	
	Sound Padding	$	1,500.00		$	-	
	Curtain Track 40'	$	1,900.00		$	-	
	Miscellaneous	$	5,000.00		$	-	
	Music Stands	$	2,500.00		$	-	
	Total	$		20,850.00	$	-	
E-OPS							
	Annex Roof Tile/Shingle Work	$	12,500.00		$	-	
	Corner Guards	$	2,000.00		$	-	
	Update Elect Eye System on Old Freight Elevator	$	2,500.00		$	-	
	Foundation Sound Issues in Office Area	$	18,000.00		$	-	
	Re-Coat Gt. Rm Balcony - Neogard	$	6,000.00		$	-	
	New Roadway Signs (x2)	$	1,675.00		$	-	
	Lighting for Ext Cars	$	4,000.00		$	-	
	Total	$		46,675.00	$	-	
TECHNICAL THEATER							
	Replace Main Stage (Summer 07)	$	49,000.00				
	Channel Deletion Filter	$	1,800.00		$	-	
	Video Switcher	$	5,500.00		$	-	
	Rear Projection Screen	$	900.00		$	-	
	Stage Camera	$	6,000.00		$	-	
	Sm Flat Screen TV's for ADA Seats (x6)	$	8,000.00		$	-	
	Moving Light Lamps (x16)	$	2,400.00		$	-	
	Re-String Main Piano	$	1,400.00		$	-	
	Total	$		75,000.00	$	-	
	Contingency	$		10,000.00			
	TOTAL CAPITAL PURCHASE	**Grand Total**	$	228,525.00	$	-	
New - Contingency							
Marketing	Projector for Exterior Ads	$	4,000.00		$	-	
Tech Ops	Piano Bench	$	900.00		$	-	
Tech Ops	Long Truck Ramp	$	1,200.00		$	-	
Eops	Fire Hose Replacment	$	4,212.96		$	-	
F&B	Slush Machines	$	1,000.00		$	-	
MIS	Acer Laptop	$	745.00		$	-	
Eops	Replace Blower Assembly Tower #2	$	3,603.85		$	-	
MIS	Copy Machine for Education	$	1,800.00		$	-	
Eops	Repair Sprinkler Pump	$	100.35		$	-	
Tech Ops	Moving Light Ballast	$	981.89		$	-	
Ticket Office	Credit Card Reader	$	680.00		$	-	
F&B	New furnature for Café	$	2,610.00		$	-	
TO	Tessitura Upgrade - Barcode	$	30,000.00		$	-	
TO	Tessitura Upgrade - Print at Home Tickets	$	10,000.00		$	-	
F&B	New chairs for Galleries	$	3,500.00		$	-	
F&B	Refrigerators for Star Suites (x2)	$	800.00		$	-	
					$	-	

BIBLIOGRAPHY

Administration for Children & Families. "Employer Services—Private Sector Employers—New Hire Reporting." *www.acf.hhs.gov/programs/cse/newhire/employer/private/newhire.htm.*

Bernstein, Alice. "Financial Management." Interview by Jessica Bathurst. Tape recording, 16 November 2005. Brooklyn Academy of Music, New York.

Blum, Debra E. "Roughly 90% of Charities Have Made Policy Changes." *Chronicle of Philanthropy*, 13 December 2007.

BoardSource and Independent Sector. *The Sarbanes-Oxley Act and Implications for Nonprofit Organizations.* Washington, D.C.: BoardSource and Independent Sector, 2006. *www.independentsector.org/PDFs/sarbanesoxley.pdf.*

Boehm, Mike, and Don Shirley. "The Play's the Thing in CTG Plan." *Los Angeles Times*, 2 September 2005.

Byrnes, William J. *Management and the Arts.* London: Focal Press, 2003.

Dobrin, Peter. "Making its debut today at the Kimmel Center for the Performing Arts: a balanced budget." *Philadelphia Inquirer*, 29 June 2006.

Farber, Donald C. *Producing Theatre.* Pompton Plains, N.J.: Limelight Editions, 2006.

Fraser, Alexander. "Commercial Producing." Interview by Kevin Condardo. Tape recording, 29 October 2005. New York.

Financial Accounting Standards Board. "Summary of Statement No. 116." *http://72.3.243.42/st/summary/stsum116.shtml.*

——. "Summary of Statement No. 117." *http://72.3.243.42/st/summary/stsum117.shtml.*

Gee, Peter. "Financial Management." Interview by Jessica Bathurst. Tape recording, 16 February 2006. Brooklyn Academy of Music, New York.

Grippo, Charles. *The Stage Producer's Business and Legal Guide.* New York: Allworth Press, 2002.

GuideStar, *www.guidestar.org.*

——. "Frequently Asked Questions." *www.guidestar.org/help/faq_990.jsp#whatis990.*

——. "Making Your 990 Work For You." *www.guidestar.org/DisplayArticle.do?articleId=854.*

——. "Nonprofit Directors and Officers Insurance: The Good, the Bad, and the Ugly." *www.guidestar.org/news/features/do_insurance.jsp.*

——. "Understanding the IRS Form 990." *www.guidestar.org/news/features/understand_990.jsp.*

Hopkins, Bruce R. *The Law of Tax-Exempt Organizations, 9th Edition.* Indianapolis: Wiley, 2007.

Horngren, Charles T., and Walter T. Harrison, Jr. *Accounting.* Upper Saddle River, N.J.: Pearson Education, Inc., 2007.

Internal Revenue Code of 1986, Section 512(b)(13).

——. Section 3121(a)(16).

——. Section 6033(a)(2)(A)(ii).

Internal Revenue Service, *www.irs.gov.*

——. "Employer ID Numbers (EINs)." *www.irs.gov/businesses/small/article/0,,id=98350,00.html.*

——. "Exempt Organizations—Documents Subject to Public Disclosure." *www.irs.gov/charities/article/0,,id=135008,00.html.*

——. "Form 990 Redesign for Tax Year 2008 Background Paper." 20 December 2007.

——. *Form 990W, Estimated Tax on Unrelated Business Taxable Income for Tax-Exempt Organizations.* Washington, D.C. *www.irs.gov/pub/irs-pdf/f990w.pdf.*

——. *Instructions for Form 990 and Form 990-EZ.* Washington, D.C. *www.irs.gov/pub/irs-pdf/i990-ez.pdf.*

——. "Instructions for Form 990 and Form 990-EZ: Political Organizations," *www.irs.gov/instructions/i990-ez/ar02.html#d0e329.*

——. *Instructions for Form 990-T. www.irs.gov/instructions/i990t/index.html.*

——. *Instructions for Form 1099-MISC. www.irs.gov/instructions/i1099msc/index.html.*

——. "IRS Releases Final 2008 Form 990 for Tax-Exempt Organizations, Adjusts Filing Threshold to Provide Transition Relief." IR-2007-204, 20 December 2007.

——. "Payroll Taxes and Federal Income Tax Withholding." *www.irs.gov/app/understandingTaxes/jsp/hows/tt/module01/tax_mod1_2.jsp.*

——. *Publication 15, Employer's Tax Guide.* Washington, D.C., *www.irs.gov/pub/irs-pdf/p15.pdf.*

——. *Publication 15-A, Employer's Supplemental Tax Guide. www.irs.gov/publications/p15a/index.html.*

——. *Publication 1635, Understanding Your EIN.* Washington D.C., October 2007. *www.irs.gov/pub/irs-pdf/p1635.pdf.*

——. *Publication 598, Tax on Unrelated Business Income of Exempt Organizations.* Internal Revenue Service. November 2007. *www.irs.gov/pub/irs-pdf/p598.pdf.*

——. "Tax Information for Charities and Other Non-Profits." *www.irs.gov/eo.*

——. "Title 26, Department of the Treasury, Section 1.6041-2(a)(1)."

——. "Unrelated Business Income Tax." *www.irs.gov/charities/article/0,,id=96106,00.html.*

Jackson, Peggy M. *Nonprofit Strategic Planning: Leveraging Sarbanes-Oxley Best Practices.* New York: Wiley, 2007.

Jackson, Peggy M. *Sarbanes-Oxley for Nonprofit Boards.* Hoboken, N.J.: Wiley, 2007.

Jackson, Peggy M., and Toni E. Fogarty. *Sarbanes-Oxley and Nonprofit Management: Skills, Techniques, and Methods.* Hoboken, N.J.: Wiley, 2006.

Jenen, Jessica R. "Annual Operating Budget." New York, 2007

——. "Balance Sheet." New York, 2007.

——. "Cash Flow Statement." New York, 2007.

——. "Financial Management." Interview by Jessica Bathurst. Tape recording, 24 May 2006. Classic Stage Company, New York.

——. "Income Statement." New York, 2007.

Larson, Kermit D., John J. Wild, and Barbara Chiappetta. *Fundamental Accounting Principles.* Boston: Irwin McGraw-Hill, 1999.

Lasher, Renee. "Financial Management." Interview by Jessica Bathurst. Tape recording, 2 December 2006. Society of Stage Directors and Choreographers, New York.

Lewis, Nicole. "Writing a New Script." *Chronicle of Philanthropy*, 12 June 2003.

Linzer, Richard, and Anna Linzer. *Cash Flow Strategies: Innovation in Nonprofit Financial Management.* New York: Wiley, 2007.

MacMillan, Kyle. "Returning an Aging Boettcher." *Denver Post*, 4 December 2006.

McMillan, Edward J. *Preventing Fraud in Nonprofit Organizations.* New York: Wiley, 2006.

Michaels, Marty. "Committee of Nonprofit Leaders Issues Set of Accountability Guidelines." *Chronicle of Philanthropy*, 1 November 2007.

Murray, Matthew. "A Study in Threes." *Stage Directions*, September 2005, 60–63.

New York State Charities Bureau. *Internal Controls and Financial Accountability for Not-for-Profit Boards*. New York: New York State Attorney General, January 2005. *www.oag.state.ny.us/charities/internal_controls.pdf*.

New York State Society of Certified Public Accountants, *www.nysscpa.org*.

New York State Workers' Compensation Board. "Understanding Workers' Compensation Insurance." *www.wcb.state.ny.us/content/main/Small_Business/understandInsurance.jsp*.

Nonprofit Coordinating Committee of New York, *www.npccny.org*.

———. "How to Read the IRS Form 990 & Find Out What It Means." *www.npccny.org/Form_990/990.htm*.

Panepento, Peter. "IRS Unveils Final Version of New Informational Tax Form for Charities." *Chronicle of Philanthropy*, 10 January 2008.

Panepento, Peter and Grant Williams. "A Question of Calculation." *Chronicle of Philanthropy*, 7 February 2008.

Papatola, Dominic P. "Ordway Balances Books." *St. Paul Pioneer Press*, 19 October 2006.

Patrick, James. "Financial Management." Interview by Jessica Bathurst. Phone interview with author, 23 November 2005.

Quotah, Eman. "A Space of Their Own." *Chronicle of Philanthropy*, 18 May 2006.

Reel, James. "Orchestral Maneuvers." *Tucson Weekly*, 20 July 2006.

Routh, Marc. *Business Management for the Performing Arts*. New York: Marc Routh, 2006.

———. "Financial Management." Interview by Jessica Bathurst. Tape recording, 10 November 2005. Richard Frankel Productions, New York.

Ruppel, Warren. *Not-for-Profit Accounting Made Easy*, 2nd Edition. Indianapolis: Wiley, 2007.

Russell, Jacob Hale. "Executive Pay Takes the Stage." *Wall Street Journal*, 11 February 2006.

Ruth Eckerd Hall. "Capital Budget." Clearwater, Fla., 2007.

Sag, Michael. "Production Budget." New York, 2007.

———. "Weekly Operating Budget." New York, 2007.

Schwinn, Elizabeth. "A Big Makeover Coming for Charity Tax Form." *Chronicle of Philanthropy*, 14 June 2007.

Strini, Tom. "Despite Financial Struggles, MSO President Stays Positive." *Milwaukee Journal Sentinel*, 27 June 2006.

TaxAdmin.org. "Individual Income Tax Starting Points." *www.taxadmin.org/fta/rate/inc_stp.html*.

Tetreault, Paul. "Financial Management." Interview by Jessica Bathurst. Phone interview with author, 3 February 2006.

United States Citizenship and Immigration Services. "About Form I-9, Employment Eligibility Verification." *www.uscis.gov*.

United States Department of the Treasury. "Treasury Regulations, Subchapter C, Sec. 31.3202-1."

Volz, Jim. *How to Run a Theater*. New York: Backstage Books, 2004.

Wakin, Daniel H. "Rare Instruments Purchase Causes Symphony's Deficit." *New York Times*, 19 July 2006.

Webb, Duncan M. *Running Theaters: Best Practices for Leaders and Managers*. New York: Allworth Press, 2004.

Widman, Robert. "Lecture on Sarbanes-Oxley Law." 21 February 2007. Brooklyn College, Brooklyn, N.Y.

Williams, Grant. "A New Form Takes Shape." *Chronicle of Philanthropy*, 28 June 2007.

Zolty, Meredith. "Financial Management." Interview by Jessica Bathurst. Tape recording, 6 February 2006. Mount Vernon, N.Y.

CHAPTER SIX

Developing a Funding Base

In this chapter, we will discuss unearned or contributed income. We will examine the role of the development director within the organization. We will then explore the creation and execution of the fundraising plan. We will also examine individual and institutional giving, followed by capital and endowment campaigns.

EARNED VERSUS CONTRIBUTED INCOME

As we discussed in the chapter on financial management, nonprofit organizations generate two sources of income to meet expenses: earned and unearned.[1] "Earned income is revenue received as a direct result of a service provided. Sources of earned income include money generated from ticket and merchandise sales; royalties; and rentals of costumes, lighting equipment, and performance spaces."[2] This chapter will focus on unearned or contributed income. This type of income is "revenue from sources not directly linked to services provided by the nonprofit organization. Sources of unearned income include gifts (also known as donations, grants, and contributions) from individuals and institutions (corporations, foundations, and the government)."[3] John Holden, director of institutional giving at New York City Center, notes: "Many people don't like the term 'unearned income,' since it implies that we don't really earn or work for it. Actually, nonprofit fundraisers or development managers work hard for this type of income."[4]

Holden is right when he says that nonprofit development managers work hard for contributed income. Depending on their size, performing arts organizations may raise between 50 and 80 percent of their income from contributed sources.[5] *Giving USA* reports that in 2006, "Americans donated $295 billion to nonprofit charities."[6] The majority of this money was contributed by individuals, followed by foundations, bequests (a donation received after the donor's death), and corporations. Donations to the arts (both visual and performing arts) rose over 6 percent from the previous year.[7] Arts and cultural organizations raised $12.5 billion.[8]

Raising money from all sources is not an easy task. Nonprofit performing arts organizations are in direct competition for donations with other nonprofit educational, social service, international, and religious organizations that provide vital services to the world. Nonprofit performing arts organizations must be savvy and strategic competitors in their efforts to secure a larger piece of the philanthropic pie. They must do a better job of presenting a compelling case for funding. Fundraising is also called "development" for a reason. When raising money, the development director is "developing relationships that result in contributed income, and this income helps develop the organization."[9]

THE DIRECTOR OF DEVELOPMENT'S ROLE

The development director is also commonly known as the director of development or the vice president of institutional advancement, because she is charged with helping to create and execute an annual fundraising strategy, or plan, with the executive director and the board of directors to help advance or move the organization forward.

An annual fundraising plan addresses the components of the organization's overall fundraising campaign: the annual fundraising campaign, capital campaign, and endowment campaign. The annual fundraising campaign (also called the annual fund) "raises money to support the operating expenses (administrative and programming) in a particular fiscal year." It can take the form of a direct mail appeal (money raised from sending mail to a targeted group of individuals); a telefunding (or telefundraising) campaign (money raised from calling individuals by phone); corporate and foundation support (targeted proposal requests); gifts from government sources (federal, state, and local); and special events—gala benefits or other parties given to raise money for the annual fund. Gifts to the annual fund can be restricted or designated for a particular purpose or project, such as commissions for new works, program startup funding, or funding to bus children to matinee performances. Unrestricted contributions may also be made to support the routine functions of the organization. These unrestricted funds are called "general operating support." General operating support may be used for whatever purpose the organization chooses, including such mundane items as utility bills.[10]

In addition to the annual fundraising campaign, the director of development is responsible for supervising capital and endowment campaigns. Richard Feiner, director of development at the World Monuments Fund (at the time of this writing, and now director of individual giving at The New York Botanical Garden), defines these terms: "A capital campaign is a specific fundraising program to secure financial resources to help effect upgrades/improvements to the physical plant of the nonprofit organization (e.g.., refurbishment of the interior or exterior of a theater, or the building of a new rehearsal studio complex adjacent to or near the theater). An endowment campaign is a specific fundraising program to secure financial resources for a separate reserve of funding that will help ensure the longevity of the nonprofit organization or a specific program of central importance to the nonprofit organization's mission. Both the capital and endowment campaigns are separate from efforts to raise annual fund contributions and also can have a lifespan of several years. All donor categories can contribute to these types of campaigns."[11]

When preparing the fundraising plan to implement these campaigns, the director of development has the following responsibilities:

- Sets fundraising goals and budgets for each category of funding (individual and institutional).
- Identifies and cultivates potential individual and institutional (corporate, foundation, and government) funding through research and board contacts.
- Designs and executes various fundraising methods (e.g., prepares applications and grant proposals requesting contributions from corporations, foundations, and the government; direct mail and online

fundraising appeals; telefundraising campaigns; and special events).
- Creates a computerized record-keeping system to keep track of donor histories, as well as proposal deadlines, status of proposal preparation/acceptance, and need for follow-up (grant calendar).
- Acknowledges every level of funding and prepares final reports for institutional funders.[12]

The director of development cannot implement this plan alone. Not only does the director of development work with her staff to implement the plan, but collaboration with the rest of the organization is essential to the fundraising process. In the next sections, we discuss the director of development's relationships with her staff, the other managers in the organization, and the board of directors.

CLASSROOM DISCUSSION

What is the difference between earned and unearned income?

What is the difference between an individual and an institutional funder?

Define the director of development's responsibilities.

Define the following terms: "annual fundraising campaign," "capital campaign," "endowment campaign," "restricted grants," "unrestricted grants," and "general operating support."

What are the major components of the fundraising plan?

Overseeing the Staff

The development department in a performing arts organization is critical in developing the relationships that will support the organization's growth. At the Minnesota Opera, Patrick Dewane, vice president of institutional advancement, creates a typical organizational chart (figure 6.1) for the development department of a large organization.[13]

As has been discussed in chapter 1, the number of positions in an organization or department depends on the budget size of the organization. In figure 6.1, there are three major directors: the director of development, the director of individual giving, and the director of institutional giving. The director of development is responsible for overseeing his staff and raising money from individuals and institutions.

The rest of the department is broken down into areas of giving. Institutional giving staff is dedicated to corporations, foundations, and the government.

Fig. 6.1. Development Department Organizational Chart, Large Organization

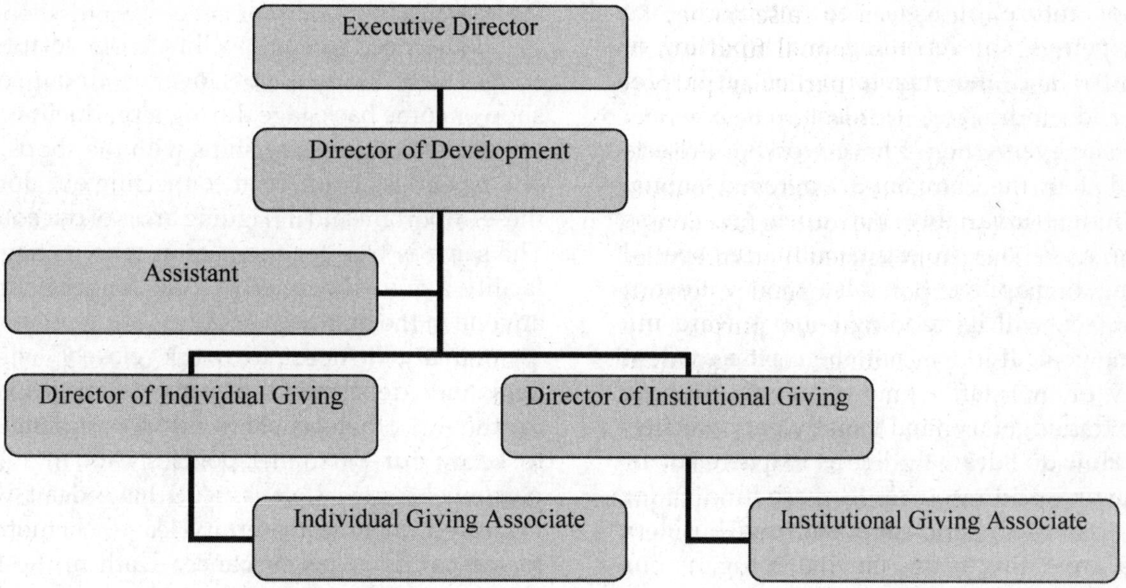

This staff identifies, cultivates, and solicits donations from these donor groups.

Individual giving staff serves all categories of individual donors, including the board and major donors, as well as small donors. The director of individual giving often conducts the annual appeal and participates in other campaigns regarding giving by individuals, including the capital and endowment campaigns. In addition, the director of individual giving may be responsible for planning and executing the annual gala benefit. This type of special event is often used by performing arts organizations to raise unrestricted money for general operating expenses. Finally, the director of individual giving may assist in planned giving. Planned gifts allow for an individual to give money to an organization as part of his overall financial and estate plan. A planned gift may be either an outright gift, in which the nonprofit organization receives the funding immediately, or it may be a deferred gift, in which the nonprofit organization will receive the gift at some future date/time.

In larger institutions, the following titles may be found in a development department: director of foundation and corporate giving; manager of special events; planned giving director; and director of capital and endowment gifts.[14]

Organizational Relationships

Beyond his duties as supervisor of his own department, the director of development has a pivotal role in interacting with other departments within the organization. Without the cooperation of the key players in an organization, the director of development will not be able to properly carry out the development plan.

Patrick Dewane discusses his relationship with his organization's staff: "At Minnesota Opera, the development department must relate well to every area of the organization. Above all, I must understand the goals and specific plans of the artistic department, as it is the heart of the organization. Good fundraisers are good storytellers, and a good storyteller must know his/her material. I must know what the artistic department is doing and why, and earn their trust and respect.

"I also have to know what the education department is doing because so many donors are interested in what we are doing for students. The cuts in school music, theater, and art programs have made this more important than ever, as arts organizations are expected to fill in the void. I must be fluent in our educational goals and programs, just as I must be able to speak compellingly about our artistic vision.

"I also work closely with marketing and public relations, as they, too, are out telling our story to the public. The information our donors read about us in the press affects their giving. And the people who buy our tickets—our subscribers and single-ticket buyers—are some of my best prospective donors. Therefore, I have a vested interest in the success of our marketing and public relations efforts.

"Our business office is another key relationship for me, as I need to be intimately involved in the creation of future budgets; the monitoring of current expenses; the recording and reporting of current gifts; and the monitoring of off-budget expenses and fundraising. This last point has been a sticky issue everywhere I have worked. Projects not included in the company's approved annual expense budget invariably crop up in the course of the year, and those projects usually need special fundraising to happen. If I raise money toward such a project, will its funding count toward my fundraising goal? If it does not, then is it a prudent use of my or my staff's time to pursue funding for this extrabudgetary (and usually very worthy) expense? How do I draw the line as to where I do or do not use time and resources to chase funding for such projects? My relationship with my business office is a great ally in this inevitable tug, as our controller understands the bigger financial picture in a way that a department head with a terrific new—and unfunded—idea may not.

"This is a huge management issue that people rarely talk about—how can you say 'yes' to one department's special funding need and then say 'no' to someone else, especially when I will need a favor from that other department sometime in the future? Or how can I keep saying 'no' to looking for funding for special projects, when one of those vetoed projects might help attract a donor who could grow into a major supporter of the organization? How to pick and choose? And I'd better not say 'no' to everything; otherwise I am an obstacle to growth. My relationship with our controller is key to making these decisions.

"Of course, so is my relationship with my boss, our president. His word is final, and sometimes he or the artistic director is the one coming up with the 'Boy, if we could just get $20,000 for this project we could . . .' ideas. I need to have a strong relationship with my boss so I can present my reasons why we should say 'no' to a project of his that, for whatever reason, does not make sense from a fundraising point of view. My relationship with the president and his assistant are probably my two most important relationships. The buck stops at the president's desk, and my job is to generate the bucks. Therefore, I need his trust and respect to do my job. He often says that his assistant is the one who 'really runs the company,' as she knows all of the board members, has a deep company history, and is well liked throughout the organization. So my relationship with her is almost as important as my relationship

with my boss. Without her cooperation, I would be sunk. Without her enthusiastic support, I would be far less effective.

"I also need to work well with our costume and scenic shops. Many donors love to tour our costume shop or come backstage during a production. If I do not have strong relationships with the shops, then I will be far less effective at connecting our donors to these important and intriguing areas of our company. The same is true for the person who manages our facility, a guy who quietly works longer hours than anyone in the building.

"Finally, I need to work closely with our personnel department because I am responsible for the five other people in my department. I need to know our personnel policies. And if I have a personnel issue—staff issues I have dealt with in my career include maternity leave, chemotherapy for cancer, poor performance, death in the family, and fraud—I had better be able to have an honest conversation about how to handle these issues with our personnel department.

"In short, I need a strong relationship with every department in our organization."[15]

CLASSROOM DISCUSSION

Discuss the importance of organizational relationships to a director of development.

Why is it important to have good relationships with the following employees: artistic director, managing director, director of finance, directing of marketing and public relations, director of human resources or personnel, facilities manager, director of education, and the managing director's or president's assistant?

Create a scenario in which the director of development collaborates with each of these important roles.

Working with the Board of Directors

Boards of directors are critical to the development effort. They are responsible for approving and helping to execute the development plan. Dewane states, "The board can open doors that the director of development can't or doesn't even know exists. The dance between the development department and the board is the key to the growth of the organization."[16] Holden agrees: "The board is the chief fundraiser and advocate for your organization. Board members need to have a passion and enthusiasm for the mission. The board should be just about the most effective advocates that your organization will have in-house. They should have an expertise in a wide range of areas, including investment, finance, marketing, and fundraising. They should have a diverse set of connections in the community, including relationships with government, business, and community leaders."[17]

Holden continues, "In addition, the board must have a give-or-get policy. In other words, they should have a set contribution that they must give or get from other sources. If they fail to meet this annual goal, their membership status should be reviewed by board leadership. The board must have the ability to contribute a significant amount of time and/or other resources to your organization, as well as be committed to a long-term vision for the company, and not just to a short-term relationship."[18]

In working with the board of directors, the director of development is the director for all board fundraising activities, working with the board chair, the president, and the board committees to achieve the fundraising goals. Dewane emphasizes, "You need to plan and know what they are doing and how you can assist them. You need to assess who is the best board member for particular donors and prospects (potential donors). You need to plan and execute cultivation events and accompany board members on solicitations for gifts. I have built strong working relationships with our board chair, our capital campaign chair, and our annual fund chair, so I am able to brainstorm, create solicitation plans, and talk to each one about what larger role they can play in realizing the goals of the company. In between meetings and solicitations, I keep all of my most important board members up-to-date with phone calls, e-mails, and scheduled meetings. My board trusts me, and I depend on them. For example, to build campaign momentum, I presented a fundraising plan to the campaign chair that included the two of us and the president soliciting the board chair for a $1 million challenge gift—which would be his second major gift to the campaign—to be matched by other new board gifts. He agreed to do $500,000, and to solicit another board member to match his $500,000 one-to-one to create the overall $1 million challenge. This proved to be successful, and we matched this $1 million. Later in the campaign, we got a boost from another challenge grant that we solicited from a board member. I scripted the ask [request], and it resulted in a $500,000 challenge gift, which helped leverage the completion of the campaign."[19]

In addition to working with the board chair, the director of development meets with members of the development and finance committees. The development committee is responsible for approving and helping to implement the fundraising plan. Once the goals have been set and approved by the entire board, the development committee will help the director of development identify, cultivate, and solicit individual and institutional donors. The director of development also works closely with the finance committee, which is responsible for monitoring the organization's budget and helping to set income goals for each year.

Since the board is considered the chief fundraising arm of the organization, Dewane believes that its size matters. He discusses his reasoning: "We have thirty-seven directors [board members]. I think that's too small. Some of our board members think it's too big. My boss thinks it's about right. My opinion (and beware of anyone who speaks in absolutes on this issue!) is that the board should be as big as the staff can handle. If it is an executive director and an assistant, then the answer might be eight. If you're a major orchestra, the answer might be eighty. I wish ours were bigger so we would have more fundraising reach in the community. We would raise more from the board members themselves than we do now, and we'd have more board members identifying, cultivating, and soliciting funds. Of course, you don't want to increase the size of your board with inferior candidates. Quality is more important than quantity. But if you are able to attract high-quality board members, I think you need to increase the size of the board to that of the largest and most successful cultural board in your community. Whom you bring onto your board this year will have a strong bearing on how successful you are three years from now."[20]

But how does a board attract new board members, especially a board for a small organization? The nominating committee is responsible for attracting new board members, and as the director of development works closely with the board in identifying, cultivating, and soliciting donations, he can make suggestions to the nominating committee. Dewane has a sound strategy: "The best sources for attracting new board members are friends and colleagues of current board members; major current donors; chief executive officers; corporate and foundation executives with influence over funding decisions; relocated senior corporate executives (get them before the competition knows they're in town); individuals of significant wealth and their family members; individuals from families known for their philanthropy; successful entrepreneurs; owners of private companies; small-business owners; printers; advertising executives who can provide pro bono [free] graphic design; established estate attorneys and financial planners; publishers and media owners; real estate developers; plaintiff attorneys; financiers; surgeons; corporate heirs apparent; and people of means whom nobody else has cultivated to be on a board."[21]

As the board grows, its relationship to the organization deepens. As in all relationships, problems do arise. Holden raises the problem of interference on a day-to-day basis. "You want a board that realizes that they are not the managers of the organization. We are the professionals, and we have degrees in performing arts management, dramaturgy, or directing. A board must take ownership of the organization without trying to run the organization."[22]

Dewane provides further insight into board management. "A board has ultimate governance power, and this power can be abused. The micromanagement of development efforts is a sensitive issue. The 'textbook' answer is that the development director must be strong and clearly communicate the boundaries of each board member's responsibilities. But what if the difficult board member is also your biggest donor? Or the chair? Or your boss's best buddy on the board? Or someone who scares the pancakes out of everyone in the organization? In these examples, and countless others, the 'textbook' answer isn't always helpful; in some circumstances, the 'textbook' advice could get you fired. How a young development director handles such problems is often far different from how a seasoned veteran does. The veteran has the benefit of past painful experiences, whereas the newcomer might be seeing this problem for the first time and cannot get past her own feelings that the situation just shouldn't be happening. It is helpful to have mentors to advise you on particularly difficult situations. You also need to have trusting relationships with your boss and with key board members so that when a problem comes up, they will guide and support you.

"With board members who try to overly control how their donations are used, I try to educate them about the bigger fundraising picture. I sometimes also have the president or other board members steer the difficult board member in the right direction. But first, I listen closely to understand exactly what the donor (board member) is saying. Sometimes, development staff members get paranoid when a donor asks what are actually innocent questions or suggestions. Trust and good listening skills are

essential tools in dealing with any donor who tries to exert too much control over his gifts.

"Several individuals on any given board are there for some sort of enlightened self-interest, and many arts boards have been used as a ladder for social climbing. But in all honesty, we wouldn't name buildings, wings of buildings, and seats after individuals if we rejected personal gain as a motivator for giving. Personal gain is not a bad motive as long as the organization benefits. The gain must be mutual. When the gain is in favor of the board member at the expense of the organization, then the development director must bring the situation to the attention of his boss, who then must decide whether it is serious enough to discuss with the chair, the executive committee, or the nominating committee. Ignoring a problem might encourage other such problems. Overreacting to a situation might damage or sever relationships. It is a sensitive issue. Still, problems arise. The species is complicated. A sense of humor can diffuse many difficult situations."[23]

Kathryn Miree, an attorney, suggests that nonprofit organizations have a written conflict-of-interest policy that can help alleviate some of the issues discussed by Patrick Dewane in this section.[24] A conflict-of-interest policy may prevent a breach of fiduciary and legal duties by the board of directors.

CLASSROOM DISCUSSION

Why does the director of development need a
    strong board of directors?
What are the characteristics of an effective board of
    directors?
What is the role of the development director in
    working with the board?
What are the roles of the development committee
    and the finance committee?
Why does the size of the board matter?
How should the board attract new members?
Discuss some of the communication problems that
    may arise between the board and the staff.
    How should the staff deal with these problems?

THE FUNDRAISING PLAN

According to Richard Feiner, "A fundraising plan provides a blueprint upon which to determine all activities of a robust, coordinated development department. There are many ways to write a development/fundraising plan, but almost all are comprised of the following four components: 1) a goal, what the development department wishes to accomplish through all coordinated activities; 2) an objective, a measurable step toward accomplishing the larger goal; 3) a strategy, what the actions will be to help accomplish the stated objective; and 4) a timeline, in which the actions will be accomplished. A budget should accompany the written plan. The annual fundraising plan should address these components for the annual fund campaign (the campaign launched each year), as well as capital and endowment campaigns, which are conducted over a period of several years and occur when the organization's leadership feels the need for strategic growth and change."[25] Let's take a look at a development plan for the annual fund created by Richard Feiner for the World Monuments Fund (fig. 6.2).[26]

Fig. 6.2. World Monuments Fund Annual Fund Development Plan, 2007

FY07 Development Plan

A.   Goal:

To expand the level of contributed income from all funding sources, with particular emphasis on unrestricted/general operating funds, in support of the organization's recognized need for increased internal capacity in the management of ongoing projects and new initiatives. This development plan will help provide cohesive direction to all fundraising efforts in support of this goal.

B.   Objectives:

To determine the types and sources of funding most important to efforts that will result in the greatest growth in general operating support [GOS]. Simultaneously, to determine the person(s) responsible for devising and implementing strategies to secure the following types of funds:

Trustee and Major Donors (including President's Council)

This constituency provides the greatest potential return on efforts to secure general operating support. A consistent approach to this constituency will require significantly increased prospecting research and out-of-office cultivation. The Development Director and major donor officers, together with input/direction from Executive Staff, will concentrate efforts to secure significant single-year and multiyear support from this constituency.

Foundation/Major Family Foundation

This constituency represents the second major potential source of increased GOS funding. Efforts will focus on New York City–based foundations to help support local-based outreach/educational programming, as well as major foundations with national/international interests in areas pertinent to the organization's core activities. The Director of Foundation Relations will head up these efforts, which include prospect identification and out-of-house cultivation.

Individual/Membership

It is vital to expand the base of lower-level individual support through a robust membership program. The Development Department already has invested in efforts that include: increased regular communication with current individual supporters (mail, e-mail) and aggressive acquisition campaigns to identify new potential members/individual supporters. Other activities/events also will help secure new individual supporters and incite current individual supporters to raise their contributions and membership levels. The Membership Manager will head up these efforts.

Corporate Support

Continue to secure new funding from corporate sources as well as to more effectively and efficiently provide "client service" support to maintain current relationships. Efforts to secure new corporate support are secondary to the above-mentioned constituencies. The Corporate Relations Manager will head up corporate solicitations.

Fig. 6.2. (continued)

Planned Giving

Continue to invest in the groundwork necessary to launch a multiphased planned giving program that includes bequests and charitable gift annuities. Current efforts will result in modest returns in the short term and should be regarded as investments for significant future returns. The Planned Giving Manager will head up these efforts together with direct Trustee involvement.

C.   Strategies:

Efforts to raise all above-identified types of funds will emphasize the organization's recognized expertise, its vast knowledge base, and its national/international credibility in the field. Areas to emphasize include the following, which will provide the framework upon which to build a consistent fundraising message to secure general operating support:

- Self-produced programming
- Collaborative presenting and coproducing activities
- Educational outreach
- Community outreach and constituency-building activities

These efforts represent the institution's most integrated/comprehensive and long-term commitments, and involve the highest level of expertise and experience. They are the most highly visible/widely recognized, and promise the greatest returns.

With these four projects/initiatives as the lens, efforts among the following constituencies include:

Major Donors:
- Cultivation events in NYC and at major cultural institutions/arts groups across the country
- Accommodation of specific requests (access/special tours, etc.) as a means of securing significant support
- Increased effectiveness of the President's Council, such as:
  o More efficient administration/cultivation of members
  o A reassessment of membership dues to help generate higher returns when measured against program administration
  o Marketing sponsorship from targeted industries with business lines pertinent to the organization's mission

Foundations/Family Foundations:
- Increased research to identify top prospects.
- Increased consistent reporting to enhance relationships with current funders.
- Leverage current foundation relationships to help support other organizational initiatives. Examples:
  o Educational outreach efforts to a specific community partner as complementary to and supportive of other departmental activities
  o Certain existing foundation GOS can be leveraged toward increased and/or new specific project support

Corporate Support:
It is increasingly difficult to identify the organization's mission with the core businesses of national/multinational corporations. (This is the current trend in corporate philanthropy.) Still, it is important to secure support from the corporate sector. Going forward, efforts will concentrate on applications/proposals to business consortia to more efficiently leverage greater funding opportunities. Additionally, greater emphasis will be directed toward corporate membership, with more highly defined benefits that will appeal to corporate employees and help solidify the relationship.

Individual/Membership:
- Increased consistent communication with current constituents: members' newsletter, e-mail blasts/updates
- Regular schedule of membership appeals (fall, spring)
- Regular annual fund appeals: calendar year-end, fiscal year-end
- Members' travel program
- Educational outreach and public programming, such as lectures/cultivation events/receptions. Examples:
  o Special lectures/talks by resident artists and project partners
  o Associations with other like-minded institutions within the community
  o Greater visibility through strategic associations with like-minded institutions across the country

D.   Timeline: 12–16 months

E.   Budget
FY07 Development Plan
Projected Revenue Budget

Earned income

Ticket sales	$1,200,000
Fees and other services	500,000
Investments/Endowment returns, etc.	300,000
Subtotal:	2,000,000

Unearned Income

Trustee giving	700,000
Major Donors	500,000
Individual Giving/Membership	225,000
President's Council	120,000
Foundation support	750,000
Corporate Support	250,000
Special Events (net: gross gala income, less gala expenses)	400,000
Planned Giving	25,000
Government	30,000
Subtotal:	3,000,000
Total:	**$5,000,000**

In Feiner's plan, the goal is to "expand the level of contributed income from all funding sources, with particular emphasis on unrestricted or general operating funds."[27] In other words, he wants to raise the type of funding that can be used for any type of project or expense. There is no restriction placed on the fund by the donor. All organizations need to raise this type of money. As organizations grow, they need to be able to expand their capacity or their "ability to do their work."[28] General operating grants may be used to support capacity-building expenses. Capacity-building income will help the organization build its management and managerial support team (hire new employees) to implement existing programs and create new ones. For example, to get to the next level, the organization may need to increase its donor base. In order to do this, the organization will need to hire a new member of the development department. A capacity-building grant will help the organization meet this goal.

As has been previously stated, the fundraiser raises money from two categories of donors: individual and institutional. In Feiner's annual fund campaign plan, individual donors are comprised of trustees (board members) and major donors, lower-level individual support (membership), and planned-giving support. Institutional support takes the form of corporate and foundation gifts. Although not indicated in Feiner's plan, performing arts organizations also raise money from the government. To reach his objectives, the director of development must determine a strategy for raising money from each type of donor. Strategies include cultivation events for major donors, proposals for corporations and foundations, direct mail and e-mail appeals for the lower-level individual members, and special gala events for both individual and institutional donors.

The strategies must all be programmed in a fundraising calendar or timeline. The fundraising calendar coordinates all dates of fundraising activities and ensures that these dates don't conflict with one another or the organization's calendar. The Minnesota Opera and World Monuments Fund use Blackbaud's The Raiser's Edge software to maintain their fundraising calendar. Dewane and his staff "input due dates for all institutional donor proposals and individual donors above $500."[29] Holden believes that "a comprehensive fundraising calendar should guide all aspects of the fundraising plan for the year," and he cites the important parts of the fundraising calendar:

- Production dates.
- Direct mail drop dates: Ensure that development mailing dates are coordinated with other mailings from the organization to avoid "mail fatigue." If donors receive too many mailings from your company in a short period of time, they may begin to ignore your communications or feel they are less urgent. For example, you wouldn't want to send an annual appeal letter in the same week that the marketing department has flooded many of the same mailboxes with a subscription renewal letter. (However, the subscription letter should also include a request for donations in the renewal form.)
- Special-event dates (including planning meetings): Be sure to check your city's "master events calendar" and call similar organizations to coordinate event dates so you aren't competing for the same pool of patrons on the same evening.
- Every proposal due date, both for the application and for follow-up when appropriate (renewals and new requests).
- Reminders to set up meetings (for introductions and regular check-ins).
- Itemized budget of projections with sources (development report).[30]

Once the calendar is set, the development director can create a development report to track the progress of the development plan. A development report provides a calendar, as well as an itemized budget with contributed income sources and projections. As the development department carries out the plan, it adds the results for each funding source. (Please see appendix A1 for a sample development calendar that lists important dates and sources. Please see appendix A2 for a sample development report.[31])

Once the calendar is set and the report is created, the organization can execute its planned strategies for each type of donor. Let's take a look at Feiner's cultivation strategy for major donors in figure 6.2. In Feiner's example, he uses cultivation events to meet prospective major donors. In other words, he plans events or gatherings where he will be able to meet donors who have the ability to fund his organization, but haven't given yet. These donors are invited to a special party where they have an opportunity to meet the director of development and the board to discuss the organization, its purpose, and its needs. Donors are not asked for money during a cultivation event. After the major donors have been "cultivated," they will be asked for money during a scheduled meeting by the appropriate person or team of individuals.

How does Feiner know whom to invite to this particular type of cultivation event? The answer is simple: research. It is in performing the necessary research that Feiner determines who may qualify as a major donor to his institution, as well as what the major donor's motivations are for giving to the organization. In researching potential major donors, Feiner might ask his board of directors to recommend potential friends or colleagues who might be interested in attending the event. Why would a friend or colleague of a trustee want to attend? Donors give for all types of reasons. Perhaps the potential donor is interested in the World Monuments Fund's good works, or perhaps he feels it's important to support his friend's charity as a gesture of friendship or obligation. Whatever the motivation, the director of development must conduct the necessary research to determine the type of funder and her motivation for giving.

Based on this information, the director of development can devise the correct timeline for hosting the event, as well as the appropriate strategy for approaching the donor. The director of development must also craft a scripted pitch or a conversation between the person requesting the donation and the prospective donor. The fundraiser must then determine the proper follow-up after the pitch for support has been made. Finally, if the World Monuments Fund receives a donation from a major donor, the director of development must aptly acknowledge the gift with a personal call or meeting, as well as a letter.

All donors, whether individual or institutional, must be researched so that their motivations for giving are determined, an approach strategy is devised, a pitch is created, follow-up is implemented, and an acknowledgement of the donation is provided. All of this information is stored on donor history files and tracked. Computer software programs such as The Raiser's Edge allow a performing organization to "capture biographic information, giving history, and telephone call reports, as well as note relationships and affiliations."[32] Both the Minnesota Opera and Alvin Ailey American Dance Theater use The Raiser's Edge to keep donor records and to track donor responses and attrition rates (the number of donors who do not renew).

New York City Center uses Tessitura. "Tessitura is an integrated fundraising and ticket inventory system with an advanced Internet interface that allows for online ticket sales. The system was developed by the Metropolitan Opera (where it is called Impressario). The Met has licensed the technology to a consortium of performing arts nonprofit organizations, including New York City Center. The consortium now markets Tessitura independently and has created a nationwide network of software clients who regularly meet to jointly implement system improvements in functionality and ease of use. Tessitura captures all important donor information—name, address(es), all family members and their associations, pertinent educational and personal data—and, of course, all giving history and types of contributions: cash and/or cash equivalents, matching gifts, pledges, bequests, etc."[33]

An important part of research is the ability to track the donors' response rates. Feiner states, "The development department tracks every donor contribution and all contact with the donor: all appeals, invitations to events, personalized solicitations, regret contributions [not able to make a contribution], etc. The database is structured to capture all data in appropriate categories that can be quickly sorted for reporting purposes. Attrition rates are tracked by detailed analysis year-to-year of individual and institutional donor records; the development department verifies when a donor misses a regular contribution, and it flags that record [donor] as 'lapsed.' A lapsed donor is a donor who has given in the past, but has not given recently. If a proposal to a foundation or corporation is rejected, the development officer responsible for the request, or perhaps some more senior member of the staff, will follow up with the donor in an attempt to understand why the proposal was rejected."[34]

Finally, maintaining excellent donor records involves also keeping hard files on each donor. Dewane emphasizes this point. "Computers crash, data gets erased, and viruses happen. Also, donors often ask for hard copies of solicitation letters, checks, thank-you letters, and proposals. They want a copy of the original, not something printed that day off of your hard drive. Plus, the people over forty will always feel more comfortable pulling out a hard copy of a solicitation or thank-you note."[35]

CLASSROOM DISCUSSION

What are the major components of a fundraising plan?

In the World Monuments Fund's fundraising plan, what types of funders are being targeted?

Why does Richard Feiner want to raise general operating support?

What are capacity-building expenses?

What types of strategies will Feiner use to raise money from each funding source (see fig. 6.2)?

Why is it important to have a fundraising calendar and development report?

What dates should be included in a fundraising calendar and development report?

What is a cultivation event?

How does a performing arts organization research prospective major donors?

Why is it necessary to research your prospective donors?

Why is it necessary to understand the motivation of a donor?

What should a donor record capture?

Why is tracking necessary?

What does attrition mean?

Why is it important to generate hard files on donors and prospective donors?

INDIVIDUAL AND INSTITUTIONAL GIVING

With a great fundraising plan in place, the organization is now ready to approach individual and institutional donors. The next section introduces individual and institutional contributors and the strategies for approaching them.

Individual Giving: Major Gifts

Amanda Nelson, deputy director of development, individual giving and government support for the Alvin Ailey American Dance Theater, explains that major gifts "may be an annual gift, or a gift for a special campaign (a capital or endowment campaign), or a planned gift. How a major gift is defined, or in other words, the level of giving that is defined as 'major,' may differ between a small nonprofit organization and a large organization. While the term 'major gift' may vary in definition, the 'ask' [request] will be shaped to meet the interests and needs of both the organization and the individual prospect.

"A major gift is more likely to come from a donor who has, or who has over time, had a relationship with the organization. In other words, a major donor could be a board member, a subscriber to your organization, or even someone who has made relatively small contributions over time to your annual fund campaign. And, while we categorize a major donor as an individual donor, in some organizations, major donors can also be corporate, foundation, and government agencies that contribute a certain amount of money. Both the board and the director of development will play a role in researching the types of individuals who will qualify as major donors." [36]

Researching Major Donors

Richard Feiner believes that "major donor research is very important and difficult. It requires a myriad of resources; a nonprofit organization should accept help from various sources, including, most importantly, referrals from trustees. Basic and consistent research should always inform the nonprofit manager's search for potential new major donors. It should never be the board's sole responsibility to identify and solicit prospects. It is part of the development department's charge to identify prospects and to bring the names of major donors to the attention of the board. Online research tools are valuable, as are newspapers, trade journals/ newspapers/newsletters, alumni newsletters, and other written sources. The best way to determine the interests of major donor prospects is to ascertain what they currently fund; where they went to school and their major academic interests; what other nonprofits they are involved with; what boards they participate in, etc. Any information is appropriate and can help identify a potential entryway that could lead to a discussion." [37]

Dewane uses this approach to research major donors. "I identify major donors by getting to know trust officers in banks and financial services companies; introducing myself to people who are wealthy and philanthropic; networking with other development directors; reading the business section and the society columns; talking to other donors; reading the lists of donors of similar organizations and looking for the overlap; identifying particularly generous individuals and creating a cultivation plan for them; getting to know the people who buy the premium seats; and getting to know people who have given consistently over many years.

"The best research is to meet someone and to get them talking about themselves. This is where a development director needs to take initiative and not be afraid of failure. It is also an area in which good people skills are very important. You must be a good listener, be able to carry on a conversation on a wide array of topics, be able to build genuine trust and rapport, and know how to identify someone's values. Also, the Internet is a phenomenal tool for researching donors. Google alone is able to get information that used to take a week for a researcher to acquire. However, getting to know someone is the absolute best way to learn someone's motivations and interests." [38]

Directors of development should heed Dewane's advice concerning the power of the Internet in researching potential major gifts. Fundraisers are using e-mail alert services, such as those offered by Yahoo (*alerts.yahoo.com*), Google (*www.google. com/alerts*), 10k Wizard (*www.10kwizard.com*), and EDGAR Online (*www.edgar-online.com*), to track a potential donor's "career changes, compensation, and positions on corporate boards. Such details can help strengthen ties with major donors, as well as figure out when best to approach them and how much to ask for."[39]

The Approach and Pitch

In approaching major donors, Nelson offers this sound advice: "The following key questions may help you determine the prospect's level of commitment to or interest in your organization: Has the prospect come to see your organization perform? Has she visited your facility? Has she participated in a program or come to an event? If not, based upon what you know of a prospect's giving history to other organizations or causes, or even her personal hobbies, would she be interested in becoming involved with your organization? As development officers, it is our job to find something in or about our organization that 'speaks' to the prospect, to find a way to reach her, to connect with her. You want to build a relationship between the prospect and the organization. Because a personal or professional connection to a prospective donor is often key in 'opening the door' to an introduction, I suggest asking board members if they know the prospect (either professionally or personally)."[40]

In approaching his major donors, Dewane maintains, "You need to understand their values and how your organization overlaps with their values. The more personalized the approach, the better. Someone needs to know or get to know the prospect. This can happen with a series of 'moves,' cultivation activities that are planned to help bring a prospect closer to the organization. The development director needs to orchestrate the 'moves' and determine when and how the approach should be made."[41]

In making a pitch to a major donor, Dewane believes that "the person with the strongest relationship generally should make the pitch. However, in some cases families have rules that family members do not solicit one another, and coworker relationships or business-partner relationships can also complicate solicitations. The development director needs to orchestrate the pitch. And often the development director is the best person to make the pitch. That is why it is important for the development director to be building relationships. The same is true for the head of the organization.

The key components are compelling answers to the two vital questions—why do you need the money, and why do you need this amount of money? You also need to make it clear what the timetable is and what next steps need to be taken."[42]

In determining who should be present at the meeting to make the pitch, Nelson notes that "who participates in the pitch depends on 'who' the prospect is. It may be appropriate for a member of the board to be present, or for the executive director or the development officer to participate."[43]

Feiner feels that the "director of development should always defer to the trustees as to who makes the pitch and how it is to be conducted. A pitch to a major donor should always be set up correctly. The conditions and situation for the pitch need to be right (at a dinner, at the intermission of a performance), and it usually takes many months of careful cultivation. Or it might come about quite suddenly. I once worked with a major donor who decided to become highly active after a single lunchtime meeting."[44]

Holden provides these key suggestions when approaching a major donor for support:

- It's best if the request originates from a peer (fellow board member or donor of similar stature). Development staff should, of course, play a crucial supporting role.
- The request should be made in person.
- Provide the prospect with a tangible result of his gift where he can take ownership.
- Fully describe the project he will be supporting.
- Outline other sources of support for the same need—where does the prospect fit into the big picture?
- Describe how you can recognize his support. Can you name a program after the prospect? Name a lounge? Will a gift of this level entitle him to an elite level of the patrons' program [donor benefits]?
- How will you measure the success of the project? How will it change/enhance your mission?
- Bring written materials that outline the project and contain answers to all the questions you can anticipate from the prospective donor. These materials might include:
  - Narrative project summary
  - Detailed budgets
  - Schematic designs/drawings (for capital projects)

o General background information on the organization

- If the prospect does not immediately commit to a gift, don't pressure him for an answer immediately—respect the fact that a major gift is a big decision. Close the meeting by letting the prospect know that the peer solicitor will follow up with him soon; ensure that the peer solicitor follows through.[45]

Follow-up and Acknowledgement

After the pitch is made, the director of development must follow up. The director of development will ask the person connected to the donor (executive director, board member) to follow up as well. Dewane follows up with personal notes and phone calls. He will schedule a follow-up meeting, if necessary. He adds, "You should send your note immediately after the initial meeting. There are no hard and fast rules for the follow-up timetable, as some donors are touchy while others need to be pushed. Know your audience, but make errors of commission rather than omission. Timidity loses gifts."[46] Feiner offers this advice: "As each cultivation case is unique, there are no set guidelines toward follow-up and/ or a schedule of repeat cultivation. Often, there will not be any tangible return on investments in major donor cultivation for many months, even years. The nonprofit organization must be willing to bide its time and entrust faith in the development department's efforts."[47]

And finally, an acknowledgement of the gift must be made. Feiner requests that "the person who initiated the contact with a major donor provides an acknowledgement letter. The nonprofit organization's president also can issue a thank-you letter, as well as the chairman and/or other trustees, depending on who knows the new major donor."[48] These acknowledgement letters should include the amount of the donation and the suggested IRS language about the tax deductibility of the donation.

CLASSROOM DISCUSSION

What is a major gift?

What type of donor gives a major gift?

How do you go about researching potential major donors?

How do you go about approaching a major donor for a gift?

Who makes the pitch and what are the key components of a pitch to a major donor?

Who follows up with a major donor and how is this done?

Who should acknowledge the gift?

Individual Giving: Membership Programs

Membership or patrons' programs are developed as a strategy for raising annual gifts from individuals. According to Feiner, "a patrons' or membership program is a series of distinct benefits that the individual donor receives in recognition of a contribution. The benefits are specific to giving level, with each level adding value as the donor's financial commitment increases. Each level of benefits builds upon the previous level so that the top level includes the highest number of benefits and provides the greatest 'bang' for the donor's 'buck.'"[49] Nelson describes the membership program at Ailey: "The 'Friends of Alvin Ailey' (which starts at $75) and 'Ailey Partners' (which starts at $1,250) have a variety of giving levels with corresponding member benefits. Members are also given the opportunity to earmark their gift to support a particular program that is important to them; for example: new works, scholarships, or arts-in-education and community programs."[50]

Members receive benefits ranging from advance notice of performances and priority seating to invitations to exclusive receptions, depending on the contribution level of support. Feiner notes that benefits programs play a key role in motivating the donor to give. "Membership benefits are of varying use in helping secure funding from various campaigns. Generally, major donors are less interested in actual membership benefits than they are in knowing that their contributions are providing value funding for specific programs or for overall general support. However, the lower-level individual donor is very interested in benefits and usually takes each benefit very seriously in any consideration of increased funding. Well-defined membership benefits that are perceived to be of real value are highly important in securing funding from lower-level patrons."[51]

Members are solicited through a direct mail appeal, a telefunding campaign, an online appeal, or a combination of all three. In addition to these solicitation methods, program inserts and subscription brochures also give the individual donor an opportunity to become a member and give to the annual fund.[52]

Direct Mail Appeal: Research and Determining Motivations

"A direct mail appeal is a targeted mailing to: a group of prospective donors who have never given before (acquisitions); a group of donors who gave in the past, but are not current donors (lapsed donors); or membership renewals. 'Targeted' is the key word.

It is important to carefully identify who on your available mailing lists will be most likely to respond to a particular mailing or solicitation, such as those who have a connection with your organization (a ticket buyer or an alumnus). At Ailey, ticket buyers from across the country are a key mailing segment [a target group] that ensures a successful acquisition campaign. An acquisition mailing may also include: people who signed up to be on a mailing list; those who requested information about the organization (by written request, e-mail, or phone); and those who are affiliated with the organization in some other way, like through a class, an event, or an outreach program."[53]

Once Amanda Nelson has targeted her potential new acquisitions, lapsed donors, and renewals, mailing lists are generated. She explains, "Expanding a mailing list for an acquisition appeal is key to broadening your base. One way to develop and expand mailing lists is name collection; you should collect the names and addresses of audience members, visitors to your facility, participants in programs and events, and visitors to your Web site.

"For a large direct mail campaign, a mail house can manage lists, print letters, mail envelopes, and even assist you in tracking your campaign. The mail house can print a code on the response mechanism (the code is assigned by mailing segment) so that we can track response rates."[54]

Determining a donor's motivations can help the fundraiser compose the proper appeal letter for the direct mail campaign. Nelson and Feiner agree that associations with the organization, and the types of benefits received, will motivate donors to give. Donors may also give when there is a challenge or matching gift given; if the nonprofit organization notes in the appeal letter that for every dollar donated, a private source (an individual or corporate donor) will match the grant, this may serve to motivate the donor to give to the annual fund campaign. According to a survey conducted by Campbell Rinker, donors who give less than $500 dollars are "more likely to be turned off by overly elaborate appeals and by charities that solicited them too frequently." Donors who give more than $500 are "more likely to stop giving if they are not treated as partners by the charities they support." In addition, the research suggests that "emergency appeals often suggest management or financial problems and 'must be carefully thought out.'" Finally, the research firm advises against using "'guilt-inducing appeals' [and coupling] a thank-you message with a repeat solicitation."[55]

Motivating an annual funder to give for the first time, to give again, or to give an increased gift is a challenge. Nelson reasons, "I think at one time or another most of us have responded to a direct mail campaign. The 'why' we respond one time and not another is the question and, I suppose, the key to a successful campaign. Perhaps the appeal compels the recipient to respond from an emotional connection to the materials (for example, an image of smiling children participating in a dance class) or to the issue seeking support (e.g., providing food or shelter for Hurricane Katrina victims or impoverished children). Or maybe the appeal elicits an intellectual response suggesting a rationale for the importance of the prospective donor's support to the particular cause (e.g., environmental protection and global warming). Or perhaps it is the member benefits or special gifts offered that are the impetus for a donation.

"In addition to bringing new donors into the fold, we also want to motivate our renewing donors to increase their giving. In a renewal appeal, it's important to remind the donor of the level that they gave last year, then explain how an increased gift can make a significant difference to a particular element or program of your organization. Use specific examples to illustrate what the donor's dollars can and will do. Remind the donor that her contribution will help effect change. (Some donors do increase their gifts for the expanded benefits that they will receive at a higher membership level.)

"Employee matching gift programs can be a simple way to increase a donor's gift. In other words, if I give $50 to an organization, my company might give $50, $100, or $150 to that organization as well. Matching gifts can be key to a successful campaign drive."[56]

Ultimately, it is the appeal letter and its message that will resonate with the donor, compelling her to make the donation. Feiner explains, "The direct emotional appeal must emphasize a compelling 'human story,' such as a little boy who now dreams of a career as a professional dancer because he attended a special school matinee produced by the theater; or a more quantitative recounting of the growth in the nonprofit organization's capacity to effect positive change in the community due to its programming. Both scenarios present success stories and imply that future increased giving on the funder's part will help ensure this upward trend."[57] In the next section, we will explore the components of the annual fund appeal letter.

CLASSROOM DISCUSSION

What is a membership program?

How are members solicited?

What is a direct mail appeal?

What does targeting mean?

Define these terms: "new acquisition mailing," "lapsed donor," and "renewal."

What is the process for creating a mailing list?

Why should an organization use a mail house?

Why is it important to determine an individual donor's motivations for giving?

What motivates a new donor to give? What turns a donor off?

What motivates a donor to increase her gift?

What is a challenge grant?

What is an employee matching gift program?

Direct Mail: The Appeal Letter

Development professionals agree that the appeal letter should be short and to the point, preferably no more than a page. Nelson begins, "We've experimented, like many organizations, with both the length and layout of the letter. We use bullet points and bolding to highlight the key points. We generally include recent accomplishments of the organization, as well as current and future projects, and clearly state what action we want the prospective donor to take (for example: renewing a membership or making a special gift).

"Finding creative ways to 'stand out' among the many appeal letters in the prospective donors' mailboxes is also important. A special message may be printed on the outside of the envelope to catch people's attention and encourage them to open the letter. For example, 'Learn more about how Ailey makes a difference in the lives of thousands of young people and how you can help.' Or, 'We were named one of the best 100 charities by *Worth Magazine*."[58]

According to Feiner, "The appeal letter should stress the unique programs and defining characteristics of the nonprofit organization and, importantly, a specific challenge that must be met. The letter should define a pressing need that will help compel a donor to give. The letter should be one page, two-sided if necessary. The copy should be substantive, yet pithy; it should make its points in punchy language that is easily understood. The letter should be signed by the nonprofit organization's president, although research has shown that the actual signature makes no real impact. The recipient understands that the signature on an appeal letter is an electronic version of the real signature. The following should accompany the appeal letter: a reply mechanism, a reply envelope (often preposted by the nonprofit organization at a special rate), and, if possible, a brochure or other promotional piece that conveys a visually compelling image of the nonprofit organization."[59]

John Holden contends that the appeal letter's pitch should do the following:

- Speak directly to the reader.
- Start with exciting news.
- Directly ask for a contribution.
- If possible, provide a specific incentive to give, such as a matching grant that will double (triple, etc.) the impact of the donor's gift.
- Describe exactly what his help will allow you to do.
- If you have a patrons' program, describe the benefits available to them for contributing.
- Highlight important elements with bold, italics, etc. (within reason).
- Keep it short—no more than one page.
- Sign in ink if possible and write a short note ("Your support will be invaluable!").
- Enclose a reply envelope (business reply if possible).
- If you're claiming every dollar counts, don't include an expensive 4-color brochure; use those brochures for high-end solicitations only.
- Hand stamp the envelope if possible.[60]

Let's take a look at two sample appeal letters on page 183 (figs. 6.3 and 6.4).[61]

After the appeal letter is written, when is the best time of the year for an organization to mail it? Nelson explains that "many people give during the last quarter of the year. People are thinking about the holidays (a time for giving) and the end of the tax year (and tax deductions for donations made to charitable organizations).

"With so much in our mailboxes (both at home and in our e-mail in-boxes), donor mail fatigue can be a real challenge to the many organizations soliciting the same people for funds. Mail fatigue occurs when an individual gets so much mail from organizations soliciting donations that she stops reading what is sent to her. Solicitations need to be carefully crafted and coordinated to ensure effectiveness and to limit donor mail fatigue.

"When creating a timetable for implementing a membership appeal, I generally allow two weeks to create my letters, decide on enclosures (e.g., brochures), and segment the mailing lists. Once all

Date
Addressee
Address
Address

Dear Salutation,

I wanted to take this opportunity to personally thank you for your continued support of the XYZ organization. **Your commitment as an *XYZ Friend* has helped us to accomplish so much!**
  • Over the summer, the XYZ took Europe by storm with three months of **sold-out performances**.
  • A record **500 inner-city children** participated in the XYZ summer program.
  • **An exciting new work will premiere** during XYZ's upcoming season.

Our performances and programs have been made possible because of the generosity of dedicated *Friends* like you.
Your membership in the ***Friends of XYZ*** program has recently expired. Please take a moment now to *renew* your membership with us. A brochure has been enclosed for your convenience.
Your gift will make a **real** difference:
  • $150 will enable an underserved student to take 12 classes at The XYZ School.
  • $300 will allow 50 inner-city children to see an XYZ performance for free.
  • $600 will cover the costs for an XYZ public school residency.

Your continued support is truly appreciated.

Sincerely,

Sally Smith
Artistic Director
XYZ Organization

Fig. 6.3. Sample Renewal Letter

Date

Dear *Friend*,
Each year the XYZ organization reaches nearly half a million people across the globe. On stage, our performers enthrall audiences through electrifying performances. In our school, professional teachers offer exceptional training to students. In the community and schools, XYZ organization works to enrich the lives of young people through innovative outreach and community programs.

In order to continue to develop and expand XYZ's artistic, cultural, and educational programs for people around the world and those just around the block, we need your help!

It is with great pleasure that I invite you to become a part of the XYZ family by joining the ***Friends of XYZ***. A membership brochure is enclosed for your convenience.

Ticket sales cover only a portion of our budget needs. We depend on contributions from Friends like you to continue and to expand our programs. Your gift will make a **real** difference:
  • $150 will enable an underserved student to take 12 classes at The XYZ School.
  • $300 will allow 50 inner-city children to see an XYZ performance for free.
  • $600 will cover the costs for an XYZ public school residency.
Aside from the joy of knowing that you've made a difference, your donation will give you *exclusive benefits* as a member of the *Friends of XYZ*, such as advance notice and priority seating, a subscription to our newsletter, and special member-only events.

Sincerely,

Sally Smith
Artistic Director
XYZ Organization

Fig. 6.4. Sample New Acquisition Letter

materials are provided to the mail house, it takes approximately three to five business days for the mailing to be sent out.

"It is important to track costs as well as income in evaluating a direct mail campaign. Mail house costs, printing, and postage can vary widely depending on the materials used and the number of appeals mailed. In terms of postage costs, the weight of the envelope and the class of mail will determine expenses for a particular mailing. Costs may be preliminarily evaluated by a ratio of cost to estimated revenue, and then adjusted when the campaign is concluded, creating the final evaluation of the ratio of cost of mailing to actual income (donations) attributed to the mailing."[62]

What kind of response rate should an organization expect and what is the rate of return on investment? Feiner reveals, "Ideally, a return rate of between 1.5 and 2 percent is normal for a new acquisitions campaign. It is hoped that a positive response rate of at least 70 percent will make the renewal campaign targeting current donors pay for the direct mail campaign. A direct mail campaign should not cost more than $0.40 of the dollar expended."[63] In fact, Nelson tries to keep costs below $0.20 on the dollar ($0.20 spent per $1 raised).[64]

Direct Mail: Follow-up and Acknowledgement

Follow-up is an important part of the direct mail appeal process. Nelson explains that "it may take three mailings, or three points of contact with your organization, before a prospect makes a gift. Successful direct mail is an ongoing process; you must refresh your approach, your letters, your style, and your brochures. Every two to three years, we redesign our brochures so that they have a new look and feel."[65]

Feiner believes that "most nonprofit organizations are too restricted in time-management pressures to follow up with any additional embellishments to a direct mail campaign. However, it is still important to take the time to update donor records with corrected address information, should there be a return of undeliverable mail pieces.

Follow-up from a direct mail campaign, if there is additional contact, should begin roughly four to six weeks after the drop of the mail pieces."[66] Holden recommends that the second letter lets the prospective donor know that the incentive outlined in the first letter is about to expire. He recommends that the letter reports on the campaign goal and its progress, as well as letting the prospective donor know how much his gift will mean in reaching the goal.[67]

Of course, all gifts, no matter what the size, are acknowledged. Feiner instructs, "Gifts are acknowledged with a letter, signed either by the development director or the nonprofit organization's president, that includes pertinent tax information for the donor. Often, for a major gift or a significant increase, the president should issue his/her own acknowledgement letter. There should be a forty-eight hour maximum turnaround time to acknowledge the donation."[68] Nelson agrees: "At Ailey, we are committed to acknowledging gifts from our donors as quickly as possible. Usually within two or three days (but no longer than a week), an acknowledgement has been written and sent to the donor.

"When possible, thank-you letters should be highly personalized, reflecting the level of the gift, as well as the area or program supported by the donation. For example, if the donor earmarked her gift for a particular fund or campaign, or if she is responding to a special campaign, the thank-you letter should reflect these points. When a donor makes a major gift, I think it is important to acknowledge the donation with both a personal note (perhaps from the executive director or the artistic director) and a second, more formal letter that contains a thank-you, as well as the required IRS language about the tax deductibility of the gift."[69]

An example of a thank-you letter is shown on page 185 (fig. 6.5).[70]

Please note that the Internal Revenue Service requires that donors obtain written acknowledgements stating the amount of the donation and the goods or services received for that amount. For a detailed description of this provision, please see chapter 3.

CLASSROOM DISCUSSION

How long should an appeal letter be? Why?

Why is it important to use bullet points and bolding in the letter?

What should the appeal letter stress? Who should sign it and why?

What should accompany the letter?

Create an appeal letter.

When is the best time to send out an appeal and why?

What is the timetable for sending out a mailing?
    When creating a timetable, what do you need to consider?

What response rate should you expect for new acquisitions and renewals?

What is mail fatigue?

What expenses do you need to consider when creating a mailing?

Fig. 6.5. New Dramatists Appeal Thank-You Letter

Date

Name
Address
City, State, ZIP

Dear Name,

Thank you for your generous contribution of $5,000. Your support will help New Dramatists to continue our multifaceted support of many of America's finest playwrights.

Support for individual artists is becoming more vital as it becomes rarer. This has caused us to appreciate, even more, our unfettered and simple mission to provide writers with an artistic home for seven years, free of charge. Of course, this is only possible because of your support.

New Dramatists is stronger than ever as we enter our 56th year. The playwrights are active and engaged, feeding the American theatre with a steady stream of new work. Meanwhile, we have continued to prove that careful management can maximize the effect of the generous gifts such as yours. We continue to operate with a balanced budget, have paid off the mortgage on our building, and continue to expand our writer development programs.

Again, thank you for helping to make it all possible.

Best regards,

Joel K. Ruark
Executive Director

In accordance with IRS guidelines concerning charitable contributions, this letter acknowledges that you received no goods or services in exchange for your gift of $5,000 on check # dated _____. Therefore, the entire amount of your contribution is tax deductible.

What are the components of an acknowledgement letter?

Write an acknowledgement letter.

When and how should you follow up a direct mail campaign? What should a follow-up letter include?

Telefundraising and Online Fundraising

As a follow-up strategy to direct mail, or as an additional method of reaching new, lapsed, and committed donors, performing arts organizations will often conduct telefundraising and online fundraising campaigns. Let's take a closer look at each fundraising strategy.

Telefundraising: Research and Determining Donor Motivations

According to Dewane, "A telefundraising campaign is a concerted effort to raise funds over the tele-phone. The calls can be made to past donors or donor prospects. The calls can be made by staff, trained professionals, or by volunteers."[71] Dewane uses a professional telefundraising company (SD&A Teleservices, Inc.) to conduct the telefundraising campaign. In the following section, Dewane shares his strategy for researching and motivating donors to give to this type of campaign. Thanks to the generosity of SD&A Teleservices, we have included a copy of the telefundraising strategy in appendix B1 of this chapter.

In the previous section, we spoke about targeting potential donors for support, as well as generating support from donors who give on an ongoing basis. How do performing arts organizations target donors for a telefundraising campaign? Performing arts organizations will use direct mail lists with telephone numbers. Dewane reveals, "The Opera is a small enough organization that we are basically calling everyone we know. That includes renewals, lapsed donors, single-ticket buyers, subscribers, and prospects.

"We run individual lists from our marketing database (e.g., single-ticket buyers to *Carmen*) and our donor database (lapsed donors since 2003), then send them to a marketing firm that specializes in list management. This firm runs a 'merge-purge' (combining all the lists and deleting duplicate records) and a 'phone append' (the compiled list is run against the phone book) on the lists. They then print each name and phone number on a separate page (called a 'lead'), which is used by the caller to record calling activity. This is an expensive process, but because we can't handle managing the lists in-house, we are left with little choice."[72] An example of a prospect sheet, which lists the names of the prospects and the requested donation amount, is on page 187 (fig. 6.6).[73]

Sounds easy, right? There are problems with calling people at home. Dewane asserts, "Certain people do not like to be called at home, especially to be asked for money. Others distrust the solicitor on the other end of the line and will not give a credit card or even make a pledge (a verbal or written promise of a gift) over the phone. Many people simply think phoning for gifts is in poor taste.

"Although there is no prototype for a 'good' telefundraising donor, the generalization seems to be that the younger and more sympathetic the audience, the better their response to telefundraising. Also, well-intentioned, but perhaps forgetful, donors appreciate receiving a call to remind them to make their gift. So it's important to segment the list by age. Sympathetic donors include audience members and previous donors.

"What else can be done to make the calling easier? Before a telefundraising campaign begins, donors with a history of giving at that time of year should receive a mailing. This gets the 'easy gifts' out of the way, and leaves the 'tougher sells' to the telefunders. During the campaign it makes sense to continue to mail to donors, but not donors who are getting a call from telefundraisers. In a small organization like the Minnesota Opera, the number of people eligible for mail solicits is very slim. We keep larger Community Donors (those who give $200 to $999) out of telefundraising and have them solicited by the president or a board member."[74]

What motivates a donor to give on the phone? Direct mail donors respond to benefits. Dewane offers this insight: "While I wouldn't give a perk or benefit to a renewal who simply made a pledge, I would offer perks that encourage individuals to renew via credit card; these perks increase the success of telefundraising campaigns by securing a higher quantity of gifts on the spot, reducing the amount of follow-up mail and the number of unfulfilled pledges. In our current campaign, donors who give via credit card over the phone receive a free season preview CD.

"However, while such benefits do confirm the gift at the time of the call, this strategy unfortunately rewards donors for using their credit card rather than for increasing their contribution. The benefit is aligned with the type of transaction rather than the level of support, and you run the organizational risk of losing money on a perk that didn't bring in an increased gift.

"Giving benefits to first-time donors, even if they only pledge, is slightly different. New-acquisition calls are very hard, and it's easier to renew a donor than to get a first-time gift. Therefore, giving benefits to those who give for the first time through telefundraising—even if they only make a pledge—can be a great strategy to increase acquisition dollars."[75]

Donors are also motivated by challenge or matching grants. Dewane explains, "We currently have a 50 percent matching grant from the Bush Foundation that applies to new and increased gifts. I think matching gifts are the untapped goldmine of individual giving. Donors who take the time to inform us that they qualify for employee matching gifts are the donors we track for matching. Including a line in a telefundraising script encouraging people to 'explore whether your employer matches gifts' is a great way to cultivate matching gifts. Also, doing a mailing to all current donors might help encourage people to inquire about matching gifts at work."[76]

CLASSROOM DISCUSSION

How does a performing arts organization target donors for a telefundraising campaign?

What can be done to support the telefundraising process before the campaign begins?

What motivates a new acquisition or a renewal to give on the phone?

Telefundraising: The Script and the Process

As we discussed, a great appeal letter is important for raising money through direct mail. In the case of telefundraising, a script given to telefundraisers can make or break a campaign. Dewane emphasizes, "The script should stress the organization's strengths; that is, the strengths that sell the organization at the

Fig. 6.6. Minnesota Opera Prospect Sheet

Opera at the Ordway - Three Year Strategy

Year One - $1,000,000 to be matched 2:1

Individual Prospects

John Fidler	$50,000
Tom Michaels	$100,000
Tim Gadzinski	$25,000
Dave Leschke	$50,000
Ann Reinbold	$50,000
Jill Kessenich	$25,000
Tim Skelton	$250,000
John Stelzer	$50,000
Jean Corrigan	$25,000
Amy Brennan	$250,000
Mark Grabowski	$25,000
Zilton Neves	$250,000
Sue Rasmusson	$25,000
Kathy Kersten	$25,000
Kevin Noskowiak	$25,000
John Tringalli	$25,000
John Stelzer	$25,000
Kathy Papineau	$25,000
Erin Marrs	$100,000
Jane Winans	$100,000
Mike Trainor	$25,000
Steve Brandl	$25,000
Rich Wingo	$25,000
Artie Green	$25,000
Mark Brouhard	$25,000
Jim Karrmann	$25,000
Dave Pleier	$25,000
Sandy Ottoman	$100,000
Dan Devine	$25,000
Dean Senglaub	$50,000
Steve Paiser	$25,000
Dan Siehr	$25,000
Will Hewer	$100,000
TOTAL INDIVIDUALS	**$2,000,000**

Corporate and Foundation Prospects

The Holschbach Family Foundation	$ 100,000
Manitowoc Industries	$ 100,000
The Susan Ross Fund	$ 25,000
Henderson and Kite	$ 75,000
Verdick Communications	$ 100,000
Hewson Corporate Foundation	$ 30,000
Thatcher, Smith and Wilson	$ 50,000
Bergman Consolidated	$ 50,000
Chiloe Corporation	$ 100,000
The Matthias Fund	$ 25,000
Klenci Power and Light	$ 50,000
The Andre Patrick Foundation	$ 250,000
The Edina Foundation	$ 200,000
TOTAL CORP AND FOUND	**$ 1,155,000**
COMBINED TOTAL	**$3,155,000**

Opera at the Ordway - Three Year Strategy

Year Two - $1,000,000 to be matched 2:1

Individual Prospects

Mitch Williams	$250,000
Mark Smith	$50,000
Leslie White	$25,000
George True	$25,000
Matt Bench	$25,000
Robert Nabotoff	$25,000
Susan Michaels	$25,000
Norman Brown	$25,000
Jennifer O'Hara	$25,000
Linda DeMaris	$50,000
Charles Stein	$25,000
Christie Page	$100,000
Eric Butler	$25,000
Sam Ross	$25,000
TOTAL INDIVIDUALS	**$700,000**

Corporate and Foundation Prospects

McKenna Foundation	$ 50,000
Stamm Corporation	$ 50,000
The Earin Fund	$ 25,000
Delaney and Sons	$ 500,000
Tyler Wireless	$ 500,000
Mitchell Foundation	$ 25,000
Grace Corporation Foundation	$ 50,000
Moates Foundation	$ 100,000
Orange Communications	$ 50,000
Marcus, Smith, and Lang	$ 25,000
Starks Foundation	$ 100,000
TOTAL CORP AND FOUND	**$ 1,475,000**
COMBINED TOTAL	**$2,175,000**

Opera at the Ordway - Three Year Strategy

Year Three - $2,000,000 to be matched 2:1

Individual Prospects

Lisa Coons	$25,000
Mary Schultz	$25,000
Mark Hammack	$25,000
Lynn Wright	$25,000
Bill Insalco	$25,000
Edward Ferrer	$25,000
Isabel Kugler	$250,000
Morgan Box	$100,000
Jennifer Mobel	$25,000
Anna Jones	$100,000
Earl Collins	$25,000
Susan Connell	$25,000
Michael Hudson	$250,000
Heather Walsh	$25,000
Philip Shapiro	$25,000
Robert Maik	$25,000
John McGlothlin	$50,000
Eric Thomas	$250,000
Richard North	$25,000
Ashley St. James	$50,000
Melissa Green	$25,000
Lisa Johnson	$50,000
TOTAL INDIVIDUALS	**$1,450,000**

Corporate and Foundation Prospects

Neptune Corporation	$ 250,000
The Jones Family Foundation	$ 50,000
Ross Communications	$ 250,000
Stine Industries	$ 100,000
Drager Corporation	$ 50,000
Butler and Smith	$ 100,000
City Industries	$ 100,000
Wexler Foundation	$ 50,000
TOTAL CORP AND FOUND	**$ 950,000**
COMBINED TOTAL	**$2,400,000**

time. If you have a matching grant, stress the grant. If you're changing output (more performances, for example), that fact is worth stressing. If you've recently received extraordinary press, stress that. In the end, the script is your commercial, so market your product as best you can in a thirty-second sound bite."[77]

Dewane illustrates the important components of an effective fundraising script:

THE SCRIPT: Tell a good story. Donors give, in part, because they understand the organization's need. The greater the intensity of the need, the more likely a donor is to give. In an annual fund campaign, the needs are generally the same year after year, but the story can change. Telling a compelling story and showing donors what their money can DO for the organization is a great motivational tool for securing increased support. Some organizations correlate giving levels to "what your money can buy" in order to put gifts into perspective (e.g., "With your $50, we can save one tree.").

THE BENEFITS: Make sure the next level of donor benefits is compelling. The basic premise is that people will give more if they get more in return, and a major motivator to secure increased gifts is to make the next giving level appealing. At The Opera, donors receive two concert tickets for donating at the $50 level and an additional two dress-rehearsal passes for donating at the $100 level, which motivates many donors to step up to the $100 level. We've also done special deals in which, if donors give in the final stretch of the campaign, they can receive $1,000-level benefits for a $500 gift. Hopefully, once they start giving at the $500 level, their support will remain at that level.

MATCHES AND CHALLENGES: Make the donor's gift count extra. Whether it's a foundation matching grant or an anonymous donor who has put up a fundraising challenge, people are more willing to give their money when the organization is able to increase the value of that contribution.[78]

In addition, the telefundraiser can use his voice to influence the donor to give. In motivating the donor to give, Dewane has this advice:

- Validate the caller in the eyes of the donor. Any steps you can take to make donors feel that the caller is "for real" (affiliated with the organization and not trying to cheat them) will make them feel more comfortable giving their credit card over the phone.
- Offer benefits to those who make credit card gifts.
- Learn your audience. You have to discover the particular culture and tendencies of your donors. In Minnesota, I've found that saying, "Now, if you're comfortable with this, we *can* put that gift on a credit card right now," works much better than "And what credit card will that be?," which would be more appropriate in other places.[79]

The Minnesota Opera uses a telefundraising company to conduct the campaign. According to Dewane, "SD&A Teleservices is responsible for hiring the callers, strategizing the calls, writing the script, tracking the campaign progress, and reporting back to the Opera. The callers are hired locally and come to make calls in our building, at which point they are supervised by an SD&A Teleservices company employee who, in turn, is supervised by an Opera staff member [please see appendix B1, B2, and B3 for the SD&A Teleservices script and caller strategy, pledge form, and acknowledgement letter]. Campaign reports are issued weekly by the telefundraising company, and include the following information: gifts raised, prospects pending, and prospects to be cultivated and/or solicited.

"Although hiring a telefundraising firm can be costly, the permanent staff of the Opera would have an extremely difficult time handling the additional human resources responsibilities of ten temporary telefundraising callers. Also, the tracking and reporting of leads and lead segments are something that, in my opinion, is best left up to the professionals.

"At the Opera, we have occasionally used board members to call for Leadership Gifts ($1,000 and above) and staff to call for Community Gifts ($200 to $999). This can be a very effective strategy for saving money and soliciting specific donors. But on the larger scale, it is very difficult to reach a large number of small donors efficiently without running a coordinated campaign. And unless the organization is willing to take on such a campaign internally, it would seem to make more sense to outsource the work to a telefundraising agency."[80]

The fundraising calendar should list your telefundraising campaign dates. Dewane advises, "It only makes sense to telefundraise when people want to give. Everyone is more likely to give right before the end of the calendar year, so I think starting a telefundraising campaign in the late fall or early winter is a great idea. No one is around during the summer, so there is not much point in telefundraising then. Any campaign that involves the period between Thanksgiving and Christmas is bound to bring in a lot of gifts."[81]

During any successful telefundraising campaign, it is important to ask for credit card gifts and to turn pledges into gifts. At the Minnesota Opera, Dewane has seen his percentage of credit card gifts increase: "In our current campaign at the Opera we're averaging about 50 percent credit card gifts, but in past Minnesota Opera campaigns, it has been considerably lower. The telefundraising firm we use aims for at least 60 percent credit card donations. Last year's telefundraising campaign had a pledge fulfillment rate of just under 50 percent.

"For those who make pledges, we have a strategy for converting those pledges into donations. We send two pieces of follow-up mail and then make a follow-up call for every person who makes a pledge. Our telefundraising firm stresses the timeliness of following up as a key to success. They insist pledge mail go out the day after the pledge is made, the second follow-up letter exactly two weeks later, and a follow-up call one week after that."[82]

Once the campaign is complete, it's time to evaluate its effectiveness. Dewane provides some financial data on a successful telefundraising campaign: "Most telefundraising agencies aim for around fifty cents spent per dollar raised. But because telefundraising is the most effective way to get acquisitions on a large scale (and new donors, once acquired, can be put on a mailing list), the acquisition gifts that a telefundraising campaign brings in are (theoretically) an investment that will continue to pay off.

"The individual-gifts division at the Opera has an overall goal of $225,000, of which $100,000 comes from telefundraising gifts. This indicates that we couldn't reach the goal without telefundraising, which makes it necessary to the success of my division as a whole. So if our current campaign only brings in $85,000, the majority of that money would have been incredibly hard to obtain without telefundraising. Therefore, even if our telefundraising campaign doesn't meet its goal, it is still an effective fundraising strategy because it

brought in gifts that wouldn't have come in without coordinated calling efforts. However, maximizing the efficiency of the campaign—bringing in more dollars in fewer hours—means that the telefundraising was more effective overall."[83]

CLASSROOM DISCUSSION
Take a look at the SD&A Teleservices script to
    answer the next few questions (see appendix B1):
        What is tone matching?
        Why is it important to listen to your donor?
        What are the important components of the
           script?
Do some role-playing: Respond to some of the
    standard objections. Convince a donor to use
    her credit card instead of making a pledge.
Why should an organization consider using a
    professional telefundraising firm?
What information should appear on a campaign
    report?
When is the best time to conduct a campaign?
How do you evaluate its effectiveness?

Online Fundraising: Research and Determining Donor Motivations
More and more charities are using the Internet to raise money. Savvy performing arts organizations like Alvin Ailey American Dance Theater and the Brooklyn Academy of Music are leading the way. Amanda Nelson reviews the process in this section.

Nelson begins with her research strategy for collecting names and creating lists. "We are constantly working to grow our e-mail lists by collecting names and e-mail addresses on our Web site (the Ailey E-Club) and at performances (Ailey Ambassadors meet and greet audience members with E-Club sign-up forms). On surveys and reply mechanisms (whether it is a donation response form or an RSVP for an event or program), a space is provided for the collection of an e-mail address. We immediately add that name to our e-mail database. For online campaign assistance, organizations have a variety of e-mail marketing services companies from which to select. Many of these companies offer design (ranging from providing e-mail templates to full-scale e-mail design services), list management, and campaign tracking. Tracking the success of an online appeal is just as important as tracking results of a direct mail campaign.

"Online fundraising can be an efficient and effective way to raise money. Once an e-mail appeal is designed (a relatively low cost compared to the design and printing of a four-color brochure), an e-mail campaign can often begin immediately; no time is needed for printing letters or brochures, stuffing envelopes, or mailing.

"Performing arts organizations need to consider donor motivation. What can a performing arts organization do to motivate the donor or potential donor to open the e-mail? I suggest using the subject line of the e-mail to entice prospects. We are careful to identify our organization and the main message of our e-mail in the subject line. For example, 'Special Holiday Offer—Give the Gift of Ailey' was the subject line of a special online campaign to promote gift memberships. With a clear and succinct subject line, we have seen open rates of up to 30 percent. Of course, not everyone who opens and reads the e-mail solicitation continues through the online donation process, but the fact that people are engaging with us is a great first step. I believe online appeals are particularly successful when done in conjunction with other mailings or communications from your organization.

"When a donor makes an online gift, an acknowledgement is automatically generated from our Web site. While some organizations provide only an online acknowledgement, Ailey also mails each donor a letter thanking her for her generosity and support."[84] Both e-mailed and written acknowledgement letters should include the amount of the donation and tax-deductibility information.

A sample of an e-mail solicitation and automatic Web response after a donation is made is shown on page 191.[85]

CLASSROOM DISCUSSION

How does a performing arts organization create
e-mail lists?
Why should you consider using a marketing
service to help you with this campaign?
Why is this an effective way to raise money?
Create an online appeal.

Individual Giving: Planned Giving

When financier Arthur Zankel died, he left Carnegie Hall approximately $22 million in his will.[86] In fact, a study conducted by the DonorTrends Project states that 40 percent of baby boomers (born between 1946 and 1964) plan to leave money to charities in their wills.[87] This type of gift is called a planned gift. Up to this point, we have been discussing "outright gifts" or "contributions that can be immediately utilized by the nonprofit organization: a cash membership gift, a foundation contribution, a corporate sponsorship, etc. A planned gift may be an outright gift,

but it may also be a deferred gift that promises contributed income at some determined date in the future. Gifts to a nonprofit organization linked to an individual's life insurance policy are examples of a deferred gift. Planned gifts are irrevocable in that the donor rescinds all rights to retrieve funds after they are transferred to a charitable organization. The Internal Revenue Service requires that all planned gifts be irrevocable to qualify for a tax deduction. This ensures that the donor cannot claim a tax deduction on a contribution and later receive a refund of the funds. It also has major benefits for a charitable organization by creating a more stable contributed revenue stream."[88]

So, what does this mean for performing arts organizations? What can performing arts organizations do to help their donors "plan" to leave part or all of their estate (money, stocks, real estate) to charity? According to Richard Feiner, there are incentives for the donor to consider this type of gift. He states, "Planned gifts, if properly structured, offer important tax savings on income tax, estate tax, gift tax, capital gains tax, or, in some instances, a combination of taxes."[89]

Richard Feiner shares his experience and insights on this very important type of fundraising. First, let's define the types of planned gifts:

• Bequests (Deferred Gift): Bequests are often the simplest and most common way to make a planned gift. They often are indicated in the donor's will. The donor may choose to leave a specific dollar amount; a percentage of an estate; or specific assets, such as stocks or real estate. The donor also can make a gift of all or part of his/her property remaining after all other bequests have been paid. Any charitable bequest is removed from the donor's taxable estate and therefore is not subject to estate taxes.

• Life Insurance (Deferred Gift): If the donor or the donor's family no longer needs the protection of life insurance coverage, the life insurance policy can provide an easy way to make a gift. The donor can irrevocably name the nonprofit as owner of the policy and receive an income tax charitable deduction. Alternately, the donor can choose to designate the nonprofit as beneficiary of the policy and receive an estate tax deduction.

• Charitable Trusts: There are two main types of charitable trusts that allow the donor to make a gift. A charitable lead trust (outright

Fig. 6.7.
Brooklyn Academy of
Music Online Appeal

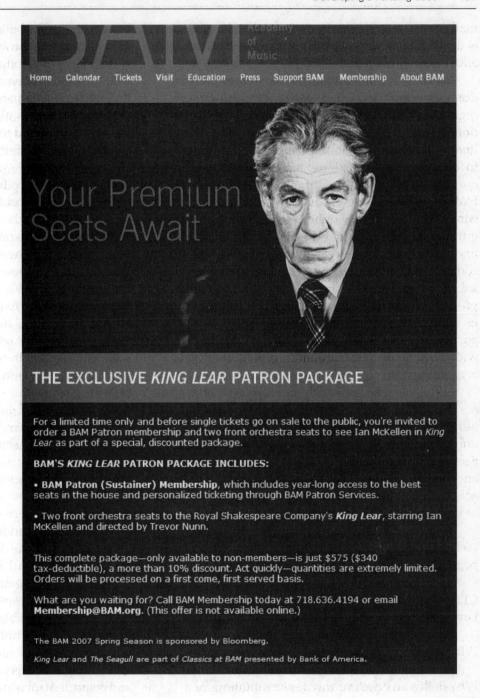

Fig. 6.8. Sample Auto Web Response Letter

Thank you for your contribution of $_____ to become a member of the *Friends of XYZ*! Your support will help to ensure our organization's artistic growth and vitality.

For your tax records, the IRS requires us to inform you that the value of goods and services received in exchange of your contribution is $_____.

Please look out in the mail for your membership materials. If you have any questions or need any assistance, please contact our membership office **by e-mail at membership@xyz.org or by phone at (555) 555-5555.**

Thank you again for your support.

gift) provides income to the nonprofit for a determined number of years, with the remainder of the assets going to the donor's heirs. The donor will receive a charitable deduction at the time of the gift equal to the present value of the total income the nonprofit will receive from the trust. This may reduce or possibly eliminate any gift tax. If the donor has substantial assets that she would like to transfer to children, grandchildren, or others, a charitable lead trust is an excellent way to do so, while reducing gift or estate taxes. A charitable lead trust may be established during the donor's lifetime or through her will.

A charitable remainder trust (deferred gift) provides the donor, or any beneficiaries designated by the donor, with income for life or for another specified amount of time. At the appropriate time (for example, the donor's death), the remaining assets in the trust are distributed to the nonprofit. The donor benefits by receiving a charitable deduction in the year the gift is made, by receiving income from the trust for the term of the trust, and by reducing the size of the donor's taxable estate. The donor may select a charitable remainder annuity trust, which pays a fixed dollar amount each year, or a charitable remainder unitrust, which pays a percentage of the value of the trust assets each year. The nonprofit organization benefits by receiving the amount remaining when the trust term ends. A charitable remainder trust is particularly well suited for gifts of appreciated securities or real estate because it may avoid or defer potential capital gains taxes. It can be established during the donor's lifetime or through his will.

- Annuity Trusts: A gift annuity (outright gift) is a contract between the donor and the nonprofit organization. The nonprofit organization receives an outright gift, and in exchange for this irrevocable charitable contribution of cash or securities, the donor or the donor's designated beneficiary will receive regular fixed payments for life. A portion of the initial gift is tax deductible for the donor as a charitable contribution to the nonprofit, and part of each annuity payment also is usually tax-free. Another type of annuity, a deferred gift annuity

(outright gift), allows the donor to make an outright gift but to delay the payout. This option allows the donor to provide a gift now and receive a generous tax deduction at the time of the gift, as well as receive generous annuity payments. When these annuity payments are no longer required (for example, at the end of the donor's life), the nonprofit organization may use the gift for general purposes or may add it to another purpose, such as an endowment fund.[90]

What motivates a donor to make a planned gift? Feiner explains, "An individual motivated to make a planned gift most likely has a great love for an institution and a desire to make a strong and recognizable contribution that can be meaningful in perpetuity."[91] The gentleman who left $22 million to Carnegie Hall had served on its board of directors and had previously given an outright gift of $10 million toward the renovation of Carnegie Hall in 1999.

How does an organization go about researching the type of individual who is most likely to make a planned gift? Feiner maintains, "Very studied and thorough research is required to identify planned giving candidates. Hospitals and universities have entire departments with dedicated staff for this purpose."[92]

Once specific individuals have been identified, it's critical to create a strategy for approaching the prospective donor. Feiner shares this advice: "This type of fundraising operates differently from securing support for programs or general operating support. It is imperative that 'the ask' be conducted in a very secure and sophisticated manner. One effective way to develop a planned giving campaign is to engage the advice of counsel from established and respected trusts and estates attorneys, either from firms already offering pro bono work or from firms associated with the trustees of the organizations. Ask these attorneys to help set up a structure to the program, and perhaps inquire whether they might be interested in serving on an advisory committee. Engage trustees from the organization. Once the groundwork is in place, there can be discussion of special event planning to be hosted by these trust and estate representatives, to which are invited a highly selective group of their clients who might be interested in learning about the organization. Through a series of very high-end cultivation events, these prospective donors can slowly be encouraged to consider a planned gift."[93]

CLASSROOM DISCUSSION

What is a planned gift?

Why do donors make planned gifts?

Define the types of planned gifts. What type of
    donor is most likely to give each type of gift?

Define the term "irrevocable."

How do you approach a potential planned gifts
    donor? When approaching this type of donor,
    why is it important to engage an attorney with
    expertise in estates and trusts?

Special Events

Development professionals use all types of events
to cultivate donors as well as to raise money from
them. New York Theatre Workshop, responsible
for developing the hit show *Rent*, used its tenth-
year anniversary to organize a gala benefit that
raised more than $2 million.[94] In this section, Patrick
Dewane provides an excellent step-by-step account
of the planning and execution of a fundraising gala
event or benefit designed to raise money from both
individuals and institutional donors.

According to Dewane, donors attend gala
fundraising events because "they enjoy the social
aspect of the event—dressing up, going to see
people and being seen by them. They like that they
can have fun and support an organization at the
same time. We develop our list of invitees from past
attendees; friends and business associates of the
gala chairs and volunteers; and people who attend
similar events."[95]

When is the best time to hold a gala event?
Before selecting a date, it's a good idea to "consult
a city or municipal area's special events calendar
to ensure that you don't schedule a major special
event or gala on the same date as a competing
nonprofit organization."[96] Holden agrees: "We all
share the same donors. It's the same people going to
a gala every weekend from February until June."[97]
Dewane contends, "It is difficult in this market
(Minneapolis) to have successful events in the
summer, as most people are away for the weekend,
or from mid-November to mid-January, when an
event would collide with the holidays. Also, in
this market you cannot count on the snowbirds
attending any event in the winter. This is significant
because if the snowbirds have the wealth to spend
winter in Florida, they also have the wealth to
support your organization. Some organizations
have snowbird events in Florida; the best time for
this is February. The four best months to hold any
event in this market are October, early November,
April, and May."[98]

Here is Dewane's blueprint for organizing the
event:

- Assign a staff person to be responsible for
  the event.
- Determine the expense budget and income
  goals.
- Pick the location for the event and have the
  staff person negotiate the rental contract and
  other site details.
- Recruit the individual and corporate co-
  chairs, giving them their job descriptions,
  the expense budget and income goals, and
  the time and location of the event.
- Recruit the other gala committee members.
- Renew past individual and corporate support.
- Work with chairs and gala committee members on generating new support through
  committee meetings and individual follow-
  up.
- Choose the theme, menu, decorations,
  graphic look, and invitations.
- Negotiate contracts with all vendors.
- Send invitations.
- Plan the logistics for the day and distribute
  assignments.
- Have the event.
- Meet to discuss what worked and did not
  work; make suggestions for the next year.[99]

Here is Dewane's timetable for organizing the gala
event:

- Eleven and a half months (before the event):
  When the previous event is still fresh in
  everyone's mind, meet to discuss what did
  and did not work; book a venue for the next
  year's gala.
- Ten months: Make a plan for the event,
  including an expense budget and income
  goals, focusing on ways to generate more
  net income; recruit co-chairs. (Please see
  appendix C for a sample event budget.)[100]
- Nine months: Have the first meeting with
  co-chairs; present a proposed budget, goal,
  and plan; discuss the theme; schedule
  regular co-chair meetings; solicit corporate
  sponsorships; and delegate responsibilities
  to other development staff members.
- Eight months: Recruit silent auction
  committee and other volunteer committees
  [if the organization has a gala committee,
  these members would also be recruited at
  this time]; begin soliciting silent auction

items; plan decorations and a contract decorator; contract valet parking; acquire search lights; and contract a designer for the printed pieces.

- Seven months: Make a presentation at a board meeting; solicit renewals of corporate tables and individual tickets.
- Six months: Send renewal letters. (We no longer create and send a formal invitation. [If you do use formal invitations, send them eight weeks before the event.] We send renewal letters. [Either the invitation/renewal letter or a receipt of contribution must provide a disclosure statement recognizing the gift amount if it is greater than $75, stating the value of the goods and services received for the gift and the amount that is tax-deductible.] We send them six months in advance and call two weeks after the letter is sent. We keep calling each week until we get an answer.) Schedule a menu tasting; choose a caterer; negotiate the caterer's contract; follow up with phone calls to individual and corporate renewals; and work with the decorator on table settings, décor, and lighting.
- Five months: Solicit new corporate tables and individual tickets/tables through targeted and personalized letters (again, we no longer send a formal invitation); continue renewal follow-up calls; work with the designer on the design for the silent auction catalogue, the menu cards, and the confirmation card; finalize décor.
- Four months: Compare the value of silent auction items secured to date with the value needed to reach your goal; determine what else needs to be secured for the silent auction; follow up with phone calls to new corporate and individual supporters; and finalize printed materials.
- Three months: Solicit the board one last time for auction items; continue follow-up with renewals and new supporters; and finalize sponsorships.
- Two months: Report on the success of the event to the board, choosing two final things you need the board to do to help you increase the net income; finalize volunteer duties for the night of the gala; begin to lay out the silent auction catalogue; and print confirmation cards.
- One month: Follow up on the myriad details; create the script for speakers/performers; plan the layout for the silent auction display; and send gala confirmation cards and tickets. [Please see appendix D for a sample confirmation card.][101]
- Two weeks: Print and mail the silent auction catalogue; give the estimated number of guests to the caterer and venue; confirm valet parking, searchlights, and decorations.
- One week: Deal with the details: design and print the silent auction catalogue insert for items that weren't secured in time; meet with staff and volunteers to go over assignments for the event; distribute a schedule of events for the day and evening.
- Day of: Arrive to the venue early; meet with the venue representative, decorator, caterer, and valet parking representative; oversee load-in and setup; make sure key staffers and volunteers arrive and are doing their assignments; trouble-shoot; go home and change; and arrive back at the venue, say a prayer, and let the event unfold.
- Monday after: Follow up on silent auction bids and any other loose ends; create a rough estimate of the income and expenses; thank everyone; identify what income still must be collected; plan post-gala assessment discussion; and input all interesting conversations into the development database and modify cultivation tracks for each entry accordingly.[102]

The Minnesota Opera charges $175 for a single ticket to the gala. Organizations usually sell tables of ten or twelve seats and charge a premium amount of money for these tables. Corporate donors and wealthy individuals can sponsor a table and receive gala tickets for their VIP guests, sponsorship listing in the program, and recognition at the gala event.

What does it cost to produce a gala event? Dewane says, "We spent $60,000 and we grossed $350,000, for a direct ROI (return on investment) of $290,000. Additionally, the gala this year honored a donor who since then gave an additional $100,000 for a commission of an opera and $25,000 to support the first production of the year. Several other gala attendees are capital campaign prospects, including one who was solicited shortly after the gala and pledged an additional $500,000. It is our signature event, and includes most of our top donors. The 'ripple-effect ROI' of the gala is about a couple million annually."[103]

Cultivating the attendees is critical to raising money. Dewane and his development staff, along with the president or co-chair (depending on who has the best relationship with the potential attendee), call every potential attendee six months before the event and say, "'I wanted to call you before our gala sells out to reserve your place. So many people think this is the most elegant night out of the year that we have a hard time fitting in our best friends. We had so much fun last year, and I so appreciate your support, that I wanted to make sure you are included. You've meant so much to the company, and this is the evening when we are at our best.'"[104]

Some organizations use consultants to organize and execute the event. Dewane has had experience working with consultants and expresses the pros and cons of using a consultant. "The cons are that consultants are expensive, and ultimately can walk away from the results, whereas I have to live with the results. I also do not like handing over important volunteer relationships to a consultant; I'd rather have someone on my staff manage those relationships so they stay with the organization, not potentially walk away with the consultant. Having an event consultant can also stunt the development of junior staff members who would grow from direct gala responsibilities.

"The big pro is that if you get a good consultant, then you don't have staff time taken up by the myriad details involved in an event. Managing a gala requires a special skill set, and it might be beyond the skills of your current staff. Like other development department decisions, it comes down to a return on investment calculation. Are you better off outsourcing this function, or keeping it in-house?"[105]

Since nonprofit organizations want to maximize the return on their investment, they use volunteers to organize and manage the event. Dewane explains, "We have co-chairs for our gala. The individual co-chair is responsible for selling individual tickets, securing silent auction items, and deciding on the theme of the gala and execution of the gala details. The corporate co-chair is responsible for selling corporate tables and securing corporate sponsorships and silent auction items. We also have a silent auction committee that helps secure silent auction items. Lastly, we have volunteers who help with mailings, the setup of the event, the running of the event, the cleanup of the event, and the follow-up. There are job descriptions for all positions, and the staff person responsible for the event trains the volunteers. The director of development also meets with the volunteers to help secure support, stress the importance of the event, and thank them for their work."[106]

Finally, Dewane lists the dos and don'ts of planning and executing a gala event:

Do:
- Plan your biggest event a year in advance and work your calendar backward.
- Plan your work and work your plan.
- Get your agreements with vendors in writing.
- Include the date, time, and place for the event clearly on everything.
- Get a variety of opinions about an event chair before recruiting one.
- Make sure the volunteers are having fun.
- Thank your volunteers *and your staff* profusely after an event.
- Make sure the staff person responsible for the event knows she has your support.
- Give your staff person as much responsibility as she can handle.
- Let your staff [members] know that their professional growth is important to you.
- Keep everything positive.
- Build word-of-mouth momentum before the event and share the successes after the event.
- Learn from last year and think about how you can make next year more successful.
- Keep your eyes open for potential volunteer and staff leadership.
- Keep your boss in the loop about problems and successes.
- Always think about the event's return on investment.
- Recruit volunteers with real clout.
- Make your events memorable and different from everyone else's.

Don't:
- Hide mistakes.
- Assume that everyone knows what is going on.
- Gossip—not about volunteers, not about your staff, not about the artists, not about anyone.
- Micromanage.
- Get in the middle of squabbles between volunteers.
- Recruit volunteers without their knowing what is expected.
- Involve people who are emotionally unstable.[107]

CLASSROOM DISCUSSION

Why do people attend gala events?

What is the best time to schedule a gala event?

Create an event and timetable for producing it.

What are the pros and cons for hiring a benefit consultant?

Name three dos and three don'ts for planning and executing a special event.

Institutional Giving: Corporations

Performing arts organizations raise money from institutions, including corporations, foundations, and the government. When asked what type of donor gives the most money to nonprofit organizations, many people believe the answer is "corporations." In reality, corporations only account for 5 percent of total giving. In this section, we will examine the ways in which corporations support the performing arts.

Corporations: Research and Donor Motivations

Why do corporations give to the arts? Richard Feiner defines "corporate motivation" for giving in the following passage: "There are some large changes influencing corporate philanthropy. Corporate America is refashioning its way of doing business with nonprofit organizations: shaking up expectations, creating challenges, and suggesting new models for nonprofit organizations to achieve goals. Whether regarded as cause marketing (donation is connected to sale of product), strategic philanthropy (donation is tied to corporate business interests), good corporate citizenship, accountability to shareholders, or a mix of such objectives, there is an underlying trend. Corporations are abandoning some long-term causes in favor of others tied more closely to business objectives—and expecting nonprofit organizations to meet their own objectives, just like businesses.

"Corporations demand effectiveness, because of the expectations placed on the private sector to fix or change problems and to reinforce a brand (product or service visibility) with its consumer base. A large reason for this changing view of philanthropic giving is the desire to reinforce and refocus it to increase shareholder value. For corporations, giving to causes that help the bottom line is no longer optional. Now it's a need-to-do thing."[108]

In his address entitled "The Current State of Corporate Philanthropy," Timothy J. McClimon, now the president of the American Express Foundation, had this to say about corporate giving trends: "American companies are increasingly interested in quantifying the business benefits that being socially responsible may generate. These can include:

- Enhanced brand image and reputation.
- Increased sales and customer loyalty.
- Increased ability to attract and retain employees.
- Improved financial performance.
- Access to capital.
- Reduced operating costs.
- Increased productivity and quality.
- Reduced regulatory oversight."[109]

According to McClimon, the "key to good corporate social responsibility depends on a company's success in *integrating* good corporate citizenship into its core business strategy, rather than treating it as an 'ad hoc window dressing.'"[110]

Keeping McClimon's view of corporate philanthropy in mind, it is imperative for the development professional to create a strategy that addresses the corporate motivation for giving. As with other donor categories, the development process in cultivating corporate support begins with research. Feiner explains, "There are many ways to research whether a corporation might consider arts funding as part of a larger corporate philanthropy program, and many ways to identify corporate prospects. Research tools include: funders' lists in programs from performing organizations; online fundraising resources that can research corporate giving by categories (especially the Foundation Center and its funding library); trade publications such as the *The Chronicle of Philanthropy* that announce major grants, etc.; and obtaining the corporation's grant guidelines and annual report online or through the mail. Once you have the corporate annual report, you can research the corporation's business objectives, as well as determine if your board of directors has an affiliation with the corporation."[111]

By conducting this research, an organization will discover that corporations give to nonprofit organizations in a variety of ways, including general operating support, project-specific grants, in-kind donations, matching gifts, challenge grants, technical assistance, multiyear grants, sponsorships, corporate memberships, and board or volunteer support. Feiner defines each type of contribution:

- General operating support (GOS): Supports annual programming that embraces the full organization and is funded through contributions to the annual fund.

- Project support: Supports specific projects, such as a specific performance or program (e.g., educational programming or special programming to commemorate a special anniversary of the nonprofit organization).
- In-kind: In-kind donations are noncash items, including services and products. Examples include: airline tickets and gift packages of products produced by the corporation.
- Matching gifts: A corporation establishes a matching gift program to augment/ supplement its philanthropic mission and to respond directly to its employees' own interests and personal charitable giving.
- Challenge grants: A corporation would provide a challenge grant (one-to-one, two-for-one match) only within a very limited situation, such as a response to a capital campaign or endowment campaign.
- Technical assistance: This falls within the area of in-kind gifts and is likely from a corporation whose products would directly benefit the general operations of the nonprofit organization. For example, IBM might provide computers and/or classes in programming languages.
- Multiyear grants: This funding can support both general operating support and specific programming, such as capacity-building efforts (GOS) or educational initiatives (program-specific).
- Sponsorship: A sponsorship is funding for a distinct, highly visible event or series of events. Sponsors may also be cultivated to pay for a specific part of the event or to donate goods and services; for example, such cultivations may result in the corporation becoming a sponsor of opening night, series sponsor, liquor sponsor, study guides sponsor, or ticket sponsor.[112] A corporation might choose to provide sponsorship support so that tangible goods and services/benefits are provided in exchange for such financial support, such as blocks of tickets; visibility on posters and in advertising; promotional outreach opportunities such as inclusion on press releases; and/or spoken acknowledgement at the premiere event for a festival.
- Corporate membership club: A corporate membership club implies gifts from for-profit businesses that wish to raise public visibility for their charitable/social work through financial support to a nonprofit organization. In exchange, this support provides the corporate member with special access that its employees can enjoy, such as free and/or reduced-price tickets; passes to dress rehearsals; and opportunities for discrete corporate parties before or after performances, often with stars and artists in attendance.
- Volunteering: Some corporations have highly sophisticated employee participation programs that complement any general operating or project-specific support. These can include programs where employees dedicate paid office time in the employ of a nonprofit organization to help implement special workshops for the organization's constituents (students, families, homebound elderly or incapacitated supporters, etc.). Corporate executives may also serve as volunteer board members.[113]

Development professionals seeking any of the above-mentioned types of support must do so by approaching one or more areas of the corporation: the corporate contributions department, the corporate foundation, or the corporate marketing department. In the following section, development professionals discuss motivations for giving, and the correct approach, pitch, and follow-up for each area of corporate giving.

Corporate Contributions Department: The Approach

Nonprofit organizations seeking funds should research whether a corporation has a corporate contributions or a community relations department. Feiner explains, "The contributions department is responsible for grant management, e.g., selecting the grantees and ensuring that the parameters of a grant are met. Corporate contributions departments may choose to fund general operating or project support. In addition, they can be asked for a multiyear grant, to meet a challenge grant, or to join a membership club where their employees receive specific benefits in return for the corporate contribution. In-kind contributions, technical assistance, and volunteer support may also be requested from this corporate area.

"The corporate contributions department does not independently choose to support the arts. Rather, it is the vehicle by which a corporation fulfills its philanthropic objectives. Again, the benefits to be accrued to a corporation for support of the arts are many and varied; these may include increased visibility/standing within the community; the generation of good will to solidify the corporation's reputation as a good corporate citizen; and public display of the corporation's dedication to responsible governance.

"Normally, there is no good or bad time to approach a corporate contributions department. It's important to check the corporation's grant guidelines, which will specify grant-making cycles and deadlines. It is normally best to make some initial approach at the start or during the fall season. This timing will allow the nonprofit organization to highlight upcoming events and provide plenty of lead time to invite corporate representatives to get to know the nonprofit organization. If there is special programming, it might be a very good idea to contact corporate representatives during the summer with invitations, updates, etc., especially as there is less competition during the slow summer months.

"All institutional funders request some type of written proposal. A proposal is a written document outlining the need for support, and in the case of a corporation, the benefits derived from supporting the organization. Before sending a detailed grant proposal and budget to a corporate contributions department, it is best to send a brief letter of inquiry to make sure that the corporation is interested in your organization. Effective letters of inquiry to a corporate community relations department and/or

contributions department are similar to other such letters: they should be short (no more than one and a half pages) and directly written, with clear objectives that are clear in their appeals."[114]

The letter should briefly include the following points:

- Introduction of the nonprofit organization, including its history, mission, and most significant accomplishments.
- Brief proposal: a summary of what you want to pitch to the corporate contributions area for its support.
- Benefits/outcomes of the project: what the nonprofit organization will achieve; what the corporate contributions area can expect to receive.
- Visibility/public acknowledgement: what the corporation can expect for its support— "bang for the corporate buck."
- Brief closing proposing a phone call or a meeting at a convenient place/time to be arranged to discuss the submission of a full proposal. Mention that you will call/follow up with the person within a few weeks.[115]

Figure 6.9 provides a sample letter of inquiry to a corporation.[116]

Date

Addressee
Address
New York, New York 10021

Dear Corporate Contributions Manager:

 It was wonderful speaking with you today about possible corporate membership support from XYZ, Inc. As we briefly discussed, the mission of the World Monuments Fund and our unrivaled expertise in cultural heritage preservation might well complement your own leadership role in [industry].

 WMF brings together public and private support to preserve individual sites, ensure their long-term maintenance, and advocate for increased public awareness of cultural heritage. As I briefly described to you, WMF is in a period of unprecedented growth, and I would welcome the opportunity to discuss how a potential XYZ partnership could help promote your business priorities.

 WMF would be delighted to extend exclusive executive and employee benefits in exchange for any corporate support. These include, but are not limited to, recognition in public materials, specially designated corporate evenings, and exclusive access to staff and recognized leaders in the field of cultural heritage preservation.

 I will call you within a few weeks to take our discussions to the next level. In the meantime, please do not hesitate to contact me with any questions or requests for additional information. Thank you very much for your interest and current consideration.

Sincerely,

Richard Feiner
Director of Development

Fig. 6.9. Sample Letter of Inquiry: Corporate Contributions Department

Feiner emphasizes the importance of benefits to a corporate contributions department. He states, "The corporate contributions person is interested in the tangible benefits that the corporation's employees can receive. Be specific: access to tickets, backstage tours, rehearsal passes, and special events/receptions that could be exclusive to the corporation and that could be marketed as a corporate evening, including appropriate signage, etc. Signage is the visual recognition of the corporation and its support for the nonprofit organization. It can include the corporate name and logo on posters and banners specific to the event/programming, or even display the corporation's product. Car manufacturers can have a model of the newest fleet on display in a plaza outside the performing arts organization, or even in the lobby or adjacent public space.

"Usually, the letter of inquiry specifies an appropriate follow-up time ('within a couple of weeks'), and it is good form to adhere to this timetable. Typically, it is important to allow the corporate contact enough time to process the letter of inquiry, but the development professional should not let too much time elapse before contact is reestablished, lest the initial momentum is lost."[117]

If the corporate contributions contact believes that a project is a good fit, he will request a written proposal and budget for the project. John Holden cites the important parts of the proposal. He begins with the cover letter (the letter that precedes the proposal; if the cover letter precedes the proposal, then the proposal is not signed):

- Open with any connections you or your organization might have to the prospective funder ("It was a pleasure to meet you at Sally's home a few weeks ago"; "Bob Smith suggested that I get in touch with you"; "Apex Theatre has been a loyal client of XYZ Corporation for over ten years and hopes that you will consider partnering with us to . . .").
- Summarize contents of proposal—highlight proposal elements that you expect to be of particular interest to the prospect.
- Close by thanking the prospect for his consideration and providing contact information—who should the prospect call if he needs more information?[118]

Figure 6.10 provides an example of a cover letter to a corporate contributions manager.[119]

Date

Addressee
Address
New York, New York 10021

Dear Corporate Contributions Manager:

   I am delighted to provide you with the enclosed proposal requesting consideration by XYZ, Inc., for corporate support for the World Monuments Fund. As you are aware from our previous conversations, WMF's unrivaled success in and expertise in cultural heritage preservation might well complement your own leadership role in [industry].

   WMF is in a period of unprecedented growth, and our commitment to projects worldwide includes a dynamic initiative-based structure with exclusive high-visibility recognition options. I would welcome the opportunity to discuss how a corporate partnership could help promote your business priorities.

   Our proposal includes exclusive executive and employee benefits, which are dependent upon any proposed level of corporate support. We would be pleased to tailor a program of benefits and acknowledgements that would best satisfy your interests.

   I will call you within a few weeks to discuss our proposal. In the meantime, please do not hesitate to contact me with any questions or requests for additional information.

   Thank you very much for your interest and current consideration.

Sincerely,

Richard Feiner
Director of Development

Fig. 6.10. Sample Cover Letter: Corporation Contributions Department

Holden outlines the key components of a proposal to a corporate contributions department:

- Mission: How is your organization unique?
- History.
- Summary of season or project.
- How it relates to the funder's priorities.
- Benefits.
- Plans for evaluating its success.
- Make it concise and compelling. It should be easy to read and understand and 3 to 4 pages long.[120]

Please see appendix E for a sample corporate contributions proposal.[121]

A proposal should include a packet of information. Here are the elements that should be included:

- IRS 501(c)(3) tax-exempt determination letter.
- Audited and unaudited financial statements from previous years.
- Detailed budget projections (organizational budget and project budget, if applicable).
- Detailed season schedule.
- A list of board members.
- Brief biographies of key collaborators, artists, etc.
- History sheet (might include mission statement, awards received, and other significant achievements).
- Recent press clippings about your organization and its work.
- Recent and relevant company publications (season brochure, company newsletters).[122]

If the corporation is interested in the proposal, the corporate contributions manager may ask for a meeting with the organizational leadership. Holden recommends that senior management (executive director or artistic director) accompany the director of development to the meeting. At this meeting, the organizational leadership will pitch the project to the corporation. Here are the important points to consider when developing a pitch to a corporate contributions manager:

- Fully describe the project the corporation would be supporting.
- Outline other sources of support for the same need (other corporations, foundations, government sources)—where does the corporation fit into the big picture?

- Describe how you can recognize the corporation's support. Can you name a program after it? Name a lounge or other public space (for a capital donation)? Promote a particular product?
- Will a gift of this level entitle the corporation to any benefits through your corporate benefits program, such as special dinners, or events where corporate officers can entertain clients?
- How will you measure the success of the project? How will it change/enhance your mission?
- Bring written materials that outline the project and contain answers to all the questions you can anticipate the corporation might have. These materials might include:
  o Narrative project summary.
  o Detailed budgets.
  o Schematic designs/drawings (for capital projects).
  o General background information on organization.
- How would you measure the success of the project and report to the corporation on the impact of its support?[123]

After sending the proposal or meeting with the grant maker, Sarah Bordy, director of development of Second Stage Theatre, advises that the organization "give the corporation a week or two and then call to ask the status of your grant."[124] Once the decision has been made, the corporate contributions department will send the organization a letter, either accepting or rejecting the proposal. If the organization is awarded a corporate contribution, thank-you letters should go out immediately. Feiner maintains, "Generally, there never is an instance of too many thank-you letters. The nonprofit organization's president should issue a personal acknowledgement letter, and it also is advisable for a trustee to issue an acknowledgement as well. The official letter acknowledging the gift with the standard tax deductibility information should be issued by the director of development, or by a director of corporate relations."[125]

A standard thank-you letter to a corporate contributions manager is shown on page 201.[126]

CLASSROOM DISCUSSION
What motivates a corporation to give support to performing arts organizations?

Fig. 6.11. Sample Corporate Contributions Acknowledgement Letter

---

Date

Name
Manager, Corporate Contributions
ABC Corporation
Address
New York, New York 10005-2858

Dear Corporate Contributions Manager:

On behalf of the Board and staff of [nonprofit name], I am delighted to thank you for the ABC Corporation $10,000 gift in support of our arts-in-education programs. These programs are a national prototype for arts-in-education instruction, and your corporation's contribution will allow us to continue to develop curriculum units for students and teachers to use in the classroom. I am grateful for the corporation's renewed support, and look forward to working with you further throughout the year.

In keeping with the Omnibus Budget Reconciliation Act of 1993,[127] I have attached the [nonprofit's] receipt of contribution. In order to ensure that the company takes full advantage of corporate membership, we also ask that you please complete the attached questionnaire and return it to [name], Manager for Corporate Relations, either by e-mail, facsimile, or regular mail. In addition, I have included our Corporate Membership brochure, which describes ABC's corporate membership benefits. You may also wish to inform employees of ABC Corporation that they can access corporate membership information on our Web site at [nonprofit Web address].

As a supporter of [nonprofit name], ABC Corporation is entitled to the enclosed 25 VIP guest/parking passes, which may be distributed to clients, community groups, or other special guests of the company. ABC Corporation is also permitted an additional 50 passes, which are available upon request. Each pass can be redeemed for complimentary admission and parking for the bearer and guest.

Thank you once again for ABC Corporation's ongoing support. I hope you will be able to take advantage of our exciting seasonal programming, as well as our many special events. In the meantime, should you have any questions, feel free to contact me at [telephone number]. Best regards.

Sincerely,

Name
Director of Corporate and Foundation Relations

Enclosures

How do you go about researching whether a corporation gives to the performing arts?

Name and define the different types of corporate funding.

How do you approach a corporate contributions department for funding?

What information should a letter of inquiry contain?

Write a letter of inquiry.

When should you follow up the letter of inquiry?

What information should be included in a proposal and proposal packet?

Write a cover letter and proposal to a corporate contributions department.

What should an in-person pitch contain?

Write a pitch.

Write a thank-you letter.

Corporate Foundations: Research and Determining Donor Motivations

While the corporate contributions and corporate marketing departments are part of the corporation, "a corporate foundation is legally a separate nonprofit operating entity within a corporation that is charged with carrying out the corporation's philanthropic mandate, if such a commitment to philanthropy exists."[128] Timothy J. McClimon maintains that "while a corporate foundation is technically and legally separate from the corporation, the entire staff and board of directors are typically corporate employees. The entire corporate foundation budget comes from its parent corporation."[129] Feiner continues, "The corporate foundation carries out its own programming that, in its execution, complements the larger societal imperative of the corporation. Many examples exist within many industry sectors, such as energy. Shell Oil operates a companywide, international foundation based in London, with programming of a very high, worldwide reputation. Simultaneously, Shell Oil headquarters in other countries also administer their own philanthropic programs, independent yet complementary to those of the international Shell Foundation.

"It can be a company's philanthropic mandate to support the performing arts. If so, a corporate foundation may choose to provide general operating support for a performing arts organization, or it may support a specific production or educational outreach/community program. The corporation would consider such support an integral part of its efforts to solidify and enhance its standing/role within a community.

"There are many resources that can provide specific information related to corporate giving programs and strategies: corporate Web sites, fundraising journals and newspapers and their associated Web sites, firsthand research of programs that list corporate funders, etc."[130]

Since a corporate foundation is a nonprofit organization, it must file a Form 990 P-F (or in some cases a Form 990) with the Internal Revenue Service. Form 990 P-F can be utilized to research the organizations that receive gifts from the foundation, the location of these organizations, and the size of the gifts. In addition to the Forms 990 database on *GuideStar.org*, the Foundation Center also provides Forms 990 P-F and 990 for all types of foundations, including corporate foundations. Corporate foundations also publish grant guidelines and issue annual reports that provide this type of information.

Feiner asserts, "Depending on the nonprofit organization's relationship with the corporate foundation's representatives, one can always request answers to specific questions, such as those regarding funding cycles and how the nonprofit organization's approach can be best timed to coincide with the company's internal schedule. Most corporate foundation people are very approachable and will gladly provide such information, as long as the nonprofit development staff demonstrates some basic research and knowledge of the corporation and its philanthropic interests.

"There is no generic 'type' of project that a corporate foundation prefers to support. It is the development department's duty to frame/present a compelling project and to research which corporate foundations might respond favorably to such a project. Corporate foundations support general operations as well as specific projects/programs. If the corporation is willing to provide general operating support funding, the corporation must believe that the benefits of such support are equivalent to their commitment, that they are receiving enough 'bang for their buck' to make such an investment worthwhile."[131] McClimon emphasizes, "The 'bang for the corporate buck' is important to a corporate foundation. Corporate foundations want to make the most of their grants from the corporate standpoint."[132]

"Corporate foundations very often provide matching gifts. It is often the easiest and most effective philanthropic program that a corporation can administer, in that it requires very little direct face time with the nonprofit organization, and it is directly responsive to corporate employees' own charitable impulses. Corporations can provide challenge grants, but usually only within the established structure of a large, multiyear effort, such as a capital campaign or an endowment campaign.

"Major support from a corporate foundation, perhaps a multiyear commitment of a six-figure gift, can take quite a bit of time to secure—one year to eighteen months is not uncommon. Each foundation functions with its own internal schedule of deadlines, but it is typical for a foundation to have a single calendar date or two calendar dates (spring and fall) by which proposals must be submitted. It is never too early to contact a corporate foundation and establish a cultivation schedule. In terms of decision-making from a corporate foundation, it is hard to generalize. Typically, a corporate foundation is respectful of a nonprofit organization's fiscal year deadlines and, if there is interest and a commitment to provide funding, the foundation will try to secure payment or provide pledge documentation by the nonprofit's fiscal year-end."[133]

Corporate Foundations: The Approach

The best way to approach a corporate foundation is with a letter of inquiry. Or, if there has been some third-party introduction, an e-mail and/or phone call can set the approach in motion, to be followed by some written communication.

The letter of inquiry should not be longer than one and a half pages. Key components of a letter of inquiry include: an introduction, background on the nonprofit organization, a specific request for the foundation's consideration of a full proposal, and some kind of follow-up, such as a meeting or a phone call to discuss the possibility of submitting the full proposal. Feiner bullets these components:

- Introduction of the nonprofit organization: its history, mission, and most significant accomplishments.
- Brief proposal: a summary of the project or initiative that you want to pitch to the corporate foundation for its support.
- The reason you have selected this foundation for its potential support, and why the nonprofit organization's mission could well complement the foundation's interests/areas of support.
- Brief closing proposing a phone call or meeting at a convenient place/time to be arranged. Also, don't be shy about enclosing supporting documents that attest to the strength of the institution or the value of the program/initiative that the corporate foundation could help support, such as recent newspaper articles on the chief executive officer or a magazine profile on the institution or the program.[134]

After sending the letter of inquiry and receiving the request for a full proposal, the organization should prepare a cover letter and a proposal. "A proposal cover letter should be short (not more than one page), especially as it accompanies and complements the proposal. It should clearly and succinctly summarize the request that is explicitly outlined and described in the proposal. It should briefly reference the previous contact you have had with the letter's recipient: initial letter or conversation; any subsequent discussion or request for a proposal; or any other pertinent action that has led to this current submission. Importantly, the cover letter should not simply repeat in the same terms/language what is presented in the proposal. Rather, it should tantalize and invite the reader to get to the proposal. Of course, the cover letter should thank the contact for his/her consideration of the proposal. It should also suggest some follow-up: a meeting, a request for the reader's input, any explanation and/or revision of the proposal, etc.

"The proposal itself should not, generally, be longer than five pages. A proposal is not signed; the cover letter should be signed by the director of development or some other executive within the nonprofit organization. Proposal packet items resemble those sent to a corporate contributions manager."[135] Richard Feiner lists the key components of a corporate foundation proposal:

- Executive summary: States the larger role of the nonprofit organization's mission within the community and acknowledges the benefits of the potential nonprofit/corporate foundation partnership for both sides. It also states the specific amount requested of the foundation.
- Introduction: Provides a brief history of the nonprofit organization and its core mission, as well as its current needs/challenges. It must request the specific amount of the hoped-for contribution from the foundation. Brief mention of the nonprofit organization's prior relationship with the foundation (if any), as well as the full impact this funding could have on the growth of the nonprofit organization. Also note the benefits to be provided to the communities served by both the nonprofit organization and the corporation.
- Description of the program for which funding is needed. Specific examples of how the corporate foundation's support would play a vital role in both the short-term and long-term success of the initiative.
- Specific parameters/metrics by which the nonprofit organization will measure and report on the success of the initiative, if funding were to be secured from the corporate foundation.
- Conclusion: Restates the requested amount of desired funding and again the larger good that this funding could engender.

It is advisable to provide support materials along with the proposal: proof of tax-exempt 501(c)(3) status; audited and unaudited financial statements from previous years; budgets; reviews; programs; student work (if applying for educational support); a list of board members; and profiles on the nonprofit organization, the artistic director, the executive director, etc. [136] Please see appendixes F1 and F2 for a sample corporate foundation proposal and budget.[137]

"After a proposal is submitted to a corporate foundation, it is advisable to follow up immediately to ensure that the materials have been received. Depending on the relationship already established, a meeting or phone call can be scheduled at this time to further discuss the proposal. Otherwise, it is advisable to recontact the foundation representatives perhaps two weeks after the submission.

"If a meeting is scheduled, the director of development should attend along with the nonprofit organization's executive director. Also, a program manager should attend if the proposal makes a specific request for programmatic funding. If invited to present to a corporate foundation representative, those staff members attending the meeting should be prepared to speak about the organization itself and the program/ initiative that requires funding. The pitch should briefly describe the proposal's [request] and should provide more details based upon the foundation's interest, as well as visibility and recognition for any support. Bring a bulleted agenda of issues/topics to be covered in the meeting. (This might not be necessary, yet might be of use in the course of the meeting.) Bring copies of the letter of inquiry, the proposal, and any other materials that had previously been submitted. Assess the tenor of the meeting and adjust the pitch accordingly. An informal yet businesslike sense of purpose is always appreciated and will raise the value of the pitch. Bring marketing materials so the corporate representative can see the professionalism of the organization. Be clear and concise in presenting the proposal and the request, and be very forthcoming in what the corporation could receive in return. However, be realistic: Don't promise the sky just to secure a commitment.

"Most often, a corporate foundation wishes for its support of a nonprofit organization to be recognized with the corporation's parent name. However, if the corporate foundation has enough visibility and stature separate from the corporation itself, the foundation can be recognized by its legal name (e.g., the American Express Foundation, as opposed to American Express). It should be noted that, unlike contributions departments of corporations, corporate foundations are not allowed to receive direct benefits, such as tickets and advertising. Corporation foundations may be given incidental sponsorship credit for their contributions to nonprofit performing arts organizations.

"If a corporate foundation provides funding, the director of development should issue the official thank-you letter with the terms and tax-deductibility information. Additionally, the nonprofit organization's executive director/president should issue an acknowledgement letter. Depending on the size of the gift and the scope of the corporate foundation's involvement with the nonprofit, the chair of the nonprofit organization's board of directors also could issue an acknowledgement letter.

"It is typical for a corporate foundation to issue a final report form at the end of a funding cycle, and the development staff should work directly with foundation representatives on answering all required questions. If no form is issued, the final report to a corporate foundation, for either general operating support or program support, should address the following quantitative and qualitative points: purpose of the funding and amount; number of constituents who benefited from the grant; and specific accomplishments resulting from this support. Reporting on measurable outcomes directly attributable to this funding deserves special consideration."[138]

CLASSROOM DISCUSSION
What is a corporate foundation?

Why do corporate foundations support the performing arts?

How do you research whether a corporation has a foundation, and whether that foundation supports the performing arts?

What should a letter of inquiry include? Who should sign it?

When and how should you follow up a letter of inquiry or a proposal?

What are the key components of a corporate foundation proposal?

Write a proposal to a corporate foundation.

How should you prepare for the meeting where you will pitch your project to the corporate foundation personnel?

What information should the final report include?

Corporate Marketing Departments: Sponsorships
Sarah Bordy defines a corporate sponsorship as "a partnership between the performing arts organization and a corporation."[139] She states, "You agree to take funds from the corporation, and in return, you are expected to provide an agreed-upon list of benefits."[140] Sponsorships can take the form of a direct contribution to underwrite or pay for an event or season. A sponsor can also underwrite the cost of goods and services or provide them to the organization. In return, the corporate sponsor will want its name associated with the item or event it supports. Corporations can sell a product and advertise that they will donate a portion of the sales to the nonprofit organization. This is called "cause marketing" or "cause-related marketing." Sponsorship deals are usually made with corporate marketing departments. The corporation receives a tax benefit for the portion of their gift that is philanthropic, in which no goods and services are

received. For a detailed discussion of corporate sponsorship's legal aspects, please see chapter 3.

Feiner speaks about the corporate trends governing corporate sponsorships: "Corporations are increasingly linking sponsorship support and philanthropic giving with their core businesses. There are several terms for this, such as cause-related philanthropy and strategic giving. Corporations are being very creative to ensure that their philanthropic commitments to nonprofit organizations support this business-minded approach to giving. For example, one major national bank has chosen primary education as a core area within its giving universe. In addition to providing financial support for nonprofit organizations with educational missions, including theaters and their performance-related educational outreach, this bank is building its philanthropic giving into the fabric of the corporate culture. The bank's employees are encouraged to dedicate paid out-of-office time to complement nonprofit organizations' efforts in schools. In addition to working with the nonprofit organization's programs, these bank employees are conducting classroom lessons in basic money management (the use of savings and checking accounts, basic accounting, etc.). The bank actually writes up and prepares these lesson plans and makes them available to all its regional branches around the country. There is a benefit to the nonprofit organization that receives this bank's philanthropic support—the nonprofit organization's staff and performers also get training in these bank-sponsored programs."[141]

Feiner contends, "It is advisable to provide plenty of lead time when approaching a corporate sponsor for a specific event—a year to two years prior to the event is advisable. It also is advisable to secure sponsorship support in advance, as such support from a highly regarded name is vital to helping leverage and secure additional support from other sources.

"The best way to first approach a potential corporate sponsor is through invitations to performances, special events, and meet-the-artist receptions. It is best to get the corporate representative to know the nonprofit organization in its best light, with all the lights and glitter intact and operating. It will provide the impression that the nonprofit organization has something of real value that the corporate sponsor should want to be in on, and that there are tangible benefits of such an association."[142] Corporate contributions and corporate foundation managers, as well as nonprofit board members with corporate affiliations, can also make introductions to corporate marketing departments.

Like other requests for corporate support, the organization should submit a letter of inquiry, followed by a cover letter and proposal, to the corporation. Feiner adds, "A letter of inquiry should be quite short, certainly no longer than two pages and preferably just a single page. Similarly, a proposal should also be quite short, also no longer than two pages; ditto for the proposal cover letter. It is appropriate for the director of development to sign each type of letter. As no one in business (or the corporate world) has time to read, the key component of a letter of inquiry and cover letter should be a distinct and short summary of the request: what the nonprofit is seeking support for, why this corporation has been targeted for such a request, and what return on investment the corporation can expect to receive.

"Visibility for a corporate sponsor is normally very important. It is most often the sole reason for a corporation's decision to provide sponsorship support. The corporation should receive prominent visual recognition, with wording consistent with its requirements and mutually determined by the corporation and the nonprofit organization. However, it is incumbent upon the nonprofit organization to keep such recognition within reasonable terms. The corporation very well might ask for the moon in terms of visibility/recognition and benefits. The nonprofit organization needs to firmly stand its ground and not give away the store in return for corporate sponsorship recognition."[143]

John Holden lists the key components that should appear in a sponsorship letter of inquiry, cover letter, proposal, and proposal packet. He then discusses the strategy for an in-person pitch, should the corporation be interested in the proposal.

Letter of Inquiry:

- Combine all the elements of a proposal cover letter with a slightly more detailed summary of a full-length proposal. Maximum length: two pages.
- Outline benefits available to the prospect at varying levels of sponsorship.
- Include only attachments that are critical for the donor to understand the key aspects of the project, and close the letter by mentioning that you would be happy to forward a full proposal packet if the sponsorship is of interest to the prospect. Mention that you will call/follow up with the person within a few weeks.

Cover Letter:

- Open with any connections you or your organization might have to the prospective funder.
- Summarize the contents of the proposal. Highlight proposal elements that you expect to be of particular interest to the prospect.
- Add that you can customize benefits to meet the corporation's specific needs and objectives.
- Close by thanking the prospect for his consideration and providing contact information: Whom should the prospect call if he needs more information?

Proposal (two pages):

- Include a short history and mission. How is your organization unique?
- Summarize the project.
- Describe how it relates to the corporation's priorities.
- Provide an overview of sponsorship benefits (include a detailed list of benefits as an attachment).
- Include a project budget.

Proposal Packet:

- Should include other background materials (reviews, board listing, company awards, newsletter, etc.)
- Typical list of attachments:
  o A list of donor benefits at different sponsorship levels.
  o IRS tax-exempt determination letter 501(c)(3).
  o Audited and unaudited financial statements from previous years.
  o The project budget (if not in proposal).
  o A detailed schedule.
  o A history sheet (might include the mission statement, awards received, other significant achievements).
  o Recent press clippings about your organization and its work.
  o Recent and relevant company publications (season brochure, company newsletters).

Pitch Strategy:

- Representatives from the organization should include development staff (it is not as important to have senior leadership involved).

- Fully describe the project the corporation would be supporting. How does it overlap with the corporation's goals/image/marketing objectives?
- Can you recognize the corporation as a "lead corporate sponsor" (meaning they won't have to share billing with others)? Outline what level of support would be needed to ensure them lead sponsorship versus cosponsorship status.
- How will you recognize the corporate sponsor's support?
- If possible, tailor sponsorship benefits to suit the corporation's specific needs and objectives. If the corporation is more interested in entertainment opportunities, offer more tickets and special receptions for clients and employees. If it is interested in profile, offer more prominent recognition in ads and the playbill. Be creative—find innovative ways of meeting the corporation's objectives in ways that are appropriate for your organization/project.
- Bring written materials that outline the project and contain answers to all the questions you can anticipate the corporation having. These materials might include:
  o A *short* narrative project summary.
  o An outline of sponsorship benefits (perhaps at different levels).
  o Detailed budgets.
  o General background information on the organization (a limited amount of material).
  o Examples of how you have credited the corporation's support in the past (if it is a renewal).
  o The method of evaluation: How would you measure the success of the project and report to the corporation on the impact of its support?[144]

After the pitch has taken place, it's appropriate to follow up with a thank-you letter (containing tax-deductibility information) and to check on the status of the project with a phone call within two weeks of the meeting. Once the deal has been made, it is appropriate to create a sponsorship deal letter that both the corporate and nonprofit representatives can sign. Because this agreement is legally binding, it must be shown to the nonprofit organization's board of directors and attorney. Figure 6.12 provides an example of this type of letter and its terms.[145]

Fig. 6.12. Sample Corporate Sponsorship Deal Agreement

November 3, 2005

To: Sponsor Contact Name
              Job Title
              Sponsor Company
              Address 1
              Address 2
              Phone: (xxx) xxx-xxxx   Fax: (xxx) xxx-xxxx   Email: xxxx@xxxxxxxx.com

From: Sponsee Name
              Job Title
              Arts Service Organization
              Address 1
              Address 2
              Phone: (xxx) xxx-xxxx   Fax: (xxx) xxx-xxxx   Email: xxxx@xxxxxxxx.com

Arts Service Organization is very grateful for the support of Sponsor Company. Please consider the following a confirmation of the sponsorship agreement between Arts Service Organization and Sponsor Company beginning in 2006:

Responsibility of Sponsor Company

At least once annually beginning January 1, 2006 for each theatre/market (see list below), Sponsor Company will provide a watch (valued at $500+) for network of theatres' promotional purposes, such as auctions, raffles or other premium programs.

Up to 200 Sponsor Company gift cards and/or gift bags shall also be made available to each theatre (select member organizations of Arts Service Organization) for each year of the sponsorship agreement. These shall be distributed as goodie bag items, or prizes or rewards to theatre donors and prospective donors only.

Responsibility of Theatres:

This donation is subject to the following:
    1) Auction/sweepstakes/premium materials will acknowledge Sponsor Company and the watch brand relating to this donation for the contribution in type face and location equal to all other donors at that level for the related event.
    2) For auctions, signage shall prominently credit Sponsor Company and the related watch brand. For live auctions, Sponsor Company and the watch brand shall be verbally credited for the donation at time of auction.
    3) In exchange for this in-kind contribution, theatre programs shall list Sponsor Company as a donor at the level equal to the value of the watch.

Participating theatres at 10/2005 (additional theatres to be added as Sponsor adds markets):
    Theatre 1 – City, State
    Theatre 2 – City, State
    Theatre 3 – City, State
    Theatre 4 – City, State
    Theatre 5 – City, State
    Theatre 6 – City, State
    Theatre 7 – City, State

Thank you once again for your support of Arts Service Organization.

_____   _____
Executive Director   Sponsor Contact Name
Arts Service Organization   Sponsor Company

CLASSROOM DISCUSSION

What is a corporate sponsorship, and what form can it take?

What is the lead time for first approaching a corporate sponsor for support?

What is the best time to cultivate a corporate sponsor?

What are the important components of the following: letter of inquiry, cover letter, proposal, proposal package, and pitch?

Take a look at the sponsorship deal letter. What information should a deal letter include?

Why must you show this letter to your board of directors and an attorney?

Institutional Giving: Foundations

According to the Foundation Center, a research library dedicated to the study of foundations, "Foundation giving increased by 6.1 percent in 2005." Gifts to arts and cultural organizations rose 3.8 percent.[146] What exactly is a foundation? Feiner explains, "A foundation is, in effect, a tax-exempt organization created to give away funds. Foundations can be national/multinational organizations (e.g., the Ford Foundation and the Kresge Foundation), or smaller, family-based organizations to help individuals distribute privately held funds in support of philanthropic causes. A foundation is federally mandated to distribute a minimum of 5 percent of its assets yearly as contributions to organizations of its choosing."[147] Let's examine the different types of foundations:

Corporate Foundation:
- Goals are consistent with corporate giving. While there may be fluctuations in the corporate contributions budget (due to stock market fluctuations, profits/loss), corporate foundations tend to keep relatively consistent levels of giving. Examples: American Express Foundation, AT&T Foundation.

Independent Foundation:
- Independent foundations are not governed by the benefactor, the benefactor's family, or a corporation. Of the largest private foundations in the United States, most are independent foundations, although they may have begun as family foundations (e.g., Rockefeller Foundation and Ford Foundation).

Family Foundation:
- Usually managed by the original donor (e.g., Bill and Melinda Gates Foundation).

Trusts:
- Typically run by friends or business associates of the original donor. Usually administered by a law firm or bank.

Community Foundation:
- Pooled gifts from many individual donors in a particular community. Can be:
  o Geographically focused (e.g., New York Community Trust)
  o Issue-focused (e.g., Rainbow Endowment)

Operating Foundation:
- Uses its endowment for its own programs (e.g., hospitals and universities).
- Does not make outside grants (e.g., Brooklyn College Foundation).[148]

Foundations: Research and Determining Donor Motivations

Since grant-making foundations are nonprofit organizations, they must file either a Form 990 or a Form 990 P-F. Forms 990 and 990 P-F list organizations that receive funding and the grant amount they received. These forms can be reviewed on *GuideStar.org*. The Foundation Center has an online service that also allows performing arts organizations to research foundations (*www.foundationcenter.org*). The large foundations (corporate and community) publish annual reports and grant guidelines that may be used to gather research on foundation giving, including the geographic area of the organizations that are funded, grant amounts, funding cycles, and proposal deadlines. Finally, it is important to review the playbill at peer institutions and study which foundations are giving to these organizations.

The Foundation Center's study reports that foundations are most likely to give to project support rather than general operating support, although unrestricted grants grew 1 percent from 2004 to 2005.[149] Holden adds, "Community foundations tend to support projects with a more civic focus; family foundations might base giving more on current relationships than on an alignment with foundation priorities. They often act more like individual donors."[150]

In approaching a foundation for support, Holden issues this critical advice:

- READ GUIDELINES.
- Use board contacts (particularly for corporate or family foundations).
- Send a letter of inquiry first, then follow up with a proposal.

- Smaller foundations often do not accept unsolicited requests. Therefore, when approaching a smaller foundation, you should:
  - Send a letter of introduction.
  - Invite foundation trustees and staff to events.
  - Try to establish a connection to the foundation board or staff through your own board members, artists, or others connected with your organization.[151]

Foundations: The Approach

In the previous section, we discussed the strategies for developing a good letter of inquiry, proposal cover letter, proposal, and proposal packet for a corporate foundation. We also examined the components of a winning in-person pitch to a corporate foundation manager. These elements are found in the organization's approach to all foundations. If the foundation accepts the proposal, it is "typically acknowledged at the appropriate level of giving in the organization's playbill, and anywhere else donors of similar stature are recognized."[152] Foundations require a report from the organization at the end of the fiscal year or project period, detailing how the funds were spent and including an evaluation of the project and financial statements.

CLASSROOM DISCUSSION

Name and define the different types of foundations. What types of grants do they fund? How do you conduct research on foundations?

How should you approach smaller foundations?

Write a sample foundation letter of inquiry.

Institutional Giving: Government

We now turn to government funding of the performing arts. Government agencies support the performing arts at the federal, state, and local levels. Robert Lynch, president and chief executive officer of Americans for the Arts, a chief national advocacy nonprofit organization supporting the arts in the United States, works closely with government agencies and elected officials. Lynch explains why the government is involved in funding the arts: "Federal, state, and local governments support arts organizations because citizens have made the case that the arts are a valuable enhancement to the community. Therefore, the community should invest money in the arts just as it does for other enhancements, like roads and sidewalks, business districts, and safety organizations."[153]

Patrick Dewane's relationship with government agencies offers this perspective: "The case has been successfully made to politicians that arts organizations are a good use of tax dollars. They improve the quality of life; are important to the enrichment of the human spirit; are important to the education of the residents; improve student test scores and achievement; and help promote economic development."[154]

Neal Brilliant, grants writer for Lincoln Center Theater, believes "these agencies were established and continue to receive annual funding because advocates for the arts have effectively lobbied and convinced legislators at all levels of government that cultural organizations merit support."[155]

Why is it important to seek support from government agencies? Lynch contends: "Even though government money accounts for less than 10 percent of the total amount of support contributed to the arts, that 10 percent is necessary for organizational survival. Government investment, which usually is awarded through a competitive process, sends a signal that the organization has passed a test for quality, making it easier to attract individual, business, and foundation dollars."[156]

Brilliant discusses the importance of government funding for small organizations or companies just getting started. "When an organization's founders (its artistic director and/or managing director) begin to look for funding, the first step is usually to ask family and friends for financial assistance. The next step in most instances is to apply for grants from city or state funding agencies. In addition to providing monetary support, these agencies can help make sure that a young company is systematizing its operations properly as it gets off the ground. Just like foundation and corporate funders, government agencies require financial statements, 501(c)(3) tax-exempt certification, and a list of the board of directors. Staff members at government agencies thoroughly vet [review] an organization and recommend funding only if all criteria have been met.

"Once an arts organization has received a grant from a government agency, its principals can start approaching foundations for contributions using its record of government funding as an imprimatur. It's important to foundation administrators—particularly if they are not familiar with the companies' work—that new companies have been scrutinized, and receipt of a government grant acknowledges that the organization has been closely inspected. Fundraising is a step-by-step process. It begins with solicitations to individuals (friends and family), proceeds to the government, then to foundations. It doesn't always happen in this orderly sequence, but that's what makes government funding important to small organizations—it serves as a stamp of approval and creates an anchor of support as a young company strives to move to the next phase of the institutional giving process."[157]

Researching and Approaching Government Agencies and Elected Officials

Funding for the arts is generated at the federal, state, and local levels. Robert Lynch provides information on the type of funding from each branch of the government:

- **Federal Funding:** Federal funding is often thought of as only the $100 million or so that is appropriated annually (by Congress) and granted out by the National Endowment for the Arts (NEA), the leading federal agency dedicated to supporting the arts. In addition to the NEA, the National Endowment for the Humanities (NEH), the Department of Education (DOE), the General Services Administration (GSA, public art investment in government buildings), and the Department of Justice (DOJ), among others, have supported the arts in this country. Our government also directly subsidizes institutions with a federal connection like the Smithsonian Institution, the Library of Congress, and the Kennedy Center. In total, the federal government's annual support for the arts at the federal level is well over $1 billion.
- **State Funding:** State arts agencies, such as the New York State Council on the Arts and the Minnesota State Arts Board, receive funds from the National Endowment for the Arts and their respective state governments. That money, in turn, is granted to arts organizations. Bond issues are another source of state support for the arts. Bonds make it possible for cities to borrow a certain amount of money at a certain rate from a bank or treasury for a variety of local projects. Similar to loans, bonds must be paid back; the interest rates of the bonds will vary, depending upon a city's bond rating (similar to a personal credit rating). Bond issues result in a wide variety of additional funding sources, such as the recent bond issue for $250 million for cultural facilities in Massachusetts. At the state and local levels, constituents may actually vote on whether to pass a bond issue. Each state has different rules. Most states have two paths: a legislative initiative brought forward by a legislator for a vote by the entire legislature,

or a citizen initiative where a petition signed by a designated number of citizens places an idea on the ballot. Constituents often vote on other kinds of ballot initiatives beyond bond issues, such as the arts lottery in Massachusetts. Fees derived by the sale of customized license plates in California and other states, which are added to the budget of the state arts council, are authorized directly by the legislature. The range of possible mechanisms to support the arts is limited only by the creativity of arts advocates who put forward the ideas for the official vote, and, of course, the enthusiasm of the voters themselves.

- **Local Arts Funding:** Local arts government funding can come from either a city's or a county's direct appropriation for the arts, usually funneled through a city government (e.g., the Department of Cultural Affairs in New York City) or a 501(c)(3) local arts agency (e.g., Brooklyn Arts Council in Brooklyn, New York), as well as from a wide variety of special designated sources like hotel/motel taxes and arts ordinances. Just as with a state ordinance, a local ordinance is a law set forth by a governmental authority; in this case, it is specifically a municipal regulation. Some cities, for example, have an arts ordinance calling for a 'Percent for Art' plan that authorizes the allocation of a certain percentage of municipal capital improvement project costs (usually around 1 percent) for the commissioning of public artwork. Other mechanisms include special taxes on hotel or motel occupancy, sales taxes, or a very specific revenue-generating mechanism, like the tax on cigarettes in the city of Cleveland, Ohio. Many local arts agencies (arts councils, arts commissions, etc.) are set up either as a part of city or county government or as a 501(c)(3) nonprofit arts organization designated by the municipality to re-grant municipal money to arts organizations. The Brooklyn Arts Council, for example, re-grants money it receives from the state, city, foundations, and corporations.[158]

Researching which federal, state, and local agencies give money to the performing arts may be done online. Agencies will issue grant guidelines and applications to organizations outlining the type of support given; the grant amounts; the deadlines; when the project may take place (dates or a timetable for carrying out the project); the information needed in the application and attachments; and when a decision will be made. If an organization is approaching an agency dedicated to supporting something other than the arts (e.g., senior citizens, employment, at-risk youth), it is important that it make in its application the case for serving this particular constituency. Please see appendix G for a sample National Endowment for the Arts proposal.[159]

In addition to these types of support, nonprofit organizations sometimes may approach their elected officials in federal, state, and local governments for a special appropriation that is earmarked for a particular organization. The earmarked organization then becomes a line item in a budget. If an organization becomes a line item in a budget, the name of the organization will appear with the amount of money appropriated to the organization. Line items can range from a few thousand to millions of dollars.[160] This money is given in addition to other monies the organization may receive from federal, state, or local government agencies. In order to become a "line item," the organization must get to know its elected officials. Terri Osborne, director of culture and tourism for the Queens Borough President, describes the process at the local level in New York City: "In researching elected officials who support the arts, you start by contacting your own elected official who represents you—city, state, federal. Very few elected officials give money to organizations outside their districts. The only time this might happen is when another elected official asks them to, or if they believe the project serves a larger audience. Therefore, building a relationship with your elected officials who represent you is the key to getting money. You can find your elected officials by visiting your city government Web site. In order to get New York City Council funding, the organization must establish a rapport with their local council representative. This means keeping her abreast of good press and letters of support from community members, awards, or special recognition that your organization has received. In other words, your organization and its activities have to be front and center in the council member's mind, leaving no question as to the many benefits the organization brings to the community. Eventually, it is as simple as writing a letter of request to the council member, or filling out a form explaining the need and the benefits the grant will provide."[161]

Ella Weiss, president of the Brooklyn Arts Council in Brooklyn, New York, offers this advice for getting to know your elected officials: "You follow the elections, see who has been elected, and see who on your board knows the elected official. Just as you get to know the corporate players, you get to know the elected officials who are players. You talk to people.

You make them aware of what you do, how you do it, why you are unique, and how you benefit their constituency. If you can't draw a line from what you do to the people they serve, you are going to have a problem. There has got to be a connection. Anybody can make that connection if he is thoughtful about it, but elected officials are not going to make it for you—you have to do it."[162]

How does an organization discover what types of projects its elected officials will be interested in supporting? Weiss responds, "That's like asking what people's favorite foods are. They all have very different agendas. Some are very interested in housing, and the arts are not on their radar. Some are very interested in job development for the unemployed, and you could come to them with a proposal if you could make the straight line between artists and job development. There are others [who have] education at the top of their list, so again if you have something that involves education, you may be able to get them interested in you, because you can make the connection between what you do and education. They are all different. There is no 'one-size-fits-all.' You have to get to know them. Some of them will say, 'That's not of interest to me. That is a luxury. I have to worry about the people in my district who don't have jobs and need money.' And so then you have to come back with an answer to these implicit questions: 'What can we do to help those people? We are not a housing agency, but what can we do to make those people's lives better?' They may or may not listen. It is a long process; it takes a long time to cultivate elected officials. It takes a long time to distinguish yourself from the pack."[163]

It is important that an elected official be approached for support in a nonpartisan manner. In other words, legally a 501(c)(3) organization cannot be supporting the elected official's political ambitions, or appear to be supporting a particular political party. (For a more detailed legal explanation, please see chapter 3.)

When initiating contact with an elected official, the organization will first send a letter of inquiry. John Holden recommends that the following components be included in a brief letter to an elected official. If granted a meeting, this information may also be used in an in-person pitch to the elected official:

- Reintroduce your organization (ideally, you have already met or been introduced to the elected official).

- Describe all the wonderful acts of public service your organization already does in the official's district.
- Outline the project you hope the official will help fund—preferably something that will enhance your public service and be accessible to the widest possible audience (it should be free or very cheap). Educational events and outreach to the public schools are very popular.
- Include only attachments that are critical for the reader to understand the key aspects of the project.
- If the official has a staff member dedicated to overseeing appropriations, or a liaison for cultural affairs, make sure you copy that person on any and all correspondence.
- If you are granted a meeting, bring written materials that outline the project and contain answers to all the questions you can anticipate. Keep these short and to the point. These materials might include:
  o A *short* narrative project summary, including *specific* information on project impact (How many students? What's the ticket price? Where are they from? What grades are they in? What's their socioeconomic makeup?)
  o A summary budget.
  o Schematic designs/drawings (for capital projects).
  o General background information on your organization (a limited amount of material).[164]

After receiving support from an elected official, what is the best way to acknowledge his support? Ella Weiss advises, "Some of them don't want recognition because they don't want other people asking them for money. Some want every bit of recognition they can get, and you have to know who should deliver that recognition. Some of it is very local, and some is much more far-reaching. If a person is a local official, but has aspirations to run citywide, statewide, or nationally, he may be interested in different forms of recognition at that point in his career. You have to be careful because if you do something for one and you don't do it for another, you can hurt rather than help your cause."[165]

CLASSROOM DISCUSSION

Why does the government support the arts?

Why is it important to seek support from the government?

Why is it important for a small organization to receive government support?

Define the various types of federal, state, and local funding.

What are the important components of a government grant (see appendix G)?

How do you get to know elected officials? How do you know what types of projects elected officials support?

What is a line item?

What does "nonpartisan" mean?

What are the major components of a letter of inquiry to an elected official? Write a letter of inquiry.

How do elected officials want to be acknowledged?

CAPITAL AND ENDOWMENT CAMPAIGNS

The annual fundraising plan raises money from individual and institutional donors to support expenses in a fiscal year. Some organizations also create a plan for a capital and/or endowment campaign. What is the difference between a capital and an endowment campaign?

Feiner explains, "As stated previously, a capital campaign is a specific fundraising program to secure financial resources to help effect upgrades/improvements to the physical plant of the nonprofit organization (e.g., refurbishment of the interior or exterior of a theater, or the building of a new rehearsal studio complex adjacent to or near the theater). An endowment campaign is a specific fundraising program to secure financial resources for a separate reserve of funding that will help ensure the longevity of the nonprofit organization or a specific program of central importance to the nonprofit organization's mission. The primary reason to conduct a capital campaign is to raise a significant amount of funds to help a nonprofit organization's overall organizational growth—to take the institution to an exciting new level of production capability and visibility. A capital campaign is, by construct, long-term, and embraces all departments of the institution. In contrast, an endowment campaign helps to establish a stable source of income for a nonprofit organization or a specific initiative/program within the nonprofit organization. An endowment has less to do with an overriding structural change in the nonprofit organization's daily operations, and more to do with providing long-term stability for the nonprofit organization's current structure. That said, an endowment campaign often can be a component of a nonprofit organization's capital campaign. The capital campaign will help fund the overall 'next phase' life of the nonprofit organization, and the endowment campaign will help ensure the long life of this 'next phase.'"[166]

Dewane has a great deal of experience with both types of campaigns. He adds, "Our current $20 million campaign is a hybrid—$12 million in endowment, $3 million in capital acquisition, and the rest in various funds to advance the company (expenses that are either one-timers, or will be supported with the added interest from the endowment). Strictly speaking, capital campaigns are for physical things—buildings, land, equipment, etc. We bought a building for $1.5 million and equipment for $1.5 million. This would be the capital portion of our campaign. The rest is endowment and bridge funding. An endowment campaign raises funds that will be invested to provide a steady stream of income from the appreciation or proceeds of the investment, with the corpus (principal) never being drawn upon. Its purpose is to provide the organization with a reliable source of income, other than what is earned or contributed. A portion of the endowment campaign may be used to fund operating expenses that will eventually be paid for by the interest of the increased endowment. This is called "bridge funding." Donors close to the organization generally contribute to capital and endowment campaigns."[167]

If an organization decides to launch an endowment or capital campaign, it will obviously coincide with the annual fund campaign. Conducting two campaigns at a time poses some challenges for fundraisers. Dewane elaborates, "You are asking many of the same people to support both campaigns. You risk losing annual support when you ask for a major capital gift. And even if you don't lose the annual fund support, it is difficult to get an increase for the annual fund while you are getting a major gift to your capital campaign. By phasing the campaign, you can manage the impact that the campaign will have on the annual fund. That is, by soliciting your insiders (board members and major donors) first, you can explain to them the importance of the continued growth of the annual fund during the early phase of the campaign. In my experience, insiders and major prospects are more likely to maintain their annual fund support while they are making their capital pledge. But I have had painful exceptions to this. It is important during the leadership and quiet phases (funds raised before the campaign becomes public) that the annual fund strategy is rigorous in securing new and increased gifts, as these donors will both mitigate any decreases to the annual fund caused by the early campaign gifts and grow the base of prospects for the later phase of the campaign. An annual fund challenge grant for new and increased gifts from individuals can be very effective in this situation. Then, as you make your way to the next phase, you can go back to early capital fund donors (if you have cultivated strong relationships) and ask them to increase their annual fund gift to cushion the impact of the donors who will give to the capital campaign at the expense of their annual fund gift.

"At all stages, it is important to effectively communicate the need for the campaign and its successes. Success begets success. You cannot have the scent of a loss on your effort. You also can't solicit broader small community gifts until you are sure you will hit your goal. These gifts should get you over the top. All four capital campaigns I have done have been situations that got off to bad starts and floundered, in which development directors before me didn't get the lead and major gifts they needed, didn't phase things correctly, and then started soliciting smaller gifts so it looked like there was some activity. All were a mess, but all got turned around.

"I have never had the luxury as a staff member of starting a campaign from scratch, but I have consulted on campaigns that have started from scratch and have followed the standard principles to success, including the challenge of raising both capital and annual funds at the same time. You have to get your big gifts from insiders first; otherwise you will languish until someone comes in and focuses you on getting big gifts first. And that languishing period will damage your annual fund. You must be strategic about it. If you are, then your annual fund can grow dramatically after the campaign is finished, as you will have a large number of donors who have become closer to you and are used to writing you big checks."[168]

In addition to addressing these challenges, the savvy director of development must also think about a strategy for raising endowment funds. According to Patrick Dewane, endowment funds are harder to raise than capital funds. Dewane reports, "People like buildings; they like stuff. If you make a good case for your building, it is far easier to get people on the periphery of your organization, even people who have never funded you, to give you big gifts. Endowments aren't nearly as appealing. However, this is where I believe arts organizations need to study how the large universities have been so successful in raising endowment gifts. Arts organizations need to focus more attention on cultivating relationships that could result in large endowment gifts, just like universities do. Endowment fundraising is a disciplined, multiyear process, but instead we spend most of our time focusing on the annual fund goal. I heard a consultant at a national arts convention facetiously describe it this way: 'Universities spend most of their time robbing the bankers, whereas arts organizations spend most of their time robbing the farmers.' Endowment fundraising takes a lot of time, but the results can be transformative."[169]

The need to conduct a campaign is determined by the strategic planning process. Even if the need is found to exist, nonprofit performing arts organizations must do the necessary research to determine whether they have the ability to launch a successful campaign. This research process often begins with a feasibility study. John Holden discusses the information that should be collected through this process. He believes that "all data should be gathered, compiled, and analyzed, preferably in partnership with a third party (consultant) to provide an impartial viewpoint." This data should include:

- A comprehensive analysis of *all* patterns in giving over the past five (perhaps ten) years in all areas of giving—individual, board, government, foundation, corporate. This data should provide an indication of the organization's areas of strength and weakness.
- Average and median gifts in all these areas of giving.
- Specific feedback from a wide sampling of current donors on their potential level of participation in a campaign, and general feedback on the organization and its effectiveness.
- Specific (and perhaps confidential) feedback from staff/board members on the organization's operations and capacity to support a campaign.
- A thorough screening (often conducted by an outside research company) of the organization's current constituency. Constituents should be compared with a well-regarded database of known contributors to identify major gift prospects who are already familiar with the organization.
- Comparison of all this data to similar organizations and campaigns. Where did they succeed? Where did they falter?

The findings of the study will help to structure a well-informed, comprehensive campaign plan.[170]

After the organization has conducted the feasibility study and determined its ability to launch a successful campaign, it must determine its campaign goal. Dewane talks about this process: "You begin by asking the question, 'What would you like to raise? What will the market support today?' Your campaign goal will be somewhere in between."[171] Once the organization determines its goal, it can develop its budget and strategy. Please see appendix H for a sample capital campaign status of funding report.[172]

The organization is now ready to organize its campaign. Dewane illustrates the important steps involved. "You need to recruit a campaign chair who makes an early stretch gift and is prepared to devote significant time and influence to securing the needed funds. A stretch gift is a gift from a donor that is significantly larger than any previous donation the donor has given in the past. The notion to 'give till it hurts' often accompanies a request for a stretch gift, just as a trainer at a gym might tell you to stretch till it hurts. I had a wonderful solicitor show up for a $1 million ask one time with a bag from a bookstore. I didn't think twice about the bag until he made the [request] and pulled out an exercise book with the large title *Stretching*. The prospect laughed heartily, especially because the solicitor was hardly an athlete.

"The chair and top staff person then need to identify and recruit the steering committee. The steering committee is the group of volunteers and staff responsible for raising the money to meet the goal of the campaign. The committee chair is the volunteer leader and works very closely with the development director on campaign strategy and execution. The committee meets regularly to review prospects and assignments, report on progress, plan cultivation opportunities, and 'bond' around the advancement of the organization. The chair should run the meetings. The development director should create the agenda with the chair and maintain all records of activities and progress reports."[173]

The strategy for raising money is as follows: "You need to secure your lead gift and many of your major gifts early in the campaign. A lead gift is your biggest gift, the most important gift to the campaign. It should be 10 to 20 percent of the goal. Major gifts are the next ten to fifteen largest gifts below the lead gift. At least 50 percent of the goal should be raised by the lead gift and major gifts. The fundraiser creates a gift table, which is a guide for how many gifts you need at what level of giving to meet your goal."[174] A sample of a gift table is shown in fig. 6.13.[175]

Fig. 6.13. Minnesota Opera Gift Table

Opera at the Ordway Initiative
Pledge Report
(as of December 20, 2006)

Contributors		Pledges To-Date
Anonymous		$ 5,000,000
Judy & Ken Dayton	(Oakleaf Trust)	$ 2,950,000
Mary Vaughan		$ 1,000,000
John & Ruth Huss	(+ virtual seat)	$ 775,000
Gus & Mary Blanchard	(+ virtual seat)	$ 625,000
Barbara Bemis	(Bemis Fund, Endow.)	$ 585,000
Andersen Foundation		$ 500,000
Target Foundation		$ 500,000
The McKnight Foundation		$ 400,000
Bigelow Foundation		$ 350,000
Dolly Fiterman		$ 300,000
General Mills Foundation		$ 300,000
3M Foundation		$ 300,000
Cargill Foundtion		$ 250,000
Al & Ingrid Harrison		$ 250,000
Medtronic Foundation		$ 250,000
Margaret & Angus Wurtele		$ 250,000
Jean Lemberg Estate	(unrest. endowment)	$ 200,000
St. Paul Foundation		$ 200,000
Wells Fargo		$ 200,000
Ecolab		$ 175,000
St. Paul Travelers		$ 150,000
Bud & Beverly Grossman		$ 150,000
Connie & Daniel Kunin	(additional $50,000)	$ 150,000
Glen & Marilyn Nelson	(virtual seat + $100K)	$ 125,000
HRK Trust (Kaemmer Fund)		$ 125,000
HRK Trust (MAHADH Fund)		$ 125,000
Mary Lee Dayton	(unrest. endowment)	$ 100,000
Karen Bachman		$ 100,000
Alexandra Bjorklund		$ 100,000
Hearst Foundation	(Education Endow.)	$ 100,000
Lucy Jones		$ 100,000
Mardag Foundation		$ 100,000
John (Smokey) Ordway		$ 100,000

Bold indicates recent pledges
Board Members are highlighted

12/20/2006 12:34 PM

Fig. 6.13. (continued)

Contributors		Pledges To-Date
Edson & Harriet Spencer		$ 100,000
RBC Dain Rauscher		$ 100,000
Virginia & Ed Stringer	(RAP endow.)	$ 100,000
Katherine B. Andersen		$ 100,000
Keller Trust	(unrest. endowment)	$ 92,500
Tom & Rebecca Binger	(unrest. endowment)	$ 75,000
Ted & Nancy Weyerhaueser		$ 50,000
Phillips Trust	(unrest. endowment)	$ 57,000
Ellie & Tom Crosby	(2 virtual seats)	$ 50,000
Heinz & Sisi Hutter		$ 50,000
Steve Rothschild	(2 virtual seats)	$ 50,000
Diana Murphy	(2 virtual seats)	$ 50,000
US Bank		$ 50,000
Frances & George Reid		$ 50,000
Thrivent Financial for Lutherans Foundation		$ 50,000
Erwin & Miriam Kelen	(virtual seat)	$ 25,000
Carolyn Foundation	(unrest. endowment)	$ 25,000
Faegre & Benson Foundation		$ 25,000
Susan & Rod Boren	(virtual seat)	$ 25,000
Richard & Darlene Carroll	(virtual seat)	$ 25,000
Jane & Ogden Confer	(virtual seat)	$ 25,000
Charles Cleveland	(virtual seat)	$ 25,000
Sara & Jock Donaldson	(virtual seat)	$ 25,000
Dorsey & Whitney LLP	(virtual seat)	$ 25,000
Chip & Vicky Emery	(virtual seat)	$ 25,000
Brad & Diane England	(virtual seat)	$ 25,000
Steve Fox & Connie Fladeland	(virtual seat)	$ 25,000
Sharon & Bill Hawkins	(virtual seat)	$ 25,000
Hella & Bill Hueg	(virtual seat)	$ 25,000
David & Perrin Lilly	(virtual seat)	$ 25,000
Tom & Barbara McBurney	(virtual seat)	$ 25,000
Molly McMillan		$ 25,000
Stephanie Simon & Craig Bentdahl	(virtual seat)	$ 25,000
Kevin & Lynn Smith	(virtual seat)	$ 25,000
Bernt von Ohlen	(virtual seat)	$ 25,000
Nicky Carpenter	(virtual seat)	$ 25,000
Southways Foundation		$ 25,000
Burt & Rusty Cohen	(virtual seat)	$ 25,000
John Andrus III	(virtual seat)	$ 25,000
Ken Latham	(virtual seat)	$ 25,000
Boss Foundation	(virtual seat)	$ 25,000

Bold indicates recent pledges
Board Members are highlighted

12/20/2006 12:34 PM

Contributors		Pledges To-Date	
Anonymous	(virtual seat)	$	25,000
Wenger Foundation	(virtual seat)	$	25,000
William & Margaret Bracken	(virtual seat)	$	25,000
Marbrook Foundation		**$**	**25,000**
Bruce & Ruth Dayton		$	20,000
Rosalie Hall		$	15,000
Debra Paterson		$	12,500
Cy & Paula DeCosse		$	10,000
Roger Hale		$	10,000
Margaret Meyers		$	10,000
Bill & Barbara Pearce		$	10,000
Lynda & Frank Sharbrough			5,000

Totals		**$**	**18,752,000**

"You need to build momentum and operate out of a position of strength. You need your early donors to make stretch gifts, the kinds of commitments that will get you closer to your goal and set a standard for subsequent donors. As a staff person, you must always be confident. You must bond with your chair and key committee members, celebrating your successes and learning from your disappointments. Your role is to motivate. I really like the use of challenge grants for this purpose, to have early donors set a challenge total for board members to meet, or for second gifts to the campaign, or for whatever goals you think are doable within your prospect base and your overall goal. In using a challenge grant, the donor is setting a particular condition that a company must meet to earn its funding. Challenge grants are used to leverage other contributions. The Kresge Foundation is the greatest example of challenge grant funding, because their challenge grants have leveraged the completion of hundreds of capital campaigns over several decades.

"For some donors, naming gift opportunities are unimportant; for others it will make the difference between a token gift and a major gift. Naming opportunities give the performing arts organization the ability to acknowledge its donors by placing the donor's name on a building, stage, or rehearsal room. As an example, a performing arts center may be named for a $5 million gift; the stage may be named for a $3 million gift; the lobby for $1 million; the education center for $1 million; classrooms for $500,000; rehearsal rooms for $250,000; dressing rooms and backstage areas for $100,000. In addition, all gifts above $100,000 may also be permanently displayed on a founders' wall in the lobby; gifts between $10,000 and $99,999 may be permanently displayed on a plaque in the lobby; gifts of $5,000 or more may be recognized with a name plaque on a seat.

You need to both be consistent in what you offer and know your audience of donors. You also need to make sure that your cash needs are not compromised by the solicitation of planned gifts. That is, if you have identified an individual as a current gift prospect, then you should not solicit her for a planned gift unless she tells you she does not have the ability to make a current gift. If you do have a planned gift component to your campaign, you need to be careful that the organization is not dependent on those planned gifts to mature in the short term. For example, if you need to raise $20 million in endowment gifts and are counting on the draw [interest] off those gifts in the short term, then you are at risk if you count $2 million in planned gifts toward your goal."[176]

Dewane notes the importance of creating various phases of a campaign, as well as a timetable for implementation. Here are the stages of the campaign:

- Leadership phase: 6 months
- Quiet major gifts phase (this term refers to your insiders, as opposed to the public): 12 months

- Public major gifts phase: 12 months
- Public broad phase: 6 months

Although these phases can overlap, and often do, three years is a typical length for a campaign. However, the length of the campaign may vary depending on the organization, its planning process, and its leadership.[177]

Dewane maintains the importance of raising at least half of the goal amount during the leadership and quiet major gift phase, before the campaign goes public. He asserts, "You want to go public with momentum, with your lead gift and many of your major gifts in place. You cannot rely on the 'kindness of strangers' to make your goal, thinking that others will do for you what your insiders should be doing. The insiders need to make stretch gifts to get you past the halfway point; otherwise, you should not take the campaign to the public."[178]

In creating a strategy to approach leaders and quiet major gifts, Dewane believes, "The donors you target should already know something about the purpose of the campaign. Ideally, they were interviewed in the feasibility study. You start your prospects from the top down, and from the inside out. That is, you start with the people closest to you who have the greatest giving potential. These prospects should be approached by the campaign chair and/or someone on staff (usually the president or the development director). Additionally, care must be taken to include the person among your major donors who will have the most influence on each prospect."[179]

The pitch to a major donor should include the following components:

- Introductions.
- Tell the story and the need.
- The volunteer who is in the solicitation meeting should talk about why she is giving to the campaign, citing the dollar amount she's committed.
- The designated solicitor asks for a specific dollar amount, citing why that amount is important.
- Answer questions and discuss, giving the prospect plenty of opportunity to talk.
- Thank the prospect for the meeting and clarify how the follow-up will occur.

- Detail how and when this donor will receive follow-up (the timetable) and who will make the contact. You should close your meeting with this point already determined. Some people make quick decisions; others draw it out. Therefore, you need to know your prospect and to talk about follow-up and the timetable in the solicitation.[180]

Please see appendix I for a sample major donor pitch.[181]

"After the campaign goes public, the quantity of solicitations increases and the availability of your top solicitors often becomes more limited because of the volume. You need to identify and train new solicitors to augment the efforts of your top solicitors. Otherwise, going public is just a variation of how you approached the donors in the quiet phase.

"Training your volunteers is critical to the success of each campaign phase. I want my volunteers to be relaxed and to speak from the heart. If I haven't solicited with a volunteer before, I want to know what kind of solicitation experience they have had. I do this informally and in a nonthreatening way, as I've had new solicitors claim they've solicited before only to be surprised at their discomfort in the [pitch]. Of course, you go over the case with the campaign volunteers and give them your materials. (Please see appendix J for a sample case statement.[182]) But what I really want them to do is articulate for me why *they* are supporting this campaign, because that is where their passion is. If they can talk from the heart, then the solicitation becomes more about making a dream happen than trying to get into someone's purse.

"I also like to script roles, but not as dialogue to be memorized. I often will write a sample dialogue for a solicitor, and submit this with my campaign material as well. In my last capital campaign I had my co-chair say during my preparation work, 'For crying out loud, I didn't prepare this much when I asked my wife to marry me.' It was a good laugh line, but I didn't want either of us going into our solicitations without an 'A' game plan.

"I also like to attend as many solicitations as possible to ensure quality control. I learned this the hard way. If I'm not there, I'm never really sure what happened, what the body language was, what follow-up was agreed on, or even if the ask was made. Early in my career, I arranged a $1 million solicitation lunch for our chair, the prospect, and someone who was more a go-between than a volunteer. After the lunch, the go-between told me that the chair never made the ask and spent most of the lunch talking about endangered apes in Africa. I scheduled another lunch with the prospect three months later for me and the chair, who assured me he would make the ask. We ate our lunch, and no ask was made. In fact, the chair didn't say one word about our project. This time the lunch conversation wasn't about African apes, it was about Florida deep-sea fishing. As the waiter brought the check, I turned the conversation to the project, and made the ask as my chair gave the waiter his credit card. The happy ending of my story is the prospect pledged $1 million and eventually joined the board. The point of the story is that you can prepare your volunteers all you want, but sometimes they just don't follow your script. So I like to be there in case the ask isn't made, or if something else goes wrong.

"During the public part of the campaign, you keep working through your prospects from the top down and the inside out, going to those who are less and less affiliated with your organization and those who you think have less capacity to give. A staff person and a volunteer closest to the prospect should make the approach. In your gift chart, you need to know what kind of success rate you need for each giving level to be successful overall.

"Once a donor has made a pledge, the organization should ask the donor to sign a gift transmittal form. [Please see appendix K for a sample transmittal form.][183] The form should include the following information: name, address, the amount the donor has pledged, and the payment schedule. Ideally, you want the gift made without any restrictions. However, if the gift is made with restrictions (e.g., it is for the scholarship endowment only), then this needs to be indicated on the pledge form. The pledge form must also state over what period of time a donor must pay his pledge. You need to have a policy so your donors don't spread their gifts out over too many years."[184]

CLASSROOM DISCUSSION
What is the difference between a capital campaign and an endowment campaign?
What is bridge funding?
What are the challenges of raising money for a capital campaign while conducting your annual fundraising campaign? How should you address these challenges?
What are the challenges of launching an endowment campaign? How should you address these challenges?

How do you research whether you have the ability to conduct a successful capital or endowment campaign?
What type of information should be captured in a feasibility study? Why is it important for a consultant to conduct the study and analyze the data?
How do you organize a capital or endowment campaign? What are the important steps?
What is the strategy for raising money from a capital or endowment campaign?
Define "lead gift," "stretch gift," "quiet phase," and "naming opportunity."
What are the phases of an endowment or capital campaign?
Why is it important to raise money for a capital or endowment campaign before the campaign goes public?
What should a pitch contain? Create a pitch.
Why should you train your volunteer solicitors?
What is the purpose of a gift transmittal form?

NOTES
1. The authors wish to thank the following contributors to this chapter: Sarah Bordy, Neal Brilliant, Patrick Dewane, Richard Feiner, Jennie Greer, John Holden, Robert Lynch, Timothy J. McClimon, Amanda Nelson, Terri Osborne, Joel Ruark, SD&A Teleservices, Megan Stevenson, Lynn M. Stirrup, Ella Weiss, and Bruce Whitacre.
2. Patrick Dewane, e-mail interview to author, January 1, 2006; Richard Feiner, e-mail interviews to author, December 1, 2005 and September 4, 2006; John Holden, "Fundraising" (lecture moderated by Tobie Stein, New York City Center, New York, November 8, 2005).
3. Dewane, "E-mail interview"; Feiner, "E-mail interview."
4. Holden, "Lecture."
5. Ibid.
6. Holly Hall, "A Record High," *Chronicle of Philanthropy*, June 28, 2007, 27.
7. Ibid, 28.
8. Holly Hall and Elizabeth Schwinn, "Behind the Numbers: How Different Types of Charities Fared Last Year," *Chronicle of Philanthropy*, June 28, 2007, 29.
9. Dewane.
10. Ibid.
11. Feiner.
12. John Holden, interviews by Jessica Johnston, November 28, 2005 and January 27, 2006.
13. The authors would like to thank Patrick Dewane for creating this sample organizational chart.
14. Dewane; Holden, "Lecture."
15. Dewane.
16. Ibid.
17. Holden, "Lecture."
18. Ibid.
19. Dewane.

20. Ibid.
21. Ibid.
22. Holden, "Lecture."
23. Dewane.
24. Holly Hall, "Written Policies Can Help Charities Steer Clear of Trouble," *Chronicle of Philanthropy*, March 31, 2005, 37.
25. Feiner.
26. The authors would like to thank World Monuments Fund for granting us permission to publish this fund-raising plan.
27. Richard Feiner, "World Monuments Fund Development Plan, FY 2007" (November 2006).
28. Dewane.
29. Ibid.
30. John Holden, e-mail interview to author, May 23, 2006.
31. The authors would like to thank Jennie Greer for allowing us to publish this development calendar and report.
32. Dewane.
33. Feiner.
34. Ibid.
35. Dewane.
36. Amanda Nelson, interview by Christina Klapper, October 7, 2005.
37. Feiner.
38. Dewane.
39. Meg Sommerfeld, "Prospecting the Web for Donors," *Chronicle of Philanthropy*, August 9, 2001, 27.
40. Nelson, "Interview."
41. Dewane.
42. Ibid.
43. Nelson.
44. Feiner.
45. Holden, "E-mail interview."
46. Dewane.
47. Feiner.
48. Ibid.
49. Ibid.
50. Nelson.
51. Feiner.
52. Nelson.
53. Ibid.
54. Ibid.
55. Holly Hall and Leah Kerkman, "Development Dollar Divide," *Chronicle of Philanthropy*, April 20, 2006, 20.
56. Nelson.
57. Feiner.
58. Nelson.
59. Feiner.
60. Holden, "E-mail interview."
61. The authors would like to thank Amanda Nelson for granting us permission to publish these appeal letters.
62. Nelson.
63. Feiner.
64. Nelson.
65. Ibid.
66. Feiner.
67. Holden, "E-mail interview."
68. Feiner.
69. Nelson.
70. The authors wish to thank New Dramatists for permission to publish this thank-you letter.
71. Dewane.
72. Ibid.
73. The authors would like to thank The Minnesota Opera for granting us permission to publish this prospect sheet.
74. Dewane.
75. Ibid.
76. Ibid.
77. Ibid.
78. Ibid.
79. Ibid.
80. Ibid.
81. Ibid.
82. Ibid.
83. Ibid.
84. Nelson.
85. The authors would like to thank the Brooklyn Academy of Music for granting us permission to publish this on-line appeal and Amanda Nelson for granting us permission to publish the auto-response acknowledgement. Photo credit: Clare Park.
86. Maria Di Mento, "Financier's Bequests Total $120 Million," *Chronicle of Philanthropy*, June 15, 2006, 10.
87. Suzanne Perry, "Baby Boomers Give More than Older Americans," *Chronicle of Philanthropy*, September 1, 2005, 14.
88. Feiner.
89. Ibid.
90. Ibid.
91. Ibid.
92. Ibid.
93. Ibid.
94. Anthony Tommasini, "Another Season of Love: The Original Cast Reassembles for a 'Rent' Anniversary," *New York Times*, April 26, 2006.
95. Dewane.
96. Feiner.
97. Holden, "Interview."
98. Dewane. "Snowbirds" are individuals who spend the winter in a warm climate.
99. Ibid.
100. The authors would like to thank The Minnesota Opera for allowing us to publish this sample event budget.
101. The authors would like to thank The Minnesota Opera for allowing us to publish this sample confirmation card.
102. Dewane.
103. Ibid.
104. Ibid.
105. Ibid.
106. Ibid.
107. Ibid.
108. Feiner.
109. Timothy J. McClimon, "The Current State of Corporate Philanthropy" (address, Donors Forum of Wisconsin, Milwaukee, Wis., April 8, 2005).
110. Ibid.
111. Feiner.
112. Sarah Bordy, interview by Sarah Stevens, November 4, 2005.
113. Feiner.
114. Ibid.
115. Ibid.
116. The authors would like to thank Richard Feiner for allowing us to publish this letter of inquiry.
117. Feiner.

118. Holden, "E-mail interview."
119. The authors would like to thank Richard Feiner for allowing us to publish this cover letter.
120. Holden.
121. The authors would like to thank Richard Feiner for allowing us to publish this proposal.
122. Holden.
123. Ibid.
124. Bordy, "Interview."
125. Feiner.
126. The authors would like to thank Richard Feiner for allowing us to publish this acknowledgement letter.
127. The Omnibus Budget Reconciliation Act of 1993 was passed by the Congress and signed into law by President Bill Clinton. It has also been referred to as the Deficit Reduction Act of 1993. Part XIII, which deals with taxes, is also called the Revenue Reconciliation Act of 1993. The Act created the 35 percent tax rate for corporations. Mention of this was included in the corporate acknowledgement letter to help the corporation establish its internal processing/calculations for any tax deductions on the contribution. It is not mandatory to include such information.
128. Feiner.
129. Timothy J. McClimon, e-mail to author, February 9, 2007.
130. Feiner.
131. Ibid.
132. McClimon, "E-mail."
133. Feiner.
134. Ibid.
135. Ibid.
136. Ibid.
137. The authors would like to thank Richard Feiner for allowing us to publish this corporate foundation proposal and budget.
138. Feiner.
139. Bordy, "Interview."
140. Ibid.
141. Feiner.
142. Ibid.
143. Ibid.
144. Holden, "E-mail Interview."
145. The authors would like to thank Bruce Whitacre and the National Corporate Theatre Fund for allowing us to publish this sponsorship deal letter.
146. Ian Wilhelm, "Giving by Big Foundations Rose 6% in 2005, Study Finds," *Chronicle of Philanthropy*, March 8, 2007, 13.
147. Feiner.
148. Holden, "Lecture"; McClimon, "E-mail."
149. Wilhelm, 13.
150. Holden, "Lecture."
151. Holden, "E-mail Interview."
152. Holden, "Interview."
153. Robert Lynch, e-mail interview to author, January 30, 2006.
154. Dewane.
155. Neal Brilliant, interview by Ladan Hamidi-Toosi, August 18, 2006.
156. Lynch, "E-mail Interview."
157. Brilliant, "Interview."
158. Lynch; Ella Weiss, interview by Sarah Stevens, April 7, 2006.
159. The authors would like to thank Lincoln Center Theater for allowing us to publish this NEA proposal.
160. Terri Osborne, e-mail interviews to author, December 30, 2005 and May 9, 2006.
161. Ibid.
162. Weiss, "Interview."
163. Ibid.
164. Holden, "E-mail interview."
165. Weiss.
166. Feiner.
167. Dewane.
168. Ibid.
169. Ibid.
170. Holden, "E-mail interview."
171. Dewane.
172. The authors would like to thank Minnesota Opera for allowing us to publish this status of funding report.
173. Dewane.
174. Ibid.
175. The authors would like to thank Minnesota Opera for allowing us to publish this gift table.
176. Dewane.
177. Ibid.
178. Ibid.
179. Ibid.
180. Ibid.
181. The authors would like to thank Minnesota Opera for allowing us to publish this major donor pitch.
182. The authors would like to thank Minnesota Opera for allowing us to publish this case statement.
183. The authors would like to thank Minnesota Opera for allowing us to publish this gift transmittal form.
184. Dewane.

APPENDIX A1: Development Calendar

Department		Subject	Date
Development	Fall Appeal	Patrons Program Brochure copy & photos to designer	Monday, October 02, 2006
Development	Fall Appeal	Letter--final draft	Monday, October 02, 2006
Development	Fall Appeal	Bid out brochure printing	Monday, October 02, 2006
Marketing	Press	Casting Press Release--Production #2	Monday, October 02, 2006
Development	Online Appeal	Copy--final draft	Monday, October 02, 2006
Development	Online Appeal	Copy & photos to designer	Monday, October 02, 2006
Development	Fall Appeal	Mailing lists to board for approval	Tuesday, October 03, 2006
Development	Foundations	Follow up with Foundation A--ask for meeting	Tuesday, October 03, 2006
Development	Online Appeal	E-mail address lists to board for approval	Tuesday, October 03, 2006
Development	Corporations	Corporation A proposal due	Thursday, October 05, 2006
Development	Major gifts	Contact Individual 1 to set up meeting	Thursday, October 05, 2006
Development	Budget	Reconcile September expenses/income with business office	Friday, October 06, 2006
Development	Gala	Initial layout of invitation	Sunday, October 08, 2006
Development	Fall Appeal	Patrons Program Brochure--first edits to designer	Monday, October 09, 2006
Development	Fall Appeal	Pull & clean up mailing list	Monday, October 09, 2006
Production	Production #2	First Rehearsal	Monday, October 09, 2006
Development	Online Appeal	E-mail design--first edits to designer	Monday, October 09, 2006
Development	Online Appeal	Pull & clean up e-mail address list	Monday, October 09, 2006
Development	Fall Appeal	Follow up with board re: mailing lists	Tuesday, October 10, 2006
Development	Online Appeal	Follow up with board re: e-mail address lists	Tuesday, October 10, 2006
Development	Theatre Events	Benefit Performance--Production #1	Wednesday, October 11, 2006
Development	Corporations	Corporation B proposal due	Thursday, October 12, 2006
Development	Fall Appeal	Patrons Program Brochure--final edits to designer	Thursday, October 12, 2006
Development	Gala	Save the Date copy to designer	Thursday, October 12, 2006
Development	Gala	Auction items--solicit board and staff	Thursday, October 12, 2006
Development	Theatre Events	Patrons Reception--Production #1	Thursday, October 12, 2006
Development	Online Appeal	E-mail design--final edits to designer	Thursday, October 12, 2006
Development	Fall Appeal	Patrons Program Brochure--send to printer	Friday, October 13, 2006
Development	Fall Appeal	Print in-house letters & begin signing	Friday, October 13, 2006
Development	Foundations	Foundation B proposal due	Friday, October 13, 2006
Development	Foundations	Foundation C proposal due	Friday, October 13, 2006
Development	Online Appeal	Send e-mail appeal	Friday, October 13, 2006
Production	Production #1	Closing Night	Sunday, October 15, 2006
Development	Major gifts	Contact Individual 2 to set up meeting	Monday, October 16, 2006
Development	Major gifts	Follow up letter to Individual 1	Monday, October 16, 2006
Development	Fall Appeal	Deliver letters, lists, & brochures to mail house	Wednesday, October 18, 2006
Development	Fall Appeal	Stuff & mail in-house letters	Wednesday, October 18, 2006
Development	Gala	Save the Date--first edits to designer	Thursday, October 19, 2006
Development	Foundations	Follow-up with Foundation B--send personal note from staff member	Friday, October 20, 2006
Development	Telefunding	Telefunding Script Draft	Friday, October 20, 2006
Development	Theatre Events	Send invitation to Patrons Reception for Production #2	Friday, October 20, 2006
Development	Gala	Table letter--mailing list compiled	Monday, October 23, 2006
Development	Gala	Save the Date--final edits to designer	Monday, October 23, 2006
Development	Gala	Committee Meeting	Tuesday, October 24, 2006
Development	Gala	Table letter--first appeal letter mailed	Tuesday, October 24, 2006
Development	Gala	Save the Date to printer	Friday, October 27, 2006
Development	Theatre Events	Send invitation for opening night Production #2	Friday, October 27, 2006
Development	Telefunding	Telefunding Script finalized	Saturday, October 28, 2006
Development	Foundations	Foundation D proposal due	Monday, October 30, 2006
Development	Gala	Save the Date--print mailing labels	Monday, October 30, 2006
Development	Major gifts	Contact Indivdiaul 3 to set up meeting	Monday, October 30, 2006
Development	Foundations	Foundation E proposal due	Tuesday, October 31, 2006
Development	Foundations	Foundation F proposal due	Tuesday, October 31, 2006
Development	Foundations	Follow up with Foundation Z	Tuesday, October 31, 2006
Development	Foundations	Foundation G proposal due	Wednesday, November 01, 2006
Development	Foundations	Foundation H proposal due	Wednesday, November 01, 2006
Development	Foundations	Foundation L proposal due	Wednesday, November 01, 2006
Development	Foundations	Schedule meeting with Foundation Y	Wednesday, November 01, 2006
Development	Government	Government A proposal due	Wednesday, November 01, 2006
Development	Major gifts	Follow up letter to Individual 2	Wednesday, November 01, 2006
Development	Telefunding	Telefunding training session with staff/volunteers	Wednesday, November 01, 2006
Development	Foundations	Foundation I proposal due	Thursday, November 02, 2006
Development	Gala	Save the Date delivered from printer	Thursday, November 02, 2006
Marketing	Ads	Announcement Ad--Production #2	Friday, November 03, 2006
Development	Corporations	Corporation C proposal due	Friday, November 03, 2006

Development	Foundations	Foundation J proposal due	Friday, November 03, 2006
Development	Foundations	Foundation K proposal due	Friday, November 03, 2006
Development	Gala	Order awards for honorees	Friday, November 03, 2006
Development	Gala	Save the Date mailed	Friday, November 03, 2006
Development	Major gifts	Phone solicitation to Individual 4	Friday, November 03, 2006
Development	Telefunding	Telefunding call list generated	Friday, November 03, 2006
Production	Production #2	Final Dress	Sunday, November 05, 2006
Development	Board	Board Meeting	Monday, November 06, 2006
Development	Telefunding	Telefunding Calls (follow-up from fall appeal)	Monday, November 06, 2006
Production	Production #2	First Preview	Tuesday, November 07, 2006
Development	Telefunding	Telefunding Calls (follow-up from fall appeal)	Tuesday, November 07, 2006
Development	Budget	Reconcile October expenses/income with business office	Wednesday, November 08, 2006
Development	Gala	Initial layout of tribute journal	Wednesday, November 08, 2006
Development	Telefunding	Telefunding Calls (follow-up from fall appeal)	Wednesday, November 08, 2006
Marketing	Theatre Events	Subscriber Reception	Wednesday, November 08, 2006
Development	Foundations	Foundation M proposal due	Thursday, November 09, 2006
Development	Gala	Auction items--follow up with board and staff	Thursday, November 09, 2006
Development	Misc	Update Guidestar profile	Thursday, November 09, 2006
Development	Gala	Begin follow up with potential table buyers	Monday, November 13, 2006
Development	Gala	Follow up letter draft	Monday, November 13, 2006
Development	Gala	Email board re: mailing lists	Monday, November 13, 2006
Marketing	Theatre Events	Talkback #1	Tuesday, November 14, 2006
Development	Gala	Menu tasting	Wednesday, November 15, 2006
Development	Major gifts	Phone solicitation to Individual 5	Wednesday, November 15, 2006
Development	Major gifts	Follow up letter to Individaul 3	Thursday, November 16, 2006
Marketing	Theatre Events	Subscriber Reception	Thursday, November 16, 2006
Development	Major gifts	Ask letter to Individual 6	Monday, November 20, 2006
Development	Theatre Events	Patrons Reception--Production #2	Monday, November 20, 2006
Development	Gala	Invitation copy to designer	Tuesday, November 21, 2006
General	Holiday	Thanksgiving--office closed	Thursday, November 23, 2006
Development	Gala	Follow up letter printed	Monday, November 27, 2006
Development	Gala	Follow up letter mailing list	Monday, November 27, 2006
Development	Gala	Invitation--first edits to designer	Tuesday, November 28, 2006
Development	Gala	Bid out invitation and tribute journal printing	Tuesday, November 28, 2006
Marketing	Theatre Events	Talkback #2	Tuesday, November 28, 2006
Development	Gala	Follow up letter mailed to potential table buyers	Wednesday, November 29, 2006
Development	Corporations	Corporation D proposal due	Thursday, November 30, 2006
Development	Foundations	Foundation N proposal due	Thursday, November 30, 2006
Development	Foundations	Follow up with Foundation C--ask for meeting	Friday, December 01, 2006
Development	Foundations	Foundation O proposal due	Friday, December 01, 2006
Development	Gala	Invitation--final edits to designer	Friday, December 01, 2006
Production	Production #2	Opening Night	Sunday, December 03, 2006
Development	Foundations	Follow up with Foundation E--ask for meeting	Wednesday, December 06, 2006
Development	Gala	Board mailing lists for invitation due	Wednesday, December 06, 2006
Development	Gala	Invitation--send to printer	Wednesday, December 06, 2006
Development	Foundations	Awards luncheon for Foundation F	Thursday, December 07, 2006
Development	Gala	Auction items--follow up with board and staff	Thursday, December 07, 2006
Marketing	Ads	Quote Ad--Production #2	Friday, December 08, 2006
Development	Board	Executive Committee meeting	Monday, December 11, 2006
Development	Gala	Pull & clean up invitation mailing list	Monday, December 11, 2006
Marketing	Mailings	Subscriber Mailing--Booking for Production #3	Monday, December 11, 2006
Development	Gala	Invitations arrive at office	Wednesday, December 13, 2006
Development	Gala	Invitations to board for personalization	Thursday, December 14, 2006
Development	Gala	Begin follow up from second table letter mailing	Friday, December 15, 2006
Development	Gala	Secure photographer	Monday, December 18, 2006
Development	Gala	Invitation stuffing	Tuesday, December 19, 2006
Development	Theatre Events	Trustee reception	Tuesday, December 19, 2006
Marketing	Theatre Events	Talkback #3	Tuesday, December 19, 2006
Development	Gala	Invitation stuffing	Wednesday, December 20, 2006
Development	Foundations	Foundation X interim report due	Friday, December 22, 2006
Development	Gala	Secure flowers	Friday, December 22, 2006
General	Holiday	Christmas Day--office closed	Monday, December 25, 2006
Marketing	Theatre Events	Talkback #4	Tuesday, December 26, 2006
Development	Planned Giving	Brochure copy & photos to designer	Wednesday, December 27, 2006
Development	Planned Giving	Bid out brochure printing	Wednesday, December 27, 2006
Development	Foundations	Foundation P proposal due	Friday, December 29, 2006
Development	Foundations	Foundation W final report due	Friday, December 29, 2006
Development	Planned Giving	Letter--first draft	Friday, December 29, 2006
Production	Production #2	Closing Night	Sunday, December 31, 2006

APPENDIX A2: Development Report

FYE06

FunderType / List As	Last Year's Gift	This Year's Request	Date Sent	Deadline	Result	Gift Amount	Program	Notes
CORPORATE								
Corporation 1	5,000.00	40,000.00	6/10/05	June	Funded	5,000.00	Staff Expansion	
Corporation 2	1,500.00	1,500.00	9/28/05	9/8	Funded	1,500.00	General	
Corporation 3		10,000.00	4/13/06	3/31			Playwrights Lab	
Corporation 4	2,000.00	3,500.00	8/2/05	August			Capital	Painting
Corporation 5	10,000.00	15,000.00	12/7/05	early December	Funded	15,000.00	Playwrights Lab	
Corporation 6	5,000.00	5,000.00	10/5/05	October	Funded	5,000.00	RNT Exchange	
Subtotals	**23,500.00**	**75,000.00**				**26,500.00**		
FOUNDATION								
Foundation 1	6,000.00	6,000.00	7/28/05	August	Funded	6,000.00	General	
Foundation 2	2,500.00	2,500.00	9/8/05	10/15	Funded	2,500.00	General	
Foundation 3	7,500.00			10/1	SUNSE		Readings/Exchanges	
Foundation 4	7,500.00	7,500.00	12/10/04	open-Nov.	Funded	7,500.00	Graduation Festival	
Foundation 5		1,000.00	7/28/05	August			General	
Foundation 6		5,000.00					Library	
Foundation 7		5,000.00	2/28/06	February			General	
Foundation 8	500.00	1,000.00	2/1/06	2/1			Working Sessions	
Foundation 9		50,000.00		10/15			Staff Expansion	
Foundation 10				10/15			Playground	
Foundation 11		10,000.00		3/1			PlayTime	
Foundation 12		1,000.00	9/8/05	September			General	
Foundation 13			11/30/05	November	Funded	5,000.00	PlayTime	
Foundation 14	5,000.00	5,000.00	10/4/05	September	Funded	5,000.00	General	
Foundation 15	5,000.00	5,000.00	7/28/05	August	Funded	15,000.00	General	Sent via email
Foundation 16		5,000.00		August			General	
Foundation 17	30,000.00	30,000.00	4/30/04	3/30	Funded	30,000.00	Fellowship	Year two of two--total gift $60,000
Foundation 18		25,000.00		April			Staff Expansion	
Foundation 19	25,000.00	25,000.00	3/31/05	January	Funded	25,000.00	Music-theatre	
Foundation 20	2,000.00	2,000.00	10/14/05	October			General	
Foundation 21				open			Working Sessions	
Foundation 22				open			Working Sessions	
Foundation 23				August	Funded	5,000.00	General	
Foundation 24				Feb. 1, Aug. 1			Fellowship	
Foundation 25	40,000.00	60,000.00	3/2/04	August	Funded	40,000.00	New Works/CLS	
Foundation 26				11/10			Working Sessions	
Foundation 27		2,000.00	11/22/05	November			Working Sessions	
Foundation 28		10,000.00		9/1			RNT Exchange	
Foundation 29				6/1	Funded	5,000.00	General	
Foundation 30	22,500.00	22,500.00		none	Funded	22,500.00	Award	
Foundation 31		5,000.00	9/8/05	September			Working Sessions	
Foundation 32	1,000.00	1,000.00	8/29/06	September			General	
Foundation 33	1,000.00	1,000.00		October	funded	1,000.00	General	
Foundation 34	12,500.00	15,000.00	12/13/05	December	Funded	12,500.00	General	
Foundation 35		32,500.00	8/12/04	August, January	Funded	32,500.00	Mentorship	
Foundation 36		5,000.00	9/20/05	October	REJECT		Working Sessions	
Foundation 37				open			General	
Foundation 38	4,000.00	4,000.00	10/4/05	October	Funded	4,000.00	General	
Foundation 39	2,500.00	2,500.00	7/28/05	August	Funded	2,500.00	General	
Foundation 40	7,500.00	7,500.00	11/29/05	December	Funded	7,500.00	Playwright Development	
Foundation 41	15,000.00			Feb	SUNSE			
Foundation 42	10,000.00	10,000.00	3/14/06	March			Playwright Development	
Foundation 43		11,000.00	8/25/05	9/15	REJECT		Capital	
Foundation 44		5,000.00	7/28/05	August			General	
Foundation 45	30,000.00	30,000.00	2/28/06	February			General/Award	
Foundation 46	15,000.00	15,000.00		none	Funded	15,000.00	Award	
Foundation 47		5,500.00	8/4/05	August	Funded	5,000.00	Award	
Foundation 48	5,000.00	5,000.00	4/20/06	April	Funded	5,000.00	Publications	
Foundation 49		10,000.00	5/5/04	April	Funded	10,000.00	General	
Foundation 50		1,000.00	7/28/05	8/1			General	
Foundation 51		5,000.00	8/31/05	August	Funded	250.00	General	
Foundation 52	5,000.00	5,000.00	4/13/06	April			Playwright Development	
Foundation 53	0.00	10,000.00	5/12/05	March	Funded	10,000.00	Library	
Foundation 54	1,000.00	2,000.00	11/22/05	November	Funded	500.00	Working Sessions	
Foundation 55	60,000.00	60,000.00	12/1/05	December			General	
Foundation 56	8,000.00	8,000.00	7/27/05	8/1	Funded	8,000.00	PlayTime	
Foundation 57	35,000.00	1,250.00	4/13/06		Reject		Staff Travel	
Foundation 58	10,000.00	10,000.00	3/2/06	February	Funded	10,000.00	Playwrights Lab	
Subtotals	**376,000.00**	**547,750.00**				**292,250.00**		
GOVERNMENT								
Government 1	50,000.00	60,000.00	3/14/04	March	Funded	50,000.00	Playwright Development	
Government 2	10,000.00	30,000.00	7/12/05	June	funded	7,500.00	Playwright Development	
Government 3	18,000.00	18,000.00	3/31/04	March	Funded	18,000.00	General	Year two of three
Government 4	11,500.00			Various	Funded	2,500.00	Capital	
Subtotals	**89,500.00**	**108,000.00**				**78,000.00**		
INDIVIDUAL								
Individual 1		10,000.00		open/summer			PlayTime	
Individual 2	10,000.00	10,000.00		open/spring	Funded	10,000.00	PlayTime	
Individual 3	5,000.00	5,000.00		November	Funded	5,000.00	General	
Individual 4		15,000.00	5/9/05	November			PlayTime	
Individual 5	10,000.00	10,000.00		November	Funded	5,000.00	General	
Individual 6		10,000.00	12/20/05	November			General	
Individual 7		1,000.00	8/30/05	September			General	
Individual 8	10,000.00	10,000.00	7/27/05	July/August	Funded	10,000.00	Playwright Development	
Individual 9		10,000.00	11/23/05				PlayTime	
Individual 10	15,000.00	15,000.00	1/5/06	open/fall	Funded	15,000.00	Working Sessions	
Subtotals	**50,000.00**	**96,000.00**				**45,000.00**		
GRAND TOTAL	**1,078,000.00**	**1,653,500.00**				**838,500.00**		

APPENDIX B1: The Minnesota Opera Telefundraising Strategy and Script

The Minnesota Opera
2005-2006 Fundraising Campaign
SD&A Teleservices, Inc.

PART I. GENERAL INFORMATION ON FUNDRAISING

A. WHY FUNDRAISING?

The Minnesota Opera needs to raise money because less than half of its operating expenses are covered by revenue from ticket sales. Fundraising efforts—like this telefundraising campaign—are vital to the Opera's artistic growth, community outreach efforts and financial stability.

B. WHY DO PEOPLE GIVE TO THE MINNESOTA OPERA?

There are several general reasons why people give: they care about the art form, they believe that it enhances their quality of life and therefore want to support its future, they believe in the educational outreach programs that The Minnesota Opera provides to the community, or they enjoy the sense of belonging they get from being members of an exclusive group. Others simply want the benefits that come with the donation, like invitations to dress rehearsals or having their name recognized in the final program of the season.

While you'll focus on a specific theme and cause in this telefundraising campaign, keep these general reasons in mind as you approach your prospects. They will help you find ways to motivate people to give.

C. SALESMANSHIP: THE STRUCTURE OF THE SCRIPT

Your skills in **communication and listening** will be your best fundraising tools. The more time you invest in listening, the better your chance of getting a large gift. *Assume two things: (1) that the prospects have a good relationship with the Opera and (2) that they WILL make a donation.* Your script will guide you with these components:

- **Legal Disclosure Requirements**
  State Law requires you to provide each prospect with the name and address of The Minnesota Opera. You must also let each prospect know that you are a professional fundraiser with SD&A Teleservices. State Law requires that you provide a clear description of the primary charitable purpose for which the solicitation is being made, and the tax-deductibility of each contribution. Federal Law also requires that you disclose The Minnesota Opera's administrative address before the close of each call. *Specific language is provided for you in the script!*

- **Opening/Building Rapport**
  Good rapport with your prospects is the foundation of every call. One way to establish good rapport is by asking open-ended questions. The questions you ask will depend on the prospect, so before you place the call, be sure to learn as much information as possible about the person you're calling! You may close and re-open a conversation several times by using open-ended questions to address and clarify any concerns the prospect may have.

- **Presentation/Purpose**
  Your success will depend on your ability to convey The Minnesota Opera's need for community support. Focus on the value of the prospect's relationship with the Opera. Make a strong case for The Minnesota Opera's role in the community, highlighting artistic excellence, educational programs and community outreach.

- **Ask High**
  You must ask prospects to give, and you must ask for a specific amount. You will only get what you ask for. Ask each prospect for a gift that is three times larger than their current or lapsed giving level. The idea is to start high and negotiate down to a gift that is comfortable for the prospect. Don't press

Appendix B1 (continued)

too hard at the beginning of the conversation, as you may not get a firm answer right away. If they say no or hesitate after the first ask, discuss the Split Payment Option (see below). If the prospect still resists, begin negotiations.

- **Negotiation/Drop**
  Drop by dollar increments, not existing donor levels. For example, after starting at the $1,000 level, drop next to $800, rather than the next benefit level of $750. This can help you close at a higher donation. *Employ sensitivity and listening techniques and avoid high pressure tactics.* In other words, *listen to the response your suggested gift receives.* If the prospect laughs at the idea of a $1,000 gift, your next drop should probably not be to $800, but perhaps $600 or even $400.

- **Benefits**
  Donor benefits are an excellent way to close a contribution. "Sell" the prospect on the campaign cause first, then use the donor benefits and the tax deduction he or she will receive as incentives.

- **Closing on a Contribution**

  1. **Your goal is to close with a credit card**. It saves the Opera money (the cost of the pledge packet, postage, etc.). Most importantly, the donation goes to work for the company immediately. Always project trustworthiness and assume a credit card close. Use a matter-of-fact tone of voice to convey that using a credit card is both convenient and routine.

  2. **Pledges**. If the prospect won't put their donation on a credit card, urge them to pledge a specific dollar amount. We have found that approximately 70% of pledges with a specific dollar amount are fulfilled. But if the prospect does NOT specify a dollar amount, the return is around 25%.

  3. **Will Considers.** Send out to prospects who will NOT pledge a specific amount and who want to think about which level of giving is best for them. If a prospect expresses interest in contributing but does not want to specify a certain amount, send the Will Consider letter and pledge card. Many donors do wish to keep their gift confidential—and some give at higher amounts than you would have asked for.

  4. **Split Payment Option.** *For gifts of $100 or more on a credit card. (Each payment must be at least $50.)* If someone is put off by the thought of giving a large gift because it seems like too much, find out how they feel about paying over a period of time. For example, paying $125 now and $125 later may seem a lot more manageable than paying $250 at once. Once an amount is established, suggest that they "bump up" their gift to the next giving level by increasing the amount of the monthly payments!

  5. **Ask open-ended questions that require more than a "yes" or "no" answer**. "How does a gift of $_sound to you?" *or* "Which of the benefits I've mentioned interests you most?"

  6. **Make them aware of this year's overall telefundraising goal of $106,000**. You may also want to mention the monthly, weekly or daily goals of the campaign

  7. **Emphasize the benefits and special premiums**

  8. **And finally, be enthusiastic**. It's contagious. Say things such as "We're reaching out to all of our friends this evening to rally support for this very important campaign. Our goal is to get 100% participation from our patrons and we're confident that we can reach our goal. How does a gift of $____ sound to you?" OR "We're grateful for the generosity of our supporters, but we still have a long way to go! If you could help us in our fundraising efforts by making a gift of $____ this evening, we would be so appreciative!"

  It also helps to smile during each call. When you're smiling, it is reflected in your tone of voice.

D. PROCESSING THE DONATION

Be sure to have the lead/pledge form in front of you at all times!

- **Confirm the prospect's name, address, phone number, and e-mail address for <u>every pledge</u>!**
  Never assume that the information on your lead sheet is correct. Always verify it. *If any of the information is incorrect, <u>neatly</u> record the appropriate changes in the notes section of the lead sheet.* If someone tells you that they'll be moving, please indicate this. If out of state, indicate the new state and whether the donor wishes to continue to receive information from The Minnesota Opera. If the donor knows his/her new address, please make note of the new information with the date that it will become effective.

- **Credit Card Order**
  Fill in the amount of the donation, the credit card number, expiration date, and the name on the card. *Always repeat this information back to the donor to insure accuracy!* Print your name and Caller ID# in the appropriate place on the pledge form.

- **Pledges**
  Fill in the amount of the contribution. Explain to the donor that you'll be sending a pledge packet that will include a return envelope for their check. Also, politely ask the donor to send in their contribution within 10 days of receiving the packet.

- **Will Considers**
  Explain to the donor that you'll be sending a pledge packet in the mail. Thank them for their consideration and encourage them to give. Also, politely ask the donor to send in their contribution within 10 days of receiving the packet.

- **Split Payments**
  If someone wishes to take advantage of the split payment option, fill in the date, their total amount of their gift, how much they're putting on their credit card now, and how much they're paying later. Before ending the call, confirm the total gift and review the payment schedule one more time. *Split payments are for gifts of $100 or more on a credit card; minimum of $50 per payment.*

- **Corporate Matching Gift**
  Remind the donor that his or her employer (or spouse's employer) may participate in a matching gift program. This is a great way to increase the amount of their donation.

- **Referrals**
  Ask if the donor has friends, relatives or co-workers who might be interested in learning more about The Minnesota Opera.

- **Tax message**
  Remind donors that all donations are tax-deductible to the extent allowed by law. Tell them that their donor packet will include a formal acknowledgment of their gift for tax purposes.

- **Thank you**
  Thank each donor for their generous contribution and assure them their (continued) support is appreciated by The Minnesota Opera. Verify and confirm the amount of the pledge and urge a prompt response. Also, be sure to thank them for their time.

- **Take the order immediately to Ernie.**

E. WHO YOU WILL BE CALLING

You will be calling people who have already shown their support of The Minnesota Opera in some way. You will be asking them for a gift in support of the Opera's artistic endeavors and educational programs. The prospect's relationship with the Opera will determine how you approach each phone call and what

Appendix B1 (continued)

you ask each person. The following is a list of the prospects you will be calling and what you should ask each one. *It is important to show each prospect that you know his/her specific relationship with The Minnesota Opera.*

- **Current Donors:** These prospects made a gift to the Opera during the 2004–2005 Annual Fund Campaign. They may be a subscriber or single ticket buyer as well. You should thank them for their support, let them know that it is time to renew their contribution, and then ask them not only to renew, but to upgrade their commitment by renewing at a higher level of giving.

- **Lapsed Donors:** These prospects are not current donors, but have given at some time in the past. They *may* be current subscribers or single ticket-buyers. Thank them for their specific support in the past and invite them to participate in this campaign by renewing their commitment to The Minnesota Opera. Ask them to become donors again, and to do so at a higher level of giving.

- **Current Subscribers / Single Ticket Buyers:** These prospects actively attend the Opera but are not currently donors. They may not be aware of the need The Minnesota Opera has for their participation as both patrons *and* donors!

- **Lapsed Subscribers / Single Ticket Buyers:** These prospects are not currently attending the Opera but have attended in the past. They may not be aware of the need the company has for their participation beyond the tickets they buy. Invite them to support the company. If you're talking to senior citizens, they may no longer be able to attend the Opera, but they may still want to support it!

- **"Magic Prospects":** These are prospects that have been professionally identified for us as individuals who are likely to have an interest in supporting The Minnesota Opera. These prospects will require a little more information from you, so be sure to exercise patience as you encourage them to participate as donors.

PART II. COMPANY BACKGROUND INFORMATION

A. OVERVIEW OF THE MINNESOTA OPERA

Since its inception in 1963 under the auspices of the Walker Art Center, The Minnesota Opera has attracted international attention for its performances of new operas and innovative productions of masterworks. On The Minnesota Opera stage, talented national and internationally known artists are brought together to create productions of the highest artistic integrity, emphasizing the balance and total integration of theatrical and musical values.

Among its most renowned world and American premieres are: Dominick Argento's *Postcard from Morocco, The Voyage of Edgar Allen Poe* and *Casanova's Homecoming*, Mayer's *A Death in the Family*, Libby Larsen's *Frankenstein, The Modern Prometheus*, Oliver Knussen and Maurice Sendak's *Where the Wild Things Are*, Conrad Susa's *Transformations and Black River*, PDQ Bach's *The Abduction of Figaro*, Moran's *From the Towers of the Moon*, Evan Chen's *Bok Choy Variations* and Poul Ruders' *The Handmaid's Tale*.

The Minnesota Opera is also recognized for its progressive and far-reaching educational programs. Residencies in schools, opera education classes and pre-performance discussions are building an audience for tomorrow and enhancing the enjoyment of audiences today.

The Minnesota Opera is guided by **President and CEO Kevin Smith** and **Artistic Director Dale Johnson**. Since Mr. Smith became the company's leader in 1984, The Minnesota Opera is now the 16th largest opera company in the nation with an annual budget of almost $7 million.
<u>2005–2006 Season Overview:</u>

Two American premieres: *Orazi & Curiazi* and *Joseph Merrick, the Elephant Man*
Three new productions: *Don Giovanni, Orazi & Curiazi,* and *Joseph Merrick, the Elephant Man*

The Minnesota Opera's 2005–2006 season opened on November 5, 2005 with Puccini's *Tosca*. The Opera will resume in March with a new production of Mozart's *Don Giovanni* and in April presents a new production and the American premiere of Saverio Mercadante's Bel Canto thriller, *Orazi & Curiazi*. These performances represent the continuation of The Minnesota Opera's commitment to repertoire from the Bel Canto period. The season closes in May with the American premiere of Laurent Petitgirard's *Joseph Merrick, the Elephant Man*, which had its world premiere in Prague in 2002.

B. CAMPAIGN CAUSE

Your call is part of a concerted effort by The Minnesota Opera to raise funds that will support the company's operating budget. Because ticket sales and earned income cover less than 50% of The Minnesota Opera's overall operating costs, the company must rely on its friends/donors/patrons to help make up the difference. Individual donations are instrumental in helping The Minnesota Opera to employ some of the world's most gifted artists. Stress to the prospect that a donation to The Minnesota Opera is a contribution to the arts as a whole and one of the best ways to participate in our community's social and cultural life. The funds you help to raise during this campaign will support the following areas:

1. <u>Financial Need:</u> The Minnesota Opera survives on strong fiscal management combined with public and private contributions. Arts organizations everywhere are straining to generate the resources they need to keep running. With increased competition for private funds, The Minnesota Opera needs community support more than ever to maintain its standards of artistic excellence.

2. <u>Artistic Excellence:</u> The Minnesota Opera has developed a national reputation for critically-acclaimed levels of performance. Donor support allows the company to reach for even greater heights of artistic excellence.

3. <u>Education:</u> The Minnesota Opera's educational outreach programs reach, teach and enrich the community. Educational outreach initiatives, all free or deeply subsidized, touch the lives of thousands of children and adults each year. Here are a few examples of The Minnesota Opera's educational programs:

•   <u>coOPERAtion!:</u> This program is designed for teachers to explore the multi-dimensional aspects of opera. We accomplish this by tailoring the residency around existing curriculum, whether it is music-specific, non-musical or interdisciplinary. This program is great for in-depth study prior to attendance at a live opera or as a separate experience. coOPERAtion! involves our Teaching Artist working directly with students. The scope and direction of the residency is based on each teacher's individual classroom objectives.

•   <u>Student Matinees:</u> Students between grades 7–12 and college are invited to attend a final dress rehearsal. Every production is fully staged with soloists, chorus and orchestra, and takes place at the Ordway Center for the Performing Arts. All rehearsals have English captions projected above the stage.

•   <u>Project Opera:</u> New for 2005-2006! The Minnesota Opera is proud to announce Project Opera, a youth opera and choral experience for girls and boys in grades 4–12. Project Opera is made up of two choirs, Ragazzi (grades 4–8) and Giovani (grades 9–12). Participants learn the fundamentals of classical and choral singing, plus skills in acting, movement, stage combat and opera. Participation is by audition only.

•   <u>Day at the Opera:</u> Send a student to Day at the Opera! Participants will experience activities such as: a master class with opera staff, movement and stage presence training, a tour the Scene and Costume Shops, lunch with the artists, passes to a dress rehearsal and more!

Appendix B1 (continued)

- **Opera Academy:** Learn the who, what, why, where and when of each production, and go away with usable classroom techniques to prepare your students for a live performance. The *Opera Academy* is also for teachers who just want to learn more about opera and gain a deeper understanding of the art form. These workshops are recommended for middle and high school teachers in any subject area.

Become familiar with all of The Minnesota Opera's education and outreach programs so that you may discuss them knowledgeably with prospects.

C. CAMPAIGN GOAL

It is helpful to mention the dollar goal of this telephone campaign (<u>$106,000</u>), which will support the Opera's artistic programming, as well as educational outreach programs.

D. BENEFITS

1. Benefits: Be familiar with all the benefits and privileges at each level of giving, and be able to discuss them knowledgeably. Remember to start high and negotiate down to a level that is comfortable for the prospect, itemizing the benefits and privileges of each new level you present.

2. Premiums: Premiums are for people who give through the telephone campaign. They may be used as an incentive to increase gift size after you've already begun negotiating, to upgrade current gifts, to reinstate members who've lapsed, or to encourage new gifts.

Current premium:

Any donor who gives $500 or more through this campaign will receive Donor Benefits at the $1,000 level.

2005–2006 DONOR BENEFITS

Member Level ($50–$99)
    -Two passes to the annual *Donor Appreciation Concert**

Friend Level ($100–$249)
Previous benefits PLUS
    -Two passes to a dress rehearsal of one opera each season (TBD)

Associate Level ($250–$499)
Previous benefits PLUS
    -Family invitation to an *Opera Open House* **NEW!**
    -Recognition in the final program of the season

Patron Circle

Silver Level ($500–$749)
Previous benefits PLUS
    -Recognition in every program of the season **NEW!**
    -An invitation to one *Meet the Artist* event at The Minnesota Opera Center
    -Personal tour of the Opera Center, Scene Shop and Costume Shop. (*To schedule a tour, donors should call 612-342-9569.*)
    -Two extra passes to the *Donor Appreciation Concert* and reception (4 total)
    -Two extra passes to one dress rehearsal each season (TBD) (4 total)

Gold Level ($750–$999) NEW!
Previous benefits PLUS
-One-year subscription to Opera News

Artist Circle ($1,000–$2,499)
Previous benefits PLUS
-One-year subscription to Opera News
-Complimentary parking to all four operas
-Invitations to all *Meet the Artist* events at The Minnesota Opera Center
-Two extra passes to a dress rehearsal of one opera each season (date TBD) (4 total)
-Two extra passes to the *Donor Appreciation Concert* (date TBD) (6 total)

Camerata Circle

Silver Level ($2,500–$4,999)
Previous benefits PLUS
-Exclusive backstage intermission receptions at every subscription performance
-Invitations to exclusive Camerata Circle dinners

Gold Level ($5,000–$7,499)
Previous benefits PLUS
-Invitation to private lunch with the President or the Artistic Director
-Copies of the Libretti for each of the season's productions
-Private backstage tour of Ordway Center for the Performing Arts

Platinum Level ($7,500–$9,999) NEW!
Previous benefits PLUS
-Personal invitation from the President to attend a Sitzprobe
-Two passes to a Minnesota Opera Education class of your choice **NEW!**

Bel Canto Circle

Silver Level ($10,000–$14,999)
Previous benefits PLUS
-Two passes to all four Minnesota Opera Education classes **NEW!**

Gold Level ($15,000–$19,999) NEW!
Previous benefits PLUS
-Two complimentary Camerata Circle dinners to the opera of your choice **NEW!**

Platinum Level ($20,000 and above)
Previous benefits PLUS
-Platinum Level members receive personalized benefits

E. TONE MATCHING YOUR PROSPECTS

Tone Matching is the practice of utilizing your tone of voice to create rapport with your prospects. The tone you use should match that of the prospect. For example:

- With **clever, fast-talking** prospects, talk fast and keep their pace. Make quick, intelligent suggestions and pay attention to their responses.

- With **polite, soft-spoken types,** lower your voice, be courteous and approach the sale gently. They may find a loud or fast-talking person abrasive.

Appendix B1 (continued)

- **Expressive, fun-loving** personalities will probably respond best to an enthusiastic voice on the line. Approach the sale with a sense of humor and informal tone.

- If your prospect is **serious and business-like**, keep a formal, business-like tone throughout the call. Impress them with your professionalism and knowledge of the season.

These are only a few of the many types of personalities you'll encounter as you go through your leads. Your tone of voice and the quality of your presentation determine how you will be received by the prospects you call. Be polite, considerate and formal until your prospect's behavior indicates that a more relaxed or casual presentation is in order. This is where **tone matching** comes in. Use it to make them feel that they're talking to a like-minded person. Adopt their tone and you should be able to direct the conversation.

The ability to tone match the many types of prospects one encounters can make the difference between a good caller and a great caller. For some, tone matching is an intuitive art, but most callers learn and develop this skill over time. You will find that using this technique will result in better rapport with your contacts and more sales in the long run.

<u>Listening Skills:</u>
One key characteristic of all top sellers is good listening skills. Take the time to listen to the patron and use responsive language such as "Uh huh," "I understand," "Oh, really?" Your goal should be to have conversations with people rather than to talk at them. This can only be achieved through listening.

INTRODUCTION

Hello, may I please speak with Mr./Ms._____? Hi, this is _____, a professional fundraiser from SD&A Teleservices calling on behalf of The Minnesota Opera. How are you today? (*Ask with sincerity, wait for reply.*)

I'm calling first of all to thank you for your support. Your generosity (*for new acquisitions, use the word* "patronage") helps to support all of The Minnesota Opera's artistic accomplishments onstage. It also supports the many educational outreach programs that we offer in the community. We really appreciate it, Mr./Ms._____.

IF THE PROSPECT GIVES A FIRM "NO," IMMEDIATELY DISCLOSE THAT THE STATE AND FEDERAL GOVERNMENT BOTH REQUIRE YOU TO PROVIDE THE MINNESOTA OPERA'S ADMINISTRATIVE ADDRESS: <u>620 NORTH FIRST STREET, MINNEAPOLIS, MN 55401.</u> IF THEY DO NOT SAY "NO," WAIT UNTIL THE END OF THE CALL TO MAKE THE DISCLOSURE (SEE LANGUAGE BELOW).

RAPPORT

(*Refer to ticket-buying history . . .*) I see that the last time you attended The Minnesota Opera was for a production of _____. How did you enjoy it?
(*If no ticket-buying history . . .*) What was the last production you attended? How did you like it?

What is it that you enjoy most about coming out for opera performances at Ordway Center?

What have you heard about The Minnesota Opera's educational outreach programs?

Did you know that our donors play a significant role in bringing each new season to life? (*Transition into . . .*)

PRESENTATION/PURPOSE

Your affiliation with The Minnesota Opera is something you can truly be proud of, Mr./Ms._____. Friends like you have helped us to build a national reputation of artistic excellence.

Our ability to bring great opera to life in Minnesota is made possible by a partnership between our donors and the performers who grace our stage. Every year, contributions from our donors provide a significant portion of our operating budget. These donations allow us to produce magnificent operas, and they also allow us to give back to the community through our educational outreach programs. We help bring opera into the schools, and that's one of the reasons why The Minnesota Opera's outreach work is so important. These programs touch thousands of young lives every year, and we have our donors to thank for this.

ASK

This is a great time to give to The Minnesota Opera, Mr./Ms._____. Right now we're in the third and final year of the Bush Foundation Matching Gift Challenge Grant. This generous grant will match all new and increased gifts up to $300,000! That means your gift this season will have an extra impact on our company!

With this in mind, I'd like to invite you to play a special role at The Minnesota Opera this season. By making a generous tax-deductible gift of **$[first ask]**, you'll be helping us to maintain our status as one of the top ten opera companies in the nation. As our way of saying thanks, you will also receive some terrific donor benefits. How does a gift of **$[first ask]** sound to you? (*Don't forget to mention the premium! If amount is too high, suggest the Split Payment Option.*)

SPLIT PAYMENT OPTION

That's understandable, Mr./Ms._____. To make things easier and more convenient, we do offer a split payment option that allows you to spread your gift out over time. You can arrange to make your donation in two or more easy installments. How does that sound? (*For gifts of $100 or more on a credit card only; minimum of $50 per payment.*)

NEGOTIATION/DROP

I can understand that, Mr./Ms._____. We really want your participation, but most importantly, we want you to be comfortable with your level of giving.

As I'm sure you know, it is very expensive to produce the caliber of operas that audiences have come to expect from our company. Unfortunately, revenues from ticket sales cover less than half of our annual operating expenses. That's why we depend on our donors. Friends like you help to fill the gap, which keeps The Minnesota Opera financially secure and thriving artistically.

With this in mind, perhaps a gift of **$[second ask]** would be more comfortable for you. In recognition of your generosity, you'll receive some wonderful benefits reserved exclusively for donors. How does a gift of **$[second ask]** sound to you? (*If amount is still too high, suggest Split Payment Option again.*)

Appendix B1 (continued)

FINAL ASK

I understand, Mr./Ms._____. Many of our donors have been showing their support for The Minnesota Opera by making a basic gift of **$[final ask]**. A gift at this level will still go a long way in helping us to continue our proud tradition of artistic excellence and service to the community. You'll also receive some great donor benefits that we know you'll enjoy.

These are extremely difficult times for arts organizations, Mr./Ms._____. The Minnesota Opera really needs your support. Does a gift of **$[final ask]** work better for you?

CORPORATE MATCHING GIFT

Thank you so much for your generous gift of $_____, Mr./Ms._____. We really appreciate your support.

Did you know that many corporations will match a gift made by an employee or their spouse, which can double or even triple the size of your gift? Does the company you work for have a matching gift program?

IF "YES": Excellent. Please be sure to notify your company's Matching Gift Coordinator about the contribution you've just made to The Minnesota Opera.

IF "NO": That's quite all right. Your gift is just as valuable to us.

CONFIRMATION

Thanks again for your generous gift, Mr./Ms._____. Before we continue, I'd like to verify your residential and your e-mail address, as well as your daytime and evening phone numbers. *(Confirm information and make changes directly into the computer if necessary.)*

For your convenience we accept MasterCard, Visa, American Express, and Discover. Which card would you prefer to use?

Enter card information into the computer. Then, read the card number, name on the card and expiration date back to the donor to ensure accuracy.

IF DONOR DOES NOT WANT TO USE A CREDIT CARD:

I understand, Mr./Ms._____. We all have to be careful in this day and age. A lot of people don't understand why The Minnesota Opera is asking all of our friends to place their gifts on a credit card this season. There are a couple of reasons for this. First of all, it eliminates the cost of paperwork, postage and processing, which means that <u>100 percent</u> of your donation will support the Opera's programs. It also puts your donation in the Opera's hands immediately, ensuring that your gift will go to work for us right away. Considering this, can you make an exception for us this evening and place your donation on a credit card?

IF DONOR STILL OBJECTS TO CREDIT CARD:

That's no problem, Mr./Ms._____. We want you to be able to take advantage of your donor benefits right away, so we're asking all of our friends to send in their gifts within 10 days of receiving the pledge acknowledgement.

ASK EVERYONE FOR REFERRALS

Okay, Mr./Ms. _____, we're just about finished. Before I let you go, there's one last thing you can do to help us. Who do you know—a friend, a relative, someone from work—who might also be interested in learning more about the great work The Minnesota Opera is doing for our community?

GIVE THEM TIME TO FLIP THROUGH THEIR MENTAL ROLODEX!

I'd be happy to wait while you find their phone numbers.

FEDERAL DISCLOSURE

And finally, Mr./Ms._____, the State and Federal Governments require that I provide you with The Minnesota Opera's administrative address. This is a new law designed to protect donors like you from fraudulent telemarketers. The address is: 620 N. First Street, Minneapolis, MN 55401.

CLOSE

On behalf of everyone at The Minnesota Opera, I would like to thank you again, Mr./Ms._____ for your generous gift of $_____. Your generosity helps to make great opera possible in Minnesota. It has been a pleasure speaking with you this evening. Have a good night.

STANDARD OBJECTIONS

- **Instant "No" or "I'm not interested."**
  (Ask if this is a bad time to call. If they say, "No, I am just not interested," politely try to find out why they are not interested and use their answer to re-open the conversation. If they say, "No, I am just busy/eating dinner/running out the door/etc.," then set up a callback.)

  I understand, Mr./Ms._____. You may not be aware of this, but your participation is very important to us no matter what size the contribution. You see, when we apply to major corporations and foundations for grants, one of the things they look at is the number of supporters we have in the community. Right now it's more difficult than ever before to attract foundation giving, so it's very important to show that we have the support of our entire community. So let me ask you, is it possible for you to participate in any way at this time? Any amount will help. How does a gift of $_____ sound to you?

- **Doesn't Attend Anymore**
  I understand, Mr./Ms._____. We have many donors who, for one reason or another, are unable to attend. But they continue to give generously because they understand that The Minnesota Opera is an important part of the cultural life of our community. They also give because they believe in the value of our education and outreach programs. Would you please consider a gift to The Minnesota Opera as part of your regular charitable giving?

- **Can't Afford**
  I certainly understand that you have to keep an eye on your expenses, Mr./Ms._____. Your support is very important to us, no matter what level you choose. You'll be entitled to some great donor benefits, plus you'll be helping out one of our community's most important artistic institutions. Isn't

Appendix B1 (continued)

that worth it? Honestly, Mr./Ms._____, without the support of friends like you, The Minnesota Opera would not be the world-class company that it is. If you could participate at a level that is most comfortable for you, we would be really appreciative. How does a gift of $_____ sound to you?

If other commitments make it inconvenient for you to make a pledge now, let me suggest that you put your gift on a MasterCard or Visa. That way, you can spread your gift over a period of months and you'll be helping us reach our goal. How does that sound to you?

- **Can you send me some information in the mail?**
  I'd be glad to send you something, but we try to keep our mailing costs down, and it's no problem for me to discuss your donor benefits right over the phone (*describe donor benefits to prospect.*) We're trying to reach our nightly goal this evening, which will push us closer to our overall campaign goal, so we're really hoping that you'll be able to join us tonight. How does a gift of $_____ sound to you?

- **I'm not sure exactly how much I can give yet.**
  I understand, Mr./Ms._____. We're glad that you're interested in supporting The Minnesota Opera. We prefer to put down a pledge amount so we can get an idea if we're meeting our projections. Is there an amount you're thinking about that I can put down for our records?

- **I need to speak with someone else.**
  If he/she is available now, I'll gladly hold. **If person is unavailable:** When would be a good time to speak with him/her? (*Set up callback time.*)

- **Won't Give Specific Amount / Wants to Think About It**

  1. Mr./Ms. _____, is there any kind of specific information you're looking for that I can clear up for you over the phone? I'd be happy to do so if that's possible.

  2. Mr./Ms. _____, if this is just a bad time to talk, I'd be more than happy to call you back. (*Set up callback time.*)

- **I give to other charities**
  That's wonderful, Mr./Ms._____. We really appreciate your understanding of the need for charitable giving. These are challenging financial times for charities and arts organizations all across the country. Considering this, could you see your way to making a gift to The Minnesota Opera that is as thoughtful as your others?

APPENDIX B2: The Minnesota Opera Pledge Form

December 2005

Dear Friend,

Thank you so much for making a generous pledge of $_____ to The Minnesota Opera!

Your contribution makes such a difference! Gifts from our loyal donors provide the resources we need to stage beautiful operas, one magnificent season after another.

The Minnesota Opera is also dedicated to enriching the community through its Educational Outreach programs. Your contribution helps The Opera introduce the beauty of opera to thousands of young people every year through programs like *coOPERAtion!*, which works with students in the schools.

As you may know, proceeds from ticket sales only cover a portion of The Opera's expenses. The support of donors like you provides the remainder of what is needed to bring great opera to life!

Please take a moment now to fulfill your pledge by sending your gift in today. In recognition of your support, you will receive exclusive benefits reserved for members of The Minnesota Opera family. Thank you for your dedicated support of the arts in Minnesota!

Sincerely,

Megan Stevenson
Individual Gifts Associate

SD&A Teleservices, Inc., a professional fundraiser, has conducted this solicitation on behalf of The Minnesota Opera.

Thank you for your pledge of $_____ in support of The Minnesota Opera!

Thank you for taking the time to speak with us on the phone. By completing this form and returning it in the enclosed envelope today, your contribution can go to work immediately to help support The Minnesota Opera!

ANNUAL FUND CONTRIBUTION:

$1,000 $750 $500 $250

$100 $50   Other: $_____

NAME_____

ADDRESS _____

CITY_____ STATE_____ ZIP_____

PHONE _____

The Minnesota
OPERA

My check is enclosed.

Please process my tax-deductible gift on my:

__Visa __MasterCard __Am. Express __Discover

ACCOUNT NUMBER_____

EXPIRATION DATE_____

Please acknowledge my gift as follows:

_____

SIGNATURE_____

Please make checks payable to The Minnesota Opera.

Please feel free to fill out the bottom portion of this letter and return it in its entirety to The Minnesota Opera in the enclosed envelope. Your acknowledgement for tax purposes will be mailed when your gift reaches us!

APPENDIX B3: The Minnesota Opera Annual Campaign Acknowledgement

December 20, 2005

Mary Smith
111 Main Street
Big City, MN 55346

Dear Ms. Smith,

Thank you for your recent gift of $105 to the Minnesota Opera Annual Campaign! We count on the support of community members like you to ensure continuing success for the Minnesota Opera—both artistically and financially.

After the wonderful success of our opening production, Puccini's *Tosca*, The Minnesota Opera's spectacular season continues with another of the world's greatest operas *Don Giovanni* followed by a fantastic bel canto piece *Orazi & Curiazi* and ending the season with the contemporary masterpiece *Elephant Man*. This season is made possible because of the generosity of our many wonderful donors—you truly help bring great opera to life onstage each season.

So, on behalf of everyone at The Minnesota Opera, let me once again express our thanks for your spectacular generosity!

Sincerely,

Megan Stevenson
Individual Gifts Associate

APPENDIX C: The Minnesota Opera Special Event Budget

Acct #	Account	Expenses	TOTALS	06-07 Projections	06 - 07 Goal	05 - 06 Actual
2006-2007 GALA BUDGET 30030						
5300	**Professional Services**			26,420.00		
	PO 82183	PA system in ballroom $100, Stage $28.80, Dance Floor $225, Floor Lecturn with microphone $25, Piano mic $15, cd player $25, Skirted tables $18, Piano $375, Pipe & Drape backdrop for check-in $20 and $58.23 tax	831.80		*$500*	125.00
	PO 82188	IATSE Stage Labor at RiverCentre $2,706.65, Electricians $752.34, Ballroom Changeover $100	3,558.99		*$2,000*	
		Design- Supplies for signage, delivery costs (on another line)	0.00		*$200*	159.72
	Beganik	Design for confirmations, signage, auctioncatalog etc. -Last year Amy Kirkpatrick's IN-KIND (accounted for in Revenue so it will zero out)	12,478.89		*$8,500*	7,780.00
	PO 82387	Rentals (tables, linens) (Linen Effects)	6,583.40		*$6,000*	4,895.50
	PO 82398, PO 82187	Silent Auction Fees ($3,570 for Ribnick fur coat items, and $3,200 for RAP Cabaret expenses ($1,200 In-Kind to be taken out) ($300 Deposit on PO 82192)	6,770.00		*$5,200*	2,575.00
	PO 82186	Coat Check (Wildside Caterers) includes staff, and $1 per item charge (this is included in Wildside bill- $491.13)	0.00		*$300*	0.00
		Piano Movers	0.00		*$0*	390.00
		Piano Tuner (RiverCentre)	0.00		*$200*	105.00
	PO 82392	Valet (Class A Valet)	2,125.00		*$2,200*	1,080.00
	PO 82189	Searchlights (6:30-8:30)	290.00		*$600*	525.00
	PO 82189	Meter Hooding (on 4th and Washington (2 meters)	75.65		*$720*	708.94
	(Beganik In-Kind) $12,478.89					
	(Rap Cabaret In-Kind) $1,200					
			32,713.73			*18,344.16*

Appendix C (continued)

2006-2007 GALA BUDGET 30030				06-07		05 - 06
Acct #	Account	Expenses	TOTALS	Projections	*06 - 07 Goal*	Actual
5320	Contract Services			*1,500.00*		
	PO 82370 &	I 1 Stip ($500 mid, $500 end)	1,000.00		*$1,000*	1,200.00
	PO 82375 &	I 2 Stip ($250 mid, $250 end)	500.00		*$500*	
			1,500.00			
5441	Development Credit Card			300.00	*$300*	0.00
	see hard file for receipt under "F"	Nicholas Font from Fonts.com for Correspondence on PD's CC 6.22.06	64.00			
	see hard file for receipt under "A"	3 Opera cd's to download to Ipods- Amazon.com on PD's CC 9.18.06	55.94			
			119.94			
5445	Interdepartmental Ticketing			11,000.00	*$11,000*	10,900.50
		Corp.$4,868.50, Indiv. $4,057.50, $808 for Russell and $870 for Beganik (C tickets to all 5 shows for Christopher and Justin, and a pair for Russell for 4 shows) (TOTAL: $10,604.00, but the $11,000 is a nonmoving number)	11,000.00		*$2,000*	
			11,000.00			*10,900.50*
5450	Front of House			1,100.00		
		Labor	0.00		*$500*	437.61
	PO 82189	Lobby production call for lighting OR labor for backstage Reception/costumer/wigs (Production Labor- House Crew $68.30 and overhead 17.08, Wardrobe $31.23, and Extra crew & wardrobe $10.31)	126.92		*$300*	276.17
		Cast Party Corkage Fee (Wildside estimate)	0.00		*$0*	
	PO 82189	Backstage Corkage Fee @ $12.00/btl with server	323.44		*$300*	
			450.36			*713.78*

Acct #	Account	Expenses	TOTALS	06-07 Projections	06 - 07 Goal	05 - 06 Actual
2006-2007 GALA BUDGET 30030						
5470	**Postage, Freight, Delivery**			270.00		
	PO 82373	Postage (for Confirmations and Auction Catalogs-originally on Linda's CC)	140.00		*$100*	87.90
	charged on our Permit #1 mailhouse acct.	Other postage- (this year postage for Bulk Mailing Auction Catalogs)	62.51		*$70*	60.34
		Delivery/Courier Services	0.00		*$100*	
			202.51			*148.24*
5550	**Renting Expense**			1,300.00		
	po 82354	Dinner/Cast Party Venue Deposit ($11,000 food and beverage minimum- cross reference with food and catering)	1,000.00		*$1,000*	2,800.00
	PO 82188	Coat Check Room Rental (Meeting Room #1)	300.00		*$300*	
			1,300.00			*2,800.00*
5640	**Supplies**			635.00		
	Went on company (Dean's) cc- marked on cc statement	Black backing, easel backs (PENCO)	280.09		*$250*	229.69
		Storage bins	0.00		*$40*	39.92
	PO 82388	Candles from Michaels	53.15		*$25*	22.45
	PO 82361	OfficeMax Envelopes #10, and #9	28.12		*$70*	65.81
	PO 82385	Gift bags, Thank you cards, Pens, Tissue paper for gift bags, coasters for gift bags	468.79	Mktg. purchased gift bags last for 2005	*$150*	135.90
	PO 85133 & PO 85134	Extras- more tissue Paper, Pens, copies, silent auction headphones etc.- or Net Litin Distributors for example	42.05		*$100*	93.15
			872.20			*586.92*

Appendix C (continued)

Acct #	Account	Expenses	TOTALS	06-07 Projections	06 - 07 Goal	05 - 06 Actual
2006-2007 GALA BUDGET 30030						
5650	Printing, Duplication, Reproduction			10,420.00		
* = Ideal Printing Costs						
	In-kind printer costs	*Ideal Printing supplies (includes everything with a star) (IN-KIND)	5,845.00		$10,000	9,984.22
	Anchor Paper	Paper-main distributor (IN-KIND)	3,389.49			
		Save the Date Printing			$0	0.00
	Beganik	FUND-A-DREAM Card Printing				
		Misc. Printing (Timeline)			$0	
	Beganik	Bid Sheets (colored backing)			$70	65.69
	Beganik/Att	Signage (mounting) (IN-KIND)	630.00		$350	238.00
		Save the Date Mailhouse			$0	0.00
		Invite/RSVP Mailhouse			$0	0.00
		Confirmations*				
	Beganik	Placecards				
		Boxes for Flower Arrangements			$0	0.00
		Evening Program*				
		Auction Catalogs*				
		Handmarbled Paper for Confirms and Programs	0.00		$0	1,040.00
		Letterpress Printing on Confirms and Even. Programs (Mary Jo Pauly)	0.00		$0	350.00
Signage (in-kind) $630						
Printing (In-Kind) $5,845						
Paper Supplier (In-Kind) $3,389.49						
			9,864.49			11,677.91
5660	Photography			100.00		
		Photographer (Theresa/Dawn)	0.00		$0	0
		Photo Development (Theresa charged on Kevin's cc)	53.37		$100	60.11
			53.37			60.11
5700	Staff Auto, Travel, Parking			700.00	$700	
		Emily Skoblik	181.67			90.40
		Linda Johnson/other staff	24.18			195.09
		Kelly Clemens	0.00			25.30
	PO 85133	Intern 1	49.94			25.00
	PO 85134	Intern 2	21.68			25.00
		Steve Mittleholz				40.50
			277.47			401.29

				06-07		05 - 06
2006-2007 GALA BUDGET 30030			**TOTALS**	**Projections**	*06 - 07 Goal*	**Actual**
Acct #	**Account**	**Expenses**	**TOTALS**	**Projections**	*06 - 07 Goal*	**Actual**
5710	Entertainment			6,350.00		
	PO for draping is 82386, PO for accordian player is 82383, PO 82391 for plywood for prows & Dean's cc for c-clamps	Decorations/Props- Shop design and supply cost $90.66 & c-clamps $23.40; Accordian player fee $250; Ceiling Clouding & equip. charge $1,455.20 (Richfield Flowers & Events)	1,819.26	draping, accordian, shop supplies	*$6,000*	463.05
		Dinner music	0.00		*$0*	0.00
	PO 82364	Florist (Wisteria)	2,604.00		*$3,500*	3,400.00
	PO 82364	Wisteria IN-KIND (glass vase fixture rental $570, delivery & set-up $124, take down $300)	994.00		*$850*	835.00
		Cast Party Music (Beasley's Big Band- 6)	0.00		*$0*	0.00
		Operations Cast Party Contribution	-4,500.00		*-$4,000*	-4,000.00
Wisteria fixtures, delivery, setup & break down(In-Kind) $994						
			917.26			698.05

Appendix C (continued)

2006-2007 GALA BUDGET 30030						
Acct #	Account	Expenses	TOTALS	06-07 Projections	06 - 07 Goal	05 - 06 Actual
5720	Food and Catering			30,965.00		
		Dinner & Wine total from 05-06 was $20,087.14				
This needs to be broken down under 5720	PO 82186	Dinner Catering (Wildside Catering- includes wine 17,610.01, volunteer lunches $517.45, bar $815.18 social hour passed hor'douvres $2,672.68 (includes bellinis), cast party food $2,510.22, Coat check $491.13)	24,850.33		$17,000	15,000.00
		(cast party food donation: $1,721.00)	1,721.00			
		Dinner Catering staffing	0.00		$5,100	5,087.14
		Dinner/Cast Party Wine (Paustis Wine Company included in Marshall Field's bill- $2,641.14) In dinner/casty party estimates	0.00		$3,300	0.00
		Cast Party Buffet Catering (2,889.00 in above number)	0.00		$3,400	2,629.00
		Cast Party Bar (1,277.58 in above number)	0.00		$0	-435.00
	PO 82186	Bar Services & Staffing (includes bar deposit if we have the wine hosted, staff, etc. -see above under dinner catering)	0.00		$1,800	1,751.60
	PO 82388	Backstage Reception Chocolates	17.98		$250	35.32
	PO 82388	Volunteer Orientation Food, Lunch with Sara or others if comes up	12.58		$100	96.45
	PO 82395	Staff food for day of set-up- meat/cheese rolls	6.95		$15	12.22
	PO 82368	RAP Cabaret 2007 Planning Lunch with Host Jane Confer on 8.24.06	31.82		$0	
Cast Party Food (In-Kind) $1,721						
			26,640.66			24,176.73
5810	Volunteer Expenses			600.00		
	PO 82395	Dev. Setup Thank you Dinner	94.48		$100	78.08
69.02 Sara's flowers & 15.96 for frame	PO 82396	Individual Co-Chair Frame and Flowers	84.98		$100	45.00
	PO 82184	Shop Thank you gifts	62.98		$300	103.38
	PO petty cas	Designer Thank you gift	100.00		$100	75.00
			342.44			301.46
	Other		0.00	375.00	$375	0.00
			0.00			0.00

2006-2007 GALA BUDGET 30030				06-07 Projections	06 - 07 Goal	05 - 06 Actual
Acct #	Account	Expenses	TOTALS			
		TOTAL EXPENSES	86,254.43	92,035.00	$94,035	70,809.15
		Less In-Kind expenses	12,478.89			7,780.00
			630.00			6,375.00
			5,845.00			897.00
			3,389.49			
			994.00			
			1,721.00			
			1,200.00			
		ACTUAL EXPENSES	59,996.05			55,757.15
		Current GROSS REVENUE	390,000.00		$370,000	355,081.00
		Less TOTAL EXPENSES	86,254.43		-$80,930	70,809.15
		NET	303,745.57		$289,070	284,271.85
		2006-2007 NET	303,745.57			284,271.85
		Less Last year's NET	$284,272			$230,935
		ABOVE LAST YEAR	19,473.72			53,336.85
		IN-KIND included in expenses breakdown				
	5300	Design $12,478.89				
	5650	Signage $630				
	5650	Printing $5,845				
	5650	Paper $3,389.49				
	5710	Wisteria flowers fixture rental, delivery, and set up/break down $994				
	5720	Wildside Catering-Portion of Cast Party Food $1,721				
	5300	Rap Cabaret $1,200				
		In-Kind = $26,258.38				
		PO 82399- Suspense account for $2,410 cash stipend on Venice trip-we will not put in expenses as determined on 11/21/06 per Jeff and PO 82187 suspense account for remaining $90 that winner should receive to bring actual cash stipend to $2,500 12/6/06				

APPENDIX D: The Minnesota Opera Gala Confirmation Card

Confirmation

We have received your reservation and
look forward to your presence at

OPERA GALA 2006

Saturday, October 28, 2006

Valet parking begins ~ 4:30 pm
Gala Festivities begin ~ 5:00 pm

Saint Paul River Centre
175 West Kellogg Boulevard
Saint Paul

Evening Program

SAINT PAUL RIVERCENTRE

Social Hour ~ 5:00 pm
Dinner and Fund-A-Dream ~ 5:45 pm

ORDWAY CENTER
for the PERFORMING ARTS

Silent Auction Opens ~ 7:00 pm
Auction closes at the end of second intermission.
Curtain for *The Tales of Hoffman* ~ 8:00 pm
Silent Auction Cashiering ~ 11:15 pm

SAINT PAUL RIVERCENTRE

Cast Party featuring Members of
Beasley's Big Band ~ 11:15 pm

Appreciation

Mary Vaughan, *Honorary Gala Chair*
Sara Donaldson, *Individual Co-Chair*
Mitchell Stover, *Corporate Co-Chair*
Target, *Sponsor*
U.S. Bank, *Sponsor*
Okabena Advisors, *Sponsor*
Beganik Strategy + Design, *Design*
Ideal, *Printing*
Anchor Paper, *Paper*

APPENDIX E: Corporate Contributions Proposal

**World Monuments Fund
Proposal to XYX, Inc. for
Corporate Support**

The World Monuments Fund (WMF) helps safeguard mankind's shared cultural heritage through the conservation and preservation of historically significant works of art and architecture around the globe. WMF brings together public and private support to provide financial and technical assistance to cultural heritage sites endangered by threats such as neglect, vandalism, armed conflict, and natural disaster. Together with local and international partners, WMF works to restore individual sites and advocates for increased public awareness of cultural heritage preservation.

The World Monuments Fund respectfully invites XYZ, Inc. to become a corporate supporter of its efforts to preserve and restore endangered cultural heritage sites. As a corporate supporter of these efforts, XYZ, Inc. would receive high visibility acknowledgment in all WMF promotional and marketing activities.

WMF would be pleased to work with company representatives to develop a recognition package that would help insure the greatest visibility for the company's support. WMF also hopes that this support would be the beginning of a new and dynamic partnership between XYZ, Inc. and WMF.

Corporate Support Benefits

WMF could offer many benefits and acknowledgment opportunities in consideration of XYZ's corporate support and would be pleased to tailor a membership package commensurate to this level of commitment. Benefits and visibility opportunities include, but are not limited to, the following:

- Acknowledgment in all reports, newsletters, and other printed materials, where appropriate.
- High visibility recognition in public promotional materials, where appropriate.
- Acknowledgment on the Web site with links to corporate site.
- Additional acknowledgements, where appropriate.
- Designated number of complimentary tickets to special events for designated executives. Quantities to be determined.
- Possibilities for special corporate membership evenings, including pre- and/or post- exclusive corporate events.
- Special access extended to XYZ employees for select events. Types of events and quantities of special ticket access passes to be determined.
- Membership privileges extended to all employees.
- Priority consideration and discounted rates for XYZ rental of event spaces for corporate use.

Appendix E (continued)

Demographics

WMF initiatives have unrivaled global impact and reach prized target populations. Significantly, WMF advocacy efforts help to serve as a catalyst to draw attention to the long-term benefits of preserving mankind's shared cultural heritage. These efforts offer unparalleled opportunities to support and complement XYZ's business interests.

The WMF operating budget is approximately $X million and includes significant community outreach efforts to raise visibility for its preservation work around the globe. As a major corporate supporter, XYZ would receive high visibility recognition in relation to these efforts.

Evaluation

WMF will provide updates on the funded project (and, if requested, on annual operations) and will work with XYZ representatives to help ensure that performance measures comply with XYZ evaluation requirements. WMF also will review with corporate representatives all appropriate and requisite benefits and will submit for approval all language and visual images that recognize XYZ support. Additionally, WMF will provide updates on employee use of membership privileges and participation in ticket programs, as well as attendance at special events.

Conclusion & Request

WMF currently is entering a new phase of dynamic growth with an initiative-based structure to major restoration and preservation commitments around the globe. This growth offers unparalleled visibility opportunities for XYZ, Inc. for its potential general operating corporate support.

WMF is hopeful that XYZ, Inc. will consider a corporate contribution at the $X level to help support its world-wide efforts to preserve endangered cultural heritage sites for future generations.

May 2006

APPENDIX F1: Corporate Foundation Proposal

**Proposal to the XYZ, Inc. Foundation
in support of the
World Monuments Fund**

The World Monuments Fund (WMF) is the foremost private international organization dedicated to helping safeguard mankind's shared cultural heritage through the conservation and preservation of historically significant works of art and architecture around the globe. Since the 1980s, the Jewish Heritage Grants Program (JHGP) of the WMF has supported the conservation of historic synagogues and advocated for the protection of Jewish culture and heritage around the world. The JHGP provides financial and technical assistance to help restore at-risk Jewish sites of significant architectural and/or historical importance. To accomplish these goals, the JHGP establishes partnerships with community and government stakeholders to bring local, national, and international attention to the importance of preserving the world's endangered Jewish heritage.

The JHGP is entering a new phase of activity that will build on its preservation work and effective partnerships. Central to this activity is technical and financial support for new project partners, as well as increased outreach to assist and advise communities to help interpret endangered sites for the general public. These efforts will help to make the preservation, maintenance, and continued use of cultural heritage sites integral to their respective communities.

WMF is hopeful that the XYZ, Inc. Foundation would consider a grant at the $X level in support of the current revitalization of the JHGP. This support would help continue to preserve cultural landmarks of Jewish life in desperate need of immediate intervention for future generations.

Rationale & Outcomes

Though the JHGP has a significant track record of effective project work to restore and sustain important Jewish cultural heritage sites, an internal assessment of the program revealed several factors that were restricting the continued success of the program. WMF currently is revising the JHGP and is hopeful that a contribution from the XYZ, Inc. Foundation would help ensure the success of all rejuvenated programmatic activities. These include:

- targeted financial assistance to support major preservation/implementation projects at endangered sites,
- smaller assistance directed towards planning and/or documentation projects and emergency interventions,
- outreach to assist communities in need.

Appendix F1 (continued)

WMF would be pleased to provide additional information specific to these activities upon request.

Education and Community Outreach

Community and educational outreach programming is central to WMF projects and to its new collaborative JHGP partnerships. This outreach includes efforts to raise overall programmatic visibility, current award funding, and strategic partnerships with local stakeholders. Additionally, WMF hopes to sponsor exhibitions and/or professional symposia and to participate in international conferences of import to cultural heritage preservation.

Evaluation

WMF employs various methods to evaluate programs, such as on-site observation and monitoring to ensure that all community outreach/educational initiatives are being carried out in an efficient and successful manner. Ongoing observation allows staff to closely interact with all partnering organizations on specific projects and to react immediately to problems. WMF encourages participants to give feedback by completion of questionnaires that help to measure levels of satisfaction and to determine whether programs are meeting expectations. This feedback also includes suggestions for improvements and modifications, as well as solicitations for new ideas. Importantly, WMF remains in regular contact with funders through periodic updates on project successes. This contact is vital to helping ensure that WMF meets specific funder expectations or requests for information on a timely basis.

Conclusion

The World Monuments Fund is in a period of unprecedented growth and its portfolio of projects worldwide is expanding. This organizational growth includes a renewed commitment to the JHGP. WMF is very grateful to the XYZ, Inc. Foundation for its consideration of general operating support for the JHGP. This funding would be a significant vote of confidence in WMF efforts to continue its effective field work and advocacy, as well as its plans for new strategic partnerships that will support cultural heritage preservation in communities around the world.

August 2006

APPENDIX F2: Corporate Foundation Budget

World Monuments Fund
Corporate Foundation Proposal
Program Budget

Expenses

Field Projects	$	250,000
- includes new awards and release of certain previous years' allocations		
Administration/management fees*	$	45,000
Research and documentation related to awards program	$	26,500
Public relations and community partnership/outreach	$	16,000
Travel	$	5,000
Printing	$	3,500
Consultancy fees	$	2,000
Supplies/materials	$	2,000
TOTAL EXPENSES	**$**	**350,000**

* Administration fee percentages range from 12% to 20%, depending on contributed revenue source

Revenue
Earned

Investment income (endowment)	$	41,000
Contributed		
Institutional support	$	130,000
Individual support	$	100,000
To Be Raised	$	79,000
TOTAL REVENUE	**$**	**350,000**

FY07 Committed and Pending Contributions

X Foundation	$	100,000	pending
Jones Family Foundation	$	20,000	pending
Major Donor (individual)	$	35,000	committed
Y Foundation	$	10,000	pending
Other family foundation grants and individuals	$	10,000	committed
Total:	$	175,000	

APPENDIX G: Lincoln Center Theater NEA Proposal

Grants for Arts Projects Application

Basic Information, Part 1

Read the instructions that follow this form before you start.

OMB No. 3135-0112
Expires 02/28/05

Applicant Official IRS name: The Vivian Beaumont Theater, Inc.

Popular name (if different):   Lincoln Center Theater

Mailing Address:
150 West 65th Street
New York, NY

Street Address (if different):

ZIP Code (9-digit number): 10023

ZIP Code (9-digit number):

Taxpayer ID Number (9-digit number): 13 – 3004747

DUNS Number: 03-781-0801

Project Field/Discipline (check one):

☐ Dance (33)	☐ Local Arts Agencies (62)	☐ Museums (44)	☐ Presenting (54)
☐ Design (42)	☐ Media Arts: Film/Radio/ Television (34)	☐ Music (31)	☐ Theater (32)
☐ Folk & Traditional Arts (55)		☑ Musical Theater (28)	☐ Visual Arts (41)
☐ Literature (52)	☐ Multidisciplinary (70)	☐ Opera (36)	

Category (check only one category -- Number 1, 2, or 3):

1 ☑ **Access to Artistic Excellence (7)**

APPLICATION DEADLINES (check one): ☑ MARCH 15, 2004   ☐ AUGUST 16, 2004
To determine the appropriate application deadline for your project, see "*Access to Artistic Excellence Application Deadlines*" or the field/discipline section that corresponds to your project.

2 ☐ **Challenge America Fast-Track Review Grants (7-78)**

APPLICATION DEADLINE: JUNE 1, 2004

For this category also select one focus area below:
☐   Professional arts programming and program enhancements (05)
☐   Arts in community development (06)

3 ☐ **Learning in the Arts for Children and Youth (8-51)**

APPLICATION DEADLINE: JUNE 14, 2004

For this category also select one focus area below:
☐ School-Based (27)   ☐ Community-Based (28)   ☐ Combination (29)

Project Director   ☑ Mr. ☐ Ms.   First: André   Last: Bishop

Title: Artistic Director   E-mail: bishop@lct.org

Telephone: (212) 362-7600 ext.   Fax: (212) 873-0761

I certify that the information contained in this application, including all attachments and supporting material, is true and correct to the best of my knowledge. I also certify that the applicant is in compliance with the federal requirements specified under "Assurance of Compliance."

Authorizing Official   ☑ Mr. ☐ Ms.   First: André   Last: Bishop

Title: Artistic Director   E-mail: bishop@lct.org

Telephone: (212) 362-7600 ext.   Fax: (212) 873-0761

Signature: Date: 3 , 10, 04

Additional Authorizing   ☑ Mr. ☐ Ms.   First: Bernard   Last: Gersten

Official (optional)

Title: Executive Producer   E-mail: gersten@lct.org

Telephone: (212) 362-7600 ext.   Fax: (212) 873-0761

Signature: Date: 3 , 10, 04

NEA GRANTS FOR ARTS PROJECTS GUIDELINES FY 2005

Grants for Arts Projects Application

Basic Information, Part 2

Read the
instructions that
follow this form
before you start.

OMB No. 3135-0112
Expires 02/28/05

Applicant (official IRS name):   The Vivian Beaumont Theater, Inc.

City, State: New York, NY   **Web Address:** www.lct.org

Individual responsible for organization and project:

The organization: **Bernard Gersten**   The project: **André Bishop**

Project Summary:

LCT will produce the world premiere of DESSA ROSE, a musical by Lynn Ahrens and
Stephen Flaherty, staged by LCT Associate Director Graciela Daniele. Scheduled for 124
performances over a 15.5-week run in the 275-seat Mitzi E. Newhouse Theater, the
production will be seen by a projected total audience of 30,180 from the NYC metro area,
including 1,000 inner-city New York City public high school students.

Intended Outcome (check one):

Access to Artistic Excellence	☑ 1. Artists and arts organizations have opportunities to create, interpret, present, and perform artistic work. (A1Z)
	☐ 2. Artistic works and cultural traditions are preserved. (A2Z)
And	☐ 3. Organizations enhance their ability to realize their artistic and public service goals. (A3Z)
Challenge America Fast-Track Review Grants	☐ 4. Audiences throughout the nation have opportunities to experience a wide range of art forms and activities. (A4Z)
	☐ 5. The arts contribute to the strengthening of communities. (A5Z)
Learning in the Arts for Children and Youth	☐ 1. Children and youth demonstrate skills, knowledge, and/or understanding of the arts consistent with national, state, or local arts education standards. (B1Z)
	☐ 2. Teachers, artists, and others demonstrate knowledge and skills necessary to engage children and youth in arts learning consistent with national, state, or local arts education standards. (B2Z)
	☐ 3. National, state, and local entities demonstrate a commitment to arts learning for children and youth consistent with national, state, or local arts education standards. (B3Z)

Performance Measurements:

Ticket sales for DESSA ROSE will be monitored by LCT's Director of Marketing to
determine whether the projected goal of 30,180 audience members has been met. We will
also assess the outcomes of teacher lesson plans and student work generated by
participants in our Open Stages education program who attend the production.

For this application, the applicant is serving as a [check if applicable; then list the one primary consortium partner (other than the lead applicant), or the group or entity on whose behalf you are applying]:

☐ Lead Member of a Consortium   ☐ Fiscal Agent   ☐ Parent of a Component

For:

Period of Support (e.g., 06/01/05 to 12/31/06):
See the "Earliest Beginning Date for Arts Endowment Period of Support" listed on the Application Calendar.

01 /04 / 05   to: 12 /30 / 05   Number of Months: 12

Project Budget Summary:

$ 150,000   PLUS $ 2,377,289   MUST EQUAL $ 2,527,289

AMOUNT REQUESTED   TOTAL MATCH FOR THIS PROJECT   TOTAL PROJECT COSTS

Total organizational operating expenses for the most recently completed fiscal year: $ 35,209,251

For year ending (Month/Year):   06 / 03

Appendix G (continued)

Grants for Arts Projects Application
Organizational Background

Read the
instructions that
follow this form
before you start.

OMB No. 3135-0112
Expires 02/28/05

Applicant (official IRS name): The Vivian Beaumont Theater, Inc. (dba Lincoln Center Theater)

Date organization was founded: 02 /21/ 1979   Date organization was incorporated: 02 /21/ 1979

Mission/purpose of your organization:

Re-established in 1985, Lincoln Center Theater (LCT) seeks to create and sustain a theater of high artistic standards, producing the work of established as well as emerging American and international playwrights, and carefully wrought revivals from the world classical repertoire. The most accomplished artists working in the theater today regularly appear on our stages.

Organization overview:

a) Overview. Now in its 19th season, LCT has achieved a reputation as one of this country's premier institutional theaters. Since 1985, some 8.4 million attendees have comprised the audiences of more than 13,000 LCT performances of over 100 productions at the Vivian Beaumont and Mitzi E. Newhouse Theaters at Lincoln Center, as well as in Broadway and off-Broadway houses.

b) Previous Activities. Among LCT's more notable premiere presentations are David Mamet's SPEED-THE-PLOW, John Guare's SIX DEGREES OF SEPARATION, Wendy Wasserstein's THE SISTERS ROSENSWEIG, Susan Stroman and John Weidman's CONTACT, and Tom Stoppard's THE INVENTION OF LOVE. The Theater's well-regarded revivals and classics have included THE FRONT PAGE, ANYTHING GOES, CAROUSEL, THE HEIRESS, A DELICATE BALANCE, TWELFTH NIGHT, and HENRY IV.

c) Community/Region/Audience. Our most immediate community consists of the 40,000 LCT Members who comprise our core audience. A survey of LCT Membership conducted last year revealed the following: over 90% of Members are white; 77% female, 23% male. Approximately 78% of Members are age 50 or over. Just over half the Membership resides in Manhattan and a significant portion lives in Westchester (10%) and Nassau (13%) Counties; the remainder live principally in NYC's other four boroughs and in Rockland and Suffolk Counties. Total annual LCT audience customarily ranges from 250,000 to 600,000.

d) Special Efforts. LCT has aggressively worked to diversify its core audience, bringing new populations to the Theater—people under the age of 45 with limited annual income or from minority backgrounds. We also make an effort to broaden our audience base by utilizing special marketing campaigns for targeted constituencies on select shows, and by offering our Open Stages education program free of charge to thousands of economically disadvantaged New York City public-school students each season.

Grants for Arts Projects Application

Organizational Activities

Read the instructions that follow this form before you start.

OMB No. 3135-0112
Expires 02/28/05

Provide a representative list of your organization's programming or activities for the following years: 2001-02, 2002-03, 2003-04. For organizations that schedule activities according to a single calendar year, use programming for 2001, 2002, and 2003. If necessary, you may attach up to two additional pages.

Applicant (official IRS name):   **The Vivian Beaumont Theater, Inc. (dba Lincoln Center Theater)**

Please see following two pages.

Appendix G (continued)

VIVIAN BEAUMONT THEATER, INC. ■ THREE-YEAR PRODUCTION HISTORY ■ PAGE 1 OF 2

2001-2002 SEASON	CREATOR(S)	KEY ARTIST(S)	PRIMARY PERFORMER(S)
CONTACT	Susan Stroman, John Weidman	Susan Stroman, director/choreographer	Boyd Gaines, Deborah Yates, Karen Ziemba
CHAUCER IN ROME	John Guare	Nicholas Martin, director	Susan Finch, Polly Holliday, Dick Latessa, Nancy McDoniel, Bruce Norris, Lee Wilkof
THOU SHALT NOT	Susan Stroman, Harry Connick, Jr., David Thompson	Susan Stroman, director/choreographer	Craig Bierko, Brad Bradley, Leo Burmester, Norbert Leo Butz, Joann M. Hunter, Kate Levering, Debra Monk
EVERETT BEEKIN	Richard Greenberg	Evan Yionoulis, director	Jeff Allin, Robin Bartlett, Jennifer Carpenter, Kevin Isola, Marcia Jean Kurtz, Bebe Neuwirth
QED	Peter Parnell	Gordon Davidson, director	Alan Alda, Kellie Overbey
MOSTLY SONDHEIM	Barbara Cook, Wally Harper	Wally Harper, music director	Barbara Cook
THE CARPETBAGGER'S CHILDREN	Horton Foote	Michael Wilson, director	Hallie Foote, Roberta Maxwell, Jean Stapleton
MORNING'S AT SEVEN	Paul Osborn	Daniel Sullivan, director	Elizabeth Franz, Julie Hagerty, Buck Henry, Piper Laurie, Christopher Lloyd, William Biff McGuire, Estelle Parsons, Frances Sternhagen, Stephen Tobolowsky
2002-2003 SEASON	**CREATOR(S)**	**KEY ARTIST(S)**	**PRIMARY PERFORMER(S)**
CONTACT	Susan Stroman, John Weidman	Susan Stroman, director/choreographer	Alan Campbell, Charlotte d'Amboise, Colleen Dunn, D.W. Moffett
MORNING'S AT SEVEN	Paul Osborn	Daniel Sullivan, director	Bob Dishy, Elizabeth Franz, Julie Hagerty, Buck Henry, Piper Laurie, William Biff McGuire, Estelle Parsons, Frances Sternhagen, Stephen Tobolowsky
MOSTLY SONDHEIM	Barbara Cook, Wally Harper	Wally Harper, music director	Barbara Cook
A MAN OF NO IMPORTANCE	Terrence McNally, Lynn Ahrens, Stephen Flaherty	Joe Mantello, director; Jonathan Butterell, choreographer	Ronn Carroll, Jarlath Conroy, Luther Creek, Charles Keating, Michael McCormick, Katherine McGrath, Jessica Molaskey, Martin Moran, Sally Murphy, Steven Pasquale, Faith Prince, Roger Rees
DINNER AT EIGHT	George S. Kaufman, Edna Ferber	Gerald Gutierrez, director; John Lee Beatty, scenic designer	Joanne Camp, Kevin Conway, John Dossett, Christine Ebersole, Enid Graham, Joe Grifasi, Byron Jennings, Anne Lange, Peter Maloney, James Rebhorn, Marian Seldes, Sloane Shelton
OBSERVE THE SONS OF ULSTER MARCHING TOWARDS THE SOMME	Frank McGuinness	Nicholas Martin, director	Richard Easton, Dashiell Eaves, Christopher Fitzgerald, David Barry Gray, Jason Butler Harner, Rod McLachlan, Jeremy Shamos, Justin Theroux, Scott Wolf
VINCENT IN BRIXTON	Nicholas Wright	Sir Richard Eyre, director	Sarah Drew, Clare Higgins, Liesel Matthews, Pete Starrett, Jochum ten Haaf
ELEGIES – A SONG CYCLE	William Finn	Graciela Daniele, director	Christian Borle, Betty Buckley, Carolee Carmello, Keith Byron Kirk, Michael Rupert
A BAD FRIEND	Jules Feiffer	Jerry Zaks, director	Jonathan Hadary, David Harbour, Jan Maxwell, Kala Savage
2003-2004 SEASON	**CREATOR(S)**	**KEY ARTIST(S)**	**PRIMARY PERFORMER(S)**
A BAD FRIEND	Jules Feiffer	Jerry Zaks, director	Jonathan Hadary, David Harbour, Jan Maxwell, Kala Savage
HENRY IV, PARTS 1 & 2	William Shakespeare, Dakin Matthews	Jack O'Brien, director	Richard Easton, Ethan Hawke, Michael Hayden, Dana Ivey, Kevin Kline, Audra McDonald
NOTHING BUT THE TRUTH	John Kani	Janice Honeyman, director	Esmeralda Bihl, John Kani, Warona Seane
BIG BILL	A.R. Gurney	Mark Lamos, director	David Cromwell, John Michael Higgins Stephen Rowe, and Margaret Welsh
KING LEAR	William Shakespeare	Jonathan Miller, director	James Blendick, Domini Blythe, William Cain, Benedict Campbell, Brent Carver, Geraint Wyn Davies, Ian Deakin, Claire Jullien, Leo Leyden, Barry Macgregor, Paul O'Brien, Guy Paul, Lucy Peacock, Christopher Plummer, Stephen Russell, Brian Tree
BARBARA COOK'S BROADWAY	Barbara Cook, Wally Harper	Wally Harper, music director	Barbara Cook
THE FROGS	Stephen Sondheim, Nathan Lane	Susan Stroman, director/choreographer	Peter Bartlett, John Byner, Moses Burke, Daniel Davis, Chris Kattan, Nathan Lane, Michael Siberry

VIVIAN BEAUMONT THEATER, INC. ■ THREE-YEAR PRODUCTION HISTORY ■ PAGE 2 OF 2

2001-2002 SEASON	THEATER	PERF. DATES	# OF PERFS.	TOTAL ATTENDANCE	% CAP.
CONTACT	Vivian Beaumont	7/3/01-6/30/02	413	344,796	78.24%
CHAUCER IN ROME	Mitzi E. Newhouse	7/3/01 – 7/29/01	32	8,107	92.80%
THOU SHALT NOT	Plymouth	9/27/01 – 1/6/02	118	91,621	77.18%
EVERETT BEEKIN	Mitzi E. Newhouse	10/19/01 – 1/6/02	91	24,199	92.66%
QED	Vivian Beaumont	10/21/01 – 12/17/01	18	18,972	98.78%
MOSTLY SONDHEIM	Vivian Beaumont	12/30/01 – 2/11/02	14	14,396	96.37%
QED	Vivian Beaumont	2/17/02 – 6/3/02	30	30,394	94.95%
THE CARPETBAGGER'S CHILDREN	Mitzi E. Newhouse	3/7/02 – 6/30/02	132	33,353	84.51%
MORNING'S AT SEVEN	Lyceum	3/28/02 – 6/30/02	108	68,534	69.89%
MOSTLY SONDHEIM	Vivian Beaumont	6/23/02 – 6/30/02	3	2,538	79.29%

2002-2003 SEASON	THEATER	PERF. DATES	# OF PERFS.	TOTAL ATTENDANCE	% CAP.
CONTACT	Vivian Beaumont	7/2/02 – 9/1/02	72	44,749	58.25%
MORNING'S AT SEVEN	Lyceum	7/2/02 – 7/28/02	32	15,249	52.48%
MOSTLY SONDHEIM	Vivian Beaumont	7/1/02 – 8/25/02	14	12,559	84.07%
A MAN OF NO IMPORTANCE	Mitzi E. Newhouse	9/12/02 – 12/29/02	124	33,810	95.00%
DINNER AT EIGHT	Vivian Beaumont	11/21/02 – 1/26/03	76	66,994	80.95%
OBSERVE THE SONS OF ULSTER	Mitzi E. Newhouse	2/6/03 – 4/13/03	76	16,512	78.72%
VINCENT IN BRIXTON	Golden	2/13/03 – 5/4/03	92	54,750	74.76%
ELEGIES – A SONG CYCLE	Mitzi E. Newhouse	3/2/03 – 4/19/03	16	3,982	90.17%
A BAD FRIEND	Mitzi E. Newhouse	5/15/03 – 6/29/03	52	13,938	97.12%

2003-2004 SEASON	THEATER	PERF. DATES	# OF PERFS.	TOTAL ATTENDANCE	% CAP.
A BAD FRIEND	Mitzi E. Newhouse	7/1/03 – 7/27/03	32	8,681	98.29%
HENRY IV, PARTS 1 & 2	Vivian Beaumont	10/28/03 – 1/18/04	78	80,398	98.45%
NOTHING BUT THE TRUTH	Mitzi E. Newhouse	11/15/03 – 1/18/04	74	18,632	85.35%
BIG BILL	Mitzi E. Newhouse	2/6/04 – 5/16/04	115	n/a	n/a
KING LEAR	Vivian Beaumont	2/11/04 – 4/18/04	49	n/a	n/a
BARBARA COOK'S BROADWAY	Vivian Beaumont	3/19/04 – 4/11/04	12	n/a	n/a
THE FROGS	Vivian Beaumont	6/17/04 – 6/26/04	11	n/a	n/a

2003-2004 SEASON

Average actors' weekly salary (range)	$775 - $1,500 (rehearsal & performance)
Artists' Fee range	$1,500 – $59,850

Appendix G (continued)

<table>
<tr>
<td>Grants for Arts Projects Application
Standard Review Grants
Details of the Project</td>
<td>Read the
instructions that
follow this form
before you start.</td>
<td>OMB No. 3135-0112
Expires 02/28/05</td>
</tr>
</table>

If necessary, you may attach up to two additional pages.

Applicant (official IRS name):   The Vivian Beaumont Theater, Inc. (dba Lincoln Center Theater)

a) Major project activities. Lincoln Center Theater (LCT) plans to produce DESSA ROSE, a new musical by Lynn Ahrens (libretto, lyrics) and Stephen Flaherty (score), directed by LCT Associate Director Graciela Daniele. The production is scheduled for a 15½-week engagement in the 275-seat Mitzi E. Newhouse Theater (February 24 – June 12, 2005) and we anticipate an audience of approximately 30,180.

Based on a novel by Sherley Anne Williams, DESSA ROSE is derived from the lives of two real women living in the antebellum Deep South. It explores the fictional meeting of these women and the impact they have on each other. Dessa Rose is a pregnant fugitive slave who escapes her death sentence after leading an uprising. Ruth is a white woman abandoned by her husband, a slave owner, on an isolated farm in Northern Alabama. At first encounter, the women's relationship is tentative and distrustful. Over time, Ruth provides refuge for other runaway slaves and gradually befriends Dessa Rose who in turn develops a deep bond with Ruth.

Ahrens and Flaherty's adaptation of DESSA ROSE is almost entirely sung. The score and its extended musical themes reveal the rarely told story of the strong-willed American women from whom our country derives much of its strength, character, and identity. It is also an account of the brutal experience of slavery seen from the African-American perspective. The composers have structured the musical as an oral history being passed down from Dessa Rose and Ruth to their children and grandchildren.

LCT has helped to develop DESSA ROSE over the past two years with a four-day reading of the musical's first act (June 2002) and a three-week workshop (June 2003), both under the guidance of Ms. Daniele. For the workshop a cast of twelve actors, including LaChanze and Donna Murphy in the roles of Dessa Rose and Ruth, was assembled for an intensive rehearsal period, culminating with two run-through performances. Impressed by the work's emotional power and resourceful story-telling technique, Artistic Director André Bishop decided to schedule a fully staged Newhouse production. To ensure the participation of the two lead actresses, Mr. Bishop accommodated their prior commitments and programmed the world premiere of DESSA ROSE for early 2005.

b) Goals. Mr. Bishop firmly believes that it is essential for not-for-profit theaters to develop and produce new musicals for the American theater if this fragile art form is to survive. Not-for-profit theaters, with their ongoing artistic programs free of commercial pressures, can provide the nurturing environment necessary for this intricate (continued)

THE VIVIAN BEAUMONT THEATER, INC. DETAILS OF PROPOSED PROJECT – FY2004
Page 2

and challenging process, given sufficient funds. The enormous expense required to do so, however, makes it imperative for organizations to secure contributed income from sources of public and private support.

Since his tenure began in 1991, the Theater's musical output has increased, encompassing presentations by established and emerging writers: MY FAVORITE YEAR, HELLO AGAIN, CHRONICLE OF A DEATH FORETOLD, A NEW BRAIN, PARADE, MARIE CHRISTINE, CONTACT, THOU SHALT NOT, ELEGIES: A SONG CYCLE, and A MAN OF NO IMPORTANCE. As a crucible for new work, LCT offers artists the opportunity to present their plays and musicals to New York audiences (customarily for 10- to 15-week engagements) in the 1,050-seat Beaumont or the 275-seat Newhouse.

New works given world premieres at LCT often play to a broader public in further productions in other venues. Susan Stroman and John Weidman's CONTACT, for example, was commissioned by LCT in 1999 and developed over several months in the Theater's rehearsal studio. After its world premiere in the Newhouse, CONTACT played an extended engagement of more than 1,000 performances in the Beaumont and was seen by audiences throughout the U.S. during a 1½-year national tour in 2001 and 2002. CONTACT was also presented in London and Tokyo, and its final performance in the Beaumont was broadcast live to some four million viewers across the country on PBS-TV's *Live From Lincoln Center*.

c) Schedule. DESSA ROSE's six-week rehearsal period is scheduled to begin on January 13, 2005. The first public performance in the Newhouse will be on February 24, 2005, and the 15½-week engagement (124 performances) will continue through June 12, 2005. Opening night is tentatively set for March 24, 2005.

d) Key individuals, organizations, and works. DESSA ROSE, the third musical by Lynn Ahrens and Stephen Flaherty developed and produced by the Theater, will be staged by LCT Associate Director Graciela Daniele. Since 1992, Ms. Daniele has guided several new musical works to fruition: HELLO AGAIN, CHRONICLE OF A DEATH FORETOLD, A NEW BRAIN, MARIE CHRISTINE, ELEGIES: A SONG CYCLE. The two lead actors in DESSA ROSE, LaChanze and Donna Murphy, have participated in the show's initial first-act reading and extended workshop and we anticipate that both women will appear in the Newhouse production, as will most of the actors who have taken part in the developmental process to date. David Holcenberg will serve as the show's Music Director and William David Brohn will provide the orchestrations. The design team (not yet confirmed) will be comprised of Loy Arcenas (sets), Toni-Leslie James (costumes), and Jules Fisher & Peggy Eisenhauer (lighting).

e) Target population. The Theater's target population is its 40,000 Members as well as the general theater-going public of the New York City metropolitan area and tri-state region. Marketing efforts for DESSA ROSE will include outreach to NYC's African-American communities similar to campaigns LCT has conducted for previous productions (SARAFINA! MARIE CHRISTINE, NOTHING BUT THE TRUTH). DESSA ROSE will also be seen by nearly 1,000 New York City public high-school students participating in LCT's Open Stages education program which works with economically disadvantaged children throughout NYC. The majority of students in the program are African-American, Asian American, or Latino. We have set as our target for DESSA ROSE a total audience of 30,180, reflecting 88.5 percent of Newhouse capacity for the show's 15½-week run.

Appendix G (continued)

THE VIVIAN BEAUMONT THEATER, INC. DETAILS OF PROPOSED PROJECT – FY2004
Page 3

f) Plans for promoting, publicizing, and/or disseminating. Several weeks prior to the first performance, LCT Members will receive newsletters that provide information about the production. Along with a synopsis of DESSA ROSE and a listing of artists involved with the project, the Theater's newsletter includes a performance calendar and ticket-ordering information. LCT Members are able to purchase tickets within a priority period before tickets go on sale to the general public.

DESSA ROSE will be publicized with a general advertising campaign in *The New York Times* and other local newspapers and magazines. As part of the Theater's efforts to attract targeted audiences, advertisements will be placed in newspapers reaching New York City's African-American communities. In addition, LCT in conjunction with Harlem cultural leader Voza Rivers will promote the show to church and social groups and encourage attendance with discount-ticket offers. The Theater will also post comprehensive information about the production on its web site (www.lct.org) which provides a link to Tele-charge, allowing web-site visitors to purchase tickets on-line.

g) Plans for monitoring and assessing. The Theater's Director of Marketing will analyze ticket sales and responses to special promotional offers to determine if the projected goal of 30,180 audience members is met and whether outreach efforts successfully attract targeted populations.

Before attending performances, all Open Stages students are prepared for their theater-going experience by participating in two pre-show classroom workshops conducted by LCT teaching artists. These interactive sessions are developed to ensure that students have an understanding of the work they are going to see and to familiarize them with theater etiquette. LCT Education Director Kati Koerner assesses students' comprehension and enjoyment of the show by evaluating feedback forms filled out by teachers and students and by reviewing the curricular projects undertaken by the students based on their teachers' lesson plans.

h) Plans for making the project accessible. Over the past several years, LCT has achieved ADA-compliant access to its two theaters, including the following improvements to the Beaumont: ramps and handrails in the theater and lobby; rebuilt elevator with a wheelchair-accessible Braille control panel; expanded assistive listening system; disabled-access restroom; wheelchair locations in the Beaumont and the Newhouse; a wheelchair lift to allow access to the box office from the Theater's 65th Street entrance.

i) Budget. The budget, which encompasses total expenditures for DESSA ROSE's six-week rehearsal period and 15½-week run, is projected at $2,527,289. Box-office revenue, estimated at $1,179,971, will offset approximately 45 percent of total expenses. Production subsidy of $1,347,318 will be covered by contributed income for DESSA ROSE, which will include special funding designated for the production along with a portion of the Theater's unrestricted grants from foundations and individuals.

If the Theater receives less than 50 percent of our requested amount from the NEA, a greater portion of unrestricted grant support will be allocated to the production. (Any remainder between amount requested and amount received from the NEA will be balanced in this manner.)

Grants for Arts Projects Application
Project Budget, Part 1

Read the
instructions that
follow this form
before you start.

OMB No. 3135-0112
Expires 02/28/05

Applicant (official IRS name):   The Vivian Beaumont Theater, Inc. (dba Lincoln Center Theater)

INCOME

1. **Amount requested from the Arts Endowment:**

   Fast-Track Review Grants $10,000   OR   Standard Review Grants $ 150,000

---

2. **Total match for this project** Be as specific as possible. Asterisk (*) those funds that are committed or secured.

   Cash (Refers to the cash donations, grants, and revenues that are expected or received for this project)   AMOUNT

The Harold and Mimi Steinberg Charitable Trust*	150,000
New York State Council on the Arts	25,000
Unrestricted Foundations	650,000
Unrestricted Individuals	372,318
Box-office Revenue	1,179,971

   Total cash a. $ 2,377,289

   In-kind: Donated space, supplies, volunteer services (These same items also must be listed as direct costs under "Expenses" below or in Part 2 of the Project Budget form; identify sources)

   Total donations b. $ 0

   Total match for this project (2a. + 2b.) $ 2,377,289

EXPENSES

1. **Direct costs: Salaries and wages**

TITLE AND/OR TYPE OF PERSONNEL	NUMBER OF PERSONNEL	ANNUAL OR AVERAGE SALARY RANGE	% OF TIME DEVOTED TO THIS PROJECT	AMOUNT
Principals	20	325,875	100	325,875
Musicians/Conduct.	8	157,925	100	157,925
Stage Crew	14	419,587	100	419,587
Stage Managers	2	35,232	100	35,232
Wardrobe Super.	1	30,451	100	30,451
Wardrobe Assts.	4	52,424	100	52,424
Hair and Make-up	1	12,400	100	12,400
Production Asst.	1	12,000	100	12,000

   Total salaries and wages a. $ 1,045,894

   Fringe benefits   Total fringe benefits b. $ 417,032

   Total salaries, wages, and fringe benefits (a. + b.) $ 1,462,926

Appendix G (continued)

Grants for Arts Projects Application
Project Budget, Part 2

Read the
instructions that
follow this form
before you start.

OMB No. 3135-0112
Expires 02/28/05

Applicant (official IRS name):   The Vivian Beaumont Theater, Inc. (dba Lincoln Center Theater)

EXPENSES, CONTINUED

2.   **Direct costs**: Travel (Include subsistence)

# OF TRAVELERS	FROM	TO	AMOUNT
2	Los Angeles	New York	5,000
		Total travel $	5,000

3.   **Direct costs**: Other expenses (Include consultant and artist fees, honoraria, contractual services, access accommodations, telephone, photocopying, postage, supplies and materials, publication, distribution, translation, transportation of items other than personnel, rental of space or equipment, and other project-specific costs)

AMOUNT

Supplies & Materials:
Scenery	220,000
Costumes	55,000
Sound & Electrics	55,000
Orchestrations & Musical Instruments	106,000
Departmental Expenses	43,250
Transportation & Cartage	7,000
Equipment Rental	127,100

Fees for Services & Other Expenses:
Artists' Fees	130,138
Advertising & Publicity	223,500
Miscellaneous Production & Operating Costs	92,375

Total other expenses $ 1,059,363

4.   **Total direct costs** (1. from Project Budget, Part 1 +2.+3.) $ 2,527,289

5.   **Indirect costs** (if applicable)

Federal Agency: Rate (%)   x Base   = $ 0

6.   **Total project costs** (4.+5.) $ 2,527,289

APPENDIX H: The Minnesota Opera Status of Funding Report

The Minnesota Opera

12/21/2006

Opera at the Ordway - Status of Funding

Institution View

Strategic Objectives	Pledges to Date	To Reach Goals	Goal	Available Funding	Expended To Date
Company Advancement	$ 2,900,000	$ -	2,900,000	$ 2,900,000	$ 2,450,000
Campaign Expenses	$ 300,000	$ -	300,000	$ 300,000	$ 300,000
Production Innovation Fund	$ 1,500,000	$ -	1,500,000	$ 1,500,000	$ 1,050,000
Prod Invent (Purchases)	$ 800,000	$ -	800,000	$ 800,000	$ 308,400
Warehouse (Princ Payments)	$ 1,500,000	$ -	1,500,000	$ 87,900	$ 32,700
Cash Reserve	$ 1,000,000	$ -	1,000,000	$ 1,000,000	$ 1,000,000
Permanent Endowment	$ 2,454,500	$ 1,595,500	4,050,000	$ 1,177,600	$ 1,177,600
Permanent Trust	$ 7,950,000	$ -	7,950,000	$ 2,723,000	$ 2,723,000
Total	$ 18,404,500	$ 1,595,500	20,000,000	$ 10,488,500	$ 9,041,700

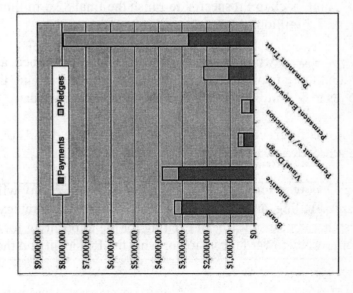

Donor View

Donor Restrictions	Pledges	Payments
Board	$ 3,335,000	$ 3,024,500
Initiative	$ 3,850,000	$ 3,153,400
Visual Design	$ 650,000	$ 410,000
Permanent w/ Restriction	$ 500,000	$ 135,000
Permanent Endowment	$ 2,119,500	$ 1,042,600
Permanent Trust	$ 7,950,000	$ 2,723,000
Total	$ 18,404,500	$ 10,488,500

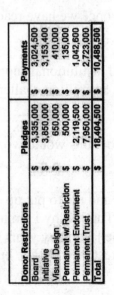

APPENDIX I: Sample Pitch to Major Donor

Proposed format for November 10 meeting with Prospect X
November 9, 2005

Campaign Chair: Thank you for meeting with us, X. And thank you for your idea to do something special around The President's 25th Anniversary. You mentioned this to me, and the more we all spoke about it, the bigger the idea became. Your comment caused us to realize that the President's Anniversary is really the culmination of a 25-year journey toward a vision for what The Minnesota Opera can become.

Board Chair: The President's 25th Anniversary year coincides with what will be a major year in the history of the company.
- We will go back to and then maintain a five production season.
- We will give "The Grapes of Wrath" its world premiere, bringing the focus of the opera world here to the Twin Cities.
- I am confident that we will be in a different situation with our landlord, the Ordway.
- And, amidst all of this, we really must finish the Opera at the Ordway Initiative, clear the table of this project so we can focus on the art and the future.

Campaign Chair: So we have an idea that can get the Initiative done by the end of the President's 25th Anniversary year. I'd like to show you how this might work.

There are two important pieces:
1. a $1 million challenge grant to leverage the Initiative to $15 million by next September 28, the President's anniversary date;
2. going back to Prospect Y to finish the final $2.5 million, once we have reached $17.5 million.

We would rally our remaining prospects, board members and institutional supporters around these two gifts. We'd like you to consider giving the $1 million challenge to get us to $15 million by the President's Anniversary date.

Development Director: I will walk you through the details of how this would work (present broad view of the plan)

Chair: X, not too long ago, they came to me and asked my wife and me to put up challenge funding, and it is working. This is a credible strategy. That's why I am here. I'm also here because it's been exciting for me to be along for the last many years of the 25 year journey toward the vision of what the President and the rest of you have built here.

Campaign Chair: For me, it is exciting to see that vision now within our grasp. Over the history we've both been involved with the President, it has been very gratifying to see the organization blossom into a tier-one arts organization. It is why I am chairing this campaign, to support that vision. Challenge gifts have helped us greatly in the past two years, particularly with the Foundation Challenge on the annual fund, your challenge last year for the Opera at the Ordway Initiative, and challenge gift from The Chair and another board member toward the Initiative. The Initiative is really the culmination of the vision that so many others have shared over the past 25 years. What we have here is a plan to conclude it, and have it be the exclamation point on the President's first 25 years.

Chair: Completing the Initiative will properly capitalize the opera, will keep us at five productions, and will be the perfect way to honor the President's 25th year. It will be a tremendous legacy. I admire the way the two of you have helped raise the local professional theatre to a new standard. It is thrilling for us to have a similar opportunity here at the Opera.

APPENDIX J: Minnesota Opera Case Statement

THE CASE FOR

THE MINNESOTA OPERA AT THE ORDWAY

I.   Overview

"Kudos to The Minnesota Opera ... how come the Met isn't bringing these works here?" **New York Times, December 28, 2003**

The Minnesota Opera's recent history is a success story of growth through innovation and agility. Its performances sell to capacity. Its work draws critical acclaim from around the world. As high schools cut music programs, The Opera is ensuring that music remains central to a quality education for Minnesota students through a series of educational programs. And The Opera is accomplishing all this while stretching a dollar farther than any other local major arts organization.

The Twin Cities community is clear about what it expects from its only opera company: great voices, quality productions, a season of at least five operas – all performed at the Ordway Center for the Performing Arts – plus financial responsibility.

The Minnesota Opera is committed to meeting these expectations. Now is the time to secure the financial resources to ensure artistic excellence *and* financial health.

With an outstanding track record of artistic acclaim and good management, The Opera must now take the next step to ensure its long-term future. It must continue its momentum, expand its buying power in the competitive marketplace for the best artists, restore a fifth production to its opera season, expand the training of young singers and enrich its education program for Minnesota's students.

II.   The Opera's Commitment to Artistic Excellence

"While most American opera companies traded risky programming for safer options this season, The Minnesota Opera has taken a different approach to the economic downturn. The company is holding to its artistic philosophy, which includes contemporary work and a bel canto work in every season. By sticking to its artistic guns in the current season, The Minnesota Opera has done 'Passion' a huge service."

Wall Street Journal, March 2, 2004

1

The Minnesota Opera's international calling card is its artistic philosophy, which is inspired by *bel canto* (Italian for *beautiful singing*), the ideal upon which Italian opera is based. *Bel canto* values, which emphasize intense emotional expression supported by exquisite technique, inform every aspect of the company's programs, from repertoire selection, casting and visual design to education and artist training.

This is an artistic point of view that answers the question, "Why do opera in 2005?" No instrument is more expressive or more powerful than the human voice. Singing can express the emotions and arouse the imagination in a way the other arts cannot. The voice makes poetry come alive. It is the interpretive power of the voice that defines the aesthetic of The Minnesota Opera.

In all of The Minnesota Opera's productions, the sets, costumes, orchestra, lighting and direction support the *beautiful singing*. It is the center of the balancing act of producing opera, the culmination of all the arts. This artistic point of view is inspired by the basic foundation of opera, dating back to the legendary technique of singing from the *bel canto* period of the early 19th century. What was beautiful and moving then remains so today.

The long-term artistic goals of the Minnesota Opera all support the fuller realization of its artistic philosophy. These goals include:

Casting
- Securing established, top-ranked singers for each production. *Beautiful singing* requires the world's best singers.
- Placing holds and contracting artists at least two years in advance of the season. The reality is that top singers are booked years in advance.

Repertoire
- Returning to five productions by FY07
- Building on the company's distinction as "the most daring programming in the nation" (Opera News, September, 2002) with a contemporary work each season, as well as a rarely seen work from the *bel canto* opera period, balanced with favorites from the standard opera repertoire.

Commissions
- Presenting the world premiere of "The Grapes of Wrath" in '07 season
- Continuing to commission and premiere a new work every few years

Resident Artist Program
- Growing the number of participants from 8 to 12 by '07
- Bringing back top graduates, like James Valenti
- Continuing to build the international reputation of the program

Appendix J (continued)

Orchestra
- Identifying and hiring a Principal Conductor

Ordway Center
- Improving the production values in the intimate Ordway Center

III. The Opera's Economic Crunch

The Opera's economic problem stems, to a large degree, from producing opera at the Ordway Center. From a financial point of view, the house is simply too small.

With only 1,767 seats, it is one of the smallest opera houses in the country, capping ticket revenue at about $85,000 per performance. Ideally, it should have another 750 seats to compete with the per-performance revenue capacity of other opera houses. Additionally, the Ordway per-seat rental cost ($7.17) is 2-4 times greater than what is paid by similar-sized opera companies in Pittsburgh ($4.40), Cincinnati ($3.00) and Portland ($1.60). This financial disadvantage is the greatest problem facing the The Minnesota Opera.

To solve this problem, the Opera Company convened an ad hoc Venue Committee that included the architecture firm Hammel, Green and Abrahamson, Inc. (HGA). After a thorough review of all possibilities in the Twin Cities, the committee suggested two options: build a new, larger facility or find a way to make the Ordway work. The cost of a new 2500-seat opera house was estimated at $125 million.

While the size of the Ordway is an economic liability, its intimate setting is an artistic virtue. The audience greatly enjoys seeing opera at the Ordway, as they are close to the stage and in a beautiful setting. It is a community treasure. And it is an ideal venue for The Opera's *bel canto* artistic philosophy. Therefore, the committee recommended that The Opera remain in the Ordway and raise an endowment to provide an income stream equal to ticket sales from an additional 750 seats.

IV. The Solution: The Opera at the Ordway Initiative

"The most daring programming in the nation." **Opera News, September, 2002**

The Minnesota Opera's artistic success has exceeded its financial strength. This imbalance must be solved to continue the standard of excellence that has drawn international praise and is valued by this community.

The **$20 million Opera at the Ordway Initiative** is the company's plan for the future. It will overcome the economic constraints of the Ordway and will expand the artistry of The Minnesota Opera. The specific components are:

A. $12 Million Endowment Fund

This fund will address the economic challenge of performing at the Ordway. It will also provide the resources to help achieve The Opera's artistic goals. Key among these goals is to consistently hire the <u>best</u> singers from the international market of talent. The endowment fund will balance the playing field, enabling The Opera to compete with its international peers.

In raising the $12 million endowment fund, The Opera has developed a novel approach to addressing the Ordway's low seat count. Ideally, the Ordway should have another 750 seats. But instead of expanding or replacing the Ordway, The Opera is raising endowment funds equivalent to 750 **virtual seats.** The endowment income stream from these **virtual seats** will be the equivalent of the income from a larger opera house. By raising $12 million in endowment funds, instead of $125 million to build a new opera house, The Opera will ensure that the community experiences outstanding opera performed in its beloved and intimate opera house. It is a ten-cent on- the-dollar solution. It will also ensure that The Opera continues to be the Ordway's most efficient tenant. An investment in this initiative is also an investment in the future of the Ordway, keeping The Opera where it belongs.

B. $3 Million Production Innovation System

The Opera's *bel canto* artistic philosophy will be advanced substantially through a $3 million Production Innovation System. This system will make the intimate Ordway Center even better suited for *beautiful singing*. In the process, the Production Innovation system will revolutionize the way opera is produced.

Already, this system has allowed The Opera to produce in a thrust stage configuration at the Ordway, bringing the singers much closer to the audience. This is a tremendous advancement in support of *beautiful singing* as it puts the focus clearly on the singers. The Production Innovation System will also fund an inventory of reusable structural scenic elements for a series of new productions. This will provide creative freedom for designers, allow the company to produce seldom-seen operas and lower overall costs for scenic construction. This is what makes it revolutionary: it is a solution to artistic and economic problems faced by all opera companies.

Of the Production Innovation System, world-renowned designer Robert Israel said, "it creates a new visual vocabulary without aesthetic or economic tyranny." The Minnesota Opera was the national leader in co-productions. But a major drawback to co-productions is the unpredictability of co-producing partners and their very different ways of producing opera. With this new system, The Minnesota Opera will again be breaking new ground. It will be able to plan repertoire without the constraint of finding co-production partners or rental productions.

Appendix J (continued)

C. $3 Million Company Advancement Fund

The Company Advancement Fund will support continued artistic growth, as well as the growth of the entire institution. The artistic product on stage already draws worldwide attention. But a lack of resources has forced the organization to cut corners in fundraising, marketing and other departments. The artistic investment must grow, but so too must the institutional platform supporting the art. Otherwise, the art is at risk. For The Minnesota Opera to become a truly great company, the enterprise must be great in all areas. Already, this investment helped increase annual fund contributions from $2 million in fiscal year 2003 to $3.2 million projected for fiscal year 2006, a 60% increase.

D. $1 Million Storage Warehouse

One problem with success is you quickly run out of room. While the company's headquarters, The Opera Center, meets many needs – costume, set and prop construction; production rehearsals; education programming; vocal instruction; office space; entertainment space – it does not have enough storage space. The short-term solution has been to rent warehouse space and store scenery in trailers. However, The Opera would save $120,000 a year in rent if it could purchase the warehouse it currently rents. That is, by raising $1 million to purchase its warehouse The Opera will save $120,000 a year. The savings is the equivalent of a 12 percent return on the $1 million purchase price.

E. $1 Million Cash Reserve

In 1992 The Opera established a $500,000 operating cash reserve to support cash flow needs during the opera production season. With an operating budget twice what it was in 1992, the need for operating capital has also increased. The cash reserve must grow to meet the needs of what is now a larger organization. The operating cash reserve will be drawn upon and replenished as cash flow adjusts cyclically.

V. Summary

The Minnesota Opera is committed to giving the Twin Cities great opera. The Opera is also committed to staying at the Ordway. And it is committed to balancing its budget. Now it must secure the financial resources to allow that to happen – to ensure a sustainable economic structure for continued growth

To date, The Minnesota Opera has raised $18.6 million toward its $20 million Opera at the Ordway Initiative goal. This is a good start. And when the remainder is raised the Opera will be transformed. In fact, this transformation can already be seen in The Opera's recent international acclaim, sold-out performances and expanding education programs. This is the right time for the right initiative. The 40-year history of The Opera has brought it to this critical moment of growth. Your generosity will have a profound impact on what will be a bright future.

5

APPENDIX K: The Minnesota Opera Gift Transmittal Form

620 North First Street, Minneapolis, MN 55401   Tel:(612) 333.2700   Fax:(612) 333.0869

The Minnesota Opera's *Opera at the Ordway* Initiative

GIFT TRANSMITTAL FORM

Date: _____

To assist The Minnesota Opera's *Opera at the Ordway* Initiative and in consideration of the gifts of others, we hereby pledge and agree to pay to The Minnesota Opera the sum of

$_____. It is our intention to pay this pledge using the following schedule:

_____

This pledge and its payments are for the general purposes of The Minnesota Opera's *Opera at the Ordway* Initiative, and may be invested or distributed within those guidelines. If the gift is restricted to a specific purpose within the goals of the Initiative, please indicate below. If the purpose of the restriction ceases to be useful, the Board may, at its discretion, redesignate the gift.

We wish our gift used for the following specific purpose within the goals of The Minnesota Opera's *Opera at the Ordway* Initiative:

_____

A portion of our gift may be used for current year bridge funding and/or Initiative campaign expenses as designated by the Board of The Minnesota Opera.

_____
Signature

Gifts are deductible under tax law and may be made in cash, securities, real or personal property, life insurance policies, collections, leases, royalties or other assets. There are a number of charitable gift techniques with income and estate tax incentives which may make it possible to increase the size of the commitment substantially. The Opera stands ready to discuss possibilities in this regard with the donor or representatives of the donor.

Please make gifts payable or transferable to: The Minnesota Opera
                                                        620 North First Street
                                                        Minneapolis, MN 55401
                                                        612-333-2700

Kevin Smith   Dale Johnson
PRESIDENT & CEO   ARTISTIC DIRECTOR

BIBLIOGRAPHY

Alexander, Douglas G., and Kristina Carlson. *Essential Principles for Fundraising Success*. San Francisco: Jossey-Bass, 2005.

Americans for the Arts. *The Future of Private Sector Giving to the Arts in America*. Washington, D.C.: Americans for the Arts, 2006.

Armbrust, Roger. "Nonprofit Theatre's Challenges, Threats, and Needs Are Real." *Backstage*, 17 November 2005.

Association of Fundraising Professionals, *www.afpnet.org*.

Barton, Noelle, Caroline Preston, and Ian Wilhelm. "Slow Growth at the Biggest Foundations." *Chronicle of Philanthropy*, 23 March 2006.

Barton, Noelle and Ian Wilhelm. "Corporate Giving Rises Modestly." *Chronicle of Philanthropy*, 23 August 2007.

Berkshire, Jennifer C. "A Volunteer's Devotion to Charity Extends to Many Organizations." *Chronicle of Philanthropy*, 27 October 2005.

Bordy, Sarah. "Corporate Support of the Arts." Interview by Sarah Stevens. Tape recording, 4 November 2005. Second Stage Theatre, New York.

Bray, Ilona. *Effective Fundraising for Nonprofits: Real World Strategies That Work*. Berkeley, Calif.: NOLO, 2005.

Brest, Paul. "Smart Money." *Stanford Social Innovation Review*, Winter 2003.

Brilliant, Neal. "Government Arts Funding." Interview by Ladan Hamidi-Toosi. Tape recording, 18 August 2006. Lincoln Center Theater, New York.

Brooklyn Academy of Music. "Online Appeal." 30 January 2007.

Cameron, Ben. "Compounding Diversity." *American Theatre*, March 2004, 4.

Ciconte, Barbara L., and Jeanne Jacob. *Fundraising Basics: A Complete Guide*. 2d ed. Sudbury, Mass.: Jones and Bartlett Publishers, 2005.

Cole, Patrick. "Orchestra of St. Luke's Receives $5 Mln Gift for Endowment." Bloomberg L.P. Web site.

Cotrone, Marion. "Special Events Fundraising." Interview by Tobie Stein. E-mail to author, 4 April 2006.

Dewane, Patrick. "Fundraising for the Performing Arts." Interview by Tobie Stein. E-mail to author, 1 January 2006.

Di Mento, Maria. "Financier's Bequests Total $120 Million." *Chronicle of Philanthropy*, 15 June 2006.

———. "Measuring Endowments: How the Survey Was Conducted." *Chronicle of Higher Education* and *Chronicle of Philanthropy*, 4–5 August 2005.

———. Compiled by "San Diego Theater Receives $20 Million from Inventor; Other New Gifts." *Chronicle of Philanthropy*, 6 April 2006.

Di Mento, Maria, Ben Gose, and Peter Panepento. "Strong Endowment Growth." *Chronicle of Philanthropy*, 31 May 2007.

Di Mento, Maria, and Nicole Lewis. "How the Wealthy Give." *Chronicle of Philanthropy*, 23 February 2006.

Downey, Roger. "Tough Love for the Arts." *Seattle Weekly*, 19–25 January 2005.

Feiner, Richard. "Fundraising for the Performing Arts." Interview by Tobie Stein. E-mails to author, 1 December 2005 and 4 September 2006.

———. "Sample Corporate Contributions Acknowledgement Letter." 2007.

———. "Sample Corporate Contributions Proposal." 2007.

———. "Sample Corporate Foundation Proposal and Budget." 2007.

———. "Sample Cover Letter: Corporate Contributions Department." 2007.

———. "Sample Letter of Inquiry: Corporate Contributions Department." 2007.

———. "World Monuments Development Plan, FY 2007." World Monuments Fund, New York, November 2006. Photocopy.

Franklin, Robert. "Charities Come Calling, a Lot; The Nation's 800,000 Charities Mail About 15 Billion Solicitation Letters a Year." *Minneapolis Star Tribune*, 1 February 2005.

Fredricks, Laura. *The Ask: How to Ask Anyone for Any Amount for Any Purpose*. San Francisco: Jossey-Bass, 2006.

Galloway, Christine K. "The Case for Outsourcing Asset Management." *Chronicle of Higher Education* and *Chronicle of Philanthropy*, 4–5 August 2005.

Gardyn, Rebecca. "Museum Fund Raiser's Prowess Earns Him Nickname 'Pickpocket'." *Chronicle of Philanthropy*, 27 October 2005.

———. "Crafting A Capital Campaign." *Chronicle of Philanthropy*, 10 November 2005.

Gose, Ben. "A Focus on Corporate Responsibility." *Chronicle of Higher Education* and *Chronicle of Philanthropy*, 4–5 August 2005.

———. "The Logic of Building an Endowment." *Chronicle of Higher Education* and *Chronicle of Philanthropy*, 4–5 August 2005.

Gose, Ben and Goldie Blumenstyk. "The Lure of Alternative Investments." *Chronicle of Higher Education* and *Chronicle of Philanthropy*, 4–5 August 2005.

Greenfield, James M. *Fundraising Responsibilities of Nonprofit Boards*. Washington, D.C.: BoardSource, 2003.

Greer, Jennie. "Development Calendar" and "Development Report." 4 November 2006 and 20 October 2006. E-mail to author.

Guenthner, L. Robert, Kathleen Nilles, and Sheldon E. Steinbach. "Investment Policies Are Not Optional." *Chronicle of Higher Education* and *Chronicle of Philanthropy*, 4–5 August 2005.

Hall, Holly. "A Record High." *Chronicle of Philanthropy*, 28 June 2007.

———. "Lobbying for Charity." *Chronicle of Philanthropy*, 21 July 2005.

———. "More Americans Are Responding to Direct-Mail Appeals, Survey Finds." *Chronicle of Philanthropy*, 14 April 2005.

———. "Much-Anticipated Transfer of Wealth Has Yet to Materialize, Nonprofit Experts Say." *Chronicle of Philanthropy*, 6 April 2006.

———. "Online Donations Similar in Size to Gifts by Cash or Check, New Study Finds." *Chronicle of Philanthropy*, 15 November 2007.

———. "Written Policies Can Help Charities Steer Clear of Trouble." *Chronicle of Philanthropy*, 31 March 2005.

Hall, Holly and Rebecca Gardyn. "Seeking Better Returns." *Chronicle of Philanthropy*, 30 September 2004.

Hall, Holly and Leah Kerkman. "Development Dollar Divide." *Chronicle of Philanthropy*, 20 April 2006.

———. "Few Signs of 'Donor Fatigue' Appear as Year-End Appeals Wrap Up." *Chronicle of Philanthropy*, 8 December 2005.

Hall, Holly, Leah Kerkman, and Cassie J. Moore. "Giving Bounces Back." *Chronicle of Philanthropy*, 27 October 2005.

Hall, Holly and Elizabeth Schwinn. "Behind the Numbers: How Different Types of Charities Fared Last Year." *Chronicle of Philanthropy*, 28 June 2007.

Hart, Ted, James M. Greenfield, and Pamela M. Gignac. *Major Donors: Finding Big Gifts in Your Database and Online.* Hoboken, N.J.: Wiley, 2006.

Hart, Ted, James M. Greenfield, and Michael Johnston. *Nonprofit Internet Strategies: Best Practices for Marketing, Communications, and Fundraising Success.* Hoboken, N.J.: John Wiley & Sons, 2005.

Hogan, Cecilia. *Prospect Research: A Primer for Growing Nonprofits.* Boston: Jones and Bartlett Publishers, 2004.

Holden, Greg, and Jill Finlayson. *Fundraising on eBay: How to Raise Big Money on the World's Greatest Online Marketplace.* New York: McGraw Hill, 2005.

Holden, John. "Fundraising Lecture." 8 November 2005, New York City Center, New York.

———. "Fundraising 101." 26 October 2004, Brooklyn College, Brooklyn, N.Y.

———. "Fundraising for the Performing Arts." Interview by Jessica Johnston. Tape recordings, 28 November 2005 and 27 January 2006. New York City Center, New York.

———. "Fundraising for the Performing Arts." Interview by Tobie Stein. E-mail to author, 23 May 2006.

Hopkins, Karen Brooks and Carolyn Stolper Friedman. *Successful Fundraising for Arts and Cultural Organizations.* 2d ed. Phoenix, Ariz.: The Oryx Press, 1997.

Hoye, Sue. "Giving 'Face' Time to Charity." *Chronicle of Philanthropy*, 7 February 2008.

Internal Revenue Service. "Instructions for Form 990 and Form 990-EZ." Washington, D.C.: Internal Revenue Service, 26. *www.irs.gov/pub/irs-pdf/i990-ez.pdf.*

———. *Publication 1771: Charitable Contributions—Substantiation and Disclosure Requirements.* Washington, D.C., May 2007. *www.irs.gov/pub/irs-pdf/p1771.pdf.*

Jensen, Brennen. "Rise in Foundation Giving Expected to Be Small This Year, Report Says." *Chronicle of Philanthropy*, 14 April 2005.

Jordan, Ronald R., and Katelyn L. Quynn. *Planned Giving: Management, Marketing, and Law.* 3d ed. Hoboken, N.J.: Wiley, 2004.

Kerkman, Leah. "Charities Urged to Do Better Job of Pitching Marketing Deals to Companies." *Chronicle of Philanthropy*, 9 March 2006.

———. "Highest Bidder." *Chronicle of Philanthropy*, 9 June 2005.

———. "A Soaring Year." *Chronicle of Philanthropy*, 4 May 2006.

Kerkman, Leah, Cassie J. Moore, and Brad Wolverton. "Growing Assets and Concerns." *Chronicle of Philanthropy*, 28 April 2005.

Klineman, Jeffrey. "Nearly 60% of Nonprofit Theaters Operated in the Red over Last Three Years." *Chronicle of Philanthropy*, 24 June 2004.

L'Ecuyer, Anne. "Public Funding for the Arts at the Local Level." *Americans for the Arts Monographs*, May 2004.

Levy, Reynold. *Give and Take: A Candid Account of Corporate Philanthropy.* Boston: Harvard Business School Press, 1999.

Lewis, Nicole. "Report Warns about Drop in Support for Arts Groups." *Chronicle of Philanthropy*, 17 May 2007.

———. "Vying for Corporate Support." *Chronicle of Philanthropy*, 23 August 2007.

Lincoln Center Theater. "National Endowment for the Arts Proposal." 10 March 2004.

Lipman, Harvy. "More New Englanders Give, but Plains Residents Give the Most, Study Finds." *Chronicle of Philanthropy*, 8 December 2005.

———. "Endowments: Big Gifts and Rising Stocks Fuel Growth." *Chronicle of Higher Education* and the *Chronicle of Philanthropy*, 27–28 May 2004.

Lynch, Robert. "Government Arts Funding." Interview by Tobie Stein. E-mail to author, 30 January 2006

Martin, Andrew. "As a Company Leaves Town, Arts Grants Follow." *New York Times*, 8 October 2007.

Martin, Patricia. *Made Possible By: Succeeding With Sponsorship.* San Francisco: Jossey-Bass, 2003.

McClimon, Timothy J. "Corporate Foundation and Foundation Funding." E-mail to author, February 21, 2007.

———. "The Current State of Corporate Philanthropy." Address made to the Donors Forum of Wisconsin, 8 April 2005. Milwaukee, Wis.

Minnesota Opera. "Acknowledgement Letter." December 20, 2005.

———. "Capital Campaign Status of Funding Report." 2006.

———. "Case Statement." 2006.

———. "Confirmation Card." 2006.

———. "Gift Table." 2006.

———. "Gift Transmittal Form." 2006.

———. "Pledge Form." December 2005.

———. "Prospect Sheet." 2006.

———. "Sample Pitch to Major Donor." 9 November 2005.

———. "Special Event Budget." 2006.

National Corporate Theatre Fund. "Sample Corporate Sponsorship Deal Agreement." 3 November 2005.

Nelson, Amanda. "Individual Giving to the Performing Arts." Interview by Christina Klapper. Tape recording, 7 October 2005. Alvin Ailey American Dance Theater, New York.

———. "Individual Giving to the Performing Arts." Interview by Christina Klapper. E-mails to Christina Klapper, 9 November 2005 and 1 March 2006.

———. "Sample Auto-Response Web Donation E-mail." E-mail to author, 13 February 2007.

———. "Sample New Member Acquisition Letter." E-mail to author, 13 February 2007.

———. "Sample Renewal Letter." E-mail to author, 13 February 2007.

Newman, Diana S. *Nonprofit Essentials: Endowment Building.* Hoboken, N.J.: Wiley, 2005.

———. "The Risk of Capital-Campaign Fatigue." *Chronicle of Higher Education* and *Chronicle of Philanthropy*, 4–5 August 2005.

Opening Night Gala. Alvin Ailey American Dance Theater Brochure. New York, 2005.

Osborne, Terri. "Government Arts Funding." Interview by Tobie Stein. E-mails to author, 30 December 2005 and 9 May 2006.

Panepento, Peter. "Connecting with Generation X: Charities Look for New Ways to Reach Out to the Under-40 Set." *Chronicle of Philanthropy*, 31 March 2005.

_____. "To Market, to Market." *Chronicle of Philanthropy*, 18 May 2006.

PatronMail, *www.patrontechnology.com*.

Perry, Suzanne. "Baby Boomers Give More than Older Americans." *Chronicle of Philanthropy*, 1 September 2005.

_____. "Charities Urged to Use Marketing to Appeal to Donors' Hopes and Dreams." *Chronicle of Philanthropy*, 1 September 2005.

_____. "More People Are Giving Online, Poll Shows." *Chronicle of Philanthropy*, 8 December 2005.

_____. "Stocks Have Bounced Back but Giving by the Nation's Wealthiest Has Not, Study Finds." *Chronicle of Philanthropy*, 4 August 2005.

Preston, Caroline. "A Sharp Rise in Grants to Charities." *Chronicle of Philanthropy*, 9 March 2006.

_____. "What Motivates People to Give Money?" *Chronicle of Philanthropy*, 26 July 2007.

Pulley, John L. "How to Gain a Competitive Advantage." *Chronicle of Higher Education* and *Chronicle of Philanthropy*, 4–5 August 2005.

Riggs, Henry and Timothy Warner. "Boards Should Reconsider What They Mean by Intergenerational Equity." *Chronicle of Higher Education* and *Chronicle of Philanthropy*, 4–5 August 2005.

Ruark, Joel. "Sample Thank You Letter." New Dramatists, New York, 2007. Photocopy.

Schwinn, Elizabeth. "How Much Fund Raising Really Costs." *Chronicle of Philanthropy*, 31 May 2007.

_____. "Lawmakers Earmarked $29 Billion for Pet Projects in 2006, Report Says." *Chronicle on Philanthropy*, 20 April 2006.

_____. "Seeking Federal Favors." *Chronicle of Philanthropy*, 21 July 2005.

_____. "Tax Watch: IRS Issues Final Rules on Charitable Trusts." *Chronicle of Philanthropy*, 14 April 2005.

_____. "Winning an Earmark Is Not Child's Play." *Chronicle of Philanthropy*, 21 July 2005.

SD&A Teleservices. "The Minnesota Opera 2005-2006 Fundraising Campaign: Strategy and Script," 2005.

Sommerfeld, Meg. "Prospecting the Web for Donors," *Chronicle of Philanthropy*, 9 August 2001.

Tommasini, Anthony. "Another Season of Love: The Original Cast Reassembles for a 'Rent' Anniversary." *New York Times*, 26 April 2006.

Trescott, Jacqueline. "With EBay Auctions, Theaters Bid on a New Brand of Fundraising." *Washington Post*, 28 December 2004.

Turegano, Preston. "$10 Million Gift Is Largest in Old Globe's 70-Year Run." *San Diego Union-Tribune*, 21 September 2005.

Wakin, Daniel J. "Joseph Volpe Bids the Met a Most Operatic Adieu." *New York Times*, 30 April 2006.

Walker, Julia Ingraham. *Nonprofit Essentials: The Capital Campaign*. Hoboken, N.J.: John Wiley & Sons, 2004.

Wallace, Nicole. "Online Donations Surge." *Chronicle of Philanthropy*, 10 June 2004.

_____. "A Surge in Online Giving." *Chronicle of Philanthropy*, 9 June 2005.

Weiss, Ella. "Government Arts Funding." Interview by Sarah Stevens. Tape recording, 7 April 2006. Brooklyn Arts Council, Brooklyn, N.Y.

Wellner, Alison Stein. "Phone Calls and Cocktail-Party Pressure." *Chronicle of Philanthropy*, 27 October 2005.

Wendroff, Alan L. *Special Events: Proven Strategies for Nonprofit Fundraising*. 2d ed. Hoboken, N.J.: John Wiley & Sons, 2003.

Wier, Mark. "Fundraising for the Arts." Interview by Jessica Johnston. Tape recordings, 10 March 2006 and 7 April 2006. New York.

Wilhelm, Ian. "Corporate Giving Rebounds." *Chronicle of Philanthropy*, 4 August 2005.

_____. "Giving by Big Foundations Rose 6% in 2005, Study Finds." *Chronicle of Philanthropy*, 8 March 2007.

Zimmerman, Robert M. and Ann W. Lehman. *Boards That Love Fundraising: A How-To Guide for Your Board*. San Francisco: Jossey-Bass, 2004.

CHAPTER SEVEN

Strategies for Selling Tickets

Nonprofit and commercial organizations must sell tickets in order to be successful.[1] Managing ticket sales requires a knowledge of both the product to be sold (ticket to a performance) and the market or audience to whom the ticket will be sold. In addition to creating tickets and constructing ticket packages, managers must be able to hire the best marketing and box office personnel to sell them. Finally, managers must be able to implement a plan that incorporates its marketing and publicity strategies for selling tickets.

TICKETS AND TICKETING PACKAGES

Performing arts organizations must sell tickets to their performances. What, exactly, is a ticket? A ticket guarantees its purchaser entry into a specific performance or specific event.[2] A ticket is considered an agreement to provide a service, so if the performance or event does not occur, the price of the ticket must be refunded (or the ticket must be exchanged for another performance). Tickets should contain the following information: the name of the production, the venue in which the production takes place, the venue's address, the performance date and time, the seat location (if seating is assigned), and the cost of the ticket.[3] The ticket should also have an audit stub, which is a portion of the ticket designed to be torn off by the ticket taker and counted at the end of the night by the house manager to determine the number of patrons in the house.

Figure 7.1a provides a sample ticket with audit stub (see page 276).[4]

In lieu of an audit stub, a ticket may display a bar code. The bar code enables the ticket to be scanned by the ticket taker when the patron enters the theater; the scanner then sends the bar code information to the computerized box office ticketing system, allowing for a more accurate count of attendance, but also for easier tracking of the details embedded in the bar code (such as the names of the ticket buyers and their seat locations). With the addition of the bar code, the tickets no longer have to be tallied by hand. The bar code also helps to prevent ticket fraud by assigning a unique code to each ticket.

On the back of the ticket, a liability waiver should be printed, informing the patron that the box office will not offer exchanges or refunds (unless the performance is canceled); that service fees will not be refunded; that the cast or program may change; photography and recording are not permitted; and the late seating policy.[5] In addition, the back of the ticket may also list rules and regulations concerning the resale of tickets and service fees.[6] (Enterprising theaters also sell advertising space on the back of the ticket [or the ticket envelope] to earn extra revenue.[7])

Figure 7.1b provides a sample ticket liability waiver (see page 276).[8]

If a ticket was sold as part of a particular discount offer, the tracking code (assigned to track the response to the discount offer) should also be printed on the ticket and the audit stub (and included in the bar code), so that the attendance count will include the number of patrons who took advantage of that particular discount.[9] Discount offers are created by marketing directors or producers (on a commercial production) and provide the ticket buyer with a specific discount, provided that the ticket buyer is part of a group that the offer is meant to target. For example, many organizations offer student discounts, which only apply to currently registered students (and may have an age restriction as well). Other discount offers target readers of particular newspapers or magazines, such as the *New York Times* or *Time Out New York*, or members of certain Web sites, such as *Playbill.com* or *TheaterMania. com*. Many theaters offer discounts during preview periods to attract audiences and create (hopefully)

Fig. 7.1a. Sample Ticket—Front

SEP 30, 2007

CTR   X 102

GIRLS CHOIR
THE LONDON

CTR   X 102
SEC   ROW   SEAT

ORCHESTRA

$38.00

NO REFUND PRICE NO EXCHANGE

Milk and Honey Productions
Presents

The London
Girls Choir

Whitman Theater • Brooklyn College
Nostrand Avenue & Avenue H

SUNDAY, SEPTEMBER 30, 2007
• 7:30 pm •

ADMIT ONE THIS DATE ONLY

CTR   X 102
SEC   ROW   SEAT

ORCHESTRA

Fig. 7.1b. Sample Ticket—Liability Waiver

LATE SEATING IS AT THE DISCRETION OF THE ARTIST AND MANAGEMENT. PATRONS ARRIVING LATE WILL BE SEATED ONLY AT APPROPRIATE INTERVALS DURING THE PERFORMANCE.

NO FOOD OR BEVERAGES ARE ALLOWED IN THE THEATRE, THE PHOTOGRAPHING OR RECORDING OF ANY PERFORMANCE IS PROHIBITED. NO CAMERAS, CAMCORDERS OR OTHER RECORDING DEVICES ALLOWED IN THE THEATRE AT ANY TIME. NO SMOKING IS PERMITTED IN THE THEATRE OR INNER LOBBIES.

THIS TICKET IS A LICENSE THAT MAY BE REVOKED AND ADMISSION MAY BE REFUSED WITH A REFUND OF THE PURCHASE PRICE. REFUSAL OF ADMISSION AND SUBSEQUENT REFUNDS ARE AT THE DISCRETION OF THE MANAGEMENT.

ALL PROCESSING FEES ARE NON-REFUNDABLE.

positive word-of-mouth. Each discount should be assigned a specific box office code in order to track both sales of tickets under that discount and, as mentioned above, actual attendance.

Tickets may be sold as single tickets, as part of a subscription series, or as part of a group sale. The process of selling single tickets is the simplest, as Gary Powers, former head box office treasurer of New World Stages (and now a treasurer for a Broadway theater), explains: "A customer comes to the box office and buys the ticket. He may pay with cash, a credit card, a money order, or a traveler's check. Some theaters may have an in-house phone sales service, in which customers are sold tickets over the phone, guaranteed seats, and charged an additional service fee [an administrative fee charged by the theater for the convenience of purchasing the tickets over the phone], usually four or five dollars per ticket."[10] In addition, if the organization's computerized ticketing system permits it, tickets may be sold online through a Web site. (If the organization's ticketing system does not permit Internet ticket sales, an organization may create a system that allows patrons to request a ticket and input payment details online, with the understanding that seats are not guaranteed and the purchase is not confirmed until a confirmation is sent by the organization.) An organization may also choose to outsource ticket sales to a ticket sales company such as Ticketmaster or Telecharge; these companies charge a fee to the customer for the use of the service, collect all of the money from ticket sales, and forward the total ticket sales (less the fee) to the organization. These ticket sales companies will mail tickets to the customer (or, in some cases, allow the customer to print out a ticket at home), but the box office may also print out tickets for those who wish to pick up tickets at the box office.[11] Using these companies provides a significant advantage to the organization: their services allow customers to purchase tickets online or by phone twenty-four hours-a-day.[12]

In addition to single tickets, organizations that produce or present more than one production in a season may sell tickets on subscription. A subscription entitles a patron to a ticket to multiple productions in the same seat. For example, if a patron has seats A1 and A3 for one production, he will also have those seats for every other production included in the subscription. Subscriptions are created by packaging the productions in different ways; these packages may include all of the shows produced or presented by an organization, or may only include a certain number (e.g., five shows in a seven-show season) or type of performances (e.g., all dance performances) in that season. Subscription packages typically mix popular events with more challenging events in order to create an audience for those less popular events. Also, some organizations include similar programs as add-ons to theme-based subscriptions (subscriptions based around a common theme, such as an "all theater" subscription), as David Kitto, vice president of marketing and sales at the John F. Kennedy Center for the Performing Arts in Washington, D.C., describes: "This year, as an add-on opportunity for our theater subscribers, we included the dance production of Matthew Bourne's *Edward Scissorhands*. Matthew Bourne is a choreographer who has worked on many theatrical pieces, and his dance works straddle the boundary between dance and theater. We try to provide our subscribers with opportunities to purchase additional art by offering performances that have logical links to their subscription package. This practice also assists in creating awareness about the breadth of the Kennedy Center's programming."[13]

Subscription tickets are sold at a discount to make them more attractive to a potential subscriber; the organization forgoes the full price of the ticket in order to secure future sales for all of its productions. Many organizations offer additional discounts by creating packages based on the day of the performance (such as an "all Tuesday evening" opera subscription, creating an audience for less-well-attended performances) or the location of the seats (such a "family circle" [the highest balcony] subscription for opera performances). In addition, subscribers who renew their subscriptions from year to year may receive a greater discount as well.[14] As an additional incentive, many organizations offer other benefits to subscribers, such as parking discounts, discounts to local restaurants, or advance notice of special events.[15] Subscription tickets may be sold by mail, on the phone, or online (if the ticketing system allows), and are typically handled by a specific staff member or department for processing.

In addition to traditional subscriptions as described above, organizations may sell "flexible" subscriptions and memberships. Flexible subscriptions allow subscribers to buy tickets in advance, but select the actual date of the performance at a time closer to that performance date. Organizations that offer flexible subscriptions assign an end date by which a subscriber must choose the date of the performance. When the subscriber chooses a performance date, he is assigned the best available seat for that date. A flexible subscription guarantees tickets to a production, but not the same seat each time as in a traditional subscription. Memberships require the member to pay an annual amount to the organization in order to purchase tickets at a discount. These memberships are completely separate from development membership programs and are solely used for ticket sales.

Finally, tickets may be sold as part of a group sale. Group sales allow the producer or organization to sell a large number of tickets at one time in one transaction. Group sales tickets are sold as a package of a certain number of tickets (typically between fifteen and twenty, but the exact number is determined by the organization or the producer); in exchange for buying a large number of tickets at one time, each ticket is given a discount off of the face value of the ticket. Janette Roush, director of ticket services for Alan Wasser Associates (and the former director of marketing for Broadway. com), notes that "it's important not to alienate the group market by charging more than the current public discount available to single-ticket buyers."[16] (The group sales discount for a popular Broadway show is typically 10 percent, but can also vary depending on the needs of the organization or producer; discounts for other productions may be significantly larger than 10 percent.)[17] The group sale may also include one or more complimentary (free) tickets for the purchase of a specific number of group tickets; for example, a producer may offer one complimentary ticket for every ten purchased tickets, with a limit of four complimentary tickets per order.[18] Producers or organizations may also put specific conditions on group sales, such as the exclusion of holiday dates or the removal of the discount for Saturday evenings.[19] For Broadway and Off-Broadway productions, group sales tickets are generally sold through licensed group sales agents, such as Broadway.com; other performing arts organizations sell group tickets directly through the organization or general management office. Licensed group sales agents receive a commission on the net amount of the sale (the ticket price less the discount) after the applicable performance has concluded.[20]

The percentage of tickets sold by each method differs with the organization or the show. Gary Powers states, "We have a complex with multiple theaters. One of our current tenants sells 75 percent of its tickets to groups and 25 percent single tickets. Another sells 5 percent to groups and 95 percent as single tickets. It all depends on the show."[21]

CLASSROOM DISCUSSION

Define the following terms: "ticket," "audit stub," "subscription," "flexible subscription," "membership," and "group sale."

Describe the process for creating subscription and group sales packages.

MARKETING AND MARKETING PERSONNEL

Marketing, in its most basic sense, is "the process of creating demand for a product."[22] In the case of the performing arts, that product is the artistic experience: the performance. Creating demand for an experience rather than an object makes marketing the performing arts a bit different than conventional marketing. Robert Friend, vice president of sales and marketing for Choice Ticketing Systems, elaborates on this difference: "The difference between selling a conventional product and marketing the arts has to do with the emotional connection to the product. In the arts, you are selling an intangible, an experience. With a tangible consumer product, such as Ivory soap, you can touch it, smell it, and wash with it before you begin planning a marketing effort. However, the arts allow for an emotional connection to the experience that provides another dimension in the sales and marketing effort."[23]

In addition to the performance itself, the product of a performing arts organization also contains all of the elements associated with the artistic experience, such as the location of the venue, the convenience of acquiring a ticket, and the comfort and cleanliness of the auditorium. These additional elements can play a major role in the success of the marketing effort, increasing the demand for the product.

The demand for the product of a performing arts organization is an expression of the level of desire that the public has for the product being offered. This demand is measured through the sale of tickets to performances. All marketing efforts must ultimately result in ticket sales to be considered successful. As Andrew Flatt, vice president of marketing at Disney Theatrical Productions, states: "At the end of day, at all of the arts organizations where I've worked in a marketing function, there's a transaction that has to occur before someone can experience the performance event on stage. It's that retail transaction that's the core of my job here, and of my entire department. Our role is to determine how we're going to make that transaction happen, and once it does, how we are going to ensure that our guest's experience here is a good one."[24]

Marketing creates demand for a product by using a variety of methods. These methods communicate the product to the public and make the product attractive to potential audience members. The combination of methods used by an organization is known as the "marketing mix." The mix consists of various marketing methods (sales techniques) that allow the most effective use of an organization's resources to reach the general public and its targeted markets (both existing and new audiences), such as mailed brochures (printed booklets that showcase an organization's performances), advertising (paid promotional announcements placed within various media, such as print, radio, or television), e-mailed ticket discount offers, and publicity campaigns (designed to get editorial—not advertising-based—exposure in various media, such as newspapers and television). As Robert Friend notes, "A mix of marketing methods is essential. Most buying decisions are made after multiple impacts of a marketing message."[25]

However, marketing methods encompass far more than sales techniques. The entire staff contributes to marketing the product and selling tickets simply by performing their jobs well. Janette Roush states, "Marketing is also the public face of your organization. It is the way that people work in your box office, the way that staff members speak to the public on the telephone, and the way that e-mails are written for outside consumption. Marketing is everything your organization does that extends outward into the world."[26] Robert Friend also believes in a more comprehensive view of marketing, noting that "everyone needs to be involved in the marketing effort—from the artistic director/executive director/managing director/board member all the way down to the custodial staff. All staff need to understand their role in marketing the institution, and they must 'own' that role in order to effectively represent the organization."[27]

Even commercial producers and theater owners may decide to focus on the customer experience. Flatt states, "Throughout the Walt Disney Company, the guest experience is an enormous focus, and we share that same emphasis in the theatrical division. From the moment the guest picks up the phone to order a ticket to the time the production ends and the guest leaves the building, that is all part of the guest experience. We spend significant time training staff members who interact with our guests. Ticketmaster is our ticket agency, and through them we have a dedicated phone number, as well as ticket staff that works specifically for Disney on Broadway; by doing this, we are able to train staff and tailor our message

in a specific way. In the theater that we operate (the New Amsterdam Theatre), we pride ourselves on the quality of our front-of-house, concessions, and box office staff; in the theaters that we rent, we work closely with our partners at the Nederlander Organization to train staff in its theaters as well. Broadway as a whole is beginning to understand that the guest experience is pivotal. Nothing beats the marketing push a show receives from someone having a good experience in your theater, driving home, and telling her friends about it. That kind of word-of-mouth marketing is easily the most successful of all the marketing efforts, and is also the one you have almost no control over as a marketer. I can change advertising and develop marketing partnerships [relationships between organizations designed to increase the impact of a marketing effort], but I can't change the words a person uses to describe the experience of the performance to other people."[28]

In the next sections, we will explore the responsibilities of marketing personnel in commercial and nonprofit organizations, as well as examine the critical role of the box office and ticket sales staff.

Marketing Personnel

For a commercial production, a producer will typically hire an outside advertising agency, which will be responsible for all advertising efforts for the production, such as advertisements in newspapers and commercials on television and radio. The producer may deem this agency sufficient for marketing purposes or, in addition, may hire a marketing firm to oversee the many dimensions of the marketing mix, including promotions (marketing efforts designed to draw attention to the production in an unconventional manner) and other tactics, such as giveaways of cast albums or other show paraphernalia. A producer may also work with a dedicated group sales agent to sell group tickets to a production. As part of the public awareness campaign, the producer will also retain a press agent. The press agent is responsible for persuading various media outlets to run news stories or editorials about the production. These media outlets include newspapers, magazines, television and radio stations, and, increasingly, Web sites. This type of media coverage is not paid for by the production, as advertising is; the press agent cultivates relationships with members of the media and pitches ideas for stories that might be of interest to them.

The marketing department in a nonprofit organization is headed by a marketing director, who is "responsible for overseeing all earned revenue generating strategies of the operation, including the sales and communication activities related to the selling, promoting, and communicating of events or productions being produced or presented by a performing arts institution to the general public."[29] Depending on the organization, the marketing director may supervise the following areas: advertising, promotions, publications, graphic design, box office, concessions, telemarketing, group sales, and communications (public relations and publicity). Many organizations, especially smaller ones, may hire outside firms to perform some or all of these marketing functions.[30]

For example, at the Brooklyn Academy of Music (BAM), the marketing division is headed by Jeff Levine, vice president of marketing and communications. He states, "I oversee four primary areas: the marketing department, the communications department, the design department, and our ticketing operations. The marketing department is responsible for direct mail, telemarketing, advertising, audience development, and interactive media (selling tickets though a Web site, e-mail, etc.).[31] The communications department encompasses public relations, press [publicity], and publications.[32] The design department handles all of our graphic design needs [e.g., images for marketing materials, ad creation, signage] and helps us develop institutional identity through our visual presentation. Ticketing operations consist of a union box office and a ticketing services department that handles information requests, as well as phone and Internet ticket orders."[33]

As the effectiveness of the marketing department is based upon communication, the marketing department of a nonprofit organization must communicate well internally, with other departments in the organization, with the artistic staff, and with the board of directors. Within the marketing department, managers typically schedule regular meetings to address marketing issues and ensure all staff are aware of current marketing initiatives and their current status. Levine describes the meetings that he schedules for his department: "I have a weekly meeting with my four direct reports [heads of marketing, communications, design, and ticketing operations]. Each department has its own staff meeting weekly or biweekly. I also have a meeting every week solely to address ticketing issues and technological issues that relate to ticketing. Finally, we have a full staff meeting every three weeks."[34]

Because marketing impacts the entire organization, the marketing director must be in constant communication with other departments. For example, the marketing director must have a good relationship with the general management, finance, and production departments, as these departments manage ticket sales revenue and determine if seats must be killed (not sold) or sold as "obstructed view" because of production elements. She works closely with the development department in assigning proper credit on printed materials for appropriate donors and arranging the best seats for the board of directors, high-level donors, and donor prospects. As another example, at BAM, the marketing and development departments use the same database (Tessitura) to record patron information. Levine notes how the staff members interact with the database: "The ticket sales representative or box office treasurer fulfills ticket orders, a fundraiser enters a donation or research information, and a marketing staff member might enter other marketing information, such as complaints received. Our IT department maintains the database as a whole and fixes any computer problems that might arise."[35] Weekly meetings are often held between the head of the marketing department and other departments to facilitate communication; e-mail may also help with this process. In addition, the marketing director is a key player at executive staff meetings and is responsible for keeping other members of the executive staff informed about current marketing efforts and their level of success.

David Kitto elaborates on the relationship between the marketing department and the rest of the organization: "We are in touch with every division in the organization. Because marketing puts the public face on the organization, the more involved all departments are with the marketing effort across the board, the more effective that effort is going to be. It's so important to develop collaborative relationships with other departments. Communication is key. At the Kennedy Center, we've put systems in place to facilitate that communication. For example, all the visual advertising that we create is routed electronically to appropriate parties. In certain cases, thirty people will see a print ad. It offers people the opportunity to respond to the ad. After the ad is placed, it is posted for the staff to see."[36]

The marketing director is also in constant contact with the artistic director or programming department to ensure that all artistic information is correct before it is released to the public. The marketing director has an impact on artistic programming, but does not guide that programming. Kitto explains: "My role is to provide realistic projections for what might happen if we decide to present a certain event, to estimate what it's going to cost for that event to be a success, and to give my opinion as to whether that event should be in the market in this jurisdiction. Based on my projections, the artistic team may decide to do one program over another. However, as a nonprofit organization, we have to be vision-based, so the artistic team has responsibility for the final decision. They make the decisions as to whether or not we're committed to taking risks. If we were to be marketing-based, much of what we do wouldn't come to our stages. Therefore, my relationship with the artistic director is about managing expectations. If he decides to present a challenging program, he needs to know a successful marketing effort may only sell half of the house."[37]

In a nonprofit organization, the board of directors is also involved in the marketing effort. Many boards have a dedicated marketing committee, which acts in an advisory role to the marketing department. Dale Edwards, marketing manager of Manhattan Theatre Club, states, "Board members come from diverse backgrounds, and many are leaders in the corporate world. Board members may serve on a marketing committee, where members strategize and share their expertise from other sectors in order to further the nonprofit organization. Members can provide great feedback and insight for marketing initiatives. It's a good practice for board members to vet [review] the marketing materials, as the members should be representative of the larger constituency of the market."[38]

Managing Ticket Sales: The Role of the Box Office

The box office and ticket sales staff play a crucial role in the marketing efforts of an organization. For most people, the first actual encounter with the theater occurs when the potential patron buys a ticket to a performance. For this reason, the marketing director or department is often responsible for supervising the ticket sales process. In a nonprofit organization, ticket sales are handled by the box office; in larger organizations, tickets that are sold by phone or over the Internet may be handled by another department.

However, in commercial theater, the box office reports to the theater owner. As an example, Gary Powers details the organizational structure of the box office at New World Stages: "The head treasurer is responsible for the operation of the box office and reports to the managing director of the complex. The assistant treasurer works for the head treasurer, and ticket sellers [box office personnel who sell tickets at the window] are also employed who report directly to the assistant and head treasurers. The box office works directly with the in-house accountant; in fact, in our complex, the head treasurer shares a separate office with the accountant to facilitate the sharing of information."[39] On Broadway and in other unionized houses (such as New World Stages), treasurers and ticket sellers are represented by IATSE, Local 751.

For the box office, selling single tickets, subscription tickets, and group tickets presents certain challenges. In selling single tickets, the box office needs to consider both the needs of the production and the needs of the ticket buyers, as Gary Powers notes: "A good treasurer will always strive to make as much money for the show as possible, while accommodating the needs of the customer at the window. At our theater, we don't want anyone to leave without purchasing a ticket. If we experience price resistance from a customer, our ticket sellers are encouraged to find out if discounts are available and to offer those discounts to the customer. We also encourage customers to check online for additional discounts in the future or visit other locations, like the TKTS discount booth, to receive discounts. Not all theaters promote this strategy, but we do; we do not want to lose a sale because the price is too high for the customer."[40]

However, lowering the price to sell tickets in advance, as subscription and group sales do, creates additional challenges. Powers continues: "Subscriptions are on the decline, as customers do not want to order tickets so far in advance; often, the discount is not a factor, as so many shows are offering other discounts. In order to entice subscribers, an organization needs to offer bigger discounts and higher levels of customer service, such as allowing tickets to be exchanged at any time. This increased customer service tremendously increases the workload for the box office. Even the discount for group sales may be complicated; producers of shows want to offer a substantial discount to encourage sales, but don't want to cheapen the show by discounting too much."[41]

Also, as subscribers purchase tickets far in advance, most organizations have specific policies and procedures for ticket exchange in the event a subscriber has a conflict with a previously purchased performance. While it is important to make ticket exchanges as easy as possible for the subscriber, the organization must take care that the subscriber doesn't wreak havoc with the box office by offering an unlimited number of exchanges. One solution is offered by Manhattan Theatre Club: subscribers are allowed one change per show; if a subscriber needs to exchange tickets more than once, a $6 fee is charged.[42]

Selling group tickets presents other challenges as well. Janette Roush states, "Student groups make up the bulk of group sales (between 50 and 55 percent), but about 35 percent of all group sales are made to groups of senior citizens. As baby boomers age into that market, they are less likely to travel in groups, and thus the senior group sales market has declined. Also, a large part of group sales used to be made up of theater parties, in which a charity would purchase a large number of seats for a performance and then resell them to raise money. The ticket might cost $100, but the charity would sell it for $1,000 and consider the difference a donation. Theater parties are not generating as much money for charities as they used to, so that part of the group sales market is declining as well."[43] To attract additional group sales, marketing professionals may use such strategies as sending postcards to tour operators (tour organizers of groups of tourists), theater educators (educational professionals involved in taking groups of students to performing arts events), and others responsible for group purchases; developing a contact list of groups to whom the production may appeal (e.g., AA groups for *Bill W. and Dr. Bob*, a play about the founders of Alcoholics Anonymous); and creating education programs and study guides to encourage student group business.[44]

Regardless of the challenges involved in selling tickets, Powers warns against the dangers of giving away blocks of complimentary tickets (a process known as "papering the house"), as many shows do when they are not selling as many tickets as expected. "You have to be careful about papering. Once a show starts to give away tickets, the perceived quality of the show diminishes. People think the show must not be any good. Also, if an audience member isn't paying for a ticket, there's no incentive for that person to show up."[45]

In addressing these challenges, the box office must remember to provide good customer service. For organizations that experience repeat customers, excellent customer service is essential. Gary Powers states, "At our box office, we strive to provide patrons with the most professional and friendly service they will ever encounter, so that they will be receptive

to visiting our complex for other productions. We encourage patrons who live in the neighborhood to identify themselves, so that we might offer them special discounts and make our complex a valuable addition to the neighborhood. We want our ticket sellers to go the extra mile to accommodate any potential customer who comes through the door. In addition, a good ticket seller has to gently educate customers. As many customers at the box office window do not know which seats are the best ones, I not only find them the best seats (which I do for *every* customer), but also assure the customers that the seats I've chosen for them are, in fact, the best ones available. A few customers are suspicious of the ticket seller, thinking the person behind the box office window is trying to sell them the worst seats. This is not true, but some customers have to be assured this is not the case. For example, I will often offer seats in either the orchestra section or mezzanine section, then say to the customer (if they can't make a decision), 'Knowing the theater the way I do, if I were going, I would sit in these seats.'"[46] Also, Powers recommends that box office managers adjust the staffing of the box office as necessary to accommodate the needs of the patrons; for example, the box office should designate specific windows for ticket pickup in the hour before a performance begins, in order that patrons may pick up their preordered tickets as quickly as possible and avoid a long line.[47]

However, even in the most service-oriented box office, conflicts with the patron will arise. In this case, Powers encourages his ticket sellers to direct the patron to another seller, in order to offer a fresh start to the transaction. If the patron has a complaint, he is directed to the head treasurer or assistant treasurer to resolve the problem; the head treasurer answers all complaints received by letter or e-mail as promptly as possible.[48]

In addition to selling tickets and interacting with customers, the box office is also responsible for providing ticket sales reports to those who need them, such as the marketing director or the company manager. Sales reports may be customized as needed, detailing sales for a specific performance, time period, discount code, ticket price, etc. (A sample box office statement, detailing the tickets sold for a particular performance, may be found in chapter 11 [figure 11.5].) Typical reports include the weekly wrap, detailing all of the sales for that particular week for all performances, and the net box office report, detailing all tickets sold for performances in a particular week minus all box office deductions (such as credit card fees and group sales commissions). The weekly wrap allows the marketing director to track all sales, including future (advance) sales, and make adjustments to marketing efforts as needed, while the net box office report provides data to help determine the success of the marketing effort on current sales.

The box office must also reconcile all ticket sales with payments received. Sales reports detailing the transactions for the day are printed at the end of the day (and sometimes midday as well) and reconciled with payments received (e.g., cash, credit card slips, group payments); if the reports and the payments do not match, the error must be found and corrected by the box office staff.[49] Payments received and deposited by the box office are reconciled with bank statements by the finance department or an accountant.[50]

CLASSROOM DISCUSSION

What is marketing?

How does marketing the arts differ from conventional product marketing?

How is demand measured for the product of a performing arts organization?

What should all marketing efforts for an organization be designed to do?

What is the marketing mix?

Name three departments that a marketing director might have to interact with and describe how those interactions might occur.

What are some of the challenges of selling single, subscription, and group tickets, and how does the ticket sales staff address those challenges?

What is the danger of papering the house?

How should ticket sales staff manage conflict?

Define "weekly wrap" and "net box office report."

THE MARKETING PLAN

The marketing director creates demand and stimulates sales of single, subscription, and group tickets through the creation of a marketing plan. The marketing plan ensures that the greatest number of tickets will be sold at the lowest possible cost to the organization. The marketing plan has five components: marketing analyses and research methods; positioning and branding of the organization and production; determining objectives and strategies for achieving these objectives; a timetable for implementation of the plan; and the marketing expense budget and revenue estimation. (The marketing plan also includes publicity, which will be discussed in the last section of this chapter.)

Marketing Analyses and Research Methods

A marketing manager must determine her existing and potential audiences. What types of analyses must be created in order to make this determination and discover the organization's target markets (existing and potential audiences)? How does a marketing manager research and collect the data to be analyzed? In this section, we will explore three different types of analyses: situation analysis, market analysis, and SWOT (strengths, weaknesses, opportunities, and threats) analysis, as well as how the data are researched and collected for each one. The three analyses are usually performed simultaneously, although the situation and market analyses may inform the SWOT analysis.

First, organizations must conduct an internal examination of their marketing trends, also called a situation analysis. The situation analysis contains data on the internal workings of the organization: sales and revenue trends, an audience profile, and a list of current operational bottlenecks and issues. Sales and revenue trends should include "detailed three-to-five-year attendance and income trends related to subscription sales, single-ticket sales, and group sales."[51] The audience profile should contain a "demographic and psychographic breakdown of existing subscribers, single-ticket buyers, and annual fund donors.[52] (Although not part of the marketing effort, annual fund donors typically overlap with subscribers, as both groups are committed to the institution as a whole and not just a specific performance. Please see chapter 6 for more information about annual funds.) Demographic data provide information on such categories as race, sex, income, and location, while psychographic data provide information about interests, attitudes, and opinions, and are thus also known as "IAO variables." An analysis of current operational bottlenecks and issues should "provide a clear picture of the areas of the operation that are stopping the organization from achieving breakthrough results in the area of marketing and sales."[53] Finally, the situation analysis ends with summary conclusions reached by examining the sales and revenue trends, audience profile, and operational bottlenecks.

Figure 7.2 provides a sample of a situation analysis for THEATER X, listing its sales and revenue trends, marketing operations and resources, audience profile, and bottlenecks and issues affecting the theater.[54]

Fig. 7.2. Situation Analysis

SITUATION ANALYSIS

SALES AND REVENUE TRENDS

Over the past five years, THEATER X has experienced unprecedented growth in both audiences and box office revenue. Below is a report of estimated revenue and attendance trends for the past five seasons. Total revenue figures for the 2003-2004 and 2004-2005 seasons are taken from THEATER X's Form 990s. Revenue for the 2005-2006 season is based on a projected overall revenue increase of 10%. Breakdowns of revenue and attendance are reasonable estimates based on these numbers. As these figures are estimates only, comparisons between 2006-2007 projections throughout this plan and these estimates may not be as useful as they would with actuals.

Marketing Trends for the Past Five Years			
Item	Households	Tickets/Subs	Revenue
Marketing Results for 2005/06 Season			
Total renewed subscribers	1,164	2,445	$232,232
# of subs renewed via telemarketing	307	645	$58,058
# of subs renewed via the Internet	873	1,833	$174,174
Total percent renewed			78%
Total new subscribers	716	1,504	$120,299
# of new subs sold via telemarketing	151	317	$30,075
# of new subs sold via the Internet	452	950	$90,225
Total # of Single Ticket Buyers	7,285	15,298	$611,900
Total # of Group Sales Buyers	1,286	2,700	$107,982
Total Paid % of Capacity			79%
Total % of Capacity			90%

Marketing Results for 2004/05 Season			
Total renewed subscribers	861	1,808	$179,002
# of subs renewed via telemarketing	258	542	$53,701
# of subs renewed via the Internet	603	1,266	$125,301
Total percent renewed			75%
Total new subscribers	631	1,326	$131,268
# of new subs sold via telemarketing	189	398	$39,380
# of new subs sold via the Internet	442	928	$91,888
Total # of Single Ticket Buyers	7,103	14,916	$596,652
Total # of Group Sales Buyers	902	1,894	$66,295
Total Paid % of Capacity			84%
Total % of Capacity			96%

Marketing Trends for the Past Five Years			
Item	**Households**	**Tickets/Subs**	**Revenue**
Marketing Results for 2003/04 Season			
Total renewed subscribers	689	1,446	$143,202
# of subs renewed via telemarketing	241	506	$50,121
# of subs renewed via the Internet	448	940	$93,081
Total percent renewed			72%
Total new subscribers	459	964	$95,468
# of new subs sold via telemarketing	161	338	$33,414
# of new subs sold via the Internet	298	627	$62,054
Total # of Single Ticket Buyers	5,676	11,920	$357,588
Total # of Group Sales Buyers	541	1,135	$39,732
Total Paid % of Capacity			80%
Total % of Capacity			96%

Marketing Results for 2002/03 Season			
Total renewed subscribers	213	447	$44,283
# of subs renewed via telemarketing	138	291	$28,784
# of subs renewed via the Internet	75	157	$15,499
Total percent renewed			70%
Total new subscribers	744	1,562	$154,608
# of new subs sold via telemarketing	483	1,015	$100,495
# of new subs sold via the Internet	260	547	$54,113
Total # of Single Ticket Buyers	6,357	13,349	$507,252
Total # of Group Sales Buyers	1,218	2,558	$89,515
Total Paid % of Capacity			82%
Total % of Capacity			96%

Marketing Results for 2001/02 Season			
Total renewed subscribers	228	479	$47,446
# of subs renewed via telemarketing	171	359	$35,584
# of subs renewed vi the Internet	57	120	$11,861
Total percent renewed			73%
Total new subscribers	76	160	$15,815
# of new subs sold via telemarketing	127	267	$13,351
# of new subs sold via the Internet	381	801	$40,052
Total # of Single Ticket Buyers	4,097	8,603	$215,087
Total # of Group Sales Buyers	723	1,518	$37,956
Total Paid % of Capacity			84%
Total % of Capacity			95%

Clearly, these numbers reflect the artistic vitality and fiscal growth of THEATER X. With this next breakdown of box office revenue, it is possible to look a little more closely at these trends.

Fig. 7.2. (continued)

Growth in Box Office Revenue and Audiences		Total Marketing Revenue	% Increase from Previous Year	Total Audience Served	% Increase from Previous Year
2005-2006 Season (projected)	Total Box Office	$1,072,414	10%	21,945	10%
	Subscriptions	$352,532	14%	3,948	26%
	Single Tickets	$611,900	3%	15,298	3%
	Group Sales	$107,982	63%	2,700	43%
2004-2005 Season	Total Box Office	$973,217	53%	19,944	29%
	Subscriptions	$310,270	30%	3,134	30%
	Single Tickets	$596,652	67%	14,916	25%
	Group Sales	$66,295	67%	1,894	67%
2003-2004 Season	Total Box Office	$635,989	-20%	15,466	-14%
	Subscriptions	$238,669	20%	2,411	20%
	Single Tickets	$357,588	-30%	11,920	-11%
	Group Sales	$39,732	-56%	1,135	-56%
2002-2003 Season	Total Box Office	$795,658	152%	17,915	66%
	Subscriptions	$198,891	214%	2,009	214%
	Single Tickets	$507,252	136%	13,349	55%
	Group Sales	$89,515	136%	2,558	68%
2001-2002 Season	Total Box Office	$316,304	no data	10,761	no data
	Subscriptions	$63,261		639	
	Single Tickets	$215,087		8,603	
	Group Sales	$37,956		1,518	

As you can see, THEATER X has come a long way since its 2001-2002 season, **more than tripling box office income in that five-year period**. Between the 01-02 and 02-03 seasons alone, total box office income doubled.

The dip in the 03-04 season is indicative of THEATER X's challenge of not having a permanent home. That season, we produced our shows at ABC Company's space, a smaller theater. Even though our overall marketing revenue declined that year, we still continued to show a strong growth in subscriptions.

Subscriptions have climbed each year, in fact. With the exception of the 03-04 season, THEATER X has shown increases in every area of marketing operations—attendance, group sales, single tickets, and subscriptions.

Looking at subscription package trends (see chart below), fluctuation in pricing is evident. THEATER X has added and subtracted packages, as well as experimented with pricing levels over the past few years. During the 2005-2006 season, THEATER X dropped the subscription price in honor of its 20th anniversary, and also removed many of the pricing levels from the year before.

Subscription Package Trends			
	Price	**Package**	**Benefts**
2005-2006 Season	$99	20th Anniversary Package	3 flexible tickets; guest tickets $47
	$60	First Performances Package	1 ticket to one of the first three performances of each show
2004-2005 Season	$135	Premium Flex Package	3 flexible tickets; guest tickets for $45
	$125	Total Package	1 ticket to each production/flexible dates; guest tickets $45
	$80	First Performances Package	1 ticket to one of the first three performances of each show
	$75	Under-30 Package	Total Package for patrons under 30
	$30	Student Subscription	1 ticket to each show with valid student ID
2003-2004 Season	$120	Total Package	1 ticket to each of 3 shows
	$75	Early Preview Package	1 ticket to one of the first three previews of each show
	$75	Under-30 Package	Total Package for patrons under 30

Stabilizing the subscription pricing, while providing pricing options to make THEATER X's subscriptions friendly for a variety of personal budgets is critical for the 2006-2007 season and beyond.

Single ticket prices (see chart on the next page), on the other hand, have remained relatively stable for the past few years. Prices for the 2003-2004 and 2004-2005 seasons stayed steady, with a slight increase for the first show of the 2005-2006 season. The top single ticket price for the next show was also raised in an attempt to offset weak sales from the first show. Unfortunately, sales for this production also flagged.

THEATER X's final production of the season will hopefully help to cover the financial gap left by the poor financial returns of the first two shows. Additionally, THEATER X was able to expand its seating to include the balcony of the QED Theatre, which not only increases the potential revenue, but also serves the equally important purpose of engaging more audience members. The show is already a financial hit. As of this report, it is selling well and has just extended for a week. If sales continue to be strong, we are projecting that the total revenue from single ticket sales will still exceed that of last year's, giving us a total increase of 10% over the 2004-2005 season.

Fig. 7.2. (continued)

Top Single Ticket Pricing Trends			
	Show 1	Show 2	Show 3
2005-2006 Season	$55	$60	$65, $70*
2004-2005 Season	$50	$50	$50
2003-2004 Season	$50	$50	$50

The balcony of the QED Theatre was used for this production, allowing for tiered pricing

MARKETING OPERATIONS AND RESOURCES

Marketing Staff

A staff of one full-time marketing director, one part-time marketing assistant, and one intern oversee marketing operations that are responsible for generating over $1 million in revenue annually. The Director of Marketing oversees and implements all marketing operations and is also responsible for overall marketing strategy. The Audience Services & Marketing Assistant is a part-time position that is dedicated to assisting the marketing director, as well as overseeing on-site box office management at the QED and customer relations. The intern serves as much-needed administrative and research support for the department.

Box Office

THEATER X outsources its online and phone ticketing to Arts Ticket Source. We provide information about shows, subscriptions, ticket prices, dates, times, accessibility, etc, and Arts Ticket Source, in return, provides customer support, data about ticket purchasing, and reports. Arts Ticket Source works directly with the marketing department at THEATER X, ensuring continual contact between marketing operations and ticket fulfillment.

THEATER X sells single tickets and subscriptions through Arts Ticket Source, and there are several heavy periods of box office traffic. The processing of subscription orders from May to mid-summer is a highly demanding time. Additionally, THEATER X has been fortunate enough to have had at least one major hit per season, so the on-sale period for those shows is quite busy. Group sales are handled in-house by the THEATER X marketing staff.

EXISTING AUDIENCE PROFILE

The typical THEATER X audience is made up of white, middle-class couples in their 40s and older, primarily from Manhattan. This information has been gathered by observation, not by empirical research. And beyond that very brief, nonscientific information, THEATER X knows very little about its audiences. This is a huge area of concern for us, as we know that an accurate audience profile is critical to knowing who those audiences are, where they live, what their economic background is, what their preferences are, and how well THEATER X's programs are serving them. This information can be utilized to implement artistic programs and sales strategies more effectively, as well as to leverage additional support from funders and corporate partners. Later in this plan, we will address this gap in our knowledge and what steps we might take to address it.

THEATER X BOTTLENECKS AND ISSUES

Earned v. Contributed Revenue

According to TCG's *Theatre Facts 2004,* "the 1,477 Theatres in the U.S. Nonprofit Professional Theatre Field in 2004 are estimated to have…received 55% of their income from earned sources." Comparatively, THEATER X Theater received only 41% of its total income from earned revenue in the 2003-2004 season. When examining earned revenue as a percentage of total expenses, THEATER X's fiscal portrait is even more dire. Among theaters in a similar budget group, total earned income was 43% when examined as a percentage of expenses; at THEATER X, that number drops considerably to 34%. Meanwhile, marketing related expenses continued to grow across the field, while the percentage of income that marketing efforts generated was on the decline.

These facts signify a problem area for THEATER X. While TCG reports that "the smaller the theatre, the more reliant it is on contributed income to support expenses," the comparatively low revenue return from marketing efforts at THEATER X highlights a major area of concern. As production costs soar, THEATER X (and indeed many nonprofit theaters in New York City) is faced with troublesome options: raise ticket prices, find a larger theater that may not be able to support riskier work, and/or expand contributed revenue, which would further widen the gap between marketing and development dollars. In this strategic plan, however, we will attempt to address this gap by focusing strategically on both short- and long-term marketing initiatives which will keep box office revenue steady and growing.

Theater Space

Mid-sized nonprofit theaters typically produce in smaller houses than their bottom lines can afford. For instance, a theater that consistently has 150 seats for every performance, season after season, cannot increase capacity and therefore revenue, even though the costs of producing plays and musicals rise each year. Their only choice is to keep raising ticket prices, which may ultimately drive some audiences away from the theater.

THEATER X, however, does not currently have a permanent home, and therefore has more flexibility than a theater that has a commitment to a particular space. This season, we will expand to the 299-seat capacity at the QED Theatre. A higher capacity

Fig. 7.2. (continued)

translates to a higher potential gross, of course, but will also have to be accompanied by strategic marketing efforts to fill those extra seats.

This is a stopgap measure only, though. One of THEATER X's long-term goals is to embark on a capital campaign and purchase a theater in which to present all of THEATER X's mainstage shows, readings, educational programs, and other events.

Single Tickets

Ticket prices at mid-sized nonprofit theaters have begun to approach or even exceed the low end of the cost of theater tickets for some commercial productions. Audiences are often unwilling or unable to pay above these prices, so again, theaters are unable to increase their revenue as expenses increase. THEATER X is no exception, with the top ticket price at $70 for the 2005-2006 season. Moreover, THEATER X's marketing staff has expressed significant discouragement with other trends in single ticket sales. They have noticed that sometimes their efforts seem futile and irrelevant: there is little they can do to sell a show that has received poor reviews and shows that get raves or have big-name stars seem to sell themselves.

These issues create two problematic situations. When a show is selling well, patrons on a tighter budget cannot afford to pay top dollar to see the production. When sales are flagging, THEATER X gives tickets away to friends and family, as well as services like Play-by-Play and Audience Extras. This has created a comp culture which not only devalues the overall THEATER X experience, but also cuts out an opportunity to capitalize on audience development efforts. Rather, THEATER X could offer tickets at a deeply discounted rate to educational, social, and religious partner organizations. We could even, in some instances, provide these tickets at no cost, while looking for ways to generate publicity through such partnerships.

Expanding into the balcony at the QED and ultimately finding a larger permanent space might also impact this issue at THEATER X—we will add multiple ticket price levels for different areas of the house. The high end of the pricing scale would quite obviously contribute significantly to the total ticket revenue. Lower priced tickets serve the equally important function of attracting a young and diverse audience. This commitment to affordable theater is vital to building our future audiences and creating a theater that opens up the door to what is for THEATER X, an untraditional audience.

Box Office

One of the major advantages of the Arts Ticket Source system is that most of the cost is passed directly on to the consumer, so THEATER X receives the benefits of a full-service ticketing system at minimal expense. Also, the administrative oversight and time that is required for an in-house system all but disappears with an outsourced system. Arts Ticket Source provides the staff that's necessary to man the phone lines and to keep the web ticketing interface functioning and up-to-date.

One disadvantage is a potential lack of connection between Arts Ticket Source employees and the mission of THEATER X. Additionally, THEATER X gives up some level of control over policies and procedures, as well as customer service training.

THEATER X sees the box office as pivotal to the marketing efforts, and, we would like to capitalize on the potential of growing the customer relationships through the point of sale. Even with all the advantages of an outside ticketing system, we want to transition to an in-house system. Over time, with minimal service fees on ticket purchases, such a system can not only pay for itself, but also generate revenue for the organization. This would give the marketing department greater control over this pivotal area of operations, with the ultimate hope that a closer collaboration between marketing and box office would lead to better customer service and increased revenues.

Human Resources

One of the biggest challenges that is preventing major strides forward in marketing is a lack of human resources. Although THEATER X's marketing income has grown significantly over the last three years, the staff for that effort has not. The marketing staff members spend most of their day trying to stay on top of pressing tasks, and have very little time or energy to focus on long-term vision and initiatives.

The marketing assistant, in one of the many catch-all components of that part-time position, is responsible for on-site box office oversight. Other than that, all other box office functions are outsourced, either to Arts Ticket Source or to QED Theatre staff. This creates two issues. One, an already overtaxed marketing assistant cannot possibly have the time to fully oversee the ticketing, financial, customer service, and other responsibilities that this position demands. Two, most of the people working for the THEATER X box office are not actually employees of THEATER X, which could possibly affect their ability to take ownership of THEATER X's mission, values, and goals, as they relate to customer service.

As part of achieving overall marketing goals, it is imperative that THEATER X expand its human potential. Collaborating with the development department could help to secure such resources. Many funders, such as TCG's New Generations program and the Robert Sterling Clark Foundation, are keenly interested in audience development. THEATER X is currently researching funding that will help us further develop audience and attendance strategies, as well as expand the marketing staff so that they will be more fully able to implement that strategy. In the meantime, three volunteer board members have each offered us 20 hours a month to help implement the strategies needed for growth in the 2006-2007 season. We hope that by the end of this season, we will have found the funding or earned the revenue necessary to increase the marketing staff.

Fig. 7.2. (continued)   <u>**Technology Resources**</u>

As for technological resources, THEATER X is unfortunately lacking. Outside of the resources provided by Arts Ticket Source, the marketing staff is tracking and managing thousands and thousands of patron records on basic spreadsheets. This severely limits or complicates the opportunities to examine trends over time, and is not an efficient way of managing this massive amount of data. As mentioned earlier, a more robust ticketing system would help to address these issues and has the potential of paying for itself over time with minimal per ticket fees.

CURRENT OPERATIONS SUMMARY

Overall, the news is good for THEATER X. We are healthy and we are growing. The significant growth in income in the last five years is encouraging and signifies that we are entering a more mature phase as an organization. Single tickets, group sales, and subscriptions have all seen increases, and expanding into a larger audience capacity will create the opportunity for even further growth.

Still, there are major issues that need to be addressed in our marketing operations, from closing the gap between earned and contributed income to finding out more about our audience demographics and psychographics to expanding our human and technological resources. It is virtually impossible for an organization to maintain the status quo—it can either move forward or fall behind. It is critical for THEATER X to immediately address issues of capacity by expanding its staff and seeking out more efficient, productive, and cost-effective ways to manage data and ticketing. We now hope to capitalize on the tremendous growth of the past few years and begin to secure the resources to enable us to achieve new heights in marketing and audience relations.

Robert Friend provides more detail on the situation analysis: "A situation analysis contains a picture of an organization's operations at a specific moment in time. The analysis should include a trend analysis of single-ticket and season ticket sales, an overview of the perceived customer base, and details about the artistic growth and managerial changes of an organization, as well as an overview of the operational bottlenecks facing the organization at this moment in time. Specifically, the trend analysis will detail information about the number of subscribers, the total capacity of the theater, the percentage of tickets that were sold for each performance, how many performances in each season, etc. Once this information is documented, a chart of growth or decline for all of these areas will be quite visible for review and will provide a framework from which to begin the strategic marketing planning process. Creating this historical background trend data for your theater is much like a forensic exercise at a crime scene. In this case, you are uncovering the bone structure of the organization."[55] Although Friend believes that there is no right or wrong way to do a situation analysis, he does think that it is imperative that all organizations create a written analysis to determine their current organizational situation. "It's amazing how writing down this kind of information changes your whole viewpoint of the organization. When something is on paper, it becomes a documented part of the planning process and provides an historical perspective of the history of the organization."[56]

How does an organization collect and organize all of the internal data that it needs for a situation analysis? Most organizations use a database to compile all information gathered from selling tickets. Many organizations use one database for both ticketing and fundraising data. Jeff Levine describes the ticketing/fundraising database at BAM: "At a place like BAM, where we're selling hundreds of thousands of tickets a year and where contributed income is 60 percent of our revenue, it is essential that we get information on both people who are buying tickets and people who are donating money so that we get a full picture of our audience. We use an integrated database called Tessitura, which was designed by the Metropolitan Opera and is specifically meant for performing arts organizations."[57] Tessitura also acts as a ticketing system, capturing information every time a ticket is sold.[58]

In addition to gathering information in-house, an organization can also choose to get additional information on its patrons by appending its database. Appending is "a process [in which] an organization works with a specialty company that has access to consumer information (e.g., phone numbers, household income, demographics) that it can pair up with names in its database."[59] Levine notes that privacy must be considered when appending a database: "You're getting information on someone that the person didn't give to you, so you have to make a judgment call about the type of information you want. Where is the line on invasion of privacy, and how close do you want to get to it?"[60]

After analyzing the internal workings of the organization, the marketing director then focuses on market analysis. A market analysis identifies primary and secondary target markets, analyzes marketing penetration, and determines target markets that have the potential for growth. Target markets are the organization's existing markets, as well as new markets that it hopes to reach. An organization's primary target market is the main focus for its marketing efforts; it is the group of people (market) most likely to buy tickets. Since an organization has already profiled its audience in the situation analysis, it may use that data to help determine its primary targeted audience. For example, a chamber music society might identify "avid fans of classical music" as a primary target market, as its analysis and research may have determined that classical music fans are most likely to buy tickets to a chamber music concert. An organization may have more than one primary target market, depending on its artistic offerings. Secondary target markets, as might be inferred, are markets that are not the main focus of the organization's marketing effort, but may still be interested in purchasing tickets. To continue with the above example, a secondary target market for a chamber music society might be "amateur classical musicians;" people who play classical music may also purchase tickets to chamber music events,

though they may be less likely to do so than avid fans of classical music. The process of separating groups of people into primary and secondary target markets that are determined by demographic, psychographic, or other factors is known as "market segmentation."

After identifying primary and secondary target markets, the marketing director must now analyze market penetration and the potential of each targeted market. Market penetration refers to the presence of the organization in the targeted market. For example, how many people in the target market buy tickets? How many know about the organization as a result of various marketing efforts? After determining the current target market penetration, the marketing director must identify those areas that have potential for growth.

In identifying potential areas of growth, the organization may choose to focus on reaching out to potential audiences that have not been part of the organization's target markets. The process of reaching out to new target markets is also known as "audience development." Donna Walker-Kuhne, president of the Walker Communications Group, defines audience development as "the process of engaging, educating, and motivating diverse communities to participate in a creative, entertaining experience as important partner[s] in the design and execution of the art. Audience development is the cultivation and growth of long-term relationships firmly rooted in the philosophical foundation that recognizes and embraces the distinctions of race, age, sexual orientation, geography, and class."[61]

Through the use of marketing strategies as described later in this chapter, an organization can help develop a new audience for its core programming. However, the organization must be truly committed to reaching out to this new audience by listening to its wants and establishing an ongoing relationship with the community. Walker-Kuhne provides this example from the Public Theater: "I took George [C. Wolfe, the former artistic director/producer of the Public Theater] to Harlem, and an African-American director said, 'We want Shakespeare. Nobody ever does Shakespeare in Harlem.' We [the Public] created a program called 'Shakespeare in Harlem,' consisting of a week of free workshops and classes. This program is now [in 2006] in its thirteenth year."[62] In this case, Walker-Kuhne and George C. Wolfe decided to target the African-American community in Harlem as an audience for the Public Theater's Shakespeare programming.

A marketing director gathers information on an organization's target markets by conducting market research. Market research is crucial, because it not only provides information on an organization's current target markets, but it also allows the organization to gather data that will lead to the identification of additional target markets. The main market research methodologies used by marketing staff are surveys and focus groups. Surveys are tools used to provide researchers with specific information on a particular topic. Thus, survey questions should be designed to give specific, quantifiable information, such as age, sex, household income, and location. If a question is designed to garner an opinion, such as an evaluation of a performance, it should contain ranking numbers or another method of rating the opinion so that the data produced can be compared to that gathered from other patrons. For example, a question may ask: "On a scale of 1 (lowest) to 10 (highest), how much did you enjoy this performance?" Formulating questions in this manner allows for the subject to express an opinion but still allow her answer to be compared with others on a quantitative basis.

The main types of surveys used by the marketing department are phone surveys, online surveys, performance audience surveys, box office ticket sales surveys, and lobby listening surveys; these surveys are defined below:

- Phone surveys are calls made from a market researcher (either in-house or hired by the organization) to customers (such as audience members, current subscribers, or past subscribers), asking specific questions to gather information. These surveys provide a broad representation of opinion and can result in a high response rate when calling those who have attended events at the organization.[63]
- Online surveys begin with a mass e-mail sent to an internal and/or external [purchased] database. Respondents are provided a link to a Web site, where an electronic questionnaire captures their responses and automatically stores responses in a database (avoiding the data-entry step required for many other survey types). "A range of information can be captured—demographic and psychographic data, as well as perceptions—and questions may take advantage of the rich media (e.g., audio and video) available on the Web. Also, technology allows the organization to identify which e-mail addresses responded and follow up accordingly."[64]

- Performance audience surveys are surveys distributed to audience members at the beginning of a performance and designed to be returned at intermission or the end of the performance; these surveys typically contain an opinion of the performance as well as demographic and psychographic information. These surveys may also be e-mailed to patrons attending the performance after that performance has concluded.[65]
- Box office ticket sales surveys consist of demographic information gathered by ticket sales staff when a customer purchases a ticket. This information tends to be limited to basic demographic information, such as a zip code, as it is part of a ticket sales service call.
- Lobby listening surveys consist of information gathered by asking questions of patrons in the lobby. As these interviews are conducted face-to-face, the interviewer must beware of bias in picking audience members to be surveyed.[66]

Please see appendix A for an example of a performance audience survey, demonstrating the typical questions asked by marketing professionals.

Focus groups are groups consisting of various types of people (or representatives of one specific market) who are questioned by the focus group leader on subjects of interest to the organization. For example, a focus group may be shown a television commercial for a production, or a series of print ads, and asked which ones appeal to them most and why; the organization would be looking for the impressions that the focus group participants have from viewing or looking at the advertisements.[67] Jeff Levine says that "focus groups can work well when you've got a good moderator and are choosing your participants very carefully to focus on a specific topic. They can be very helpful if you're trying to get a sense of how your attendees are reacting to your marketing materials or your positioning (how an organization defines itself in the marketplace), but you have to be careful about extrapolating your findings. A focus group is not necessarily representative of your audience as a whole."[68]

Surveys and focus groups may be conducted whenever an organization feels that more audience research is necessary. At BAM, Levine conducts performance audience surveys every three years. "Our programs do change, but gradually, so we've discovered that if we do audience surveys more often, we are just wasting money."[69]

In addition to conducting in-house research efforts, marketing directors may also use outside market research and consulting firms to conduct research. AMS Planning and Research and ArtsMarket are two organizations that conduct focus groups and other market research efforts for arts organizations. These organizations use an organization's data and compare it to other similar arts organizations or to national arts audiences to determine how the organization's data is similar to or differs from the average data. Other organizations that have general market research data on different types of audiences include The Broadway League, Theatre Development Fund, and the Alliance of Resident Theatres/New York; these organizations provide general arts industry data to interested organizations.

The final analysis conducted by the marketing director is a SWOT analysis. A SWOT analysis is a study of the organization, exploring its "strengths, weaknesses, opportunities, and threats" to help determine its current market position. Strengths and weaknesses refer to the internal strengths and weaknesses of the organization. A large subscription base might be a strength for an organization, while a budget deficit might be noted as a weakness. Opportunities and threats arise outside the organization. If the local economy is in recession, then the organization would note that threat, while the opening of a university in town might provide new opportunities for the organization. "A SWOT analysis consists of conclusions reached by the marketing director after reviewing a variety of sources, including: data within the situation and market analyses, past quantitative and qualitative research conducted by the theater, and a review of the internal and external factors that might affect the success of any given marketing campaign."[70] An example of a SWOT analysis for THEATER X is shown on pages 296 and 297.[71]

Positioning and Branding the Organization or Production

After an organization has defined its target markets, it can create a position for itself within the marketplace in order to sell more tickets. An organization positions itself by defining its unique place in the market and stressing the advantages it has over its competition. Competition includes all businesses that may attract the performing arts organization's potential ticket buyers to spend money on their products and services. This competition may be performing arts– and entertainment-related, such as other performing

arts events/organizations, cinemas, sporting events, and casinos, or it may include other businesses or activities that compete with the organization for "leisure time and dollars" (time and money set aside for nonessential purchases), such as staying in and renting a movie or going to the beach.[72] By defining its position, the organization can create strategies to sell its tickets by stressing the benefits it offers to consumers versus the benefits offered by its direct competitors.

Positioning is also known as "branding."[73] When an organization brands itself, it creates an institutional image that defines its unique position in the marketplace. Jeff Levine describes BAM's brand: "I'd say we're one of the more successful organizations in terms of branding. Part of our brand success is luck: We have a memorable name (BAM) that perfectly mirrors our mission, which is to present events that have impact. However, we made a strategic decision to use our acronym (BAM) instead of the full 'Brooklyn Academy of Music.' This was one of the decisions we made to help develop a personality for our organization and contribute to a psychological understanding of our programming."[74]

Levine continues, "Effective brands accurately reflect your product. There can't be any disconnect between people's perception of your brand and the experience that they have with your product. The most successful brands are the ones that have figured out a way to communicate the experience that people are going to have—and consistently deliver that experience; they use every contact point that a person can have with the organization to communicate the brand. Branding encompasses everything from visual design to copywriting, customer service to programs [playbills]. If the experience with your product does not match the expectations you've given customers, your branding efforts will fail."[75]

Disney is another organization that uses "every point of contact" to communicate its core brand on a global scale, including its theatrical division. Andrew Flatt states, "The theatrical division is lucky enough to be a part of a large company that is known for its core brand association: high-quality entertainment for audiences of all ages, rooted in the spirit of innovation, imagination, and magic."[76] The organization keeps a keen eye on brand awareness through ongoing research initiatives, resulting in a handful of adjectives that consistently reappear when research subjects discuss their perceptions of the company's Broadway shows, including "magical,"

Fig. 7.3. SWOT Analysis

SWOT ANALYSIS

While we may not have a wealth of information about our patrons' behavior in the marketplace at our fingertips, we do have in-depth knowledge of THEATER X's own strengths, weaknesses, opportunities, and threats, which is highly valuable. The following SWOT Analysis is based on conversations with current and former THEATER X board members, staff, artists, and friends.

Strengths	Weaknesses
Commitment to new work	Board in transition
Artistic integrity	Unwillingness to allow the board to help lead the organization
Track record of both artistic and financial success with productions	No permanent theater
Providing engaging and thought-provoking theater to our audience	Too reliant on contributed income
Profile of artistic leadership	Artistic leadership often not accessible
Excellence in arts education	Budgetary constraints on number of productions per year
National recognition of education programs	Small season makes THEATER X dependent on financial hits
Support of writers through development program	Artistic integrity can be obscured when a show is failing financially
Highly respected literary office	Inability to reach a larger audience
Strong, collaborative staff team	Lack of funds for sufficient advertising
Twenty year track record	No consistent institutional message and image
Reputation for producing 'intelligent' theater	Poor technology for contact/constituent management
High renewal rate for subscriptions	Website is too low of a priority
Strong record of success in development	Inadequate press coverage on the theater and some productions
Ability to attract well-known artists	Little to no corporate sponsorships
Nurturing emerging artists	Institutional life cycle—been around too long to be the hot new theater and too short for institutional stability
Providing opportunities for mid- and late-career artists to stretch and challenge themselves	Very little data on our audiences demographics, psychographics, or market behavior
Cultivating a sense of belonging and self-worth in students through our youth programs	

Opportunities	Threats
Expansion of potential audiences served	Increasing costs of producing theater
Increased theatrical offerings	Box office revenue increases unable to keep up with overall revenue needs
Growth of education programs	Saturated market—many nonprofit theaters in local area, including several at our budget size
Branding	
Sponsorships—financial and advertising	Audiences unwilling to pay higher ticket prices
Finding a new space that works artistically and financially	Current staff is maxed out
Build a board that is fully engaged in the life of THEATER X without being overly involved in day-to-day affairs	Staff retention
	Anticipated drop in foundation income
	Tight real estate market for new theater space
Increasing relationships with local businesses and industries	
Developing closer relationships with government agencies and representatives	
Ticket programs and events for specific audiences (young, singles, gay, student, etc)	
Tickets with a lower price point	
Resource sharing with other theaters	
Staff expansion through major funder underwriting	
Increase retention by taking steps to make THEATER X a more "human" place to work (added vacation, comp time, generous maternity/paternity policies, health care, retirement contribution)	
Learn more about our audience demographics, psychographics, and market behavior	
Organizational maturity	

"vibrant," "meaningful," "unforgettable," and "fun." Flatt explains that it's important to keep in touch with the public's perception of one's brand while developing and executing marketing campaigns: "In today's fast-moving information age, perceptions can change on a dime, so keeping the brand's core attributes at the forefront of your mind helps to determine appropriate messaging in a campaign, through both language and design. Our attributes shape the way we speak to our consumers on a variety of levels."[77]

One way for an organization to effectively brand itself is through the use of graphic design. Good graphic design helps create a visual institutional image that supports the identity that the organization wishes to put into the outside world. If an organization has a consistent graphic identity, any publication from the organization is linked to every other publication from that organization. In addition to printed marketing materials used in direct mail campaigns, graphic design may also be used in programs, newsletters, study guides, and other printed materials. Graphic design is also a vital part of any Internet presence; a well-designed Web site is crucial to the success of an organization's Internet marketing effort.

An organization may have an in-house design department, or it may choose to use an outside graphic design firm or advertising agency. Jeff Levine describes the pros and cons of this decision: "We have a substantial in-house design department. If the graphic designers are in-house, then they work for you and have a deeper understanding of your needs than an outside agency, which is typically juggling multiple clients. In fact, an agency may be working with your competitors. However, external firms may have more staff expertise and will look at the design from an outsider's perspective. The decision to use an external firm depends on the needs of your organization. If you only need to place a few ads a year and design a couple of brochures, it may not make sense to hire a full-time designer."[78]

An organization may choose to use a word or image to represent the organization, using it on all marketing and printed materials. This word or image is known as a "logo." A logo should create an immediate association between the visual image and the organization. For example, the logo for *The Lion King* is displayed in fig. 7.4.[79]

Since this image is so immediately identified with Disney's *The Lion King*, its presence on any marketing materials immediately invokes the name of the show in the mind of the public, as well as

Fig. 7.4. *The Lion King* Logo

brand associations about the production that have developed during its run: strong, majestic, and powerful.[80]

CLASSROOM DISCUSSION

What does a situation analysis contain? How do you obtain the data for a situation analysis?

What is a market analysis? How is market research conducted?

What types of surveys might a performing arts organization use?

What is a SWOT analysis?

Define the following: "demographic data," "psychographic data," "appending," "primary target markets," "secondary target markets," "market penetration," "audience development," "focus groups," "competition," "positioning," "branding," and "logo."

Marketing Objectives and Strategies

The next part of the marketing plan involves determining the specific objectives that will allow the marketing director to reach his goal of selling tickets, as well the strategies used to accomplish these objectives. As defined in chapter 2, an objective is a definite endpoint toward which efforts are aimed; objectives have measurable, tangible results. Examples of typical marketing objectives may include increasing subscriptions, attracting new target markets to particular programs, and increasing student ticket sales. Strategies are methods created to help the marketing director fulfill the objective. A marketing plan includes a number of strategies in its mix, all designed to sell tickets; the strategies may include direct mail, advertising, and promotions that will attract attention to the production or organization. Robert Friend provides an example of an objective and strategies: "When I worked at the Long Wharf Theatre in Connecticut, our objective was to increase our subscriber base by 5 percent through expanding our student subscriber base. We created a flexible student subscription at an attractive price with a special ID card. We then asked students who worked in the theater department to become part of a special board of student advisors to serve as the on-campus ambassadors to the theater and implement our strategies to sell this subscription. So, examples of strategies that could support these objectives include: distributing marketing materials promoting this subscription via a Web site and through hand-to-hand distribution at heavily trafficked student areas; creating banners and other displays to inform students of the new flexible subscription; and placing advertisements in campus papers."[81]

These next sections will examine marketing strategies in detail, dividing them into three major areas: direct marketing, advertising, and promotional partnerships.

Direct Marketing Strategies
Direct marketing strategies include those strategies that are targeted to specific people via mail, e-mail and text messaging, and telephone.

Direct Mail
Direct mail involves the mailing of marketing pieces to specified postal addresses. A direct mailing may occur as the first part of a subscription campaign, in which the marketing director mails information on the new season to attract subscribers. The subscription campaign is divided into two parts: the renewal campaign, which focuses on retaining current subscribers, and the acquisition campaign, which focuses on acquiring new subscribers. New

subscribers may be acquired from lapsed subscribers, from donors who do not subscribe, from single-ticket buyers, or from people affiliated with similar organizations. However, those potential subscribers who have the strongest relationship with the organization are most likely to become or remain subscribers, as they have already decided that the organization is one that interests and appeals to them. A direct mailing is usually sent to current subscribers (for the renewal), lapsed subscribers, single-ticket buyers, and any other groups determined to be good targets for a subscription campaign by the marketing director (e.g., ticket buyers from a similar arts organization). This mailing takes place about six months before the start of the next season; at BAM, Jeff Levine states that direct mail for a subscription campaign is sent three to four months before the start of the next season.[82]

A direct mail piece may also be sent to sell single tickets. Subscription-based organizations may mail a single-ticket brochure featuring the entire season. In addition to a single-ticket brochure, individual direct mail pieces for various productions or series of productions may also be created. For each individual direct mail piece, the marketing director should determine the goal of the direct mail offer and its target audience. For example, a marketing director may want to increase audiences for a particular dance performance by offering a two-for-one ticket discount to people who have purchased tickets to dance events at that organization. A single-ticket direct mail campaign typically begins about six to eight weeks prior to the first performance, or two months later than the subscription campaign.[83]

To begin a direct mail campaign, the marketing director must acquire lists of addresses. These lists are acquired by compiling subscriber and ticket sales information from his own organization, purchasing mailing lists from other organizations or a list house, or trading mailing lists with another organization (e.g., an opera house might trade mailing lists with a symphony orchestra). These lists are compiled and managed by the marketing director; the lists must be organized, purged of duplicate or incomplete addresses, and marked with their category of origin (e.g., current subscriber, trade with X organization).

Jeff Levine notes the importance of having clean mailing lists: "It's a waste of money if you're sending materials out to someone who doesn't live at that address. Besides merging and purging your lists in-house, you can also send your database out to the U.S. Postal Service National Customer Support Center to match the information with the National

Change of Address database. It ensures that your addresses are all up-to-date, and that your mail is getting to the person to whom it is addressed. Keeping your mailing lists clean is just common-sense marketing."[84]

After the lists are compiled, the organization creates a direct mail package or single piece to send to the targeted addresses. For a subscription campaign, the package would contain the subscription brochure; an order form; a reply envelope; and a letter from an executive staff member (e.g., the executive or artistic director). (Please see appendix B1–B4 for a sample subscription package.[85]) The subscription brochure details the upcoming season, using the most eye-catching graphics and marketing copy, as well as seating and pricing details. The brochure provides instructions on how to subscribe by phone or by Internet if the organization offers these services; it includes any discounts available to subscribers, as well as any other information necessary. The brochure will also be coded to allow for the tracking of responses to the mailing. The renewal form allows the renewing or prospective subscriber to fill out his subscription request and return it with payment in the preaddressed reply envelope. The renewal form may also have a space for the subscriber to make a donation to the organization. Letters included in the subscription package contain an appeal for renewal or an acquisition, depending on the target of the letter. For example, a letter for a renewing subscriber may offer that subscriber the opportunity to upgrade her seats.

Single-ticket direct mail campaign packages may consist of a single-ticket brochure, summarizing the entire season's offerings. (These brochures are typically first mailed to anyone who did not respond to the subscription mailing.) At BAM, single-ticket brochures are less extensive than subscription brochures. Jeff Levine explains, "With subscribers, we tend to give lots of information to help them make their decision. We tend to be briefer with the single-ticket buyers, because we don't want to put anyone off by sending a huge brochure. For a single-ticket brochure, we're looking to create a piece with catchy marketing angles that is easy to pick up and scan through."[86] Single-ticket pieces may also be postcards or small brochures that feature specific productions, as in fig. 7.5a and 7.5b, which promotes single tickets for the Sondheim Celebration at the Kennedy Center.[87] This brochure provides information about these productions, as well as instructions on how to order tickets. Single-ticket mailings are also often coded to track

responses to the mailing, especially if discounts are offered.

Direct mail may be sent at the regular first-class postal rate or, if the mailing is big enough, at the bulk mail rate. Bulk mail rates require that at least 200 pieces be mailed at one time, and that the organization must sort and bundle the mail to the bulk mail center specifications. In addition to the bulk mail rate, nonprofit organizations may also mail at a special discounted nonprofit rate. All information about postage rates may be found at the U.S. Postal Service's Web site, *www.usps.com*; organizations should choose the postage rate that will be the most cost-effective for their particular mailing. For a fee, a mailing house may be hired to compile and post the mailing.

When constructing a direct mail campaign, it is important to coordinate the mailing dates with the mailing dates of other departments in the organization. If a person gets too many mailings from one organization, that person may experience "mail fatigue." Jeff Levine explains mail fatigue: "Mail fatigue is just what it sounds like. If people get five mailings in five days from the same organization, these mailings are becoming less effective and border on annoying. The marketing director must be aware of the amount of communication the organization is having with an individual."[88]

Results for a direct mail campaign can vary widely depending on the lists used. The list with the most defined relationship to the organization will produce the best result. Therefore, a direct mail subscription renewal appeal to current subscribers may have a success rate of between 10 and 50 percent, while an acquisition mailing to a new list of names may have a success rate of less than 1 percent.[89] Typically, standard response rates to a new acquisition direct mail campaign are: 2 to 4 percent for in-house lists, .25 to 1 percent for purchased lists, and .5 to 2 percent for traded lists.[90] Measuring results for single-ticket direct mail campaigns is slightly more difficult than measuring results for subscription direct mail campaigns. The marketing director is dependent on the self-reporting of ticket buyers; the ticket buyer needs to remember that he saw a particular direct mail piece when he is asked about it during the ticket purchase. For a typical single-ticket direct mail campaign, 2 percent is considered a good return rate.[91]

As responses can be tracked by coding each mailing, small-scale tests can be done with inexpensive pieces to test the response for that

Fig. 7.5a. Single-Ticket Mailing—Cover

Fig. 7.5b. Single-Ticket Mailing—Inside

particular piece. The average response for a single-ticket direct mailing is .5 percent; if the response is any less than that, the list should be considered marginal and should not be used again. All lists used should be evaluated based on the cost benefit to the organization; the direct mail campaign for a particular list should not cost more than the amount of ticket sales that it brings in.

E-mail and Text Messaging

In addition to mailing printed pieces, subscriptions and single tickets may also be sold using e-mail. The timetable for an e-mail campaign is flexible, as e-mails may be sent out whenever the organization desires. E-mail lists are generated from the general ticketing database, along with any e-mail information requests that may have been sent to the organization. In addition, someone can also request to be put on an organization's e-mail list. Since e-mail is far less expensive to distribute than direct mail, the marketing director can choose to use a wider variety of lists for an e-mail campaign than he might choose to do otherwise. Eugene Carr, president of Patron Technology, suggests that organizations send mailings featuring other organizations to their own lists as part of a swap: "For example, the X Theater and the Y Theater are both located in the same town. The marketing manager for the X Theater calls the Y Theater and offers a 25 percent discount to people on the Y Theater's e-mail list, in exchange for the same discount for its own e-mail list. The Y Theater then sends out its own e-mails to its list offering the discount to X Theater, and the X Theater does the same with the Y Theater discount. These theaters are able to maintain the integrity of their lists, and those e-mails are not considered spam because they come from a list that the recipient signed up for."[92]

After a list is generated, the e-mail must be designed. Carr recommends that organizations use "e-newsletters" for distributing information on the organization, and shorter "e-Postcards" for action-oriented e-mails, such as those that offer a discount.[93] E-newsletters are designed to build the relationship between the organization and its patrons, offering news and other information about the organization, as well as links back to the organization's Web site.[94] E-Postcards are designed to provoke an action in the reader, such as clicking through to a Web site and purchasing tickets online.[95] The subject lines for both kinds of e-mail should be direct, clear, and short; all e-mail sent from the same organization should have similarly structured subject lines so that the e-mail can be immediately identified.[96] All information sent via e-mail should be relevant and have value to the potential reader. Carr states, "Your e-mail campaign should ideally offer value in one of the following ways: more detailed information than is available to the public; early notice of events or offers; or private offers or discounts."[97]

Jeff Levine describes the process of designing an e-mail for BAM: "We're very careful about keeping the visual design of our e-mail similar to our Web site design. Our e-mail template mirrors our homepage, so that when people go from the e-mail to [our] Web site, it's the same visual experience. We try to be direct in e-mail, because a lot of people just read the subject line, and no one wants to get into a detailed e-mail message. The first step is getting people to open the e-mail, and once they do that, hitting them with something that is engaging. E-mail gives you the ability to link to different Web sites, which you can't do in a direct mail piece. You can go a step further than a postcard, because your prospect is immediately plugged into your Web site with one click."[98] Figure 7.6. provides an example of an e-mail from the Kennedy Center promoting performances of the National Symphony Orchestra.[99] This e-mail gives the patron a discount on ticket purchases; the discount code on the e-mail allows the Kennedy Center to know the number of tickets sold using that discount offer.

After the e-mail is sent, the organization is able to track its status. The organization is able to tell when an e-mail has been opened, when a link has been clicked on, and, by coding all e-mail offers, when an e-mail has resulted in a ticket sale. This extensive reporting makes the evaluation of e-mail marketing efforts the most accurate. The percentage of patrons who open an email is known as the "open rate;" Carr states that the open rate among his clients averages 30 percent.[100] "The click-through rate refers to the percentage of patrons who receive an e-mail and click on any link within that e-mail. The average click-through rate for all [Carr's] clients...was 3.9 percent."[101] If only half of these click-throughs led to ticket purchases, the success of the e-mail campaign equals that of a direct mail campaign, but costs much less. Carr makes this point emphatically; he states, "If you can't afford to conduct an e-mail marketing campaign, what kind of marketing can you afford to do? I've met marketing directors who tell me that their marketing budgets are set for the year, and they don't have any additional money to spend on an e-mail campaign. I tell them to take some of the money from their direct mail campaign and put it toward e-mail, because the return on the investment is so much greater."[102]

Fig. 7.6. Kennedy Center E-mail

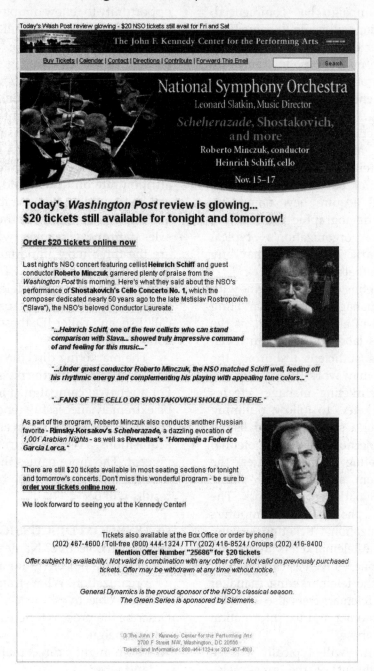

Although e-mail has become an established method of direct marketing, text messaging is becoming a popular way to get information directly to interested potential consumers. "In a text messaging campaign, an organization or production partners with a wireless telephone marketing partner (such as Sprint) to create a dedicated telephone number for the campaign. Interested consumers may text special code words to that number and receive a ticket discount or other promotional prize from the organization or production."[103] For example, at certain performances of the Broadway musical *Spring Awakening*, audience members were instructed to send a text message to a special number during intermission for a chance to win a backstage visit after that performance. The audience members provided their e-mail addresses and phone numbers to be used in a marketing database and received a ringtone and a photograph in response.[104] In a text messaging campaign, marketing managers may see exactly how many texts were sent and evaluate the success of the campaign based on those numbers.

Telemarketing

After a subscription campaign has commenced, responses from the mailing will begin to come back to the organization. After three or four weeks have passed, the organization may choose to contact by phone those who have not responded. The process of contacting these potential buyers by phone is known as "telemarketing."

In addition to contacting these nonresponders, the organization may also choose to acquire additional phone lists (either by purchase or by trade) of likely potential subscribers. Often, a marketing director will acquire new names by buying lists based on demographic information; after determining the organization's typical customer profile, the marketing director may buy lists of names that match that profile.

Typically, a telemarketing campaign begins with hiring a telemarketing manager. The telemarketing manager is usually part of an outside firm, as the telemarketing process is labor-intensive; however, if the organization has sufficient resources, the telemarketing manager may work directly for the organization. The telemarketing manager creates a script for the telemarketers to follow, outlining the benefits of becoming a subscriber and listing responses to common objections raised by potential buyers. The telemarketing manager hires the telemarketers, trains them, and creates a "phone room" in which the telemarketers will work. The phone room contains phones and computers connected to the organization's ticketing system. The computers allow the telemarketers to process subscriptions on the phone, as well as capture data for future analysis by the telemarketing manager and marketing director. Telemarketers also use their computers to correct customer and list information in the organization's database.

A telemarketing firm will typically charge between 29 and 33 percent of the gross sales achieved through the telemarketing effort, as well as a fixed amount to pay the telemarketers.[105] Telemarketers are usually paid an hourly salary with commission on sales. If the projected gross sales of the telemarketing effort do not sustain the cost of hiring a telemarketing firm, then the organization should not conduct this campaign.

The telemarketing sales effort must be undertaken with a great deal of sensitivity. A performing arts organization relies on its relationships with its ticket buyers, and a too-aggressive telemarketing campaign can alienate those customers. However, if the organization frames the telemarketing effort as a service, providing potential subscribers the opportunity to renew or upgrade right on the phone, the telemarketing effort will be more successful.[106]

David Kitto remarks, "Telemarketing works because the telemarketing agent engages the consumer in a conversation about the product. If the agent is effective, he can communicate to the consumer, 'This is something very interesting that I'd like to share with you.' The consumer becomes engaged by the conversation. It's a social and educational process. The problem with telemarketing is that the attrition rate on tickets sold through telemarketing can be very high, because it's an impulse buy. The quality of your leads, the training and ability of the sales staff, and a manager [who] can inspire that staff are the three most important components of your telemarketing campaign. Timing is important, in terms of the sales cycle. Telemarketing is becoming increasingly difficult because of all of the 'do not call' lists and caller ID; these can wreak havoc with contact rates."[107]

The marketing director receives reports nightly and weekly tracking the progress of the campaign.[108] For a renewal campaign, a telemarketing effort can be extremely successful; renewal rates are generally between 60 and 70 percent. However, for new acquisitions, a typical return rate is between 5 and 6 percent. The more names that an organization gets from its in-house lists, the better the telemarketing results will be.

CLASSROOM DISCUSSION

What is an objective? Name three examples of typical objectives for a performing arts organization. What strategies might support these objectives?

Describe the process for creating a direct mail campaign.

To whom might a direct mail campaign be targeted, and why?

How are mailing lists acquired?

What is the importance of making sure a mailing list is "clean"?

Describe the process for creating an e-mail campaign.

What sort of responses can an e-mail campaign track?

Describe the process for creating a telemarketing campaign.

For what sort of patron is a telemarketing campaign most effective?

What should an organization consider before beginning a telemarketing campaign?

Advertising

Although advertising doesn't target an individual in the way that a mailing or telemarketing campaign does, it is still designed to appeal to a specific target audience. Advertising consists of paid promotional announcements placed in various media. Advertising is typically used in conjunction with other strategies. For example, at the same time that a direct mail subscription campaign begins, many organizations place ads in newspapers, in magazines, on the radio, and on the Internet, describing their new season and offering contact information for potential subscribers. For a single-ticket campaign, an advertising push might begin two to four weeks before the performance, in conjunction with direct mail and e-mail marketing.[109]

Before beginning an advertising campaign, the marketing director needs to know the objective of the advertising campaign and its target market. She especially needs to know how that target market uses media, so that she may purchase her advertising in the media that will garner the most benefit for the organization. For example, if an organization wishes to target a student population, it may want to spend more money on Internet advertising, but if it wishes to target a commuter population, it might be better off purchasing advertising on drive-time radio.

Andrew Flatt describes his process for determining his advertising needs: "At Disney, we project advertising and related marketing costs for a full year (fifty-two weeks) of performances. We set a net box office goal for each week, and then determine the type of media that we'll need to support those goals. We work with Serino Coyne, our advertising agency, to put together a strategic plan with detailed expenses, which includes a combination of print, radio, television, outdoor, and online advertising, plus direct response efforts as required. The important thing is to plan as far in advance as possible, but to allow ourselves enough flexibility so that we can change the media at a moment's notice depending on ticket inventory and sales needs. We may find ourselves selling better (or worse!) than originally planned, so we build in enough breathing room to alter specific media placement to allow for natural shifts in sales patterns. For example, this week [in July 2006], we have a lot of *Beauty and the Beast* tickets to sell, which is not surprising: this time of year, the week of the Fourth of July, our advance sales from the local New York audience are lower than at other times of the year, so we're really dependent on walk-up sales from the tourist audience. We decided that we needed to be running more print ads than we had originally anticipated, so we put five or six different print ads in motion for this week; tourists are inundated with print ads when they come to New York, whether it's guidebook magazines in the hotel lobbies or newspapers delivered directly to their hotel rooms. We also ran some early-morning television spots during shows like *Good Morning America*, because tourists watch those programs in their hotel rooms before they go out for the day (as do the locals, who are deciding how to spend their leisure time, too). These changes are within our budget, because we've planned for flexibility."[110]

An advertisement should contain a "call to action" (in the form of a ticket purchase) for the consumer; most advertisements contain a "call to action" with a box office phone number or Web site address.[111] (The advertisement may also include the address of the venue and the date and time of the production, as necessary.) This information should be prominent and easily understandable. The advertisement should also be consistent with the institutional image of the organization. For an advertisement highlighting a specific production, the tone and manner of the ad should reflect not only the personality of the organization, but the personality of that specific production as well.[112]

Advertisements consist of five types: print (newspapers and magazines), radio, television, Internet, and outdoor advertising (e.g., billboards). Print advertisements are placed by calling the newspaper or magazine and reserving a spot for the ad. Jeff Levine notes that most print media outlets ask for advertisements to be sent electronically, so the ad is either sent by e-mail or uploaded onto an FTP site.[113] For most publications, the price of the ad is directly related to the size of the ad (generally determined as a percentage of page size or number of column inches) and the frequency of the ad placement.[114] (Also, nonprofit organizations may be able to negotiate a discount with the media outlet.) For print advertisements, the layout should be simple and clear; the graphics should be compelling; and the copy should contain a headline to aid in targeting audiences and telling the story of the production. David Kitto remarks that, with the advent of graphic design programs, it is easier than ever for organizations to create advertising in-house. "Smaller organizations are best served by developing an ad template. This template is a grid onto which images can be rotated as needed. You can create effective advertising this way, and you won't have to use an outside advertising agency."[115] Appendix C provides an example of an advertisement.[116]

However, if an organization does choose to work with an advertising agency or graphic designer to create an ad, the organization should not dictate the content or the design, but should be very clear about the goal of the advertisement. Andrew Flatt explains, "It's not my job to tell a designer what to do in terms of logo placement or color or design, but it is my role to clarify the goal and expected outcome of the ad. We write a creative statement for each ad campaign about the intended audience, the projected sales that the ad needs to deliver, and the strategic positioning of the ad. Each production has its key assets—the title, the author or director, the creative team or cast, or the subject matter, among others—and emphasizing one asset over another is a decision in the development of an advertising piece. A good example of utilizing different assets can be found in our production of *Beauty and the Beast*, which used casting as a key asset on numerous occasions over its thirteen-year run on Broadway. Most recently, Donny Osmond played Gaston, and his appearance in the show became the focus of a successful three-month marketing campaign."[117]

A radio or television advertisement should also tell the story of the event. As with print advertising, radio and television ads are placed by contacting the radio or television station directly and determining a price based on the number of listeners/viewers and the number of spots (ad repetitions) the arts organization wants to purchase. In creating these types of ads, the copy should be clear and concise, mentioning the event at the beginning of the spot and repeating phone numbers and Web site addresses for greater clarity.[118] The radio or television ads should have consistent audiovisual elements to help create institutional identity for the organization; music and sound effects may be used to enhance the spot.

Internet advertising includes banner and pop-up ads purchased on Web sites, as well as the organization's Web site itself. Banner and pop-up ads are placed by contacting the host Web site. The price for a banner or pop-up ad is usually determined by the amount of traffic a particular Web site receives. A common method of pricing online ads is CPM (cost per thousand); for example, if a Web site charged $30 CPM, the arts organization would pay $30 for every 1,000 page views.[119] Banner ads, which traditionally run across the top of the Web page, but have morphed into an increasing number of shapes and sizes as Internet advertising trends continue to evolve,

consist of eye-catching graphics and text; banner ads may use Flash animation, video, or sound to attract the viewer's attention. Pop-up ads display in a new browser window and also use graphics, animation, and sound to grab attention. These ads allow the viewer to click through to a Web site for more information on the advertised production or organization. In many cases, click-through information (such as the number of click-throughs that result in a ticket purchase) is used as a benchmark of success for a given online advertising campaign.

Although not an advertisement in a traditional sense, a Web site provides an organization with a dedicated portal to promote itself using graphics, sound, and video. Web sites may contain such promotional elements as production photographs or rehearsal video footage, historical information on the production or organization, and podcasts of interviews conducted with members of the creative team.[120] A Web site should be well designed: easy to navigate, clear, and with an easy-to-follow link system for purchasing tickets. Jeff Levine describes how a Web site works for a performing arts organization: "A Web site is a huge resource of information, so you want to put all of the information on your Web site that someone might want to know. You want to set the Web site up so that it's easy to find that information. For instance, the most visited page on our site is the calendar, so clearly people are curious about what we're doing day-to-day; therefore, we want to make sure that the calendar is readable and easily found from the homepage. Give people the information they're looking for in the simplest way possible and then move them into purchasing a ticket. You want to create a site that has a nice balance of information and persuasive marketing that can get someone who just happens to be visiting the site to stop, look at a preview or article, and then decide to buy a ticket."[121]

Outdoor advertising includes billboards, transit signs, and other point-of-entry advertising (such as airports and train stations). Outdoor advertisements are placed by contacting the owner of the area where the ad would be placed (e.g., the billboard owner; the local transportation authority for subway or bus advertising) and negotiating a price for ad placement. Outdoor advertisements should be simpler than print, television, and radio advertising. Signage should use bold lettering and arresting visuals. Due to its static presence, outdoor advertising is not efficient for date-related events; it works best for advertising long-running productions or institutions.

The rate of return on an advertising campaign can range from 1 percent to 5 percent. Although advertising is often the single biggest expense in the marketing budget, a marketing director will find it difficult to assess how well that money was spent. Jeff Levine explains, "At BAM, advertising is close to 50 percent of our marketing budget. However, it's almost impossible to track the return on an advertising campaign. You try to track the response by asking people who buy tickets how they found out about the show, but that method is not reliable. Your patrons can't remember what spurred them on to order a ticket, or they remember a number of different factors, but they're only choosing one. The tracking is sketchy at best."[122]

CLASSROOM DISCUSSION

Define "advertising." What is the "call to action" of an advertisement?

What information should an advertisement include?

Describe the major characteristics and pricing policies for print ads, radio and television ads, Internet ads, and outdoor advertising.

What elements should an organization's Web site contain to make it a more effective ticket sales tool?

Promotional Partnerships

In addition to direct mail and advertising, marketing directors often create promotional partnerships to help sell tickets. Promotional partnerships are partnerships created between the performing arts organization and another corporation/organization that allows the performing arts organization to reach potential ticket buyers at a cheaper cost than direct mail or advertising. Andrew Flatt explains, "The primary purpose of creating [promotional] partnerships is to help defray our marketing costs. We want to find [promotional] partners who are trying to achieve their goals of reaching our audience, which is viewed as an asset by partners looking to reach the same target. An automotive company may want to sell its cars to our audience, or another producer may want to cross-promote and have our audience see his show. Financial service companies like Visa or American Express are great examples of [promotional] partners looking to reach our ticket buyers, who tend to have luxury dollars at their disposal. So a company like Visa may decide to share the expense of media, like radio or print ads, in which we can feature a promotional message such as, 'Purchase your *Mary Poppins* tickets using a

Visa card,' or 'Visa gets you special access to *The Lion King*.' This shared media reduces my bottom line, so I'm very happy to create this sort of [promotional] partnership—and it can be good for the brand as well."[123]

In some cases, a performing arts organization may partner directly with a media outlet. This type of promotional partnership is known as a "media sponsorship." Jeff Levine defines this relationship: "A media sponsorship is a [promotional] partnership between your organization and a media outlet, such as a radio station, publication, or Web site, to help promote an engagement. A media sponsor commits to some exposure via its outlet to help you advertise or promote your product."[124] For a nonprofit organization, this sponsorship assistance may be donated to the organization by the media outlet; in this case, the marketing director would work closely with the development department to ensure that both the marketing and development needs are being met.

Andrew Flatt states, "However, not every [promotional] partnership is media-focused. We've also done many retail partnerships over the years. For example, Marshall Field's in Chicago is using the artwork of *Mary Poppins* as the inspiration for its holiday windows. We're involved in this in several different ways. We'll have logo displays in the windows, and the original cast recording of *Mary Poppins* will be the environmental music inside and outside the store during the holiday season. Marshall Field's is also running a 'trip to New York' sweepstakes, and we're providing the prize package. It's a perfect [promotional] partnership: Marshall Field's is looking for something unique and newsworthy for its holiday windows, and we need to distribute the message nationally that *Mary Poppins* is a new Broadway blockbuster."[125]

Flatt describes the process of evaluating a potential promotional partnership: "Before beginning a partnership, you must ask, 'What does that potential partner bring to the table?' It might be media, access to that company's core audience or demographic, or inclusion in its own advertising. And we use that exact same criteria internally to determine what we are bringing to the table. Our audiences, our shows, and our brand are valuable. We use the expression 'experiences that you can't buy' to help describe what we can offer to [promotional] partners—primarily hospitality experiences, like backstage tours or meetings with actors or the creative team. Distribution is our key challenge, so we hope our partners will bring distribution to the table. Having a [promotional] partner—Visa, a retail company, an automotive company—say 'Go see *Beauty and the Beast*' is valuable to us. It not only helps to endorse us, but it also helps us get the eyeballs that we may not get otherwise.

"As an example, last year, we had just finished the cast recording of *Tarzan*, and we wanted to sell it online on iTunes. Apple did a fantastic presale campaign for us, including exposure on their home page and in e-mails. We would never have been able to afford to purchase a campaign like this. In return, Apple wanted *Tarzan* to do a cast appearance in the Apple Store in Soho. Although the appearance took some effort, it was a small price to pay relative to the promotional exposure from the iTunes campaign, so it was worth it."[126]

However, Flatt cautions against a too-intrusive partnership campaign. "At the end of the day, our purpose is to entertain people. If a [promotional] partnership were to impede that experience in any way, or feel intrusive, it would become problematic. We are constantly evaluating our partnerships to make sure that all aspects of that partnership are in line with our entertainment goals."[127]

In some cases, pieces of the promotional partnership that seem of little benefit to the show itself may add to the value of the partnership as a whole. Flatt states, "The trickiest part of a partnership is managing the amount of time it takes to execute it. If marketing is about the details, then partnerships are about the minutiae. Add to this the fact that, more often than not, the net gain of a promotional partnership is hard to quantify. The Marshall Field's partnership with *Mary Poppins* seems like the right thing to do, given the level of exposure, but because I can't really determine how well the partnership is selling tickets, I keep an eye on the staff time required to make it come together. We need to find the right balance between proven sales-driven strategies and brand-driven efforts such as these."[128]

Affinity, Viral, and "Guerrilla" Marketing

In addition to promotional partnerships, organizations utilize affinity, viral, and "guerrilla" marketing strategies to bring the organization into direct contact with desired audiences. Affinity marketing is "peer-to-peer marketing," in which an organization forms a partnership with an individual to bring information into a targeted community."[129] David Kitto describes the development of affinity marketing at the Kennedy Center: "We identify groups and organizations within our community and work through community leaders to establish and build meaningful relationships with these organizations. We then develop listservs so that we can quickly and efficiently communicate with these groups. We are now at the point where, with certain performances, we can rely exclusively on disseminating messages to these constituencies and let peer-to-peer marketing do the work. We have examples of this working so well that no paid media campaign is required to take us to sold-out status.

"For example, when we presented the China Festival, we worked with the Embassy of China to identify a particular community leader. (Our community leaders are compensated.) We drew up a contract, and he acted as a consultant for us. Our community leader for the China Festival was extraordinary. He assisted in determining the appropriate print and electronic media. He assisted with making connections to Chinese-American groups within the region. In an unusual move, he was very involved with acting as a front person for our group sales department. He delivered in excess of $70,000 worth of group sales."[130]

As another example of affinity marketing, Shorey Walker, marketing manager, creates relationships with "tastemakers" to create "buzz" around certain productions. She states, "I create lists of people who are considered tastemakers, who have a lot of influence in particular communities. Tastemakers are people like hairdressers, personal trainers, concierges, or resident assistants [RAs] in a college dorm: anyone who is in contact with many different kinds of people and who is in a position to recommend entertainment options to those people. These tastemakers are invited to see our productions so that they will tell others about how wonderful the shows are; we are explicit about this purpose in our invitation. For example, as part of my promotional campaign for an Off-Broadway musical, I sent a packet to RAs in all New York City colleges, along with posters, flyers, and buttons from the show. The package contained a cover letter with instructions for the RAs, as well as an invitation to see the show and talk to their residents about it."[131] The letter sent for this campaign can be found in appendix D.[132]

In contrast to affinity marketing, viral marketing messages are spread voluntarily by an organization's core supporters, or fans. Most viral marketing techniques utilize the Internet to spread marketing messages to the widest possible audience. For example, *Xanadu*, a Broadway musical, has created both MySpace and Facebook sites for its production, as well as dedicating space on its Web site (*http://xanaduonbroadway.com/index2.html*) for a "fANADu" photo blog and video submission contest. As fans of *Xanadu* "friend" its social networking sites or submit images to its blog, they spread the word about the musical to their online acquaintances and make more people aware of the show's existence.

Finally, marketing directors may utilize direct distribution techniques, generally known as "guerrilla" marketing. Guerrilla marketing, or grassroots marketing, typically involves giving out printed materials on the organization's programming to targeted businesses and individuals; it may also include putting up posters in targeted areas. Jeff Levine describes the distribution program at BAM: "We have inserted brochures into magazines and newspapers. We also do hand-to-hand distribution, where we send someone out with printed materials and give them out person-to-person. We do neighborhood drops, where we go to a particular neighborhood, drop [our materials] into each shop or restaurant, and see if they'll let us display our posters or leave postcards."[133]

At Disney, Andrew Flatt has a similar program: "We have street teams distributing postcards and other printed material hand-to-hand. Our street teams operate fifty-two weeks a year, but in summer we triple the staff to try to reach the increased number of tourists in New York. It's very important to us to have a face on the street saying, 'Check out this show. It's fantastic.' A street team staff member can engage in one-on-one dialogue with the potential customer and talk about which of our shows is going to be the most appropriate for that customer and why."[134]

CLASSROOM DISCUSSION

Define the following: "promotional partnerships," "affinity marketing," "viral marketing," and "guerrilla marketing."

How should you determine if a potential promotional partnership is right for your organization? How can you evaluate the success of a promotional partnership?

The Timeline for the Marketing Plan

Typically, the marketing plan is created a year before the start of the applicable season. David Kitto describes the planning process at the Kennedy Center: "Right now [July], we are receiving the final details about presentations from all of our ancillary [resident] organizations [e.g., the National Symphony and other organizations that perform in the Kennedy Center]. We then take several weeks to determine [ticket] pricing. The [marketing] planning process will take eight months, and then we'll deliver the season announcement in the form of a press

release in March."[135] However, timelines can vary from organization to organization, depending on the programming. As Jeff Levine notes, "Marketing and programming are tied at the hip. In opera, for example, the stars book up years in advance, and the audiences (or at least the subscribers) are used to buying tickets very far in advance, so you would need to begin that marketing initiative much earlier than for a dance or theater event."[136] Any form of calendar program can be used to create the timeline for the marketing plan; at BAM, the marketing director uses Microsoft Project to assign dates to steps in the marketing plan. A sample timeline for a marketing plan, including timetables for brochure production, single-ticket mailings, and advertisement creation, may be found in appendix E.

The Marketing Expense Budget and Ticket Sales Estimation

Since the goal of a marketing plan is to increase ticket sales, a ticket sales estimation must be created to generate a sales goal for the plan, and a marketing expense budget must be created to estimate the costs for implementing that plan. (Please see appendix F for a sample marketing expense budget.) The expense budget details all costs incurred on marketing activities for the organization or the production. These costs include direct mail campaign expenses, advertising costs, and promotional campaign expenses.

Once the marketing plan is created, all aspects of it are broken down into elements, with each element having an associated estimated cost. For example, if the marketing plan states that a postcard mailing will take place in October, then the cost might be estimated as follows:

$3,000 for design: Graphic element (e.g., design or photo)

$1,200 for 10,000 cards: Postcard printing (1,000 for $120)

$2,600 Postage ($0.26 for each card)

$6,800 Total cost for mailing

As with any budget, the more specific the cost estimation, the more useful the budget will be as a planning document. Also, as a planning document, the expense budget is subject to review throughout the year and may be modified if the assumptions behind the cost estimations change.

David Kitto gives an example: "For the China Festival, we were going to expand our media purchasing. We were going to be advertising in new publications, so we needed to have an understanding of the ad rates of those publications. We were planning to have television and radio advertising as well. To budget expenses for these strategies, we acquired information on the rates for these media and projected out the frequency with which we felt the ads were going to run. We then factored in the costs of creating these ads to come up with the total budget for the initiative."[137]

In order to estimate revenue, marketing directors make sales goal projections based on prior year information and a reasonable estimate for increases. The revenue from subscriptions is estimated by noting the current number of subscribers, projecting the renewal and new acquisitions rates, and determining the new goal for subscriptions. For single tickets, revenue is projected by determining the total number of single tickets available (less projected subscription sales), determining the average ticket price by show, and estimating any ticket discounts that will need to be applied for each particular show.[138] Group sales are estimated using a similar system; the marketing director projects a goal for group sales based on prior year sales and the specifics of the current season.

The concept of pricing deserves a special mention here. Effective pricing balances the perceived benefits to the consumer against the cost of the product.[139] If the consumer believes that the experience of attending the performance is worth the cost of the ticket, then she can be expected to purchase the ticket. However, if the ticket is priced too high, then the consumer may choose to attend a different event (or attend no event at all). In order to effectively create a pricing strategy, the marketing director must have a clear understanding of the mission and vision of the organization, as well as awareness of the ticket-purchasing behavior of the targeted markets. He should be aware of the expectations of sales revenue: Does the ticket sales revenue need to cover expenses for this particular performance only, or is the goal to make as much revenue as possible? The marketing director should also take into consideration the capacity of the venue, the potential market size, the type of performance being priced, and competitors' pricing policies. After determining a pricing structure, the marketing director will then scale the house, creating different prices for different areas within the venue. For example, orchestra seats for a Broadway production may cost as much as $120, but balcony seats for the same production may be $65. Typically, when pricing performances, the marketing director will also create some discounts (such as subscription discounts or discounts during a preview period) to provide an incentive to buy tickets. (Many productions may also raise prices during certain periods if ticket demand warrants, as most Broadway shows do during the holidays and other peak seasons.[140])

As an example of revenue estimation, at Manhattan Theatre Club, Dale Edwards projects a subscription goal as follows: "We know the current number of subscribers at a given point and we look at our historic rate of retention [the number of subscribers who renew from year to year] and assume a similar rate. Then we look at the percentage of new subscribers [who] we obtained in the past few years, as well as the percentage of subscribers [who] did not renew. That gives us a baseline figure for the next season. We then look at new information for the upcoming year. If we are doing a production with mass appeal, then we would anticipate that we would get more new subscribers than we did the year before. We also look at other productions in our market that are competing with us; this year [2005], the Broadway production of *The Odd Couple* [starring Nathan Lane and Matthew Broderick] has been selling very well, so we knew it would impact the market for playgoers. Lastly, we look at new marketing initiatives that we have in place for the upcoming year and try to estimate how many more subscribers [those efforts] might bring in for us. Once we come up with an estimated number of subscribers, we multiply that number by the anticipated average price of a subscription (also determined using historical data and any planned increases) to determine our budgeted revenue."[141]

Andrew Flatt describes the process for projecting ticket sales for *Mary Poppins*, which opened on Broadway in 2006: "We project sales on a fifty-two-week basis, and we have a net box office goal for every single week. The very first thing we start with is our capacity. We have X number of seats for Y performances per week for fifty-two weeks a year. If we were to sell every single seat, how much money would that bring in? Then we work backward, trying to factor in things like group sales discounts and required comps, resulting in what we hope is a realistic number of how many tickets we think we can sell. We drill down to the numbers on a performance-by-performance basis, and we use prior seasons to assess seasonal trends. We'll go back twelve years and look at *Beauty and the Beast* in its first season. Although ticket prices have changed dramatically, capacity hasn't, so that first-year history is still useful. We also look at outside factors, such as the other shows that will be opening around the same time as *Mary Poppins*. A firm understanding of the competition, which isn't restricted to other theater events, is an important factor when projecting sales."[142]

When creating revenue projections, Robert Friend cautions that these projections must be realistic: "You've got to be honest with your revenue projections. You can't be in a situation where you're making projections just to meet management's overall revenue goal in order to make management happy. You must present real sales projections, because the worst thing that can happen is for you to not meet your projected sales goals due to overzealous sales forecasting."[143]

In a nonprofit organization, after the marketing director creates the marketing expense budget and revenue estimation, it is submitted to the finance department for incorporation into the annual operating budget. At the Kennedy Center, David Kitto creates his budget at the same time that all of the other departments create their budgets. "All of our budgets are submitted to the finance department. That department is responsible for putting the entire annual budget together. Typically, all of the budgets do not align, so the budgets are reviewed and returned to the various departments, including ours, and we need to revisit our numbers. We generally go through two to three cycles of reviewing and changing, and then the budget balances. Tweaks can be made—you can tweak pricing, and you can tweak capacity—but I've learned in my time that the marketing department may be pushed to raise percentage capacity to allow more earned revenue to be added to the budget. I will make adjustments to my budget, but I am very, very careful not to exaggerate my sales projections."[144]

CLASSROOM DISCUSSION

How does an organization create a marketing
    expense budget?
How is revenue estimated?
How does an organization price its tickets?
Why is it important that the sales predictions be
    accurate?

PUBLICITY

A critical part of the marketing plan that deserves special attention is publicity. Publicity is "the media relations arm of the organization. Publicity efforts seek out positive editorial coverage in newspapers, magazines, radio, television, and online media."[145] Publicity is part of an organization's or production's overall public relations effort. Public relations is "the act of instilling a point of view about an organization or a production within the public's mind. It gives the organization or production greater visibility and helps to brand [position] the organization or production within the marketplace."[146] An organization or production may choose to create a public relations campaign "to further the positive image of the organization or production itself, to promote arts attendance in general, to support a nonprofit organization's fundraising efforts, or to emphasize the importance of art and culture in young people's lives. Individuals working on public relations campaigns work very closely with the marketing department."[147]

Publicity differs from advertising in that publicity is not paid for; the editorial coverage originates from the media outlet itself. Sandy Sawotka, director of communications at the Brooklyn Academy of Music, defines the advantage of publicity efforts over paid marketing: "Publicity has greater credibility because it is not bought. We can buy an ad for a BAM show, get a nice chunk of space in the *New York Times*, and let everyone know that we are having a show, yet the reader of the newspaper looks at that ad and knows that we bought it. Whereas if the same amount of space is taken up by editorial coverage, that means that the *New York Times* made the choice to put it there. Our show is valuable in the mind of the critic [who evaluates the performance], journalist [who writes for a magazine or a newspaper], or editor [who determines which stories run in a newspaper or magazine]. It gives us that extra credibility that advertising doesn't."[148]

However, that credibility comes at a cost: The organization cannot control the content of the editorial coverage. Tom D'Ambrosio, first associate at Richard Kornberg and Associates, points out: "When you're doing publicity, you are trying to convince a writer, an editor, or a television booker of the merits of your work. You're selling them an idea. If the person takes your idea, that's wonderful, but you are not guaranteed any results."[149] Nancy Hereford, press director of the Center Theatre Group in Los Angeles, states, "With publicity, there are no guarantees that the media will be interested in the story being pitched, or that the story being written will contain only positive messages, or that the story will run in a timely manner."[150]

Publicity strategies for an organization are typically carried out by a publicity department, headed by a publicity director or director of press. For a commercial production, a press agent is engaged to provide publicity services to the production. Nonprofit organizations that do not have their own in-house publicity department may also hire an outside press agent. For most Broadway and Off-Broadway productions (and in some nonprofit organizations), the press agent is a member of the Association of Theatrical Press Agents and Managers (ATPAM). (Please see chapter 9 for more information about ATPAM.) The responsibilities of the publicity director or press agent include: creating the publicity campaign; researching the production or organization to be promoted; researching media markets and creating a press list; writing all press releases; pitching ideas to selected media markets; creating photo and video images for use in promoting the product; arranging interviews with the creative team, press conferences, and media appearances by the cast; and working with critics and organizing press night. The following sections provide an overview of these responsibilities, as well as a timetable for a typical publicity campaign and strategies for controlling the message that the organization or production puts into the marketplace.

Creating the Publicity Campaign

To begin with, the publicity director is responsible for creating the publicity campaign for the institution or production. Depending on the needs of the campaign, the publicity director may choose to focus on different aspects of the organization or the production. For example, at BAM, Sandy Sawotka may focus on BAM "as a wide-ranging performing arts institution. We have theater, dance, and music performances, and we have community events as well, such as a trick-or-treat celebration for neighborhood children on Halloween. However, when we are working on an individual production as opposed to our organizational publicity, we focus on getting the message out about the strengths of that particular dance or theater engagement."[151]

Peter B. Carzasty, founder and principal of Geah, Limited, describes the questions he asks when creating a public relations/publicity campaign: "First, you have to have product. What are you promoting? As a public relations director, you are dealing with news, and the root of news is 'new.' What is new about your product? Is it an event? Is it a milestone for your organization? In short, why would the public, and for that matter, the media, care? After you've identified what is newsworthy about your product, you need to find out what will make it appealing to the marketplace. How will you articulate that appeal? What will be the method of communicating your articulation to the public?"[152] In answering these questions, the publicity director will be able to create the specific elements of the publicity campaign.

Researching the Production or Organization

Publicity directors must undertake research to "familiarize themselves with what is going to appear on the stage." Sawotka explains the process of researching a performance at BAM: "Let's say that we were going to present a dance company from Japan. The first step for me is to find out what the performance is all about. I would contact the company for a videotape or DVD of the performance (if one exists), as well as any written reviews or photographs. Then you start your research. It's very academic. You view the tape/DVD and read background information about the performance and the company. If the reviews are in a foreign language, then you get them translated. You may talk to journalists to see if they know anything about this company; if a journalist likes its work, you would ask her what she liked specifically."[153] Adrian Bryan-Brown, partner at Boneau/Bryan-Brown, reads the scripts, listens to demo recordings of new musicals, talks to all members of the creative team about their ideas for the production, and researches the subject of the show and other projects by the creative team. He uses the library as well as Web sites such as *Google.com*, *Broadway.com*, *Playbill.com*, and *IBDB.com* (the Internet Broadway Database) to conduct this research.[154]

Researching Media Markets and Creating a Press List

In addition to researching the production, the publicity director must also research potential media markets for pitching his ideas. Publicity directors should read all magazines and newspapers that may be interested in their organization or production. Peter B. Carzasty states, "When I was still engaged exclusively in public and media relations, I would read and review thirty to forty publications per month, from daily newspapers to monthly publications, to see the style, nuance, and elements of these publications. They all run on a template format, with slight variations. You learn the rhythm of the publication, and you get in sync with it. You learn when the publication comes out, what its emphasis is, what sections are most appropriate for you, etc. The more you know which publications are a good fit, the more efficient you become with your time and the editor's time."[155]

Adrian Bryan-Brown describes his process for researching media markets: "First, we buy all the newspapers and magazines that cover entertainment and get the names of writers of pertinent articles and reviews. When the magazine has a masthead [displaying the magazine's staff], we add the editors in different relevant departments. We then call the appropriate desk at the paper and ask where and how the editors and writers would like to receive press materials. Many reporters work from their homes and would prefer to get invitations and solicitations by e-mail since they rarely go into the office to pick up their mail. Web sites often have contact information for writers as well. As you build a relationship with a writer, you can determine the best way to approach him. We also video-record the closing credits of programs like NBC's *The Today Show* or *CBS Evening News* on Thursdays or Fridays, when the crawl [the credits] runs the complete staff. Sometimes, when a production is in early previews, you have a lot of tickets to sell, so you may want to ask anyone who works at an important news program to see the show, because that person will talk about it in the workplace. We also call the shows to find out if they have an internal system for extending invitations and sharing information with the staff."[156]

If a publicity director is working with a company that is touring, such as a dance company, she will need to conduct this research on every market in which the company performs. In this case, the publicity director may rely on the knowledge of the publicity directors at the venues where the company will be playing.

As the publicity director researches media markets, she will begin compiling a press list for use in distributing her pitches. A press list contains contact information for journalists and editors, including phone numbers and e-mail addresses. Most organizations use a database program to compile and organize their lists; Adrian Bryan-Brown uses ContactEase to manage his list, while BAM uses a database called ACT, which also allows the publicity director to print mailing labels and e-mail press releases directly from the database.[157] In addition to compiling their own lists, organizations may find contact information for journalists, as well as information on the areas that they write about, in publications such as *Bacon's Media Directories* (and the associated Bacon's Media Database), the *PartyLine*, and the *Bulldog Reporter*. Adrian Bryan-Brown notes, "If a campaign involves a specific geographical market where our shows don't usually

play, it is sometimes helpful to build a list using these publications."[158] Journalists and editors may also contact an organization directly and ask to be placed on the press list.

Although most organizations compile contact information for press lists over many years, the press list must be constantly updated to add new publications, as well as to ensure that the contact information in the list is accurate and that all publications still belong on the list (e.g., they have not gone out of business). Sandy Sawotka notes the importance of a "clean" and detailed list, stating, "It's a waste of time if your list is reaching people who are no longer working for that publication, or have no interest in your organization. You also want to know what your journalist writes about before you pitch the story, because otherwise you're going to sound like a fool. You don't want to waste anyone's time, and you don't want to insult anyone."[159]

Writing the Press Release

After the press list has been compiled, the publicity director creates the main tool of her pitch: the press release. A press release provides basic information about a production or organization and communicates the newsworthy aspects of the work. Figure 7.7 is an example of a press release announcing the new Broadway production of *Wicked*.[160]

Nancy Hereford describes the ideal press release: "The press release is the basic tool for communicating with the media, and its style should be basic and clear and concise. Flowery prose and exaggerated pronouncements should not be in a press release. The 'rules' of a good release are to use the four 'Ws' and one 'H': Who, What, Where, When, and How? Answers to these questions should occur in the first few paragraphs. Perhaps most importantly, the press release has to be newsworthy. If there is no news, or the press release is poorly written or organized, the release is likely to be tossed in the trashcan. The press release should always contain a name and phone number/e-mail address that the media can use to follow up on the information in the release. It's usually better if the press release is one page long, but there are times (season releases, major announcements) when the press release can be longer to accommodate all of the information."[161]

Peter B. Carzasty adds, "Once you get the basics [who, what, where, when, and how] out of the way, the press release becomes a more nuanced advocate of your product. The narrative contains the descriptive element of the event that might make it of interest to a writer or editor. You need to answer

Fig. 7.7. Sample Press Release

July 1, 2003   From: Bob Fennell, Marc Thibodeau

<u>For immediate release, please</u>

SO MUCH HAPPENED IN OZ BEFORE DOROTHY DROPPED IN . . .

* * *

"WICKED"

A NEW MUSICAL
BY STEPHEN SCHWARTZ AND WINNIE HOLZMAN
BASED ON THE NOVEL BY GREGORY MAGUIRE
BEGINS PREVIEWS AT BROADWAY'S GERSHWIN THEATRE
ON TUESDAY, OCTOBER 7, 2003

* * *

KRISTIN CHENOWETH AND IDINA MENZEL STAR
WITH CAROLE SHELLEY, NORBERT LEO BUTZ
AND ROBERT MORSE AS THE WIZARD

* * *

WITH CHOREOGRAPHY BY WAYNE CILENTO,
THE PRODUCTION is DIRECTED BY JOE MANTELLO
And Will Have its official opening on THURSDAY, October 30

WICKED, a new musical with music and lyrics by **Stephen Schwartz** (*Godspell*, *Pippin*, Academy Award winner for *Pocahontas* and *Prince of Egypt*) and book by **Winnie Holzman** ("My So Called Life," "Once And Again" and "thirtysomething") based on the 1995 novel by Gregory Maguire, will begin Broadway previews on Tuesday, October 7 at the Gershwin Theatre (242 West 51st Street). The musical is directed by 2003 Tony Award-winner **Joe Mantello** (*Take Me Out*, *Frankie and Johnny in the Clair de Lune*, *A Man of No Importance*) and choreographed by **Wayne Cilento** (*Aida*, *The Who's Tommy*, *How To Succeed . . .*). **WICKED**, the untold story of the witches of Oz, is being produced by Marc Platt, Universal Pictures, The Araca Group, Jon B. Platt and David Stone and comes to Broadway following a sold out, smash-hit San Francisco engagement (May 28–June 29). The new musical will have its official Broadway opening on Thursday, October 30.

WICKED stars Tony Award winner **Kristin Chenoweth** (Broadway's *You're a Good Man Charlie Brown* and Marian in the recent Disney television presentation of "The Music Man") as Glinda and Tony Award nominee **Idina Menzel** (Maureen in the original cast of *Rent*, she was also seen on Broadway in *Aida*) as Elphaba. Two-time Tony Award winner **Robert Morse** (the original *How To Succeed in Business . . .* and *Tru*) plays the Wizard. **WICKED** also stars Tony Award winner **Carole Shelley** (the original Broadway production and film of *The Odd Couple* as well as the original Broadway *The Elephant Man*) as Madame Morrible; Tony Award-nominee **Norbert Leo Butz** (Broadway's *Thou Shalt Not* and Off-Broadway's *The Last Five Years*) as Fiyero; **Michelle Federer** as Nessarose; **John Horton** (recently on Broadway in *Noises Off* and *Kiss Me, Kate*) as Doctor Dillamond; and **Kirk McDonald** (Broadway's *Boys from Syracuse* and *Parade*) as Boq.

Long before Dorothy drops in, two other girls meet in the land of Oz. One, born with emerald-green skin, is smart, fiery and misunderstood. The other is beautiful, ambitious and very popular. **WICKED** tells the story of their remarkable odyssey, how these two unlikely friends grow to become the Wicked Witch of the West and Glinda the Good Witch.

WICKED features set design by **Eugene Lee** (*Ragtime*, *Show Boat* and the original Broadway production of *Sweeney Todd*), costume design by **Susan Hilferty** (the recent *Into the Woods*), lighting design by **Kenneth Posner** (*Hairspray*) and sound design by **Tony Meola** (the current *Man of La Mancha*). **Stephen Oremus** is the show's musical director. Orchestrations are by **William David Brohn**, with dance arrangements by **Jim Abbott**.

Also featured in the cast of **WICKED** will be **Ioana Alfonso**, **Ben Cameron**, **Cristy Candler**, **Mellissa Bell Chait**, **Marcus Choi**, **Kristoffer Cusick**, **Kathy Deitch**, **Melissa Fahn**, **Rhett George**, **Kristen Lee Gorski**, **Manuel Herrera**, **Kisha Howard**, **LJ Jellison**, **Sean McCourt**, **Corrine McFadden**, **Mark Myars**, **Jan Neuberger**, **Walter Winston ONeil**, **Andrew Palermo**, **Andy Pellick**, **Michael Seelbach**, **Lorna Ventura** and **Derrick Williams**.

WICKED begins Broadway previews on Tuesday, October 7 at the Gershwin Theatre, 242 West 51st Street, and will have its official press opening on Thursday, October 30. The performance schedule is Tuesday evenings at 7 PM; Wednesday through Saturday evenings at 8 PM; matinees on Wednesdays and Saturdays at 2 PM; Sundays at 3 PM. The scale of prices is $40–$100. Tickets are available through Ticketmaster, 212-307-4100 (or you may visit www.ticketmaster.com) beginning June 29. The Gershwin Theatre box office opens on August 18.

# # #

the question, 'What are the virtues or the inherent characteristics of this production that separate it from other events that are happening?' This builds the case as to the 'news value' and therefore supports the call for coverage. A successful media person is like a good lawyer: Each has to build a case to gain the confidence of the individual(s) whom they are trying to convince to reach a positive outcome."[162]

Pitching to the Media

As part of obtaining media coverage of his production or organization, a publicist must pitch to a writer, critic, or editor. The purpose of the pitch is to convince a media outlet to provide editorial coverage on the desired product. A pitch may be made on the telephone, by e-mail, or by mail. If a pitch is made by e-mail or mail, it may take the form of a pitch letter. A pitch letter outlines the main points of the pitch, detailing the reasons that a journalist or editor should write a story about a particular production or organization. Peter B. Carzasty believes that "a pitch letter should be short and succinct. It should contain compelling information structured in a format that the editor can potentially see as the basis for an editorial story. E-mail should be structured the same way as regular mail, as a formal letter. You should use complete and discernable sentences, as well as proper punctuation."[163]

Figure 7.8 provides a sample of a pitch letter.[164] Carzasty provides a note on this particular letter: "The basis of the letter is presented as a narrative story—supplying history and facts, as well as the aspirational aspects of the new New Jersey Performing Arts Center. Like a good story, it has a past and present, and raises potential issues for the future. A successful pitch letter, like a good lawyer in the courtroom, should raise questions while always knowing what the potential answers might be. This letter resulted in a page-one story in the *New York Times*, a 14-minute feature on *CBS News Sunday Morning*, and stories in *USA Today* and the *Wall Street Journal*."[165]

Fig. 7.8. Sample Pitch Letter

Dear [name],

Near the shores of the Passaic River in Newark, New Jersey, one of the nation's most maligned cities, rises the last major American arts complex to open in the 20th century. It has been built through an extraordinary leap of faith, undertaken by a unique partnership between the public and private sectors.

Newark is a city where 26.3 percent of families live below the poverty level and 12.8 percent of the population is unemployed; a city still branded with the memory of the 1967 riots. And yet, just one decade after then-governor Thomas Kean announced plans to create the New Jersey Performing Arts Center (NJPAC), the $180 million complex will open in downtown Newark on October 18, 1997. As the first in a series of urban renewal projects slated to cost another quarter of a billion dollars, NJPAC qualifies as more than a symbol of civic optimism. In a very real sense, the future of Newark itself rests on NJPAC.

How did a new, untested cultural institution take on this leading role, supported not only by government but by the private sector as well? Apart from Prudential Insurance, Newark has few corporate citizens. Yet NJPAC has attracted a host of powerful CEO's and business leaders: Dr. P. Roy Vagelos (Merck & Co., Inc.), Percy Chubb III (The Chubb Corporation), Albert R. Gamper (The CIT Group, Inc.), Melvin R. Goodes (Warner-Lambert Company), Jon S. Corzine (Goldman, Sachs & Company), among others.

On the heels of the successful downtown revitalization of the city of Cleveland, ignited by the arts, Newark is attempting to repeat that city's success. This project is but one example of how America's urban environments are trying to address their relevance. Newark is trying to address their divergent community, their past, and the need to reach ahead into the future—at the close of this century. How are they doing it, and what will the impact be on the people who remember the city's past? Is there a relationship between the old, troubled perception of the city and the future embodied in this center?

A troubled city; a daring group of investors, public and private; a high-risk plan that lays everything on the arts: these are the elements of an exciting and far-reaching story, whose outcome has yet to be decided.

Hopefully the national implications of this story will be of interest to your readership. To that end, I will be contacting you shortly to check your interest.

Sincerely,

Peter B. Carzasty

The publicity director may also choose to distribute the press release directly to begin the pitching process. (Some public relations professionals may choose to send a "tickler" [teasing preview] e-mail in advance of a press release, but such e-mails are generally saved for events that the journalist or editor may need to reserve on his calendar, such as a gala.[166]) Many media outlets prefer to receive press releases by e-mail, but some do require the releases to be sent by regular mail. The publicity director should note the preference of the journalist or editor and mail accordingly. The press release may also be sent via a service like PR Newswire, which sends the press release to an enormous number of media outlets. "Services like PR Newswire serve as an effective insurance policy. The reach of the service means that Yahoo, Google, and other search engines are likely to pick up the information in the release. However, for most arts groups and shows, PR Newswire is too expensive to be a practical tool."[167]

In addition to the press release, the publicity director may compile a press packet. Nancy Hereford details the contents of a press packet: "The press packet can take on many forms. It can be as simple as a few production photos and an information sheet that contains the basics of the production (play title, billing, actors), the performance dates and times, and the ticket prices. If a program (playbill) exists, the combination of photos, an information sheet, and a program is a fairly comprehensive press packet. More detailed press packets are developed for large events such as the anniversaries or opening of a new theater, or the establishment of a major new program. These kits should provide as much background as possible about the subject and contain visuals that support the subject."[168] Press packets may be compiled and sent by either regular mail or e-mail.

The pitch may begin with the press release and press packets, but the publicity director must also personally pitch the production or organization to the specific journalist or editor. Tom D'Ambrosio describes his process for pitching a production: "You need to know the specific tastes of the writer [who] you're pitching to. You need to read everything by that writer. If you think that a project is going to appeal to his specific taste, then you should pitch to that writer, appealing to his own aesthetic or his reader's aesthetic. You need to use your relationship with the writer to make a specific plea to see the show. You must be honest with the writer, stating truthful reasons that your production is worth seeing, and (if you mean it) you should also add that

your show is very good. Once you've been working with writers long enough, you develop a relationship with them, and they listen to your opinion; even if a writer doesn't agree with you, it's fine, as long as you continue to be truthful in your relationship with that writer."[169]

Bob Fennell, co-owner and press representative at The Publicity Office, agrees and adds a note about trust: "You can't misrepresent yourself with a writer because that will come back to haunt you. You can't promise somebody something that you're not going to deliver. For example, if you were pitching an interview with a star, your job is to be accurate and let the writer know what the parameters of the interview would be, and at the same time make them realize that this interview could be an interesting story and one that is appropriate for their outlet. But you should never say 'This person's going to give you a tour of her home' if this person has absolutely no intention of letting the writer into her house. The writer won't take your call the next time. The relationship between the publicist and the writer has got to be a trusting one. And you've got to always remember that when you're selling a story, you're going to be trying to sell stories to the same person for the rest of your career—you've got to make sure you don't close the door on that relationship by being untruthful."[170]

Publicists should try to be as creative as possible when thinking of ideas to pitch, as coverage of the arts in mainstream media has become more competitive and more performing arts organizations are trying to get editorial coverage. Philip Rinaldi, at Philip Rinaldi Publicity, provides an example of a creative pitch: "My associate, Barbara Carroll, and I were working on *The Light in the Piazza* and *The Glass Menagerie* at the same time, and Barbara came up with the idea of going to the *New York Times* with a story about actors playing characters who were mentally or physically challenged. We partnered with *The Pillowman*, and the story went forward, with Michael Stuhlbarg, Sarah Paulson, and Kelli O'Hara interviewed about playing these particular parts in a feature story in the Sunday Arts & Leisure section."[171]

Although a publicity director should be aggressive in pitching the story to carefully researched media outlets, he should be wary of harassing the journalist or editor and discouraging her from writing about the production. Tiki Davies, vice president of the press office at the Kennedy Center, provides some guidelines for follow-up in pitching a story: "You make a pitch, either by e-mail or by phone, and you hopefully wait for an answer for a day or two—obviously you do this with enough lead time that it's not a problem—and then you follow up with a phone call. You say, 'I hope you got my e-mail, and I wanted to check with you to see if you're really interested.' You need to speak to the other person directly, so obviously you would never leave this message on voice mail. And then you wait a couple of days, and then you go [call] again. If you've got any level of sensitivity, you're going to know when you're starting to stalk the writers. Basically what you're looking for is a 'yes' or a 'no.' Don't ask for anything more complicated than that, because to tell the truth, the writer knows if he wants to do it or not. If he's saying to you, 'You know, it does sound interesting but I don't think I know enough,' he'll give you a hint if he really wants to do it. But if he's saying 'I'll get back to you, I'll get back to you,' he doesn't want to do it, and he just doesn't know how to say no to you. When dealing with writers and editors, you have to decide when your drop-dead response date is, and what your backup plan is going to be if you don't get a commitment for a story by that time."[172]

As a summation of all of these points, Peter B. Carzasty shares his dos and don'ts of a successful pitch:

DO:

Know the outlet before you pitch it.

Make sure your communication has the correct name and title.

Know who you are pitching and his/her position.

Reduce your story to key points—three at most.

State clearly and succinctly why your story is relevant and newsworthy.

Demonstrate if there is a trend to pick up on.

Relate other examples of coverage, if needed as references.

Know when it's best to contact the media person.

Write handwritten thank-you notes.

DON'T:

Misspell or use improper grammar.

Present sloppy materials.

Call unless you've thought it through.

Leave long, unfocused messages.

Overstate your case.

Act like a person of entitlement.

Nag.

Plead or beg.

React negatively to rejection.[173]

Creating Photo and Video Images for Distribution

Most press packets contain photos, if they are available. For example, at BAM, Sandy Sawotka obtains photos initially by requesting them directly from the company, as most of BAM's productions have been previously produced; these photos are used for promotion of the engagement before the company arrives at BAM.[174] However, if no photos exist, the publicity director will need to arrange a photo call or photo shoot. Adrian Bryan-Brown describes the process of arranging photo shoots and gives some tips for a successful shoot:

"If a show is in rehearsals or previews, we hire a photographer to take photographs. We try to do this in two ways. Ideally, the photographer shoots the show at a run-through in the rehearsal and/or on stage at the theater in full costume. We will also arrange a setup session under controlled conditions. There may be an aesthetic and artistic preference for images that capture the 'real' live moment of performance; however, there are often many variables that may make it impossible to catch striking, attractive images, so that we need to do setups. For example, the show may be literally too dark, with very low lighting levels, meaning that supplemental lighting is required. The stage makeup may be too extreme for a close-up photograph (but look great to an audience in the theater). With a setup, head microphones can be removed, and costumes and hair can be set correctly.

"The photographer can shoot on film or digitally. Sometimes the quality of the lighting may dictate that film must be used to show a warmer image; for example, if the light is too blue, it may not be easily corrected in a digital image.

"On a theatrical production, you need to first discuss, with the director and stage management, a good time to take photographs—either during a dress rehearsal or from the audience (quietly) during an early preview. You will be under pressure to get the images as soon as possible to make them available for as many press deadlines as you can. It is also smart to check with the designers that their sets, costumes, lighting, and hair are far enough along in the creative process to be photographed. Ideally, the photographer will see a run of the show before shooting it.

"The regulations for dealing with a photo shoot vary depending where and how the production is being shot. The labor rules for shooting on Broadway, Off-Broadway, and in a rehearsal room are all slightly different. The basic rule is that the company and house staff must be given twenty-four hours' notice (even for a 'candid' run-through shoot).

"Ideally, the photographer should shoot a run-through and do setups at a later time, filling in the gaps of what wasn't possible during the run. A shot list should be prepared describing who is in a scene and the particular moment or blocking. Sometimes it is helpful to have a line of dialogue from the play so the actors can run the moment as if performing it in the show. The actors should be notified in advance of what the shot list is, and a stage manager should work out the running order to make efficient use of everyone's time. The order he comes up with should involve the minimal amount of set and costume changes and may not be in the chronological order of the actual show.

"Don't be too ambitious on the list. The time taken for a photo call is considered very valuable— you are often cutting into precious rehearsal time. There is a temptation to try to cover everything that happens in the show. Focus on what you really need—key moments and images with the principal actors. If you rush the process, chances are you won't get some of the important photographs you need.

"In our office, all images are converted to digital images as the end result. We e-mail images directly [as JPEG files]. We may also send out a CD-R with images. We can also upload images to a secure site, where photo editors can retrieve them. If you do use a site, make sure you know who is taking the images, so you have an idea of where and how they are being used."[175]

In some organizations, photographers from major media outlets may take photos of the production alongside the organization's photographer. Nancy Hereford describes how this process works at Center Theatre Group: "Prior to the run-through, a half-hour of setup photos takes place. Certain key scenes from the production are selected (again, after discussions with the director and the production stage manager). To avoid a stagy, static 'setup' look to the photos, the actors run through these scenes (which are really just portions of scenes). And, when necessary, a brighter light cue is used for the setups than what is used in the actual production. Several major newspapers are invited to the setups to shoot their own art alongside our photographers. (The *Los Angeles Times'* policy is that they must shoot their own art.) By choosing the setups and with optimum lighting conditions, we can somewhat control what photographs the papers use and the quality of these photographs. After the setups, the newspaper photographers leave and only our photographer shoots the run-through."[176]

For television and radio coverage, publicity directors may create video news releases (VNRs). "A VNR is almost equivalent to a press release on videotape [or DVD]."[177] The organization or production will arrange for part of the production to be filmed and distributed to various media outlets. Adrian Bryan-Brown describes the benefits of creating VNRs: "VNRs are an important tool in marketing theater, especially for larger plays and musicals. Broadcast TV and radio, cable, and online sites are able to play clips of a show to literally millions of people, with clearance from labor unions under various conditions and with a minimal financial cost. By providing footage, rather than allowing crews to come in and shoot the show, you are able to maintain a quality of sound and audio, and determine which moments from the show will be seen. Since the play or musical is not being staged for filming, it is important not only to choose telegenic moments from the show, but also to make sure, especially on a musical, that you have a good feed from the sound board as well."[178] As with photo shoots, it is important to follow Actors' Equity and IATSE regulations on using recordings of the production (usually referred to as B-roll footage); typically, no more than thirty minutes of the production may be filmed, and only two or three minutes may be aired without compensation to the union members.[179]

In addition to VNRs, publicists may also arrange for public service announcements (PSAs) to be created and run on television or radio stations. PSAs are five-to seven-second noncommercial announcements that are run free of charge on television or radio stations as a service to the public; the publicist will work with the organization's advertising agency or marketing director to negotiate a certain number of PSAs in addition to the advertising purchased from the television and radio stations. Bill Miller, publicist at AWA Touring Services, states, "I negotiate PSAs as much as I can, knowing television stations have PSA time in their logs [airtime dedicated to PSAs]. For example, I'll contact the CBS station in a local market: 'We're bringing in *The Phantom of the Opera* for a monthlong engagement to your city. I'd like to negotiate a schedule of PSA spots to run beginning four weeks prior to the engagement through closing.'

I'll arrange to attach the *Phantom* mask and logo to the visual on these announcements that tell viewers that they're watching CBS. That kind of exposure translates into a lot of added value."[180]

Arranging Interviews, Press Conferences, and Media Appearances

If a pitch is successful, the publicity director may need to arrange an interview with an artist or a member of the production's creative team. Bob Fennell describes the process of arranging an interview: "You begin by giving the appropriate background information on the production and on the interviewee to the person who's doing the interview. You might also have a conversation with the interviewee and give him a couple of talking points. If you know that there are sensitive issues that might come up in the interview, you might discuss those with the interviewee. You make sure that the interview is scheduled for an appropriate amount of time to suit both parties; you don't want to schedule a half-hour interview and fear that the person being interviewed is going to skip out after twenty minutes. You then check in with both parties sometime after the interview. I like to call the interviewee first and ask, 'How did it go? Any issues?' Then I might call the person who's done the interview and say, 'So-and-so said she had a great conversation with you. One thing she mentioned was that she wanted to make sure that a certain portion of it was off the record (not for publication).' I do advise people not to go off the record, because you just never know. If something is said, it's said, and it can be difficult to pull it back afterwards. You have to know the interviewer and really trust her before you should go off the record."[181]

Adrian Bryan-Brown adds some specifics for scheduling interviews: "Scheduling interviews is a very time-consuming and labor-intensive process. No one is usually contractually obliged to do every interview you might want him to do. Actors normally recognize that it is important for their own profile and that of the show to do press, but they are also under a lot of pressure at the time you need them. Actors rarely want to do press on their day off (the day when there are no performances or rehearsals, usually Mondays). They often don't want to do interviews on matinee days because they want to rest between performances. It's important to work with stage management on the schedule. Plan a convenient location for the interview and a place that is quiet and without distraction. The actor may not want to reveal his home or dressing room to a stranger."[182]

In lieu of an individual interview or announcement, an organization or production may schedule a press conference. In a press conference, representatives from various media outlets meet and are presented with an announcement or a significant individual; at the end of the presentation, the representatives may ask questions of designated personnel. Nancy Hereford notes that press conferences in the performing arts are rare and should only be used on notable occasions: "Press conferences should be used rarely, and only if the news is major. Most of the time a big story can be handled better on a one-on-one basis with the media outlet. This manner allows in-depth questions and answers that wouldn't be possible in a group environment. And, in a city as large and spread out as Los Angeles, if the news is not extraordinary, you'll anger those journalists who had to fight traffic to arrive at the press conference. However, there are some circumstances where a press conference makes sense. We had a major celebrity, Al Pacino, who was appearing in one of our productions, and he wanted to talk with all the press at the same time. With the status of Pacino, even in Hollywood, the press conference made sense."[183]

In addition to interviews, publicists may also schedule television and radio appearances in which scenes or musical numbers from a production may be performed. Although performers and other needed staff members (such as wardrobe and makeup crew) are usually compensated for such media appearances, the promotional benefits of appearing on radio or television can be extensive, as Adrian Bryan-Brown notes: "When the Broadway cast of the musical *Titanic* appeared on Rosie O'Donnell's morning talk show, the stirring performance and lavish words of praise from Rosie lead to a boost in ticket sales, countering the mostly negative reviews the show had received from the Broadway newspaper critics. More recently, an extended cast appearance by *The Color Purple* on Oprah Winfrey's show (who is widely known as a producer of the musical) led to more than $1 million in single-ticket sales in the days following. The national appearances, which still carried production costs for the performers, dressers, and other show crew members, cost much less than it would to run a typical thirty-second television commercial on these particular shows—in 2005, a national spot on Oprah would cost over $100,000."[184]

Creating the Program or Playbill

As well as dealing with the press, the publicity director is often responsible for creating the playbill or program for the production. Publicists must obtain production information from the creative team, as well as biographical information for all performers and creative staff working on the show. William Nedved, publicist at Steppenwolf Theatre Company, describes the creation of the program at his theater: "We do our programs in-house. It allows us to control the content and get relevant information to our audience. We request the biographies from the artists or their agents several weeks in advance. Copy is distributed to our marketing and communications team, and then to the entire staff for proofing to ensure that the information is correct. It receives an additional round of proofing from senior staff before going to our graphic designer for design and printing."[185]

Adrian Bryan-Brown shares his process for creating the *Playbill*® for a Broadway production: "Get confirmation from your general managers and producers on who is contractually entitled to a biography in the *Playbill*® program. You need to determine how much space you have in the program to allocate for biographies. For example, taking the standard of the Broadway *Playbill*®, you have a certain number of pages you can use for the 'Who's Who' (bios), beyond which there is a supplemental weekly cost. Check with general management and stage management that no one has been left out and no one has a contractual biography length. (Actors' Equity mandates that every member must have a biography that should be distributed in a free program to an audience member. The length of the biography is not stipulated by the union.) Ask the actors and other members of the production team (or their representatives) for their biographies, letting them know how many words they can have. You may want to offer to write the bio for them from résumé information. Make sure you allow yourself enough time to collect and edit biographies, if necessary, to meet your deadlines. You must always get approvals on any edits or cuts."[186] In addition to the biographies, the publicist determines which unions must be mentioned in the program whenever their members are employed on a production. These unions must be credited with logos or other contractually specified wording.

Working with Critics and Organizing Press Night

Also, in addition to pitching writers and editors, publicity directors pitch critics, who are responsible for reviewing the production. A good review will spur ticket sales, while a bad review may cause a production to lose ticket sales. Many media outlets may assign a critic to review a production automatically, especially if the production is a major one; however, for many smaller organizations and those in crowded performing arts markets (like Chicago or New York City), critics must be pitched in the same manner as writers and editors.

Critics are typically invited to a production's press night, a performance specifically dedicated for reviewers. Nancy Hereford describes her strategies for ensuring a successful press night: "Press night is all about seating the press in the best seats possible, making sure that they have been given a press kit (with photos) and a program, that they have been able to easily pick up their tickets at the press table, and that they have been welcomed warmly to the theater. The key to success in all this is to be very careful with everything. Do the seating yourself; do not have the box office do it. Make sure the [ticket] envelopes are marked neatly with the correct spelling of the names. Make sure that the press table is manned with enough people so that a long line does not form. Have enough press kits and programs at hand. Greet the press with a smile. You can briefly chitchat, but don't ignore the next person in line. Handle any problem with a smile and a solution. Keep extra tickets available if someone shows up without having made a reservation. Keep it all flowing. If a major critic is going to be late, try to have the stage manager hold the curtain a few minutes (but not too long). At intermission and after the show, be visible in the lobby or outside the theater in case the critics have any questions, but do not ask them what they thought of the play! You may also receive phone calls the next morning with questions. Sometimes the critic will ask to read a script. Permission must be obtained from the playwright for this. If changes have been made in the script during rehearsals, be sure to give the critic the most current version of the script."[187] Although the publicity director can control the quality of the critic's experience during press night, she cannot control the critic's opinion; in the end, only the quality of the production and the critic's own taste determine whether a review is positive or negative.

The Timetable of a Publicity Campaign

Nancy Hereford provides a description of a typical publicity campaign in a nutshell:

• The publicity campaign begins with pitching, pitching, pitching . . . and more pitching. The major job of a press agent is to pitch story ideas to a journalist (either a writer or an editor). For long-lead magazines (magazines which require that stories be pitched far in advance of publication date), pitching can start as early as six months in advance of the presentation if the information about the presentation is available (selection of the play, performance dates, casting, etc.).

- In order to begin the long-lead pitching, research and gathering of materials need to happen, and an overall strategy should be developed that outlines the strengths of the production, what is 'sellable,' what makes a good story. Through this process, language is developed that describes the production; this is used in all the press releases.
- Magazines with three-month leads or less are next for pitching stories, followed by newspapers, then television and radio as the time draws nearer to the presentation dates.
- Photographs are important tools of publicity. At CTG [Center Theater Group], 90 percent of the time the productions are new, so production photos don't exist at the beginning of the publicity campaign. [Actor] headshots or photos taken in rehearsal can be used with early press releases. As soon as the production photo call takes place, there should be a distribution of these photos.
- Invitations to the press should be mailed four weeks (not later than three weeks) in advance of the press night/opening night.
- If social or celebrity coverage is possible, those journalists should be contacted two to three weeks in advance of the opening (as soon as the guest list starts to gel). A candid photographer should be hired for the opening to supply photos to these journalists.
- Video of the show should be taken during the preview period and distributed around the opening night.
- Once a show opens, the press agent's job is not over. Keep on pitching.[188]

Controlling the Message

Although publicity directors try to control the message that they are communicating, the process of dealing with writers, editors, and critics ensures that they are not always able to control that message. As Nancy Hereford states, "There is no real way to 'control' how the message will appear in the media. But you can increase the odds that the message will be handled fairly if: the message is clear and accurate and honest; the actions of the theater match up with the rhetoric (actions do speak louder than words); and the journalist has a relationship with the theater

and has been regularly fed information and invited to see the productions.

"However, if 'bad' news is anticipated, and this news affects the public in any way (canceled performances, canceled production, etc.), it is best to take control of the news and release it before a reporter discovers it. Gather the information, including what remedies the theater plans to put into place, and move swiftly. Select a journalist you trust as fair and objective and tell the story as openly as possible. Do not lie. If you can't talk about certain issues, explain why you can't discuss those issues.

"If bad news leaks out and appears in the media before you are prepared to deal with it, move quickly to respond, but don't respond in a 'defensive' mode. Follow the steps in the previous paragraph, provide the facts and the plans, and set up interviews with key artistic and/or management personnel.

"When the news improves, make sure that the positive information is released. Perhaps most importantly, make sure that the operating decisions made by the management of the theater are in line with good public relations for the theater. Speak out if there is a discrepancy. Try to stop the bad news before it has time to form."[189]

One of the most successful methods of distributing information to a vast quantity of people is also the most uncontrollable: the Internet. Bob Fennell describes the positive and negative sides of the Web: "The Internet is sort of a wonderful monster: You can put something out there immediately, but at the same time, if something's being put out there that's not factual, you have to react very quickly to stop it from spreading. The Internet has the news outlets, but then there are also the chat rooms, in which you've got people posting anonymously and sometimes irresponsibly. In chat rooms, many people don't want to be responsible—that's part of the thrill of those Web sites. So you've got to monitor that stuff, and you've got to react quickly if someone's putting something out on the Internet that's not true.

"We do keep an eye on the chat rooms. Our office checks in sometimes, and there are also people in general managers' and producers' offices who will contact us if they see something on a chat site that they think is problematic. I've had many occasions when there's been something posted that's really problematic for no other reason than that it's not true. It could be casting information that's not true, or it could be casting information that's premature; [for example,] the actor's in the middle of negotiating a contract. Those things can be problematic, because it's not just us who's reading this news, but it's also reporters. Then we get a call: 'I hear so-and-so has been cast in such-and-such.' You've then got to say to the reporter, 'Well, actually that actor has not been cast yet, and he might not be at all.' And, if this premature casting gets written about, that might be an even worse problem because the reporter is making the casting more of a done deal than the producers want it to be, and more of a done deal than the actor and his reps want it to be.

"If a situation like this happens, the first thing you can do is deal with calls as you get them and deal with them intelligently. You can then contact the administrators of the Web site and say that the information posted is problematic and untrue. A lot of times they want to have good relationships with the press agents, so they'll deal with it [take down the information]. There's also been a couple of times where I've sent a statement to the administrators and asked them to put it up on the Web site.

"However, if somebody posts information that's actually true, most people understand that there's not a lot of action to be taken. Even inflammatory or negative reviews are opinions, and as far as I'm concerned, there's not much we can do about that. If, in somebody's review, she says that an actor was obviously drunk on stage, that's a different matter. But if her review consists of, 'I didn't like the costumes, I didn't like the color of the sets,' that's someone's opinion, and we're never going to be able to stop that. That's just part and parcel of the way the game is played. It's about word of mouth that is now posted in a public forum for everybody to see. It used to be that somebody would leave a show in previews and talk to their five friends about it, and now they can post anonymously on a message board and it's seen by five thousand people. That's just part of life now and there's nothing we can do about that."[190]

CLASSROOM DISCUSSION

Define the following: "publicity," "public relations," "press release," "pitch letter," "VNR," and "PSA."

How does publicity differ from advertising?

What resources might a publicist use to research media markets?

What is the importance of having a clean press list?

What should a press release contain?

What might a press packet contain?

Name the dos and don'ts of a successful pitch.

What factors should be considered when setting up a photo or video shoot?

What is the process for setting up and following up an interview?

What is the process for creating a playbill for a production?

What strategies help ensure a successful press night?

How does a publicist "control the message"?

How should a publicist handle "bad publicity"?

NOTES
1. The authors wish to thank the following contributors to this chapter: Adrian Bryan-Brown, Eugene Carr, Peter B. Carzasty, Tom D'Ambrosio, Tiki Davies, Dale Edwards, Bob Fennell, Sean Patrick Flahaven, Andrew Flatt, Robert Friend, Jennie Greer, Richard Grossberg, Nancy Hereford, David Kitto, Jeff Levine, Bill Miller, Will Nedved, Amanda Pekoe, Gary Powers, Philip Rinaldi, Janette Roush, Sandy Sawotka, Shorey Walker, and Donna Walker-Kuhne.
2. Janette Roush, interview with Christopher Thomasson, October 26, 2005.
3. Gary Powers, interview with author, June 7, 2006.
4. The authors would like to thank Richard Grossberg for allowing us to reproduce a copy of this ticket.
5. Dale Edwards, interview with Christopher Thomasson, November 10, 2005.
6. Powers, "Interview."
7. Edwards, "Interview."
8. The authors would like to thank Richard Grossberg for allowing us to reproduce a copy of this ticket liability waiver.
9. Powers.
10. Ibid.
11. Ibid.
12. Ibid.
13. David Kitto, interview with author, July 13, 2006.
14. Edwards.
15. Ibid.
16. Roush, "Interview."
17. Ibid.
18. Powers.
19. Ibid.
20. Ibid.
21. Ibid.
22. Jeff Levine, interview with Elizabeth Coen, Aimee Davis, and Jean Sidden, November 2, 2005.
23. Robert Friend, interview with author, January 26, 2006.
24. Andrew Flatt, interview with author, July 6, 2006.
25. Robert Friend, *Marketing the Non-Profit Performing Arts*, (New York: Robert Friend, 2004).
26. Roush.
27. Friend, "Interview."
28. Flatt, "Interview."
29. Friend, *Marketing the Non-Profit Performing Arts*. Earned revenue is "income earned as the result of specific programs, goods, or services." (Jim Volz. *How to Run a Theater: A Witty, Practical, and Fun Guide to Arts Management* [New York: Backstage Books, 2004], 146.)
30. Ibid.

31. Telemarketing is the process of selling subscription tickets (tickets to multiple events at the organization) over the telephone. "Audience development is the process of engaging, educating, and motivating diverse communities to participate as a partner in the artistic experience." (Donna Walker-Kuhne, interview with author, January 4, 2006.)
32. Public relations is the creation and management of a public image of the organization. The publications department creates all printed material, such as playbills and newsletters.
33. Levine, "Interview."
34. Ibid.
35. Ibid.
36. Kitto, "Interview."
37. Ibid.
38. Edwards.
39. Powers.
40. Ibid.
41. Ibid.
42. Edwards.
43. Roush.
44. Ibid.
45. Powers.
46. Ibid.
47. Ibid.
48. Ibid.
49. Ibid.
50. Ibid.
51. Robert Friend, *Marketing Plan* (New York: Robert Friend, 2007).
52. Ibid.
53. Ibid.
54. The authors would like to thank Jennie Greer for allowing us to publish this situation analysis.
55. Friend.
56. Ibid.
57. Levine.
58. Ibid.
59. Ibid.
60. Ibid.
61. Walker-Kuhne, "Interview."
62. Ibid.
63. Levine.
64. Ibid.
65. Edwards.
66. Levine.
67. Edwards.
68. Levine.
69. Ibid.
70. Flatt.
71. The authors would like to thank Jennie Greer for allowing us to publish this SWOT analysis.
72. Friend, *Marketing Plan*.
73. Jim Volz, *How to Run a Theater* (New York: Backstage Books, 2004), 128.
74. Levine.
75. Ibid.
76. Flatt.
77. Ibid.
78. Levine.
79. The authors would like to thank Disney Theatricals for allowing us to publish this logo.
80. Flatt.
81. Friend.
82. Levine.
83. Ibid.
84. Ibid.
85. The authors would like to thank the Kennedy Center, the Alvin Ailey American Dance Theater, and Tania Pérez-Salas Compañia de Danza for allowing us to publish this subscription package. (On brochure cover: photo of Clifton Brown/Alvin Ailey American Dance Theater by Andrew Eccles. On main brochure page: photo on right: Linda Celeste Sims/Alvin Ailey American Dance Theater by Andrew Eccles.)
86. Levine.
87. The authors would like to thank the Kennedy Center for allowing us to publish this brochure. (Images © Fraver/rave! 2001 under license to the Kennedy Center. Set designs on brochure cover by Derek McLane.)
88. Levine.
89. Friend.
90. Friend, *Marketing the Non-Profit Performing Arts*.
91. Levine.
92. Eugene Carr, interview with author, May 9, 2006.
93. Eugene Carr, *Wired for Culture: How E-mail is Revolutionizing Arts Marketing* (Third Edition) (Patron Publishing: New York, 2007).
94. Ibid.
95. Ibid.
96. Ibid.
97. Ibid.
98. Levine.
99. The authors would like to thank the Kennedy Center for allowing us to publish this e-mail. (Image on masthead © 2007 The John F. Kennedy Center for the Performing Arts. Photo of Roberto Minczuk by Chris Lee. Photo of Heinrich Schiff by Klaus Rudolph.)
100. Carr, *Wired for Culture*.
101. Ibid.
102. Carr, "Interview."
103. Amanda Pekoe, e-mail interview with author, January 30, 2008.
104. Andrew Adam Newman, "During Intermission, Cellphones are Brandished in Promotion," *New York Times*, June 18, 2007. *Spring Awakening* had partnered with Broadway Phone for the promotion.
105. Kitto.
106. Ibid.
107. Ibid.
108. Ibid.
109. Friend.
110. Flatt.
111. Kitto.
112. Ibid.
113. Levine. A media outlet is a specific communication medium, such as the *New York Times* (print media outlet) or Fox Television (television media outlet). FTP stands for "file transfer protocol" and is used to transfer files from one computer to another.
114. A column inch is a measurement used by newspapers with multiple columns per page; it is a space one inch high and one column wide.
115. Kitto.

116. The authors would like to thank the Kennedy Center for allowing us to publish this advertisement. (Graphic © Fraver 2005 under license by the Kennedy Center.)
117. Flatt.
118. Kitto.
119. Levine.
120. Nancy Hereford, e-mail interview with author, January 11, 2006.
121. Levine.
122. Ibid.
123. Flatt.
124. Levine.
125. Flatt.
126. Ibid.
127. Ibid.
128. Ibid.
129. Kitto.
130. Ibid.
131. Shorey Walker, interview with author, July 11, 2006.
132. The authors would like to thank Shorey Walker for allowing us to publish this letter.
133. Levine.
134. Flatt.
135. Kitto.
136. Levine.
137. Kitto.
138. Friend, *Marketing the Non-Profit Performing Arts.*
139. Kitto.
140. Flatt.
141. Edwards.
142. Flatt.
143. Friend.
144. Kitto.
145. Hereford, "Interview."
146. Peter B. Carzasty, interview with Andrea Stover, November 25, 2005.
147. Hereford.
148. Sandy Sawotka, interview with Nadeisha Williams, November 3, 2005.
149. Tom D'Ambrosio, interview with Gillian Fallon, November 22, 2005.
150. Hereford.
151. Sawotka, "Interview."
152. Carzasty, "Interview."
153. Sawotka.
154. Adrian Bryan-Brown, e-mail interview with author, December 16, 2005.
155. Carzasty.
156. Bryan-Brown, "E-mail."
157. Bryan-Brown; Sawotka.
158. Bryan-Brown.
159. Sawotka.
160. The authors would like to thank The Publicity Office for allowing us to publish this press release.
161. Hereford.
162. Carzasty.
163. Ibid.
164. The authors would like to thank Peter B. Carzasty for allowing us to publish this pitch letter.
165. Carzasty.
166. Ibid.
167. Bryan-Brown.
168. Hereford.
169. D'Ambrosio, "Interview."
170. Bob Fennell, interview with author, January 20, 2006. Bob Fennell passed away on November 12, 2006.
171. Philip Rinaldi, interview with author, March 20, 2006.
172. Tiki Davies, interview with author, January 13, 2006.
173. Carzasty.
174. Sawotka.
175. Bryan-Brown.
176. Hereford.
177. Sawotka.
178. Bryan-Brown.
179. Hereford.
180. Bill Miller, interview with author, November 15, 2005.
181. Fennell, "Interview."
182. Bryan-Brown.
183. Hereford.
184. Bryan-Brown.
185. Will Nedved, interview with author, November 23, 2005.
186. Bryan-Brown.
187. Hereford.
188. Ibid.
189. Ibid.
190. Fennell.

APPENDIX A: Performance Audience Survey

> **Audience Survey Instructions:** Darken ovals completely using a #2 pencil or dark pen. Please do not fold or make stray marks on the form.

1. **Welcome! Is this your first time at a Broadway show in New York City?**

   ☐ Yes   ☐ No

2. **Indicate which of the following shows you've seen before today.** (mark all that apply)

   ☐ Mary Poppins   ☐ Grease
   ☐ The Lion King   ☐ Chicago
   ☐ Spring Awakening
   ☐ Hairspray
   ☐ Phantom of the Opera
   ☐ Legally Blonde
   ☐ The Drowsy Chaperone   ☐ Grey Gardens
   ☐ Les Miserables   ☐ Rent
   ☐ 110 In The Shade
   ☐ Mamma Mia!

3. **How many times have you attended Broadway shows (including this performance) in the past 12 months?** (mark one)

   ☐ 1 time   ☐ 5 to 9 times
   ☐ 2 to 4 times
   ☐ 10 or more times

4. **In what section of the theater are you seated?**
   ☐ Orchestra (main floor)   ☐ Balcony
   ☐ Mezzanine

5. **What is the face value of your ticket—not including service charges?** (mark one)

   ☐ $100 ☐ $75 ☐ $55 ☐ $35

6. **What role did you play in the decision to purchase tickets for today's performance?**

   ☐ I made the decision
   ☐ I participated in a joint decision
   ☐ Someone else decided

7. **How was your ticket purchased?** (mark one)

   ☐ By telephone through Ticketmaster
   ☐ At a Ticketmaster outlet
   ☐ In-person at this theater's box office
   ☐ At the "TKTS" booth in Times Square
   ☐ Hotel concierge or ticket broker
   ☐ Online—through any web site
   ☐ Organized group or package deal

8. **Do you recall when your ticket for this performance was purchased?** (mark one)

   ☐ Today   ☐ Within the past week
   ☐ 1–2 weeks ago
   ☐ 2–4 weeks ago
   ☐ 1–2 months ago
   ☐ 2–4 months ago
   ☐ 4–6 months ago
   ☐ More than 6 months

9. **How many people are in your party today, including yourself?**

   ☐ One (just me) ☐ Two ☐ Four ☐ Six ☐ Eight ☐ Ten or more
   ☐ Three ☐ Five ☐ Seven ☐ Nine

10. **Going to the theater is a fun way to spend time with family and friends. What relationships do you have with the other people in your party?**
    (mark all that apply)

    ☐ Spouse/partner   ☐ My children   ☐ Other family   ☐ Co-workers
    ☐ Parent(s) ☐ Other children   ☐ Friends   ☐ A date

11. **If there are any children or teenagers in your party today, what are their ages?** (mark all that apply)

    ☐ Age 5 and Under   ☐ Age 7   ☐ Age 9   ☐ Age 11   ☐ Age 13   ☐ Age 15   ☐ Age 17
    ☐ Age 6   ☐ Age 8   ☐ Age 10   ☐ Age 12   ☐ Age 14   ☐ Age 16

12. (NY, CT and NJ residents only) **Indicate which of the following media you read regularly, listen to regularly, or watch regularly.** (mark all that apply)

☐ The New York Times   ☐ WLTW-FM— Lite FM 106.7   ☐ Morning News (e.g., Today Show)   ☐ The (Newark) Star Ledger   ☐ WPLJ-FM-95.5 (Good Morning America)

☐ The (Bergen) Record   ☐ WKTU 103.5   ☐ Daytime TV
☐ The Journal News   ☐ BLINK—WNEW-FM 102.7   ☐ Evening News (5–7PM)
☐ Newsday   ☐ CD 101.9 (WQCD)   ☐ Late News (10–11:30PM)
☐ WCBS-FM— NY's Oldies   ☐ Late Night Sitcoms   ☐ WCBS-AM (880)
    Station 101.1   (Channels 5 or 11)
☐ WINS-AM (1010)

13. Did you use any of the following web sites to find out about this production? (mark all that apply)

☐ The show's website   ☐ Broadway.com   ☐ Playbill.com   ☐ Google search
☐ Ticketmaster.com   ☐ TheaterMania.com   ☐ New York Times online   ☐ Yahoo search

14. How influential were each of the following on your decision to attend?

	Very Influential	Moderately Influential	A Little Influential	Not A Factor
…The story	☐	☐	☐	☐
…The music and songs	☐	☐	☐	☐
…Someone in the cast I wanted to see	☐	☐	☐	☐
…It's from a producer I trust	☐	☐	☐	☐
…Tickets were available for the date I wanted	☐	☐	☐	☐
…Discount price of tickets	☐	☐	☐	☐
…The children wanted to see it	☐	☐	☐	☐

Please tell us a little about yourself. Of course, your answers are anonymous and confidential.

A. Your gender: ☐ Female   ☐ Male

B. Your age: ☐ 13–17   ☐ 35–49
☐ 18–24   ☐ 50–64
☐ 25–34   ☐ 65+

C. Your racial or ethnic background:

☐ Asian American   ☐ White, not Hispanic
☐ African American   ☐ Native American
☐ Hispanic/Latino   ☐ Other

D. Your annual household income:
☐ Under $50,000
☐ $50,000 to $100,000
☐ Over $100,000

E.   Are you a U.S. resident?
☐ Yes   ☐ No

F. Home ZIP Code:
Write in your home ZIP code in the top five spaces, and then darken in the corresponding number in the column below.
(U.S. residents only)

0	0	0	0	0
1	1	1	1	1
2	2	2	2	2
3	3	3	3	3
4	4	4	4	4
5	5	5	5	5
6	6	6	6	6
7	7	7	7	7
8	8	8	8	8
9	9	9	9	9

Thank you! Please exchange your completed survey for a free poster at the front lobby bar after the show.

APPENDIX B1: Subscription Brochure Cover

APPENDIX B2:
Subscription
Brochure

Embark on a journey of discovery and experience...

the passion and drama of Latin social dance,

the energizing fusion of urban American and African culture,

the hypnotic art of Japanese butoh,

the explosive spirit of Pacific Islander dance,

the intersection of Chinese art and movement,

...a world of motion.

This season, some of the world's greatest dance companies and visionaries take you on a global tour of contemporary movement, with works of dynamic athleticism, sensuous beauty, and provocative new directions. Your voyage begins at the Kennedy Center—the nation's center for the performing arts.

2007-2008 SEASON

ALVIN AILEY AMERICAN DANCE THEATER

DANA TAI SOON BURGESS & CO.

BALLET HISPANICO and the AFRO-LATIN
JAZZ ORCHESTRA with ARTURO O'FARRILL

TANIA PÉREZ-SALAS COMPAÑÍA DE DANZA

URBAN BUSH WOMEN and COMPAGNIE JANT-BI

JO KANAMORI'S NOISM 08

SANKAI JUKU

AKIRA KASAI

SHEN WEI DANCE ARTS

BLACK GRACE

DISNEY'S THE LION KING

Many of last season's performances sold out.
Only subscribers can guarantee great seats in advance of public sale, and also save on each performance in their series.

CHOOSE FROM FIVE CONVENIENT SUBSCRIPTION PACKAGES
AND ORDER YOUR SUBSCRIPTION TODAY!

RENEWAL DEADLINE FRIDAY, JUNE 8

Dear Subscriber,

It is my pleasure to announce our new season of contemporary dance, a season that takes you on a journey of discovery through a world of motion.

Making their Kennedy Center debuts, Mexico's **TANIA PÉREZ-SALAS COMPAÑIA DE DANZA** brings a mixed repertory program of alluring and visually arresting works, while New Zealand's all-male **BLACK GRACE** presents an exciting mixed repertory program that displays its fusion of traditional and contemporary dance forms.

The Kennedy Center festival, *JAPAN! culture + hyperculture*, showcases three of Japan's leading contemporary dance ensembles: **SANKAI JUKU** in *Kinkan Shonen*, **AKIRA KASAI** in *Pollen Revolution*, and **JO KANAMORI'S NOISM 08** in the world premiere of *NINA materialize sacrifice*.

Returning favorites include resident Kennedy Center dance company **SHEN WEI DANCE ARTS**, which presents a remarkable fusion of painting and movement in *Connect Transfer*. **ALVIN AILEY AMERICAN DANCE THEATER** performs the classic *Revelations* and other exciting works. D.C.-based **DANA TAI SOON BURGESS & CO.** explores the Asian American aesthetic with a mixed repertory program that celebrates its 15th anniversary. Brooklyn's all-female **URBAN BUSH WOMEN** joins with Senegal's all-male **COMPAGNIE JANT-BI** to perform *The Beauty of Little Things*. Traveling back to the Golden Age of Latin Jazz, New York's **BALLET HISPANICO** teams with the acclaimed **AFRO-LATIN JAZZ ORCHESTRA** with **ARTURO O'FARRILL** to perform *Palladium Nights*. And the dynamic choreography of Garth Fagan is featured in the Tony Award®–winning Broadway sensation, **DISNEY'S *THE LION KING***.

As a renewing subscriber, you can guarantee seats for all of these performances. Choose from five subscription packages for the first chance to reserve the best seats available before general public sale and **SAVE UP TO 20%**.

Please review our new brochure and send in your personalized renewal order form today. You may also renew online at **kennedy-center.org/subscribe**. We look forward to seeing you at the Kennedy Center.

Sincerely,

Alicia Adams
Vice President of Dance Programming
The Kennedy Center

P.S. Questions? Please call our Subscription Office at (202) 416-8500, Monday-Friday, 10 a.m. – 5 p.m. The TTY number is (202) 416-8518. A subscription representative will be happy to assist you.

Kennedy Center
CONTEMPORARY
DANCE 2007 2008

2007–08 SUBSCRIPTION RENEWAL INVOICE

PATRON ID

○ I would like to renew my Contemporary Dance subscription as listed below:

Series Name	# of Subscribers	Series Price		Total
		x $		= $
		x $		= $

○ In addition to my series, I would like to order tickets for the following optional performance(s):

Company	Date/Time	Section	# of Seats	Price	Total
Ballet Hispanico	Nov. 5/8 p.m.	Orchestra	x	$45.00	= $
ABT's *The Nutcracker*	Dec. 18/7:30 p.m.	Orchestra	x	$79.00	= $
ABT's *The Nutcracker*	Dec. 19/7:30 p.m.	Orchestra	x	$79.00	= $
Jo Kanamori's Noism 08	Feb. 7/7:30 p.m.	Orchestra	x	$32.00	= $
Jo Kanamori's Noism 08	Feb. 8/7:30 p.m.	Orchestra	x	$32.00	= $
Sankai Juku	Feb. 12/7:30 p.m.	Orchestra	x	$45.00	= $
Akira Kasai	Feb. 16/7:30 p.m.	Orchestra	x	$32.00	= $
Akira Kasai	Feb. 17/7:30 p.m.	Orchestra	x	$32.00	= $
Alvin Ailey American Dance Theater	Feb. 20/7:30 p.m.	Orchestra	x	$61.00	= $
McCoy Tyner/Savion Glover	Feb. 24/7 p.m.	Orchestra	x	$45.00	= $
Disney's *The Lion King*	Jul. 13/7:30 p.m.	Orchestra	x	$85.00	= $

SUBTOTAL =$ _____

○ I want my seating coordinated with other subscribers. (*Please include their information on the reverse side.*)

○ I need seating to accommodate my wheelchair.

○ I have written more detailed seating requests on the reverse side of this form.

○ Tax-deductible voluntary contribution to the Kennedy Center Annual Fund* $ _____

Please make your check payable to the Kennedy Center or complete the credit card information below.

Contribution of $60 automatically enrolls you as a Kennedy Center Member

GRAND TOTAL $ _____

○ Enclosed is my check payable to the Kennedy Center

○ Visa ○ MasterCard ○ American Express ○ Diners Club

Card Number   Exp. Date   Signature

Appendix B4 (continued)

Your canceled check or credit card charge will serve as confirmation of receipt of your order.

Please use the enclosed business reply envelope or mail your renewal to:
CONTEMPORARY DANCE RENEWAL
KENNEDY CENTER SUBSCRIPTIONS
PO BOX 101510
ARLINGTON, VA 22210

OR FAX TO **(202) 416-8585**

OR RENEW ONLINE AT **kennedy-center.org/subscribe**

Questions about your order? Call the Subscriptions Office at **(202) 416-8500**
Monday-Friday 10 a.m.-5 p.m.

I would like my seating to be coordinated with the following person(s) who subscribe separately:

Name _____   Phone _____

Address _____

_____

Name _____   Phone _____

Address _____

_____

Additional notes about my renewal request:

_____

_____

_____

_____

APPENDIX C:
Advertisement

APPENDIX D: Letter to RAs

September 29, 2005

Enclosed are some Student Discount Offers for our new Off-Broadway show.

Please assist me in my efforts to get this information to your students ASAP. The show has been a tremendous success with college students for the last few weeks! I can't believe how much they seem to LOVE this show!!! We are only running Off-Broadway for 9 weeks— closing November 13th.

Please post this information in the Student Union area or around the school.

Feel free to contact me for more information on the show or **to book a group.**

ALSO—please accept this as a formal invitation to see the show. We are just finishing up our preview performances, but I have limited ticket availability over the next two weeks. Please call me to arrange your complimentary pair of tickets.

If you have any questions about the content of the show call me or look to our website for more information.

Thank you for your assistance. I look forward to hearing back from you.

Warm regards,

Shorey Walker
Group Sales & Marketing

The American Theatre of Actors
314 West 54th Street- btwn 8th & 9th Ave
NEW YORK CITY

APPENDIX E: Marketing Timeline

	bus days	start	finish
Season Brochure - Turn in word count/initial text to design department	0 days	1/17/07	1/17/07
Season Brochure: Season information meeting with artistic director		1/24/07	1/24/07
Season Brochure: Create binders, gather information, images	14 days	1/24/07	2/12/07
Season Brochure - Initial design creation	5 wks	1/29/07	3/5/07
Season Brochure - Copywriting (create text)	3 wks	2/13/07	3/6/07
Season Brochure - Initial design review by marketing	3 days	3/1/07	3/5/07
Season Brochure - Second design review by marketing	3 days	3/6/07	3/8/07
Season Brochure - Presentation to artistic director	3 days	3/9/07	3/13/07
Season Brochure - Billing information due for companies	0 days	3/12/07	3/12/07
Season Brochure - Finalize text	2 days	3/13/07	3/15/07
Season Brochure - Full brochure design	3 wks	3/14/07	4/4/07
Season Brochure - Text routed to building for approval	3 days	3/15/07	3/20/07
Season Press Release - Begin long-lead pitching for magazines, etc.		3/15/07	ongoing
Season Brochure - Text routed to companies for approval	3 days	3/23/07	3/28/07
Season Brochure - Copy from other departments (e.g. fundraising) due	0 days	3/28/07	3/28/07
Season Brochure - Final program copy sent to design department	0 days	3/28/07	3/28/07
Season Brochure- Brochure routed to marketing for changes	4 days	4/4/07	4/10/07
Season Brochure - Sponsorship pages routed to sponsorship for approval	2 days	4/4/07	4/6/07
Season Brochure - Brochure routed to building for approval	2 days	4/10/07	4/12/07
Season Brochure - Brochure corrections due	4 days	4/12/07	4/18/07
Season Brochure - Make changes from 1st route to building	3 days	4/18/07	4/23/07
Season Brochure - Final brochure routed to building, companies for approval	2 days	4/23/07	4/25/07
Season Brochure - Final route corrections due	4 days	4/25/07	5/1/07
Season Brochure - Make final changes/send off to printer	3 days	5/1/07	5/4/07
Show Posters - Text sent to design department	0 days	5/3/07	5/3/07
Show Posters - Posters back from design department	7 days	5/3/07	5/14/07
Season Brochure - Brochure prints	3 wks	5/4/07	5/25/07
Show Posters - Route to building for approval	3 days	5/14/07	5/17/07
Show Posters - Route due from building	3 days	5/17/07	5/22/07
Single Ticket Brochure - Request copy from departments	0 days	5/18/07	5/18/07
Season Brochure - All mailing lists due to marketing department	3 days	5/21/07	5/24/07
Show Posters - Final proofing	2 days	5/22/07	5/24/07
Show Posters - Send to printer	2 days	5/24/07	5/29/07
Season Brochure - All lists due to mailhouse	0 days	5/25/07	5/25/07
Season Brochure - Brochures arrive at mailhouse and development department	0 days	5/25/07	5/25/07
Single Ticket Brochure - Copywriting, text sent to design department	0 days	5/25/07	5/25/07
Single Ticket Brochure - First draft from design department	7 days	5/25/07	6/6/07
Season Press Release - Sent to printer			5/30/07
Season Brochure - Mailhouse preps for mailings	4 days	5/25/07	5/31/07
Show Posters - Posters arrive in-house	1 wk	5/29/07	6/5/07
Season Brochure - Priority (High-level Donor) brochures drop (are mailed)	1 day	6/4/07	6/5/07
Season Press Release - Release emailed/mailed			6/5/07
Single Ticket Brochure - Route to sponsorship for approval	1 day	6/6/07	6/7/07
Single Ticket Brochure - Edits sent to design department	4 days	6/6/07	6/12/07
Season Brochure - Regular brochures drop	0 days	6/7/07	6/7/07
Single Ticket Brochure - Sponsorship route due	3 days	6/7/07	6/12/07
Show Posters - Hang posters	0 days	6/8/07	6/8/07
Season Brochure - Priority Donor brochures hit (arrive at destination)	0 days	6/11/07	6/11/07
ON SALE DATE FOR PRIORITY DONOR SUBSCRIPTIONS	0 days	6/11/07	6/11/07
Single Ticket Brochure - Second draft from design	2 days	6/12/07	6/14/07
Single Ticket Brochure - Route to building for approval	3 days	6/14/07	6/19/07
Season Brochure - Regular brochures hit	0 days	6/18/07	6/18/07
ON SALE DATE FOR REGULAR SUBSCRIPTIONS	0 days	6/18/07	6/18/07
Single Ticket Brochure - Building route due	1 wk	6/19/07	6/26/07
Single Ticket Brochure - Final proofing	2 days	6/26/07	6/28/07
Single Ticket Brochure - Send to printer	3 days	6/28/07	7/3/07
TELEMARKETING CAMPAIGN BEGINS			7/2/07
Single Ticket Brochure - Brochure arrives in-house	2 wks	7/3/07	7/18/07
Mailing to Lapsed Subscribers - Write letter	1 wk	7/16/07	7/20/07
Mailing to Lapsed Subscribers - Send letter copy to design for typesetting	0 days	7/20/07	7/20/07
Single Ticket Brochure - Request mailing lists for single tickets brochure	0 days	7/23/07	7/23/07
Mailing to Lapsed Subscribers - Letter back from design department	3 days	7/23/07	7/25/07
Mailing to Lapsed Subscribers - Letter sent to mailhouse	3 days	7/26/07	7/30/07
Postcards for Show #1 - Text to design department	0 days	7/27/07	7/27/07
Postcards for Show #1 - Card back from design	4 days	7/27/07	8/2/07
Mailing to Lapsed Subscribers - Letter drops	4 days	7/31/07	8/3/07
Postcards for Show #1- Route to building for approval	3 days	8/2/07	8/7/07
Newspaper Season Announcement Ad - Text to design department	0 days	8/3/07	8/3/07
Newspaper Season Announcement Ad - Back from design department	8 days	8/3/07	8/15/07
Postcards for Show #1- Corrections due	2 days	8/7/07	8/9/07
Postcards for Show #1- Final proofing	2 days	8/9/07	8/13/07
Single Ticket Brochure - Priority (High Level) Donor Mailing	3 days	8/13/07	8/16/07
Postcards for Show #1 - Send to printer	1 day	8/13/07	8/14/07
Postcards for Show #1- Postcards arrive in-house	1.2 wks	8/14/07	8/22/07
Newspaper Season Announcement Ad - Route to building for approval	3 days	8/15/07	8/20/07
Single Ticket Brochure - Standard mailing	3 days	8/20/07	8/23/07
Newspaper Season Announcement Ad - Ad corrections due	3 days	8/20/07	8/23/07
Postcards for Show #1- Postcards mailed	3 days	8/22/07	8/25/07
Newspaper Season Announcement Ad - Final proofing	2 days	8/23/07	8/24/07
Newspaper Season Announcement Ad - Send to newspaper	0 days	8/24/07	8/24/07
ON SALE DATE FOR PRIORITY DONOR SINGLE TICKETS	0 days	8/27/07	8/27/07
ON SALE DATE FOR REGULAR SINGLE TICKETS	0 days	9/4/07	9/4/07
SEASON BEGINS/SHOW #1 OPENS			10/3/07

APPENDIX F: Marketing Budget

	DESC.	BUDGET
PART-TIME PERSONNEL EXPENSE		
Part-Time Employee	4 weeks	$2,000.00
		$2,000.00
INTERN EXPENSE		
Interns	16 weeks	$8,000.00
		$8,000.00
TRANSLATION OF MARKETING MATERIALS (into another language)		
Estimated		$400.00
		$400.00
POSTAGE		
Season Brochure mailings	**Amount Mailed**	
Season Subscription Brochure Mailing	70K	$18,000.00
Single Ticket Brochure Mailing	120K	$17,000.00
Postcard mailings		
Show #1	15K	$2,100.00
Show #1 in Chinese	5K	$700.00
Show #2	10K	$1,400.00
Show #3	10K	$1,400.00
Show #4	15K	$2,100.00
Show #5	10K	$1,400.00
Show #6	5K	$700.00
Show #7	10K	$1,400.00
Show #8	10K	$1,400.00
Show #9	10K	$1,400.00
Show #10	15K	$2,100.00
Monthly postage expense		
Jul-Dec Estimated		$5,000.00
Other		
Estimated		$200.00
		$56,300.00
PRINTING EXPENSE		
Postcards		
Show #1	20K	$1,650.00
Show #1 in Chinese	10K	$850.00
Show #2	15K	$1,250.00
Show #3	15K	$1,250.00
Show #4	20K	$1,650.00
Show #5	15K	$1,250.00
Show #6	10K	$850.00
Show #7	15K	$1,250.00
Show #8	15K	$1,250.00
Show #9	15K	$1,250.00
Show #10	20K	$1,650.00
Posters		
Season announcment posters	2K	$1,800.00
Production posters (6)	qty 500= $250	$1,500.00
Program Inserts		
Estimated $2000		$2,000.00
Outdoor Banners		
Estimated $8000		$8,000.00
		$27,450.00
ELECTRONIC PROMOTION		
Online Ads/Third-Party Email Campaigns		
Major News Ad - Season Announcement		$20,000.00
Major News Ad - Show-Specific	3 @ $8500 per show	$25,500.00
Newspaper Online Ticket Information		$4,700.00
Magazine #1		$10,000.00
Other		$20,000.00
Electronic Asset Development (sign, website, lobby, video previews)		
Estimated		$10,000.00
		$90,200.00
PHOTOGRAPHY EXPENSE		
Rights for photos		$500.00
		$500.00
TELEMKTG EXPENSE		
Estimated		$25,000.00
		$25,000.00
MAILHOUSE EXPENSE		
Season Brochure mailings		
Season brochure	70K	$4,000.00
Single ticket brochure	120K	$8,000.00
Postcard mailings		
Show #1	15K	$1,000.00
Show #1 in Chinese	5K	$600.00
Show #2	10K	$750.00
Show #3	10K	$750.00
Show #4	15K	$1,000.00
Show #5	10K	$750.00
Show #6	5K	$600.00
Show #7	10K	$750.00
Show #8	10K	$750.00
Show #9	10K	$750.00
Show #10	15K	$1,000.00
		$20,700.00
RADIO ADVERTISING		
Radio Station #1 Advertising		$18,000.00
Target radio:		
Chinese Radio		$2,500.00
		$20,500.00

PRINT ADVERTISING

Major Newspaper #1

	Size of Ad	
Season announcement ad	4 x 14	$36,000.00
Ad #1 (for Show #1)	2 x 7	$10,300.00
Ad #2 (for Show #1)	2 x 5.25	$6,600.00
Ad #3 (for Show #2)	2 x 5.25	$6,600.00
Ad #4 (for Show #3)	2 x 5.25	$6,600.00
Ad #5 (for Show #3)	2 x 7	$10,300.00
Ad #6 (for Show #4)	2 x 5.25	$6,600.00
Ad #7 (for Show #4)	2 x 5.25	$6,600.00
Ad #8 (for Show #5)	2 x 5.25	$6,600.00
Ad #9 (for Show #6)	2 x 7	$10,300.00
Ad #10 (for Show #6)	2 x 5.25	$6,600.00
Ad #11 (for Show #7)	2 x 7	$10,300.00
Ad #12 (for Show #7)	2 x 5.25	$6,600.00
Ad #13 (for Show #8)	2 x 7	$10,300.00
Ad #14 (for Show #8)	2 x 5.25	$6,600.00
Ad #15 (for Show #9)	2 x 7	$10,300.00
Ad #16 (for Show #9)	2 x 5.25	$6,600.00
Ad #17 (for Show #10)	2 x 5.25	$6,600.00
Ad #18 (for Show #10)	2 x 5.25	$6,600.00

Local Weekly #2
1/4pg: $1,111.80/$833.85; 1/3pg: $1482.40; 1/2pg: $2,224.45

Ad #1 (for Show #1)	1/4 page	$1,100.00
Ad #2 (for Show #1)	1/4 page	$1,100.00
Ad #3 (for Show #2)	1/4 page	$1,100.00
Ad #4 (for Show #2)	1/4 page	$1,100.00
Ad #5 (for Show #3)	1/4 page	$1,100.00
Ad #6 (for Show #3)	1/3 page	$1,500.00
Ad #7 (for Show #4)	1/4 page	$1,100.00
Ad #8 (for Show #4)	1/4 page	$1,100.00
Ad #9 (for Show #5)	1/4 page	$1,100.00
Ad #10 (for Show #5)	1/4 page	$1,100.00
Ad #11 (for Show #5)	1/4 page	$1,100.00
Ad #12 (for Show #6)	1/4 page	$1,100.00
Ad #13 (for Show #6)	1/2 page	$2,200.00
Ad #14 (for Show #6)	1/3 page	$1,500.00
Ad #15 (for Show #7)	1/4 page	$1,100.00
Ad #16 (for Show #7)	1/4 page	$1,100.00
Ad #17 (for Show #8)	1/4 page	$1,100.00
Ad #18 (for Show #8)	1/4 page	$1,100.00
Ad #19 (for Show #9)	1/4 page	$1,100.00
Ad #20 (for Show #9)	1/4 page	$1,100.00
Ad #21 (For Show #10)	1/4 page	$1,100.00
Ad #22 (for Show #10)	1/4 page	$1,100.00
Ad #23 (for Show #10)	1/4 page	$1,100.00

Magazine #2

Season announcement ad		$5,000.00
Ad #1 (for Show #1)	1/4 page	$1,500.00
Ad #2 (for Show #1)	1/4 page	$1,500.00
Ad #3 (for Show #2)	1/4 page	$1,500.00
Ad #4 (for Show #2)	1/4 page	$1,500.00
Ad #5 (for Show #3)	1/4 page	$1,500.00
Ad #6 (for Show #3)	1/2 page	$2,500.00
Ad #7 (for Show #4)	1/4 page	$1,500.00
Ad #8 (for Show #4)	1/4 page	$1,500.00
Ad #9 (for Show #4)	1/4 page	$1,500.00
Ad #10 (for Show #5)	1/4 page	$1,500.00
Ad #11 (for Show #5)	1/4 page	$1,500.00
Ad #12 (for Show #5)	1/4 page	$1,500.00
Ad #13 (for Show #6)	1/2 page	$2,500.00
Ad #14 (for Show #6)	1/2 page	$2,500.00
Ad #15 (for Show #6)	1/4 page	$1,500.00
Ad #16 (for Show #7)	1/4 page	$1,500.00
Ad #17 (for Show #7)	1/4 page	$1,500.00
Ad #18 (for Show #7)	1/4 page	$1,500.00
Ad #19 (for Show #8)	1/4 page	$1,500.00
Ad #20 (for Show #8)	1/2 page	$2,500.00
Ad #21 (For Show #9)	1/4 page	$1,500.00
Ad #22 (for Show #9)	1/4 page	$1,500.00
Ad #23 (for Show #10)	1/4 page	$1,500.00
Ad #24 (for Show #10)	1/4 page	$1,500.00
Ad #25 (for Show #10)	1/4 page	$1,500.00

Other

Magazine #1 - Fall Season announcement ad		$14,000.00
Local Newspaper - Show #3 Ad		$350.00
Local Newspaper - 3 ads @ $400		$1,200.00
		$266,250.00

TV ADVERTISING EXPENSE

Chinese TV		$2,500.00
Production of Ad Spot		$200.00
Video Transfer of Ad Spot		$75.00
		$2,775.00

BROCHURE EXPENSE

Season Subscription Brochure- Printing	75k, 48 pages	$62,000.00
Single Ticket Brochure- Printing	200K - 36 pages	$70,000.00
		$134,730.00

DESIGN EXPENSE

Estimated		$50,000.00
		$50,000.00

DISTRIBUTION

Fall Announcement - Outdoor Poster Campaign	qty 1000	$4,000.00
Single Ticket Brochure Inserts in Newspaper	65K	$18,000.00
		$22,000.00

MAILING LIST EXPENSE (Rentals/Purchase)

Estimated		$1,500.00
		$1,500.00

TOTAL		$726,940.00

BIBLIOGRAPHY

Armbrust, Roger. "Broadway Sees Cash, Sales Up." *Backstage*, 5 January 2005.

Arnold, Laurence. "Arts Pumped $21.2 Billion into NYC Economy in 2005." Bloomberg.com, 30 May 2007. *www.bloomberg.com/apps/news?pid=20601088&refer=muse&sid=aMgxG0lmeNC8*.

Arts Journal, *www.artsjournal.com*.

ArtsMarketing.org, *www.artsmarketing.org*.

Bellafante, Gina. "Examining Black-Latino Relations, Gently." *New York Times*, 20 June 2007.

Bernstein, Joanne Scheff. *Arts Marketing Insights*. New York: Wiley, 2006.

Boehm, Mike. "Now That's Rich." *Los Angeles Times*, 2 December 2006.

———. "Survey Finds a Decline in Attendance." *Los Angeles Times*. 2 November 2006.

Bryan-Brown, Adrian. "Publicity." Interview with Jessica Bathurst. E-mail to author, 16 December 2005.

Cameron, Ben. "School Dazed." *American Theatre*, April 2004, 4–5.

Carr, Eugene. "E-mail Marketing." Interview with Jessica Bathurst. Tape recording, 9 May 2006. Patron Technology, New York.

———. *Sign Up for Culture*. New York: Patron Technology, 2005.

———. *Wired for Culture: How E-mail Is Revolutionizing Arts Marketing* (Third Edition). New York: Patron Technology, 2007.

Center for an Urban Future. *Creative New York*. December 2005.

Carzasty, Peter B. "Publicity." Interview with Andrea Stover. Tape recording, 25 November 2005. New York.

———. "Sample Pitch Letter." New York, 1997.

Commanday, Robert P. "Come to the Aid of Music Journalism." *San Francisco Classical Voice*, 17 October 2006.

Confessore, Nicholas. "Theater Association Support Dismantling of Scalping Laws." *New York Times*, 20 March 2007.

D'Ambrosio, Tom. "Publicity." Interview with Gillian Fallon. Tape recording, 22 November 2005. New York.

David, Cara Joy. "How Much Does It Cost to Buy a $100 Theater Ticket?" *New York Times*, 10 February 2007.

Davies, Tiki. "Publicity." Interview with Jessica Bathurst. Phone interview with author, 13 January 2006.

Disney Theatricals. "*The Lion King* Logo." New York, 2007.

Dobrin, Peter. "Orchestra on the Move Proves Itself Neighborly." *Philadelphia Inquirer*, 25 June 2006.

Dobrzynski, Judith H. "Unsuccessful Overtures." *Wall Street Journal*, 18 November 2006.

Dunn, Julie. "Arts Make Big Impact on Local Economy." *Denver Post*, 28 October 2006.

Dunning, Jennifer. "Rule No. 1: Avoid the Same Old Song and Dance." *New York Times*, 15 May 2005.

Eccles, Jeremy. "Finding the Post-Rationalist Audience." Realtimearts.net, 13 December 2005. *www.realtimearts.net/article/70/7993*.

Edgers, Geoff. "Filling the Seats." *Boston Globe*, 14 November 2004.

Edwards, Dale. "Marketing." Interview with Christopher Thomasson. Tape recording, 10 November 2005. New York.

Fennell, Bob. "Publicity." Interview with Jessica Bathurst. Phone interview with author, 20 January 2006.

Flatt, Andrew. "Marketing." Interview with Jessica Bathurst. Tape recording, 6 July 2006. Disney Theatricals, New York.

Friend, Robert. "Marketing." Interview with Jessica Bathurst. Tape recording, 26 January 2006. New York.

———. *Marketing the Non-Profit Performing Arts*. New York: Robert Friend, 2004.

———. *Marketing Plan*. New York: Robert Friend, 2007.

Gallagher, David F. "What to Expect of 'Spamalot'? A Lot of Spam." *New York Times*, 12 March 2005.

Goodwin, Joy. "New Audiences Fall for Dance." *New York Sun*, 8 September 2006.

Green, Jesse. "Producers Use the Web to Romance Audience and Bring Them Back." *New York Times*, 9 July 2006.

Greer, Jennie. "Situation Analysis." New York, 2007.

———. "SWOT Analysis." New York, 2007.

Grossberg, Richard. "Sample Ticket—Front." Brooklyn, N.Y., 2007.

———. "Sample Ticket—Liability Waiver." Brooklyn, N.Y., 2007.

Hereford, Nancy. "Publicity." Interview by Jessica Bathurst. E-mail to author, 11 January 2006.

Hill, Elizabeth, Catherine O'Sullivan, and Terry O'Sullivan. *Creative Arts Marketing*, 2d ed. Oxford (UK): Butterworth-Heineman, 2003.

Hirsch, Lisa. "The (High) Price of Music." *San Francisco Classical Voice*, 21 February 2006.

Holland, D.K. *Branding for Nonprofits*. New York: Allworth Press, 2006.

International Association of Assembly Managers, Inc. "Taking Inventory: Teaming Up to Move Tickets." *Facility Manager*, February/March 2004. *www.iaam.org/facility_manager/pages/2004_Feb_Mar/Feature_1.htm*.

Ives, Nat. "Guerilla Campaigns Are Going to Extremes, but Will the Message Stick?" *New York Times*, 24 June 2004.

Jack, Carolyn. "Studies on Arts Examine Turnouts, Impact in Schools." *Cleveland Plain Dealer*, 18 November 2005.

Jacobs, Leonard. "League: B'way Sales Rise, Other Stats Stubbornly Stagnant." *Backstage*, 19 January 2005.

The John F. Kennedy Center for the Performing Arts. "Advertisement." Washington, D.C., 2007.

———. "E-mail." Washington, D.C., 2007.

———. "Single Ticket Postcard." Washington, D.C., 2007.

———. "Subscription Package." Washington, D.C., 2007.

Jones, Chris. "Non-Profit, Commercial Divisions Melt: Broadway Producers Take On Subscription Business." *Chicago Tribune*, 16 December 2007.

Jones, Kenneth. "Broadway's Major Producers Join with Regional Presenters for Audience Rewards Program." Playbill.com, 28 June 2007. *www.playbill.com/news/article/109186.html*.

Kitto, David. "Marketing." Interview with Jessica Bathurst. Tape recording, 13 July 2006. Kennedy Center, Washington, D.C.

Kotler, Philip and Joanne Scheff Bernstein. *Standing Room Only: Strategies for Marketing the Performing Arts*. Boston: Harvard Business School Press, 1997.

Kozinn, Allan. "Check the Numbers: Rumors of Classical Music's Demise Are Dead Wrong." *New York Times*, 28 May 2006.

Kuchwara, Michael. "Broadway Sees Profits in Female Buying Power." Associated Press, 3 March 2005.

———. "Coyne Knows the Art of Selling Broadway." Associated Press, 17 August 2005.

Lauro, Patricia Winters. "Videos in Lobby Help Nonprofit Theaters Keep Actors in Stage." *New York Times*, 8 November 2006.

Lemire, Jonathan. "A Dismal Play Date." *New York Daily News*, 5 June 2006.

Levine, Jeff. "Marketing." Interview with Elizabeth Coen, Aimee Davis, and Jean Sidden. Tape recording, 2 November 2005. Brooklyn Academy of Music, Brooklyn, N.Y.

MacMillan, Kyle. "Showing Ticketing Services the Door." *Denver Post*, 30 September 2005.

Manly, Lorne. "Revue Seeks to Attract Latinos to Broadway." *New York Times*, 26 October 2005.

Marder, Dianna. "The Wedding Zinger." *Philadelphia Inquirer*, 25 July 2006.

Marketing Pilgrim. *Online Reputation Monitoring Beginners Guide.* 12 September 2006. *www.marketingpilgrim.com/online-reputation-monitoring-beginners-guide.pdf.*

McKinley, Jesse. "Bucking a Trend: Theater for $15." *New York Times*, 23 June 2005.

———. "Lincoln Center Goes A-Courting." *New York Times*, 12 July 2005.

———. "'Spamalot' Discovers the Straight White Way." *New York Times*, 10 April 2005.

McNulty, Timothy. "Ticket Fees Going Up at Smaller Theaters." *Pittsburgh Post-Gazette*, 21 June 2007.

Miller, Bill. "Publicity." Interview with Jessica Bathurst. Tape recording, 15 November 2005. New York.

Nance, Kevin and Mike Thomas. "Chicago Arts Attendance Holding Its Own." *Chicago Sun-Times*, 7 June 2006.

Nedved, Will. "Publicity." Interview with Jessica Bathurst. Phone interview with author, 23 November 2005.

Newman, Andrew Adam. "During Intermission, Cellphones Are Brandished in Promotion." *New York Times*, 18 June 2007.

Page, Tim. "Live Opera to Come to Movie Theaters." *Washington Post*, 7 September 2006.

Passi, Peter. "Arts Pack Financial Punch." *Duluth News Tribune*, 30 March 2006.

Pekoe, Amanda. "Direct Marketing." Interview with Jessica Bathurst. E-mail to author, 30 January 2008.

Perry, Suzanne. "Marketing the Message." *Chronicle of Philanthropy*, 23 June 2005.

Pincus-Roth, Zachary. "Great Not-Just-White Way: Ethnic Shows Eye New Marketing Strategies." *Variety*, 7 March 2004.

Pitz, Marylynne. "Analyst Helps Arts Groups Target Likely Ticket Buyers." *Pittsburgh Post-Gazette*, 30 December 2004.

Playbill.com. "Producers of *Dirty Rotten Scoundrels* Sow Seeds of Score by Giving Away 50,000 Cast Albums April 27–May 31." Playbill.com, 20 April 2005. *www.playbill.com/news/article/92472.html.*

Pogrebin, Robin. "Operas for $20? New Audiences Hear Siren Song." *New York Times*, 9 October 2006.

Powers, Gary. "Box Office and Ticket Sales." Interview with Jessica Bathurst. Tape recording, 7 June 2006. New York.

The Publicity Office. "Sample Press Release." New York, 2003.

Roush, Janette. "Group Sales and Marketing." Interview with Christopher Thomasson. Tape recording, 26 October 2005. New York.

Rinaldi, Philip. "Publicity." Interview with Jessica Bathurst. Phone interview with author, 20 March 2006.

Robertson, Campbell. "Enter Stage Right: Live Advertisements." *New York Times*, 24 May 2006.

———. "Nielsen Brings a New Marketing Strategy to Broadway." *New York Times*, 1 August 2006.

———. "We All Got Together and Put On a . . . Brand." *New York Times*, 2 July 2006.

Rose, Marla Matzer. "A Fresh Face for Arts Groups: Competition Forces New Emphasis on 'Branding'." *Columbus Dispatch*, 26 July 2007.

Ruhe, Pierre. "Will the Atlanta Opera Solve Its Problems by Moving to Cobb?" *Atlanta Journal-Constitution*, 16 July 2006.

Russell, Jacob Hale. "The Great Green Way." *Wall Street Journal*, 22 October 2005.

———. "Orchestras Ponder Their Future." *Wall Street Journal*, 4 June 2006.

Sawotka, Sandy. "Publicity." Interview with Nadeisha Williams. Tape recording, 3 November 2005. Brooklyn Academy of Music, Brooklyn, N.Y.

Schneider, Keith. "Brands for the Chattering Masses." *New York Times*, 17 December 2006.

Sisario, Ben. "Walking the Line, Stalking Bargains on Broadway." *New York Times*, 15 September 2006.

Sparta, Christine. "Selling Your Season." *Stage Directions*, September 2005, 44–47.

Stabler, David. "Striking the Right Notes with 'Voters'." *Oregonian*, 6 November 2005.

Strini, Tom. "Symphony Boosts Subscriber Rolls." *Milwaukee Journal Sentinel*, 29 November 2006.

Taylor, Kate. "The BAM Example: Art Around Town." *New York Sun*, 11 July 2007.

———. "Performances in Print." *New York Sun.* 14 August 2006.

———. "Reaching a New Audience." *New York Sun.* 28 August 2007.

Teachout, Terry. "What Young Audiences Want." *Wall Street Journal*, 23 June 2007.

Topcik, Joel. "Yes, They Can Give 'Em Away." *New York Times*, 24 April 2005.

Urban Insitute. "Motivations Matter: Findings and Practical Implications of a National Survey of Cultural Participation." November 2005. *www.wallacefoundation.org/WF/Community/MotivationsMatter.*

Volz, Jim. *How to Run a Theater.* New York: Backstage Books, 2004.

von Rhein, John. "CSO Returns to Radio, Gets Own Record Label." *Chicago Tribune*, 30 November 2006.

Wakin, Daniel J. "A Butterfly (With Pipes) Lands in Times Square." *New York Times*, 15 September 2006.

———. "The Multiplex as Opera House: Will They Serve Popcorn?" *New York Times*, 7 September 2006.

Walker, Shorey. "Affinity Marketing." Interview with Jessica Bathurst. Tape recording, 11 July 2006. New York.

———. "Letter to RAs." New York, 2005.

Walker-Kuhne, Donna. "Audience Development." Interview with Jessica Bathurst. Tape recording, 4 January 2006. Brooklyn, N.Y.

———. *Invitation to the Party: Building Bridges to the Arts, Culture, and Community.* Theatre Communications Group: New York, 2005.

Weisstuch, Lisa. "With Subscribers Aging, Stage Companies Offer College Discounts and Free Nights." *Christian Science Monitor*, 14 October 2005.

Wilburn, Robert C. and Peter Rogovin. "Misconceptions Often Undermine Charity Marketing Efforts." *Chronicle of Philanthropy*, 4 October 2007.

Wolf, Thomas. "The Search for Shining Eyes: Audiences, Leadership, and Change in the Symphony Orchestra Field." John S. and James L. Knight Foundation. September 2006.

Wren, Celia. "At the Intersection of Optimism and Uncertainty." *American Theatre*, November 2006, 36–42.

CHAPTER EIGHT

Performing Arts Education

In this chapter, we will examine presenting and producing organizations that use both the performance and performance-related education programs to make curricular connections with public schools—prekindergarten through the twelfth grade.[1] We will also discuss best practices in developing performing arts education programs.

This chapter distinguishes performing arts education programs from family programs. Family programs, for the most part, are open to the public and serve the entire family. While there may be an educational component attached to a family program, this component isn't necessary.

WHAT IS PERFORMING ARTS EDUCATION?

What is performing arts education within the context of producing and presenting performing arts organizations? Producing organizations, such as Making Books Sing and Inside Broadway, and presenting organizations, like The New Victory Theater and the Brooklyn Academy of Music, use their productions and production-related education programs to integrate the arts into nonarts disciplines (math, science, literacy), or to teach students a particular art form, such as dance, music, playwriting, design, or acting.

What types of producing and presenting performing arts organizations have a performing arts education component? Producing organizations, such as theaters, opera and dance companies, and symphony orchestras, may all have performing arts education programs. Examples of such producing organizations include the Brooklyn Philharmonic Orchestra, Roundabout Theatre Company, Alvin Ailey American Dance Theater, Lincoln Center Theater, and New York City Opera. Presenting organizations with strong educational components

include Playhouse Square Center (Cleveland, Ohio), the Ordway Center for the Performing Arts (St. Paul, Minnesota), Urban Gateways: Center for Arts Education (Chicago, Illinois), and The New Victory Theater (New York, New York).[2]

In addition to these organizations, Darrell Ayers, vice president for education at the Kennedy Center, and his colleague Kim Peter Kovac, director of theater for young audiences, introduce us to a type of production called "theater for young audiences": "'Theater for young audiences' (TYA) seems to be the term most preferred for theatrical performances produced by adult professional performers that are intended for ages about 3 through 18 years old. It is also called 'children's theater,' as well as 'theater for young and family audiences.'"[3] TYA productions may be performed within schools, and may have additional educational components as well. Many of the large organizations producing theater for young audiences operate under the Actors' Equity TYA Contract, which defines a theater for young audience production as "a production of plays expressly written, created, or adapted to be performed for children. Performances are generally done during normal school hours and are limited to ninety minutes in length. In addition to performances, the agreement allows associated 'artist activity,' such as classes with the students."[4] "Theatre for Young Audiences/USA (the U.S. chapter of ASSITEJ, the International Association of Theatre for Children and Young People), the national service organization of professional producing theaters for young audiences, has a Web site (www.assitej-usa.org) that contains a listing of what most of the member theaters are producing each season."[5]

In any organization, performing arts education programs are managed by a dedicated director of education who creates and orchestrates the relationship between the school and the organization;

the director also hires and trains teaching artists. Suzanne Youngerman, director of the department of education and humanities at the Brooklyn Academy of Music, emphasizes that "teaching artists are working professional artists who are also experienced teachers. Teaching artists, along with either a classroom teacher or arts specialist, offer multiple workshops during a residency."[6]

Dr. Edie Demas, director of education at The New Victory Theater, explains the purpose of workshops as follows: "Experiential workshops enhance the performance experience and increase understanding of the art forms and themes presented in each New Victory presentation. The individual presentation's artistic sensibility, themes, and theatrical style form the basis for the design of each pre- and post-performance workshop plan. Partner schools receive developmentally appropriate workshops, taught by a team of specially trained teaching artists and education staff and adapted to meet the particular interests, needs, and schedule of each participating class."[7]

Multiple workshops may be presented as part of a residency. Paul King, director of theater programs at the New York City Department of Education, states that a "residency, in general terms, involves a teaching artist who spends an extended amount of time in the classroom with the teacher or arts specialist (a dance, music, or theater teacher) with a residency plan designed to teach students the art form or provide a connection through the arts to another discipline." The best type of residency can also be called a "partnership." King explains, "In a partnership, classroom teachers and teaching artists are trained together with support from both the performing arts organization and the school. There is a great deal of co-planning and there is a mutual accommodation of schedules. It's like a marriage. You are true partners."[8]

Debra Sue Lorenzen, cofounder and executive director of Making Books Sing, explores literature through theater arts, working exclusively with elementary school children. She distinguishes a residency from a partnership in this way: "Partnerships open many doors, making a significant impact on diverse stakeholders—from teacher to child, parent to administrator. Partnerships allow for so many precious opportunities that set the stage for exemplary teaching and learning, such as developing in-depth relationships between teachers and teaching artists or sequential curricula (curricula that build on previously learned curricula) that follow students as they proceed from one grade

to another. School reform through the arts can be among the great achievements of well-honed visionary partnerships."[9] King agrees: "When an arts organization develops a partnership with a school, the arts organization is really supporting the learning that is integral for that art form or for a particular discipline."[10]

Arlene Jordan, director of education at New York City Center, discusses her partnership experience. "Partner schools are looking for school change through the arts. New York City Center has been in partnership with a particular school for ten years. Our missions are aligned. The language of dance is something you feel the minute you walk through the school doors. Not only the teachers talk about it—the security guard and custodian know about it and talk about it. It's part of the identity of the school. Principal Joyce Bush, who sits on New York City Center's Education Advisory Committee, says, 'the partnership is sewn into the fabric of our school community.' Each year we reimagine and reinvigorate our work. We refine our goals, expand programming, and discover new ways to connect to the curriculum, assess student work, engage parents, and leverage additional funding. Over time, we have built a new culture within the school. Recently, we invited two other arts and cultural organizations to join us in an effort to deepen the learning and inspire students to create and showcase interdisciplinary original pieces that integrate dance, video, and spoken word."[11]

To assist teachers in preparing for workshops, residencies, and partnerships, performing arts organizations prepare study guides, which often include specific lesson plans that are connected to the learning standards established by the city or state. "Study guides generally include historical or cultural background about the performance work being studied, in addition to a bibliography, synopsis, biographies of the artists, and other supporting and background information. Study guides may also include individual or sequential lesson plans that teachers may use in the classroom."[12] Study guides are used by teachers and teaching artists to prepare students for the performance they will see.

For example, The New Victory Theater calls its study guide the *School Tool*. Demas explains, "In preparing the study guide, we follow the same structure for every guide. Teachers who have been with us for more than one season understand our format. There are always connections to the New York City Department of Education's *Blueprint for Teaching and Learning in the Arts*, state and national learning standards, as well as a section on what to do before the show. If the school is not planning a workshop with one of our teaching artists, the classroom teacher is able to follow the guide on his own. Each guide includes dramaturgical context, or information that gives theater history, criticism, and literary context, as well as information on the company, a synopsis of the production, focus questions, and hands-on activities that are designed to be used by the classroom teacher as a point of departure when planning his own lessons and/or units."[13]

In-school workshops, residencies, partnerships, and study guides are designed to prepare students for a professional performance either inside the school or at the performance venue. Inside Broadway's residency prepares students for Inside Broadway's adaptations of Broadway musicals, which are presented in public schools throughout New York City.[14] New York City Center's *Encores! in Residence* provides students with the opportunity to write their own original song and perform it before a community audience at New York City Center. The students also see a performance of *Encores!* at New York City Center.[15] Performing arts education activities at the professional venue can include talk-back sessions with the cast and crew, pre-performance or post-performance workshops with teaching artists, and backstage tours. Every professional venue activity is linked to the student's curriculum.

All education programs should also include a professional development component, in which teaching artists and classroom teachers can learn the best possible methods for implementing performing arts education programs. King believes, "Directors of education should carefully consider aligning the content and delivery of professional development with the goals and vision of the education program. In so doing, the process should be developed to answer these questions: How can the professional development deepen the learning in the art form for students by empowering teachers with a new understanding or experience in the art? How can teaching artists become more effective classroom practitioners through learning effective classroom management and pedagogical (teaching) skills?"[16]

Finally, performing arts education managers create evaluation and assessment tools. Program content may be evaluated and assessed by students, teachers, and/or teaching artists. Evaluation questions to students, teachers, and teaching artists center on the degree to which the program met its intended goals and objectives. "Assessment focuses on the degree to which the student [and teacher and teaching artists, as participants in professional development programs] has learned the content, can use specific skills, and demonstrates an understanding of the material, themes, and ideas that were embedded in the arts education learning experience."[17]

CLASSROOM DISCUSSION

What is performing arts education?

What is the role of the performing arts education manager?

What types of producing and presenting organizations have an educational component?

What does "theater for young audiences" mean?

Define these terms: "workshop," "residency," "partnership," "study guide," "teaching artist," "professional development," "assessment," and "evaluation."

Why is a good teacher–teaching artist relationship important?

PERFORMING ARTS EDUCATION PROGRAMS: BEST PRACTICES

Performing arts organizations that have established performing arts education programs create workshops and residencies that work inside and outside of the schools; have a strategy for approaching the schools and establishing curricular connections with the schools; produce professional development for teaching artists and teachers; and build ongoing evaluation and assessment tools. In the following section, we examine some of the best practices conceived and executed by leaders in the field.

Workshops and Residencies

Performing arts education programs are multi-faceted. In addition to the actual performance, the performing arts organization creates performance-related workshops and residencies that support the relationships among the students, teacher, and teaching artist. Performing arts managers at The New Victory Theater, Inside Broadway, Lincoln Center Theater, and New York City Center discuss some of their best practices in this section.

The New Victory Theater

Cora Cahan, president of The New 42nd Street, Inc. (which operates The New Victory Theater), describes The New Victory's commitment to its educational programs as such: "The heart and soul of The New Victory Theater is to bring young people to the New Vic who might not otherwise ever have the opportunity to get to a theater; for them to come to the heart of the city and find themselves in a place where the lights go down, the curtain goes up, and something magical happens . . . [Instantly] they are changed a bit forever. That's why from the beginning the education program was always so important, because those kids might not otherwise make this discovery."[18] "The New Victory is founded upon a close synergy between its public and its arts education and outreach components,[19] each of which centers around the dynamic productions presented onstage throughout the season.

"In order to achieve this synergy, The New 42nd Street has contractually required every company or artist presented by The New 42nd Street in a New Victory season to perform for student audiences as well. This has resulted in 513 school performances between the 1995–1996 and the 2006–2007 seasons, introducing over 193,000 pre-K to twelfth-grade students and teachers to a broad spectrum of the performing arts. The New Victory Theater Education Program has experienced ongoing expansion, with school memberships growing by over 400 percent in just eleven seasons.

"The New Victory Education Program has the following three components:

1. Education Membership and Performances enable pre-K to twelfth-grade schoolchildren and teachers to see acclaimed New Victory productions via $2 student tickets, accompanied by free tickets for teachers.
2. *New Vic School Tools* (study guides) are a resource for pre-K to twelfth-grade teachers demonstrating arts-based thematic units and presenting concrete, comprehensive connections to city, state, and national standards.
3. New Vic In-the-Classroom and Residency Programs are provided at no additional cost to member teachers. Taught by New Victory Education staff and teaching artists, these interactive workshop sessions are designed to promote active engagement with the performances, increase art-form literacy, and stimulate students to listen, look, observe, and write critically. In addition, participating teachers gain valuable, firsthand experience working with performing arts education methods in their own classrooms while collaborating with trained teaching artists.

"In order to execute the workshops and residencies, the New Victory collaborates intensively with a team of professional, highly skilled, and creative [teaching] artists. Currently, this team consists of thirty-seven artists, whose skills range from commedia dell'arte to contemporary dance; from world puppetry to playwriting; from classical to hip-hop to avant-garde theater and beyond. [Teaching] artists participate in both season-related and general training sessions throughout the year. Our workshops, residencies, training sessions, and other activities rely upon the ongoing collaboration between full-time staff and teaching artists, participating classroom teachers, and the artistically nourishing resources of The New Victory Theater's presentations."[20]

Inside Broadway

Inside Broadway is "a professional New York City–based children's theater company committed to producing Broadway's classic musicals in a contemporary light for young audiences. Our aim is to pass down the rich legacy of America's musical theater to future generations so that the magic, music, and universal themes of the genre are not lost, but rediscovered and made relevant for today's youth."[21] Executive Director Michael Presser and Program Director Katie McAllister feel strongly about the importance of live performance in an arts education program. Presser contends that "you just can't sit in a classroom and discuss theater and feel that you know theater unless you see it. School programs must have a performance component that exposes students to theater at the highest possible level."[22]

For true learning to occur, there must be a link between classroom learning and the professional performance. To prepare students for viewing the professional performance, McAllister creates a teaching artist residency. She explains the residency: "Our teaching artist residencies are all curriculum-based. They meet all of the English language arts, social studies, and math standards. Our most popular programs are called "Build a Musical" and "Song and Dance." The only difference between the two is that "Song and Dance" is a shorter residency than "Build a Musical." After the school selects the residency, the students will receive scripts to a show like *Bye, Bye Birdie* (or whatever show we are doing), and they'll learn songs and dances with the help of the teaching artist. It's a complete tie-in. Students learn songs and dances through modeling, which means that you demonstrate the work, and then they do it. If students are learning choreography, teaching artists show them the choreography and students repeat it. Or teaching artists will sing part of the song, and the children will repeat it. For small children, this is the best way to learn a song.

"They also get a study guide that lists background information on the show and the era when the show was first produced. A couple of seasons ago, we did a rock-and-roll show, *Smokey Joe's Cafe*. Our teaching artists taught students about what was going on in the 1950s. Student learned about the inventions of the fifties, including Barbie, Kraft singles, and ballpoint pens. They also learned that Disneyland opened in California, and that the Port Authority in New York City was created as well.

"Most of our relationships with schools have been ongoing, anywhere from five to ten years. We have an incredible amount of repeat business. I'm proud of that because there are lots of arts organizations that offer performing arts education programs. When developing a relationship with a school, we study its curricula. Some schools want us to focus on the curricula of every grade. In one of our schools, we work with students from kindergarten to eighth grade. That's a lot of residency programming, because you can't do with kindergarteners what you do with eighth-graders.

"We also do programs for children with special needs. When working with this type of student, we want to know what the needs are. Do the students have physical or mental disabilities? Do they have behavioral problems? We do a site visit with the school; I'll observe the children and advise the school with regard to the right type of residency. I will work with the principal, or whoever's in charge. I will ask, 'What do you think is really going to work?'"[23] In seeking a relationship with a particular school, the organization must always keep in mind that what will work for one school may not work for another. Thus, McAllister's question to the school officials— "What do *you* think is really going to work?"—is central to creating a successful partnership between a performing arts organization and a school.[24]

Lincoln Center Theater
Kati Koerner, director of education for Lincoln Center Theater (LCT), "considers school programs as those that are coordinated with the principals and teachers of a school and involve students during school hours. These may be pre-show workshops, residencies, or attendance at matinee performances. LCT generally does not schedule all-student matinees, but prefers to integrate student audiences into the 'regular' patron audience. Lincoln Center Theater doesn't produce plays specifically for young audiences. Therefore, all education activities at LCT are extrinsic to the act of presenting/producing. This does not make the education work any less meaningful to the organization; it is merely a different point of departure.

"LCT's mission states that it 'strives to create and sustain a theater of high artistic standards, producing the work of established as well as emerging American and international playwrights, as well as carefully wrought revivals from the world's classical repertoire. The most accomplished artists working in the theater today regularly appear on Lincoln Center Theater's stages.' Although the word 'education' does not appear in this mission statement, LCT's education programs enable students from schools that are under-resourced in the arts to have access to LCT, a major New York City cultural institution. As theater is a uniquely effective means of teaching critical and creative thinking skills, learning in and through the art form supports teacher creativity and effectiveness and allows students of widely different educational needs and learning styles to become more engaged in their learning process."[25]

Koerner introduces her programs: "LCT's Open Stages education program includes our core high school and middle school programs, which provide both pre- and post-show in-class workshops, visits to the theater, and a series of teacher professional development workshops; long-term residencies that support particular areas of learning, such as our Songwriting in the Schools Program; and the LEAD Project (Learning English & Drama), an extended residency program that pairs a theater teaching artist with an ESL (English as a Second Language) classroom teacher and uses theater to support English-language instruction among recent immigrants. In all, LCT's education programs serve approximately three thousand students and fifty-five teachers in twenty-eight schools across the New York City public school system."[26]

Koerner describes her partnership with the schools: "Before we begin working with a school, we communicate clearly all expectations of our collaboration to both the participating teachers and the principal. Generally, we have a kickoff meeting at the theater attended by all participating teachers, in which the show being studied that semester is introduced, and we talk through all logistics.

"The lesson plans for LCT's pre-show workshops are created through a collaborative process with our team of teaching artists. We collectively articulate two or three themes from the play that the students will be seeing, choosing ones that we feel young people will find most compelling, or that encapsulate some information that will be vital to the students' enjoyment and comprehension of the performance. We then develop a series of lesson plans that offer a common frame of reference for all students attending our shows.

"Pre- and post-show lesson plans are presented to all of the teachers in our program during a professional development session at LCT. (Subsequently, teaching artists meet at the school with each teacher in whose classroom they will be working for a forty-five-minute planning meeting. This meeting is less about curriculum design and more about tailoring the lesson to suit the needs and curricular interests of a particular class.) The initial professional development session is part of a series of four two-hour professional development workshops per semester at LCT that give them insight into the production being studied and allow them to make curricular connections. The workshops frequently introduce teachers to basic classroom drama techniques as well.

"For students, the teaching artists execute four pre-and post-show workshops per show in both the high school and middle school programs. Over the course of a school year, participants in the Open Stages high school program will see two shows and experience a total of eight in-class workshops. Participants in the semester-long Open Stages middle school Shakespeare program attend one performance.

"Residencies obviously include a lot more planning time and a lot more involvement with the school's administration. Residencies, such as our LEAD Project, have an explicitly curricular connection that is determined by the school. Because the LEAD Project requires such an extensive time commitment on the part of teachers (the planning time is equal to the time spent in the classroom), and also requires the willingness to integrate drama into the ELL (English Language Learner) curriculum, I spend a considerable amount of time in discussions with the administration prior to starting the project in their school. We also call all LEAD Project participants (teaching artists, teachers, and LCT education staff) in for meetings at LCT four times a year. These are opportunities for everyone involved in the project to share what they've been doing, as well as opportunities for professional development. The group can help to brainstorm possible solutions and share ideas with one another. The teaching artists meet alone an additional two times per semester to share strategies and problem-solve together. Schools currently assume approximately one-third of the cost of the LEAD Project. The rest is supported by grants from education funders."[27]

New York City Center

New York City Center is renowned for its presentation of world-class companies, as well as its acclaimed, Tony Award–honored *Encores!* series that celebrates one of America's indigenous art forms—musical theater. Through this series, audiences rediscover the rarely heard music of America's greatest composers and lyricists as performed by today's top Broadway talent. As an educational complement, *Encores! in Schools* offers two programs that engage students in the musical, movement, and theatrical components of the stage, while having an impact on teaching and learning in the schools: *Encores! Putting It Together*, a model that offers students an introduction into the world of musical theater, and *Encores! In Residence*, a more in-depth learning experience.

Arlene Jordan meets with school administrators and teachers to craft a program that meets the unique needs of each school. Jordan notes, "We believe it is essential for New York City Center and the schools to align our missions, identify clear expectations, and establish open communication among the teaching artists, arts specialists, and classroom teachers. All bring their own unique talents."[28] *Encores! Putting It Together* cultivates the next generation of audiences and gives students firsthand experience in singing, dancing, acting, and creating. The goal is to instill a respect for the creative collaboration necessary to produce works in musical theater and to empower students to create their own work. Students learn and polish numbers from an *Encores!* show and work with a composer/lyricist intern team from New York University's Graduate Musical Theatre Writing Program to write lyrics to an original song. In the more extended *Encores! in Residence*, in addition to rehearsing a scene and musical number from a current *Encores!* show, students create and rehearse an original scene and song based on themes generated by the class.

The residency program is rich and rigorous. Jordan explains: "Students explore the historical context for specific musical theater productions, while building a vocabulary within musical theater and making literacy connections to the school curriculum. By making and reflecting on personal artistic choices, students articulate their own goals and speak thoughtfully about the collective theater-making process. Embedded in the creative work are multiple opportunities for students to self–assess and engage in ongoing dialogue and reflection with their peers and teachers about how they can use their skills to make their pieces better."[29]

Key to the success of the program is professional development. Each year begins with an intensive day, in which teachers come together to build performance skills and confidence. The session gives them a hands-on opportunity to write a one-minute play and go through the process of experiencing how a dramatic moment becomes musical theater. According to Jordan, "It's inspiring to witness the creativity and willingness of teachers to take risks, use their imagination, and identify applications to their respective disciplines."[30] On-site professional development occurs throughout the year as City Center's veteran teaching artists model professional practices.

Most exciting is the cross-school Sharing Sessions, where students from four schools meet in a City Center studio to perform for each other, ask questions, and provide feedback. Jordan says, "The energy in the studio is palpable as over one hundred students from across the city have their moment to shine."[31] The evening concludes as all students see what artistic choices the professionals have made for their own performance of the *Encores!* show at City Center's dress rehearsal.[32]

CLASSROOM DISCUSSION

Why is it important for performing arts education to have an arts-making component for students and/or teachers?

Why is it important for a performing arts organization to have a performance attendance component for teachers and students? Why might it be important for the organization itself?

What does "modeling" mean?

What kind of information should go into a study guide?

Discuss the various types of workshops and residencies developed by producing and presenting organizations.

Approaching the School and Developing Curricular Connections

The New Victory Theater, Inside Broadway, Lincoln Center Theater, and New York City Center have all developed strong workshops and residencies, in which curricular connections with their partnering schools are essential. Curricular connections are not made in a vacuum. True partnerships between the schools and performing arts organizations involve crafting an approach whereby both parties contribute to the process. In the next section, we discuss this process in greater detail with the help of Darrell Ayers and Kim Peter Kovac from the Kennedy Center and Debra Sue Lorenzen of Making Books Sing.

The Kennedy Center

The Kennedy Center is well known for its performing arts education programs. Reaching over 11 million people each year, the Kennedy Center's programs focus on presenting performances for young people, school-based education programs, and developing resources for arts managers, students, teachers, principals, and teaching artists.[33] For more specific information about all of these programs, please visit the Kennedy Center's Web site (*www.kennedy-center.org*) and see the bibliography at the end of this chapter.

Darrell Ayers and Kim Peter Kovac have this advice for those performing arts managers who want to establish a relationship with a school. "Before beginning a relationship, it is important to establish what each partner hopes to gain from the relationship. Creating a written document that defines the relation between the organizations is important. (Please see appendix A for a sample partnership agreement.)[34] These established benchmarks help to ensure that both partners' needs are met, or if they are not, they state what steps can be taken to rectify the situation or dissolve the partnership. Both organizations' money and time are valuable. Don't allow a partnership to flounder. Address any concerns immediately. If mutual agreement cannot be reached, then the partnership should be dissolved. Move on; there are too many potential school partnerships out there to waste each other's precious time and resources.

"It is always better to create a plan together than to take prepackaged or pre-formed programs into the schools. There is no program that can be exactly replicated from community to community. It must be adapted to the individual needs and desires of the specific school and classroom.

"Meet with someone high in administration, preferably the superintendent in smaller school systems or the appropriate senior staff in a large school system. First and foremost, it is necessary to determine the level of interest for your organization to work in the school system.

"If there is interest, get the superintendent (or senior staff) to assign the most appropriate person with whom you can work. With that staff person, develop a list of schools that may be appropriate or have a level of interest in your program. Next, meet with the principal of each school and determine his level of interest, his need, his past participation in partnerships, and other organizations with whom the school is working. Be careful not to select a school that has too many partnerships. Also determine the type of art(s) being taught in the school.

"If all parties are in agreement, a formal, written partnership plan should be developed, listing what the performing arts organization will provide and what the school will provide, as well as what will be accomplished by the partnership. It should include dates by which tasks will be completed. This document allows each partner to know what is expected, and it will be used to evaluate the effectiveness and success of the partnership. And finally, careful planning with the specific teacher(s) is imperative."[35]

Performing arts organizations and schools develop relationships based on the assumption that there will be curricular connections made between the performing arts educational programming and the school curricula. Ayers and Kovac maintain that "if specific curricular connections are being made, the connections should be significant rather than superficial. It is easy to arbitrarily say something is connected to the curriculum, e.g., using a song to memorize the fifty states and saying that is arts education or arts integration. True arts integration and arts education need to be sequential and in-depth. Arts for arts' sake are important, as is the need for arts integration. Arts integration allows the organization to connect with more than just the arts teachers; it allows work to be accomplished with classroom teachers as well."

The Kennedy Center has done significant work in both arts education and arts integration. Amy Duma, director of teacher and school programs at the Kennedy Center, defines their arts integration approach in fig. 8.1.[36]

Fig. 8.1. Arts Integration, The Kennedy Center Model

THE CHANGING EDUCATION THROUGH THE ARTS (CETA) PROGRAM'S
Definition and Characteristics of Arts-Integrated Instruction

There are many approaches to arts-integrated instruction and each has its own merit. The CETA program focuses on teaching other subject area(s) *through* the arts in a school that also has an active arts curriculum (arts for arts' sake). The program defines arts integration as instruction that makes natural and significant connection(s) between a subject area (e.g., science, social studies, language arts, and/or mathematics) and an art form. Arts-integrated instruction complements discipline-based instruction. The goal of the CETA program is to help students learn more fluently and with greater motivation. Students master learning objectives in *both* the subject area and the art form.

The following checklist describes the characteristics of effective arts-integrated instruction. The characteristics can be used as criteria for determining effectiveness.

Characteristics of Effective Arts-Integrated Instruction

❏   Connections between the subject area(s) and the arts are natural, significant, and developmentally appropriate. Overlapping content and/or skills from both the subject area and the art form ensures that a connection is natural and significant but not forced.

❏   Each subject area and art form included in the integrated unit/lesson(s) has clearly defined and developmentally appropriate instructional objectives. These objectives are the basis for both instruction and assessment and are linked to national and/or state standards of learning. Objectives identify what students will know, be able to do, and appreciate in each discipline.

❏ Instruction involves students in active learning by drawing on students' multiple intelligences and various learning styles. Students are involved in learning arts processes and/or in making arts products.

❏ Learning activities require students to solve problems similar to those that choreographers, designers, composers, and visual artists wrestle with in their work. These real-life problems are complex, have no single answer, and require multiple steps to solve.

❏ Teachers use inquiry methods for instruction. Teachers pose open-ended questions to guide student learning.

❏ Arts-integrated instruction involves students actively; they observe and respond, imagine, analyze, hypothesize, create, reflect, revise, evaluate, and revise again.

❏ Teachers play different roles depending on the instructional need. Sometimes teachers play the role of director, while at other times teachers are facilitators. Still other times, teachers play the role of encourager, coach, or critic.

❏ Classroom management strategies support intensive, creative work.

❏ Performance assessments (e.g., reviews of student portfolios or arts products, such as plays, visual artworks, poetry, songs, dances, storytelling, and puppet shows) and criterion-referenced assessments are used to evaluate student learning.

❏ Students have roles in assessment. They help design tasks, criteria, and/or descriptors on which their work will be judged. Students engage in self-assessment and peer assessment.

Developed by Amy Duma, Director, Teacher and School Programs, The Kennedy Center ©2005
Do Not Photocopy or Distribute without Permission.
© January 2005 The John F. Kennedy Center for the Performing Arts

Making Books Sing

"Making Books Sing adapts books into plays and musicals for the professional stage, which serve as a model for children to adapt other books into plays and musicals. Since books are a vitally important part of a literacy curriculum, the connection is clear and direct."[37] Debra Sue Lorenzen of Making Books Sing shares her process for establishing curricular connections: "Curricular connections should not be viewed as an unfortunate necessity to validate the devotion of precious instructional time to drama. Theater arts are organically intertwined with the language arts curriculum (which covers speaking, listening, reading, writing, and viewing), as well as other art forms, history, culture, and so much more. The performing arts also help kids develop a long list of cross-curricular skills such as research, teamwork, social development, higher-order thinking, creativity, and risk-taking. In my opinion, these natural connections should be embraced and celebrated.

"The creation of theater is a prime opportunity for project-based learning, during which children are immersed in layered, substantive, and exciting learning across many content areas. Theater opens the door for children who think and learn in different ways to develop their potential as creative, literate team players, allowing them to succeed in life.

"In order to make curricular connections, we have to know the New York City curricula. We make it our business to familiarize our staff and teaching artists with Balanced Literacy (New York City's standardized literacy curriculum); the recommended social studies curriculum; and the arts curriculum at each school. We strive to be well versed in the New York State Learning Standards in English Language Arts, the Arts, and Social Studies. New York City also has a wonderful *Blueprint* for each arts discipline that denotes what children should know and be able to do at distinct benchmarks (second grade, fifth grade, eighth grade, and commencement). We give great care to aligning our work with these standards.

"We learn about these programs through various channels. For example, our school partners share information with us and offer us tutorials, and we (Making Books Sing staff and teaching artists) attend professional development workshops on these curricula. The art and music curricula are different from school to school, so we routinely meet with our schools' arts specialists to learn about their work with the children and to discover possible connections.

"In selecting books to adapt, we choose illustrated children's books, since our target audience is primary school children, their teachers, and families. Books are selected with New York City's standardized core curriculum in literacy and social studies in mind. For example, we choose literary genres studied by the students, such as historical fiction or memoirs; we also select books that might illuminate areas of study in social studies, such as family, Native America, immigration, and post–Civil War America. Historical figures might be prominent characters in our adaptations. The books always have children as central characters, so kids can make text-to-self connections readily. Connections to art and music curricula are also possible.

"However, the primary goal in selecting a book is its potential to adapt into an excellent play or musical. The book must have literary merit, with beautiful illustrations, rich language, and meaningful content. It should have exemplary literary elements, such as strong characters, the potential for conflict (not always present in children's books), and a great theme. Equally as important, the books and the stage production should never be didactic or pedestrian.

"We provide Making Books Sing Curriculum Packets to the schools attending our productions. The packets include a copy of the adapted book, a Teachers' Resource Guide with information that will help teachers make curriculum connections, and a CD of music relevant to the production. In addition, we engage in professional development with all our school partners and many of our ticket-buying schools to illuminate and discuss curriculum connections.

"The planning process for a residency includes a workshop that focuses exclusively on curricular connections. Teachers and Making Books Sing staff explore their curriculum map, a calendar of the main topics in their curriculum throughout the year. We also discuss what the students have studied before the residency begins, and what they will be working on during the residency. We examine specific skills the residency program might support, such as sequencing, understanding a character, writing dialogue, or reading between the lines of the book.

"During this workshop, teachers are asked to choose books for their classes to adapt. We recommend books germane to their social studies or literacy curriculum; illustrated books; books related by theme, genre, or author to our professional adaptation; and especially books they and their children will enjoy working on for the next four to six months. While we provide a list of recommendations, they have tremendous freedom of choice. We encourage them to choose many books, and during in-depth planning sessions, we review them and make a final selection—based on which one has the most potential for adaptation. Later, each teacher will meet with the teaching artist to tailor his lesson plans to the book, as well as the academic and arts-based needs of each class."[38]

CLASSROOM DISCUSSION

What are the important components of a partnership agreement between a performing arts organization and a school? (See appendix A.)

What is the Kennedy Center's process for approaching a school?

What is arts-integrated instruction?

What are the characteristics of effective arts-integrated instruction?

Describe the process of making curricular connections with schools.

Professional Development

Professional development, involving the training of teachers and teaching artists, is a critical part of all performing arts educational programming. In this section, we review Making Books Sing's professional development program.

Making Books Sing

The selection and training of teaching artists is an important part of performing arts education. Debra Sue Lorenzen states, "Teaching artists are your front line. They represent your organization and are largely responsible for the realization of your pedagogy (educational philosophy) and curriculum. Making Books Sing hires trained, working theater artists who can impart their craft to young people in an effective and caring way. They are directors, actors, performance artists, musicians, composers, lyricists, playwrights, and dramaturgs, and any combination thereof. Most of our artist educators fall within three or four of these categories. I often find that, for the most gifted teaching artists, their work as artists is informed by their work with children, and their work with children is informed by their work as artists.

"Making Books Sing teaching artists must have: the ability to write a cohesive lesson plan, a sensitivity to the inner workings of and demands placed on schools, classroom management skills, and working knowledge of core curriculum areas supported by Making Books Sing. They must also love children and be driven to serve kids and share their artistry.

"Being a teaching artist is a very difficult profession. Being a good teaching artist is even harder, and it takes commitment to hone your craft. Teaching artists require tremendous energy, stamina, artistry, and intellect.

"The quality of your programs depends highly on the quality of your teaching artists. Helping your teaching artists develop the skills they need to be successful is crucial. Making Books Sing strives to provide a great deal of ongoing support and differentiated training for our teaching artists. New teaching artists must enroll in a three-part 'course' in which they are immersed in Making Books Sing's pedagogy, curriculum, and lesson-planning strategies. We take them through the process of writing lessons and require them to teach a sample lesson in a classroom before they are placed in a residency.

"Returning teaching artists also participate in training. Since they have firsthand experience with our pedagogy and curriculum, they receive skills-based training on topics of interest or need, such as child development, tailoring a lesson to a special-needs class, and serving the English-language learner. We also do cross-discipline training, so the musical theater and drama teaching artists can learn from each other.

"In addition, we work one-on-one with all of our teaching artists to develop their lesson plans. We conduct site visits during their classroom teaching and provide feedback and advice. We help them set personal and professional goals related to their teaching artistry.

"Throughout this process, I focus on teaching artists' strengths. For example, if a teaching artist can effectively lead a host of engaging drama games but has limited lesson planning ability, I will ask: 'How can we take your favorite activities and modify them into a well-written lesson with clear goals?'"[39]

Lorenzen has a professional development program for her partnering teachers as well. She describes the process: "My ideal educational program for any child is one in which all teachers consider themselves arts specialists. They would have received excellent training in the arts in their own primary and secondary education. They would have the training, from undergraduate school on, to teach any and all academic curriculum through the arts. Elementary and secondary school teachers would have the freedom and skill to create short- and long-term theater arts projects that engage children in writing, performing, designing, building, and marketing a theater production.

"Making Books Sing has two approaches with regard to the professional development of classroom teachers. The first strategy engages teachers in the process of discovering the potential, relevance, and value of theater education in their core academic curriculum. This strategy is folded into the planning for teaching artist residencies. Training can range from three to eight hours with residency teachers at a given school. The time is divided into at least three workshops, arranged in a whole group (all the teachers participating in the program), small groups (e.g., all teachers in the same cluster or section or all second-grade teachers), and one-on-one training with each teacher.

"The workshops concentrate on guiding teachers through discovering the impact of the production on them and their students. Through hands-on activities and discussion, we explore their personal connections to and interest in the book under study; our adaptation and the residency; curriculum connections, particularly in literacy and social studies; and targeted skills in areas such as language arts, theater, music, or social development. We also offer skills-based workshops that train teachers to use specific theater games, improvisation, or music activities to reinforce student learning about a book's literary elements.

"Lesson planning, which occurs one-on-one with each teacher, allows the teaching artist and teacher to negotiate the ways in which the teacher can actively participate during residency sessions and reinforce arts learning in between residency sessions. Teachers set personal goals for the residency, so that they can strive to grow and learn. Then, throughout the residency, teachers are encouraged and guided toward meeting their professional academic goals."[40]

CLASSROOM DISCUSSION
What are the qualities of a good teaching artist?
What type of training should a teaching artist receive?
What type of training should a teacher receive?

Evaluation and Assessment
According to Darrell Ayers and Kim Peter Kovac, "Evaluation and assessment must go hand-in-hand in order to determine the true success of a program. One cannot simply evaluate the success of a program without assessing what the participants have learned. In-depth evaluation and assessment are expensive. Most organizations cannot afford to have an outside evaluation, so internally, staff must focus on being brutally honest about the true impact and success of the program through observation and formal written feedback. This can be done with quantitative [numerically based] and qualitative [narrative-based] measures. Some questions to think about include:

Quantitative Measures:
• How many people attended the program?
• How many people completed the evaluation/ feedback form?

Qualitative Measures:
• What did the participants write about the program?
• As you observed the program, were the participants engaged throughout the entire process?"[41]

Arlene Jordan also believes that evaluation and assessment techniques must be closely linked. "Assessing the performance of students, teachers, and teaching artists is a way of evaluating the program. We attempt to triangulate the data by using at least three sources. In our Choreography Residencies, for instance, teachers and teaching artists use a rubric[42] three times a year to assess each student; students complete pre- and post-attitudinal surveys and use journals and a rubric to self-assess their progress; a master teaching artist observes the style and methodology of the teaching artists and provides them with detailed suggestions for improvement; and teachers give New York City Center feedback on the success of the program from

their perspective. As education director, and a former Department of Education supervisor, I observe instruction with the principals. An assessment team then meets to analyze the qualitative and quantitative data, reflect on burning questions that have arisen in the process, and determine adjustments that will result in a more effective program."[43]

In the next section, Debra Sue Lorenzen from Making Books Sing and Cathryn Williams from the Lincoln Center Institute for the Arts in Education share their evaluation and assessment strategies. Making Books Sing provides samples of evaluation and assessment tools. We also share a letter from a teacher evaluating and assessing the strength of The New Victory Theater's education programs.

Evaluation
Regarding the difference between evaluation and assessment tools, Debra Sue Lorenzen states, "Cultural institutions must be sensitive to the many demands placed on public school teachers' time. Program evaluation forms such as the one on pages 353–355, created by Making Books Sing, strive to gather feedback and anecdotes that will inform future program decisions. This practice is different from assessment, which is intended to capture the progress made by students, teachers, and teaching artists in developing understanding, knowledge, and skills."[44]

Fig. 8.2. Making Books Sing Program Evaluation

PROGRAM EVALUATION FORM [FOR TEACHERS]: 2005–06

SCHOOL: _____   GRADE: _____

1=POOR   2= FAIR   3= GOOD   4= EXCELLENT

Overall rating of Residency.   1   2   3   4

What worked well?	Why?
What did not work well?	**Suggestions for Improvement.**

Fig. 8.2. (continued)

Overall rating of Teaching Artist.   **1**   **2**   **3**   **4**

What worked well?	Why?
What did not work well?	**Suggestions for improvement.**

Overall rating of Teachers' Guide.   **1**   **2**   **3**   **4**

What worked well?	Why?
What did not work well?	**Suggestions for improvements.**

Overall rating of **The Orphan Singer** *production.*   **1**   **2**   **3**   **4**

What worked well?	Why?
What did not work well?	How could we improve?

Overall rating of Planning Sessions.   **1**   **2**   **3**   **4**

What worked well?	Why?
What did not work well?	Suggestions for improvements.

Assessment

Cathryn Williams is the director of strategic alliances for the Lincoln Center Institute for the Arts in Education (LCI). "For more than thirty years, LCI has developed and refined its own distinctive approach to the arts and education, one that challenges all students to learn about and through the arts. Working in partnership with pre-K through grade-twelve educators, as well as college teacher education programs, the Institute develops experiential studies focusing on works of art, including dance, music, theater, visual arts, film, and architecture. Since its inception, LCI has served over 20 million students, educators, parents, and community members worldwide."[45] (For more information about LCI, please visit their Web site at *www.lcinstitute.org*, and see the bibliography at the end of this chapter.) Williams defines the major components of an assessment tool below:[46]

Fig. 8.3. Making Books Sing Student Assessment Tool

SKILL	4	3	2	1
Creating character with body, voice, and gesture	Uses body, voice, and gesture to depict a character	Uses a combination of body, voice, and gesture to depict a character	Uses either body, voice, or gesture to depict a character	Does not use body, voice, or gesture to depict a character
Depicting character emotions	Always creates a clear emotion for his/her character	Usually creates a clear emotion for his/her characters	Tries to create an emotion for a character, but unclear	Character emotions are unclear or nonexistent
Working well with others in small groups	Actively participates, contributes many ideas, and remains focused throughout a small-group session	Maintains focused for most of a small-group session, but offers few ideas	Loses focus and interest during small-group work; contributes little.	Refuses to participate in a small-group session
Sequencing	Retells story using accurate sequencing	Retells story in sequence, but misses a few important details	Retells part of story in sequence, misses most details	Retells story out of sequence and without details
Using proper script format	Uses standard script format properly throughout his/her written work	Uses some elements of standard script format in his/her written work	Inconsistently or improperly uses standard script format	Does not use standard script format
Being an attentive, invested audience member	Sits quietly and attentively as an audience member	Sits quietly and attentively for most of a performance; may lose concentration but does not distract others	Begins by sitting quietly and attentively, but becomes noisy, restless, and distracting over time	Restless and disruptive as an audience member
Reflecting on other students' work	Offers a lot of clear and constructive feedback to peer groups on characters, plot, or dialogue	Offers some constructive feedback to peer groups	Offers feedback that does not reflect a clear understanding of the task	Offers no feedback

- Student-generated work—evidence of learning.
- Review and assessment meetings between teachers and teaching artists; between teachers and students; [and] between teaching artists and students.
- Assessment surveys and tools completed by teachers, teaching artists, and students. [In assessing professional development programs, teachers and teaching artists will also be assessed by the performing arts organization.]
- End-of-unit written reflections to a set of questions.
- Written and verbal communications between LCI staff and school leaders, as well as LCI staff and teaching artists.

Page 356 shows a rubric for assessing individual students in a class in which students work in whole and small groups to create a scene with clear characters, plot, and dialogue. The small groups share their work with one another. In this rubric, a "4" reflects mastery of the skills, "3" is approaching mastery, "2" indicates developing skill, and "1" indicates no evidence of skill.[47]

As an important part of the education department's reflective process, teachers are often asked to write letters commenting on the program. Marjorie Damashek Levine, the drama director at Beach Channel High School in Rockaway Park, New York, wrote the letter shown in fig. 8.4 to The New Victory Theater.[48]

Tuesday April 20, 2006

Dear Edie:

The School Membership has enabled hundreds of economically and academically challenged students to experience the wonders of live theater in Manhattan. Our school is Title I, which means we are eligible for Free Lunch due to the economic makeup of our students. And we are a Corrective Action Year I school, which means we are not making the grade in terms of numbers of students passing the English Regents and Math Regents and the percentage of students graduating in four years. We are also cited for poor attendance. The variety of your season has enabled not only the drama classes, but also the dance and even the history classes to enjoy and learn about different genres in the theater. The students have a powerful motivation to attend their classes regularly in order to be included in this wonderful opportunity. Next year, we will have more delineated Small Learning Communities, and one of them will be "The Arts." I will work closely with the Team Leader to include the New Victory into our CEP again and into the design of the Drama and Dance Institutes.

The In-Classroom Workshops have taught experienced teachers a thing or two about Interactive Strategies and have reinforced the Blueprint principles that improve Theater Literacy, Playmaking, Acting, Directing, Choreography, Set Design, and many of the various strands. Many students had never before been to the theater and some have never been to the city. Living out on the peninsula can be a bit isolating, but it doesn't have to be if you are a member of The New Victory Theater. Thank you all for your hard work and the wonderful services that you provide.

Sincerely,

Marjorie Damashek Levine
Drama Director/UFT TC Professional Developer Beach Channel High School

Fig. 8.4. Teacher's Letter of Support

CLASSROOM DISCUSSION

What is the difference between evaluation and assessment? Why must evaluation and assessment go hand in hand?

What do evaluation tools measure?

What do assessment tools measure?

Why is performing arts education program evaluation important to an arts organization?

Why is performing arts education program evaluation important to a school?

Why is assessment of student learning important?

How can assessment of student learning shape the education program structure and delivery?

Why is it important for a performing arts organization to receive support letters from teachers and students?

NOTES

1. The authors would like to thank the following contributors to this chapter: Darrell Ayers, Dale Byam, Cora Cahan, Dr. Edie Demas, Denis Guerin, Arlene Jordan, Paul King, Kati Koerner, Kim Peter Kovac, Marjorie Damashek Levine, Debra Sue Lorenzen, Katie McAllister, Dr. David Morris, Michael Presser, Nicole Novy Schneider, Cathryn Williams, and Suzanne Youngerman. Curricular connections are connections made from the art to a particular course of study.
2. Darrell Ayers and Kim Peter Kovac, e-mail interview to author, January 9, 2006.
3. Ibid.
4. Actors' Equity Association, "Theatre for Young Audiences National Agreement," *www.actorsequity.org/agreements/agreements.asp?code=080*.
5. Ayers and Kovac, "E-mail interview."
6. Suzanne Youngerman, interview by Lynn Hyde, November 4, 2005.
7. Edie Demas, Mary Rose Lloyd, and Lisa Lawer Post, "Performing Arts Education." Interview by Tobie Stein, tape recording, May 22, 2006, The New Victory Theater, New York.
8. Paul King, interview by Cristin Kelly, October 25, 2005. The terms "workshop," "residency," and "partnership" may vary in content, depending on the organization and the school district.
9. Debra Sue Lorenzen, e-mail interviews to author, November 30, 2005 and May 3, 2006.
10. King, "Interview."
11. Arlene Jordan, interview by Cristin Kelly, October 3, 2005.
12. King.
13. Edie Demas, Mary Rose Lloyd, and Lisa Lawer Post, "Interview."
14. Michael Presser and Katie McAllister, interview by Kristen Miles, October 7, 2005.
15. Jordan, "Interview."
16. King.
17. Ibid.
18. Edie Demas, "Identifying the Role of The New Victory Theater's Education Department." Ph.D. diss., New York University, 2006.
19. Outreach consists of community-based programs without a formal education component.
20. Edie Demas, Mary Rose Lloyd, and Lisa Lawer Post, "Interview."
21. Inside Broadway, *www.insidebroadway.org*.
22. Presser and McAllister, "Interview."
23. Ibid.
24. Ibid.
25. Kati Koerner, e-mail interviews to author, December 9, 2005 and April 21, 2006.
26. Ibid.
27. Ibid.
28. Jordan, "Interview."
29. Ibid.
30. Ibid.
31. Ibid.
32. Ibid.
33. Barbara Rich, Jane L. Polin, and Stephen J. Marcus, eds, *Acts of Achievement: The Role of Performing Arts Centers in Education* (New York: Dana Press, 2003), 46.
34. The John F. Kennedy Center for the Performing Arts, "Letter to the Principal" and "Partnership Initiative Acceptance Form." The authors would like to thank the Kennedy Center for granting us permission to reproduce this letter and sample partnership agreement.
35. Ayers and Kovac, "Interview."
36. Amy Dumas, *The Changing Education Through the Arts (CETA) Program's Definition and Characteristics of Arts-Integrated Instruction* (Washington, D.C.: The Kennedy Center, 2005). The authors would like to thank the Kennedy Center for granting us permission to reproduce this publication.
37. Lorenzen, "E-mail interview."
38. Ibid.
39. Ibid.
40. Ibid.
41. Ayers and Kovac, "E-mail interview."
42. Debra Sue Lorenzen notes that "rubrics establish evidence of progress and may be used for program evaluation or assessment. An evaluation rubric measures the success of the program utilizing a four-part scale, such as excellent, good, fair, and poor. An assessment rubric gauges a child's progress in learning or applying a skill, gaining knowledge, or developing an understanding. Usually, an assessment rubric measures using four achievement levels (e.g., far below grade level, approaching grade level, at grade level, exceeding grade level)."
43. Jordan, "Interview."
44. Lorenzen, "E-mail interview." The authors want to thank Making Books Sing for allowing us to publish this evaluation tool.
45. Cathryn Williams, e-mail interview to author, December 20, 2005.
46. Williams, "E-mail interview."
47. The authors would like to thank Making Books Sing for allowing us to publish this sample assessment tool.
48. Marjorie Damashek Levine, "Letter to The New Victory Theater," April 20, 2006. The authors would like to thank Marjorie Damashek Levine and Beach Channel High School for granting us permission to reproduce this letter.

APPENDIX A: Sample Partnership Agreement

The Kennedy Center

THE JOHN F. KENNEDY CENTER FOR THE PERFORMING ARTS

WASHINGTON, D.C. 20566-0001

(Date)

(Principal)
(School)
(Address)

Dear «Salutation»:

This letter represents the understanding between the (arts organization) and (school) for a one-year commitment to participate in the (name of partnership) Partnership Initiative for the 200x-200x School Year.

The purpose of the (name of partnership) Partnership Initiative is to provide arts education programming for select (name of school system) schools through professional development and artist resources to support skill-based arts learning and arts-integrated teaching across the curriculum. The partnership schools will have an opportunity for students to attend performances/exhibitions at the (arts organization) or other cultural institutions, and access to in-school arts programming. Teachers and administrators will participate in introductory professional development sessions on arts integration and select teachers will have an opportunity to engage with artists to design and implement introductory arts integrated teaching strategies in their classrooms.

The responsibilities of the (arts organization) follow:
    I. Provide In-School Artist Resources and Performance Attendance Opportunities
        1. Assistance with registration for in-school student programs (lecture/demos or performances) and events at cultural institutions.
        2. Tickets and transportation for 2 (arts organization) weekend performances for up to 45 participants per performance (selected from [name of brochure] brochure).
        3. Priority advanced registration for (arts organization) in-school programs.
        4. Arts-integrated, professional development/modeling residency for at least one (1), and no greater than four (4), teachers with a (arts organization) teaching artist. Teachers selected to participate in the artist-in-residence program must meet the eligibility requirements, complete an application process, and participate in all professional development activities and meetings associated with the residency.

Appendix A (continued)

«Principal», Principal   August 31, 2004
«School»

II. Provide Professional Development for Teachers
   1. Assistance with registration for community site and/or school hosted professional development workshops
   2. $10 off each workshop that has a fee over $10 for any partnership school staff attending (arts organization) after school/weekend professional development workshops (selected from workshops listed on pages xx-xx in the [name of brochure]).
   3. Arts Integration Summer Institute for a team of up to six (6) teachers to assist teachers in the development of arts-integrated lesson planning and effective teaching artist-teacher residency collaborations.
   4. Arrangement for one on-site professional development workshop for partnership school faculty with a (arts organization) teaching artist upon principal request.

The responsibilities of (school) follow:
   1. Designation of <u>one</u> school coordinator to liaise with (arts organization) staff for all programming activities. The coordinator is required to attend scheduled partnership coordinator meetings at the (arts organization) and respond to telephone and fax communications from (arts organization) staff in a timely manner.
   2. Completion of all evaluation materials for programming activities.
   3. Participation in all activities arranged as part of the partnership, including performances, professional development sessions, residency activities, and meetings. Notification of the cancellation of activities, with the exception of inclement weather, must be provided no less than five (5) business days prior to the scheduled activity.
   4. Payment of the (Partnership Fee) non-refundable annual partnership fee by (date).

Upon the successful completion of the one-year partnership agreement for the (date) school year, (school) will be invited to continue the partnership for a period of two school years (SY200x-200x and SY200x-200x) with the possibility of an additional one year extension (SY200x-200x). Failure to meet the responsibilities of the Partnership could result in dissolution of the Partnership and (school) ineligibility for Partnership for a period of two school years. If during the year, the responsibilities of the school are not being fulfilled, written notification will be sent. If there is no improvement in fulfilling responsibilities, the principal will be notified of termination of the program within 30 days after the last official class of the school year.

To confirm your acceptance of the partnership, please provide your signature at the conclusion of this letter and send back via fax to (xxx)xxx-xxxx.

(Name of manager of program) and (his/her) staff will serve as the contact with the school for partnership activities. (He/She) can be reached at (xxx)xxx-xxxx or (email address)

If I can be of any assistance, please contact me at (xxx)xxx-xxxx. We look forward providing valuable arts education resources to support your curriculum.

Sincerely,

cc:

The Kennedy Center

THE JOHN F. KENNEDY CENTER FOR THE PERFORMING ARTS

WASHINGTON, D.C. 20566-0001

200x-200x (name of partnership) Partnership Initiative Acceptance Form

_____   (School) is pleased to accept the invitation to participate in the (name of partnership) Partnership Initiative Program for the 200x-200x school year, and agrees to abide by the responsibilities of Partnership outlined in the letter. I understand that failure to meet the responsibilities as outlined will result in dissolution of the partnership and (school) will be ineligible for consideration of partnership for two years.

The following individual will be the partnership coordinator for the 200x-200x school year:

_____
Name (please print)

_____
Title

_____   (School) is not interested in participating in the (name of partnership) Partnership Initiative.

Principal Signature: _____ Date: _____
«Principal», Principal
«School»

BIBLIOGRAPHY

Actors' Equity Association. "Theatre for Young Audiences National Agreement." Actors' Equity Association. *www.actorsequity.org/agreements/agreements.asp?code=080*.

American Alliance for Theatre and Education. *AATE Newsletter*, 7 February 2005.

Americans for the Arts. E-mail to author, 8 November 2006.

Americans for the Arts and National School Boards Association Online Resource Center: Arts Education in Pubic Schools. *ww3.artsusa.org/services/arts_education/resource_center*.

Arts Education Partnership. "Arts Education Links." Arts Education Partnership Web site.

———. *Teaching Partnerships: Report of a National Forum on Partnerships Improving the Arts*. Washington, D.C.: Arts Education Partnership, 2003.

———. *Visions of the Future: Education in the Arts*. Produced by Arts Education Partnership, 12 min. Arts Education Partnership, 2006. DVD.

ArtServe Michigan. *ArtServe Michigan's Best Practices in Arts Education 2003*. Washington, D.C.: Americans for the Arts, 2003.

Association of Teaching Artists, *www.teachingartists.com*.

Ayers, Darrell and Kim Peter Kovac. "Performing Arts Education." Interview by Tobie Stein. E-mail to author, 9 January 2006.

Backstage. "Breaking in to Arts Education." *Backstage.com*, 12 November 2004.

Bauernschub, Mary Beth and Kingsford Elementary School of Mitchellville, Md. "A Character Lifebox." The Kennedy Center ARTSEDGE. *http://artsedge.kennedy-center.org/content/2164*.

Brantley, Ben. "The Kiddie Show Goes Dark." *New York Times*, 1 May 2005.

Brooklyn Arts Council, *www.brooklynartscouncil.org*.

———. "Arts in Education Coordinator Job Description." Brooklyn, 2005.

Brooklyn Information & Culture and the Brooklyn Arts Council. "Brooklyn Information & Culture and the Brooklyn Arts Council Arts in Education Regrant Program Application." Brooklyn, N.Y., 2005. Photocopy.

Cameron, Ben. "School Dazed." *American Theatre*, April 2004, 4.

———. "The Art and Education Conundrum." *American Theatre*, July/August 2004, 6.

Campbell, Kim. "Theaters Get 'Em While They're Young: Kids Are Offered Special Ticket Deals and Other Perks to Help Turn Them into Lifelong Fans of the Theater." *The Christian Science Monitor*, 11 February 2005.

The Center for Arts Education. "About CAE." The Center for Arts Education, Inc. *www.cae-nyc.org/general/about.htm*.

———. "CAE in the News." The Center for Arts Education, Inc. *www.cae-nyc.org/general/news.htm#PA06*.

———. "Career Development Program." The Center for Arts Education, Inc. *www.cae-nyc.org/pages/career-development-program*.

———. "Impact." The Center for Arts Education, Inc. Web site.

Community Works. "Our Programs." Community Works New York City. *www.communityworksnyc.org/our_programs*.

Creating the Magic: Little Shop of Horrors. Inside Broadway Program. New York, 2003.

Creativity and Collaboration: Arts in Education Programs. Brooklyn Arts Council Brochure. Brooklyn, N.Y., 2006.

Demas, Edie, "Identifying the Role of The New Victory Theater's Education Department." Ph.D. diss., New York University, 2006.

Demas, Edie, Mary Rose Lloyd, and Lisa Lawer Post. "Performing Arts Education." Interview by Tobie Stein. Tape recording, 22 May 2006. The New Victory Theater, New York.

DiFarnecio, Doris, Ric Oquita, and Debra Sue Lorenzen. *Making Book Sing's Resource Guide: The Orphan Singer*. Edited by Barbara Zinn Krieger and Debra Sue Lorenzen. New York: Making Books Sing, 2005.

Duma, Amy. *The Changing Education Through the Arts (CETA) Program's Definition and Characteristics of Arts-Integrated Instruction*. Washington, D.C.: The Kennedy Center, 2005.

Dziemianowicz, Joe. "Hey Kids: It's Play Time!" *New York Daily News*, 2 May 2005.

Fineberg, Carol. *Creating Islands of Excellence*. Portsmouth, N.H.: Heinemann, 2004.

———, ed. *Planning an Arts-Centered School*. New York: Dana Press, 2002.

Foundation Center. "Growth in Funding for Arts Education Surpasses Arts Giving Overall, Report Finds." 3 October 2005.

Gordon, Dan. "ArtsConnection Shares Model for Education Partnerships." *The Dana Foundation's Arts Education in the News*, May 2005.

Hughes, Kristine. "The Art of Testing." *The Dana Foundation's Arts Education in the News*, February 2005. First published in *Teacher Magazine*, 1 January 2005, 7–8.

Inside Broadway, *www.insidebroadway.org*.

———. *Extra! Extra! On the Town: A Broadway Musical Classic for Children Study Guide*. New York: Inside Broadway, 2005.

———. *Gilbert & Sullivan's The Pirates of Penzance Study Guide*. New York: Inside Broadway, 2004.

Institute for Education and the Arts. "Arts for Young People Education Initiative." E-mail to author, 11 January 2006.

———. "Community Partnerships." Institute for Education and the Arts. *www.edartsinstitute.org/community/index.htm*.

———. "Grants and Other Opportunities." E-mail to author, 28 March 2006.

———. "Music Education." E-mail to author, 20 July 2006.

———. "Online Resources for Arts Education." E-mail to author, 4 January 2006.

———. "Publication: Third Space: When Learning Matters." E-mail to author, 3 February 2006.

Johnson, Nikki, Paul King, Debra Sue Lorenzen, Margie Salvante, Steve Tennen, and Suzanne Youngerman. "Education Roundtable." MFA class discussion moderated by Dale Byam. 25 September 2006. Brooklyn College, Brooklyn, N.Y.

Jordan, Arlene. "Performing Arts Education." Interview by Cristin Kelly. Tape recording, 3 October 2005. New York City Center, New York.

Jordan, Arlene, Diana Feldman, and Lisa Dennett. "Facilitating the Arts of Today for the Minds of Tomorrow: Building, Coordinating, and Maintaining Educational Arts Programming." Discussion moderated by Lori Ann Laster and Padma Sundaram. 10 May 2004. Richard Frankel Productions, New York.

Jordan, Arlene, Paul King, and Debra Sue Lorenzen. "Performing Arts Education Lecture." 20 September 2005. New York City Center, New York.

Kaiser, Michael M. "Strategic Planning in the Arts: A Practical Guide." The Kennedy Center. *www.artsmanager.org/strategic*.

King, Paul. "Performing Arts Education." Interview by Cristin Kelly. Tape recording, 25 October 2005. New York.

Kiss Me, Kate Tour Guide. Inside Broadway Brochure. New York, 2004.

Koerner, Kati. "Performing Arts Education." Interview by Tobie Stein. E-mails to author, 9 December 2005 and 21 April 2006.

Levine, Marjorie Damashek. Letter to The New Victory Theater, 20 April 2006.

Lincoln Center Institute. "About LCI." 2007. *www.lcinstitute.org*.

———. "LCI's Practice." 2007. *www.lcinstitute.org*.

———. "News & Ideas." 2007. *www.lcinstitute.org*.

———. "Resources." 2007. *www.lcinstitute.org*.

Lincoln Center Theater. "Open Stages High School Program Spring 2005 Teacher Survey." New York, 2005. Photocopy.

———. "Student Response Form for *The Light in the Piazza*." New York, 2005. Photocopy.

———. *Study Guide for Teachers: The Light in the Piazza*. New York: Lincoln Center Theater, 2005.

———. *Welcome to Lincoln Center Theater: A Brief History of Theater and a Guide to the People Who Make It*. New York: Lincoln Center, 2005.

———. "What to Say When You Greet the Student Groups." New York, 2005. Photocopy.

Lind, Vicki R. and Elizabeth Lindsley. *Creative Collaboration: Teachers and Artists in the Classroom Pre-K–Grade 12*. Pasadena: California Alliance for Arts Education and San Bernadino City Unified School District, 2003.

Lorenzen, Debra Sue. "Performing Arts Education." Interview by Tobie Stein. E-mails to author, 30 November 2005 and 3 May 2006.

Macrides, Kalle, Cara Marcous, and Susan Willerman, eds. *Public School 255: Anthology: 2005*. New York: Making Books Sing, 2005.

Making Books Sing. *Crescendo!* 1, no 2, Spring 2005.

———. "Student Assessment." 2007.

———. "Teacher Evaluation." 2006.

Marks, Peter. "Children's Theater Comes of Age at Kennedy Center." *Washington Post*, 9 December 2005.

McCaslin, Greg. "Performing Arts Education." Interview by Tobie Stein. E-mail to author, 23 November 2005.

McKenna, Sheila. "Books Set the Stage for Theater; Children's Arts Education Program 'Making Books Sing' Turns Novels into Plays, Musicals and Operas." *Newsday*, 8 February 2005.

Moore, John. "Room with a Viewpoint." *The Dana Foundation's Arts Education in the News*, February 2005. First published in *Denver Post*, 22 November 2004.

National Endowment for the Arts. "About Shakespeare in American Communities." National Endowment for the Arts. *http://arts.endow.gov/national/shakespeare/About.html*.

New York City Department of Education. *Blueprint for Teaching and Learning in the Arts: Theater Grades PreK–12*. New York: New York City Department of Education, June 2005.

New York State Council on the Arts. "Arts in Education." New York State Council on the Arts. *www.nysca.org/public/resources/spec_education.htm*.

NYC Arts in Education Roundtable. "About the NYC AIE Roundtable." NYC Arts in Education Roundtable. *www.nycaieroundtable.org/about.htm*.

———. "Career Services." NYC Arts in Education Roundtable. *www.nycaieroundtable.org/career.htm*.

———. "Events." NYC Arts in Education Roundtable. *www.nycaieroundtable.org/events.htm*.

———. "Roundtable Membership." NYC Arts in Education Roundtable. *www.nycaieroundtable.org/members.htm*.

———. "The Roundtable Reading Room: Arts Education Policy." NYC Arts in Education Roundtable. *www.nycaieroundtable.org/rr_artsedpolicy.htm*.

———. "The Roundtable Reading Room: Arts Research." NYC Arts in Education Roundtable. *www.nycaieroundtable.org/rr_artsresearch.htm*.

———. "The Roundtable Reading Room: Classic References." NYC Arts in Education Roundtable. *www.nycaieroundtable.org/rr_classic.htm*.

———. "The Roundtable Reading Room: Curriculum & Standards." NYC Arts in Education Roundtable. *www.nycaieroundtable.org/rr_curriculum.htm*.

———. "The Roundtable Reading Room: Journals." NYC Arts in Education Roundtable. *www.nycaieroundtable.org/rr_journals.htm*.

———. "The Roundtable Reading Room: Serving the Field." NYC Arts in Education Roundtable. *www.nycaieroundtable.org/rr_thefield.htm*.

Paige, Rod and Mike Huckabee. "Putting Arts Education Front and Center." *The Dana Foundation's Arts Education in the News*, February 2005. First published in *Education Week*, 26 January 2005.

Payne, Joyce. "A Guide to Authentic Assessments." The Kennedy Center ARTSEDGE. *artsedge.kennedy-center.org/content/3337*.

Presser, Michael, and Katie McAllister. "Performing Arts Education." Interview by Kristen Miles. Tape recording, 7 October 2005. Inside Broadway, New York.

———. "Performing Arts Education." Interview by Jennie Greer. Tape recordings, 7 October and 18 November 2005. Inside Broadway, New York.

Project Arts. "Theater Resources." The New York City Department of Education. *schools.nyc.gov/projectarts/Media/PA%20PAM/theater/resources/theaterresourcepage.htm*.

Renz, Loren and Josefina Atienza. *Foundation Funding for Arts Education: An Overview of Recent Trends*. New York: The Foundation Center, 2005.

Rich, Barbara, ed. *Partnering Arts Education: A Working Model from ArtsConnection*. New York: Dana Press, 2005.

Rich, Barbara, Jane L. Polin, and Stephen J. Marcus, eds. *Acts of Achievement: The Role of Performing Arts Centers in Education*. New York: Dana Press, 2003.

Rossi, Rosalind, and Art Golab. "Test Scores Soar Higher after Arts Push." *The Dana Foundation's Arts Education in the News*, February 2005. First published in *Chicago Sun-Times*, 15 December 2004.

Rousuck, J. Wynn. "$125 Million for Performing Arts Education." *Baltimore Sun*, 17 February 2005.

Salamon, Julie. "A Children's Troupe, Homeward Bound." *New York Times*, 8 July 2005.

Silverman, Rachel. "Mozart Opera Leaves Kids Full of Smiles." *The Dana Foundation's Arts Education in the News*, May 2005: First published in *The Princeton (NJ) Packet*, 6 May 2005.

Smokey Joe's Cafe: The Songs of Leiber and Stoller. Inside Broadway Program. New York, 2003.

Smyth, Laura, and Lauren Stevenson. *You Want to Be a Part of Everything: The Arts, Community, & Learning*. Washington, D.C.: Arts Education Partnership, 2003.

Soloway, Seth. "Performing Arts Education." Interview by Jennie Greer. E-mail to Jennie Greer, 28 January 2006.

Sotto, Theresa. "Creative Conflict: Resolving & Avoiding Conflict in Group Art Projects." The Kennedy Center ARTSEDGE. *http://artsedge.kennedy-center.org/content/3905*.

Stevenson, Lauren M. and Richard J. Deasy. *The Third Space: When Learning Matters*. Washington, D.C.: Arts Education Partnership, 2005.

The John F. Kennedy Center for the Performing Arts. "Kennedy Center Alliance for Arts Education: State Alliance Information." The John F. Kennedy Center for the Performing Arts. *www.kennedy-center.org/education/kcaaen/statealliance/home.html*.

———. "Kennedy Center Alliance for Arts Education: Tools and Resources." The John F. Kennedy Center for the Performing Arts. *www.kennedy-center.org/education/kcaaen/resources/home.html*.

———. "Kennedy Center Education." The John F. Kennedy Center for the Performing Arts. *www.kennedy-center.org/education/home.html*.

———. "Kennedy Center Education and Outreach: New Visions/New Voices." The John F. Kennedy Center for the Performing Arts. *www.kennedy-center.org/education/nvnv.html*.

———. "Kennedy Center Partners in Education." The John F. Kennedy Center for the Performing Arts. *www.kennedy-center.org/education/partners*.

———. "Letter to the Principal." Washington D.C., 2007. Photocopy.

———. "Partnership Initiative Acceptance Form." The John F. Kennedy Center for the Performing Arts, 2007.

———. "Performing Arts Series: Arts-Based Programming via Satellite/Web." The John F. Kennedy Center for the Performing Arts. *www.kennedy-center.org/education/pwtv*.

———. "The John F. Kennedy Center for the Performing Arts Commits $125 Million for Arts Education." The John F. Kennedy Center for the Performing Arts. *www.kennedy-center.org/education/announcement.html*.

The Kennedy Center Alliance for Arts Education, and Kathi Levin. *A Community Audit for Arts Education: Better Schools, Better Skills, Better Communities*. Washington, D.C.: The John F. Kennedy Center for the Performing Arts, July 2001.

The Kennedy Center ARTSEDGE. "How-To's." The Kennedy Center ARTSEDGE. *http://artsedge.kennedy-center.org/teach/hto.cfm*.

———. "Lessons." The Kennedy Center ARTSEDGE. *http://artsedge.kennedy-center.org/teach/les.cfm*.

———. "Standards." The Kennedy Center ARTSEDGE. *http://artsedge.kennedy-center.org/teach/standards.cfm*.

———. "Standards: Theater K-4." The Kennedy Center ARTSEDGE. *http://artsedge.kennedy-center.org/teach/standard.cfm?standard_id=74&view=full*.

The Pirates of Penzance. Inside Broadway Brochure. New York, 2004.

Theatre Communications Group. "Arts Education." *www.tcg.org/tools/education/*.

———. "Study Guide Database." *www.tcg.org/tools/education/protected/search_sg.cfm*.

———. "Theatre Education Research, Resources and Advocacy Tools." *www.tcg.org/tools/education/edu_links.cfm*.

Theatre for Children and Families 2005–2006 Season. Inside Broadway Brochure. New York, 2005.

Theater for Young Audiences. "Our Productions." Theater for Young Audiences. *www.tyasheboygan.org/index_files/page0001.htm*.

Theatre for Young Audiences/USA. *www.assitej-usa.org*.

Toumani, Meline. "Get Them in the Seats, and Their Hearts Will Follow." *New York Times*, 26 February 2006.

Trescott, Jacqueline. "Kennedy Center Adds a Theater for the Kids; Arts Education Gains Emphasis, Funding." *Washington Post*, 17 February 2005, final edition.

University of the State of New York. "New York State Learning Standards." New York State Education Department. *www.emsc.nysed.gov/ciai/arts/artls.html*.

Williams, Cathryn. "Performing Arts Education." Interview by Tobie Stein. E-mail to author, 20 December 2005.

Youngerman, Suzanne. "Performing Arts Education." Interview by Lynn Hyde. Tape recording, 4 November 2005. Brooklyn Academy of Music, Brooklyn, N.Y.

———. "Performing Arts Education." Interview by Laura E. Miller. Tape recording, 7 November 2005. Brooklyn Academy of Music, Brooklyn, N.Y.

CHAPTER NINE

Labor Relations

In this chapter, we will explore labor relations.[1] We will begin with the basic concepts of contract creation. We will then define collective bargaining and explore basic labor law. We will examine each major national performing arts union, guild, and multi-employer bargaining group. Finally, we will explore human resources policies and procedures in the workplace.

CONTRACTS

In order to commit the specific duties and obligations of a labor relationship to writing, a contract must be drawn up and executed by both parties. A contract is "an agreement between two or more parties creating obligations that are enforceable or otherwise recognizable at [by] law."[2] A contract consists principally of three essential elements: the offer, acceptance, and consideration. An offer is "the manifestation of willingness to enter into a bargain."[3] The offer must be definite, specifying all key or important details, such as price. The person offered the bargain is invited to assent to the terms of the bargain; the act of assenting to a bargain is called "acceptance."[4] (An acceptance must be made in the manner required by the offer, such as in writing; silence does not normally qualify as acceptance.)[5] However, a contract has not been created just because an offer has been made by one party and accepted by the other. The parties must also exchange "consideration." Consideration concerns "a performance or a return promise [that] must be bargained for."[6] Simply put, consideration is a bargained-for exchange—a benefit conferred or a service done by one party for the other. For example, if an actor is paid $200 to perform in *Hamlet*, then the performance is consideration for the $200.

Like other contracts, employment contracts consist of the offer, acceptance, and consideration. Let's examine a sample contract for a director (see page 366).[7] This contract shows the offer (the producer offers a certain amount of money for directing the play at a certain point in time), acceptance (the director must signal his assent to the terms of the offer by affixing his signature to the bottom of the contract), and consideration (the directing services promised by the director in exchange for payment). In addition, this contract shows such common contract provisions as salary and dates during which the director is expected to perform the duties specified under the contract.

A contract is legally binding and enforceable against all parties to the contract. In other words, if one of the contracted parties does not fulfill his obligations under the contract, that party has "breached" the contract. When any key or material terms of a contract have been breached [not fulfilled], the nonbreaching party may treat the contract as being at an end and may sue for any damages that it has incurred as a result of the breach.

In the event that one party to a contract claims that the contract has been breached, the party accused of breaching may show that no breach has occurred, and that he has fully performed all his obligations under the contract. However, if the party claiming breach of contract can prove that a breach has occurred, the breaching party may raise a defense against the validity of the contract. Under these defenses, the breaching party claims that there was some irregularity in the formation of the contract, and hence the contract should not be enforced. Some of these defenses include fraud (one party misrepresented what the contract was about, or the essential terms of the contract), duress (agreement was entered into under some kind of threat or undue influence), or unconscionability (when terms of the contract are so unfair and unbalanced to one party that no reasonable person should be expected to be bound by those terms). If successful, these defenses invalidate the contract as though no contract ever existed.

Fig. 9.1. SSDC—LORT Director Contract

SSDC society of stage directors and choreographers

1501 Broadway, Suite 1701   New York, NY 10036   Tel 212 391 1070   Fax 212 302 6195
Info@ssdc.org

This contract must be signed in quintuplicate. Attach all riders to each copy. The Theatre and the Director/Choreographer each must file one copy of this contract and any riders with SSDC within five business days after signing or prior to the first rehearsal, whichever first occurs. Each party may retain one copy. One copy is for the agent or attorney of the Director/Choreographer.

The following constitutes our agreement:

1. This contract is subject to all terms and conditions of the Agreement between the Society of Stage Directors and Choreographers, Inc. (SSDC), and the League of Resident Theatres (LORT), effective April 15, 2005, or its successor Agreement, and binds the Theatre to its terms for the duration of said Agreement.

2. The Theatre, _____, LORT stage category _____, hereby engages the services of _____ as **Director** and you accept such engagement with respect to the Production _____. Your services shall be rendered during rehearsals of the Production from _____ through _____. The Production
    shall be performed through _____.
                      (final performance)   (starting date)   (opening performance)

3. In consideration of full and timely performance by you hereunder, the Theatre agrees to compensate you as follows:

    SALARY/FEE AND PAYMENT SCHEDULE:

    A Salary of $ _____   (at $ _____   per week _____ for weeks)
    A Fee of $ _____   Fee Schedule: $ _____ upon signing this contract
                                                     $ _____ upon first day of rehearsal
                                                     $ _____ upon first day of the last week of rehearsal

    The Theatre is authorized to send compensation to:

    _____

    _____

4. EFFECTIVE FOR SSDC MEMBERS ONLY:

    Effective immediately, the undersigned assigns to the SSDC, two and one-half percent (2 1/2 %) of all monies earned and to be earned as Director and/or Choreographer of the above-named Production and authorizes and directs the Theatre to deduct such amounts and remit same to the SSDC. This assignment shall be irrevocable for the term of the above-named Production.

5. RIDERS: (Attach additional riders to each copy of this contract.)

Accepted:	Theatre must sign contract first.
DIRECTOR/CHOREOGRAPHER	THEATRE _____
_____ (Signature)	By _____ (Signature)
Please type name _____	Please type name _____
Date _____	Date _____
Address _____	Address _____
_____ Zip _____	_____ Zip _____
Phone _____	Phone _____
Email address _____	Email address _____
Social Security No. _____	Employer Registration No. _____ (for Unemployment Insurance)
Member of SSDC in Good Standing: yes _____ no _____	

Revised 7/8/05

LORT

A party may also defend against a breach of contract on the grounds that performance was made impracticable or was otherwise frustrated. These defenses acknowledge that the contract was valid and enforceable, but that the breach of the contract was justified or excusable under the circumstances. One example of impracticability occurs when a contract for a vocal performance specifies that the performance is to take place at a particular venue. If that specific venue burns down, and no other venue is available or appropriate, the artist cannot sing and is technically in breach of contract. However, because the venue specified in the contract burned down, and no other space was available or appropriate, performance under the contract would be impracticable, and the breaching party is excused from performance.

A person accused of breach may also claim that no contract was ever formed to begin with. For example, if the parties did not reach an agreement on the essential terms of the contract, and hence there was no "meeting of the minds," then no contract was formed. An example of a lack of meeting of the minds occurs when one party thinks he is contracting for a performance of *Hamlet*, to be performed by seven dwarves, and the other party thinks he is contracting for a performance of *Snow White and the Seven Dwarves*, to be performed by a Danish prince named Hamlet. The parties fail to reach a firm agreement on the essential terms of the contract, and therefore, no contract comes into existence.

CLASSROOM DISCUSSION

Define "contract."

What are the three parts of a contract?

What is breach of contract, and what are the
    defenses against it?

COLLECTIVE BARGAINING AND LABOR LAW

Although an employment contract may be enacted between individuals, employees working in the same industry may elect to form a collective bargaining unit. A collective bargaining unit consists of a group of employees who join together to engage in collective bargaining; this collective bargaining unit is known as a "union." Employers may also choose to join collective bargaining units, which are known as "multi-employer collective bargaining groups." Collective bargaining is the process by which a union and an employer (or multi-employer bargaining group) "meet and negotiate the minimum terms under which an employee will work for that employer. These terms can include salary, pension and health benefits, working conditions (clean, safe facilities, etc.), hours worked, dispute resolution, termination procedures (covering the firing of an employee), and many others. The final document is called a "collectively bargained agreement," and it is usually in effect from two to four years."[8]

Through the negotiation of collectively bargained agreements, unions protect employees by providing minimum conditions that must be met for employment. When an employer hires an employee represented by a union, that employer must use the appropriate union contract and cannot reduce or subvert the terms in that contract. As Alan Eisenberg, former executive director of Actors' Equity Association, states, "By law, the employer is prohibited from reducing the conditions below that which have been negotiated in a collectively bargained agreement. If an agreement provides that the minimum salary for an actor is $1,000 per week, it is illegal for the employer to say, 'We're only going to pay you $900.'"[9]

Although unions have existed since the nineteenth century, their right to organize (form in the workplace) and collectively bargain has often been challenged by employers. Employers discriminated against workers in unions, locking them out of their places of employment and forcing new employees to sign "yellow dog" contracts, promising that the employees would not join a union.[10] In fact, the Sherman Antitrust Act of 1890, which controlled monopolies by prohibiting "restraint of trade," was often applied to control union organizing.[11]

However, legislation favorable to labor was finally passed in 1914. The Clayton Antitrust Act "is intended to diminish union exposure to antitrust laws" and "affirms the right of unions to strike [stop their members from working as an act of protest], boycott [prohibit their members from buying goods from a particular business], and picket [patrol in front of businesses undergoing strike activity to discourage others from engaging with the business]."[12] In 1932, the Norris-LaGuardia Act (also known as the Anti-Injunction Bill) was passed. This act "restricts the power of federal courts to issue injunctions"; these injunctions [court orders] prevented workers from engaging in strikes and other organizing activities by issuing fines or jail terms to those workers.[13]

Three years later, the National Labor Relations Act (also known as the Wagner Act) was passed. "Congress approved the National Labor Relations Act [NLRA] in 1935 to encourage a healthy relationship between private-sector workers and their employers, which policy makers viewed as vital to the national interest. The NLRA was designed to curtail work stoppages, strikes, and general labor strife, which were viewed as harmful to the U.S. economy and to the nation's general well-being. The NLRA extends many rights to workers who wish to form, join, or support unions, also known as 'labor organizations'; to workers who are already represented by unions; and to workers who join together as a group (two or more employees) without a union seeking to modify their wages or working conditions, which is known as 'protected concerted activities.' The NLRA also extends rights to employers, protecting commercial interests against unfair actions committed by labor organizations, and extends rights to labor organizations, protecting organizational and collective-bargaining representative interests against unfair actions committed by employers."[14] The NLRA only applies to employees, employers, and unions involved in privately owned businesses; federal, state, and local employees, as well as airline and railroad employees, are not covered by this act.[15]

The NLRA protects the following specific rights for employees, employers, and unions:

Employees have the right to form, join, support, or assist unions, also known as labor organizations, who may bargain collectively with the employer on the employees' behalf seeking to modify wages or working conditions. Employees also have the right to engage in other protected concerted activities without a union seeking to improve their wages and other working conditions. Employees also have the right to refrain from engaging in these activities or to seek removal of a union from the workplace. (However, a union and employer may, in a State where such agreements are permitted, enter into a lawful union-security clause.) Employees covered by the NLRA are protected from employer and union discrimination, also known as unfair labor practices.

Employers are also afforded rights under the NLRA protecting them from certain unlawful activities. For example, labor unions may not limit their productivity and insist that more workers be hired.

Unions are protected by the NLRA from unfair labor practices, and guaranteed the right to organize, or attempt to form a bar-gaining unit in private-sector workplaces covered by the Act. Unions, chosen as employee representatives, are entitled to engage in collective bargaining with an employer on behalf of employees to modify their wages and other working conditions.[16]

To protect these rights, the NLRA provides for the establishment of the National Labor Relations Board (NLRB). "The NLRB investigates unfair labor practice allegations made by employees and unions."[17] (Unfair labor practice allegations may also be made by employers against unions.)[18] "All cases are submitted to a regional NLRB office with jurisdiction over the concerned parties. The Board office investigates the charge by requesting information from both parties. Following a review of the information, the Regional Director [head of the regional office] decides whether or not to issue a complaint. If a complaint is issued, the charge is prosecuted; the regional office tries the case before an administrative law judge on behalf of the party filing charges. If the Regional Director refuses to issue a complaint, the party filing charges has the right to appeal to the General Counsel of the NLRB [who represents the entire organization]."[19]

After the NLRA lifted restrictions on union activities, unions were able to strike at will and thus acquire huge gains for their members. To counteract this union advantage, Congress passed the Taft-Hartley Act (also known as the Labor-Management Relations Act) in 1947. "The Act amends the NLRA to prohibit certain union activities and establishes unlawful labor practices for unions, including secondary boycotts [boycotts against a business working with a business boycotted by the union] and jurisdictional strikes [strikes conducted over job-assignment disputes]."[20] The Taft-Hartley Act also prohibits closed shops, which permit only union members to be hired. Because of this act, new employees do not have to be members of a union to work in a union shop (union-organized workplace), but they do need to join the union within thirty days after they are hired.

To protect union members, the Labor-Management Reporting and Disclosure Act (the Landrum-Griffin Act) was passed in 1959 as a measure to promote good governance in unions. This act "creates a bill of rights for union members, requires financial disclosure by unions, creates procedures for the election of union officers, and establishes remedies for financial abuse by union officers."[21] In addition, a federal law was passed in

1974 to regulate pension and health plans established by unions and private employers. (Please see the last section in this chapter for more information about pension and health plans.) The Employee Retirement Income Security Act (ERISA) "requires [pension and health] plans to provide participants with plan information, including important information about plan features and funding; provides fiduciary responsibilities for those who manage and control plan assets; requires plans to establish a grievance and appeals process for participants to get benefits from their plans; and gives participants the right to sue for benefits and breaches of fiduciary duty."[22]

CLASSROOM DISCUSSION

Define the following: "union," "multi-employer collective bargaining group," and "collective bargaining."

Name the major provisions of the following labor laws: Sherman Antitrust Act of 1890; Clayton Antitrust Act of 1914; Norris-LaGuardia Act (Anti-Injunction Bill) of 1932; National Labor Relations Act (Wagner Act) of 1935; Taft-Hartley Act (Labor-Management Relations Act) of 1947; Labor-Management Reporting and Disclosure Act (Landrum-Griffin Act) of 1959; and the Employee Retirement Income Security Act of 1974.

What is the National Labor Relations Board, and how is a case submitted for review and prosecution?

UNIONS AND GUILDS

The following sections describe the major national unions encountered in the performing arts: Actors' Equity Association; American Federation of Musicians; American Guild of Musical Artists; Association of Theatrical Press Agents and Managers; Society of Stage Directors and Choreographers; International Alliance of Theatrical Stage Employees; and United Scenic Artists. We will also examine the Dramatists Guild, distinguishing the guild from unions.

Actors' Equity Association (AEA or Equity)

"Actors' Equity Association (AEA or Equity), founded in 1913, is the labor union that represents more than 45,000 Actors and Stage Managers in the United States. Equity seeks to advance, promote and foster the art of live theater as an essential component of our society."[23] Equity is part of the Associated Actors and Artists of America (4As), which is a group of performing arts unions that organize under the umbrella of the American Federation of Labor and Congress of Industrial Organizations (AFL-CIO).[24] The other unions that comprise the 4As are the Screen Actors Guild (SAG, representing actors working in film, television, and digital media), the American Federation of Television and Radio Artists (AFTRA, representing actors and announcers working in television, radio, and digital media), the American Guild of Musical Artists (AGMA, representing singers and dancers in opera, dance, and concert performances), and the American Guild of Variety Artists (AGVA, representing entertainers in such areas as variety shows and some job categories at theme parks).[25]

Equity is governed by a council, a governing body elected by the membership, which is Equity's "ultimate decision-making body, particularly regarding finance [and] policy. . . . It also has the authority to adopt rules supplementing [the union's] constitution and bylaws."[26] The Council employs an executive director, who is "responsible for primary oversight and implementation of national policy, contract negotiations, and general communications with members and the public."[27] Equity also employs three regional directors, responsible for overseeing Equity contracts and policy in their regions; these regional offices are located in New York, New York; Chicago, Illinois; and Los Angeles, California; with subsidiary offices in San Francisco, California, and Orlando, Florida.

Actors and stage managers become members of Equity by qualifying through the Equity Membership Candidate Program, which requires a certain number of workweeks at Equity theaters before membership is granted. Individuals may also become members if they are hired under Equity contracts (e.g., hired for a Broadway production), or have been a member of one of the other 4A unions for one year and have worked as a performer under that union's jurisdiction. Equity members pay an initiation fee, as well as semiannual dues and work dues. Semiannual dues are paid twice yearly by the member, while work dues are paid out of earnings and are capped (stopped) after a specific amount has been paid. Dues collected by a union support the work of that union, including collective bargaining negotiations and organizing.

Equity members enjoy certain contractual benefits, such as health and pension benefits, which are available to members after the completion of a certain number of weeks worked. Equity has also established a system of auditions for Equity members, ensuring that all Equity members have an equal opportunity to compete for jobs. To help its members secure employment between acting jobs, Equity has created an actors' work program. A related service helps dancers transition from performing to nonperforming careers. (Both of these initiatives are now administered by the Actors Fund of America, a service organization that helps those individuals in the entertainment industry.)[28] Equity provides other services to its members as needed, including assistance with tax preparation and filing unemployment and disability claims.[29]

In addition to programs administered by the union directly, Equity has also established a foundation, the Actors' Equity Foundation, to raise money and distribute grants to support actors and promote live theater.[30] These grants support such projects as the Non-Traditional Casting Project (which supports diversity in casting and is now known as the Alliance for Inclusion in the Arts) and the Actors Fund of America ("for aid to actors and the maintenance of the Actors' Residence and Nursing Home in Englewood, New Jersey, and the Aurora Residence on West 57th Street [in New York City]").[31] Another charitable organization associated with Equity is Broadway Cares/Equity Fights AIDS (BC/EFA), serving individuals affected by HIV/AIDS. BC/EFA supports services provided to workers suffering from HIV/AIDS in the entertainment industry by raising money through performances and other fundraising events.[32]

Collectively bargained agreements negotiated by Equity cover a wide variety of theaters, including Broadway productions and national tours (under the Production Contract), Off-Broadway productions, regional theaters (under the League of Resident Theatre [LORT] contracts), stock theaters, and theater for young audiences.[33] In addition to these collectively bargained agreements, Equity also uses promulgated contracts, in which terms are determined by the union without going through the collective bargaining process. If an employer wishes to hire an employee under that contract, then he must abide by those terms; examples of promulgated contracts include the Workshop Agreement, used to develop new works, and the Los Angeles 99-Seat Theatre Plan.[34] Alan Eisenberg notes, "We're constantly trying to expand the number of theaters covered by Equity contracts, because those are the only theaters in which Equity members may work. If you're an Equity theater, you have access to our membership, so you can hire what we believe to be the best talent in the country. Also, many plays are only licensed to Equity theaters, not non-Equity theaters."[35] Equity contracts cover many different types of workplaces, so the wages and fringe benefits offered in these contracts range widely (up to the maximum bargained rates in the Production Contract). However, certain terminology is common to each contract, as defined by Equity:

- Contracts: There are several individual employment contracts that cover Equity's three job categories: Principal, Chorus, and Stage Manager. Each individual employment contract is referenced to and incorporates all the terms of a specific rulebook.
- Standard Minimum (Principal) contract: This contract (often referred to as the "white" contract) is used for all principal actors, and most stage managers.[36] (Production and Off-Broadway agreements use separate stage manager contract forms.)
- Understudy (Principal contract): Understudy assignments are required in some agreements in order to provide coverage for other principal performers' roles or parts. An actor may perform as an understudy only if the individual employment contract provides for this additional responsibility. A "general understudy" is hired to understudy one or more roles and does not regularly perform in the show.
- Term contract (formerly run-of-the-play contract: a contract established for a fixed guaranteed period of employment, as agreed between an employer and an individual actor. During this period of time, neither party may end the contract. In exchange for this guarantee, a term contract requires a higher rate of pay than a standard minimum contract.
- Chorus Minimum contract: This contract (often referred to as the "pink" contract) is used for Actors whose primary function is chorus.
- Swing (Chorus contract): A Swing is a nonperforming member of the chorus who substitutes for absent chorus members. (A Swing may also be assigned to understudy principal roles and/or chorus parts and specialties.) A Partial Swing is a performing member of the chorus who is assigned to "swing" specific production numbers for absent chorus members.

- Favored Nations: This term refers to a specific contract rider provision that may be negotiated between an actor and an employer. Such a rider generally provides that if other specified actors receive better terms or conditions than the individual actor, then the actor signing the contract is entitled to the same terms or conditions (including, for example, level of compensation, transportation, and/or housing).

- Fight Captain: Some agreements require a Fight Captain, who is the company member responsible for maintaining the fight choreography and the safety of those engaged in staged fights.

- Extra: Where agreements permit the use of extras, an extra may only provide atmosphere and background. An extra may not be identified as a specific character, and may not be required to change makeup. The extra receives a reduced salary, usually 50 percent of the minimum.

- Dance Captain: The Dance Captain is the member of the company who maintains the artistic standards of all musical staging and choreography in the style, intent, technique and energy level of the original production. The Dance Captain is responsible for rehearsing and preparing all understudies, swings, and replacement performers, and works in tandem with the Stage Manager in conveying and maintaining the creative intention of the artistic staff.

- Deputy: The Deputy works in conjunction with the Stage Manager as the elected company member responsible for facilitating communication between Equity and the rest of the company. The Deputy is selected by majority vote of the company, usually on the first day of rehearsal. This election is conducted by the Stage Manager. The Deputy advises performers on procedures and rules, and directs problems to the Stage Manager and/or the Equity staff. Deputies and members should not take grievances or questions about working conditions or rules directly to management. Once alerted to a problem, the Stage Manager or the Equity business representative will contact management on your behalf. The Deputy and the Stage Manager advise Equity of possible rule infractions, complaints, or any questions that company members may

have. However, changes or modifications to any work rule may not be made without prior written authorization from Equity. The Deputy and the company members should always avoid direct confrontation with management, and should work with the Stage Manager in an attempt to resolve immediate issues.

- Just Cause: Most agreements provide for some form of "just cause" termination provision. This rule provides that if, after specified time periods, a person is terminated without just or sufficient cause (valid reasons), the employer is liable for substantial penalty payments.

- Nudity Code: A set of guidelines and limitations for the use of nudity by performers at auditions, rehearsals, and performances exists in most agreements. These rules are specifically designed to reduce the possible risk of sexual harassment in the entertainment industry.

- Stage Manager: Responsibilities of the Stage Manager include: coordinating a production during rehearsal and performance periods; maintaining the artistic intentions of the director after the opening of the show; scheduling understudy or brush-up rehearsals; and, with the Deputy, maintaining order within the company. The Stage Manager also assembles and maintains the prompt book (the accurate playing/stage business text), cue sheets, plots, and other necessary daily records. Additionally, the Stage Manager maintains records of attendance, illness, injury, changes in duties, and other work-related issues.[37]

Even though Equity is active in providing services and attempting to secure work for its members, getting work as an Equity member is always a challenge. Alan Eisenberg states, "As an actor, you're always trying to get a job. You're always auditioning, and employment is very intermittent. The average number of workweeks [per year] is seventeen. We are always trying to increase the number of workweeks for our actors. For example, to counteract the increasing number of tours that were going out with non-Equity actors, we created the Experimental Touring Program, which provides for lower rates than the Production Contract for shows that qualify for these reduced rates. [More information on non-Equity tours and the Experimental Touring Program may be found in chapter 10.] We also protect jobs by regulating the number of alien (non-U.S.-citizen) actors who are employed in this country, especially on Broadway. As a foreign actor, you must either be a recognized star, have a specific skill that cannot be duplicated here [e.g., the African performers in *The Lion King*], or create an exchange; an exchange provides equal employment for American actors in the host country in exchange for allowing the foreign actor to perform here."[38]

For more information on Equity, please visit its Web site, *www.actorsequity.org*.

American Federation of Musicians (AFM)

The American Federation of Musicians (AFM), formed in 1896, represents musicians employed in live and recorded performances throughout the United States and Canada. Its mission statement reads, in part:

We must engage in direct action that demonstrates our power and determination to:

- Organize unorganized musicians, extending to them the gains of unionism while securing control over our industry sectors and labor markets;
- Bargain contracts and otherwise exercise collective power to improve wages and working conditions, expand the role of musicians in workplace decision-making, and build a stronger union;
- Build political power to ensure that musicians' voices are heard at every level of government to create economic opportunity and foster social justice;
- Provide meaningful paths for member involvement and participation in strong, democratic unions;
- Develop highly trained and motivated leaders at every level of the union who reflect the membership in all its diversity;
- Build coalitions and act in solidarity with other organizations that share our concern for social and economic justice.[39]

The AFM is governed by an International Executive Board. "AFM International officers [who serve on the Executive Board] are elected every three years by delegates to the AFM Convention. The delegates who elect International officers are themselves elected as representatives by the memberships of their locals."[40] The AFM is comprised of over 250

"locals," which are local unions that have jurisdiction over a specific geographic area.[41]

Musicians may join AFM by filing an application form with their local union and paying the required initiation fee; no other qualifications are needed to join the union. Upon joining AFM, the member will also have to pay annual dues and working dues. Members of AFM are eligible to receive pension and health benefits through their local unions, depending on the contract under which the member is working. Members also receive assistance in looking for work through such services as GoProMusic (AFM's online booking and referral program) and industry audition ads.[42] Union membership also provides for the opportunity to network and make professional contacts with other members. In addition, AFM provides inexpensive instrument insurance to its members.[43]

Since AFM represents all musicians, many different types of musicians choose to become members. As Patrick Glynn, director of touring, theater, and booking at AFM, states: "Our members include musicians working in Broadway or touring theater shows, orchestral musicians, musicians working in opera, touring musicians backing other performers, and jazz musicians. Even some rock-and-roll artists become members of the union, to take advantage of the services we offer."[44] Because of its varied membership, AFM is divided into separate departments. These departments include the department of touring, theater, and booking, which covers musicians who tour, such as those performing in touring theatrical shows, concert tours, and circuses.[45] The symphonic services division supports classical musicians who perform in symphonies and operas.[46] To administer recording contracts, AFM also has an electronic media services division.[47]

The wide range of its membership also means that not all AFM members are covered under collectively bargained agreements. Patrick Glynn notes that some members may not even be full-time musicians. "One of our members may be a schoolteacher during the week, and on weekends he plays for weddings or the restaurant down the street. For those members, we have model contracts available to use as a guide for pay rates and working conditions. On the other hand, we have members who work thirty-six or fifty-two weeks a year as professional musicians, so we have collectively bargained agreements to protect these members."[48] For example, a collectively bargained agreement known as Pamphlet B is negotiated with The Broadway League to cover theatrical tours. While Pamphlet B is bargained for the union as a whole, local unions may create their own collectively bargained agreements as well. As an example, Local 802, the local union representing musicians in New York City, has a collectively bargained agreement with The Broadway League to cover work on Broadway productions, while Dallas–Fort Worth Local 72-147 has collective bargaining agreements with orchestras, operas, and theaters in Texas and Oklahoma.[49] Some AFM contracts permit substitution, which allows musicians to find replacements for themselves for a specified number of performances; substitution helps to alleviate the repetitive nature of long-running engagements (such as working in the orchestra pit of a long-running Broadway or touring show) and allows musicians to take other gigs that are more challenging or lucrative.[50]

As mentioned in chapter 4, Broadway contracts also require that a minimum number of musicians be hired for musicals; this minimum number is specific to the particular Broadway theater. AFM believes that this minimum is the number required for a full, "Broadway" musical sound; producers contend that they do not need to hire as many musicians as the union mandates and thus refer to the minimums as "'featherbedding,' or requiring them [the producers] to use more players than are actually needed."[51] In order to address the concerns of the producers, Local 802 and The Broadway League reached an agreement in 1993 that allowed for smaller orchestras, based on the artistic and musical needs of a particular show. The agreement put in place a panel composed of Broadway orchestrators, arrangers, and music directors, who reviewed the musical needs of any show seeking to utilize a smaller orchestra. This procedure continued for ten years, and shows like *Smokey Joe's Cafe*, *Footloose*, and *Mamma Mia!* were granted the right to use much smaller orchestras because of the musical requirements of these shows.[52] In the collective bargaining negotiation with Local 802 in 2003, producers wanted to eliminate all minimums, as well as the review procedure. Unable to come to an agreement regarding minimums, Local 802 went on strike, joined by IATSE, Local One and Actors' Equity; the strike was settled after four days, with producers agreeing to retain minimums, and the union agreeing to reduce the number of musicians required.[53]

Like other unions comprised of performing artists, AFM works to increase employment opportunities for its members and must address practices that limit that employment, such as nonunion tours and virtual orchestras, in which some musicians are replaced by computerized recordings. Patrick Glynn explains the reasons that employers should hire professional union musicians for a performance: "When producers use nonunion personnel or replace musicians with computerized sound, they lower the standard of performance. If we could have audiences sit down and listen to a full orchestra versus a reduced orchestra or recorded performance, they would hear the difference clearly. As a union of musicians, we want to provide the audiences with the best musical experience possible, not just an adequate one."[54]

For more information on AFM, please visit its Web site at *www.afm.org*.

American Guild of Musical Artists (AGMA)

Founded in 1936 by opera singers, the American Guild of Musical Artists (AGMA) represents musical artists in opera, concerts, and dance, including the casts of Broadway and Off-Broadway productions consisting primarily of dance or operatic music (such as the 2002 Broadway production of *La Bohème*). Like Equity, AGMA is part of the Associated Actors and Artists of America under the AFL-CIO umbrella.[55] AGMA covers singers and dancers, as well as stage managers, directors, and choreographers employed in dance or opera companies. Opera performers in AGMA, like actors in Equity, have specific job functions based on casting. Opera performers work as principal artists (soloists), choristers (chorus), and supernumeraries (extras). In ballet companies, AGMA members are employed as principal dancers, soloists, and corps de ballet (a chorus of dancers) members.

AGMA's Board of Governors, consisting of union members and elected by the membership, establishes the union's basic goals and policies and "is responsible for oversight of the union's contracts, management of union funds, and protecting all members from unfair or unsafe practices and conditions. Any active member in good standing is eligible to run for a seat on the Board. Elections for the Board are held in three-year cycles, and elections of all officers (a National President, five Vice Presidents, a National Secretary and a Treasurer) are held biennially."[56] Representation on the Board of Governors is determined by geographic area; each geographic area is represented proportionally based on the number of members in that area.[57] AGMA has regional offices and professional staff in New York, New York; Philadelphia, Pennsylvania; Washington, D.C.; Miami, Florida; Chicago, Illinois; Los Angeles,

California; San Francisco, California; and Seattle, Washington.

Like AFM, potential AGMA members must file an application to join the union and must pay initiation fees, annual dues, and working dues. Alan Gordon, national executive director of AGMA, notes the unique nature of its membership: "First, AGMA does not prohibit its members from accepting nonunion work. Second, admission to AGMA is entirely open and nondiscriminatory. Live performance artists can join AGMA at any point in their careers to take advantage of members-only benefits and auditions. It is not necessary for performers to have a union job before joining AGMA. And finally, AGMA recognizes that opera and dance are international in scope, and welcomes foreign performers into its membership and allows them to perform at American companies, rather than excluding them."[58]

AGMA has collectively bargained agreements with over one hundred individual opera and dance companies, such as the Metropolitan Opera, the Boston Ballet, and the San Francisco Opera.[59] Contracts are negotiated by AGMA's negotiators, who are assisted by negotiating committees from each bargaining unit. When an artist is hired by a company covered by an AGMA collective bargaining agreement, under federal law, membership in AGMA becomes compulsory.[60] Benefits offered to members of AGMA include: "rehearsal and overtime pay; regulated work hours; vacation and sick pay; [and] access to low-cost health benefits."[61] AGMA members who need financial or social services assistance may receive help from the AGMA Emergency Relief Fund, the Actors Fund of America, and Career Transition for Dancers, all of which are partially funded by AGMA's members. AGMA members also participate in AGMA-only auditions at most AGMA signatory employers.[62]

AGMA also feels that it is important to provide services to performing artists who are not yet union members. Alan Gordon expresses AGMA's policy this way: "We believe that what hurts one singer or one dancer anywhere hurts all singers and dancers everywhere, so we're prepared and willing to help any performer who's in trouble without regard to his membership status. Our obligation to the advancement and protection of singers and dancers transcends the bounds of union membership. Also, nonunion singers and dancers whom we help invariably seek to unionize and become members."[63]

For more information on AGMA, please visit its Web site at *www.musicalartists.org*.

Association of Theatrical Press Agents and Managers (ATPAM)

The Association of Theatrical Press Agents and Managers (ATPAM) was established in 1928 to represent press agents, company managers, and house managers. ATPAM is affiliated with the International Alliance of Theatrical and Stage Employees (IATSE) as Local 18032; in this case, ATPAM is a local union distinguished from other local unions in IATSE by its jurisdiction over press agents, company managers, and house managers, not by geographic location.

ATPAM is divided into two chapters: a Manager chapter and a Press Agent chapter. Members are assigned to the chapter under which they gained eligibility, and they may not accept employment in the other chapter for three years after gaining membership.[64] The operations of ATPAM are overseen by a Board of Governors, which consists of ten members (five from each chapter). The officers and members of the Board are elected by the membership for a one-year term.[65]

ATPAM negotiates the following collectively bargained agreements with The Broadway League: the Minimum Basic Agreement, which covers company and house managers on Broadway and on national tours, and the Memorandum of Agreement, which covers press agents working on Broadway and on national tours. In addition, "ATPAM negotiates individual agreements outside of the MBA or MOA with several institutional and regional theatrical venues, including the Kennedy Center, Brooklyn Academy of Music, and Carnegie Hall, among others."[66]

Company and house managers may become members of ATPAM by beginning as a Non-Member Apprentice Manager. "A Non-Member Apprentice Manager (NMAM) may be employed when a member is hired per the Minimum Basic Agreement (MBA) between ATPAM and The Broadway League [for a Broadway or national tour engagement]. [The NMAM is hired in addition to the ATPAM member.] A contract must be filed by the employer and, at the same time as the contract filing, the NMAM must pay a nonrefundable registration fee. . . . To be eligible for membership in the Union, NMAM candidates must accumulate at least 52 credit weeks on valid contracts over a period of not less than two and not more than three consecutive seasons. No fewer than ten credit weeks must be accumulated in each season and no more than 42 credit weeks may be accumulated in one season. Any NMAM who fails to complete the program within three consecutive seasons shall be removed from the program. Each season shall be considered as starting on Labor Day. Following accumulation of 52 credit weeks, all NMAMs must pass an oral and written test for Union admission."[67] In addition, any press agent or manager employed under a standard ATPAM contract may become a member of the union, but must be approved by the Board of Governors.[68] ATPAM members must pay an initiation fee (NMAMs get a credit toward membership for attending training seminars), annual dues, and working dues. Benefits received by ATPAM members include health and pension benefits, as well as training seminars and scholarships for further management training.[69]

For more information on ATPAM, please visit its Web site at *www.atpam.com.*

International Alliance of Theatrical Stage Employees (IATSE)

The International Alliance of Theatrical Stage Employees (IATSE) received its union charter in 1893.[70] Although IATSE represents stagehands nationwide in various local unions (designated by location), it also has locals that represent other theatrical personnel, such as press agents and managers in ATPAM (IATSE, Local 18032). For the purposes of this section, we will examine IATSE representation of stagehands, including stagehands involved in construction, lighting, props, and flying production elements (production elements that hang on bars above the stage).

"The supreme governing body of the IATSE is the Quadrennial Convention. Every four years convention delegates, elected by their local unions, review the progress of the organization; its policies are affirmed or altered; plans for the future are formulated; and its Constitution and By-Laws are kept up to date."[71] IATSE is divided into fourteen districts, each covering specific regions of the United States and Canada. These districts monitor regional areas of interest and hold conventions that immediately precede the Quadrennial Convention. "Between Conventions, the [IATSE] government is entrusted to its General Executive Board— consisting of the International President, General Secretary-Treasurer, and thirteen Vice Presidents. The Board meets at least twice each year. Day-to-day administration of IATSE affairs is in the hands of the International President, whose staff includes Assistants to the President and a corps of International Representatives working throughout the United States and Canada."[72]

Stagehands become members of IATSE by joining their local union. They may either be hired by an organization that has a collective bargaining agreement with IATSE or, if the local union has an apprenticeship program, they may become membership candidates through an apprenticeship. William Ngai, trustee of IATSE, Local One (the local representing stagehands in Manhattan and other areas near New York City), states, "For Local One, a test is administered to potential apprentices that acts as an objective measurement of math skills and other general knowledge areas. We then take the top scorers and place them on an apprentice list. As openings come up in the various shops [workplaces] that we have, they become apprentices for a minimum of two to three years. When they complete their apprenticeship, they receive their full union cards."[73]

Upon joining the union, members will have to pay an initiation fee and annual dues; some locals also require working dues as well. Depending on the local, IATSE members may be eligible for pension and health benefits, and may have access to training programs or tuition reimbursement for classes designed to enhance their skills as a stagehand. William Ngai stresses the importance of acquiring these additional skills, especially as production elements become more technologically advanced: "You can't survive in this business if you think that all you need to know as a carpenter is how to wield a hammer or a screw gun. If you're working with automated scenery, you have to know about electricity, you have to know some physics to do the calculations to see what power is required to move the scenery. For lighting technicians, a light is not just a Leko [a type of light] anymore; lights have gotten a lot more complicated. You need to have more between your ears than in your shoulders and your hands to get the show up and keep it running."[74] Also, due to the nature of the stagehand's job, safety is a high priority for IATSE; a safety committee meets regularly to update safety procedures for IATSE members.[75]

IATSE locals have collectively bargained agreements with various employers. For example, IATSE, Local One has a collectively bargained agreement with The Broadway League (for Broadway productions), as well as agreements with the Metropolitan Opera and Carnegie Hall.[76] Across the country, IATSE, Local 15, representing stagehands in western Washington, has contracts with the Pacific Northwest Ballet, the Seattle Opera, and the Intiman Theatre.[77] Many IATSE contracts require a minimum number of "house" stagehands (those employed by the theater owner, rather than the production) be called to work whenever work is done in the theater; these minimums typically consist of the heads of the carpentry, lighting, props, and fly departments, known as "basics."[78] (Additional stagehands hired in addition to the basics are known as "extras.") In addition, many contracts mandate that stagehands be paid for a minimum of four or eight hours of work for every work call [when the stagehand is called to work], even if the work does not require that much time. IATSE contends that minimum calls allow the member to "get a decent day's pay every time that member is called to work;" however, minimum calls are sometimes viewed by management as a requirement that demands payment for hours worked that are not necessary for the production.[79] William Ngai notes that it is the responsibility of management (e.g., the production supervisor) to arrange for the appropriate amount of labor to cover the task at hand in a safe manner.[80]

In November of 2007, IATSE, Local One went on strike after its negotiations with The Broadway League came to an impasse over work rules, minimum call times, and tasks performed during work calls. The strike lasted for nineteen days, and closed all but four commercial Broadway productions.[81] An agreement was reached with the following points: a lower daily minimum number of stagehands required during the load-in period (replacing a requirement stating the number of stagehands hired on the first day of the load-in had to be maintained during the entire length of the load-in); an extension in the work call before each performance (known as the "continuity call") from one hour to two hours; and "yearly [salary] raises well above the 3.5 percent that the League had been offering."[82]

For more information about IATSE and a list of its local unions, please visit its Web site at *www. iatse-intl.org*.

Society of Stage Directors and Choreographers (SSDC)

The Society of Stage Directors and Choreographers (SSDC) was incorporated in 1959. "SSDC was established to be a national independent labor union with the broad purpose of elevating the standards of the art of stage direction and choreography; to develop communication among the Director and Choreographer craftspersons; to establish means for the dissemination and exchange of ideas of directorial and choreographic interest to the profession; to aid the development and training of

Directors and Choreographers; [and] to increase the professional and public esteem of these arts and to develop all conditions which encourage them."[83] The union was first recognized as the collective bargaining representative of theatrical directors and choreographers in 1962, when Bob Fosse refused to go into rehearsal for the Broadway production of *Little Me* without an SSDC Director/Choreographer contract.

SSDC is governed by a thirty-member Executive Board, comprised of board members and officers elected by the membership. The Executive Board includes at least one regional representative from the Northeast, Southeast, Midwest, Southwest, and Northwest regions; the states qualifying in each region are determined by the Board prior to the nomination of candidates.[84] The Executive Board appoints an Executive Director, "responsible for the management of the staff and operation of the Society."[85]

Directors and choreographers become members of SSDC by obtaining employment under an SSDC contract or demonstrating professional experience. Barbara Hauptman, executive director of SSDC, and Renee Lasher, contracts administrator, state, "SSDC does not deny membership to any professional directors and choreographers, but we advise applicants that their investment in joining will be most worthwhile if they are working regularly in professional venues."[86] By filing a contract, SSDC members are eligible for pension and health benefits. In addition to full membership, an associate membership is also available. An associate membership is for educational and informational purposes; associate members do not file contracts or receive any of the benefits of full membership. "Associate members receive the SSDC newsletter, invitations to and discounts for Stage Directors and Choreographers Foundation events, and access to the SSDC online directory. The online directory contains contact information for all members (full and associate), as well as job listings. Producers may also subscribe to the directory."[87] The Stage Directors and Choreographers Foundation (SDCF) is a separate nonprofit organization created "to foster, promote and develop the creativity and craft of stage directors and choreographers. SDCF's goals are to provide opportunities for exchange of knowledge among directors and choreographers; to provide opportunities to practice the crafts of directing and choreography; to promote the profession to emerging talent; to gather and disseminate craft and career information; and to increase the awareness of the value of directors' and choreographers' work."[88] SDCF accomplishes these goals through such programs as the observership program (which pairs an emerging director with a more established mentor director to observe the process of directing a show), director/choreographer networking meetings, and director/dramatist exchanges.

SSDC has collectively bargained agreements with such multi-employer bargaining groups as The Broadway League (Broadway and national tours), the League of Resident Theatres (LORT), the Association of Nonprofit Theatre Companies (ANTC, representing small theater companies in New York City), and stock theaters. In addition, SSDC has Independent Producer Agreements with individual producers, which are usually tied to a collectively bargained agreement and reflect those negotiated terms.

One of SSDC's biggest issues is the protection of its members' property rights. SSDC has had a longstanding interest in protecting the intellectual property of its members. Because the work of directors and choreographers does not have permanent tangible form, copyright is difficult to prove; typically, any copyrightable work must have a "tangible expression," such as a manuscript or a recording. Pamela Berlin, president of SSDC, explains how directors and choreographers express their creative work. "No one can own the idea or concept of an artistic work. What we can own is how we take those concepts and embody them—the execution of those ideas, provided the execution is original or unique. We cannot own setting a play in a particular place or staging *Hamlet* in modern dress, but how these choices are executed in the fuller work—stage movements, specific props, even decisions made in collaboration with the designers—rises to the level of property rights."[89]

As of 1983, directors and choreographers were determined to own their own work, to be licensed to or used by a producer in return for a royalty payment.[90] All SSDC collectively bargained agreements have a property rights clause detailing how the producer may use the work of the director or choreographer. For example, in the collectively bargained agreement with LORT, the property rights clause reads: "All rights in and to the direction and/or choreography conceived by the Director and/or Choreographer in the course of the rendition of his/her services hereunder shall be, upon its creation, and will remain the sole and exclusive property of the Director and/or Choreographer; it being understood, however, that the Theatre and its

licensee(s) shall have a perpetual and irrevocable license to use such direction and/or choreography in any stage production of the play for which the Director and/or Choreographer receives a recognition payment (or royalty) under an applicable SSDC minimum basic agreement. Any additional use or license of the direction and/or choreography by the Theatre shall be subject to further agreement between the Theatre and the Director and/or Choreographer."[91] The theater may not publish the stage directions and/or choreography. Finally, the property rights clause also gives the director and/or choreographer the right to copyright the work.

Choreographers may copyright the dance steps they use in a theatrical piece, but a copyright for direction has been more difficult to obtain. However, the case involving the play *Love! Valour! Compassion!*, in which unpublished stage direction was copied from the Broadway production and reproduced in a regional theater, further established the intellectual rights of directors by causing the issuance of "a summary judgment ruling which indicated that stage directions could be protected under copyright law."[92] This potential copyright protection has caused some friction with the Dramatists Guild, which believes that the copyright issued to directors may infringe on the authors' copyright.

For more information about SSDC, please visit its Web site at *www.ssdc.org*.

United Scenic Artists (USA 829)

United Scenic Artists (USA 829) was founded in 1897. "The members of USA 829 are scenic, costume, lighting, and sound designers; scenic artists; coordinators; and craftspeople working in film, theater, opera, ballet, television, industrial shows, commercials, and exhibitions. Through the Union, they work together to protect standards, working conditions, wages, and creative rights. In an industry plagued by high unemployment, tight work schedules, and loose payment practices, such protection is greatly needed."[93] Cecilia Friederichs, business representative for legitimate theatre for USA 829, adds a note about designers as working professionals: "Designers are not just hobbyists; they are working professionals who often work on two or three shows simultaneously to make a decent living. The contribution of designers to live performance is essential. We live in a cinematic world. People spend their lives staring at television. The visual and aural designers of the show are integral to the performance experience."[94] Like ATPAM, USA is an IATSE Local (Local USA 829), distinguished as a local union by its jurisdiction over designers, rather than by geographic location.

USA 829 is governed by a National Executive Board and three Regional Boards that oversee area issues and entrance examinations. The operations of USA 829 are conducted by the National Business Agent out of the main office in New York, and two regional business representatives: Central (Chicago, Illinois) and Western (Los Angeles, California).[95] In addition to the New York staff, the Eastern Region has business representatives in Boston, Massachusetts; Washington, D.C.; and Miami, Florida.

Because USA represents so many different types of designers, it has a number of membership categories. Members are allowed to belong to and work in multiple categories. The membership categories for live performing arts are:

Scenic Designers/Art Directors: Design, sketching, drafting, and supervision of scenery for all media

Costume Designers/Stylists: Design, selection, painting, and dyeing of costumes for all media

Lighting Designers: Design and direction of lighting for all media except network television and motion pictures

Sound Designers: Create the aural environment in tandem with other design elements of the production, including the selection and implementation of sound effects and music

Scenic Artists: Layout, surface decoration, sculpting, mold making, casting, and painting of scenery and properties for all media

Computer Artists: Recently created to address the evolving visual needs of the entertainment industry

Allied Crafts: Covers costume painters, storyboard artists, computer skills, etc.

Industrial Members: Assist the Scenic Artist in shops, in studios, and on location[96]

Designers and Scenic Artists may become members of USA 829 by the use of a professional membership application, the scenic artist apprenticeship program, and individual category exams and interviews:

- **PROFESSIONAL MEMBERSHIP APPLICATION:** Local USA 829 currently has collectively bargained agreements that cover employment in the following areas: Broadway, Regional Theatre, Network Television, Metropolitan & New York City Operas, Feature Films, Regional Opera, Major Ballet, Television Commercials, and Scenery Suppliers. Professionals who get a job under many of these Agreements must make application for membership by contacting the USA 829 Business Office. Proof of employment must be submitted along with a résumé, letters of recommendation, and prepayment of the Initiation Fee. This prepayment is held in escrow until the application can be proposed to a General Membership Meeting for acceptance.[97] The applicant may be asked to present his/her portfolio for review by an Oversight Committee, at the discretion of the Business Agent. The Business Agent will then present the applicant's credentials and current job status at the next General Membership Meeting for an acceptance vote. Should the application be denied, the Initiation Fee is refunded.

- **EASTERN REGION SCENIC ARTIST APPRENTICESHIP PROGRAM:** The Scenic Artist Apprenticeship Program is a three-year program that is sponsored by the Eastern region of USA 829 and is partially funded by the New York State Department of Labor. An Apprenticeship Exam will be offered periodically as dictated by the availability of work. Interested parties must have the following minimum qualifications *before* making application to the program:

1) Applicant must show proof of being at least 18 years of age and have a valid Social Security number.
2) Applicant must have earned a high school diploma or G.E.D.
3) Applicant must have reliable transportation or means of transportation to job sites and related training locations.
4) Applicant must supply a physician's statement confirming the applicant's agility & physical ability to:
   A) Lift 5 gallons of paint, joint compound, and/or other materials on the job.
   B) Work on ladders and scaffolding.

C) Work outdoors on locations under various weather and temperature conditions.

5) Applicant must be able to pass an aptitude test in English (read & write in English).

The program is looking for applicants with a working knowledge of art, theater, film, and related industries, but with less than three (3) years of experience. The Apprenticeship Committee reserves the right to reject applicants possessing too much experience as a working Scenic Artist, and would recommend TRACK A [the Professional Membership Application] or the OPEN EXAM [see below].

- **ADMISSION INTERVIEWS AND EXAMINATIONS:** The Union usually gives Exams or Portfolio Review/Interviews in seven categories of membership: Scenic Artist (Painting), Costume Designer, Lighting Designer, Scenic Designer/Storyboard Artist, Sound Designer, Art Department Coordinator, and Computer Artist. The Exams look for the specific skills required of each category. Getting experience in the profession is the best way to prepare, and applicants from academic or fine-arts backgrounds are encouraged to work in the field before applying to the Union. The Exam Committees of each category determine what skills they need to see from each applicant and how to best reveal those skills that prove the applicant's ability to successfully meet the demands placed on working professionals in the industry. Some categories use a practical or written Exam, while others use an Interview and/or Portfolio Review process. Applicants are asked to inquire of the nearest regional office for specific Exam information for their category and region. Exam applications, schedules, and requirements are available for download at *www.usa829.org*.[98]

USA 829 members must pay an initiation fee, as well as annual and working dues. Members are eligible for health and pension benefits, as well as other retirement benefits, such as a 401(k) plan and an annuity plan.[99] (401[k] plans and annuity plans are described in the last section of this chapter.) USA 829 also provides availability lists of members looking for work, which it provides to employers.[100]

For more information on USA, please visit its Web site at *www.usa829.org*.

Dramatists Guild of America

The Dramatists Guild of America, formed in 1919, "advances the interests of playwrights, composers, lyricists, and librettists writing for the living stage."[101] The Dramatists Guild is not a union; it does not engage in collective bargaining on behalf of its members. Rather, the Guild functions as a professional association for playwrights, composers, lyricists, and librettists, providing contracts for them to use in negotiations with producers. The producer is under no obligation to use these contracts; it falls to the member to ensure that the contract is utilized.

Christopher Brockmeyer, director of labor relations at Live Nation, further defines the distinction between a union and a guild. "The main distinction between a union and a guild is that a union has a legal right to collectively bargain with employers on behalf of its members. A guild such as the Dramatists Guild, on the other hand, does not represent statutorily defined employees and cannot legally establish minimum terms and conditions under which their members may be employed. As such, producers have a right to freely bargain with individual playwrights, composers, lyricists, and others without being bound by minimum terms and conditions."[102]

The Dramatists Guild is governed by a Council, which acts as a Board of Directors and is responsible for "the general management, direction, and control of the affairs, funds, and property of the Guild."[103] In addition, the "Council shall have the authority to formulate and negotiate Minimum Basic Production Contracts with respect to the production of dramatic and dramatico-musical works."[104] The Council consists of active members and ex officio members, who are either past presidents of the Council, or who have served on the Council for a total of fifteen years.[105] The Council is elected by active members of the Guild.

Active membership in the Guild is obtained by a vote of the membership committee. Prospective members must have a work produced on Broadway, Off-Broadway, or in a resident theater, or must be determined by the membership committee to have achieved a comparable professional status.[106] The membership committee also votes on the membership status of associate members, who must be engaged in writing dramatic or musical works (or be the author of a work adapted for the stage); associate members do not have voting rights.[107] Both active and associate members must pay annual dues, as well as working dues on royalties received and some subsidiary rights.[108] Dramatists Guild members "have access to our business affairs department, which provides model contracts and agreements as well as advice in negotiating contracts with theaters, collaborators, publishers, and others. [They] receive our bimonthly magazine, *The Dramatist*, and our annual *Resource Directory* for all aspects of the theater business nationwide, along with full access to our Web site, with links to virtually every theater Web site in the country, and exclusive access to the wide-ranging symposia and seminars which we sponsor dealing with the art, craft, and business of writing for the stage."[109]

In addition to these benefits, the Dramatists Guild acts as an advocate for the rights of its members as authors of their work. As mentioned earlier, the potential copyright protection granted to directors has caused some concern for the Dramatists Guild. As a response to these concerns, as well as others, Ralph Sevush, executive director of the Guild, has articulated the following authorial rights:

If your rights as an Author are to be protected, you should always have a written contract with your Producer. The following eight points are fundamental, and language protecting those rights should appear in all your contracts with Producers. You will also want to educate yourself further in specifics, and consult with an attorney as appropriate to fully protect your rights and interests.

1. ARTISTIC INTEGRITY. No one can make changes, alterations, and/or omissions in your script without your prior consent. This is called "script approval." You should never permit this provision in your contract to be diluted by phrases such as "such prior consent not be unduly or unreasonably withheld," or by settling for "consultation" rather than "approval" of such changes.
2. OWNERSHIP OF INTELLECTUAL PROPERTY. You own the expression of the ideas embodied in your script. You should grant your Producer only a particular license for a particular production, not general rights to produce your script in many arenas. If you so choose, however, you may grant a Producer specific rights (Future Options, Subsidiary Rights) for carefully delineated periods of time in specific venues. However,

only you should have the right to formulate contracts for all other productions and uses of your script.
3. APPROVAL OF PRODUCTION ELEMENTS. You have the right to select the cast, designers, choreographers, conductors, and director (including replacements) for your production. This is called "artistic approval." Together, you and the Producer will also confer on other elements of the production (i.e., costumes, advertising, etc.).
4. OWNERSHIP OF INCIDENTAL CONTRIBUTIONS. You own all contributions made by other participants in the production to your script. You do not owe anyone any money for these contributions unless you have a written agreement providing for such payment.
5. SUBSIDIARY RIGHTS. In the first instance, you own not only your script, but also the rights to all exploitations of your script. If you agree to grant your Producer a monetary share of subsidiary rights (motion pictures, television, stock, amateur, etc.) from future exploitation of your script, you should grant it only after the aforementioned Producer has presented your script for an agreed-upon number of performances. Any grant of subsidiary rights should only be for a limited period of time, and should generally be limited to income received by you from a well-defined geographic area (e.g., the United States and Canada).
6. FORMULA FOR RESOLVING DISPUTES. If you and your Producer disagree, you both agree to arbitrate the dispute, and not to litigate. [Arbitration is described later in this chapter.]
7. ASSIGNING YOUR RIGHTS. Your Producer cannot assign or license the rights acquired by him or her in the contract with you to a third party without your prior written consent.
8. DIRECTOR/DRAMATURG AGREEMENTS. Although a director or dramaturg may work with you over time to shape your script, such development never makes that person an "Author" unless they have actively collaborated with you as an author. No director or dramaturg should have a right of first refusal for productions after the initial production by them, or be entitled to receive a percentage of your income from future productions.[110]

For more information on the Dramatists Guild, please visit its Web site at *www.dramatistsguild. com*.

CLASSROOM DISCUSSION

Define "promulgated contract," "substitution," "basic," and "extra."

How do unions in the performing arts increase work opportunities for their members?

Who does AGMA represent, and how does its membership differ from Actors' Equity and SSDC?

What is the difference between ATPAM's Minimum Basic Agreement and Memorandum of Agreement?

Why is it important for IATSE stagehands to increase and improve their skills with ongoing training?

What strategies does SSDC use to address the issue of property rights for its members?

How do designers become members of USA?

Why is the Dramatists Guild not a union?

What are the rights of an author as defined by the Dramatists Guild?

MULTI-EMPLOYER COLLECTIVE BARGAINING GROUPS

Like individual employees, employers may decide to form multi-employer collective bargaining groups. Seth Popper, director of labor relations at The Broadway League, describes some of the advantages of belonging to a multi-employer collective bargaining group: "Producers and theater owners gain cost certainty by belonging to a multi-employer bargaining unit [group]; they know that their 'competitors' will not be paying any less for labor than they are. A member also gains exposure to the history and practices of the labor agreements by working with other members in negotiations."[111]

In this section, we will examine the major multi-employer collective bargaining groups: The Broadway League, the Off-Broadway League of American Theatres and Producers, and the League of Resident Theatres. (These multi-employer collective bargaining groups are also known as "employer trade associations" or simply "employer associations."[112]) Other multi-employer collective bargaining groups also exist, such as the Council of Resident Stock Theatres (for summer stock theaters with resident companies); these groups operate in much the same way as other multi-employer collective bargaining groups. Most operas, dance companies, and symphony orchestras do not form multi-employer collective bargaining groups, but engage in collectively bargained agreements individually with unions.

The Broadway League

"The Broadway League was born in 1930 when Broadway theater operators came together to promote their common interests and negotiate collective bargaining agreements with theatrical unions and guilds. In subsequent years, the organization's mission expanded to include serving the various needs of theatrical producers in New York and of national touring shows, as well as presenters of touring productions in cities throughout North America."[113]

A Board of Governors supervises the operations of The Broadway League. The Board of Governors is elected by the membership. Before progressing to full membership, theater owners, producers, presenters, and general managers must apply to become Associate members. "In general, candidates must have been associated with a qualifying production as defined by the League's bylaws. Associate members will be reviewed on an annual basis [by the Board of Governors] to determine if they meet the requirements for promotion to Full Membership. Full members enjoy all League benefits [as do Associate members], and are also eligible for Tony Awards voter status."[114] Associate and full members must pay annual dues, as well as "weekly dues on paid attendance for current Broadway and touring Broadway productions."[115] In addition, any person or company that engages in business with The Broadway League members may apply for Affiliate membership. Affiliate members must pay annual dues.

As mentioned in chapter 4, The Broadway League has collective bargaining agreements with many theatrical unions, including:

- Actors' Equity Association.
- Society of Stage Directors and Choreographers.
- AFM, both with the international union (touring productions) and with Local 802 (Broadway).
- Service Employees International Union, Local 32BJ, representing maintenance and cleaning personnel.
- International Union of Operating Engineers, Local 30, covering operators of heating, air-conditioning, and ventilation systems.
- International Alliance of Theatrical Stage Employees (IATSE), an international union covering the United States and Canada, with

local unions representing employees in specific jobs or geographic areas. The Broadway League has a collective bargained agreement with the international IATSE union to employ "pink contract" stagehands on touring productions, as mentioned in chapters 4 and 10.[116] On Broadway, The Broadway League negotiates collectively bargained agreements with the following locals:

o Local 1, representing stagehands in Manhattan.
o Local USA 829, USA.
o Local 18032, ATPAM.
o Theatrical Wardrobe Union, Local 764, covering all wardrobe personnel.
o Hair and Makeup Union, Local 798, covering all hair and makeup artists.
o Treasurers and Ticket Sellers Union, Local 751, representing all box-office personnel.
o Ushers, Ticket Takers, and Doormens' Union, Local 306.

For unions organized under IATSE, The Broadway League negotiates separate collective bargaining agreements with each local.

In addition to its responsibilities as a collective bargaining unit, The Broadway League "supports its members through an array of programs and events designed to promote Broadway as a vibrant national entertainment medium. These include special events, industrywide marketing initiatives, and corporate sponsorships, as well as numerous programs geared to making Broadway tickets and show information more accessible to the consumer. Other key services include overseeing government relations for the Broadway industry, maintaining extensive research archives and databases, investing in the future through audience development programs, and supporting charitable efforts benefiting the theatrical community."[117]

For more information about The Broadway League, please visit its Web site at *www.livebroadway.com*.

League of Off-Broadway Theatres and Producers

The League of Off-Broadway Theatres and Producers "was founded in 1959 to foster theatrical productions produced in Off-Broadway theatres, to assist in the voluntary exchange of information among its members, and to serve as the collective voice of its membership in pursuit of these purposes."[118] The Off-Broadway League members include both commercial and nonprofit organizations.[119] Marc Routh, president of the Off-Broadway League from 1999 to 2007, illustrates how these organizations work together within the Off-Broadway League: "Commercial producers may enhance productions at nonprofit theaters, and nonprofit theaters may want their productions to transfer to a commercial run. So our members are very concerned that working conditions remain fair for both types of organizations, in order to make sure these relationships continue. Both commercial and nonprofit organizations are very much on the same team in our League."[120] The Off-Broadway League Board of Directors, which governs the organization, consists of commercial producers, general managers, and representatives from nonprofit organizations and theater owners.

Membership in the Off-Broadway League is gained by sending an application to the Off-Broadway League office, along with an annual dues payment. Members may join as one of three categories: as a "Theatre" (commercial theater owners and nonprofit theaters; theaters must be between 100 and 499 seats); as a "Production" (covers commercial and nonprofit productions; nonprofit productions have reduced dues); or as an "Individual" member (e.g., a general manager or producer; dues are reduced).[121] All members must abide by the collectively bargained agreements negotiated by the Off-Broadway League; these agreements are with Equity, ATPAM, and SSDC. Off-Broadway League members also informally consult with one another about individual negotiations with AFM.[122]

Some benefits for members of the Off-Broadway League include:

• Representation at the negotiation table for collective bargaining agreements with Actors' Equity Association, the Association of Theatrical Press Agents and Managers, and the Society of Stage Directors and Choreographers.
• Support at grievance proceedings under those agreements, as well as information and guidance regarding the history of the agreements and past industry practices.
• Shared information at membership meetings with regard to member experiences and concerns, and trends within the industry.
• Promotional display racks for flyers and brochures provided to member theaters, which producers (member or nonmember) may use to advertise their shows to Off-Broadway audiences. These racks are maintained by the League, free of charge to

member theaters, in cooperation with the Theatre Development Fund [a nonprofit organization that supports and advocates for live theater].

- Automatic registration for the Lortel Awards, assuming other eligibility requirements are met.[123]

Also, "[t]he League is active in developing ideas for the creative marketing of Off-Broadway, which in past years has included such projects as the Lucille Lortel Awards, recognizing excellence on Off-Broadway stages, and, in conjunction with TDF [Theater Development Fund], sponsorship of ART/NY's Passport to Off-Broadway [offering 50-percent discounts to Off-Broadway shows]."[124] Future projects will include a Web site specifically tailored to showcase Off-Broadway productions, an Off-Broadway season kickoff party, and a series of roundtable discussions for Off-Broadway League members.[125]

For more information about the League of Off-Broadway Theatres and Producers, please visit its Web site at *www.offbroadway.org*.

League of Resident Theatres (LORT)

The League of Resident Theatres (LORT) is a collective bargaining group comprised of nonprofit resident theaters, which are theaters that produce a full season of work and reside physically in a particular community. (Most of these theaters are located outside of New York City, and thus are also sometimes known as "regional theaters.") In addition to its work as a collective bargaining unit, LORT also acts as an advocacy group for resident theaters, as described in its objectives:

- To promote the general welfare of resident theaters in the United States and its territories;
- To promote community interest in and support of resident theaters;
- To encourage and promote sound communications and relations between and among resident theaters in the United States and between resident theaters and the public;
- To afford resident theaters an opportunity to act for their common purpose and interest;
- To act in the interest and on behalf of its members in labor relations and related matters:

- o To serve as bargaining agent for its members in bargaining collectively with unions representing employees of its members;
- o To establish and maintain stable and equitable labor relations between its members and unions representing employees of its members;
- o To provide guidance and assistance to its members in administering collective bargaining agreements;
- o If requested by a member, to handle disputes between members and their employees and/or union representatives; and
- o To represent its members before government agencies on problems of labor relations.
- To carry on all lawful activities which may directly or indirectly contribute to the accomplishment of such purposes; and
- To communicate with the Federal Government through the National Endowment for the Arts and the American Arts Alliance [an organization that advocates on behalf of nonprofit arts organizations] and to keep those agencies apprised of the needs and status of its membership.[126]

LORT is governed by an Executive Committee, which consists of elected officers (a president, two vice presidents, a secretary, and a treasurer), a representative from each member category, and not more than five at-large representatives who may be appointed by the president.[127] The Executive Committee "conducts the business of the League between Annual Meetings [where the general membership is present], appoints committees as it deems necessary, acts upon applications for membership in the League by resident theaters, and negotiates and administers collective bargaining agreements between the League and unions."[128]

Theaters must be approved by the Executive Committee before they can join LORT. In order to qualify for membership, a theater "must be incorporated as a nonprofit IRS-approved organization. Each self-produced production must be rehearsed for a minimum of three weeks, [and] the theater must have a playing season of twelve weeks or more."[129] After a theater joins LORT, it is assigned to a member group based on its operating expenses, which determines its initiation fee and annual dues payment.[130]

LORT theaters are bound by the organization's collectively bargained agreements with AEA, SSDC, and USA. To determine rates and other payments due to these unions, the LORT theaters are assigned to a member category based on the total weekly gross box office receipts as averaged over several years; from highest to lowest, these categories are A, B+, B, C1, C2, and D.

LORT also has an A+ category, which covers nonprofit theaters considered "Broadway" productions, as described in chapter 4. LORT members may have individually negotiated contracts with other unions, such as IATSE.

As an organization of nonprofit theaters, LORT feels a special obligation to help train nonprofit managers. For example, at its annual meeting LORT presents seminars on such issues as fundraising. Adam Knight, management associate at LORT, elaborates: "LORT is increasingly concerned about developing the next generation of managers. We try to make sure that new managers or junior staff in LORT organizations have all of the information that they need to interpret contracts, work with the union business representatives, and understand the collective bargaining history between LORT and the unions."[131]

For more information about LORT, please visit its Web site at *www.lort.org*.

CLASSROOM DISCUSSION

Who does The Broadway League represent?
What unions have collectively bargained agreements with The Broadway League?
What other benefits does The Broadway League offer its members?
What unions have collectively bargained agreements with the Off-Broadway League of Theatres and Producers?
What other benefits does the Off-Broadway League offer to its members?
Who does LORT represent?
What unions have collectively bargained agreements with LORT?
What other benefits does LORT offer to its members?

NEGOTIATING COLLECTIVELY BARGAINED AGREEMENTS

Collectively bargained agreements last for several years, but at the end of that period, the agreement must be renegotiated. How do employers and unions negotiate these agreements? They begin by doing research. Research for collective bargaining

negotiations encompasses a review of previous negotiations and a review of the experience of the prior contract period. The bargaining groups will also collect internal data, such as a salary and benefits history, and external data, such as the rate of inflation, to be used in creating a negotiating strategy.

Alan Eisenberg elaborates on the research he gathers for collective bargaining agreements: "A history of what's been accomplished in past negotiations is reviewed. A history of proposals both sides rejected is reviewed, as is the history of concessions, which are modifications made to the agreement after negotiations end. We get figures on employment, as well as information on wages, pension, and health payments, under the current contract. We'll look at the cost of living for the term of the agreement. We will try to determine the general economic health of the particular segment of the industry. For example, we'll examine information released in trade papers (like *Variety*) and press releases to determine how Broadway is doing. *Variety* reports Broadway grosses every week, as well as the length of each show's run, so you have some idea of success or failure."[132]

Adam Knight adds, "We start preparing for future negotiations at the end of the present negotiation. If it's 2007, we'll already be preparing for the 2010 or 2011 negotiations. We'll set up files to examine issues that come up between our organization and the union, and as correspondence (memos, letters, etc.) comes in regarding these issues, we'll copy that correspondence to the appropriate file so that we have the information in place as the negotiation gets closer. We compile employment information, such as actor workweeks or wages, from our theaters on an annual basis, so that we know what would most benefit our members during a negotiation. For example, if we find that most "D" stages are paying actors at or very close to minimum salaries, then it stands to reason that a significant increase in minimum salaries could have an adverse effect on actor workweeks and cast sizes: More accurate information helps us know where to draw the line. We also collect anecdotal information from our members, describing the challenges they face as nonprofit organizations, like the shrinking of subscription audiences. These challenges are different from the challenges faced by commercial producers, and the unions need to know that."[133]

After the research is completed, the collective bargaining units formulate strategies to address the most important issues for the negotiation session.

At SSDC, negotiating committees are created to work with staff in formulating strategy. Barbara Hauptman and Renee Lasher state, "The negotiating committee is chaired by and made up of members who have worked in the relevant jurisdiction.[134] The staff prepares some preliminary data, such as statistical information and jurisdictional trends. The committee and staff then have a strategy meeting to discuss what issues should be discussed at the negotiation and prioritize those issues."[135]

At AGMA, Alan Gordon works with a "wish list" to help him determine his strategy. "AGMA has a national 'wish list' called 'Negotiating Priorities for AGMA Contracts,' so our strategy involves achieving as many items on the list as possible in each negotiation. AGMA also has national policies for certain health and safety issues, such as the use of smoke and fog effects, and we try to implement those policies on a national basis in our negotiations. Because opera companies plan their productions five or more years in advance, our negotiators are equally concerned with the current negotiation and with the subsequent negotiation. In fact, our strategies sometimes include making proposals that we know can't be accomplished during the current negotiation; we want to get employers familiar with our long-range goals so that during the following negotiation they are more comfortable with them."[136]

Once strategies are formulated, the union and management are ready to meet each other at the negotiating table. Each side presents the changes that it would like to make to the existing agreement or, if no previous agreement exists, lists terms and provisions that it would like to see included in the agreement. Typically, the union presents its demands first, followed by the employer. Alan Eisenberg describes the exchanges that occur after each side has presented its proposal: "After listening to the other side's proposal, you try to marshal your arguments as to why the proposal is acceptable or not acceptable. You listen to the arguments of the other side, and then you go back in to caucus. "Caucus" means you are discussing the state of the proposal with your own negotiating team, away from the main negotiating table. You return to the table and rebut the arguments provided by the employer, or you acknowledge the legitimacy of his position. You also have to gauge the area of compromise that's available to both sides, and you proceed from there to inch closer and closer to that compromise. Sometimes you'll make an argument for a proposal that you know is 'not gettable,' because if you don't

get it this time, maybe you'll get it next time. If you don't get it the next time, you'll get it the time after that. Negotiation is a continuing process: because of changing times, you'll get something that was initially rejected twelve, fourteen, or sixteen years later."[137] Alan Eisenberg advises that all negotiating teams maintain and keep copies of bargaining notes, so that points discussed in the bargaining session are recorded. (Notes are kept by each party; the bargaining sessions are not recorded on tape or digitally in order that all participants may feel comfortable with speaking freely.)

Many collectively bargained agreements include similar provisions, regardless of the union or employer involved. An integration clause notes that the current agreement incorporates all prior oral or written agreements. A separability clause states that "it is not the intent of either party hereto to violate any laws or any rulings and regulations of governmental authority or agency. The parties agree that if any provisions of the agreement are held or constituted to be void or as being in contravention of any such laws, rulings, or regulations [i.e., illegal], nevertheless, the remainder of the agreement shall remain in full force and effect."[138] A "no strike/no lockout" clause prohibits the union from striking or the employer from "locking out" union members (prohibiting them from entering the building to work) for the duration of the agreement. (However, once the agreement expires, strikes or lockouts may occur at will.) Since, under this provision, strikes or lockouts are not permissible for settling disputes, most agreements have a grievance and arbitration clause in the contract. The grievance and arbitration clause provides for disputes between the union and the employer to be handled by filing an official grievance. The grievance is heard by the grievance committee, comprised of representatives for both the union and the employer; the grievance is either settled by the committee or, if the committee members cannot come to an agreement, passed on to arbitration. In an arbitration, an independent, neutral person (known as the "arbitrator") hears both sides of the grievance and makes a decision to settle the grievance. The decision either becomes a "common-law" part of the agreement, generally accepted by all parties as binding, or is modified or reversed in the next negotiation.[139] Alan Eisenberg describes the selection of arbitrators: "Most of our contracts have specific individuals named as potential arbitrators. When a grievance goes to arbitration, the union and the employer agree upon one arbitrator. If you think the arbitrator is making bad decisions, then you can fire that arbitrator either on the annual date of the contract (for multiyear contracts) or when the agreement expires. If you don't have a named arbitrator in your agreement, you can also use independent organizations such as the American Arbitration Association or the Federal Mediation and Conciliation Service, but this takes more time."[140]

Both union and management need to be aware that both sides of the negotiating table want the agreement to be negotiated and, thus, they will need to compromise. Alan Eisenberg advises: "You build up a certain kind of relationship with the bargainers. You stay in touch during negotiations to maintain a satisfactory working relationship. Most chief negotiators know that you've got to make a deal if you want to continue working. A strike is easy enough to achieve, but in order to make a deal, a chief negotiator has got to get his own negotiating team ready for a certain amount of disappointment. The negotiators have got to find areas where they can compromise, and this requires a great deal of trust between negotiators."[141] Adam Knight agrees: "Both the unions and management have the same objective: to put on as many productions as possible. We need a deal that we can live with, and they need a deal that they can live with."[142]

After the negotiation concludes, the parties have agreed on a deal, which must be written into a formal agreement. The agreement is sent to the board of directors of the union, as well as the employer, for approval or revision. This approval process can take months, depending on complications in the union ratification process and the drafting of the final document.[143]

CLASSROOM DISCUSSION

Define the following: "caucus," "integration clause," "separability clause," "no strike/no lockout," and "grievance and arbitration clause."

What is the process for negotiating a collectively bargained agreement?

What research must be done before negotiations commence?

Why is compromise essential to the bargaining process?

PERSONNEL POLICIES AND PROCEDURES

For both employees and managers, clearly defined personnel policies and procedures are essential to good workplace practice; these policies and procedures provide rules and regulations governing employment, and must be followed by managers and employees. These policies and procedures should be described in an employee handbook given to the employee on her first day of work. The employee handbook may include the following information: organizational mission and vision, employment information (e.g., job description), compensation (e.g., salary, overtime payments), time off (e.g., holidays, vacation, sick leave, and personal days [days off for personal use that are neither sick leave nor vacation]), employee benefits, and resignation/termination procedures.[144] In addition, employee handbooks should contain information on the following topics: pension benefits offered, health benefits offered, federal equal opportunity employment laws, sexual harassment policies, and family and medical leave. An example of an employee handbook may be found in appendix F of chapter 11.

Pension Benefits

Pension benefits provide income to an employee after that employee retires. Pensions may be considered either defined benefit plans or defined contribution plans. "A defined benefit plan promises a specified monthly benefit at retirement. The plan may state this promised benefit as an exact dollar amount, such as $100 per month at retirement. Or, more commonly, it may calculate a benefit through a plan formula that considers such factors as salary and service—for example, 1 percent of average salary [or a dollar amount] for the [last] five years of employment for every year of service with an employer. The benefits in most traditional defined benefit plans are protected, within certain limitations, by federal insurance provided through the Pension Benefit Guaranty Corporation (PBGC).

"A defined contribution plan, on the other hand, does not promise a specific amount of benefits at retirement. In these plans, the employee or the employer (or both) contributes to the employee's individual account under the plan, sometimes at a set rate, such as 5 percent of earnings annually. These contributions generally are invested on the employee's behalf. The employee will ultimately receive the balance in [his] account, which is based on contributions plus or minus investment gains or losses. The value of the account will fluctuate due to the changes in the value of the investments. Examples of defined contribution plans include 401(k) plans, 403(b) plans, employee stock ownership plans, and profit-sharing plans."[145] In a 401(k) plan, the employee is able to contribute a set amount of money to an investment fund for her use at retirement. This contribution is often matched by the employer and is exempt from federal, state, and local income tax. The investments in a 401(k) plan are typically managed by the employee. Though they are similar to 401(k) plans, 403(b) plans are used only by nonprofit organizations, like schools and hospitals. In an employee stock ownership plan, the employee possesses investment in company stock; this investment may either be granted by the employer or created by salary contributions from the employee. Profit-sharing plans use company profits to determine the amount contributed to the plan, with each employee receiving a certain percentage of the profits.[146] Defined contribution plans are also known as "annuity plans."

Typically, an employee must be vested in the pension plan to receive full benefits. "Vesting" means that an employee has worked for an employer (or has worked during enough plan years if covered by a union plan) to qualify for a pension benefit. For example, under current requirements, an SSDC member is vested in the pension plan and eligible for a pension if she works for five years under SSDC contracts that require employer benefit contributions.[147] If an employee leaves the employer before completing the vesting period (or if a union member has a break in qualifying years of service), he may lose his eligibility for pension benefits.

When an employee becomes a participant in a pension plan, she must be given a summary plan description (SPD). "The summary plan description is an important document that tells participants what the plan provides and how it operates. It provides information on when an employee can begin to participate in the plan, how service and benefits are calculated, when benefits become vested, when and in what form benefits are paid, and how to file a claim for benefits."[148]

Health Benefits

In the workplace, health benefits consist of group health plans. "A group health plan is an employee welfare benefit plan established or maintained by an employer or by an employee organization (such as a union), or both, that provides medical care for participants or their dependents directly or through insurance, [medical] reimbursement [plans], or otherwise."[149] Health insurance allows employees to receive medical benefits paid for by the insurance company. These medical benefits can include visits with doctors, dental services, vision services, hospital care, and mental health services. The employee

may be required to make a payment (known as a co-payment) for some medical services, such as an office visit with a doctor. Medical reimbursement plans allow employees to be reimbursed for covered medical expenses as outlined in the plan document, such as prescription medication and visits to a chiropractor. In addition to group health plans, employers may also choose to offer flexible spending accounts. An employee contributes a set amount of money through payroll deduction to the flexible spending account for covered medical expenses; the contribution is not subject to income or Social Security taxes. The employee may not change the amount deducted or drop out of the flexible spending account plan during the year unless she experiences a change in family status (e.g., marriage, birth of a child), and must spend all of the money in the account by the end of the plan year, or the money will be forfeited back to the employer.[150]

To gain eligibility in a group health plan, employees often need to work for a certain period of time or earn a certain amount of wages. For example, Equity requires its members to have "at least twelve (12) weeks of covered employment in the previous four quarters (12 months) to qualify for six (6) months of coverage;" if the member has twenty weeks or more of employment, he is covered for twelve months.[151] Participants in a group health plan are also required to receive a summary of benefits outlining the major components of the plan.

If an employee becomes ineligible for health coverage, she may be eligible to purchase coverage at her employer's group rate through the Consolidated Omnibus Budget Reconciliation Act (COBRA) of 1986. COBRA "gives workers and their families who lose their health benefits the right to choose to continue group health benefits provided by their group health plan for limited periods of time under certain circumstances such as voluntary or involuntary job loss, reduction in the hours worked, transition between jobs, death, divorce, and other life events. Qualified individuals may be required to pay the entire premium for coverage, up to 102 percent of the cost to the plan. COBRA generally requires that group health plans sponsored by employers with 20 or more employees in the prior year offer employees and their families the opportunity for a temporary extension of health coverage (called 'continuation coverage') in certain instances where coverage under the plan would otherwise end."[152] COBRA beneficiaries are eligible to continue health benefits for eighteen months after the loss of participation in the group health plan.

Equal Employment Opportunity Laws

All employers are required to abide by federal equal opportunity laws, which prohibit discrimination in the workplace.

The Federal laws prohibiting job discrimination are:

- Title VII of the Civil Rights Act of 1964 (Title VII), which prohibits employment discrimination based on race, color, religion, sex, or national origin;
- The Equal Pay Act of 1963 (EPA), which protects men and women who perform substantially equal work in the same establishment from sex-based wage discrimination;
- The Age Discrimination in Employment Act of 1967 (ADEA), which protects individuals who are forty years of age or older;
- Title I and Title V of the Americans with Disabilities Act of 1990 (ADA), which prohibit employment discrimination against qualified individuals with disabilities in the private sector, and in state and local governments;
- Sections 501 and 505 of the Rehabilitation Act of 1973, which prohibit discrimination against qualified individuals with disabilities who work in the federal government; and
- the Civil Rights Act of 1991, which, among other things, provides monetary damages in cases of intentional employment discrimination.

The U.S. Equal Employment Opportunity Commission (EEOC) enforces all of these laws. EEOC also provides oversight and coordination of all federal equal employment opportunity regulations, practices, and policies.[153]

When working with performers, it is often difficult to determine if an artist is not hired or terminated due to artistic preference or discrimination. Alan Gordon describes AGMA's policies for dealing with discrimination in opera and dance companies. "In the opera world, ageism is a continuing problem. In the ballet world, discrimination based on body weight necessitates a constant vigilance, particularly when a performer becomes pregnant but can still perform. Once it looks like someone has been subjected to age, race, sex, sexual orientation, or other prohibited discrimination, there's no negotiation with the employer: Either the employer complies with the law, or we sue. Our policy results in employers being extraordinarily careful that their midlevel supervisors and artistic personnel don't make inappropriate decisions based on inappropriate considerations."[154]

Sexual Harassment

Sexual harassment is a form of sex discrimination that violates Title VII of the Civil Rights Act of 1964. [As such, it is subject to prosecution; a company may be held liable for the action of its employees if it is demonstrated that no action was taken by the company to prevent or address the harassment.]

Unwelcome sexual advances, requests for sexual favors, and other verbal or physical conduct of a sexual nature constitute sexual harassment when this conduct explicitly or implicitly affects an individual's employment, unreasonably interferes with an individual's work performance, or creates an intimidating, hostile, or offensive work environment.

Sexual harassment can occur in a variety of circumstances, including but not limited to the following:

- The victim as well as the harasser may be a woman or a man. The victim does not have to be of the opposite sex.
- The harasser can be the victim's supervisor, an agent of the employer, a supervisor in another area, a coworker, or a nonemployee.
- The victim does not have to be the person harassed, but could be anyone affected by the offensive conduct.
- Unlawful sexual harassment may occur without economic injury to or discharge of the victim.
- The harasser's conduct must be unwelcome.

It is helpful for the victim to inform the harasser directly that the conduct is unwelcome and must stop. The victim should use any employer complaint mechanism or grievance system available.

Prevention is the best tool to eliminate sexual harassment in the workplace. Employers are encouraged to take steps necessary to prevent sexual harassment from occurring. They should clearly communicate to employees that sexual harassment will not be tolerated. They can do so by providing sexual harassment training to their employees and by establishing an effective [written] complaint or grievance process [set forth in employee handbook]; [designating an appropriate staff member to receive complaints;] and taking immediate and appropriate action when an employee complains.

It is also unlawful to retaliate against an individual for opposing employment practices that discriminate based on sex or for filing a discrimination charge, testifying, or participating in any way in an investigation, proceeding, or litigation under Title VII.[155]

Family and Medical Leave

The Family and Medical Leave Act of 1993 provides for protected unpaid leave for medical and child-related reasons. Under the terms of this act:

Covered employers [with more than fifty employees] must grant an eligible employee [employed at least twelve months] up to a total of 12 workweeks of unpaid leave during any 12-month period for one or more of the following reasons:

- For the birth and care of the newborn child of the employee;
- For placement with the employee of a son or daughter for adoption or foster care;
- To care for an immediate family member (spouse, child, or parent) with a serious health condition; or
- To take medical leave when the employee is unable to work because of a serious health condition.[156]

CLASSROOM DISCUSSION

Why is it important to have clearly defined personnel policies?

Define the following: "defined contribution plan," "defined benefit plan," "annuity plan," "vesting," "group health plan," "flexible spending account," and "COBRA."

List the major provisions of: Equal Employment Opportunity Laws, Sexual Harassment Law (as defined in Title VII of the Civil Rights Act of 1964), and the Family and Medical Leave Act of 1993.

NOTES

1. The authors wish to thank the following contributors to this chapter: Terry Byrne, Christopher Brockmeyer, Bill Dennison, Alan Eisenberg, Cecilia Friederichs, Patrick Glynn, Alan Gordon, Nur-ul-Haq, Barbara Hauptman, Adam Knight, Renee Lasher, William Ngai, Seth Popper, Marc Routh, Ralph Sevush, Harriet Slaughter, and Sarah Wiseman.
2. Bryan A. Garner, ed., *Black's Law Dictionary*, 8th ed. (Eagan, Minn.: West Publishing, 2004). An obligation is an act that a person is required to perform.
3. Restatement of Contracts, 2d ed. (Philadelphia: American Law Institute, 1981), Section 24.
4. Ibid., Section 24.
5. Ibid., Sections 50 and 69.
6. Ibid., Section 71.
7. The authors thank SSDC for allowing us to reproduce this contract.
8. Barbara Hauptman and Renee Lasher, interview by author, January 23, 2006.
9. Alan Eisenberg, interview by author, November 23, 2005.
10. Christopher Brockmeyer, *A Brief History of Labor in America* (New York, Christopher Brockmeyer, 2005).
11. Ibid.
12. Ibid.
13. Ibid.
14. National Labor Relations Board, "What Is the National Labor Relations Act?" *www.nlrb.gov/Workplace_Rights/i_am_new_to_this_website/what_is_the_national_labor_relations_act.aspx*.
15. Railroad and airplane employees are covered by the Railway Labor Act.
16. National Labor Relations Board, "What Are My Rights?" *www.nlrb.gov/Workplace_Rights/i_am_new_to_this_website/what_are_my_rights.aspx*.
17. National Labor Relations Board, "How Do I File a Charge against an Employer or a Union?" *www.nlrb.gov/Workplace_Rights/i_am_new_to_this_website/how_do_i_file_a_charge_against_an_employer_or_a_union.aspx*.
18. Brockmeyer, *A Brief History of Labor in America*.
19. Ibid.
20. Ibid.
21. Ibid.
22. United States Department of Labor, "Employee Retirement Income Security Act," *www.dol.gov/dol/topic/health-plans/erisa.htm*. "Plan fiduciaries include, for example, plan trustees, plan administrators, and members of a plan's investment committee." (United States Department of Labor, "Health Plans and Benefits: Fiduciary Responsibilities," *www.dol.gov/dol/topic/health-plans/fiduciaryresp.htm*.)
23. Actors' Equity Association, "About Equity," *www.actorsequity.org/AboutEquity/aboutequityhome.asp*.
24. "The American Federation of Labor and Congress of Industrial Organizations (AFL-CIO) is a voluntary federation of 55 national and international labor unions." (American Federation of Labor and Congress of Industrial Organizations, "This is the AFL-CIO," *www.aflcio.org/aboutus/thisistheaflcio*.)
25. Actors' Equity Association, *About Equity* (New York: Actors' Equity Association, 2006), *www.actorsequity.org/docs/about/aboutequity_booklet_06.pdf*, 5.
26. Ibid., 11–12.
27. Ibid., 10.

28. Eisenberg, "Interview."
29. *About Equity*, 8–9.
30. Actors' Equity Association, "AEA Foundation," *www.actorsequity.org/AboutEquity/aeafoundation.asp*.
31. Ibid.
32. Broadway Cares/Equity Fights AIDS, "Mission Statement," *www.broadwaycares.org/about/missionstatement.cfm*.
33. The Production Contract is negotiated between Actors' Equity and The Broadway League and covers Broadway production and national tours. "A stock theatre presents consecutive productions of different shows with no lay-off or hiatus between the productions." (*About Equity*, 19.)
34. The Los Angeles 99-Seat Theatre Plan is used by theaters in Los Angeles County with 99 or fewer seats.
35. Eisenberg.
36. A "principal actor" is defined by Equity as any actor not engaged in Chorus, Stage Managerial, or Extra work (and thus, not covered by those contracts).
37. *About Equity*, 16–18.
38. Eisenberg.
39. American Federation of Musicians, "Mission Statement," *www.afm.org/about/mission-statement*.
40. American Federation of Musicians, "International Executive Board," *www.afm.org/about/international-executive-board*.
41. American Federation of Musicians, "Locals," *www.afm.org/about/locals*.
42. American Federation of Musicians, "Why Join?," *www.afm.org/why-join*.
43. Patrick Glynn, interview by author, April 30, 2007.
44. Ibid.
45. American Federation of Musicians, "Touring, Theater, and Booking," *www.afm.org/departments/touring-theatre-and-booking*.
46. American Federation of Musicians, "Symphonic Services Division," *www.afm.org/departments/symphonic services*.
47. American Federation of Musicians, "Electronic Media Services Division," *www.afm.org/departments/electronic-media-services-division*.
48. Glynn, "Interview."
49. Local 802, "Wage and Contract Info," *www.local802afm.org/frames/fs_wage.htm*; Dallas-Fort Worth Professional Musicians Association, "Collective Agreements," *www.musiciansdfw.org/pages/collective_bargaining.htm*.
50. Glynn.
51. "Broadway musicians union sets strike deadline," *CNN.com*, March 2, 2003.
52. Bill Dennison, e-mail to author, August 2, 2007.
53. "Musicians strike hits Broadway," *CNN.com*, March 8, 2003, *www.cnn.com/2003/SHOWBIZ/03/08/broadway.strike.ap/index.html*; "Musicians reach tentative agreement with producers," *CNN.com*, March 11, 2003, *www.cnn.com/2003/SHOWBIZ/03/11/broadway.strike/index.html*.
54. Glynn.
55. At the time of this writing, AGMA was considering a withdrawal from the 4As to allow it more opportunity to organize in other, nontheatrical venues.
56. American Guild of Musical Artists. *New Member Information Booklet* (New York: American Guild of Musical Artists, 2007), *www.musicalartists.org/MemberInfo/Handbook%205-29-07.pdf*, 5.
57. Ibid. (The states comprising specific areas are detailed in this document.)
58. Alan Gordon, interview by author, July 30, 2007.
59. *New Member Information Booklet*, 7.
60. Gordon, "Interview."
61. *New Member Information Booklet*, 4.
62. Gordon.
63. Ibid.
64. Association of Theatrical Press Agents and Managers, "Constitution and By-Laws," *www.atpam.com/Resources/Constitution.htm*.
65. Ibid.
66. Association of Theatrical Press Agents and Managers, "ATPAM Agreements," *www.atpam.com/Services/contract.htm*.
67. Association of Theatrical Press Agents and Managers, "How to Join," *www.atpam.com/Services/Membership.htm*.
68. Ibid.; Tom Walsh, interview by author, June 16, 2006.
69. Association of Theatrical Press Agents and Managers, "About ATPAM: An Overview," *www.atpam.com/About/About.htm*.
70. International Alliance of Theatrical Stage Employees, "About IATSE," *www.iatse-intl.org/about/about.html*.
71. Ibid.
72. Ibid.
73. William Ngai, interview by author, May 31, 2007.
74. Ibid.
75. Ibid.
76. IATSE Local One, "About Us," *www.iatselocalone.org/about/aboutus.html*.
77. IATSE Local 15, "About IATSE Local 15," *www.ia15.org/about.html*.
78. "The minimum number of stagehands required is different when the house is dark (no production) and when a production is running or loading in/out. When the house is dark, the minimum number of stagehands is determined by knowing what can be minimally accomplished in the facility in a safe manner." (Ngai.)
79. Ngai, "Interview." "When production on a show is just beginning, minimum calls may not take the whole four or eight hours, especially if the call is to measure the space or discuss some peculiar aspect of the incoming show." (Ngai.)
80. Ibid.
81. Four nonprofit Broadway productions were also running during this time, and a fifth, *How the Grinch Stole Christmas*, was granted an injunction (order) from a judge and allowed to run.
82. Campbell Robertson, "Stagehands End Walkout on Broadway," *New York Times*, November 29, 2007.
83. Society of Stage Directors and Choreographers Web site, *www.ssdc.org*.
84. Society of Stage Directors and Choreographers, *Bylaws and Work Rules* (New York: Society of Stage Directors and Choreographers, 2005).
85. Ibid.
86. Hauptman and Lasher, "Interview."
87. Ibid.
88. Society of Stage Directors and Choreographers, "SDC-Foundation," *www.ssdc.org/sdcf.php*.

89. Pamela Berlin, "Our Union Property Rights," *SSDC Notes*, May/June 2007.

90. Society of Stage Directors and Choreographers, "SDC-Foundation," *www.ssdc.org/sdcf.php*.

91. Society of Stage Directors and Choreographers, *LORT Collective Bargaining Agreement, April 15, 2005–April 14, 2009* (New York: Society of Stage Directors and Choreographers, 2005), *www.ssdc.org/LORT_05-09.pdf*, 27–28.

92. Hauptman and Lasher.

93. United Scenic Artists, *General Entrance Information – Eastern Region* (New York: United Scenic Artists, 2007), *www.usa829.org/USA/pdf/Exams/Eastern/2007-General-Entrance-Info-East-B.pdf*, 1.

94. Cecilia Friederichs, interview by author, June 26, 2006.

95. United Scenic Artists, *General Information* (New York: United Scenic Artists, 2007).

96. Ibid.

97. Money in escrow is held by a third party (usually a bank) until certain conditions are fulfilled.

98. *General Entrance Information.*

99. Friederichs, "Interview."

100. United Scenic Artists, *Member Orientation Book* (New York: United Scenic Artists, 2006).

101. Dramatists Guild "About," *www.dramatistsguild.com/about.aspx*. A librettist composes the text of a musical or operatic work. Although the Dramatists Guild mainly represents theatrical authors, composers and librettists of operatic works may become members as well.

102. Christopher Brockmeyer, e-mail to author, September 5, 2007.

103. Dramatists Guild, "Constitution and By-Laws," *www.dramatistsguild.com/about_constitution.aspx*.

104. Ibid.

105. Ibid.

106. Ibid.

107. Ibid.

108. Ibid.

109. Dramatists Guild, "Member Benefits," *www.dramatistsguild.com/mem_benefits.aspx*.

110. Ralph Sevush, "Dramatist's Bill of Rights," *www.dramatistsguild.com/about_rights.aspx*.

111. Seth Popper, interview by author, June 29, 2006.

112. Brockmeyer, *A Brief History of Labor in America.*

113. The Broadway League, "About the League," *www.broadwayleague.com/index.php?url_identifier=about-the-league-1*.

114. The Broadway League, "Membership," *www.broadwayleague.com/index.php?url_identifier=membership-1*.

115. Ibid.

116. Stagehands employed under a pink contract work directly for the producer, as opposed to the theater owner.

117. The Broadway League, "About the League."

118. League of Off-Broadway Theatres and Producers, "FAQ," *www.offbroadway.org/faq.html*.

119. Marc Routh, interview by author, February 8, 2006.

120. Ibid.

121. League of Off-Broadway Theatres and Producers, "FAQ," *www.offbroadway.org/faq.html*.

122. Routh, "Interview."

123. League of Off-Broadway Theatres and Producers Web site.

124. Ibid.

125. Terry Byrne, interview by author, August 7, 2007.

126. League of Resident Theatres, "LORT Objectives," *www.lort.org/mission.htm*.

127. League of Resident Theatres, "The By-Laws of the League of Resident Theatres," *www.lort.org/by-laws.htm*.

128. Ibid.

129. League of Resident Theatres, "LORT Membership Requirements," *www.lort.org/newmembership.htm*.

130. League of Resident Theatres, "The By-Laws of the League of Resident Theatres."

131. Adam Knight, interview by author, May 8, 2007.

132. Eisenberg. The "cost-of-living adjustment" is a yearly adjustment made by the federal government that increases some government benefits (like Social Security) to keep pace with inflation. This adjustment may be used as a base increase for wages and other compensation in negotiations.

133. Knight, "Interview."

134. A "jurisdiction" refers to all employers employing members under a particular collective bargaining agreement, such as LORT or Off-Broadway.

135. Hauptman and Lasher.

136. Gordon.

137. Eisenberg.

138. Society of Stage Directors and Choreographers, *Off-Broadway Collective Bargaining Agreement, July 1, 2005–June 30, 2010* (New York: Society of Stage Directors and Choreographers, 2005), *www.ssdc.org/OB05-10book.pdf*, 33.

139. Eisenberg.

140. Ibid.

141. Ibid.

142. Knight.

143. Brockmeyer, "E-mail."

144. Society for Human Resources Management, *Module 5: Employee and Labor Relations* (Alexandria, Va.: Society for Human Resources Management, 2006), 5–107.

145. United States Department of Labor, "Retirement Plans, Benefits & Savings: Types of Retirement Plans," *www.dol.gov/dol/topic/retirement/typesofplans.htm*.

146. Ibid.

147. Society of Stage Directors and Choreographers, *Spotlight on Benefits* (New York: Society of Stage Directors and Choreographers, 2007).

148. U.S. Department of Labor, "Health Plans and Benefits: Plan Information," *www.dol.gov/dol/topic/health-plans/planinformation.htm*.

149. U.S. Department of Labor, "Health Plans and Benefits," *www.dol.gov/dol/topic/health-plans/index.htm*.

150. Haneefa T. Saleem, "Health Spending Accounts," *Compensation and Working Conditions Online* (Washington, D.C.: U.S. Department of Labor, Bureau of Labor Statistics, October 22, 2003), *www.bls.gov/opub/cwc/cm20031022ar01p1.htm*.

151. Actors' Equity Association, "Actors' Equity Association Benefits," *www.actorsequity.org/Benefits/healthinsurance.asp*.

152. United States Department of Labor, "Continuation of Health Coverage—COBRA," *www.dol.gov/dol/topic/health-plans/cobra.htm*.

153. Equal Employment Opportunity Commission, "Federal Equal Opportunity Laws," *www.eeoc.gov/abouteeo/overview_laws.html*.

154. Gordon.

155. Equal Employment Opportunity Commission, "Sexual Harassment," *www.eeoc.gov/types/sexual_harassment.html.*

156. United States Department of Labor, "Compliance Assistance–Family and Medical Leave Act," *www.dol.gov/esa/whd/fmla.*

BIBLIOGRAPHY

Actors' Equity Association, *www.actorsequity.org.*

———. "About Equity." *www.actorsequity.org/AboutEquity/aboutequityhome.asp.*

———. *About Equity.* New York: Actors' Equity Association, 2006. *www.actorsequity.org/docs/about/aboutequity_booklet_06.pdf.*

———. "Actors' Equity Association Benefits," *www.actorsequity.org/Benefits/healthinsurance.asp.*

———. "AEAFoundation." *www.actorsequity.org/AboutEquity/aeafoundation.asp.*

Adler, Andrew. "Agreement Reached to Save Orchestra." (Louisville, Ky.) *Courier-Journal,* 20 March 2006.

American Federation of Labor and Congress of Industrial Organizations, *www.aflcio.org.*

———. "This is the AFL-CIO." *www.aflcio.org/aboutus/thisistheaflcio.*

American Federation of Musicians, *www.afm.org.*

———. "International Executive Board." *www.afm.org/about/international-executive-board.*

———. "Locals." *www.afm.org/about/locals.*

———. "Mission Statement." *www.afm.org/about/mission-statement.*

———. "Electronic Media Services Division." *www.afm.org/departments/electronic-media-services-division.*

———. "Symphonic Services Division." *www.afm.org/departments/symphonic-services.*

———. "Touring, Theater, and Booking." *www.afm.org/departments/touring-theatre-and-booking.*

———. "Why Join?" *www.afm.org/why-join.*

American Federation of Musicians Local 802. "Wage and Contract Info." *www.local802afm.org/frames/fs_wage.htm.*

American Guild of Musical Artists. *www.musicalartists.org.*

———. *New Member Information Booklet.* New York: American Guild of Musical Artists, 2007. *www.musicalartists.org/MemberInfo/Handbook%205-29-07.pdf.*

Armbrust, Roger. "Roundabout Exits League." *Backstage,* 16 February 2005.

Associated Press. "Radio City Show Goes On without Musicians." Associated Press, 3 November 2005.

———. "Radio City, Union Reach Tentative Deal." Associated Press, 17 November 2005.

Association of Theatrical Press Agents and Managers. *www.atpam.com.*

———. "About." *www.atpam.com/About/About.htm.*

———. "ATPAM Agreements." *www.atpam.com/Services/contract.htm.*

———. "Constitution and By-Laws." *www.atpam.com/Resources/Constitution.htm.*

———. "Becoming a Member." *www.atpam.com/Services/Membership.htm.*

Ayer, Julie. *More than Meets the Ear: How Symphony Musicians Made Labor History.* Minneapolis, Minn.: Syren Book Company, 2005.

Barbeito, Carol L. *Human Resources Policies and Procedures for Nonprofit Organizations.* New York: Wiley, 2006.

Berlin, Pamela. "Our Union Property Rights." *SSDC Notes,* May/June 2007.

Boroff, Philip. "Broadway Contract Full of Costly, Arcane Rules, Producers Say." *Bloomberg.com,* 19 July 2007. *www.bloomberg.com/apps/news?pid=20601088&sid=aT.k1D2IeleU&refer=muse.*

Breslauer, Jan. "Playing to a Bigger Crowd." *Los Angeles Times,* 17 September 2006.

Broadway Cares/Equity Fights AIDS. "Mission Statement." *www.broadwaycares.org/about/missionstatement.cfm.*

The Broadway League, *www.broadwayleague.com.*

———. "About the League." *www.broadwayleague.com/index.php?url_identifier=about-the-league-1.*

———. "Membership." *www.livebroadway.com/index.php?url_identifier=membership-1.*

Brockmeyer, Christopher. *A Brief History of Labor in America.* New York, Christopher Brockmeyer, 2005.

———. "Labor Relations." E-mail to author, 5 September 2007.

Byrne, Terry. "League of Off-Broadway Theatres and Producers." Interview by Jessica Bathurst. E-mail to author, 7 August 2007.

Cantrell, Scott. "Musicians Picket Fundraiser." *Dallas Morning News,* 26 October 2006.

CNN.com. "Broadway Musicians Union Sets Strike Deadline." *CNN.com,* 2 March 2003. *www.cnn.com/2003/SHOWBIZ/Music/03/02/broadway.strike.ap.*

———. "Deal Reached to End Broadway Strike." *CNN.com,* 11 March 2003. *www.cnn.com/2003/SHOWBIZ/03/11/broadway.strike/index.html.*

———. "Musicians Strike Hits Broadway." *CNN.com,* 8 March 2003. *www.cnn.com/2003/SHOWBIZ/03/08/broadway.strike.ap/index.html.*

Cox, Gordon. "More 'Urinetown' trouble." *Variety,* 6 December 2006.

Dallas-Fort Worth Professional Musicians Association. "Collective Agreements." *www.musiciansdfw.org/pages/collective_bargaining.htm.*

Dennison, Bill. "Local 802 and Musician Minimums." E-mail to author, 2 August 2007.

Dramatists Guild, *www.dramatistsguild.com.*

———. "Constitution and By-Laws." *www.dramatistsguild.com/about_constitution.aspx.*

———. "Member Benefits," *www.dramatistsguild.com/mem_benefits.aspx.*

Druckenbrod, Andrew. "Pact with Union Likely to Boost Live Recordings by PSO, Others." *Pittsburgh Post-Gazette,* 8 August 2006.

Eisenberg, Alan. "Actors' Equity Association." Interview by Jessica Bathurst. Tape recording, 23 November 2005. Actors' Equity Association, New York.

Elliott, Susan. "Atlanta Ballet Season to Open with a CD, Protest." *Atlanta Journal-Constitution,* 26 October 2006.

Equal Employment Opportunity Commission, *www.eeoc.gov.*

———. "Federal Equal Opportunity Laws." *www.eeoc.gov/abouteeo/overview_laws.html.*

———. "Sexual Harassment," *www.eeoc.gov/types/sexual_harassment.html.*

Feuer, Alan. "Music Isn't Live, but Rockettes Keep Kicking." *New York Times,* 4 November 2005.

Friederichs, Cecilia. "United Scenic Artists." Interview by Jessica Bathurst. Tape recording, 26 June 2006. United Scenic Artists, New York.

Garner, Bryan A., ed. *Black's Law Dictionary*. 8th ed. Eagan, Minn.: West Publishing, 2004.

Gerard, Jeremy. "Broadway Union, Management Agree on One Thing: Higher Prices." *Bloomberg.com*, 26 July 2007. *www.bloomberg.com/apps/news?pid=20601115&refer=muse &sid=alEloGWmSOK0*.

Glynn, Patrick. "American Federation of Musicians." Interview by Jessica Bathurst. Tape recording, 30 April 2007. American Federation of Musicians, New York.

Gordon, Alan. "American Guild of Musical Artists." Interview by Jessica Bathurst. E-mail to author, 30 July 2007.

Green, Jesse. "Exit, Pursued by a Lawyer." *New York Times*, 29 January 2006.

Greenhouse, Steven. "Seven Unions Ask Labor Board to Order Employers to Bargain." *New York Times*, 15 August 2007.

Hauptman, Barbara, and Renee Lasher. "Society of Stage Directors and Choreographers." Interview by Jessica Bathurst. E-mail to author, 23 January 2006.

International Alliance of Theatrical Stage Employees, *www.iatse-intl.org*.

———. "About IATSE," *www.iatse-intl.org/about/about.html*. International Alliance of Theatrical Stage Employees Local 1. "About Local 1." *www.iatselocalone.org/about/aboutus.html*.

International Alliance of Theatrical Stage Employees Local 15. "About IATSE Local 15." *www.ia15.org/about.html*.

Jepson, Barbara. "Where Stagehands Clean Up in More Ways than One." *Wall Street Journal*, 17 November 2004.

Jones, Chris. "'Urinetown' Battle Roils the World of Musicals." *Chicago Tribune*, 19 November 2006.

Kaufman, Sarah. "Ballet Rejects Offer by Michael Kaiser to Mediate, Returns to Bargaining Table." *Washington Post*, 7 January 2006.

———. "Dancers, Ballet Out of Step in Pas de Deux." *Washington Post*, 22 December 2005.

———. "Dancers, Company Agree on Contract." *Washington Post*, 7 March 2006.

———. "Seeking Their Balance." *Washington Post*, 1 March 2006.

———. "Tonight's 'Nutcracker' Canceled in Dispute." *Washington Post*, 15 December 2005.

———. "Washington Ballet Cancels 'Nutcracker' Run." *Washington Post*, 17 December 2005.

Kaufman, Sarah and Darragh Johnson. "All Toes Point to the Picket Line." *Washington Post*, 16 December 2005.

Kiehl, Stephen. "BSO Agrees to 2-Year Contract." *Baltimore Sun*, 16 September 2006.

Knight, Adam. "League of Resident Theatres." Interview by Jessica Bathurst. Tape recording, 8 May 2007. League of Resident Theatres, New York.

League of Off-Broadway Theatres and Producers, *www. offbroadway.org/index.html*.

———. "FAQ." *www.offbroadway.org/faq.html*.

League of Resident Theatres, *www.lort.org*.

———. "The By-Laws of the League of Resident Theatres," *www.lort.org/by-laws.htm*.

———. "LORT Membership Requirements," *www.lort.org/newmembership.htm*.

———. "LORT Objectives." *www.lort.org/mission.htm*.

McClernan, Nancy. "The Strange Case of Edward Einhorn v. Mergatroyd Productions." *Dramatist*, September/October 2006.

McKinley, Jesse. "Musicians' Union Files Complaint against Radio City Owner." *New York Times*, 5 November 2005.

Morris, Stephen Leigh. "Squinting into the Sun." *LA Weekly*, 9–15 December 2005.

National Labor Relations Board, *www.nlrb.gov*.

———. "How Do I File a Charge against an Employer or a Union?" *www.nlrb.gov/Workplace_Rights/i_am_new_to_ this_website/how_do_i_file_a_charge_against_an_employer_ or_a_union.aspx*.

———. "What Are My Rights?" *www.nlrb.gov/Workplace_ Rights/i_am_new_to_this_website/what_are_my_rights. aspx*.

———. "What is the National Labor Relations Act?" *www. nlrb.gov/Workplace_Rights/i_am_new_to_this_website/ what_is_the_national_labor_relations_act.aspx*.

Ngai, William. "International Alliance of Theatrical Stage Employees." Interview by Jessica Bathurst. Tape recording, 31 May 2007. International Alliance of Theatrical Stage Employees Local One, New York.

Pitz, Marylynne. "Pre-'Carmen' Concerts Planned Outside Benedum to Protest Ballet Cuts." *Pittsburgh Post-Gazette*, 5 October 2005.

Popper, Seth. "The League of American Theatres and Producers." Interview by Jessica Bathurst. Tape recording, 29 June 2006. League of American Theatres and Producers, New York.

Restatement of Contracts, 2d ed. Philadelphia: American Law Institute, 1981.

Robertson, Campbell. "Actors at American Girl Place Store Go on Strike." *New York Times*, 4 August 2006.

———. "American Girl Place Returns Fire in Legal Skirmish with a Union." *New York Times*, 2 November 2006.

———. "Bitty Bear and the Secret Ballot." *New York Times*, 20 November 2006.

———. "The Broadway Strike, Now Starring the Grinch." *New York Times*, 22 November 2007.

———. "Creative Team of 'Urinetown' Complains of Midwest Shows." *New York Times*, 15 November 2006.

———. "Stagehands Bracing for Broadway Showdown." *New York Times*. 26 July 2007.

———. "Stagehands End Walkout on Broadway." *New York Times*, 29 November 2007.

Routh, Marc. "League of Off-Broadway Theatres and Producers." Interview by Jessica Bathurst. Tape recording, 8 February 2006. Richard Frankel Productions, New York.

Saleem, Haneefa T. "Health Spending Accounts." *Compensation and Working Conditions Online*. Washington, D.C.: U.S. Department of Labor, Bureau of Labor Statistics, 22 October 2003. *www.bls.gov/opub/cwc/cm20031022ar01p1. htm*.

Salomon, Andrew. "Actors Return to Work at American Girl." *New York Times*, 7 August 2006.

———. "NY Actors Exit Theatre to Stage Protest." *Backstage*, 3 August 2006.

Sevush, Ralph. "The Dramatist's Bill of Rights." *www. dramatistsguild.com/about_rights.aspx*.

Smith, Tim. "BSO's Dedicated Musicians, Richlin Instrumental in Reaching Deal." *Baltimore Sun*, 19 September 2006.

Society for Human Resources Management. *Module 5: Employee and Labor Relations*. Alexandria, Va.: Society for Human Resources Management, 2006.

Society of Stage Directors and Choreographers, *www.ssdc. org*.

———. *Bylaws and Work Rules*. New York: Society of Stage Directors and Choreographers, 2005.

———. *Off-Broadway Collective Bargaining Agreement, July 1, 2005–June 30, 2010*. New York: Society of Stage Directors and Choreographers, 2005. *www.ssdc.org/OB05-10book. pdf*.

———. "SDCFoundation." *www.ssdc.org/sdcf.php*.

———. *Spotlight on Benefits*. New York: Society of Stage Directors and Choreographers, 2007.

Tagami, Kirsten. "Ballet to Scrap Orchestra." *Atlanta Journal-Constitution*, 21 July 2006.

Trescott, Jacqueline. "Labor Dispute Jeopardizes Ballet Troupe's 'Nutcracker'." *Washington Post*, 14 December 2005.

———. "Opera House Forgoes 'Virtual Orchestra' in Kennedy Center Contract." *Washington Post*, 18 October 2005. United Scenic Artists, *www.usa829.org*.

———. *General Entrance Information—Eastern Region*. New York: United Scenic Artists, 2007. *www.usa829.org/USA/ pdf/Exams/Eastern/2007-General-Entrance-Info-East-B.pdf*.

———. *General Information*. New York: United Scenic Artists, 2005.

———. *Member Orientation Book*. New York: United Scenic Artists, 2006.

United States Department of Labor. *www.dol.gov*.

———. "Compliance Assistance–Family and Medical Leave Act." *www.dol.gov/esa/whd/fmla*.

———. "Continuation of Health Coverage–COBRA." *www. dol.gov/dol/topic/health-plans/cobra.htm*.

———. "Employee Retirement Income Security Act." *www. dol.gov/dol/topic/health-plans/erisa.htm*.

———. "Health Plans and Benefits." *www.dol.gov/dol/topic/ health-plans/index.htm*.

———. "Health Plans and Benefits: Fiduciary Responsiblities." *www.dol.gov/dol/topic/health-plans/fiduciaryresp.htm*.

———. "Health Plans and Benefits: Plan Information." *www. dol.gov/dol/topic/health-plans/planinformation.htm*.

———. "Retirement Plans, Benefits & Savings: Types of Retirement Plans." *www.dol.gov/dol/topic/retirement/ typesofplans.htm*.

Wakin, Daniel J. "Orchestra Musicians Reach Agreement over Control of Live Recordings." *New York Times*, 4 August 2006.

Walsh, Tom. "Association of Theatrical Press Agents and Managers." Interview by Jessica Bathurst. Tape recording, 16 June 2006. Association of Theatrical Press Agents and Managers, New York.

CHAPTER TEN

Touring Productions

In this chapter, we will discuss touring productions.[1] Touring productions can take any form found in live performance, from Broadway musicals to chamber orchestras to dance companies. We will first examine the different types of touring productions, as well as the ways in which the market is determined for each show. We will then examine types of touring productions as determined by both the length of the engagement and union personnel employed. Finally, we will explore the creation, booking, and presentation of touring productions.

Touring productions are created by acquiring the appropriate license (rights) for the property, forming a producing entity, creating a budget, securing financing, and hiring administrative, creative, and production staff. When the tour is created, a booking agent is hired to negotiate engagement dates for the tour by planning the route (the itinerary) for the tour, securing dates and negotiating contracts with presenters, and acting as the representative of the touring production in its dealings with presenters.[2] Presenters own, operate, or rent performance spaces and are responsible for finding works to present in their spaces, creating the schedule for their venues, negotiating contracts with booking agents, supervising the ticket sales and marketing efforts for the engagement, and managing the engagement while it is at the venue.[3]

TOURS AND TOURING PRODUCTIONS

Simply put, a tour is a production or work that travels from one place to another. A tour may also be considered a production that travels outside of its home base.[4]

Touring productions may be created from any theater, dance, or music work. Touring theatrical productions originate from existing Broadway or Off-Broadway productions, and can also originate in nonprofit theaters. Theatrical tours can also be created directly for the road (presenters in the touring market). Touring dance and music productions typically consist of a combination of new works and existing repertory.[5]

Touring productions adapted from current or recently closed Broadway shows are the most common theatrical touring productions. In the 2006–2007 season, Broadway productions on tour grossed $950 million and sold 16.7 million tickets.[6] Large-scale Broadway musicals such as *Cats*, *Les Misérables*, and *The Phantom of the Opera* have toured quite successfully for many years. More recently, *Rent*, *Chicago*, *The Lion King*, and *Wicked* have also shown that they are hits on tour as well as on Broadway. (In fact, the *Chicago Tribune* published an article entitled "How 'Wicked' Run Has Broken Chicago's Curse," noting that the sold-out Chicago sit-down production of *Wicked* typically grosses $1.2 million in weekly ticket sales, comparable to the Broadway ticket grosses.[7]) While Broadway plays also tour, they do not sell as many tickets as musicals and are seen as a greater challenge to tour.[8] Touring plays tend to be star-driven; for example, the national tour of *Doubt* starred Cherry Jones, who won a Tony Award for her role on Broadway.

A successful Broadway production may ensure a successful tour, but even less-successful Broadway productions may have a life on the road. As Ron Gubin, a partner and booking agent for Avid Touring Group, states, "Without a doubt, the best way to have a successful tour is to have a successful Broadway run. However, there are different definitions of 'successful Broadway run.' Some shows have run 'successfully' on Broadway for years and never made a penny in profits, but have toured. There are also shows that did not do well in New York but made money on the road."[9] For example, the musical *Singin' in the Rain* did not succeed on Broadway, but did well on tour and in regional productions; Gary McAvay, president of Columbia Artists Theatricals, notes, "It sold on the road because middle America recognized the title from the movie and bought tickets."[10]

Off-Broadway productions may also tour. For example, *Stomp* began as an Off-Broadway attraction and has toured extensively. Josh Sherman, a booking sales agent at Columbia Artists Theatricals, states, "Off-Broadway shows can tour in a lower price range than Broadway shows and may also require less equipment and load-in/load-out time [time required to set up or take down the production in the venue]. Presenters purchase these shows as a programming alternative to the standard Broadway fare."[11] However, because Off-Broadway theaters are by definition fewer than 500 seats, these productions may need to be booked into smaller theaters that do not diminish the aesthetic experience of the production.[12]

Although they mount tours less often than Broadway and Off-Broadway productions, nonprofit theaters may decide to tour a production. Nonprofit organizations such as regional theaters may tour their most successful productions, as the Theater of the Stars in Atlanta, Georgia, did with its production of *White Christmas* in the fall and winter of 2007/2008; the tour included engagements in Nashville, Tennessee and Fort Myers, Florida. If the production is deemed a good commercial prospect, these organizations may work with veteran commercial touring producers to help them produce the tour, or the nonprofit organization may produce the tour itself. For example, the Roundabout Theatre Company produced a national tour of *Twelve Angry Men*, starring Richard Thomas and George Wendt, without any participation from commercial producers; the nonprofit theater assumed the entire financial risk of the tour.[13] (It should be noted that the Roundabout Theatre Company is an exception rather than the norm with regard to touring nonprofit productions.) A few nonprofit theater companies exist mainly as touring companies, and tour regularly with several different productions during the same season, as the SITI Company did with *Hotel Cassiopeia*, *A Midsummer Night's Dream*, and *bobrauschenbergamerica* during the 2006–2007 season.

Some theatrical touring productions bypass a Broadway, Off-Broadway, or nonprofit run entirely and are created directly for the touring market. Many of these tours are revivals of Broadway musicals or plays. Ron Gubin provides an example: "We just recently toured Cathy Rigby in *Peter Pan*; it's been on Broadway before, but not in several years. However, it's a classic title, it's well priced and well produced for that price, and Cathy is America's sweetheart. These factors make it an appealing production."[14]

The majority of incorporated dance companies or orchestras are nonprofit organizations. Unlike touring theatrical productions, most tours of dance or music works are created directly for the touring market, as many dance companies and musicians do not have a venue of their own as a "home base." (Some larger dance companies, such as the Mark Morris Dance Group or the Alvin Ailey American Dance Theater, do own their own performance spaces and still tour extensively.) These tours consist of existing repertory work and new work created for a particular tour. The creation of new work for one venue may stimulate the desire for a tour, as was the case with Philip Glass's *Orion*, created for the 2004 Cultural Olympiad in Athens.[15]

DETERMINING THE ROAD MARKET

Before planning to tour any production, a producer or artist must first consider the potential road market for the title. Harold Norris, founder of H-Art Management, states, "I don't think the power is in the artist's hands to decide when he wants to tour. I think the power is in the hands of the market. When the demand exists for that artist to tour, then he should tour."[16]

How does an artist or producer determine if market demand exists? By conducting "road" research: interviewing booking agents and presenters to see if audiences on the road would be interested in the work. Josh Sherman explains: "One of the things that Columbia Artists Theatricals does well is market analysis. The producers check the titles with the booking agents before they decide what shows to take on the road, because the agents are the ones who are on the front lines, working with presenters and determining what shows the presenters want. For example, this past summer [of 2005], the booking agents were presented with five different potential titles to take on tour. Out of the five, we selected *Wonderful Town* as the strongest title, because of its classic Leonard Bernstein score, its Broadway pedigree, and the fact that we could use some of the design elements from the recent Broadway production. We thought this title, because it was more established than some of the others that we were considering, would fit in well with our presenters' seasons."[17]

Regarding research with presenters, John Starr, director of booking at Big League Theatricals, notes,

"Like most booking agencies, we survey titles with presenters. We have twelve or fifteen presenters whose judgment we rely upon. We'll ask them about their responses to particular titles. Also, a couple of years ago, we did an e-mail survey on a potential tour of a musical revival. We sent e-mails out to 150 presenters and gave them four choices of response: I definitely want it; I'm interested, but it depends on what else is being offered; I'm unsure; and No, I don't want it. We got sixty or seventy responses back. Twelve presenters wanted it, another twelve were pretty sure they wanted it, and the rest weren't really interested. I thought, 'Based on these responses, we've got a 50 percent chance of actually booking this tour, and that percentage does not warrant putting this title out there.'"[18]

If the market for a touring production is not as strong as the producer or artist would like, producers may work with booking agents to increase the project's profile on the road. Ron Gubin states, "We do work with producers on making projects roadworthy. We might book an engagement in a national market (such as Chicago, Los Angeles, San Francisco, or Boston) to help build a profile for a show. We would also arrange for presenters to see the production, so that the presenters might look at it and think, 'My audience will want to see this.' One example of a show that needed U.S. market exposure was *Blast* [a music/performance piece]. That show was very successful, even though it didn't play in New York until after it had been on the road. (In fact, Broadway was a stop for it after the tour had already begun; it won the first Tony Award ever given for a 'Special Theatrical Event' on Broadway, so for the remainder of the tour, we could advertise as a Tony winner.) The producers of the show thought that it could be a successful touring production, and they created a market for it that didn't necessarily include New York by booking engagements in national markets and creating a public television special for the piece."[19]

CLASSROOM DISCUSSION

What is a tour?

What types of productions may tour?

What Broadway productions are most successful on tour?

What are the advantages of presenting an Off-Broadway production?

How do nonprofit theaters tour a production?

What types of dance and music works are presented on tour?

How can the road market for a potential tour be determined?

What sort of research do booking agents do to determine whether a road market exists?

Give some examples of factors that a booking agent must take into consideration when determining the potential road market of a tour.

TYPES OF TOURING PRODUCTIONS

After a producer or artist decides to tour a work, he must determine the right type of tour for the production. Tours are primarily classified by the length of their engagements, but may also be defined by their use of union personnel.

Touring Engagements

Touring engagements may run for multiple weeks; for one week; for a part of a week (a "split-week engagement"); or for one or two nights (a "one-nighter" or "bus-and-truck" tour). A tour may also consist of one engagement only; such tours are known as "run-outs." In addition, a touring company may stay "in residence" for a period of time in one community, often working with local artists and community members on activities beyond the performance. Finally, an engagement may be organized as a separate production designed solely for one market (a "sit-down production"), meaning that a production will open in a city and will either have a set closing date or will run as long as ticket sales support it.

Generally, multiweek engagements play in one location for more than one week, while weeklong tours play one location for one week. Typically, weeklong tours travel and load in all day Monday and on Tuesday morning, in time to play eight performances between Tuesday night and Sunday evening, and load out on Sunday night; multiweek tours follow the same basic schedule, with more performing weeks between load-in and load-out.

If a particular market will not support a full week of performances for a particular production, the production may play for half of the week in one location, and the other half in a different location. This type of engagement is known as a "split-week" engagement. Finally, a tour that consists mainly of one- or two-night engagements is called a "one-nighter" tour. (One-nighters are also sometimes referred to as "bus-and-truck" tours, referencing the primary mode of transportation for the company and freight.)

Many touring productions are reducing the length of their engagements due to market factors. Josh Sherman states, "Because nearly every Broadway musical now spawns a U.S. tour, the number of shows jockeying for bookings has increased, and shorter engagements are becoming more common. With an excess of viable product available for a limited number of size-appropriate venues, and because audiences no longer view a show touring into their town as a 'must-see' event, it has become much more difficult to justify and sustain engagements of longer than two weeks in most markets (Boston, Chicago, San Francisco, Los Angeles, Toronto, and Washington, D.C., being the notable exceptions) unless a show is a megahit on the order of *The Lion King*.[20]

All of these touring models suppose that one engagement will follow another, regardless of how long the engagement itself lasts. However, a producer, artistic director, or artist may decide to tour a production to a single venue away from the production's home base. This type of tour is called a "run-out;" it lasts for one engagement only, but the engagement itself may run one or more days.[21] A run-out differs from a sit-down production in that the touring production is not organized specifically for one market.

In addition to touring performance works, nonprofit orchestras, dance companies, and theater companies may take up residency with one or more presenters in a community. A residency typically contains performances from the touring company, as well as ancillary activities with members of the hosting organization or the community.[22] These activities may include workshops, classes, or the development of new works. Residencies may last from one week to several months, depending on the scope of performances and activities involved.

Finally, productions that are created solely for one market, such as *Wicked* in Chicago or Blue Man Group's *Tubes* in Boston, are known as "sit-down" productions. A sit-down production is not typically part of a traditional tour (meaning that the production does not travel from one venue to another), and thus may be considered a new commercial production, requiring separate capitalization. A sit-down production may have a specific closing date determined at the beginning of the run, as *Jersey Boys* did in San Francisco, running from December 2006 through September 2007. However, the Chicago production of *Jersey Boys* began as an open-ended run in October 2007; it will continue to run as long as ticket sales support it.[23] In the next section, we will examine an attractive destination for sit-down productions with open-ended runs, Las Vegas, in further detail.

Las Vegas

One particular market for open-ended runs has received renewed attention in recent years. Although theatrical productions have played in Las Vegas for many years, the current trend of presenting new musicals in theaters attached to casinos has led to a recent boom in touring productions on the Strip. Most of the productions are cut to run 90 minutes, without intermission (known as a "tabbed" version, after "tabloid," a smaller newspaper layout), allowing tourists to attend the production and still have plenty of time in the evening to dine out, shop, and gamble. Because of this shortened running time, shows in Las Vegas typically play ten to twelve performances in one week.

Although the 2003 production of *Mamma Mia!* at the Mandalay Bay Resort and Casino inaugurated the current Vegas theatrical boom, the historic agreement drawn up by the producers of *Avenue Q* in 2004 put Las Vegas at the center of the Broadway touring map. The producers of *Avenue Q* decided to forgo a national tour in order to give the Wynn Las Vegas Resort the exclusive right to present the production. Even though this production of *Avenue Q* closed in nine months (playing at 50 to 75 percent capacity), other productions soon followed, such as *Hairspray* (closed after four months), *The Phantom of the Opera*, *Spamalot*, and *The Producers*.[24]

Following the exclusivity deal that *Avenue Q* negotiated with the Wynn Casino, other productions have also struck exclusivity agreements before opening in Las Vegas. In particular, *Spamalot*, which opened at the Wynn Casino in March 2007, agreed to a semi-exclusive agreement, preventing it from touring to California, Nevada, or Arizona while the Las Vegas production is running. This semi-exclusive arrangement is quickly becoming a industry standard; as shows (such as *Stomp*) negotiate for productions in Las Vegas, their producers now negotiate an exclusive period of time to exclude them from the touring markets in these Western states.[25]

Casino owners present theatrical productions as a service to their guests and other tourists, providing them with one more entertainment option that induces them to spend money in the casino. Unlike typical commercial touring productions, casinos are not solely dependent on ticket sales to make the majority of their income, so the production may be partially subsidized by the other activities of the casino. (This arrangement allows for expensive production elements and custom-built theaters, as the Wynn provided for *Avenue Q*.)

However, Las Vegas casinos are still a business and are usually not willing to subsidize an unsuccessful production for a long period of time, especially when the production can be replaced with something the casino views as a more attractive entertainment option. More importantly, because none of the casinos have a subscriber base to provide advance sales, ticket sales are more unstable than they would be for a normal touring production. Therefore, productions in Las Vegas casinos are not as much a "sure bet" as some producers had believed; the same amount of market analysis that any touring production must undertake is still required to determine if a production is suitable for the Las Vegas market.

Productions that succeed in Las Vegas tend to emphasize spectacle and fun. Josh Sherman states, "Casinos don't have an art mindset, they have an entertainment mindset. That's the casino market."[26] As an example, Cirque du Soleil, the Montreal-based modern circus company, has five productions running in various casinos as of 2007. Simma Levine, president of On the Road, believes that the majority of live attractions that succeed in Las Vegas are geared toward adults, and notes, "Attractions that seem to work in Las Vegas are ones that are exclusive to Vegas, e.g., Celine Dion or Cirque du Soleil—shows that are unique and can't be seen 'back home.'"[27]

Despite the risks, a Las Vegas run can be quite successful for the right production. Josh Sherman states, "I believe in Las Vegas as a destination for Broadway-type entertainment. It's a city with a massive amount of tourist dollars, and if the casinos continue to view the productions in their spaces as another attraction to offer to their guests, then I think there's a future for the right theatrical productions, like *Mamma Mia!*, *Stomp Out Loud*, or *Phantom*. I think the neon glows pretty bright."[28]

CLASSROOM DISCUSSION

Define the following: "split-week tour," "run-out," "residency," and "sit-down production."

What is the typical playing schedule for a weeklong tour?

What is a one-nighter tour, and why is it sometimes referred to as a "bus-and-truck" tour?

What determines the engagement length of a tour?

Why do Las Vegas casinos choose to present theatrical productions?

How does an engagement in Las Vegas affect touring routes in Western states?

What are the risks involved in producing a production in Las Vegas?

Equity, Non-Equity, and Nonunion Tours

As well as determining the desired length of the tour engagements, a theatrical producer must decide if a tour will include Actors' Equity Association (AEA or Equity) actors or will be non-Equity. Although touring companies may employ members of other unions, tours may also decide to be completely nonunion, which means that no member of the touring company belongs to a union. Non-Equity and nonunion tours can and do play in venues that employ union personnel; the designations apply only the touring company itself.

Productions that employ Equity actors use the Production Contract negotiated between the union and The Broadway League. Tours produced under the full provisions of the Production Contract are known as "first-class tours"; typically, first-class tours are the first or second national tour of a Broadway production, playing major markets such as Boston, Chicago, and San Francisco. The Production Contract requires that first-class touring productions pay on the same scale as the Broadway production, including per diems (payments made to members of the touring company to cover the daily costs of food and housing). For touring productions, the Production Contract sets strict rules for the amount of travel allowed on a daily and weekly basis, and any violation of these travel regulations results in overtime payments to Equity members. These requirements cause first-class tours to be very expensive, so tours produced in this fashion are considered to have excellent potential in the touring market; to cover these costs, first-class productions generally play weeklong or multiweek engagements (like *Spamalot*), or sit down in one city for a substantial amount of time (as *The Phantom of the Opera* did in Toronto).

Touring productions that want to utilize Equity actors but cannot afford to tour first-class may petition Actors' Equity to be considered under the Split-Week Contract. Tours employing actors under this contract must fulfill the following requirements: "(a) A majority of the total weeks of the tour are engagements of less than one week; (b) at least 80% of the total weeks of the tour shall be engagements of one week or less; (c) no more than 20% of the total weeks of the tour are engagements longer than one week; (d) no single engagement is more than four weeks; and (e) no Actor's total compensation for any week of the tour is more than $10,000 per week."[29] The Split-Week Contract has lower salary minimums than the Production Contract and also has slightly altered work rules to address performances in split weeks.

Even under the Split-Week Contract, producers may determine that a particular production costs too much money to tour with Equity actors. In such cases, a producer may choose to cast the tour using non-Equity actors. Touring a show as a "non-Equity" production allows producers more leeway in the negotiations involving weekly salaries, per diems, and health and pension contributions, and does not force the producers to abide by all of the Equity regulations concerning work rules, travel time, and performance schedules.

Producers of non-Equity tours explain this decision as a purely economic one. John Starr states, "We're not opposed to Equity as a union. It's all about economics. In the one-nighter market, there is a limit to how much a presenter can afford to pay for a show (usually determined by the size of the venue). Because of the minimum salaries, per diems, and economic implications of the rules and regulations of an Equity contract, certain projects would be financially unfeasible. It's different if you are producing a first national tour that plays mostly full and multiweeks, but many of our tours play mostly one-nighters. We load in, set up, perform, load out, and travel two hundred to three hundred miles to the next venue and repeat the process. We may have five to six one-nighters in a row. Under an Equity contract, the cost (including all the overtime) would be prohibitive."[30]

Starr continues, "However, as it turns out, we closely mirror the Equity rules and regulations, especially with regard to daily travel, breaks, and days off. A rested company is a happy company and gives better performances given the constraints of constant travel."[31]

Actors' Equity agrees that actors should be protected, but feels that Equity membership and Equity productions are the only ways to guarantee that protection. Furthermore, Equity believes that non-Equity tours, which are often placed on "Broadway" subscription series, are misleading to the audience, because these tours are not employing "professional" union actors. Equity has fought what it views as the encroachment of non-Equity tours into major markets by prohibiting its members from accepting employment on non-Equity tours in any capacity. In Equity's *Theatre News*, Executive Director Alan Eisenberg states, "The ban is an important step in our battle with non-Equity producers, who claim to present a 'Broadway' production without paying their actors a decent living wage or adequate benefits. To that, we say, 'If it's not Equity, it's not Broadway.'"[32] Indeed, Equity has been most concerned in recent years with musical revivals who go directly from the Broadway production to a non-Equity tour, without having a first-class tour at all. For example, the 2000 Broadway revival of *The Music Man* went out as a non-Equity tour; due to its large cast, it was seen as too expensive to produce as an Equity tour.

In order to address some of the concerns raised by producers of non-Equity tours, Actors' Equity created the Experimental Touring Program (ETP) in 2004 as part of the Production Contract (covering Broadway and first-class productions).[33] The ETP only applies to musicals with more than forty people in the touring company, and most of the tour must consist of engagements of one week or less (engagements of more than four weeks are prohibited, with specific exceptions for certain cities). It provides a tiered salary structure for Equity members based on the amount of the guarantee (per-performance payment guaranteed to the producer by the presenter), plus 10 percent of the net adjusted gross box office receipts (as described in chapter 4); these salaries increase after recoupment, regardless of tier. The ETP also provides separate rules for such provisions as housing and benefit contributions, and requires that all actors earning less than three times the Production Contract minimum participate in the producers' share of the profit.[34] Finally, the ETP requires that all touring productions produced by members of The Broadway League display the "Live Broadway" logo on playbills, Web sites, and advertisements to promote the ETP and other Equity-League productions. At the time of this writing, some non-Equity producers have started to produce tours under this model, but time will tell if it provides a solution to each party's concerns.

In addition to Actors' Equity, touring producers also need to decide whether to hire other union personnel. Most union tours employ members of IATSE (stagehands), AFM (musicians), and ATPAM (company manager) in the touring company. Tours that employ union stagehands are known as "yellow card" tours, after the yellow card that those members have to sign at each engagement and give to the IATSE local with jurisdiction over the presenter.[35] (Thus, touring productions that do not use IATSE stagehands are called "non–yellow card" tours.)[36] Yellow card tours require that the presenter hire at least as many union stagehands for the venue as are in the touring company, even if the presenter has no signed agreement with IATSE. If the local union does not have enough available members to fill the tour's requirements, then the local union can negotiate an arrangement for nonunion stagehands to fulfill the call requirements.[37] Arrangements have also been made for certain one-nighter or split-week tours, in which the touring stagehands are covered by an IATSE contract (a pink contract, as mentioned in chapter 4), but the local presenter is not absolutely required to fill the call with local IATSE stagehands. (Such arrangements only apply to theaters that do not have a collectively bargained agreement with a local stagehands union.)[38] Union musicians traveling with a production are covered under the Pamphlet B Theatrical Touring Agreement; any other musicians needed to fill the requirements for the production are hired from local unions in accordance with any agreement that may be in place with the presenter. Theatrical company managers who are members of ATPAM are contracted individually in the same way they are contracted for any commercial production. Orchestras and dance companies tour with the union affiliation of their organizations; if these companies are organized by the American Guild of Musical Artists (AGMA) or AFM, those unions have jurisdiction over the tour.

If a producer decides to tour a nonunion production, he must arrange to hire all nonunion personnel as necessary. Producers may also decide to hire members of one union and not another; for example, Big League Theatricals hires union stagehands, but nonunion musicians on some projects.[39] Nonunion tours (and non-Equity tours) may play in venues with union contracts, if the presenter agrees.

Nonunion tours, like non-Equity tours, also meet resistance from the affected unions, although these unions do not typically bar members from accepting nonunion employment (in some cases, members must seek permission from the union to work with specific producers or organizations). Like Equity, these unions argue that nonunion tours are marketed as "Broadway" product, but do not contain the elements of the Broadway production. Some local unions have picketed nonunion productions that play in their areas, as AFM, Local 72 did to a nonunion touring production of *The Will Rogers Follies*.[40]

CLASSROOM DISCUSSION

Define "first-class tour," "non-Equity tour," and "yellow-card tour."

What contract does Equity require of first-class tours, and what does this contract require?

What is a Split-Week Contract, and how does a production qualify for it?

What are Equity's objections to non-Equity tours?

What is the Experimental Touring Program, and what does it consist of?

Besides Equity, what other unions are typically involved in touring productions?

How does a producer determine if a show would be better served by not using union personnel?

CREATING THE TOURING PRODUCTION

Once a producer, artistic director, or artist decides to tour, the touring production must be created. The producer, managing director, or artist needs to negotiate the appropriate license (rights) agreement with the artist or attraction, form a producing entity, create the budget for the production, raise money for the tour, and hire all required personnel.

License agreements are obtained in the same manner described in chapter 4. The producer must determine who holds the rights for the production and obtain a license to tour it.

For nonprofit companies and individual artists, the producing entity is generally the company or artist herself. (Individual artists may form personal corporations for tax purposes, but this incorporation is not done solely for touring purposes.) Commercial touring productions must form a separate entity for the touring production; most often, this entity takes the form of a limited partnership (as described in chapter 4). Even if the production is still playing on Broadway, the touring production must usually have a different corporate producing entity in order to raise the capitalization for the tour and operate its business separately from the Broadway production.

After the producing entity is determined, a budget must be created for the tour. Nonprofit organizations and individual artists may use one engagement budget for all touring expenses, while commercial productions will divide expenses into a capitalization budget and a weekly operating budget as described in chapter 4.

All touring budgets begin by estimating all of the expenses involved with touring the production and are created using the procedures outlined in chapter 5. Certain budget items are unique to touring productions. Touring productions must estimate travel expenses, including airfare, hotel costs, ground transportation (buses and cars) and per diem payments.[41] Costs to transport freight (which includes all elements of the physical production, such as set pieces and costumes) must also be estimated. Any publicity materials that the company must provide, such as photographs or DVDs, must be accounted for in the budget, as well as any fees that must be paid to a booking agent or manager. Finally, the budget should include any royalties that must be paid to the creative team; a detailed explanation of royalties and royalty pools for commercial productions may be found in chapter 4.

Once the total touring costs are determined, the producing entity can determine the guarantee needed for each engagement. On tour, the production does not receive the income from ticket sales directly; this income goes to the presenter, who then pays the touring production a guaranteed payment (the "guarantee") of a certain amount of money per performance. The presenter must pay the full amount of the guarantee regardless of the amount of ticket sales the show generates. The guarantee may be a flat fee (known as a "flat deal"), or it may be a fee plus a percentage of the net adjusted gross box office receipts (as described in chapter 4; this is known as a "terms deal").[42] As production expenses are amortized over the length of the tour, the guarantee covers the cost of the engagement itself (salaries, load-in expenses, hotel costs, etc.), plus a percentage of the production/capitalization costs.[43] (If the tour is an existing production, such as a previously performed work from a dance company, the creation costs are not amortized over the run of the tour.)[44]

The guarantee is often the deciding factor in determining the total amount of the production's budget. Producing entities and booking agents will sometimes call presenters to ask if a certain guarantee amount is feasible for a certain production. If the presenters think the guarantee is too high, the producing entity and booking agent may try to modify the budget so that the project is more attractive financially, and thus more viable to tour.[45]

While the producing entity is creating the budget for the production, it is also searching for funds to mount the tour. For nonprofit companies and individual artists, grants and contributions must be obtained to raise the needed funds to tour. Harold Norris states, "Presenters will only pay a certain amount of money for an engagement. In the case of smaller, riskier work, that amount is not high. In this case, the touring production needs to raise money to remedy the shortfall. For artists like David Dorfman or Meredith Monk, this can be quite a bit of money."[46]

Commercial productions raise money by acquiring investors, as detailed in chapter 4. Often, investing in touring productions is seen as less of a risk than investing in other commercial productions.

John Starr states, "Because we sell a show a year in advance, I'll know by January if the tour that I plan to start in September is viable. I'll have a solid idea of what the guarantees are, and how long the tour will last, so I'll know how much money the tour will make and budget accordingly. So, in terms of investors, I'm not speculating. I've designed the show so that it's within the amount of money that I sold it for, so it's going to make a certain amount of profit. It's not a risk."[47] Also, investors from an original Broadway or Off-Broadway production may be interested in investing in a tour of that production. The creation and promotion of the tour may increase the visibility of the title; this increase in visibility may lead to additional licenses for other productions (e.g., other tours, and amateur and school productions) and more income for the investors in the original Broadway or Off-Broadway production.[48]

In conjunction with determining the budget and securing the financing, the producer must hire appropriate administrative, creative, and production staff for the tour. Nonprofit companies will typically use their own administrative staff for touring productions, occasionally hiring additional personnel if needed. Individual artists will either self-manage their tour or hire a tour manager to handle all contract negotiations, travel arrangements, and other administrative duties. Commercial producers will first hire a general manager, who will create budgets, negotiate contracts, and perform all other administrative duties of a general manager, as detailed in chapter 4. The general manager will supervise the company manager, who makes all travel arrangements for the company, processes payroll, and acts as the producer's representative on the tour. The company manager will travel with the company, addressing any personnel issues as they arise. Also, the company manager is responsible for reviewing and signing the box office settlement with the presenter at the end of each performance; the box office settlement details all tickets sold for the engagement and is used to determine the amount of money owed to the producer. (Nonprofit companies may engage company managers as well; these company managers may perform some or all of the duties of a commercial company manager.) On a union tour, the company manager is a member of ATPAM.

Other administrative personnel are hired as needed. A press agent may be engaged to coordinate publicity for the tour in conjunction with the presenter. (For first-class tours and other union productions, the press agent is a member of

ATPAM.) On commercial productions, lawyers, accountants, and bankers may also be engaged, as described in chapter 4.

After the tour is confirmed, the creative team must be assembled. For nonprofit companies and individual artists, the creative team is already in place; occasionally, additional performers may need to be hired as replacements, but the creative team remains the same. On a commercial touring production, the producer and general manager will work together to assemble the creative team. They must hire a director (and choreographer, if needed), designers, and performers; these creative personnel may be the same people who worked on the original Broadway or Off-Broadway production.[49] The directors and designers may be members of SSDC and USA, respectively. Depending on the union affiliation of the tour, the performers may be members of Actors' Equity or AFM. For organizations or productions under the jurisdiction of AGMA (e.g., dance companies), performers, directors, and choreographers will be members of that union.

For theatrical productions, casting for a touring production is as important as casting a Broadway production. Especially in the case of revivals, a star is seen as essential to the success of the tour. Ron Gubin states, "The question of star casting doesn't come up frequently with Broadway titles like *Wicked*. Many of the current new Broadway titles are strong enough to push ticket sales . . . or at least strong enough to encourage presenters to buy the show. However, stars are generally considered a requirement for revivals. There are very few exceptions to this 'rule.' When we're booking a revival, the first question a presenter will ask is, 'Who is the star?' The star has to make sense to the presenters in terms of the role; the presenter needs to be able to connect the star to the role and imagine the star as a good fit, as opposed to star X just slotted into a production. Also, stars on Broadway aren't necessarily stars on the road. Generally, Broadway stars haven't branded themselves on the road; presenters may tell their audiences, 'This actor won a Tony Award, and we are fortunate to have this artist here on tour,' but that may not be enough to sell tickets."[50]

Gary McAvay agrees: "Casting can sometimes make the difference between a production being commercially viable or not. If you want to tour a regional theater's production of *Blithe Spirit* with some of their great actors, that tour may have a limited life on the road. However, if you've cast Richard Chamberlain in your tour of *Blithe Spirit*, then your tour has a longer life."[51]

The process of casting a star may be more difficult than the typical casting process. Ron Gubin notes, "Star casting is an enormous challenge in terms of scheduling because the producer is trying to get a star to commit to a tour that may last roughly a year or more, and the producer is trying to get this commitment perhaps a year and a half before the tour opens. The star wants to leave his schedule as open [for] as long as possible to accommodate potential television shows or movie offers. This conflict is not impossible, but it is very, very difficult to solve."[52] Also, a star may receive a percentage of the net adjusted gross box office receipts as part of his compensation for participating in the tour, which reduces the profit for the producer.[53]

Finally, the producing entity must hire all necessary production and technical staff for the touring production. A technical supervisor or production manager is hired to supervise the construction of the physical production (if it does not already exist) and to manage the transfer, load-in, and load-out of the production on tour. The production manager will also supervise any stagehands hired as part of the touring company; these stagehands may be members of IATSE, depending on the union affiliation of the tour. The producer may also hire a stage manager to coordinate pre-tour rehearsals and manage all aspects of the production onstage, including scheduling rehearsals in the space and other performance-related duties. Depending on the tour's union affiliation, the stage manager may be a member of Actors' Equity or AGMA.

CLASSROOM DISCUSSION

How does a nonprofit organization form a producing entity for a tour?

How does a commercial production form a producing entity for a tour?

What factors must be taken into consideration when budgeting expenses for a tour?

What is a guarantee, and how is it determined?

How do nonprofit organizations raise money for a tour?

How do commercial productions raise money for a tour?

What are the responsibilities of a general manager on a touring production?

What are the responsibilities of a company manager on a touring production?

Why is casting important for a theatrical touring production? What are the advantages and disadvantages of hiring a star for a touring production?

BOOKING THE TOUR

When a producer, nonprofit organization, or individual artist decides to tour a production, a booking agent must be hired. The booking agent acts as the producer's representative in negotiating touring engagements.[54] (It is possible for a tour to be booked in-house, but such an arrangement is not recommended unless the organization has significant booking experience.) Booking agents plan the route (itinerary) for the tour, sell the tour to presenters and promoters, negotiate deal memos and contracts between the producers and the presenters, and assist the producer in working with presenters once the tour is en route.

Typically, booking agents take a percentage of the guarantee as payment for their work in booking the tour. This percentage can range from 3 percent for the first tour of a Broadway production to as much as 20 percent for small dance companies and lesser-known performance works.[55] Booking agents may also take a flat fee, paid weekly. When working on an international tour, booking agents may receive a set fee per performance rather than a percentage or weekly fee.[56]

Booking agents acquire clients (touring productions) in various ways. Ron Gubin states, "As booking agents, we are engaged by producers to represent their shows. We may approach those producers to solicit their business, or we may be selected by the producers to book the show."[57] Josh Sherman adds, "Often the choice of booking agent is determined by the agent's prior relationship with a specific producer. For example, Columbia Artists Theatricals has a relationship with Troika Entertainment, so we book their nonunion tour of *Cats* every year. Because of these prior relationships, the booking agents for a Broadway show may be contracted (or at least agreed upon) before the production even opens in New York."[58]

Booking agents also research potential artists and productions to tour by reading applicable publications, using the Internet, and talking to colleagues in the field. Harold Norris states, "For research, I read *Variety* and the *New York Times*. I actually read the print publications less because I've started using Google Alerts, which send me news Web links on specific artists. It allows you to follow artists through the news. You can see where a dance company is touring, or you can find out that a choreographer set a piece on another company that you never heard of. I also talk a lot on the phone to presenters to find out what they think is exciting in the performing arts world. We just signed an Israeli artist whom I learned about from talking to a couple of presenters. Once you've heard about someone from more than one presenter, you know there's a kind of buzz out there about this artist."[59]

Other booking agents may choose to develop touring projects as well as book them. Alisa E. Regas, associate director of Pomegranate Arts, describes the process by which her company selects projects: "Pomegranate is a very small, specific boutique company with a contemporary focus. We don't just book tours; we also manage the tours and often produce them as well. The perfect Pomegranate client is an artist or company without existing representation that has created a cool new piece that they feel can have a touring life and want to see if there's a market for it. We work with artists with whom we have had long relationships, like Laurie Anderson and Philip Glass. Often, these artists will have an idea about a project or a collaboration that they'll bring for us to develop, or we will come up with a new project idea together. Also, we continually go out to performances and develop relationships with artists whose work we admire. We mainly see work in New York City, but we also travel to international festivals."[60]

Regas continues, "An example of a project that we saw, fell in love with, and decided to tour is *Charlie Victor Romeo*. It was a series of dramatic recreations of cockpit recordings during airplane crashes, and it was produced by Collective Unconscious, a small theater company in New York City unknown to the touring market. The company had never toured before, and the piece needed shaping before it could become a viable touring work. We took them under our wing and worked with them for about two years. We brought in a highly experienced team to help the theater company beef up the show: a set designer, a lighting designer, a sound designer, and a seasoned director to help adapt the show for each touring situation, in consultation with the original creators. Because the piece was so unconventional, we could really think creatively about what kind of organizations would be suitable presenters for the tour. We researched potential partners such as major aeronautical organizations, medical institutions, and presenters located in towns with aeronautical businesses (which we approached for sponsorships and audience development projects). In the same season, we played a theater festival in Perth, Australia, and then we performed a corporate gig for Boeing. *Charlie Victor Romeo* on tour was the same show as it was in New York, but by knowing how to shape it as a touring piece, we could play all of these different spaces with it. These artists began by playing to 60 people in their downtown storefront theater, and ended up working with us to adapt the show to reach 2,500 people in a hotel ballroom for a medical convention."[61]

Occasionally, booking agents will be approached by potential clients who believe that they have a show that will make a successful tour. If the project is of interest to the booking agent, he may attempt to book a tour for that show. However, the production may not be suitable for a tour. In that case, the best practice is to decline representation. Ron Gubin states, "Sometimes, we are asked to book a tour for a production that isn't a good fit for this office. We may be asked to work on a tour for a production that we don't have any faith in; we don't believe that the market exists for that particular show on tour. We always try to tell our producer clients that we are not in the business of creating markets for a show. We are in the business of exploiting a title [of the show]. So, if a producer comes to us with a title that is virtually unknown, we usually don't book the tour, because there's no existing market for that title. It's the producer's job to create the market; as booking agents, we manage the market on the road."[62]

The booking process begins early. For Avid Touring, it begins about a year and a half before the season starts. Ron Gubin explains: "Right now, it's June of 2006, and we are working primarily on the 2007–2008 [September 2007–summer 2008] season. From May through December, the majority of our work focuses on booking: talking to presenters, routing our shows, making our deals, and attempting to fill the route. By January or February 2007, most presenters will be sending their season brochures to print, so they need to have their titles, their dates, and their deals in place by that time. From January through the spring, we'll negotiate and sign the full version of the contracts and handle any other issues that arise after the deal is made. In May 2007, we'll begin the process again for the 2008–2009 season."[63]

The booking process begins with planning the tour. However, before the booking agent can begin to contact potential presenters and secure engagement dates, he must know all the applicable facts about the production and the potential market for it. Josh Sherman lists some important variables a booking agent must keep in mind when planning the tour; although the list is specific to commercial tours, booking agents for other types of tours must also know this information:

- How expensive is the production to mount? Since the goal of a commercial production is to recoup expenses and turn a profit, knowing the dollar amount of the total production expenses [capitalization expenses] of a show will help determine how many weeks the tour must run in order to be successful, and what size venues the show can be booked into. For example, booking a very expensive show into theaters with too few seats will extend the time it takes the production to recoup, perhaps extending it to a time frame longer than its touring life.

- How expensive is the production to run? The running expenses [weekly operating expenses] of the show, in addition to helping to determine the size of the theaters into which the show must be booked, will help determine how much the producer must be guaranteed to earn for each engagement week.

- How extensive is the show's physical production? If the sets are very large or complex, or require substantial wing (side of the stage) and/or fly (above the proscenium) spaces, some venues will be struck from consideration immediately, because their stage dimensions will not be adequate for the needs of the show.

- How much load-in and load-out time does the show need, and how difficult is it to transport the physical production? The standard time allotted to a production is six to twelve hours for load-in and two to five hours for load-out. Shows requiring extensive load-in and load-out time must either minimize traveling distances between venues or increase the hours allotted to move the production from one market to another. The amount of load-in and load-out required will also impact the expense of running a tour, as additional stagehands may be required or stagehands will have to work overtime at higher rates of pay.[64]

After these variables are determined, the booking agent may begin considering potential presenters for the tour and tentatively constructing the touring route.

When considering potential presenters, the booking agents should know the presentation history of the venue and its technical specifications. Many booking agents use databases to help organize this information. At Columbia Artists Theatricals, Josh Sherman uses a database to keep track of information about presenters, as well as copies of all of the contracts negotiated by his organization. This information allows each agent to have such information as ticket prices and expenses for specific markets on hand before contacting presenters.

Harold Norris believes that a booking agent should not only know the production specifics of the venue, but the interests of the presenter himself. He states, "Every presenter is an individual human being with likes and dislikes. You can't just categorize them. I call the presenter and ask a lot of questions: 'What's in your season?' 'What are you interested in?' I try to find out as much as I can about the presenter, because once I know what he's looking for, I can find something on my roster (list of artists represented) that he might want. For example, if a presenter likes Liz Lerman, he'll probably like David Dorfman, one of my artists. Liz and David are nothing alike choreographically, but as a matter of taste, people who like one tend to like the other. So that allows me to talk to a presenter about David Dorfman, if the presenter has no idea who David is."[65]

As the tentative touring route is being created, the booking agent is also in contact with presenters to sell the touring production to them. (In some cases, a booking agent may deal with a promoter instead of a presenter; a promoter assumes all obligations of the presenter, as well as the financial risk of the presentation, but does not own the venue in which the performance is presented.[66] For example, live pop music events are often negotiated with promoters.[67])

For Ron Gubin, this selling process begins with a phone call. "The first thing we do at the beginning of the season is arrange a call with each of the presenters and go through the entire roster of our shows. As we focus on Broadway tour markets for single and multiple weeks, we typically have five or six titles a season; other offices may take on single-night non-Equity engagements and have more shows to offer. During this first phone call, we'll take notes on presenters who are interested in our shows, and some presenters may hold some time for a show as a preliminary measure. At this stage, everything is very tentative: a presenter might say, 'I'm kind of interested in this title, and I am penciling you in for this particular week, but you should also know that I'm in talks with two other shows.' After the initial phone call, we follow up by sending the presenter promotional materials, such as a sampler CD of songs from a musical, and the tech rider [a list of

the technical requirements of a touring production, created by the general manager in conjunction with the production manager; a sample tech rider may be found in appendix J of chapter 11]. We're trying to keep the conversation ongoing by sending the presenters information as soon as we receive it. We also use a database to keep track of the bookings each venue is making on other tours, so we know what the presenters are looking at and for which dates."[68]

Although the main business between booking agents and presenters is conducted by phone, the Internet is an indispensable aid to their relationship. Harold Norris states, "We use the Internet constantly in my office. I'm usually looking at a presenter's Web site when I'm talking to him on the phone, looking at his season and information about his theater, and he's on his computer looking at the artists on our Web site. We put reviews of our artists on our Web site, so while I'm talking to a presenter about an artist, he can look at the review and ask me questions about the work. We also have technical riders and other information available on our Web site, because we want to be service-oriented to the presenter."[69]

In lieu of initiating the process with a phone call, some booking agents mail a season brochure detailing all of the touring productions being offered. At Columbia Artists Theatricals, this season brochure is mailed to potential presenters in the summer a year before the season begins (for example, the brochure mailed in the summer of 2005 listed the productions for the 2006–2007 touring season). By mailing this brochure in the summer, the presenters will receive it before the booking conferences that take place in the fall and winter.

Booking conferences allow booking agents and presenters to meet face-to-face to discuss potential touring projects. The major regional conferences are sponsored by the following organizations: Western Arts Alliance (covering the western United States, Alaska, and Hawaii); Arts Midwest (covering Illinois, Indiana, Iowa, Michigan, Minnesota, North Dakota, Ohio, South Dakota, and Wisconsin); Southwest Performing Arts Presenters (covering Arkansas, Louisiana, New Mexico, Oklahoma, and Texas); the Consortium of Eastern Regional Theatres (known as ConsERT, representing historic theaters and presenters in the Northeast); and the Southern Arts Federation (covering the southern, mid-Atlantic, and New England regions; the conference is known as the Performing Arts Exchange). Other organizations that sponsor conferences include the Association of Performing Arts Presenters (APAP), a national organization representing all states and some international organizations that meets annually in New York City in January; the Canadian Arts Presenting Organization (CAPACOA), an organization representing Canadian presenters; and the International Society for the Performing Arts (ISPA), an organization that promotes international work.

Regarding booking conferences, Josh Sherman states, "Although telephone and e-mail are the booking agent's lifelines, nothing truly beats the value of a face-to-face conversation between a presenter and a booking agent. Booking conferences serve to bring booking agents, presenters, and many arts organizations together in a hotel or convention hall, where booking agents set up elaborate booths, offer short presentations of their shows, and hand out DVDs and brochures to browsing presenters, who are there to scout the shows they may wish to present. Press releases, free merchandise, and show-branded tchotchkes fly out of the booking agents' hands at these conferences as they attempt to convince presenters to remember their titles when the presenters are programming the season."[70]

When approaching a presenter, the booking agent needs to focus on filling the needs of that presenter. Ron Gubin states, "In order to sell a show to a presenter, it's helpful to imagine what the specific appeal of a specific title might have for a specific presenter. You have to analyze your show and determine what it might provide for the presenter's season."[71]

Gubin continues, "Since we begin the process so early, we are selling shows that don't have a firm selling price. Many elements are not in place at this point. For example, we may not know how many musicians we might need for a show, or we don't have a tech rider available. We've sold shows where we said that there would be a star involved, and it might take six or eight months for us to find out who the star is. As new information becomes available and is confirmed, we continue to talk to presenters, who hopefully will be excited about the new details."[72]

As the booking agent gathers interest and tentative bookings from presenters, he creates a "ghost route," the first (tentatively planned) route of the tour. The ghost route allows the booking agents to consider the markets that have expressed the most interest in the tour and the ideal route placement of these interested markets.[73] The ghost route will change significantly as presenters drop out or are added; as commitments firm up and deal memos are signed, the ghost route evolves into a "firm route."[74] Please see appendix A for an example of a touring route.[75]

When routing the tour, a booking agent may decide to focus his attention on one particular presenter, hoping that the presenter will commit and provide the touring production with financial or artistic benefits. These engagements are known as "anchor engagements," as Harold Norris explains: "For me, the first step in booking a tour is finding an anchor. An anchor may be a prestigious institution like the Brooklyn Academy of Music that will lend your tour its cache. An anchor may also be financial; that presenter may have a lot of money and end up subsidizing the rest of the tour. Anchors typically have less flexibility in terms of dates. I have conversations with my potential anchors to see if there is any interest in the production. I try to get them to commit to dates. Anchors help tell other presenters that your tour is going to happen, that it's a solid deal."[76]

Norris continues, "After my anchors are settled, the tour routing becomes much easier, because I know what my available dates are and what institutions are committed. I can use these anchor dates to sell the tour to other presenters, which are called fill-ins, because you're filling in holes between your anchor dates."[77] However, as engagements are added, booking agents must maintain the integrity of the route by avoiding "bad jumps," market- or calendar-specific conflicts, and unnecessary layoffs.[78]

A "bad jump" is "a move from one city to another city requiring the physical production to travel over 1,100 miles in 48 hours (for a weeklong engagement) or 350 miles in 24 hours (for one-nighters)."[79] Bad jumps, in addition to being hard on a company, cost the production money, both in increased travel expenses and in the loss of any engagements that the production might have had while traveling. Bad jumps should be avoided as much as possible, and special consideration should be paid to engagements that may create delays leading to bad jumps, such as performances in northern cities in winter (because of potential bad weather) and engagements that require border crossings (potential bad traffic and time-consuming customs inspections).[80]

Booking agents must keep national holidays and regional events in mind when routing the tour.[81] These market- or calendar-specific conflicts may impact the number of people who will come to the performance. For example, audiences are typically small on Super Bowl Sunday, so booking agents would be wise to schedule that day as a travel day or dark day, if possible.

Layoffs are weeks in which no performances occur. Typically, during a layoff, the company is flown to the tour's point of origin (the city where the tour was organized and, generally, rehearsed), and the freight travels to the next engagement; when the tour resumes, the company is flown from the point of origin to the next engagement.[82] This arrangement can often save the touring production money, as it often does not have to pay salaries and per diems for the week that the show is dark. Most tours have a negotiated and scheduled amount of layoff weeks, due to both company fatigue and the reality of the touring route. The booking agent must attempt to minimize the amount of layoff weeks by scheduling the tour in such a way that large jumps or dark weeks do not occur, or that they occur over major holidays.[83]

Although booking agents hope to route a show in the most efficient way possible, such efficiency is not always feasible. Ron Gubin states, "Sometimes, you need to have an 'inelegant' route, because the choice is between inelegant routing or no routing at all. You want to avoid layoffs and long travel distances, so if you have an open week in your routing, you try to arrange for bookings in other cities to fill it. Or you might move a booking from one slot to another, if the travel logistics support it. Another option is accommodating presenters who have open dates because another tour has collapsed. If you can't fill that open week, you may have to face a layoff."[84]

When routing a tour, even a hit show can present a booking agent with challenges. Ron Gubin states, "We represent *Spamalot* [the winner of the 2006 Best Musical Tony Award], so presenters are calling us and competing for dates. For this show, the booking process is more about managing the interest in the title, rather than exploiting it. This comes with its own set of issues. We need to deal with competing presenters from the same area. If a presenter on one side of town wants the show, and a presenter from the other side also wants it, then we need to determine which presenter gets the production. We bring the presenting options to the producer and explain the advantages and disadvantages of their offers. This determination can be very subjective. The presenters are all going to pay the same guarantee, so we need to look at which presenters have the best track record, will take the best care of the show, and will deliver what they've promised. (Obvious advantages such as a larger audience capacity or subscription base can also play a role in determining an appropriate presenter.) Recommending one presenter over another can be difficult sometimes, because you may be looking at two presenters with equal or similar strengths and weaknesses. In that case, we take a neutral stance and tell the producers, 'Pick one.'"[85]

Gubin continues, "Invariably, even if you present it with champagne and chocolate on a silver tray, telling a presenter that he has not been awarded the show makes him very unhappy. There's not a whole lot you can do about this reaction; nobody likes to hear the word 'no.' But over the long haul, you try to take care of people and their business interests as best you can. You might not make them happy today, but you might be able to make them happy tomorrow."[86]

If initial interest in a tour fizzles, and not enough presenters commit to the production, an offered tour may be canceled. If a tour must be canceled, booking agents prefer to make this announcement as early as possible, so that presenters holding dates for the production will have enough time to replace the hole in their schedules. John Starr provides an example: "Last year [in 2004], we canceled *Urinetown*. Some presenters wanted that show passionately, but not enough of them would commit to a tour to make it viable. At the end of January, we canceled the proposed six-to-seven-week tour, which would have been financially unprofitable."[87]

After a presenter has expressed interest in a production, the booking agent begins to negotiate the terms of the engagement. Ron Gubin describes this process: "We negotiate the deal with such terms as the expenses of the engagement, ticket prices, types of ticket discounts, allowable box office deductions, and so on. We confirm the engagement with a deal memo, which lists these points. We draft the deal memo in a form approved by the producers and general manager of the production; we report all of the specific deal points for the engagement to them for approval before we issue the deal memo."[88] Please see appendix B for an example of a deal memo.[89]

After the deal memo is issued, full contract negotiations may commence between the booking agent and the presenter. Issues may arise between the drafting of the deal memo and the acceptance of the full contract, but generally, once the deal memo is agreed to, the engagement will proceed. Ron Gubin explains: "The deal memo is meant to be the bullet-point confirmation of the major areas of the engagement. The contract is more expansive. The majority of presenters that we work with have dealt with us frequently, so they know what our contracts look like. That's not to say that issues don't come up—they do—but you don't have to walk the presenter through all of the parts of the contract. For example, presenters know that they need to provide pure and ample drinking water backstage for the actors because it's part of the Actors' Equity sanitary code, so you don't have to mention in the deal memo that this requirement will be in the contract."[90]

A major component of the deal memo negotiations is the specific financial arrangements made for the tour. The producer, with assistance from the booking agent, has determined the quoted price for the production. The quoted price consists of the guarantee, any percentage guarantee paid off of the net adjusted gross box office receipts to the producer, and a percentage of the overage.[91] The "overage" is the amount of money left over after the presenter has recovered the expenses of the engagement as well as a presenter profit (the amount of money given to the presenter beyond engagement expenses), if applicable, from the net adjusted gross box office receipts. This overage is divided between the production and the presenter and is based on some negotiated percentage, ranging from a 50/50 split to a 90/10 split, respectively.

For example, assume that an engagement has a guarantee consisting of $350,000 plus 10 percent of the net adjusted gross. The production expenses are $200,000. The presenter profit of the engagement is negotiated at $5,000, and the overage will be split 60 production/40 presenter. If the net adjusted gross is $650,000, then the settlement of expenses is:

$650,000 net adjusted gross
− $350,000 guarantee (to production)
− $65,000 royalty (10 percent of net adjusted gross; to production)
− $200,000 production expenses (presenter)
− $5,000 presenter profit (to presenter)
= $30,000 overage

This overage will be split so that 60 percent ($18,000) goes to the production and 40 percent ($12,000) goes to the presenter.

Another negotiated deal point is known as "middle money" (or "next monies"). Middle money is an amount of money taken from the net adjusted gross before the overage is split, which will go to the production or presenter (depending on the negotiation).[92] As presenters feel that they are taking a substantial risk on the engagement, and producers feel that they are risking a great deal on the tour, both believe that they should be entitled to additional funds. Next monies (or middle money), as

Josh Sherman notes, "are serious negotiating points, because though these payments are not guaranteed, they can be the difference between profit and loss on an engagement."[93]

Because they are used to determine the overage, expenses incurred by the presenter are negotiated as part of the contract. Ron Gubin remarks, "At this point, if we have not given the presenter the tech rider, we do so now. The tech rider helps the presenter understand all of the expenses involved in presenting the production, such as the personnel required for the load-in, and it is included with the contract. The deal memo may state that the show costs $300,000, but the technical rider is going to tell the presenter exactly how expensive it's going to be to present the production. We consult with the general manager on the tech rider, noting elements that may not work for our presenters or suggesting things that we think should be included."[94]

Presenter expenses are listed on a schedule, which is part of the contract.[95] The schedule of expenses divides the presenter's expenses into fixed expenses and documented expenses. "Fixed expenses" consists of the house package (which includes such items as rent, security, and front-of-house staff salaries and benefits), as well as other costs agreed upon between the producer and the presenter.[96] These expenses are negotiated from season to season. "Documented expenses" are carefully budgeted estimates that will be supported by bills and invoices. Documented expenses include some variable expenses, which are estimated based on projected audience attendance and will only be exact when the engagement is concluded; these expenses include such items as insurance and ticket printing. Please see appendix C for a sample schedule of expenses.[97]

The final financial piece of the contract is the ticket pricing scale and performance schedule; this information is also listed on a schedule in the contract.[98] The schedule includes house seat provisions and allowable box office deductions. A booking agent may use the information in the schedule to determine potential ticket sales for an engagement, based on the terms agreed to and his knowledge of the market.[99] Please see appendix D for a sample schedule of ticket prices and discounts.[100]

Although the financial terms are meant to be the same for every presenter, in some cases it is necessary for the booking agent to be flexible regarding the needs of a specific presenter. Ron Gubin states, "If the presenter really wants the show, but he finds some component to be too much of a burden, you allow him to make his case to you and express why he needs an exception. You then bring his reasons to the attention of the producer or general manager of the tour. There are some points that are nonnegotiable; rarely, if ever, do we reduce the guarantee for a show. However, you might decide that, even though you have a show that is a very big hit and has absolutely no discount policy, you will give a discount for a weekday matinee in [a] particular market. This is no small part of our day: exceptions to the rules."[101]

The booking agent's job does not end after the tour is completely booked. Ron Gubin states, "We remain the liaison between the show and the presenter through the end of the engagement. We also are responsible for distributing the wraps [the amount of ticket sales tallied daily after the show goes on sale] to the producers, the general manager, and the press agent. In addition, issues invariably arise after the contract is signed, and the producer or general manager may ask us to talk with the presenter about them. For example, the presenter might not be marketing the show aggressively enough, and we might need to speak with the presenter because the producer feels that the presenter isn't cooperating with him. Or a presenter might come to us and say, 'The producer turned down our promotional request. Why can't your cast come to the Thanksgiving Day parade in our town?' We represent the producer's interest, as he or she is the party that engages us, but we want to be sure the engagement goes well and that the interests of both parties are well served."[102]

Josh Sherman agrees: "Without the relationships you have with your presenters, you have nothing. You don't want to sell someone a bad engagement where he loses money, because then you lose him as a potential presenter for another tour. However, even though these presenter relationships help you book the tour, and you may be trying to work in the best interests of everyone, you do have to remember that you're not working for the presenter; you're working for the producer."[103]

CLASSROOM DISCUSSION
What is a booking agent, and what are the responsibilities of a booking agent on a tour?
How do booking agents acquire productions to represent?
What variables should a booking agent keep in mind when planning the tour?
What strategies do booking agents use when contacting presenters about booking their production?

What strategies do booking agents use to solidify their relationships with presenters?
For a booking agent, what is the advantage of attending a booking conference?
Define the following: "ghost route," "firm route," "bad jump," "layoff," "deal memo," "documented expenses," and "fixed expenses."
What is an anchor, and what is its use when routing a tour?
How do booking agents avoid bad jumps and unnecessary layoffs?
What are the challenges of booking a hit show?
What is the process for canceling a tour?
What is middle money (next monies), and why is it important in a deal negotiation?
What are the responsibilities of the booking agent after the tour is booked?

PRESENTING THE TOUR
As a tour is created, and a booking agent begins to create a route for it, the presenter enters into the touring process. A "presenter" is an entity (either commercial or nonprofit) that owns or rents a space for the purpose of presenting previously produced work. The presenter decides which works to book into his space, plans his season by negotiating engagements with various booking agents, supervises the marketing efforts for the presentation, and "manages the entire engagement while the show is in town."[104]

Many presenters operate as nonprofit corporations. As in other nonprofit organizations, nonprofit presenters have an artistic mission and program their seasons in support of that mission. Tom Gabbard, president of the North Carolina Blumenthal Performing Arts Center in Charlotte, North Carolina, states, "As a nonprofit presenter, you are driven by a unique mission and purpose, with attributes and values that extend beyond just making a profit. These may be artistic values or community development values that are about doing good in some respect. We are frequently judged by the good we do in the community: Do we enrich the community in some way? Do we lift it up culturally in some way? Do we enhance the quality of life in our community?"[105]

However, some for-profit presenters exist, and some theaters that present touring productions are owned and operated by commercial entities (such as the Key Brand Entertainment [formerly Live Nation] theaters). These presenters aim to earn a profit in each of their engagements. This goal does not necessarily preclude other priorities, as Mike

Isaacson, vice president of programming at the Fox Theatre in St. Louis, Missouri, notes: "We're sort of an unusual institution, because even though we're a private organization, we act publicly. There's a history for the Fox in St. Louis; there's a relationship between the theater and the community that crosses generations. Coming to the Fox is often an emotional decision, not a logical one, and because of that fact, we need to act in a more community-minded way. We do a certain amount of free events each year, and we make sure that there's a wide variety of ticket pricing to appeal to different types of people. When people find out we're for-profit, they tend to be surprised, which is a good thing."[106]

Regardless of how the presenter is incorporated, each one chooses works to present according to its own criteria. Some presenters program a single season, choosing five or six productions from a variety of genres, and then offer other events on a one-off basis. Other presenters program their season with several series made up of the same type of performances, such as a chamber music series or a contemporary dance series.

As a commercial presenter, Mike Isaacson wants to present shows that sell tickets, but his first concern is quality. "My foremost question: 'Is it a good show?' I've certainly presented shows like *Contact* [a fully danced work that won the 1999 Tony Award for Best Musical] that I knew weren't going to be extremely popular, but were extraordinary artistically and would please a dedicated segment of our audience. We did very well with *Contact*, but there was a portion of our audience questioning the programming of what they considered to be a modern ballet. I am aware of shows on the radar, and I track the ones that I'm interested in, looking at their success on Broadway and other factors. Clearly, we want big, popular, wonderful hit Broadway musicals, but there's only one or two of those a season (if we're lucky), so we need to look at other shows as well. Because we sell tickets on subscription, we have a price ceiling for ticket sales, which determines how much money we have to spend on programming, so we need shows that vary in cost in order to fit this model. Subscribers also want variety in the season, so we don't want to book six events within the same genre. I'm located in the middle of the country, so I get a lot of calls early from agents as they try to route their tours from one coast to the other; because of this fact, I need to look with a very discerning eye on the credibility of the tour and determine if the property is viable or not."[107]

If a presenter has a particular interest in a specific kind of work, such as new plays or experimental performance, that interest will dictate the type of work that the organization presents. Vallejo Gantner, artistic director of P.S. 122 in New York City, describes his programming process as follows: "P.S. 122 is looking at a diverse range of contemporary work in many disciplines and performance styles, including cross-disciplinary work such as dance-theater or multimedia work. Because so many of our presentations are not created when we agree to present them, we have to look at the history of the artist and his work and whether we think the work is any good. Innovation and the level of artistic ambition in the work are the first considerations, not potential sales or a simplistic assessment of good or bad. Video documentation of previous work or the working process often plays a major role in this evaluation. We also look at the suitability of the work for our spaces (we have two theaters, of 145 and 80 seats) and in the context of the entire season; if an artist proposes a piece that is too similar to other works in the season, we may choose not to present it or to move it to another season."[108]

Presenters find properties to present by accepting submissions through the mail, talking to booking agents, and attending booking conferences to see performances and learn about potential presentations. Also, presenters travel to festivals and other performance spaces to see if suitable works can be found for their own venues. Some presenters even look at work in their own cities to research new artists. For P.S. 122, Vallejo Gantner estimates that he sees eleven shows a week when he is in New York. "I'll see a work or something in development and talk to the artist about his next project, or whether he wants to have a piece presented at P.S."[109]

In addition to selecting previously produced work, presenters may also help to create work for presentation. Presenters may commission a work, providing funds to an artist or company in exchange for the right to present the finished piece. In addition, presenters may decide to produce a work directly. For example, in recent years, the Independent Presenters Network (IPN), an association of presenters, has also acted as a producer of various Broadway shows and touring attractions (such as Matthew Bourne's *Edward Scissorhands*); by producing these works, IPN members gain productions for their seasons as well as an additional revenue stream from profits and royalties.[110]

Tom Gabbard states that it is important for presenters to consider their audience when selecting works to present. "It's not difficult to come up with ideas that you personally might be interested in; the greater challenge is finding new ideas that will excite the public's interest. I am looking for projects and presentations that this community, in its broadest sense, is going to find relevant. I need a range of shows, some of which are more traditional, others that appeal to those looking for something hip and edgy, as well as everything in between. We are constantly searching for new presentations, for things that will keep our offerings fresh and pleasantly surprise people. We don't want anyone to look at a brochure and say, 'Yeah, yeah, yeah: same old, same old.' We want them to look at our season and say, "Oh! That sounds really interesting. I don't know what it is, but this place has a habit of doing things that surprise, intrigue, and delight me.'"[111]

Gabbard continues, "We're constantly on the prowl for exciting new productions, but we have to carefully balance that with financial viability. We want to find work that is artistically interesting for our community, but that is also affordable. A production may look like a good idea, but after we create the budgets, we may find that it is too expensive for the value that we think it brings to the community. If that turns out to be the case, we will not present the production."[112]

Presenters can only find out what value a work has to the community by reaching out directly to this community. A presenter may do this by conducting audience surveys or creating focus groups made up of members of a target market to get feedback. However, Mike Isaacson notes that there's an easier way to know what the community is thinking: "You can find out what an audience wants by being in the house before the show or during intermission, by talking to subscribers, and by talking to different people in the community as you go about your day. The great thing about this business is that the audience tells you what it wants—they either buy tickets or they don't. After getting this audience feedback, you can analyze all of the elements that went into the engagement to get the bigger picture."[113]

Presenters begin to program a season between two and four years before the season is to start, depending on the availability of productions. Many presenters use calendar or scheduling programs to assist in programming, such as ArtsVision; some presenters even use Excel spreadsheets as preliminary season calendars.[114] Seasons that are two or three years away from the current date contain only lightly held or "penciled" dates, and as the season gets closer, these penciled holds await

confirmation. Most seasons are confirmed during the year preceding the start of the season; if the season begins in October, the presenter will begin to solidify the schedule in the fall of the previous year. However, some touring productions are announced several years in advance, and if a presenter is interested in such a production, he may hold tentative dates on his calendar for it, even though the majority of productions scheduled for that touring season have not yet been announced. If dates are held more than a year in advance, the presenter understands that there is a good possibility that these dates will change as the tour route is finalized. Other attractions, such as pop music acts, do not announce tours in advance, and may be programmed into the season three months to six weeks before the performance date.[115]

Much like booking agents, presenters begin to program their seasons by setting dates for anchor productions. "Anchor productions" are the main events that presenters feel will spark audience interest in the presenter's season. For example, in a Broadway touring series, an anchor production may be a successful Broadway show such as *Wicked* or *Spamalot*. Although these productions are held on specific dates, these dates may change; if the anchor production is valuable enough to the presenter, he may move or cancel other presentations to accommodate it.[116]

After determining the dates for anchor productions, presenters then begin to slot other productions of interest into the season, making certain not to saturate the market with similar works at the same time. Tom Gabbard gives an example: "Every dance company on tour seems to want to come to Charlotte in February or March. I've had years when I could do a six-show dance mini-season in those months, but then it's famine the rest of the year. You need to get a handle on this kind of bunching early on and nudge companies to look at other alternatives to avoid clogging your schedule."[117] In addition to scheduling the main performance season at the venue, the presenter must also hold dates on the schedule for any other groups that have arranged to use the space. These groups may include organizations that have agreed to rent the space or other presenters that also share the venue. Many presenters, especially nonprofit organizations, have arranged with local arts organizations (such as symphonies and theater companies) to provide free or reduced-rent space for performances; these organizations are known as "resident companies." (Presenters may also offer rehearsal space and administrative support to these organizations.)[118] These resident companies typically have a standard season that the presenter must work around when programming the main events into his space.

At the Blumenthal Performing Arts Center, Tom Gabbard must include the schedules of nine different organizations in his programming season. He begins by holding dates for each resident company's typical season, as he explains: "Tradition plays a huge role in scheduling resident companies. If these companies have the same schedule year to year, then that creates a template that gives you a lot of guidance. We do provide some deferential consideration to resident companies; we try to accommodate their needs first and then we schedule around that, considering exceptions as we go. For example, Opera Carolina usually needs one week for their productions, but one year they decided to produce *Porgy and Bess* for two weeks. We needed to go to our other resident companies and tell them that the season schedule needed to be altered to allow this, because Opera Carolina believed, rightfully, that the market was deep enough to support two weeks of this production. We limit that sort of preference to three of the resident companies. We support a host of other nonprofit groups, to which we give discounted rental rates, but we don't give them that sort of priority scheduling."[119]

At this point, presenters are only holding dates for their season, but these dates are not confirmed. As touring arrangements are finalized (and as tours that are not financially viable drop out of the marketplace), presenters firm up these holds, creating the first version of the finalized season schedule. Although these dates may still change, this version of the season calendar is the one the presenter works with when negotiating the deal memo with the booking agent.

The booking agent begins the negotiation by quoting the price of the production to the presenter. (The quoted price is a starting point in the determination of the asking price, and may be modified based on the titles available in the market, the national or local economic climate, or the position of the production within the presenter's season.)[120] In most cases, the quoted price is the amount that the presenter will actually pay, and expenses are negotiated for the engagement.

The presenter then prepares an estimation of all documented and fixed expenses related to the presentation, creating the initial version of the schedule of expenses. He negotiates with the booking agent, reviewing every estimate until both parties agree on the numbers. As these expenses are deducted from the net adjusted gross before the overage is determined, the amounts are very important to both parties. The presenter must estimate these expenses as accurately as possible, or he may find himself paying additional money out of his own organization's budget to cover the difference.

The negotiation continues as the ticket prices for the engagement are determined, along with allowed box office deductions (found in the schedule of ticket prices and discounts in the contract). Presenters usually determine ticket prices by looking at their presentation history for similar projects and the quoted price of the show, using those figures as a base for figuring out current prices; however, ticket prices must be established with an eye to making a certain amount of money for the engagement. The booking agent and presenter will also negotiate arrangements for presenter profit, middle money, and the overage, if applicable.

Although presenters need to consider their own financial advantage when negotiating, they must also keep in mind the need of the booking agent and the producer to make a profit. Tom Gabbard elaborates: "My philosophy is that a deal needs to be fair. I think some people want to get the best deal possible, and they love hammering agents down to the lowest possible price. I don't want to overpay for something, but in my experience, if the deal is not fair, it is not going to hold up over time. In the case of a touring artist or a show, they may cancel the tour or go elsewhere; in some cases, you may drive them out of the business completely. Negotiations have to be equitable to both sides—artist and presenter."[121] Mike Isaacson agrees, but notes: "You have to have constant conversations and point out what your priorities are and why certain deal points matter to you. If it's really important and you can't give it up, you have to be willing to walk away. It's the biggest hammer you have during a negotiation, but very rarely does it get to that point."[122]

After the deal is agreed upon, the full contract is negotiated, and the engagement is considered confirmed. The presenter receives the full technical rider and begins to make preparations for the load-in of the physical production, including holding time on the schedule to accommodate this process and arranging for needed crew members. (If the presenter has an agreement with IATSE, these stagehands will be part of that union. If not, the presenter will use nonunion stagehands unless the attraction is a yellow-card tour.) The presenter also begins to work on marketing the engagement and the season as a whole.

For most presenters, the marketing process begins with the production of a season subscription brochure. Ticket subscriptions provide ticket discounts in exchange for the purchase of tickets to multiple events; for presenters, subscriptions constitute advance sales that provide a measure of security for an engagement. From a producer's perspective, a large subscription audience makes an engagement more attractive, as it provides some additional financial assurance; as Josh Sherman notes, "If a production plays an engagement at a presenter with a substantial subscriber base, it has a much better chance of reaching overage than if it plays an engagement with a small number of subscribers."[123]

Subscription brochures are typically mailed between April and June for a season beginning in the fall, so the season must be confirmed by the time the brochure goes to print. The brochure contains information about all of the attractions offered by the presenter, along with photos and ticket information. These brochures are mailed to current subscribers for renewal, as well as lapsed subscribers and others on selected mailing lists. In conjunction with the brochure mailing, e-mails may be sent to potential subscribers; the presenter's Web site will also display this information, along with online subscription creation or instructions on subscribing by mail or telephone.

The structure of a ticket subscription differs among presenters. At P.S. 122, ticket buyers may join a membership program that entitles them to $10 tickets to every performance.[124] Other presenters offer season subscriptions, which allow ticket buyers to buy one ticket to every show presented in the season, or a series subscription, in which ticket buyers may purchase a ticket to every show in a similar genre, such as dance or "Broadway." At the Fox, subscribers are offered a six-show series, with individual events sold off-series as single tickets; since the theater has 4,100 seats, subscribers are willing to commit to a full season to hold on to desirable seat locations.[125] Subscriptions may also be offered for specific evenings or performances, as many opera companies and symphonies do.

Like many arts organizations, presenters have seen subscriptions decline in recent years. Tom Gabbard notes, "Subscriptions make up about 35 to 40 percent of our audience, so it's a substantial piece of our ticket revenue. We've been seeing an overall attrition of about 5 to 10 percent per year, which is a large reduction when added up over a few years (although recently we've seen a turnaround and an increase in subscriptions). Clearly, however, there's been a move toward more last-minute purchases."[126] Mike Isaacson feels that time is the issue: "Our audience's lives are such that it's very hard to look at the coming year and plan for six nights when you know you're going to be available."[127] To address this concern, some presenters have begun to offer flexible subscriptions, allowing subscribers to buy tickets to productions without committing to specific dates until just before the engagements.

The membership program at P.S. 122 provides another method of addressing this challenge. After the subscription campaign begins, other marketing efforts are also put in place. Many presenters begin a single-ticket campaign a month or two before the season begins, in order to sell tickets in advance to those who may not wish to commit to a subscription. As specific engagements get closer, marketing for individual events comes to the fore, with direct mail, e-mail, and advertising campaigns beginning several weeks before the engagement and continuing until the presentation is finished. If a presenter is not selling as many tickets as he would like, he may create discount ticket offers, such as a two-for-one ticket purchase offer; however, he must be careful about developing a reputation in his community for frequent discounting, as this may cause potential ticket buyers to wait to purchase tickets in anticipation of a discount.[128]

All marketing efforts must address the events competing with the presenter's engagements. In some markets, presenters compete with each other and with other venues offering live entertainment, such as casinos. Tom Gabbard notes, "Casinos throw outrageous sums of money at singers and comedians to get them to perform in their venues, and they often charge bargain prices to ticket buyers. If you've got one of those casinos within driving distance of your theater, as presenters in Providence, Rhode Island, or Hartford, Connecticut, do with Foxwoods and Mohegan Sun, you've got a huge competitive challenge on your hands."[129] Also, presenters are competing with all of the forms of entertainment available to people at home—such as movies, television, video games, and the Internet—and must make a special effort to emphasize the value of live entertainment and the merits of their particular presentation.

As part of the marketing campaign, the presenter also creates a publicity strategy for the season and for individual engagements. The entire season is written up in a press release and distributed to various media outlets at the same time that the subscription information is released. As the season progresses, the publicity campaign continues, with the focus shifting to individual events. Typically, press releases are sent out three months to six weeks before the event (depending on the publication); from that time until the opening of the presentation, the presenter attempts to get as much press coverage as possible for the presentation. In conjunction with the production's publicist (if there is one), the presenter arranges for interviews with the creative team and the attendance of critics at the performances.

Finally, after all of the pre-engagement preparation has been completed, the production arrives at the venue. The presenter must load in and set up the production as quickly and efficiently as possible. In most venues, a production manager is responsible for supervising the load-in, the load-out, and all the technical needs of the engagement while it is in the venue. (In unionized venues, the personnel responsible for loading the scenery in and out [known as "loaders"] may be either members of IATSE or the International Brotherhood of Teamsters; loaders are contracted to the venue, not the production.) As the technical rider has been sent to the presenter many months prior, all of the staff involved with the load-in should know the requirements for the production; however, the tech rider may not always be entirely accurate, especially at the beginning of a tour, when technical needs and the load-in process may be adapting to the actuality of life on the road. In this situation, Tom Gabbard recommends that both presenter and producer communicate their expectations, especially if changes to technical requirements may result in additional costs. "I've done a lot of new shows where the production may only have been teching for two weeks or so, and I always try to define the parameters of what they can expect from me. You try to be specific, saying things like, 'Here are the limits of what I'm willing to do. I'm willing to provide X number of people for X number of days.' If they exceed that amount, there is an explicit understanding in advance of the additional costs for personnel or services. If you can have a clear paper trail of expectations, that goes a long way to making sure that things go smoothly."[130]

Beyond the load-in, the presenter needs to make the touring company feel welcome in his venue. The presenter should welcome the company to his space and communicate that he is pleased to present them to his audience. Tom Gabbard states, "Just showing up and being around makes a difference. It's amazing how often I hear from performers that they never see presenters. Right away, that communicates to the company that the presenter doesn't really care."[131] Presenters may also provide refreshments backstage for the performers; in some contracts, food and drink are required, but even if they are not, inexpensive items like coffee, tea, and cookies are appreciated by the company. The presenter may also throw an opening-night party for the engagement, inviting people who are important to his organization to celebrate the company.

At the end of the engagement, the production will load out of the space to travel to the next stop on the tour. The presenter must settle the finances of the engagement with the company manager or other representative of the producer. This settlement is created by adding up all of the tickets sold for the engagement. Allowed box office expenses (as agreed to in the schedule of ticket prices and discounts) are then deducted to determine the net adjusted gross. The guarantee amount, local expenses, presenter profit, and any middle money agreed to in the contract are subtracted from the net adjusted gross to obtain the overage amount. Finally, the overage is split between the presenter and producer as agreed to in the contract. The responsibility for payment of additional expenses that the engagement incurred will be determined during the settlement process. Both the presenter and the company manager must agree on all figures and sign the settlement. An example of a settlement may be found in appendix K of chapter 11.

CLASSROOM DISCUSSION

What is a presenter?

What criteria might a presenter consider when deciding to present a production?

How do presenters find out about potential productions?

How do presenters determine their local market interest in a particular production?

Define the following: "held date" and "anchor production."

What strategies do presenters use to accommodate other organizations that may need to use the space?

What is the process for negotiating the financial aspects of an engagement with the booking agent?

How does a presenter determine ticket prices?

What are some of the elements of the marketing campaign for a presenter?

How do presenters sell ticket subscriptions?

Why are subscriptions important?

What are the responsibilities of the presenter during the load-in and while the production is in the space?

How might a presenter make a touring company feel welcome in his space?

What is a settlement, and how is it determined?

NOTES

1. The authors would like to thank the following individuals for their contributions to this chapter: Tom Gabbard, Vallejo Gantner, Ron Gubin, Mike Isaacson, Simma Levine, Gary McAvay, Kent McIngvale, William Ngai, Harold Norris, Alisa E. Regas, Josh Sherman, and John Starr.
2. Josh Sherman, "Booking and Touring the Commercial Production: A Look Inside Columbia Artists Theatricals," MFA thesis, Brooklyn College, 2003.
3. Mike Isaacson, interview by author, November, 7, 2005.
4. Harold Norris, interview by author, November 17, 2005.
5. In this context, a "repertory" is a collection of works that the company is prepared to perform.
6. The Broadway League, "Touring Broadway Statistics," www.broadwayleague.com/index.php?url_identifier=touring-broadway-statistics.
7. Chris Jones, "How 'Wicked' Run Has Broken Chicago's Curse," Chicago Tribune, August 13, 2006.
8. Gary McAvay, "Booking and Touring," (lecture moderated by Tobie Stein, Brooklyn College, Brooklyn, N.Y., October 18, 2005).
9. Ron Gubin, interview by author, June 13, 2006.
10. McAvay, "Booking and Touring."
11. Josh Sherman, interview by author, November 29, 2005. Currently, Josh Sherman is the director of booking at On the Road.
12. McAvay.
13. Chris Jones, "Non-Profit Is Banking on 'Twelve Angry Men,' Chicago Tribune, January 28, 2007.
14. Gubin, "Interview."
15. Alisa E. Regas, interview by author, November 11, 2005.
16. Norris, "Interview."
17. Sherman, "Interview."
18. John Starr, interview by author, October 26, 2005.
19. Gubin.
20. Sherman, "Booking and Touring the Commercial Production."
21. Rena Shagan, Booking and Tour Management for the Performing Arts (New York: Allworth Press, 2001), 1.
22. Ibid., 1-2.
23. Sherman, "Interview;" Kent McIngvale, interview by author, January 28, 2008.
24. Canadian Broadcasting Company, "'Spamalot' to Replace 'Avenue Q' in Las Vegas," CBC.ca, February 17, 2006, www.cbc.ca/arts/story/2006/02/17/avenue-q-vegas.html; Norm Clarke, "'Hairspray' Won't Stick in Vegas," Las Vegas Review-Journal, June 6, 2006.
25. Sherman, "Interview."
26. Sherman, "Interview."
27. Simma Levine, interview by author, August 14, 2007.
28. Sherman, "Interview."
29. Actors' Equity Association, Agreement and Rules Governing Employment under the Equity/League Production Contract (June 28, 2004–June 29, 2008) (New York: Actors' Equity Association, 2004). www.actorsequity.org/docs/rulebooks/Production_Rulebook_League_04-08.pdf, 123.
30. Starr, "Interview."
31. Ibid.
32. Actors' Equity Association, "Theatre News – January 29, 2004," www.actorsequity.org/NewsMedia/archive/equity_bans_bignettroik_jan29_04.html.
33. Actors' Equity Association, Agreement and Rules Governing Employment under the Equity/League Production Contract (June 28, 2004 –June 29, 2008).
34. Ibid.
35. Booking and Tour Management for the Performing Arts, 178. The exact number of stagehands required on the yellow card is determined by such factors as the complication of the set construction, the time allotted for the load-in before the first performance at that venue, and any advance work that must be done to mount the show (e.g., a crew and possible truckload of equipment to prepare the venue prior to the actual arrival of the set). (William Ngai, interview with author, August 14, 2007.)
36. Sherman, "Interview."
37. Booking and Tour Management for the Performing Arts, 178.
38. Starr.
39. Ibid.
40. Dallas/Fort Worth Professional Musicians Association, "Newsletter Aug.–Sept. 2005," www.musiciansdfw.org/newsletter/Vol14Issue34c.pdf.
41. Per diem payments are made to members of the touring company to cover the daily costs of food and housing.
42. Sherman, "Interview."
43. Sherman, "Booking and Touring the Commercial Production."
44. Norris.
45. Regas, "Interview"; Sherman, "Interview."
46. Norris.
47. Starr.
48. Sherman, "Interview."
49. Ibid.
50. Gubin.
51. McAvay.
52. Gubin.
53. Sherman, "Booking and Touring the Commercial Production."
54. Ibid.
55. Norris.
56. Ibid.
57. Gubin.
58. Sherman, "Interview."
59. Norris.
60. Regas.
61. Ibid.
62. Gubin.
63. Ibid.
64. Sherman, "Booking and Touring the Commercial Production."

65. Norris.
66. Sherman, "Booking and Touring the Commercial Production."
67. Tom Gabbard, interview by author, June 1, 2006.
68. Gubin.
69. Norris.
70. Sherman, "Booking and Touring the Commercial Production."
71. Gubin.
72. Ibid.
73. Sherman, "Booking and Touring the Commercial Production."
74. Ibid.
75. The authors would like to thank Columbia Artists Theatricals for allowing us to reproduce this sample route.
76. Norris.
77. Ibid.
78. Sherman, "Booking and Touring the Commercial Production."
79. Ibid.
80. Ibid.
81. Ibid.
82. Ibid.
83. Sherman, "Interview."
84. Gubin.
85. Ibid.
86. Ibid.
87. Starr.
88. Gubin.
89. The authors would like to thank Columbia Artists Theatricals for allowing us to reproduce this sample deal memo.
90. Gubin.
91. Sherman, "Booking and Touring the Commercial Production."
92. Ibid.
93. Ibid.
94. Gubin.
95. Sherman, "Booking and Touring the Commercial Production."
96. Ibid.
97. The authors would like to thank Avid Touring Group, Ltd. for allowing us to reproduce this sample schedule of expenses.
98. Sherman, "Booking and Touring the Commercial Production."
99. Ibid.
100. The authors would like to thank Columbia Artists Theatricals for allowing us to reproduce this sample schedule of ticket prices and discounts.
101. Gubin.
102. Ibid.
103. Sherman, "Interview."
104. Isaacson, "Interview."
105. Gabbard, "Interview."
106. Isaacson.
107. Ibid.
108. Vallejo Gantner, interview by author, August 11, 2005.
109. Ibid.
110. Gabbard.
111. Ibid.
112. Ibid.
113. Isaacson.
114. Gabbard.
115. Ibid.
116. Ibid.
117. Ibid.
118. Ibid.
119. Ibid.
120. Sherman, "Interview."
121. Gabbard.
122. Isaacson.
123. Sherman, "Interview."
124. Gantner, "Interview."
125. Isaacson.
126. Gabbard.
127. Isaacson.
128. Gabbard.
129. Ibid.
130. Ibid.
131. Ibid.

APPENDIX A: Sample Touring Route

ROUTE AS OF AUGUST 08, 2005 / TENTATIVE AND SUBJECT TO CHANGE

calendar wk	playing wk	layoff wks	layoffs	begin	end	Scenario 1	Scenario 2	Scenario 3	Notes
1	1			8/2/05	8/7/05	PITTSBURGH: Benedum			
2	2			8/9/05	8/14/05	PITTSBURGH: Benedum			
3	3			8/16/05	8/21/05	ST. PAUL: Ordway			
4	4			8/23/05	8/28/05	ST. PAUL: Ordway			
5		1	1	8/30/05	9/4/05	layoff			
6	5			9/6/05	9/11/05	GREEN BAY			
7	6			9/13/05	9/18/05	MEMPHIS: Orpheum			
8	7			9/20/05	9/25/05	PHILLY, PA: Acad.			
9	8			9/27/05	10/2/05	HERSHEY, PA			Open on Wed, Thu mat.
10	9			10/4/05	10/9/05	CHICAGO			
11	10			10/11/05	10/16/05	CHICAGO			
12	11			10/18/05	10/23/05	DES MOINES			
13	12			10/25/05	10/30/05	CLEARWATER			
14	13			11/1/05	11/6/05	PADUCAH, KY / HUNTSVILLE			Open on Wed.
15	14			11/8/05	11/13/05	HARTFORD			7 performance week
16	15			11/15/05	11/20/05	CHARLOTTE			
17		2	2	11/22/05	11/27/05	layoff			
18	16			11/29/05	12/4/05	SEATTLE: 5th Avenue			
19	17			12/6/05	12/11/05	SEATTLE: 5th Avenue			
20	18			12/13/05	12/18/05	SEATTLE: 5th Avenue			
21		3	3	12/20/05	12/25/05	layoff			
22	19			12/27/05	1/1/06	SACRAMENTO			Open on Wed.
23	20			1/3/06	1/8/06	SACRAMENTO			
24		4	4	1/10/06	1/15/06	layoff			
25	21			1/17/06	1/22/06	HOUSTON: Hobby			
26	22			1/24/06	1/29/06	HOUSTON: Hobby			
27	23			1/31/06	2/5/06	DENVER: Buell			
28	24			2/7/06	2/12/06	DENVER: Buell			
29	25			2/14/06	2/19/06	BOSTON: Wang			Open on Wed.
30	26			2/21/06	2/26/06	BOSTON: Wang			
31		5	5	2/28/06	3/5/06	layoff			
32	27			3/7/06	3/12/06	SAN DIEGO: Civic			
33	28			3/14/06	3/19/06	TUCSON: Civic			
34	29			3/21/06	3/26/06	COSTA MESA			
35	30			3/28/06	4/2/06	COSTA MESA			
36	31			4/4/06	4/9/06	travel / WILMINGTON, DE			5 performance week
37	32			4/11/06	4/16/06	WILMINGTON, DE			
38	33			4/18/06	4/23/06	CLEVELAND			
39	34			4/25/06	4/30/06	CLEVELAND			
40	35			5/2/06	5/7/06	PROVIDENCE			
41	36			5/9/06	5/14/06	RALEIGH			
42	37			5/16/06	5/21/06	ST. LOUIS			
43	38			5/23/06	5/28/06	ST. LOUIS			
44	39			5/30/06	6/4/06	SCHENECTADY			Open on Wed.
45	40			6/6/06	6/11/06	GRAND RAPIDS			
46	41			6/13/06	6/18/06	KANSAS CITY			
47	42			6/20/06	6/25/06	ATLANTA			
48	43			6/27/06	7/2/06	FAYETTEVILLE, AR			
49		6	6	7/4/06	7/9/06	layoff			
50	44			7/11/06	7/16/06	LOS ANGELES			
51	45			7/18/06	7/23/06	LOS ANGELES			
52	45			7/25/06	7/30/06	Dallas	(Les Mis)		
53	46			8/1/06	8/6/06	Dallas	(Les Mis)		
54	47			8/8/06	8/13/06	San Francisco: Golden Gate			unconfirmed
55	48			8/15/06	8/20/06	San Francisco: Golden Gate			unconfirmed
56	49			8/22/06	8/27/06	San Francisco: Golden Gate			unconfirmed
57	50			8/29/06	9/3/06	San Francisco: Golden Gate	Vienna, VA		unconfirmed
58				9/5/06	9/10/06	tbd			
59				9/12/06	9/17/06	tbd			
60				9/19/06	9/24/06	tbd	San Jose		unconfirmed
61				9/26/06	10/1/06	tbd			
62	51			10/3/06	10/8/06	Detroit: Fisher			unconfirmed
63	52			10/10/06	10/15/06	Detroit: Fisher			unconfirmed
64	53			10/17/06	10/22/06	Detroit: Fisher			unconfirmed
65	54			10/24/06	10/29/06	East Lansing			unconfirmed
66				10/31/06	11/5/06	tbd	San Jose		unconfirmed
67	55			11/7/06	11/12/06	Norfolk	San Jose		unconfirmed
68	56			11/14/06	11/19/06	Richmond			unconfirmed
69				11/21/06	11/26/06	tbd			
						TARGETS (06-07)			
						Phoenix/Mesa	Newark	Oklahoma City	Montreal
						Buffalo	Ft. Myers	Milwaukee	Greenville
						Tulsa	Dayton	Rochester	NYC ( )
						Ft. Worth	Las Vegas	Spokane	Wash DC/Vienna, VA
69	56	6	6		as of 7/20/05				

CAPS = confirmed dates, **Bold = on 1st hold**, plain text = available or on 2nd hold, ( ) = speculative/tentative

5/7/08

APPENDIX B: Sample Deal Memo

COLUMBIA ARTISTS THEATRICALS, LLC.
ENGAGEMENT CONFIRMATION AND COMMITMENT OF TERMS

Columbia Artists Theatricals, LLC., acting solely as an Agent for the production herein, hereby confirms on this Thursday, August 16, 2007 the engagement of **PRODUCTION ABC** on the dates, times, venues and terms outlined below. This document, when signed in the space provided, will be binding upon the parties so noted and shall be evidence of an agreement until such time, if ever, as the parties enter into a more formal contract.

PRESENTOR: State University

CITY/STATE: Anytown, USA

VENUE: State University Performing Arts Center

DATES OF PERFORMANCES: Wednesday, October 10, 2007

PERFORMANCE SCHEDULE: 1 performance at 7:30pm

COMPENSATION TO BE PAID BY PRESENTOR: $23,000 flat guarantee. Special and confidential.

PLEASE SIGN AND FAX BACK ACKNOWLEDGEMENT/AGREEMENT WITH ABOVE TERMS.

By:_____   By:_____
          (Presenter)   (Company)

APPENDIX C: Sample Schedule of Expenses

NAME OF SHOW
THEATRE
ENGAGEMENT DATES

Schedule A

ESTIMATE OF DOCUMENTED & SUBSTANTIATED EXPENSES	Weekly	Engagement
Stagehands (includes 20% payroll taxes)	$50,400.00	$50,400.00
Forklift & Operagor	$1,500.00	$1,500.00
Labor Catering, if needed	$1,500.00	$1,500.00
Musicians	$18,000.00	$18,000.00
Rider/Misc (Dry Ice - 200 lbs./performance)	$2,400.00	$2,400.00
Signed Performance Interpreter, if needed	$550.00	$550.00
Star Rider Requirements	$5,400.00	$5,400.00
Telephone/Internet		TBD
	$79,750.00	**$79,750.00**
Advertising	$50,000.00	$50,000.00
(TV, Radio, Print Media, Posters/Heralds)		
	$50,000.00	**$50,000.00**

TOTAL WEEKLY DOCUMENTED & SUBSTANTIATED EXPENSES	$129,750.00	

TOTAL ENGAGEMENT DOCUMENTED & SUBSTANTIATED EXPENSES		$129,750.00

VARIABLE DOCUMENTED EXPENSES

Insurance $0.23   (per **paid** ticket)($XXX at capacity)

FIXED/UNDOCUMENTED EXPENSES

Shall include all of Presenter's obligations and operating expenses to operate Theatre as a first-class theatre suitable in all respects at all times during the Term for the presentation of the PRODUCTION at the Theatre.
Includes, but not limited to:

Bottled Water for Company	League Dues (Presenter's Share)	Security/Doormen/Police
Box Office Preliminary	Legal and Accounting Fees	(load in/out, strip/restore, performances,
Box Office Running	Licenses/Permits (inc. Pyro)	wardrobe/hair daywork and workcalls)
Catering (Talent)	Local & Regional Overhead	Sound/Lights (in-house)
Cleaning	Medical	Strip/Restore
Electrician	Miscellaneous	Telephone Installation (Company Phone)
In-House Equipment Rental	Moving Orchestra/Band Shell	Theatre Rental Charges
Follow Spots (2)	(if necessary)	(performance/rehearsals/daywork/workcalls)
General and Administrative	Opening Night	Ticket Printing
Group Sales Expenses	Piano/Piano Tuning (1 each/wk)	Ticket Sellers and Takers
Houseman/TD	Program (9.5 pages)	Ushers
House Manager	Public Relations	Utilities
House Staff		Washers/ Dryers (2 each; non-coin operated)

Additional Contractual Local Labor Requirements Not Required By Production

WEEKLY FIXED/UNDOCUMENTED EXPENSES	$67,975.00	

TOTAL ENGAGEMENT FIXED/UNDOCUMENTED EXPENSES		$67,975.00

Presenter Profit	$15,000.00	$15,000.00

TOTAL WEEKLY EXPENSES (Excl. Variable)	$212,725.00	

TOTAL ENGAGEMENT EXPENSES (Excl. Variable)		$212,725.00

PRESENTER shall furnish all items specified above and PRODUCER shall not be charged
for any item other than specified above. Advertising and Fixed Expenses are not to be in amounts in
excess of those specified above without the prior written approval of PRODUCER. Any increases
to the estimated documented expenses are to be subject to discussions between both the
PRODUCER and the PRESENTER.

PRESENTER hereby advises PRODUCER that company payments are subject to a 0% Withholding Tax (rate current as of 3/19/07).

Presenter Initials   _____

APPENDIX D: Sample Schedule of Ticket Prices and Discounts

PRODUCTION X
SCHEDULE B -- TICKET INFORMATION AND SALE OF TICKETS

A)   **TICKET SCALE: Tuesday-Saturday Eves, Saturday & Sunday Mats**

Seating Area	# of seats	Adults	Totals
Level A	1485	$65.00	$96,525.00
Level B	311	$55.00	$17,105.00
Level C	293	$45.00	$13,185.00
	2089		$126,815.00
	# of performances	8	
Gross Potential Ticket Sales			**$1,014,520.00**

TOTAL ENGAGEMENT GROSS POTENTIAL: $1,014,520.00

To be supplied to Producer in advance for approval

B)   <u>20 pair</u> of House Seats located between the third and tenth rows in the center section
section of the orchestra per performance will be reserved for purchase at regular
box office prices for PRODUCER

C)   Complimentary tickets for legitimate press only for opening night, to be approved by
PRODUCER's press agent.

D)   Opening night seating shall be under the supervision of the PRODUCER's designated
representative, such seating to be mutually approved by PRODUCER, PRESENTER and Theatre,
subject to previously sold subscription and group sale tickets and local press allocations.

Such tickets shall be held until fifty (50) hours before the advertised curtain times for each performance,
unless payment therefore is guaranteed by PRODUCER.

TICKET COMMISSIONS:

SUBSCRIPTION (INCLUSIVE OF CREDIT CARDS)	12%
GROUPS (INCLUSIVE OF CREDIT CARDS)	10%
PHONES (INCLUSIVE OF CREDIT CARDS)	6%
WINDOW BOX OFFICE (CREDIT CARDS)	4%

ALLOWABLE DISCOUNTS:

SUBSCRIBERS	10%
GROUPS	10%

BIBLIOGRAPHY

Actors' Equity Association. *Agreement and Rules Governing Employment under the Equity/League Production Contract (June 28, 2004–June 29, 2008).* New York: Actors' Equity Association, 2004. *www.actorsequity.org/docs/rulebooks/Production_Rulebook_League_04-08.pdf.*

———. "Theatre News—January 29, 2004." *www.actorsequity.org/NewsMedia/archive/equity_bans_bignettroik_jan29_04.html.*

Armbrust, Roger. "Broadway Tours Reap $700 Million." *Backstage,* 25 May 2005.

Avid Touring Group, Ltd. "Sample Schedule of Expenses." New York, 2007.

The Broadway League, *www.broadwayleague.com.*

———. "Broadway Season Statistics." *www.broadwayleague.com/index.php?url_identifier=touring-broadway-statistics.*

Campbell, Drew. "Making a Connection." *Stage Directions,* December 2005, 72–76.

Canadian Broadcasting Company. "'Spamalot' to Replace 'Avenue Q' in Las Vegas." *CBC.ca,* 17 February 2006. *www.cbc.ca/arts/story/2006/02/17/avenue-q-vegas.html.*

Clarke, Norm. "'Hairspray' Won't Stick in Vegas." *Las Vegas Review-Journal,* 6 June 2006.

Columbia Artists Theatricals. "Sample Deal Memo." New York, 2007.

———. "Sample Touring Route." New York, 2005.

———. "Sample Schedule of Ticket Prices and Discounts." New York, 2007.

Cox, Gordon. "Live Nation Sells Off Theater Division." *Variety,* 24 January 2008.

Dallas/Fort Worth Professional Musicians Association. "Newsletter, Aug.–Sept. 2005." *www.musiciansdfw.org/newsletter/Vol14Issue34c.pdf.*

Dezell, Maureen. "Clear Channel Giving Up Its Lease on Wilbur." *Boston Globe,* 1 December 2005.

Fagg, Ellen. "SLC as Broadway a Hard Sell, Even in Arts Circles." *Salt Lake Tribune,* 3 July 2006.

Friess, Steve. "Broadway on the Strip." *Newsweek,* 13 January 2006.

———. "Broadway Puts On a Show for Las Vegas." *USA Today,* 26 August 2005.

———. "Las Vegas Builds its Own Great White Way." *Christian Science Monitor,* 11 February 2005.

Gabbard, Tom. "Presenting." Interview by Jessica Bathurst. Phone interview with author, 1 June 2006.

Gantner, Vallejo. "Presenting." Interview by Jessica Bathurst. Phone interview with author, 11 August 2005.

Green, Jesse. "Live on the Strip: Broadway's Second City." *New York Times,* 2 October 2005.

Gubin, Ron. "Touring Productions." Interview by Jessica Bathurst. Tape recording, 13 June 2006. New York.

Herring, Hubert B. "A City Plots Its Future by Reaching into the Past." *New York Times,* 29 August 2006.

Isaacson, Mike. "Presenting." Interview by Jessica Bathurst. Phone interview with author, 7 November 2005.

Johnson, Lawrence A. "Classical Groups Being Pushed out of Broward Center by Broadway Shows." *South Florida Sun-Sentinel,* 19 June 2006.

Jones, Chris. "How 'Wicked' Run Has Broken Chicago's Curse." *Chicago Tribune,* 13 August 2006.

———. "Indie Presenters Rewrite Road Rules." *Variety,* 1–7 December 2003.

———. "Non-profit is Banking on 'Twelve Angry Men.'" *Chicago Tribune,* 28 January 2007.

———. "Is Vegas the New Broadway?" *Chicago Tribune,* 6 February 2005.

Jones, Kenneth. "Broadway's Major Producers Join with Regional Presenters for Audience Rewards Program." *Playbill.com,* 28 June 2007. *www.playbill.com/news/article/109186.html.*

Kurtz, Sandra. "Artists, Go Home." *Seattle Weekly,* 19 April 2006.

Leonhardt, David. "Broadway's Touring Shows Find Seats Harder to Sell." *New York Times,* 20 August 2006.

Levine, Simma. "Touring Productions." Interview by Jessica Bathurst. E-mail to author, 14 August 2007.

McAvay, Gary. "Lecture on Booking and Touring." 18 October 2005. Brooklyn College, Brooklyn, N.Y.

McIngvale, Kent. "*Jersey Boys* on Tour." Interview by Jessica Bathurst. E-mail to author, 28 January 2008.

McKinley, Jesse. "Sales Slow, Las Vegas 'Avenue Q' Will Close." *New York Times,* 16 February 2006.

McNulty, Timothy. "While Some Cities Take Do-It-Yourself Approach, Pittsburgh Books Broadway Tours with the Big Boys." *Pittsburgh Post-Gazette,* 7 May 2007.

Micocci, Tony. *Booking Performance Tours.* New York: Allworth Press, 2008.

Ngai, William. "Touring Productions." Interview with Jessica Bathurst. E-mail to author, 14 August 2007.

Norris, Harold. "Touring Productions." Interview by Jessica Bathurst. Tape recording, 17 November 2005. New York.

Pacheco, Patrick. "Rescripting the Strip." *Los Angeles Times,* 11 September 2005.

Rawson, Christopher. "Puttin' on the Glitz: Las Vegas Theater Scene Embraces the Big, the Brief and the Beautiful." *Pittsburgh Post-Gazette,* 8 July 2007.

Regas, Alisa E. "Touring Productions." Interview by Jessica Bathurst. Phone interview with author, 11 November 2005.

Robertson, Campbell. "'Hairspray' Is to Close in Las Vegas, Following 'Avenue Q,' Another Broadway Offshoot." *New York Times,* 1 June 2006.

Rousuck, J. Wynn. "Making a Broadway Show Portable Is a Challenge." *Baltimore Sun,* 10 September 2006.

Salomon, Andrew. "'Hairspray' Won't Stay in Vegas." *Backstage,* 6 June 2006.

Shagan, Rena. *Booking and Tour Management for the Performing Arts.* New York: Allworth Press, 2001.

Sherman, Josh. "Booking and Touring the Commercial Production: A Look Inside Columbia Artists Theatricals." MFA thesis, Brooklyn College, 2003.

———. "Touring Productions." Interview by Jessica Bathurst. Phone interview with author, 29 November 2005.

Spindle, Les. "Give Our Regards to Vegas?" *Backstage,* 29 November 2004.

Starr, John. "Touring Productions." Interview by Jessica Bathurst. Tape recording, 26 October 2005. Big League Theatricals, New York.

Stryker, Mark. "Theater Has New Energy." *Detroit Free Press*, 15 September 2006.

Wakin, Daniel J. "Tighter Security Is Jeopardizing Orchestra Tours." *New York Times*, 15 August 2006.

Ward, David. "Trouble and Cost of Visas Halts Hallé's US Tour." (London) *Guardian*, 30 March 2006.

Weatherford, Mike. "In Depth: Giving Regards to Broadway." *Las Vegas Review-Journal*, 29 January 2006.

Wolf, Thomas. *Presenting Performances: A Basic Handbook for the Twenty-First Century*. Washington, D.C.: Association of Performing Arts Presenters, 2000.

CHAPTER ELEVEN

Facility Management

This chapter is dedicated to the facility manager—the manager who oversees the operations of the building.[1] Depending on the organization, the facility manager could hold the following titles: general manager, theater manager, or director of operations. For the purposes of this chapter, we will define "operations" as duties related to general management, front-of-house management, box office and ticketing management, ancillary income, backstage operations, and building maintenance (please see appendixes A, B, and C for sample job descriptions, and appendixes D and E for sample organizational charts).[2] General management duties may include all activities related to staffing and training the staff; financial management and technology; negotiating, administering, and following all union contracts; managing the calendar and the scheduling of events; renting and booking the theater; and event management. Front-of-house duties consist of staffing and training all front-of-house personnel (all personnel who work in front of the proscenium, including house managers, ushers, ticket takers, security, box office employees, and cleaners). Box office and ticketing duties involve selling tickets, as well as creating box office settlements and box office statements. Ancillary income is income generated from non-production-related activities, such as concessions (food, beverage, and merchandise) and parking. Backstage operations duties consist of working with the production manager or technical director to make sure that the technical requirements (sound, lighting, staging, etc.) are being met for the shows being produced or presented. Building operations and maintenance requirements include making sure the building's management has complied with code enforcement and secured all necessary permits for operation; working with systems engineers to ensure that systems are sound; ongoing maintenance, cleaning, and setup of the building and equipment; and consulting on renovations or capital improvements.

Not all facility managers are charged with all of the activities mentioned in this chapter, though knowledge of most of these items is helpful. Responsibilities, as well as reporting orders, vary from one organization to another. For the purposes of this chapter, we will examine the various operational duties that comprise this vital position in producing, presenting, and rental facilities.

GENERAL MANAGEMENT

Since the facility manager is responsible for the day-to-day operations of the facility, she will be responsible for administering general management duties on behalf of the organization. General management duties may include all activities related to staffing and the training of staff; financial management and technology; negotiating, administering, and following all union contracts; managing the calendar and the scheduling of events; renting and booking the theater; and event management.

Staffing and Training of Personnel

Facility managers are responsible for hiring and providing training for front-of-house staff, cleaners, security personnel, engineers, the production manager or technical director, and the box office manager. (Depending on the size of the facility, the facility manager may be responsible for hiring supervisory management, who will then hire the staff listed above.) Facility managers who employ best practices develop employee staffing and training guides or manuals. Terry Byrne, general manager of the Westside Theatre, has created a manual that outlines employee responsibilities (see appendix F).[3] The director of finance or the human resources manager may also be responsible for creating these documents. Hiring processes must comply with all federal and state equal opportunity employment requirements and guidelines, and must conform to all state labor laws concerning legal working status, workweek hours, etc.[4]

Gina Vernaci shares her hiring processes for executive managers and part-time and full-time employees, as well as her orientation process for new employees: "Playhouse Square enjoys unusually long tenures from its staff, particularly the executive staff. We have only had two presidents in the past twenty-five years, one starting in 1980 and the other in 1990. The following process is typical of searches at that level. A headhunter [a consultant hired to research potential new executive personnel] is engaged; he conducts the search. Qualified candidates are forwarded to a search committee, comprised of trustees, [that] conducts the interviews and makes the decisions. Prior to the search, there is an evaluation of the organizational needs, the duties of the position, and any changes to the job description.

The search for other executives would be a similar process:

1. Conduct exit interviews with the outgoing executive to gather any points of view for improvements or changes that should be considered with a new candidate.
2. Review the job description. Make changes if needed.
3. Establish salary range.
4. Conduct a national search with the aid of industry publications and Web sites. Organizations such as APAP (Association of Performing Arts Presenters), TCG (Theatre Communications Group's ArtSearch), IAAM (International Association of Assembly Managers), and ISPA (International Society for the Performing Arts) are helpful.
5. Network in the industry. Send the job description to colleagues. Make calls or send e-mails to others in a similar position to see who may know of a candidate to recommend. Booking agents are a good source of information. They talk to a lot of people, all over the country. You need to launch a campaign to attract quality candidates. For marketing and sales, you can look to other types of venues for candidates, such as arenas and sports teams.
6. We conduct a local search via ads in the newspaper, posting the ad on our Web site, and posting on other local sites such as *Cleveland.com.*

7. Human resources (HR) screens the inquiries, reviews résumés, and forwards appropriate candidates along to the supervisor. For most of the executive staff, this person would be the president. In some cases, the vice president(s) would be responsible for interviewing appropriate candidates.
8. The supervisor reviews the résumés and further sorts through any additional information provided by the candidate, including brochures, writing samples, and so forth.
9. Human resources makes appointments with the candidates and the supervisor. The interview consists of these three individuals: the candidate, the supervisor, and HR.
10. In instances when the position needs to work extensively with other departments, the executive in charge of that department may participate in the interviewing process.
11. When the field is narrowed to two or three candidates, HR checks references. We ask for three business-related references who can give a fair evaluation of the quality of the candidate's work.
12. Although the supervisor is the final decision maker, she seeks the input of the HR director (who interviews people for a living) and any other colleagues who are a part of the process. If someone has a strong point of view, especially if it is a negative impression of the candidate, it is important to get to the bottom of the issue. Pass on [do not hire] the person if necessary.
13. Human resources makes the offer to the candidate and may negotiate salary within the approved range. They meet with the individual to coordinate a start date and review the organization's benefit package.

Here are the hiring processes for part-time and full-time members of the staff:

Part-Time
1. Jobs are posted internally first.
2. [Playhouse Square] encourages staff members to make referrals. This has been quite successful.
3. The local search begins. Ads are placed in local papers, on [the Playhouse Square] Web site, and on *Cleveland.com.*
4. Candidates are screened by phone. Communication is important. If the prospective candidate has difficulty selling herself over the phone, being a good listener, and articulating a solid response, she will not be invited to send in a résumé or apply for the position."

5. The interviewing and hiring process is as outlined in the section above [see steps 9–13].

Full-Time
1. Jobs are posted internally [first].
2. The search is local.
3. When the position is an entry-level position, [Playhouse Square has] had success with asking college and university programs in the area to refer recent graduates for the position. This is particularly true with the development, human resources, and marketing positions.
4. Submitting a résumé and salary requirements is necessary. If salary requirements are not included, we most often put the résumé aside. Should the initial search not bring qualified candidates forward, we may then review the résumés with incomplete information (such as salary) and contact them to give them the opportunity to submit the needed data.
5. The direct supervisor has final approval for the hires. As stated above, it is wise to seek the counsel of the HR director before making a final selection.

The organization's approach to new hires (orientation process):
1. On his first day, the new hire is greeted by his supervisor. The supervisor will then introduce the new employee to the department and to key staff members.
2. The new employee will meet with HR for a photo ID, fringe benefits discussion, and review of any questions.
3. The new hire is given a formal tour of the facility.
4. The supervisor conducts any cross-departmental briefings.
5. New hires all have a ninety-day probationary period.[5]

Andrey Shenin, director of operations at New York City Center, explains that "New employees must understand the facility's overall goals and objectives and what their role is in the process. All new employees start with the orientation process—a session that introduces them to the physical plant and all the locations (restrooms, concessions, and the seating section of the theater). Ushers are taught our safety requirements and how to assist in seating. It is very important to explain what guest service entails. A new employee will work anywhere from a few days to a few weeks alongside the 'old-timers.' After that, I count on the house manager and building

manager to keep up with the training on an ongoing basis. It's also important to provide employees with written materials, bulletin boards, a newsletter, and staff meetings. I update the employee manuals and schedule staff meetings. The annual employee evaluation is also a helpful training tool. Keeping job descriptions up-to-date is also important."[6]

Since most performing arts organizations employ a number of part-time employees, training them properly is an important concern. Richard Grossberg, general manager of Brooklyn Center for the Performing Arts at Brooklyn College, states: "Part-time workers are trained by department heads on-the-job or in specific training sessions, usually led by each department head. At the beginning of each year, we have formal training sessions for ushers and front-of-house staff. Production, box office, and our cleaners are trained in ongoing sessions as they are learning to use new equipment or new methods of performing their jobs."[7]

Valerie Simmons, theater manager of Manhattan Theatre Club's Biltmore Theatre in New York City,[8] details her training for part-time employees: "The ushers, stage crew, and security guards for the Biltmore train for at least one performance before assuming the positions they will hold. In addition, the ushers receive an information packet that includes seating charts, sample tickets, and any information about the theater that they may need. New engineers ([who work with] heat, ventilation, and air-conditioning, known as HVAC) work with the head engineer for at least a week, during the day, to become familiar with the equipment and controls before training on a performance or working alone. The security guards receive post orders outlining their responsibilities. Box office staff is trained to use the Telecharge system (ticketing system) and the Tessitura system, a ticketing and database system used for subscribers and patrons."[9]

CLASSROOM DISCUSSION
What is the role of the facility manager?
Name the facility manager's primary responsibilities.
What are the general management duties of the facility manager?
Why is it important to create an employee manual?
Develop a search strategy for finding a facility manager. How does the search for full-time and part-time employees differ?
Why is it important to orient new employees?
Why is it important to develop training processes for both full-time and part-time employees?

Financial Management and Technology

Financial management may include all or some of the following duties: creating, forecasting, and controlling the budget; preparing monthly and annual financial statements; preparing and overseeing the audit process; reviewing settlements; overseeing payroll, purchasing, and billing; dealing with insurance and legal issues; and making sure that the technology systems are current and working properly.

The facility budget expenses may include:

- Labor costs: salaries for full-time and part-time personnel—backstage, box office, information technology, front-of-house, cleaners, security, finance, engineers, marketing and sales, development, and education staff—and benefit costs.
- Front-of-house and production expenses: concessions, the box office computer system, tickets, postage, backstage sound and lighting equipment, and technology expenses.
- Stage and building maintenance expenses: cleaning service fees, exterminator charges, electricity, gas, rubbish removal, cleaning supplies, permits (fire department, annual boiler inspection report, state liquor license, etc.).
- Equipment contracts: for lighting and sound systems, the sprinkler system, the fire alarm monitor, elevators, air-conditioning, etc.
- Software contracts: for the box office, scheduling, and the phone system.

Income is generated from outside rentals, ticket sales, and ancillary income. Robert Freedman, president and chief executive officer of Ruth Eckerd Hall, states, "Each department head prepares his budget and submits it to the chief executive officer and chief financial officer for review. They review the total budget and determine the next steps. If the budget presented isn't balanced, the chief executive and chief financial officers will meet with the department head to review and recommend modifications to the budget. Once the initial draft is complete, the budget is submitted to the board's finance committee.

"The finance committee reviews the budget in some detail, reviewing in particular the underlying assumptions of the budget. The finance committee recommends changes that they might like to see accomplished in the budget. Once these changes, if any, are made, the finance committee recommends the adoption of the budget by the full board of directors.

"Once the budget is adopted, the chief executive officer and the chief financial officer monitor the budget and watch for any significant variations in performance. It is up to the individual department head to monitor his income and expenses. As part of monitoring the financial condition of the organization, the chief financial officer should prepare monthly financial statements, including a balance sheet, a profit and loss statement, and sometimes a cash flow statement. The profit and loss statement should compare actual to budgeted expenses for the current month, actual to budgeted expenses for the year to date, and any variances.

"The chief financial officer and chief executive officer should present these statements to the board's finance committee and the board each month. The board and staff can then monitor the organization's financial health. The chief financial officer also prepares all financial documents and records for independent auditors that represent the financial activity of the organization for the completed fiscal year."[10]

Robyn Williams, executive director of Portland Center for the Performing Arts in Portland, Oregon, monitors the overall facility budget. She expects monthly reports from all of her department heads so that she can closely monitor and forecast (estimate) potential problems. She states, "If we see a major problem, such as a significant drop in a funding stream, we will assess the need to take corrective steps through cuts, or we will determine that our reserves are adequate to 'ride out' the problem. We try to avoid 'slash-and-burn' cuts and figure a way to manage the problem through finding creative ways to increase earned revenues."[11] It is also the responsibility of the facility manager to review settlements or the "reconciliation of income and expenses for a particular performance, activity, or rental of organizational space."[12]

Facility managers are also involved in preparing payroll and in the purchasing of supplies and equipment. If the manager is charged with renting the facility, she will also be involved in the billing process. Valerie Simmons explains, "I prepare the payroll for the house manager, engineers, and box office staff. In the first season, I also prepared the stage crew payroll. Because the production department is responsible for the stage crew budget, they now prepare that payroll. I oversee the usher payroll. I also process the invoiced payroll for the security and cleaning staff. In terms of purchasing, all nonperformance purchases for the Biltmore are approved by me, and I process and track invoices. Once I have approved the invoices, I forward them to our business office for payment. Finally, rentals are invoiced either by me or by the finance department."[13]

As was discussed in the law and financial management chapters, theaters must carry insurance in case there are accidents in the theater that cause harm to property (general liability insurance) or the public (public liability insurance).[14] "Fire and theft insurance [property insurance] allows the full replacement value of all scenery, costumes, electrical and sound equipment, literary and musical material, and all other properties and material owned, rented, or brought to the premises. Most facility managers require that all producers renting their facilities properly insure themselves and their attractions, as well as provide a certificate of insurance before they appear in the theater."[15]

Facility managers also must be aware of legal issues that might occur within their facilities. Simmons maintains, "As theater manager, I try to protect the organization legally in the manner in which I handle employee and audience problems. For example, if an audience member is sick, I fill out an incident report form that documents what happens and can be kept on file in case there are future problems that require legal or medical follow-up [see appendix G]."[16] Shenin agrees that it is important for the facility manager to anticipate problems before they happen. He asks the following questions: "Should I have anticipated the problem? What was done to prevent it? Based on the past, does this event present any danger to the public?"[17] Shenin also notes the importance of having language in the rental contract, "such as negligence and indemnification clauses, which hold the facility and employees harmless from any liability or financial responsibility associated with injury or loss of property. This way, the facility is able to transfer the risk to the user. In other words, [these clauses state that] the client or renter of the facility assumes full responsibility for any and all negative occurrences during the rental period."[18]

In many organizations, the facility manager is responsible for maintaining and upgrading technology within the organization. Robert Freedman describes this responsibility: "My personal knowledge of ticket office and stage technology is maintained through direct discussion with staff involved in these areas of operations, reading industry publications, discussions with colleagues around the country, and information learned at professional conferences. For the ticket office operation, the organization recently decided

to review our combined ticketing and development system and find a new software system. All levels of staff are involved in the use of ticketing software: ticket office managers, IT (information technology) staff, development and marketing staff, etc. The chief executive and chief financial officers participated in presentations from several leading providers of ticketing software."[19]

Grossberg also reads stage technology journals and publications produced by the United States Institute for Theatre Technology (USITT) and the International Association of Assembly Managers (IAAM) to learn about recent advances in lighting and sound technology. The manufacturers of these technologies attend the IAAM and USITT trade shows, where facility managers view the equipment and ask questions that pertain to utilizing the equipment in a particular facility.[20]

CLASSROOM DISCUSSION

What are the main expenses and sources of income in a facility manager's budget?

How can a facility manager anticipate and prevent potential lawsuits?

What kind of information should be captured in an incident report form? (See appendix G.)

What can a facility manager do to make sure he has up-to-date information concerning the latest stage and box office technology?

Union Contracts

Many facility managers engage in contract negotiations with unions representing the stagehands, engineers, ticket takers, ushers, house managers, musicians, custodians, and so forth. Other facility managers, while not directly involved with negotiations, must make sure that all contract rules are enforced. Ruth Eckerd Hall works with two unions: IATSE (International Alliance of Theatrical Stage Employees, representing stagehands) and AFM (American Federation of Musicians). Freedman's director of operations handles negotiations with IATSE. Freedman states, "For IATSE, a contract is negotiated that takes into account all pay scales and working conditions, stage operations conducted by union members, overtime provisions, potential meal penalties when a particular amount of continuous working time takes place, and safety issues.[21] It is the responsibility of the operations director and his staff to ensure that the organization complies with IATSE contract conditions.

"We don't have a specific contract with AFM, but hire AFM musicians when it is required by contract with an artist to supply local musicians. For example, when the promoter is responsible for hiring the orchestra pit musicians for a touring Broadway show, or hiring backup musicians for a pop artist, we hire local AFM musicians. Many artists only play with a music director and some key musicians, which might include a pianist, drummer, and bass player. The presenter might be responsible for hiring the remaining musicians locally for the show. We work with a union music contractor to find the appropriate players. We also rely on the music contractor to ensure that we comply with union requirements. The contractor interfaces with the show and helps us determine the number and specific musicians needed. With our approval, the music contractor also helps us determine the rehearsal time, as a rehearsal needs to take place with the music director of the touring show."[22]

CLASSROOM DISCUSSION

What is the facility manager's role in negotiating and complying with union contracts?

What is a music contractor, and what is she responsible for providing?

Managing the Calendar and Scheduling Events

Facility managers maintain computerized scheduling systems to keep an accurate accounting of all events. Walter Thinnes, a facility management consultant, advises that the "calendar be maintained by one office or manager with support from other staff. All calendar changes, additions, or deletions must be processed through this office. My rule for the calendar is simple: Everything on the calendar must be true, and everything true must be on the calendar."[23] Ruth Eckerd Hall uses an automated calendar software system—the Artifax system. Freedman describes the process of managing the calendar and scheduling events for his presenting organization: "The majority of the entries are made to the calendar by the operations department. They add all events that are programmed by the organization and all rental activity in the main hall. On a weekly basis, the operations department electronically distributes the upcoming facility calendar with information on the use of all spaces in the theater. The individual responsible for a particular room in the building is accountable for ensuring that the data is scheduled in Artifax. Virtually everyone in the building has access to viewing the schedule."[24]

Valerie Simmons describes the process for maintaining the calendar for a producing organization. "The calendar is a negotiation among the production, general management, artistic, and marketing departments. The production department creates a line calendar based on the number of productions and the scheduling of design, construction, and rehearsal for those productions. The line calendar will show overlaps among the various production schedules. For each production, tech rehearsals, preview performances, press performances, patron nights, opening nights, etc. all have to be planned. The line calendar coordinates all of these things."[25]

At New York City Center, which is primarily a rental house, "the director of bookings maintains the calendar. This computerized calendar is essential to avoiding conflicts with the load-in and load-out (bringing the production in and out of the theater) of various productions."[26] In addition, Andrey Shenin notes that the calendar helps New York City Center avoid swing time. "'Swing time' occurs when the crew doesn't have the required eight-hour rest between their work calls (the time in which they are called to work). Having an eight-hour rest protects the workers. If they have to work straight through (without a break), they go into overtime, which results in financial penalties. The same is true with holidays. If the work call falls on a holiday, the pay rate is much higher (doubled in most cases). Before a booking contract is signed, a responsible booking manager should point out to the attraction that by avoiding working on certain dates, or at a certain time of the day, the attraction (and the presenter or rental house) can save money."[27]

CLASSROOM DISCUSSION

What is the purpose of having a calendar?

Name three scheduling conflicts that might be avoided through the use of a facilitywide calendar.

Renting and Booking the Theater

As has been discussed in previous chapters, presenting organizations have directors of programming who program their seasons. They do this by booking events and attractions that they believe their audience will want to see. Ruth Eckerd Hall and Playhouse Square Center are presenting organizations that book a season of events for their subscribers and single-ticket buyers. A presenting organization has 100 percent control over the season's programming, contracts, insurance, budget, marketing, development, and staff.

In contrast, a rental house, such as the Portland Center for the Performing Arts, has no control over the rental production's budget. Portland Center provides the rental production with utilities, concessions, limited marketing, equipment, box office staff, front-of-house staff, cleaners, engineers, and stagehands. A rental house will bill ("bill back") the renting organization or producer for all labor and extra services, such as overtime, security, special events, equipment and space rentals, etc.

Some presenting organizations present *and* rent their facilities. When this is the case, they give their presented attractions and their resident companies first priority. If the organization is strictly a rental facility, and it works with resident companies, it is customary to give these resident companies first crack at the dates.[28] This next section will only focus on the process by which performing arts organizations rent their facilities.

Freedman describes the process: "For those wishing to rent the facility, we have a policy that they can book the building in season (from October through April) sixty days out (sixty days before the event), or ninety days out if it's out of season. Rental inquiries are directed to the assistant director of operations. If it is a new client, a space request information form is requested (see appendix H).[29] We use this form to determine if the user has the ability to meet the financial conditions of renting Ruth Eckerd Hall. A hold is put on the rental date requested. The assistant director of operations reviews the potential date requested with the director of entertainment ([who] programs the presenting series), director of education ([who] programs the education events), and chief executive officer, if that is necessary to resolve a conflict. Once this check is done, and it is ensured that Ruth Eckerd Hall itself has no plans for the requested date, that date is released to the renter requesting it."[30]

Shenin discusses New York City Center's booking process for rentals: "Booking depends on aggressive marketing. You don't wait for the clients to come to you; you want to establish relationships with clients and seek their return business. The booking calendar has the following categories: on hold (the initial inquiry is on hold for thirty days; no contract or deposit is required), tentative (waiting for the contract and the deposit to come to the facility), and confirmed (the signed contract and deposit have been received by the facility). Establishing deadlines is important. Once you agree on a date, the producer assumes that the date is his, and he will book the rest of his tour around this date. Once the booking manager secures the date, the contract is issued. The contents of a typical contract are outlined below."

1. Outline:
    It lists the title of the show, dates, performance schedule, capacity, and on-sale date.

2. Theater's obligations:
    Theater agrees to provide cleaning, heating, air-conditioning, and all other physical elements that go along with renting a facility (e.g., toilet tissue, soap, light bulbs, and dressing room fixtures).
    Theater also provides all stage equipment and employs (on Company's behalf) stagehands, house manager, box office personnel, ushers, ticket takers, porters, cleaners, matrons, elevator operator, security, and engineering personnel.
    List hours when Theater is available for load-in/out, tech and dress rehearsals, and performances.
    List Box Office and CityTix [in-house ticket center] hours.

3. Company's obligations:
    Company is responsible for all artistic elements of the production. Company also has to give Theater a description of the show at least two weeks before the on-sale date.
    Company pays its own salary, and any social security withholding, workers' compensation, unemployment, and disability insurance. Company also pays all royalties due in connection with its performance.
    Company must provide a technical/production manager, and all performers, dressers, and musicians for the Engagement. Company must also provide artistic, supervisory, production, technical, rehearsal, and management personnel. Company must also provide all elements necessary for the presentation of Company's performances; for example, costumes, scenery, lighting, and sound equipment (beyond Theater's inventory).
    Company must provide a technical rider on or before the production meeting, which must take place no later than two weeks before the first performance.

4. Special access programs:
   Theater is in compliance with the American with Disabilities Act (has assisted listening devices, wheelchair access, and certain seats held for use by physically challenged patrons).

5. Deposits, fees, and box office receipts:
   Company must deliver a deposit by X date.
   Box Office receipts are proceeds from the sale of the tickets less all credit card charges. Company will have access to these receipts after the performances are finished.
   On the settlement after the engagement, Theater will deduct: rent, charges for front-of house personnel, stagehand labor, additional security, ticket printing costs, and postage.

6. Tickets:
   Except for TDF [Theatre Development Fund], Theater is the only agent selling tickets to the Engagement. Patrons can purchase tickets using cash, Visa, MasterCard, and American Express credit cards. A service charge of $X on each ticket is charged from all purchasers of tickets by telephone or Web. A service charge of $X on each order is charged from all purchasers of tickets by mail or fax.
   Theater can purchase X seats to each performance and have X comp tickets.

7. Advertising:
   Company is fully responsible for all advertising of the Engagement.

8. Concessions:
   Theater will operate bars and coat check.

9. Broadcasting, recording, and photograph policies:

10. Company may not broadcast, telecast, or reproduce any performance or rehearsal without Theater's prior consent.

11. Theater's warranties:
    Theater can legally enter into all aspects of the contract.

12. Company's warranties:
    Company can legally enter into all aspects of the contract.

13. Use of premises and equipment:
    Company can't make any alterations or repairs to the building without Theater's approval. Company is responsible for any equipment brought to the theater and for all physical damages to the premises.

14. Insurance
    Company must provide Theater with a copy of the public liability and general aggregate insurance policies.[31]

15. Breach of agreement, destruction of premises:
    Theater has the right to cancel the Engagement if Company fails to observe any term of the Contract.
    Contract can be terminated only due to Act of God, civil tumult, or strikes or labor disputes involving either party's employees.

16. Distinct remedies:
    Theater and Company can dispute and enforce any aspect of the contract.

17. Signature page

18. Appendixes:
    Stage equipment inventory; union list (list of unions with whom we work); logo; FOH costs chart (e.g., wages and benefits for house management, security, ushers and ticket takers, cleaners and porters, box office personnel).[32]

When the rental agreement or contract is issued by the organization, it will include a usage policy (see appendix I), which outlines the rules that must be followed when utilizing the facility.[33] "It is also important for stating what type of event is taking place, so a lessee can't switch from a classical concert to a rap show without notifying the theater."[34] When returning the contract to the organization, the producer or renter will provide a technical or production rider that outlines her expectations (see appendix J).[35] Before signing the contract, it is critical that the facility manager carefully read the technical rider to make sure that there are no hidden expenses or technical specifications that cannot be provided.

Shenin states, "If the contract is not signed by the due date, the booking director will give the renter a 'twenty-four-hour challenge.' In other words, the booking director will give the renter twenty-four hours to sign the contract and make a deposit, or lose the dates."[36]

Without the execution of a contract, no deal exists. Richard Grossberg explains his strategy for executing the contract: "When we receive an inquiry for rental of the theater, we ask the client to come in for a meeting or, if need be, have the meeting on the phone. We discuss in as much detail as possible the requirements of the show and the very specific schedule that will take place on the day of the show. For example, we discuss that load-in starts at 9 A.M.; technical work goes until 6 P.M.; dinner starts at 7 P.M.; the show runs from 8 P.M. to 11 P.M., and then loading the show out goes on until 1 A.M. Based upon the requirements of the show, I check with the production manager as to the estimated stage crew staffing; receive an estimate for front-of-house staff, security, and equipment costs; and prepare an estimate of all expenses for the client. We prepare the contract upon receipt of the deposit for the event. The client receives, signs, and returns the contract to the facility, and the event is then scheduled in the calendar. Further production meetings are arranged, additional payments are made according to the contract schedule, and the event takes place on the scheduled date."[37]

CLASSROOM DISCUSSION

What type of information is captured in a space request form?

Discuss the contract items provided in the sample contract. Why is it important to include each of these items in a contract? Justify the importance of each item.

Review Ruth Eckerd Hall's usage policy (see appendix I) and discuss the importance of each area of the policy.

Review the sample technical rider provided by the producer of an event (see appendix J). If a facility manager doesn't carefully review the technical rider, what might go wrong?

Event Management

What is event management? Richard Grossberg states: "It is the planning, coordination, communication, and execution of a show or event, serving the needs of the client, the performers, and the audience attending the show."[38]

Robert Freedman gives an overview of how an event is executed in his facility: "The staffing of a public event must take into account all aspects of building operations. All operations should lead to a positive experience for the patron arriving at your facility. All systems should be such to ensure that the primary focus is making the guest comfortable, making it easy for him to move around the facility, making it easy to find his seat location, having pre-performance and intermission functions readily accessible and easy to use, and, at the end of a performance, allowing for a safe and quick exit from the facility to the patron's means of transportation away from the facility."[39]

Robyn Williams agrees, but stresses safety as well: "Staffing, in my opinion, is more about the safety of the patrons in your facility. How many staff does it take to move people around your facility? How many are needed to handle a variety of safety or security issues? The primary responsibility of the facility manager is the safety and security of the people who work and attend events in the venue."[40]

Freedman continues, "Also, at Ruth Eckerd Hall, artists are treated as special guests in our facility. The entire production services area, including backstage catering, ensures that the artist and the artist's crew have all the tools that they need to put on the best show they can. If all aspects of an artist's experience in your hall are positive, it will lead to the artist having a positive feeling about your facility and organization. At Ruth Eckerd Hall, each show is meticulously advanced as described below, primarily by the organization's technical director or production manager.

"Through working with the artist's advance personnel, the technical director and/or production manager determines: the exact time of load-in; the number of crew required; the technical needs of the artists (e.g., sound and lighting instruments); the time of sound check, if needed; the time the artist will arrive; and any catering needs. (Ruth Eckerd Hall has a function room and a full kitchen. This allows us to hire our own in-house backstage catering crew that reviews the needs of the artist's technical rider.) The production manager also ensures that all technical equipment is in place for the artist's show that day, and that any meet-and-greet requirements of either the artist or the organization are met. In conjunction with marketing, he arranges any press requests, including any potential interviews, as well as permission for the house photographer to shoot the beginning of the artist's shows for our archives.

"A typical day of an event would probably take on the following characteristics. Usually, first at the hall would be the security staff. The security staff opens the facility and ensures that access to the facility and backstage areas are secure, while allowing all working staff (including the office administration staff) and show staff access to the facility. Prior to this day, and at the conclusion of any previous events, the cleaning and/or maintenance staff would clean all areas of the theater, including dressing rooms and backstage areas. Our goal is to make sure no one at any part of the facility enters an area that is not clean and ready for use. A facility that is not clean gives the impression to guests that the facility is not well cared for, and that this lack of care might translate into other areas of the operation.

"The technical staff arrives at the theater and does final stage preparations for the arrival of the artist. The technical staff might have prepared some aspects of the load-in, such as a pre-hang of lighting equipment, clearing all equipment and drapes from the stage pipes, etc., the day or evening before the actual load-in of the show. Ruth Eckerd Hall does not have an engineering staff member on duty for shows, but he is available during normal business hours to review and be sure all the facility equipment is operating properly. Our security staff monitors the HVAC system during performances and responds to changes needed in the HVAC system as they arise. For example, the company may request changes to room temperatures in dressing rooms, or the house management staff may report comments from audience members on the theater being too cold or too warm.

"Most likely the ticket office staff would be the next to arrive, usually opening at 10 A.M. House management is next to arrive. The house management staff, along with the cleaning supervisor, would perform a house check, testing all lighting and safety equipment, and reviewing the building for cleanliness. The usher staff, including head ushers, arrives at approximately 6 P.M. for an 8 P.M. performance. The house manager (also called our "patron services manager") would have a meeting with all ushers and review the nature of the performance that evening, including such details as the time that doors to the lobbies and auditorium will open; the length of the performance, including intermissions (if any); the length of intermissions; sales of artist's merchandise or other merchandise that might take place during the course of the evening in conjunction with the show; and any special conditions that might exist for that evening. The house manager would also review evacuation and security protocols.

"In addition, the development staff has a manager on duty to handle any questions or concerns of the Ruth Eckerd Hall donors and to oversee the operation and entry into the Dress Circle Room—a room specifically set aside for use by major donors prior to the performance, at intermission, and after the performance. This room has its own bar and bar staff, serves light refreshments, and has its own private restroom facilities.

"Ruth Eckerd Hall has paid parking on our grounds. The parking staff arrives next to set up their equipment and to prepare to accept parking payments and to direct people to the correct parking lots. The collection of funds is done by a contracted parking company, but the directional parking guards are Ruth Eckerd Hall staff employees.

"Show managers who are to be on duty for the specific performance arrive and will include programming staff, marketing staff, and accounting staff, if a settlement with the artist is required that evening. For presented performances, the accounting staff or programming staff prepares the settlement reports (the amount of money owed to the facility and to the renter/artist), if required. Rental performances are generally settled after the fact and prepared by the accounting department. In many facilities that are not presenters, the show settlement would be prepared by the house manager or event manager. The distinction here is that if the facility is primarily a rental facility, the settlement is for the building costs only. If the facility is a presenter, the settlement would be for the building costs and any other costs, such as marketing costs associated with presenting the performance that have been agreed to contractually between the presenter and the artist.

"During the event, key staff members have two-way radios with specific channels on which they are to communicate. Typically, the patron services/house manager, technical director, ticket office, marketing staff, food and beverage staff, and cleaning/maintenance staff are all on radio."[41]

Figure 11.1 shows a sample event timeline for a gala event, including a pre-performance reception and a dinner following the performance.

Fig. 11.1. Event Timeline[42]

EVENT TIMELINE
date

TIME	TASK	VENDOR/CONTACT
12 midnight–6 A.M.	Tent installed	
9:00 A.M.	Power run to kitchen tent	
10:00 A.M.–1 P.M.	Rentals arrive	
12:00 P.M.–12:30 P.M.	Volunteer meeting	
1:00–2:00	LUNCH	
1:00 P.M.–5:30 P.M.	Setup staff arrives (coat check, reception)	
5:00 P.M.	Setup of check-in tables	
5:30 P.M.	READY for reception	
5:30 P.M.–5:40 P.M.	Photographer arrives Press arrives	
5:45 P.M.	Volunteers in places	
6:00 P.M.–7:00 P.M.	Cocktail reception	
6:45 P.M.–6:55 P.M.	Reception patrons go to their seats	
7:00 P.M.–7:10 P.M.	Awards presentation on stage	
7:00 P.M.–9:00 P.M.	Dinner setup	
7:10 P.M.–7:57 P.M.	ACT I	
7:57 P.M.–8:12 P.M.	Intermission	

8:12 P.M.–9:17 P.M.	ACT II	
9:00 P.M.	READY for Dinner	
9:17 P.M.	Dinner	
10:00 P.M.	Gift-bag distribution starts	
11:30 P.M.	Dinner ends Load-out starts	
1:00 A.M.– 5:00 A.M.	Kitchen tent removal	

Robyn Williams uses the form on page 437 (fig. 11.2) to critique her events.[43–45]

CLASSROOM DISCUSSION

Define "event management."

Using Freedman's event management process as a model, create your own event and outline your process for executing it.

Create a sample event timeline.

Create a sample event critique.

FRONT-OF-HOUSE DUTIES

Front-of-house (FOH) duties include staffing and training the house manager, ushers, ticket takers, cleaning staff, and security staff.

The house manager is "responsible for the operation and maintenance of the theater during the performance, including the supervision of the front-of-house staff; providing assistance to the audience; verifying box office statements; preparing weekly payrolls; and supervising the security, maintenance, and emergency protocols of the premises during performances."[46] A facility manager "meets with the house manager on a regular basis to ensure that there is an ongoing high level of service to guests. He discusses staffing and the ongoing training of assistant managers and ushers by going over scheduling, special events, FOH budgets, cleaning, and security needs."[47]

Ushers "organize and distribute programs and inserts; greet and seat patrons; seat latecomers at appropriate times; answer patron questions; maintain a post in the lobby and in the theater at all times; keep management informed of the condition of the public areas of the theater; and report all accidents, hazards, trash, and unusual conditions immediately. Ticket takers take the tickets before patrons enter the theater and direct them to the appropriate seating location."[48] While Grossberg doesn't supervise the ushers directly, he "greets them on a regular basis at shows and ensures that they are: wearing proper uniforms; greeting and handling guests in a friendly and professional manner; and properly doing their jobs, such as tearing tickets and showing people to their seats. He also points out issues or problems to the house manager, so that he can take corrective action or give additional training to the ushers."[49]

The facility manager also hires the cleaning staff, processes their payroll, provides their schedules, and discusses the details of the specific event and its requirements with them. Shenin notes that, because the cleaning staff are often part-timers, "we need to budget for the dark period (days without shows), so we don't lose people. Housekeeping is critical to the operation. A clean facility is key to how the public sees you."[50] Grossberg says of his facility, "cleaners report to the house manager. I often tour the building with the cleaning supervisor and/or the house manager to ensure that all areas of the building are being properly maintained. I sometimes have meetings with all or part of the cleaning staff to resolve issues or questions that arise. I ensure that they are wearing proper uniforms at performances. If need be, I will request that special projects be undertaken by communicating with the house manager's office. It's important to make sure that water leaks, snow, ice, and slippery areas are cleared in a timely fashion."[51]

Fig. 11.2. Event Critique

EVENT: Rob Thomas   PROFILE: 5443
PERMITTEE: House of Blues Concerts, Inc.
DATE: 11/8/05   DAY: Tuesday
LOCATION: Arlene Schnitzer Concert Hall   TYPE OF EVENT: Concert

****

OF EVENT DAYS: 1   # OF PERFORMANCES: 1
OF INGRESS & EGRESS DAYS: 0[43]

ATTENDANCE: 2447
RESERVED OR NONRESERVED: Reserved
TICKETED OR NONTICKETED: Ticketed

TIME DOORS OPEN: 6:33 P.M.   TIME EVENT(S) STARTED: 7:25 P.M.
TIME INTERMISSION STARTED: 8:05 P.M.   TIME INTERMISSION ENDED: 8:33 P.M.
TIME EVENT ENDED: 10:28 P.M.   TIME FACILITY CLEAR: 11:36 P.M.*

WEATHER CONDITIONS: Partly cloudy and cool.
REPAIRS NEEDED: ATM machine went down at the end of intermission. (See below under "Special Problems.")
REQUEST SUBMITTED (YES OR NO): No
COMPLETENESS OF SETUP: Complete

EVENT PERSONNEL
TENANT HOUSE MANAGER: N/A   ADMISSIONS LEAD: Carol
FACILITY AGENT (NAME): Gene
PEER SECURITY (SUPERV. NAME & # OF AGENTS): Rod & 20
STAGEDOOR: Don   BOX OFFICE SUPERVISOR: Louise
ENGINEER: Lynn   OPERATIONS COORDINATOR: N/A   CUSTODIAN: Mary
CONCESSIONS SUPERVISOR (ARAMARK): Sara
FRONT-OF-HOUSE CATERING (COMPANY & MANAGER NAME): N/A
BACKSTAGE CATERING (COMPANY & MANAGER NAME): T.R.Y. Ventures/Toni
ADMISSIONS/COMMENTS: All Present
VOLUNTEERS/COMMENTS: N/A

OF INFRARED[44] USED: 0   W/AID: W/OUT AID: 0
OF RADIOS USED: 3
TIME BOX OFFICE TICKETS TURNED IN: 7:45 P.M.
SOUVENIR SALES: $2,220.00

DAMAGE TO FACILITY: None noted or reported
INJURIES OR ACCIDENTS: None reported
SPECIAL PROBLEMS: *Lengthy clear time due to CD signing by opening performer. 1. A woman using the ATM machine when it went down had requested $100.00 and received only $60.00 without a receipt. She was worried that the transaction would be listed as a $100.00 withdrawal. She was given the PCPA business number and was told to contact the box office if there is a discrepancy between what she received and what the bank records end up showing.
REPORT ON FILE (YES OR NO): No
AUDIENCE BEHAVIOR, COOPERATION OF PERMITTEE & COMMENTS: Good/Good/None
CONCESSIONS COMMENTS (ARAMARK): 1 bar on Orchestra, 1 bar on Mezzanine, both concessions stands open, and 1 beer station.
FRONT-OF-HOUSE CATERING COMMENTS: N/A
BACKSTAGE CATERING COMMENTS: No complaints.
CONTRACTORS OR OUTSIDE SERVICES COMMENTS: N/A

HOUSE MANAGER: Emerson Scott   DATE: 11/8/05   SHIFT: Evening

The Biltmore Theatre's theater manager, Valerie Simmons, issues post orders for the theater's security officers. At the Biltmore, "security officers are responsible for monitoring activities in the building to protect persons and property; preventing vandalism and other crimes; and monitoring fire alarm and security systems."[52]

At the end of the performance, the house manager submits a house management report to the facility manager. Two sample house management reports are shown in figs. 11.3 and 11.4.

Fig. 11.3. Ruth Eckerd Hall House Management Report[54]

House Management Report

EVENT Performer ABC
HALL Main Auditorium
DATE 11.19.05
PERFORMANCE TIME 8:00 P.M.
EVENT TYPE Opera
SEATING Reserved
DROP COUNT 1283[53] **ATD*** 1407

House Proper Open	7:31 P.M.
Act I—Curtain	8:05 P.M.
Intermission	8:35 P.M.
Act II	8:50 P.M.
Intermission	9:20 P.M.
Act III	9:50 P.M.
Show Ends	11:12 P.M.
Merchandise Sales**	$xxx.xx
Hall Closed	11:25 P.M.

On Duty

Police	Jones
Education	n/a
Finance	n/a
Food & Beverage	Pete Johnson
House Management	Sally Vickery
Marketing	May James
PAC Foundation	George Williams
Security	Casey/Dorian/Denver
Technical Operations	Kurt Seagrams
Ticket Office	Jane Mayflower

COMMENTS The show was busy with the two intermissions; however, everything went smoothly.

OCCURRENCES n/a

MAINTENANCE Blue Collar Comedy Poster in West Lobby needs to come down.

*ATD=Actual Tickets Distributed (paid and comp)
**For merchandise sales, this represents the amount of dollars (commissions) received by Ruth Eckerd Hall

Fig.11. 4. Westside Theatre House Management Report[55]

HOUSE MANAGER'S REPORT

SHOW:

WEATHER:

DAY/DATE:

TIME:

RUNNING TIME		
	Begin	**End**
ACT I		
INTERMISSION	mins.	
ACT II		
INTERMISSION	mins.	
ACT III		

ATTENDANCE BREAKDOWN		
Ticket Type	**Price**	**Amount**
Regular		
B - School		
E - Blast		
J - TKTS		
TOTAL		

HEADSETS:

LATE COMERS:

AIR CONDITIONING: ☐ Yes ☐ No

SUPPLY NOTES	TECHNICAL NOTES

GENERAL NOTES:

HOUSE MANAGER:

All of the facility managers interviewed for this chapter stressed the importance of providing customer service in the house. Simmons explains, "My main responsibility during the performance is customer service. Unlike in commercial Broadway theaters, half of our audience subscribes to Manhattan Theatre Club's season at the Biltmore, and Stages I and II at New York City Center. Because we rely on return customers, we endeavor to create an environment that will encourage them to renew and return each season. We train our front-of-house staff to be as helpful, knowledgeable, and polite as possible. We try to accommodate our audience by changing their locations, if preferable seating is available; offering a private lounge for patrons; and opening the lobby to give the audience an opportunity to socialize prior to the performance. Also, as is the case in most subscription-based organizations, a portion of our audience is older. As a result, they require more time and patience from the staff."[56]

Robyn Williams believes the tone for customer service begins at the top of the organization. "Since customer service starts at the top, I try to promote it as a facility philosophy in everything we do. Everyone is looked upon as a customer: those who patronize our facility, those who lease our facility, and every employee who serves these two groups. I encourage each staff member to create 'moments of magic,' to try to exceed each other's expectations."[57] Grossberg agrees: "The general manager should set the standard for customer service by example. At Brooklyn Center, each department head does customer training for its staff. I meet with the department heads, and we spend significant time going over customer service and making it a priority in all areas of the organization and facility. Any business is dependent on repeat customers. We have had clients that have been using our facility for ten, fifteen, and even over twenty years. We take care of everyone coming into our building as efficiently and as professionally as we can. We aim to resolve complaints and problems as well, and have a happy client or guest leaving a show or event."[58]

CLASSROOM DISCUSSION
What do front-of-house duties entail?
Why is customer service so important?
Give some examples of good customer service.
Give some examples of poor customer service.

BOX OFFICE AND TICKETING
Good customer service extends to the box office staff, which may be the first theater staff a customer encounters. Facility managers often have duties that extend to the box office. Purchasing and providing training on the latest software, reconciling box office statements and settlements, and protecting against theft are considered common box office duties.

Andrey Shenin notes that box office personnel must be familiar with the latest box office software. Robert Freedman specifies the ticketing systems at his facility: "Ruth Eckerd Hall uses the Tessitura computerized ticketing system for its ticket-selling services. Tickets from this system can be purchased in person at the ticket office, by phone to the facility, or through the Internet. (The amount of Internet sales has doubled over the last four years.) Ruth Eckerd Hall also takes advantage of remote outlet sales and contracts with Ticketmaster."[59] At the Biltmore, "the box office reports to the company manager. (However, house management works with the box office pre-curtain to resolve ticketing issues.) Each day's sales are reconciled (confirmed) in a 'wrap and advance report' prepared by the company manager, and monies are deposited daily via a security service. This report totals sales from all outlets—Telecharge, box office, and subscription income for the day (the 'wrap'), adds it to income for upcoming performances (the 'advance'), and compares it to previous productions and against current budget projections. To protect against theft, the box office statements are signed off on by the theater manager and the company manager, along with the box office treasurer for the day's performance and daily sales. Statements and deposit information are then forwarded to the finance office, where they are rechecked."[60]

Figure 11.5 provides a sample box office statement for a presenting or rental house. Note that the box office statement includes the following information: the season, production, and performance(s); the price code, number of seats sold in each price code, and revenue earned; payment methods, the number of seats sold by each payment method, and the revenue earned; the mode of sale, number of seats sold by each mode, and the revenue earned; gross sales, credit card commission, and net sales for the current performance and previous performances; the total gross and net sales of all performances; and the signatures of the company representative and venue representative.

Facility managers also work with the box office to generate settlements for the rental of the facility. Robyn Williams explains, "A settlement itemizes

Fig. 11.5. Sample Box Office Statement[61]

BOX OFFICE STATEMENT

Season: 2003-2004
Production: XYZ Dance Company
Performance(s): May 1, 2004

Price Code	Seats	Revenue
Comp	820	-
Discount A	2	$190
Discount B	3	$285
Discount C	9	$460
Regular	1135	$77,165
Student	10	$100
Senior	5	$50
TKTS	2	$100

Payment Method	Seats	Revenue
AMEX	65	$5,210
CASH	44	$2,185
MC	121	$10,313
VISA	119	$8,100
Misc	1637	$52,542

Mode of Sale	Seats	Revenue
Box Office	1125	$35,300
Phone	212	$10,600
Web	397	$19,850
Outlets	252	$12,600

	Gross Sales	Credit Card Commission	Net Sales
This Perf	$78,350	$1,315	$77,035
Played	$78,350	$1,315	$77,035
TOTAL	$78,350	$1,315	$77,035

Signature of Company Representative

Signature of Venue Representative

all of the expenses: rent, labor, equipment charges, and other event-related costs that are owed to the building. It will show any money paid, such as a deposit, or any ticket revenue we are holding. After subtracting the costs from the revenues, we will know if we owe the producer or if the producer owes us."[62] Freedman adds, "The settlement is accompanied by a box office statement, showing the sales for the event. The cost of the event (the billable settlement cost) will be deducted from the box office sales revenue being held by the facility, and a check will be issued to the lessee (renter). If the amount of box office revenue does not cover the cost of the event, then the user will be billed for the difference."[63] Please see appendixes K and L for sample settlements provided by the Portland Center for the Performing Arts and the Westside Theatre.[64]

CLASSROOM DISCUSSION

Prepare a sample box office statement. What information must be included?
What is a settlement? What information must be included? Prepare a sample settlement.

ANCILLARY INCOME

Ancillary income is earned income from nonperformance activities, such as concessions (food and beverage), parking fees, gift shops, rentals for receptions and other special events, merchandising (the selling of merchandise), and on-site restaurants. Grossberg states, "The house manager at Brooklyn Center is responsible for all of the areas that are considered ancillary income. He schedules staff, orders supplies, and coordinates merchandising with clients. [As general manager,] I am directly involved with all large special events or receptions for a client, and stay in close touch with the house manager to orchestrate a general policy for concessions, merchandising, and parking. I also handle the coordination of parking with the college security department so that there are no conflicts or problems with the parking on a college campus."[65]

Robyn Williams recommends that a facility manager "should not limit her thinking about the numerous ways to earn income. What was 'taboo' years ago is acceptable practice now, such as allowing your patrons to drink in the theater. With funding streams becoming more and more limited, we have to be creative and aggressive to capture every dime we can."[66]

Walter Thinnes remembers creating an ancillary revenue stream for the Philharmonic Center for the Arts in Naples, Florida: "I often hung out in various parts of the facility, trying to observe patterns and problems for patrons and performers. We made many small adjustments based on my observations. As I watched the intermission bars one night, I noticed a patron who had just gotten his coffee after a bit of a wait, but, as we only allowed water in the auditorium, he couldn't finish the hot beverage before returning to the hall and had to throw it away. I talked that night to our catering manager, as we were always looking for ways to improve service, and suggested we set up a coffee bar that sold little else to help people like this. He took it one step further, setting up two dedicated coffee bars that sold gourmet coffee, some liqueurs to provide a shot in the coffee (but no other mixed or bottled drinks), and some pastries like biscotti for dunking. We notified our patrons through program inserts and with signs at the regular bars, and it proved a big hit (and still is, some seventeen years later). The next month, the catering manager happily informed me that alcohol sales were up more than 30 percent. It turns out that by clearing some of the intermission bar lines of those who just wanted coffee, we were serving more regular drinkers at the intermission bars, where the lines were not as daunting. And as we controlled liquor sales in-house, rather than using an outside caterer, we were able to keep the considerable markup. The lesson to me as a young manager: Finding ways to better serve your patrons is rewarding in more ways than one."[67]

When considering ancillary income sources, a facility manager must also think about protection against theft. Richard Grossberg, Valerie Simmons, and Robyn Williams share their strategies for protecting against theft when employees and outside vendors are dealing with cash sales, and the facility is entitled to a percentage of the money collected. Grossberg states, "With regard to concessions and merchandising, we carefully control inventory by comparing it against sales. At the beginning of each show, we count all merchandise to be sold, and at the end of the show, we compare the remaining inventory against sales. Parking has consecutively numbered tickets that are issued for each car, so we can compare the number of tickets distributed against the cash that is collected from our parking operations. All cash is handled and counted by at least two staff people and deposited in a lockbox by a manager."[68]

Simmons shares her strategy: "The Biltmore has an agreement with an outside vendor to service the public bars. Each week, the bar manager provides me with a statement of income for the week. I receive a settlement and invoice for their total sales every month. After I have reconciled the statements, they are forwarded to the business office for payment or deposit. The concession company is responsible for any losses of product or money. The Biltmore also has a small gift shop. Its modest sales are handled by the theater's intern. Each day's sales are individually accounted for and held until the end of the week. An inventory report is then prepared to account for and reconcile the week's sales. The report is double-checked by the assistant house manager and then forwarded, with the deposit, to the business office. A copy of the inventory report is also given to the marketing office, as they are responsible for replenishing the inventory."[69]

And finally, Williams provides a procedure that is based on accounting principles: "Basically, we make sure that all the necessary checks and balances are in place. We follow generally accepted accounting procedures [GAAP]. This is particularly important when it comes to money handling. For example, you don't want just one person handling all of the cash. So if a concession worker closes out his till [cash drawer], you wouldn't want the same person verifying his sales and making the deposit. You want another person, preferably a manager or supervisor, to verify the sales with the worker. Both the manager and the worker will sign a sheet with the total cash listed. A third person will collect the money and deposit it. You need to have enough people involved to keep everyone honest. You need to have a written policy for reconciliation and deposit. Periodic audits will ensure that correct protocols are being followed. Unscheduled audits focus on how well we follow our own policies and procedures, and they are generally conducted by our finance department. This includes a review of receipts, inventories, contracts, settlement documents, payroll practices, deposits, and payment to vendors—anything involving money."[70]

CLASSROOM DISCUSSION
What is ancillary income?
How do facility managers protect against theft?

BACKSTAGE OPERATIONS
Facility managers must have a close working relationship with their production or technical manager. At Brooklyn Center, the production manager reports to the general manager: "The production manager is a senior staff person and one of the most critical members of my team. He ensures that all shows are supported technically and professionally, assigns all IATSE staff to the show, handles the production budget for the show, and ensures the artistic and technical quality of the show. All complex and large shows must be approved by the production manager before a contract can be finalized. Some shows may not physically fit or be technically possible within a facility. The production manager is often asked to sit in on final negotiations with a client before the rental contract is realized."[71] At the Biltmore, "the production manager oversees all aspects of getting the shows physically in and out of the theater. He coordinates the production schedule with me so that I can arrange security, cleaning, and maintenance coverage. The production managers schedule the stagehands for the shows. However, if I have a rental, a special event, or a building maintenance call, I must coordinate these activities with our stagehands."[72]

To ensure good communication with the production department, Grossberg has "regular staff meetings with the full-time staff members of the production department. We go over the production requirements for each large show, discuss any conflicts that might occur (e.g., an afternoon show running overtime and holding up the load-in for an evening show). We discuss problems that may have arisen at or during a show, and how to avoid those problems in the future. We talk about procedures and protocols that need to change to ensure smoother operations. If there are any particular security or safety questions, we discuss these as well."[73]

Grossberg also talks about his relationship with the stagehands: "I am one of the negotiators for the IATSE union contract and its renewals. I get to know all of our IATSE stagehands who regularly work for us, and treat them as important team members,

even if they are only part-time. It is important for the general manager to respect the stagehands for their skills and effort in putting on all of our shows and events. They are critical to having a satisfied client and a good show. I carefully monitor production labor expenses with the production manager. We honor and follow our contract with IATSE to ensure good labor relations. It pays off in mutual respect and good working conditions."[74]

Williams's involvement with production matters also concerns safety and the proper training of her crew. She explains, "I need to make sure that safety rules are followed. My crew heads must be well trained and need to stay current with the latest technical knowledge. The backstage is a dangerous place, so your staff must know what they are doing. Don't forget the backstage crew when it comes to training."[75]

Robert Freedman recognizes the importance of his technical director in describing the load-in and load-out process: "The load-in/load-out activity is that part of an event in which the traveling show brings its equipment off the trucks and onto the stage and sets up for the performance, and then at the end of the show breaks down the equipment or set and loads these items back onto the trucks.

"Typically a Broadway musical travels 'intact,' which means that the show will bring in the scenery, costumes, lighting, and sound equipment. Sometimes the show will use in-house lighting, particularly the front-of-house permanent positions. It is vital to review the technical riders for Broadway shows to understand the length of time that will be needed to load the show in to your theater. Most major Broadway shows, which typically might play an eight-performance-week, require the day before the first performance to bring the show in to the venue. Therefore, it is imperative that no event is scheduled in the theater the day before opening, and that the day be reserved as a load-in day for the show.

"A Broadway show will require the theater to do a fair amount of preparation prior to its arrival. Since the production is bringing all the scenery, mechanical, sound, and lighting equipment, it is required that the theater take out all its in-house equipment, such as the house hanging lighting equipment, sound towers (also called "stacks," which are several speaker boxes stacked on top of one another) and other speakers, stage curtains (with the exception of the house curtain), etc. This process is usually called a "strip." Many times the time and labor involved in the strip is borne by the theater entirely, but not in our case; we consider it a show expense. Similarly, the process of putting all the theater's equipment back in place once the show leaves is called the "restore." The cost of the restore is also most often assumed by the theater. In other words, at settlement time, you may not be allowed to deduct the strip and restore as local expenses. This item is subject to negotiation between the presenter and the show."[76] In contrast, at the Portland Center for the Performing Arts, the rental charges include the strip and restore.[77]

Freedman states, "Every show should be advanced by your technical staff. It is important to review the entire rider to be sure the amount of space needed for the show can be accommodated. Pay particular attention to the breakdown of the crew, determining how many stage carpenters, lighting technicians, sound technicians, wardrobe [staff], riggers, and loaders are required for the show. Loaders ([who] may be members of IATSE or the International Brotherhood of Teamsters) typically only unload or load the trucks before and after the show, and do not participate in the setup of the show. This will depend on whether you are a union (IATSE) house and the nature of the working conditions in the union contract. Pay attention to the length of each period of the load-in, and how it matches with your labor contract.

"You should be aware of when the trucks for the show will arrive. Sometimes the show could send the trucks early, and if you have another event that is loading in to your theater, this could cause a traffic jam. Therefore, it is necessary to be specific about when trucks and buses will arrive. If the show has a number of trucks greater than can be accommodated in your parking area, be sure to make the show aware that the trucks will have to move from the loading dock area once they are unloaded to allow additional trucks and the company's bus access to the loading dock and stage door. It is the theater's responsibility to have a place for trucks and buses to park.

"When buses are in your loading dock, it is best to have 'shore power'[78] available so that the buses and trucks do not have to 'run' their motors, which is not particularly good for the environment or neighbor relations, particularly if you are in an area that is residential or close to a residential area.

"Many times the same crew that serves as running crew for a show also loads out the show. Usually following the performance, the crew will need a break prior to beginning the load-out. There are ways to begin the load-out sooner, either by providing a meal (half an hour in length) to the running crew, or by paying a meal penalty to the crew. The tech director should be able to determine the best course to take in this regard."[79]

CLASSROOM DISCUSSION
Why is it important for the facility manager to have a good relationship with the production manager and the stagehands?

What is the role of the facility manager in production?

What is the role of the production manager or technical director?

What does the process of loading in and loading out the show entail?

Why is the production or technical rider important to backstage operations?

BUILDING OPERATIONS AND MAINTENANCE
The facility manager is responsible for the building's operations and its maintenance. Her duties may include all or some of the following: complying with codes and securing the necessary permits; working with systems engineers to make sure the systems are working properly; ongoing maintenance of the building and equipment; and consulting on renovations or capital improvements.

Complying with Codes and Securing Permits
Complying with codes (city and state rules and regulations, and the Life Safety Code[80]) and securing the necessary permits from the city and state to operate the facility coincide with maintaining the safety and security of the building for all occupants. James L. Harding, senior building construction engineer for the New York State Codes Division, recommends that "when you are developing an operations or construction plan for a building, it's best that you consult with a design professional (registered architect or professional engineer)."[81] The International Code Council (ICC) has created a series of codes that most cities and states have adopted. (Please see their Web site for more information, at *www.iccsafe.org*.) "The ICC offers a searchable version of the building codes in electronic form."[82] Each city's and state's code requirements may vary. The facility manager should check with the local code and permit authorities. Buildings in New York State (those buildings outside the New York City metropolitan area) must adhere to the following codes: Building Code of New York State, Fire Code of New York State, Residential Code of New York State, Plumbing Code of New York State, Mechanical Code of New York State, Fuel Gas Code of New

York State, Property Maintenance Code of New York State, and Energy Conservation Code of New York State.[83] In complying with the New York state and city codes, Simmons obtains the following permits for the Biltmore: the New York City Department of Buildings Public Assembly Permit, the Fire Department of New York (FDNY) Fire Alarm Permit, the FDNY HVAC Permit, the Marquee Permit, and the Department of Buildings Elevator Inspection report. "All permits are kept on file, readily accessible in the theater manager's office."[84]

"In New York State, all front-of-house personnel must have Public Assembly Fire Guard Certificates. These certificates are required in places of public assembly. Fire guards are responsible for making sure that all fire safety regulations are obeyed. They must have a good working knowledge of basic firefighting and fire protection. The fire safety director is responsible for maintaining the facility according to the latest fire codes. He conducts monthly training in evacuation procedures for the rest of the front-of-house staff."[85]

Meeting the fire safety codes is serious business. The Uniform Fire Prevention and Building Code (Uniform Code) is available from the International Code Council. At Brooklyn Center, Richard Grossberg complies with the code by making sure that "the use of open flame and fireworks on stage conforms to New York City regulations, and that a New York City Fire Department permit is obtained for all use of open flame or fireworks. All of the older curtains are treated so that they are flameproof. All newer curtains are now inherently flameproof for the life of the curtain, according to New York City regulations."[86]

At the time of the completion of its renovation in 2003, the Biltmore's "fire safety equipment was the most 'state-of-the-art.'" Simmons "maintains contracts with the fire alarm and fire extinguisher service companies to ensure that the system is regularly checked and serviced when needed to maintain required standards of operation. At the first technical rehearsal of each production, I give a presentation to the new company about emergency procedures at the Biltmore, and give each member a handout detailing the location of the exits, how to reach people, and what to do for different emergencies."[87]

Facility managers must also be aware of how the Americans with Disabilities Act (ADA), a federal regulation, impacts their facilities, and they must make sure they are in compliance. Newly constructed, renovated, or restored theaters occupied after January 26, 1993 must meet the architectural standards for accessibility. (The ADA Accessibility Guidelines can be found on the ADA Web site, *www.ada.gov*.) The Biltmore, a newly renovated facility, is ADA-accessible. Simmons states, "We possess an infrared listening system and a wheelchair lift to allow seating in the front of the orchestra; we also have separate wheelchair locations in the orchestra and mezzanine levels of the theater. When we have a wheelchair-bound person, a work order is distributed to the house manager, box office staff, and our prop head to remove the seat and install the wheelchair platform and companion chair if needed. While it's easier to do this if we have the information in advance, sometimes we have wheelchairs arrive without prior notice. We are fortunate that our seating and platform are relatively easy to remove and install. We try to hold a wheelchair location until the last moment, but because the platform absorbs four seat positions, we may sell those seats if the show is popular. That may require us to relocate audience members to accommodate the wheelchair."[88]

Working with Systems Engineers

The Biltmore Theatre "has three full-time building engineers who oversee and maintain the physical plant. Their responsibilities include the operation, daily monitoring, and/or maintenance of the HVAC system, hot water heaters, fire alarm system, electrical system, etc. They perform any minor repairs to the heat and hot water supply. All major equipment is under service contract to ensure regular maintenance and warranty compliance. The engineers are responsible for determining whether repairs can be done in-house or require outside service. For example, with the opening of the theater, there were initially some problems with maintaining water temperature and water pressure in the dressing room and wardrobe areas of the theater. It was deemed necessary to bring in professional plumbing assistance to investigate, identify the problems, and repair or replace the sections of the various plumbing systems in the building."[89]

Ongoing Maintenance

Robyn Williams has a building maintenance supervisor with the following responsibilities:

- Perform routine maintenance and repair on doors and door hardware.
- Repair and maintain locks and locksets and assist with access control, key duplication, and log maintenance.

- Perform routine maintenance and repair of seats, including anchors and seat hardware.
- Repair Sheetrock, plaster walls, ceilings, and moldings.
- Perform routine facility inspections; make notes and recommendations.
- Repair handrails, concrete moldings, marble, and stair treads.
- Assist with and supervise various maintenance projects.
- Supervise and assist with painting projects and maintain paint charts and coating inventories.
- Perform routine maintenance and repair of roofs, decks, carpets, and flooring.
- Supervise, review, and assist with contracted maintenance, as well as providing requests for proposals of contracted maintenance.
- Perform related duties and responsibilities as required.[90]

At the Biltmore, "any painting or repair of walls or building fixtures is done by the props department; any repair of doors or hardware is done by our carpenters. Depending on the extent of the work, it is scheduled to be done either on the pre-show call, or on a separate work call during the day. Cleaning work (e.g., windows, upholstery, carpet cleaning) is done on a periodic basis by the building cleaners per my instructions. Specialized work is done by outside vendors (electricians, plumbers, etc.)."[91]

Building Renovations and Capital Improvements

Because facility managers have an in-depth understanding of the day-to-day operations of the building, they must be involved when the theater is scheduled for renovations and capital improvements. The consequences of disregarding the facility manager's advice can lead to design flaws that compromise the integrity and successful operation of the building's intended use. This involvement should begin at the top of the organization. Robyn Williams explains, "I am highly involved. Currently, I'm in the feasibility stage of such a project. I have selected the consulting team, written the scope of the study, developed the budget, participated in all meetings, selected the architect, and signed all of the contracts. In particular, the facility manager has to pay attention to the design phase; she must analyze and understand the design. Design flaws cost you money or business. Since project monies are generally exhausted by the end of the project, you end up living with the problem."[92]

Richard Grossberg has been involved with the renovation and restoration of two theaters at Brooklyn Center. He emphasizes, "The facility manager must be involved in any and all renovation work done in the space he or she manages. No one knows better what needs to be done, what the priorities are, and how the available renovation budget can be most effective. I was in all of the meetings with the architects and budget people to discuss priorities, the time schedule, and what specific work needed to be accomplished; I was also in the weekly meetings to monitor the progress of the work. I gave input as to what was needed, the use of materials, the priority of the work, and how the available budget was to be spent. When something needed to be cut for budget reasons, I was also consulted as to what part of the budget should be eliminated."

"A serious design flaw in a building can be costly from many points of view. It can cost much more in labor expenses to make up for the design flaw. For instance, if a truck does not have direct access to a stage, you would need more labor hours to load and unload the show. A really bad design flaw, like the wrong size doors or hallways, could prevent a piano or key piece of scenery from being able to be loaded onto the stage. And how do you get heavy costume trunks and equipment to the second-floor dressing rooms without an elevator?"[93]

At New York City Center, Andrey Shenin is expected to sit in on meetings with his colleague, the senior director of facilities and capital planning, when they meet with architects designing the renovation or restoration of the building. Shenin is asked to provide input as to how to make the theater "more patron-friendly, and how to make the visiting companies' spaces feel more like home." He suggested that they consider "adding another elevator, creating more restrooms, and enlarging the lobby space."[94] The original theater, built many years ago, did not provide "enough legroom, restrooms, catering spaces, elevators, or stage left wing space. These design flaws limit our ability to provide the best service possible."[95]

Working in theaters that were once operating as movie theaters, or theaters deemed to have historical significance and given landmark status by the city or federal government, raises challenges for facility managers. Valerie Simmons has experience working in theaters that fit this definition. She reveals that the "renovation and restoration of these types of buildings may be confined to the structure that already exists. However, an architect's design can improve the auditorium areas for better viewing of dance and theater; create new spaces that allow for better audience accommodations, such as more restrooms and lounge areas; and provide state-of-the-art technical equipment."[96]

For newer theaters, Walter Thinnes adds, "A theater architect must understand how the Americans with Disabilities Act will influence the design of an auditorium and the arrangement of the seats in the auditorium. In addition, when designing a new theater, the needs of every staff member must be taken into consideration. For example, stagehands and ushers need locker rooms so that they can store their personal items and change into their uniforms. Without designing personal space for these essential employees, you may have to use other space in the theater that was originally designed for other uses."[97] Also, Grossberg notes, "the design of a theater should consider the proximity of the scenery, props, costumes, and storage area to the stage and performance areas."[98]

Robert Freedman has overseen the construction or renovation of a facility in every position he has ever had. "At Ruth Eckerd Hall, I directly oversaw the construction of a performing arts institute attached to Ruth Eckerd Hall, as well as the renovation of a twenty-year-old facility designed, with Frank Lloyd Wright's architectural concepts and ideas, by his son-in-law, William Wesley Peters.

"The renovation process occurred in several phases. Phase one was hiring an architect and a theater consultant to review the facility and to make recommendations to me and the key Ruth Eckerd Hall staff, based on programmatic outcomes and needs. We formed a facilities committee that served as a board oversight committee during the entire construction process; it reviewed construction budgets and made recommendations to the board regarding necessary motions needed during the construction process, such as the engaging of the construction manager, the approval of construction budgets, and the review of any architectural programmatic changes.

"My role included reviewing initial architectural drawings and recommending changes as needed; reviewing construction documents; and generally overseeing the total construction and renovation process with the architect and theater consultant. This included review of all technical systems, including: lighting, sound, stage equipment, functional capabilities of the various rooms in the performing arts institute, HVAC issues, life/safety issues, and ADA compliance. This could not have been accomplished without a terrific and knowledgeable staff, which was included in every part of the process.

"The program—the types of performances and activities in the facility—for Ruth Eckerd Hall was already established. So my primary role was to ensure that the renovation of Ruth Eckerd Hall was going to meet the programmatic needs of the organization, taking into account audience amenities, backstage amenities, technical upgrades, and the construction of the Marcia P. Hoffman Performing Arts Institute. 'Amenities' can be defined as anything that helps increase the comfort of your patrons, employees, clients, and artists. Improvements in patron restrooms, additional standing areas around concession stands, and comfortable seats are all examples of audience amenities. Backstage amenities include additional star dressing rooms, improved load-in and load-out capabilities, better catering facilities, and so forth.

"In our case, a great deal of attention was paid to the look and feel of the facility. We upgraded our interior design to improve the audience and artist response to the facility. Attention was given to improving the lobby areas, including creating significant additional rest rooms and lobby spaces; by creating a Grand Concourse connecting the two sides of the theater, we doubled lobby space and concession areas. My operations knowledge was useful in understanding audience traffic flow, intermission procedures, and the need to improve concession and merchandising services.

"As design flaws can impact operations to a major degree, a year was spent in planning the new construction and the renovation of Ruth Eckerd Hall. Every level of staff involved in operations was involved in the process. That factor, combined with an excellent theater consultant, helped create a project that had the most minimal of design flaws and significantly improved the operation of the facility. We have had nothing but significant praise for this project from audience [members], artists, our board of directors, and the staff who use the facility.

"But I have seen instances where design flaws can impact an operation. There are stories in the industry of designing acoustical shells that are so heavy that the stage floor cannot support the shell. In another facility, I saw where the design of the third balcony did not allow patrons to see most of the stage. In this instance, it was necessary to significantly reduce the ticket pricing in that area of the theater. Obviously, this affects the earned income ability of the organization."[99]

CLASSROOM DISCUSSION

With regard to building operations and maintenance, what are the primary responsibilities of a facility manager?

What is the International Code Council?

What types of codes are enforced in theater buildings?

What types of permits must a theater have to operate?

What is a Public Assembly Fire Guard Certificate?

What is the ADA, and how does it apply to public facilities?

What is the role of the systems engineer?

What types of ongoing maintenance must be managed in a facility?

Why must a facility manager be involved in building renovations and construction?

Describe the process of a well-managed renovation. Name three serious design flaws and discuss their consequences.

NOTES

1. The authors would like to thank Terry Byrne, Robert Freedman, Richard Grossberg, David Kissel, Andrey Shenin, Valerie Simmons, Walter Thinnes, Gina Vernaci, and Robyn Williams for their contributions to this chapter.
2. The authors would like to thank Manhattan Theatre Club, Portland Center for the Performing Arts, and Ruth Eckerd Hall for granting us permission to reprint these job descriptions and charts.
3. The authors would like to thank Westside Theatre for granting us permission to reprint this manual.
4. Richard Grossberg, e-mail interview to author, September 1, 2006.; Valerie Simmons, e-mail interviews to author, March 7, 2006 and August 22, 2006.
5. Gina Vernaci, e-mail interviews to author, November 1, 2005, February 16, 2006, and February 20, 2006. A "probationary period" is a trial period during which the new employee is evaluated in his fitness for the job.
6. Andrey Shenin, e-mail interviews to author, December 12, 2005 and April 27, 2006.
7. Richard Grossberg, "E-mail interview."
8. At the time of publication, Valerie Simmons is the director of operations for Frederick P. Rose Hall, home of Jazz at Lincoln Center.
9. Valerie Simmons, "E-mail interview."
10. Robert Freedman, e-mail interviews to author, November 27, 2005, April 19, 2006, and April 20, 2006.
11. Robyn Williams, e-mail interviews to author, November 21, 2005 and April 20, 2006.
12. Robert Freedman, e-mail message to author, February 28, 2007.
13. Simmons, "E-mail interview."
14. Ibid.
15. Shenin, "E-mail interview."
16. Simmons. The authors would like to thank Manhattan Theatre Club for granting us permission to reproduce this document.
17. Shenin.
18. Ibid.
19. Freedman, "E-mail interview."
20. Grossberg, "E-mail interview."
21. A meal penalty is the financial penalty incurred by a venue when work exceeds a certain period of time and runs into contractually stated meal times.
22. Freedman.
23. Walter Thinnes, e-mail interview to author, September 1, 2006.
24. Freedman.
25. Simmons.
26. Shenin.
27. Ibid.
28. Williams, "E-mail interview."
29. The authors wish to thank Ruth Eckerd Hall for granting us permission to publish this form.
30. Freedman.
31. Andrey Shenin defines aggregate insurance: "Insurance against all losses and claims for personal injuries, and fire and theft insurance for full replacement value of all scenery, costumes, electrical and sound equipment, literary and musical material, and all other properties and materials owned, rented, or brought into the Premises by Company."
32. Shenin.
33. The authors want to thank Robert Freedman for granting us permission to publish the Ruth Eckerd Hall theater usage policy.
34. Williams.
35. The authors want to thank Andrey Shenin for creating a sample technical rider.
36. Shenin.
37. Grossberg.
38. Ibid.
39. Freedman.
40. Williams.
41. Freedman.
42. The authors wish to thank Andrey Shenin for creating this sample event timeline.
43. Robyn Williams defines the terms "ingress/egress days" as load-in and load-out days.
44. Robyn Williams defines the term "infrared," as "infrared hearing impaired devices."
45. The authors wish to thank Portland Center for the Performing Arts for granting us permission to publish this event critique.
46. Shenin.
47. Grossberg.
48. Shenin.
49. Grossberg.
50. Shenin.
51. Grossberg.
52. Manhattan Theatre Club, Biltmore Theatre Post Orders, January 2006.
53. Robert Freedman defines the term "drop count": "A drop count is a standard industry term. It derives from when ticket stubs were (as they still mostly are) dropped into a ticket box. The ticket stubs are then counted to determine the drop (the stubs dropped in the box) count.

Drop counts are important for many reasons. As part of your insurance premiums, you pay a cost for each person attending your facility. For any given show, there may be people who purchased tickets or were given a complimentary ticket but did not attend the performance. You want to pay the insurance premium on the number of people that actually attended the performance, and not necessarily on the number of tickets printed and distributed. Also, when you are 'settling' with a show, insurance costs can be a deducted itemized expense. The show will usually only allow the deductions on the drop count, ranging these days from 20 to 40 cents per person attending. The drop count is also a way of assessing the accuracy of a ticket report or box office statement. There should not be a large discrepancy between the drop count and the ticket office settlement or statement. If it seems there are more people attending than reported on the ticket office report, then one might consider that not everything is being reported on the amount of ticket sales."

54. The authors wish to thank Ruth Eckerd Hall for granting us permission to publish this form.

55. The authors wish to thank Westside Theatre for granting us permission to publish this form. Ticket types: R: Regular price or full box office price; B: School or school ticket discount program (those discount slips that are mailed to educational institutions); D: Telecharge e-mail blast or discount to frequent theatergoers who buy through Telecharge; F: Rush, a discount offered to students with a valid ID at curtain time; J: TKTS discounts of either 25 or 50 percent offered at the Theatre Development Fund's Duffy Square booth on the day of the show; M: Mania, a discount offered through TheaterMania to their loyal buyers; N: Blast, a discount e-blasted through another theater club, like *Playbill* Online; W: Staff, a discount offered to friends and family of the cast, crew, and staff of the show; X: TDF, a ticket sold at a discount through Theatre Development Fund to seniors, students, teachers, and other qualifying members; Y: NCTD (National Corporate Theatre Fund), a discount offered to large corporations (ticket buyers must present card or code); Z: SVM (SVM Corporate Marketing, now Plum Benefits), a corporate discount program similar to NCTD.

56. Simmons.

57. Williams.

58. Grossberg.

59. Freedman.

60. Simmons.

61. The authors wish to thank Andrey Shenin for creating this sample box office statement.

62. Williams.

63. Freedman.

64. The authors wish to thank Portland Center for the Performing Arts and Westside Theatre for granting us permission to publish these settlement reports.

65. Grossberg.

66. Williams.

67. Thinnes, "E-mail interview."

68. Grossberg.

69. Simmons.

70. Williams.

71. Grossberg.

72. Simmons.

73. Grossberg.

74. Ibid.

75. Williams.

76. Freedman.

77. Williams.

78. Robert Freedman defines the term "shore power": "Shore power is a seafaring term. When a ship or boat docks, it plugs its electrical system into a power source on land, at the dock, or on shore. Similarly, when a bus or truck is parked in your loading dock, it can plug its electrical system into the theater's electrical outlets if the theater has made provisions for this. This way the bus or truck can use its lights and air-conditioning systems without running its motor."

79. Freedman.

80. Robyn Williams defines the Life Safety Code: "It was established by the National Fire Protection Association, which sets standards for fire safety. (For example, keeping the aisles free and clear, or having the minimum number of ushers needed for an evacuation in case of fire.)"

81. James L. Harding, e-mails to Tobie Stein and Cristin Kelly, February 6, 2007 and February 17, 2005.

82. Ibid.

83. Ibid. New York City codes are available through the New York City Department of Buildings.

84. Simmons.

85. Shenin.

86. Grossberg.

87. Simmons.

88. Ibid.

89. Ibid.

90. The authors would like to thank Robyn Williams for providing us with the building maintenance supervisor job description.

91. Simmons.

92. Williams.

93. Grossberg.

94. Shenin.

95. Ibid.

96. Simmons.

97. Thinnes.

98. Grossberg.

99. Freedman.

APPENDIX A: Theater Manager Job Description, Manhattan Theatre Club/Biltmore Theatre (Producing Organization)

PROPOSED JOB DESCRIPTION
THEATRE MANAGER (as of 6/30/03)

REQUIREMENTS:
> Certified CPR/First Aid
> Certificates of Fitness for Fire Guard, Fire Drill Conductor, Sprinkler System and Fire Alarm System

OBJECTIVE:
The Theatre Manager's main responsibility would be the supervision and management of the Biltmore Theatre's staff and operations and the continual upkeep and maintenance of the theatre, constantly monitoring and maintaining the facilities in terms of safety, federal and state law compliance, and staff, audience and artist comfort.

FACILITIES MANAGEMENT/BUILDING OPERATIONS

Develop, monitor and implement functional management systems for all theatre operations.

Oversee all front of house and backstage operations, maintenance staff and outside contractors and workers.

Supervise maintenance, engineer/building supervisor and cleaning staff at the Biltmore: prepare and coordinate schedules; monitor quality of cleaning, order and maintain cleaning supplies; authorize, coordinate and supervise repairs; prepare and authorize payroll

Establish and maintain communications with other departments to determine facilities and operations needs.

Review and monitor relationships with building vendors and service contractors on annual maintenance agreements and building repairs

Prepare and oversee theatre maintenance annual departmental operating budgets with General Manager, Director of Finance and Production Manager/Director of Capital Projects.

Ensure compliance with building department and fire department codes, DEP, health department, where applicable

Ensure ongoing compliance with ADA

Monitor, maintain and ensure building security needs at the Biltmore

Maintain current operations permits
The many permits required to operate the facilities must be maintained. Expiration dates must be monitored or fines can be levied by the dispensing organizations. In addition to Certificates of Fitness or Dept. of Health Food Certificates for staff members and permanent copies of the buildings' Certificate of Occupancy, we are required to have current:

@ The Biltmore Theatre

Place of Assembly Permit
Fire Department Permits for Boiler and Roof AC units
Marquee Permit
State Liquor License
Department of Health Retail Food Permit
Special Tax Stamp for Retail Liquor Sales
DEP Certificate of Boiler Operation
Annual Boiler Inspection Report
Petroleum Bulk Storage Registration Certificate

Develop, monitor and maintain annual operations, maintenance and capital budgets for the Biltmore in conjunction with the General Manager, Director of Finance and Production Manager/Director of Capital Projects.

Work closely with contractors and architects on improvements and changes to the facilities. Participate in the coordination and oversight of capital and maintenance projects and the planning of future additional facilities with Production Manager/Director of Capital Projects.

Appendix A (continued)

<u>FRONT OF HOUSE</u>

Oversee all Front-of-House Operations in concert with House Manager (Assistant House Manager?), including hiring, training, scheduling and supervision of FOH staff: Assistant House Manager, ticket takers and ushers; supervision of maintenance of bar and concessions at performances and liaison with concessions/merchandise operator; ordering and maintaining of all supplies and equipment.

Prepare and oversee Front-of-House annual departmental operating budget with General Manager, Director of Finance, and Production Manager/Director of Capital Projects

Establish and maintain communications with other departments

Coordinate operations with production staff and box office; ensure smooth operations and prompt starting time

Monitor air temperature

Ensure first-rate customer service to all donors, subscribers, and single ticket buyers

Handle patron complaints and problems

Calculate daily payroll and approve concessions, bar and merchandising statements from concessionaire

Submit weekly payroll for FOH, building staff and stage crew

Approve weekly bar, concessions and merchandise reconciliations

Review and amend, where appropriate, departmental policies and procedures

Coordinate and supervise receptions, special events (including dark night events), and rentals, including invoices and collection

Ensure building is empty and secure before departing

Handle emergencies relating to the building and/or audience.

In absence of House Manager (Asst House Manager?), serve as House Manager at performances and assume all related responsibilities.

APPENDIX B: Operations Manager Job Description, Portland Center for the Performing Arts

A SERVICE OF METRO

Classification Description

OUR VISION:
To be the acknowledged leader in public assembly venue management in the region

OUR MISSION:
To enhance the livability and economic vitality of the metropolitan region through sound stewardship, expert management and creative development of the region's public assembly venues

OUR VALUES:
Respect ~ Excellence ~ Teamwork ~ Innovation ~ Community

Job Title	Operations Manager - PCPA	Bargaining Unit	Non-represented
Functional Job Family	Operations	Classification #	8165
FLSA	☒ Exempt ☐ Non-Exempt	Salary Grade #	326
Position Status	☒ Full-time ☐ Part-time	Revision Date	May 2007

Summary:

Manage the daily operations of building maintenance, grounds maintenance, custodial services and security. Oversee event setup and teardown. Develop and implement appropriate policies, programs and services to ensure effective utilization of resources and regulatory compliance. Serve as member of management team.

Essential Functions:

- Manage, supervise and coordinate the activities of staff involved in all aspects of building maintenance, grounds maintenance, custodial services, security and stage-related services.

- Oversee and manage the setup and tear-down of events and shows; oversee the coordination of events/shows with clients, promoters, exhibiters, vendors and contractors.

- Plan, direct, coordinate and review department plan; monitor and evaluate processes, methods and procedures; document and prepare reports.

- Manage and participate in the development of goals and objectives, policies and priorities of assigned programs and functions.

- Coordinate and manage capital projects with vendors, contractors and consultants; obtain bids and quotes; negotiate contracts.

- Prepare and manage department budget.

- Ensure work is performed in compliance with codes, ordinances, regulations, and other requirements, including but not limited to, Leadership in Environmental and Energy Design Certification (LEED), and OSHA.

Secondary Functions:

- Conduct organizational studies and recommend modifications to maintenance programs, policies and procedures.

- Other duties which may be necessary or desirable to support the agency's success.

APPENDIX C: Director of Operations Job Description, Ruth Eckerd Hall

JOB DESCRIPTION
RUTH ECKERD HALL, INC.

POSITION:	Director of Operations	**STATUS:**	Exempt
DEPARTMENT:	Operations	**PAY GRADE:**	
REPORTS TO:	President	**MINIMUM:**	
EFFECTIVE DATE:	August, 2003	**MAXIMUM:**	

POSITION CONCEPT:

Direct and supervise event services, food and beverage, and all technical mechanical and physical plant systems for mainstage and education productions including the facility's general day-to day operation, event auxiliary services such as security, parking services, maintenance staff, contracted housekeeping.

DUTIES:
> *Indicates essential functions of the position.*

> Plan, direct and oversee the delivery of services in the areas of Technical Operations, Environmental Operations, Security, Event Services and Food & Beverage.

> In conjunction with subordinate staff establish goals and objectives.

> Ensure preparation and adherence to expense and revenue budgets for assigned departments as well as specific show budgets.

> Provide the President of Ruth Eckerd Hall, Inc. and its Board, as well as the Board of the Foundation, with routine reports as required to ensure smooth operations.

> Works closely with Director of Entertainment and Director of Education to ensure facility and technical requirements are met.

> Assist President with oversight of construction project.

> Administer the union labor contract as to daily usage, interpretation and long-term effect. Negotiate contract renewals.

> Advance events with road personnel and respond to requests for support services from appropriate subordinate staff as well as accounting or other departments.

> Professionally represent Ruth Eckerd Hall, Inc. at all times.

> Complete all other duties as assigned.

APPENDIX D: Organizational Chart, Manhattan Theatre Club, Biltmore Theatre

MANHATTAN THEATRE CLUB
BILTMORE THEATRE
ORGANIZATION CHART

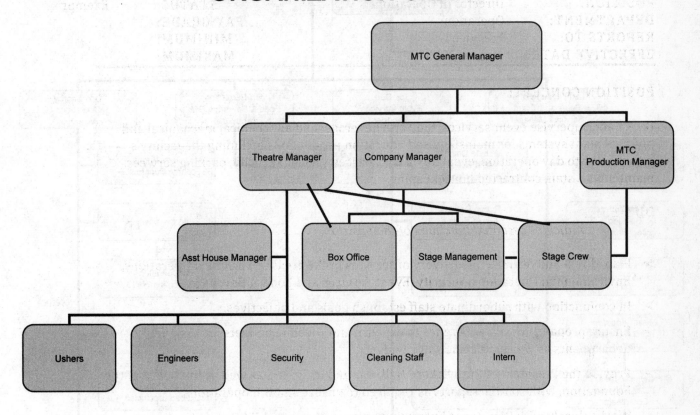

APPENDIX E: Organizational Chart, Portland Center for the Performing Arts

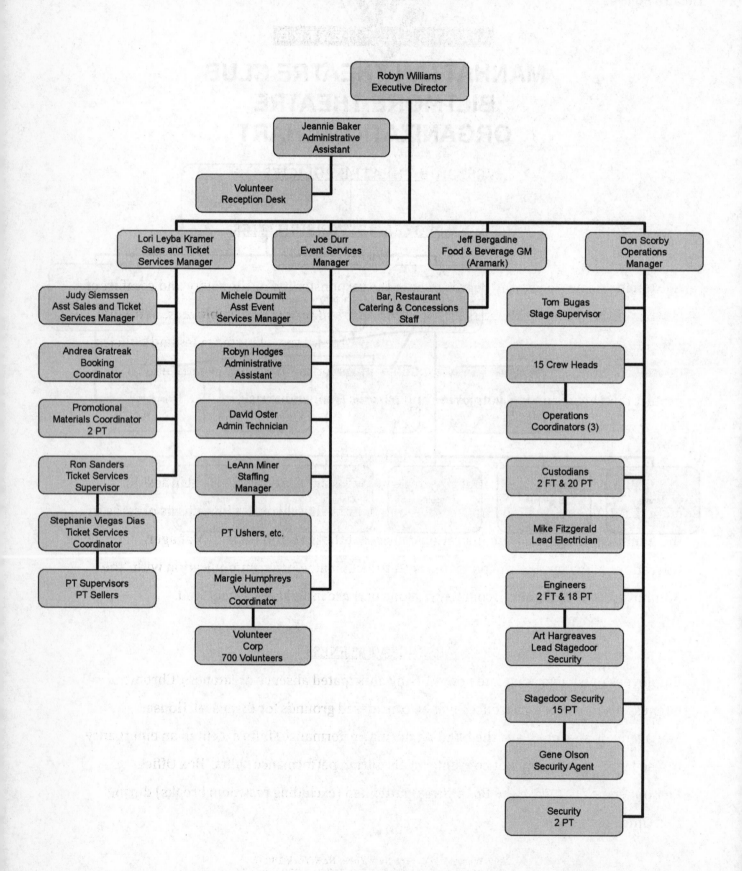

**APPENDIX F: Westside
Theatre Policies**

WESTSIDE THEATRE POLICIES

PART I: EMPLOYEE RESPONSIBILITIES

GENERAL

All staff members, to varying degrees, share the responsibility for the safety and comfort of
patrons of the Westside Theatre, fellow employees, and production employees. Westside
Theatre employees are expected to adhere to and enforce the following rules and policies
in order to project a proficient and hospitable image for the Westside Theatre and to
protect the Theatre and its employees and patrons from undue risk.

HOUSE RULES

See "Exhibit A: House Rules" attached. All employees are expected to do their best to
enforce compliance with the House Rules and to immediately report infractions of same to
the Administration. The Administration consists of the Director, General Manager,
Operations Manager. For the purposes of this document, when communication with "the
Administration" is required, contact with one of these individuals is required.

ABSENCES/LATENESS

Employees must give adequate notice of any anticipated absence or lateness. Chronic
lateness or unapproved absences will be considered grounds for dismissal. House
Management may not leave the building during performance shifts except in an emergency.
House Management may not consume meals during performance shifts. Box Office
Personnel may not leave the Box Office unattended (excluding restroom breaks) during
Box Office hours.

Appendix F (continued)

RECORD KEEPING AND REPORTING

Administration will inform each department of the reports or records which are required. Reports are expected to be accurate, complete, and to be filed in a timely manner, with a signature when required. Time sheets are required for payment of overtime hours and substitute's hours, and must be signed by a member of the Administration.

DRESS CODE

Box Office and House Management staff are expected to be dressed appropriately. Suggested attire includes comfortable shoes, neat pants, collared shirts, ties, jackets or sweaters for men; comfortable shoes, neat pants, skirts, dresses, jackets, sweaters for women. Almost anything that is not blatantly controversial is fine but blue jeans, tee shirts, athletic footwear and sandals are excluded. Hair style and facial hair should be well kept. Identifying badges, provided by the Theatre, must be worn prominently by all House Management staff and Ushers during working hours.

NON-DISCRIMINATION AND ANTI-HARASSMENT POLICY

The Administration of The Westside Theatre is committed to a work environment in which all individuals are treated with respect and dignity. Attached (Exhibit B: A Non-Discrimination and Anti-Harassment Policy) is a document defining harassment on the job, and outlining the complaint procedure for individuals to follow who have experienced conduct which they believe is contrary to the Theatre's policy.

ALCOHOL AND DRUG USE

The consumption of alcoholic beverages and/or the use of illegal drugs or controlled substances while on duty is unacceptable. Likewise, coming to work under the influence of alcohol or illegal drugs is equally unacceptable. Any violation of this policy is grounds for immediate dismissal.

Westside Theatre POLICIES
June 2006

TERMINATION

Employees should make best efforts to give at least two weeks= written notice of resignation. The Administration will make best efforts to give two weeks' written notice of termination, except when a production gives less than two weeks' notice, or when circumstances require the immediate dismissal of an employee. In either case, it should be understood that each party will be better prepared for the future when more notice is given.

PART II: EMPLOYEE BENEFITS

Intentionally deleted.

PART III: THEATRE ADMISSION POLICIES

SHUBERT TICKETING SERVICES BAR-CODE PDA SCANNERS

Shubert Ticketing Services (aka. Tele-Charge.com) has provided the Westside Theatre with 6 PDAs which scan Bar-Code information on tickets and e-tickets. The scanners establish the validity of tickets and e-tickets presented for admission and display admissions information which is shared with the Box Office through the Tele-Charge computer system. The PDAs can only be operated after signing on with Barcode Cards issued by Shubert Ticketing Services. The General Manager, Operations Manger, as well as each House Management Staff member, are issued Barcode Cards. In addition, two cards have been issued for use by substitutes. It is the Shubert Ticketing Policy and the Westside Theatre Policy that only the individual who has signed on to a PDA should operate it. By way of example, a House Manager should not give his/her card to a Substitute Assistant House manager to sign on to a PDA. The House Manager must give the substitute a substitute card and note the substitute's name on the House Management report.

No PDA should be left unattended, and the House Management offices should always be locked in order to secure the Shubert equipment, as well as the Theatre's property.

Appendix F (continued)

Westside Theatre POLICIES
June 2006

ADMISSION/REFUND/EXCHANGE GUIDELINES

Every individual (including children—no "lap sitting") entering the Theatre must have a valid, bona-fide ticket for admission to any performance or attraction. Admitting an individual to the Theatre without a ticket is considered grounds for dismissal. It is the responsibility of the ticket taker (generally the Assistant House Manager) to verify that the ticket is valid for the performance in question by scanning the ticket prior to admitting the patron. Only the Box Office may issue a **Location Pass** after verifying the patron's right to use the seats in question. Patrons presenting tickets for seats occupied by Location Pass holders take precedence, unless the Location Pass holders can produce adequate proof of purchase.

No standing or sitting in the aisles is permitted. Latecomers will be seated at the discretion of the House Manager.

No refunds or exchanges of tickets are permitted for a performance that takes place on schedule. The Theatre does have a **"Past Date Policy,"** which is a courtesy to patrons who have been unable to attend the performance. Those patrons interested in "past-dating" their tickets must call the Box Office after 12:00 noon on the day of the performance they wish to attend to ascertain the availability of tickets. If, **at the reasonable discretion of the Box Office staff**, seats will be unused at curtain time, the patron may come to the Box Office to **replace** their "past-date" tickets with complimentary tickets for that performance. **They must have the "old" tickets with them or confirm that the Box Office is holding their tickets in the "past-date" file. No past-date arrangements may be made in advance.**

BLIND PATRONS

For obvious reasons, special attention must be paid to blind patrons. House Management should confirm that blind patrons are adequately escorted to and from their seats. Ideally, the Box Office or Tele-charge will be informed that tickets are being purchased by or for a

Westside Theatre POLICIES
June 2006

blind patron, and the party can be sold tickets on an aisle, and near an exit. However, this is not always the case, so the House Manager and Box Office should make best efforts to rearrange seating as necessary when the blind patron arrives so that the individual is as close to an aisle and exit as possible. Seeing Eye Dogs may be admitted when they accompany blind patrons. Best efforts should be made to arrange for an empty seat next to the blind patron, so that the dog may have as much room as possible to lie down. For the safety of all, please try to avoid putting the dog in the aisle.

HEADSETS

Both Theatres are equipped with Sennheiser Infrared sound reinforcement systems. House Managers and Box Office staff should inform patrons that the headsets only operate well from the 3rd row back. There are some dead spots in the Downstairs Theatre. House Management and Box Office staff should determine where the headsets do not work well and inform patrons. The headsets are available free of charge to patrons on a first-come, first-served basis. Patrons must present some sort of valid I.D. with their address (such as a driver's license.) If their I.D. does not have an address, an address and phone number must be obtained. Please do not accept credit cards, due to security reasons.

CHILDREN IN THE THEATRE

House Rule #12 states that "no children under the age of sixteen shall be brought into the Theatre." This rule applies to individuals other than ticket holders. With respect to ticket holders, and in order to insure an atmosphere free from distractions, no child under four years of age may be admitted to the Theatre at any time unless approved in advance by the Administration. Patrons may be issued a refund or an exchange if they arrive at the Theatre with a child under four. Consult the Company Manager for each production's policy on the sale of a ticket or admission to the Theatre of children over four. For children between the ages of four and sixteen, it is appropriate to speak to the parent/guardian prior to curtain and to advise them that a disruption caused by the child may result in the expulsion of their party. A patron who has elected to attend the performance and is subsequently asked to

Appendix F (continued)

Westside Theatre POLICIES
June 2006

leave because of a disruptive child is not eligible for a refund. A patron may be issued a refund if he/she deems the show inappropriate for an older child (aged 4–16), but must make the request to the House Manager or Box Office before the show begins. Refunds in this instance will be at the discretion of the Company Manager. A patron who has elected to attend any portion of the performance with an older child is not eligible for a refund.

PHOTOGRAPHS/RECORDING

Patrons who are caught in the act of **taking pictures of the stage, with or without actors present, or making a sound/video recording during a performance** should be handled as follows:

1. Inform the patron that they are in violation of copyright laws. There is a warning in the PLAYBILL, as follows:

WARNING:

The photographing or sound recording of any performance or the possession of any device for such photographing or sound recording inside this theatre, without the written permission of the management, is prohibited by law. Violators may be punished by ejection and violations may render the offender liable for money damages.

2. Ask for the patron to turn over the film, disposable camera, videotape or audio tape. Warn them that they may be asked to leave if they refuse. In general, do not put yourselves at any physical risk on such an issue. Most people will comply with your request, but if you meet with resistance, do not force an altercation.

3. Sound or videotape recordings will not be returned under any circumstances. Inform the patron that they may retrieve the camera or recording equipment from you after the performance. When the patron comes for the device, ask them to delete the photo or recording or remove the film or tape for you. It is important that you do not operate the equipment so that they cannot claim that you damaged it. Explain that you are required by the producers and theatre management to confiscate the film, video or recording tape, and it cannot be returned to them under any circumstances.

Westside Theatre POLICIES
June 2006

4. Patrons who have taken photographs in the theatre before the show or after the curtain call should be asked to refrain from doing so; however, it is not necessary to confiscate the film. If the photographer has taken shots before the show, ask to hold the camera until the end of the performance, at which time you may return it.

CELL PHONES

The use of cellular phones within the Theatres during performances is prohibited by New York City law. Cell phones may be used in the Lobby and Lounge areas.

UNRULY PATRONS

Any staff member has the authority to call the police for assistance when anyone is causing a disturbance on the premises.

ACCIDENTS/ACCIDENT REPORTS

Assess the situation and immediately call for back-up assistance from another staff member if possible. Avoid leaving any injured or ill person alone. Immediately offer to summon emergency medical attention for the injured or ill party. Staff members have the authority to call for emergency services (911) whether or not such medical attention is requested.

An accident report must be filled out whenever an accident occurs. The accident report should be as detailed as possible, and fully completed. Please note the condition of the area (including lighting), in or outside the Theatre, where the accident occurred.

EMERGENCY PROCEDURES

All staff should understand that they have the authority and obligation to take appropriate measures to evacuate the public from the building in the event of any life threatening emergency, or when the Fire Alarm sounds. It is crucial that the building be evacuated immediately if the Fire Alarm sounds. Time should not be wasted in attempting to find the cause of the alarm. (If the Trouble Bell rings, though, the building does not have to be evacuated. Be sure you know the difference.) In the event of an evacuation, a designated

Appendix F (continued)

Westside Theatre POLICIES
June 2006

House Manager or Fire Guard is the last to leave the building. The members of the House Management staff should identify themselves to emergency personnel to describe the nature and location of the problem.

CANCELLATION OF PERFORMANCE

House Managers have the authority to stop or cancel a performance because of a fire, fire alarm, or other life threatening situation. House Managers also have the authority to cancel a performance due to a Theatre related issue such as a security problem, a failure of building systems (A/C, plumbing, heating etc.) or any unsafe condition. The Producer, General Manager, or Company Manager of the show must authorize the cancellation of a performance if such cancellation is due to a production related issue, such as a performer's illness or technical problem. In any case, best efforts must be made to contact the Administration prior to the cancellation of a performance.

REFUNDS FOR CANCELLED PERFORMANCES

ARefund Information for Cancelled Performance@ slips, which contain the following information, should be distributed to patrons who are present. In the event of a cancelled performance, all tickets scanned in to the theatre must be scanned out. If the tickets are not scanned out, refunds can be delayed or will be more difficult.

Telecharge.com, Broadwayoffers.com and **TDF** tickets will be refunded automatically with no further action required on the patron's part (if the tickets were scanned out).

Broker tickets (including those from **Broadway.com**) will be refunded by the broker. The Box Office will inform the ticket broker on the day following the cancelled performance, and instruct them to refund tickets.

TKTS tickets must be taken back to the TKTS booth for a refund. If the booth is closed (8:00 p.m., 7:30 p.m. on Sunday), this can be done at a later date. If the patron is leaving town and is unable to get to the booth, the instruction slip contains the information they will need for securing a refund by mail.

Westside Theatre POLICIES
June 2006

Group Sale tickets will be refunded or rescheduled by the group agent. The Box Office will inform them on the day following the cancelled performance and instruct them to issue a refund.

Box Office tickets should be returned to the Box Office. If the performance is cancelled after the Box Office is closed, patrons may contact the Box Office after 12:00 noon the following day.

CONCESSIONS/MERCHANDISE

Food and Beverage Concessions, when offered, are controlled and operated by the Westside Theatre. When the production elects to sell show-related merchandise, the vendor employed by them is solely responsible for all aspects of their business, including stocking and selling the merchandise and the security of all monies. Production merchandise must be sold from behind the bar, in space shared with concessions, before the show, during intermission and after the show. The Westside Theatre has agreed that the production may store its locked cash box in the Auxiliary Box Office safe. The House Managers are responsible for locking and unlocking the safe only, and are not responsible for the contents of the merchandise cash box. As a courtesy to the merchandise vendors, House Managers may (but are not required to) transport the cash box to and from the safe. The merchandise vendor is responsible for maintaining its own "bank" and supply of change; therefore, vendors should not ask the Box Office for change.

Generally, Westside Theatre concession will operate whenever there are productions booked in one or both theatres. It is expected that the concession stand will be open for business at least one hour before curtain and at intermission.

The Theatre holds a license for the sale of Wine and Beer which is displayed on the wall of the concession stand. While it is the responsibility of the Bartender to abide by New York State laws regarding the sales of alcoholic beverages, we expect the House Management to enforce the law as well. Specifically, the Bartender, the House Manager and/or the Assistant House Manager should object to the sale of alcohol to a minor or a visibly intoxicated individual. Any incident or violation must be reported to the Administration.

Appendix F (continued)

Westside Theatre POLICIES
June 2006

EXHIBIT A: House Rules

1. No pets or animals shall be brought into the Theatre.

2. No food shall be brought into the Theatre. The foregoing notwithstanding, however, Licensee may permit its cast to take meals into the dressing rooms during the interval between performances if said interval is less than two hours and Actors' Equity Association requires that Licensee provide meals; or during photo calls. In such event, Licensee shall immediately clear all remains and rubbish resulting from such meals from the dressing rooms.

3. There shall be no smoking in the Theatre at any time. There shall be no smoking anywhere in the building: including lobbies, dressing rooms, rest rooms, support areas, hallways and stairways.

4. There shall be no open flames used in the production without the prior consent of Licensor. Licensee will be responsible to pay for any Open Flame Permit or similar permit as may be required by the Fire Department.

5. There shall be no visitation backstage except upon terms agreed to by Licensor.

6. Onstage and backstage areas, dressing rooms and actors' washrooms shall be kept clean.

7. At the end of each day, Theatre and dressing room doors and windows shall be locked and all mechanical equipment and lights (except the stage ghost light) shall be shut off.

8. Licensee shall not have access to or utilize the Theatre unless Licensor has a representative at the Theatre and Licensee pays all costs and expenses relative to such representative.

9. Unauthorized persons are not allowed onto the stage or in the backstage areas.

10. The cast and crew shall not be permitted behind the counters of the concession areas or any other areas which the Licensor maintains for its own use.

Westside Theatre POLICIES
June 2006

11. The auditorium shall not be used for storing, setting up or temporarily placing stage, sound, lighting, prop, set or wardrobe materials in the aisles and public seating areas of the house. Nor shall the Licensee load into the Theatre any of the above materials through any other than the west door without the express consent of Licensor.

12. Other than ticket holders, no children under the age of 16 shall be brought into the Theatre. Regardless of whether they are ticket holders, no children under the age of four will be permitted into the Theatre.

13. No bicycles shall be brought into the Theatre and bicycles may not be parked in front of the Theatre.

14. For purposes of interpreting these Rules, the "Theatre" shall refer to the premises in which the Theatre is contained as well as the Theatre itself.

15. These House Rules apply to all employees and independent contractors, including without limitation persons stopping by for brief periods to supervise or check on the progress of work in the theatre.

APPENDIX G: Manhattan Theatre Club Incident Report Form

Manhattan Theatre Club
INCIDENT REPORT FORM

1.   DATE OF INCIDENT:_____   TIME OF INCIDENT:_____
2.   <u>INJURED PARTY:</u>   <u>GENERAL PHYSICAL DESCRIPTION</u>

NAME:_____   AGE:_____SEX:_____

ADDRESS:_____   APPROX. WEIGHT:_____

_____   <u>OTHER RELEVANT INFORMATION:</u>

TELEPHONE:_____   _____

3.   EXACT LOCATION OF INCIDENT:_____

_____

CONDITION OF LOCATION (i.e. wet floor, well-lit, carpeted, etc.)_____

_____

4.   DESCRIBE INDIVIDUAL'S ACTIVITY AT TIME OF INCIDENT:_____

_____

WAS INDIVIDUAL SICK:_____   INJURED:_____ (check one)
DID INDIVIDUAL CLAIM PROPERTY DAMAGE? (i.e. torn coat, stolen wallet):

YES:_____NO:_____   TYPE:_____

DESCRIBE, IN DETAIL, THE EXTENT OF THE INJURY OR ILLNESS:_____

_____

DID YOU OFFER MEDICAL ASSISTANCE?   YES:_____NO:_____
DID INDIVIDUAL ACCEPT?   YES:_____NO:_____

WAS FIRST AID ADMINISTERED OR AMBULANCE CALLED?_____

IF YES, EXPLAIN:_____

_____

HOW DID INDIVIDUAL LEAVE PREMISES? (i.e. walk, taxi, ambulance) :_____

_____

5.   DESCRIBE ANY OTHER DETAILS:_____

_____

6.   WITNESSES:

NAME: _____   TELEPHONE:_____

NAME: _____   TELEPHONE:_____

REPORT COMPLETED BY:_____   DATE:_____

REPORT SENT INSURANCE COMPANY   YES_____NO:_____

APPENDIX H: Space Request Form, Ruth Eckerd Hall

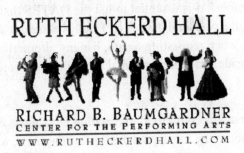

Thank you for your interest in Ruth Eckerd Hall. As a member supported theater, Ruth Eckerd Hall is proud to showcase a diverse group of artistic talents. The Programming, Education and Event Services departments work in sync to present many artists & groups. Before calling or making an appointment, it is necessary to review and complete the following:

Application

Since its 1983 opening, Ruth Eckerd Hall (REH) has established itself as an industry leader in the southeast United States. REH is consistently presenting nationally and internationally renowned artists and artistic companies in the Bay area. The Event Services department is in place to assist all Outside Productions (i.e., Rentals that are not presented via Mainstage/Programming and Education Departments). Therefore, the first step is to complete an Application. Please remember to be very detailed. More importantly, include any fliers, brochures and/or video footage that can be reviewed, and forward these materials to **Lisa Taylor, Asst. Director of Operations**.

Scheduling Procedures

❖ All Outside Production/Rental held dates are secondary to Ruth Eckerd Hall Programming & Education department performance holds.

❖ **Under no circumstances is any date confirmed until the Lease Agreement has been countersigned by Ruth Eckerd Hall, Incorporated.**

❖ Please note: a 501-c-3 Letter of Determination must be presented to Ruth Eckerd Hall, Incorporated to receive Non-profit/Community rental rates and tax exemption on ticket revenue.

While reviewing the packet, it is necessary to understand the components in presenting a production at Ruth Eckerd Hall:

☐ Technical   ☐ Marketing   ☐ Ticketing   ☐ Food & Beverage   ☐ Administrative

Appendix H (continued)

Ruth Eckerd Hall showcases its Events in Seasons: **Act I** (October–January); **Act II** (January–May); **Act III** (May–September). It is essential to list the DATES that are key to making the Event a success. Of course, the weekend days (i.e., Friday– Sunday) are the most requested & *in-demand* days. Therefore, when requesting a date, list any alternative days and dates. Please note that dates will not be made available for rental opportunities more that two (2) months in advance.

Finally, Ruth Eckerd Hall remains committed to reaching new levels of artistic excellence. We thank you in advance for continuing to support the Performing Arts, which is essential to enhancing the future of our community.

RUTH ECKERD HALL, INC.
1111 McMullen Booth Road • Clearwater, Florida 33759
(727) 791-7060 • Fax (727) 724-5976

RUTH ECKERD HALL

RICHARD B. BAUMGARDNER
CENTER FOR THE PERFORMING ARTS
WWW.RUTHECKERDHALL.COM

The Undersigned hereinafter referred to as the applicant, hereby makes application for permission to use Ruth Eckerd Hall, hereinafter referred to as Ruth Eckerd Hall, Inc., as indicated below, on the date(s) and specified purposes.

Ruth Eckerd Hall, Inc. reserves the right to approve which events will be presented at the facility.

COMPLETION OF APPLICATION DOES NOT GUARANTEE INSSUANCE OF A LEASE AGREEMENT

Requested dates and time

Month and Year	Requested Day and/or Dates	Load In/Event Time/Load Out

Event Information

➢ Please attach a detailed description of the Event. Please also include any video footage, programs, fliers, inserts, etc.

Organization/Business Name	
Event Title	
Corporation/Partnership/Sole Proprietor?	
Profit/Non-Profit?	

Appendix H (continued)

IRS Tax ID#	
Registered in the State of/County of?	
Business Address	
City/State/Zip	
Business Phone Number—Main	
Business Fax #	
Business Website Address	
Primary Contact Name	
Primary Contact Phone# + Email Address	
Secondary Contact Name	
Secondary Contact Phone# + Email Address	

Financial Information

#1 Bank Name	
Bank Address	
City/State/Zip	
Phone Number	
Account Number	
#2 Bank Name	
Bank Address	
City/State/Zip	
Phone Number	
Account Number	

Business References (and/or) Venues

Business/Venue Name (I)	
Personal Contact	
Phone#	

Business/Venue Name (II)	
Personal Contact	
Phone#	
Business/Venue Name (III)	
Personal Contact	
Phone#	

RELEASE OF INFORMATION

I hereby authorize the release of any financial information necessary to provide assurance of financial ability to Ruth Eckerd Hall, Inc. to process this application.

_____   _____

Signature & Title   Date

RUTH ECKERD HALL, INC.
1111 McMullen Booth Road • Clearwater, Florida 33759
(727) 791-7060 • Fax (727) 724-5976

Appendix H (continued)

RUTH ECKERD HALL

RICHARD B. BAUMGARDNER
CENTER FOR THE PERFORMING ARTS
WWW.RUTHECKERDHALL.COM

- ❏ All rates are subject to change without notice
- ❏ Commercial and Community rates are versus 10% of (GTS) Gross Ticket Sales
- ❏ Other rooms and Reception spaces may be available at an additional cost
- ❏ An Additional $150/hr fee applied to all events that exceed their Inclusive timing
- ❏ A FLAT Rental Rate of up to $4000 can result if the possibility of GTS is nonexistent

2180-seat Auditorium Fee Structure

Inclusive Time	Days	Commercial	Community (501-c-3)
8:00am–11:00pm	M-R	$3,000	$1,700
8:00am–11:00pm	F, Sa, Su	$3,200	$2,500
5:00pm–11:00pm	M-R	$2,175	$1,500
5:00pm–11:00pm	F, Sa, Su	$2,300	$1,700
8:00am–5:00pm	M-R	$1,475	$1,175
8:00am–5:00pm	F, Sa, Su	$1,550	$1,275

Ticket Office Expenses	Rate	Detail
Base Charge	$500	Ticket Printing, Tickets on sale (4) weeks in advance; $50/per add week
Ticketmaster	$250 + 3%	Set up fee + % Service Charge
Ticket Printing	**	Included in base charge; $150 if set up only and consignment
Advanced Sales	$50	Flat rate each additional week
Day of Show Sales	$200	Fee for personnel to sell consigned date of the show
Credit Card Fee	5%	Flat % based on charges sold

Administrative Expenses	Rate	Detail
MDS: Maintenance & Depreciation	$1.00	Per Ticket Tickets below $10
MDS: Maintenance & Depreciation	$2.00	Per Ticket Tickets $10 and above
Sales Tax	7%	% Mandated by the State of FL
Police	$25.hr	4hr minimum requirement*
Security Guards	$15/hr	Min (1) guard, based on Inclusive timing *
Parking Guards	$12/hr	Min (3) guards, based on Inclusive timing
Custodial	$350	Clean up Flat Rate
ASCAP	TBD%	% based on Ticket Price
BMI	TBD%	% x Gross Ticket Sales
SESAC	TBD%	% based on tickets distributed
Merchandise	25% Net + 7% tax	Tax collected + Net Sales

* Ruth Eckerd Hall reserves the right to mandate more than one Police Officer and/or Security guard.

Appendix H (continued)

RUTH ECKERD HALL

RICHARD B. BAUMGARDNER
CENTER FOR THE PERFORMING ARTS
WWW.RUTHECKERDHALL.COM

TECHNICAL EXPENSES

All Labor supplied by:

I.A.T.S.E. Local 321
Paul Paleveda, BA
7211 N. Dale Mabry Hwy. #209
Tampa, FL 33614

[EFFECTIVE October 1, 2005]—Hourly Rates and Union Stipulations:

HOD's, Steward & Riggers	$25.00/ per hour
Additional Stagehands	$24.00/per hour

- Minimum of four (4) hours, minimum four (4) stagehands per call.
- Any part of an hour is considered one hour
- An **overtime** rate of *time and one half* is charged for all hours worked in excess of eight (8) hours in one day {Inclusive—between 12:00am and 8:00am, and all hours worked on holidays}
- There is a meal requirement after five (5) consecutive hours of work; overtime will result in a meal penalty.
- Please note that if an Audio or Video stagehand is needed for recording purposes, the hourly rate will be <u>increased</u> by $1 per hour

Equipment	Rate	Detail
Piano—Grand	$250	Flat rate
Piano—Baby Grand	$150	Flat rate
Piano—Upright	$ 75	Flat rate
Piano Tuning	$100	Flat rate
Audio Recording	$150	Flat rate
Video Recording	$300	Flat rate
Marquee: Computer Road Sign	$250	Day of Event only; Wording is limited AND per approval of Marketing Director
6 foot Table	$5	(4) Complimentary 6' tables; $5 per table thereafter
Table linens	$4	Per linen table cloth
Table Skirting	$12	Per Skirt
Easels	$2	(4) Complimentary; $2 per easel thereafter

APPENDIX I: Theater Usage Policy, Ruth Eckerd Hall

USAGE POLICY

SECTION 1
INTRODUCTION

This Usage Policy is a part of the Lease Agreement for Ruth Eckerd Hall, Incorporated (herein after referred to as the Hall), and rules herein must be adhered to absolutely by the Lessees of the Hall.

The Lease Agreement and Usage Policy are governed by the laws of the State of Florida. Lessee irrevocably submits itself to the jurisdiction of the Courts of Pinellas County and the State of Florida for the purpose of any suit, action or other proceeding arising out of or based upon this agreement or the subject matter thereof.

Should Lessee be found in violation of any of the provisions of this Usage Policy, the Hall will immediately consider the Lease Agreement null and void, and Lessee will forfeit all advance payments made to the Hall and be liable for all rental fees and other expenses incurred, including attorney's fees, whether or not the performance actually occurs.

The aforementioned Lease Agreement and the Usage Policy are the only agreement between the parties relative to Ruth Eckerd Hall, Inc., and no oral statements or prior written matter shall have any force or effect.

The facilities on the site of the Richard B. Baumgardner Center for the Performing Arts, at 1111 McMullen-Booth Road, Clearwater, Florida 33759, are managed by Ruth Eckerd Hall, Inc. which has its offices in the Hall at 1111 McMullen-Booth Road, (727) 791-7060.

IT SHALL BE THE RESPONSIBILITY OF THE LESSEE TO COMPLETELY INFORM THE PROPER AGENTS, EMPLOYEES OF LESSEE, CONTRACTORS, AND SUBCONTRACTORS HIRED BY THE LESSEE, CONCERNING THESE RULES AND REGULATIONS. FOR CLARIFICATION OF INDIVIDUAL RULES, CALL THE HALL'S ASST. DIRECTOR OF OPERATIONS (727) 712-2776.

Due to the varied nature of the Hall, all requirements and production costs cannot be completely defined within these pages. Additional specifications and costs will be determined after arrangements for each event have been established with Ruth Eckerd Hall, Inc. management.

Appendix I (continued)

CHECKS: Checks for deposits, rent, maintenance and depreciation surcharge, and other expenses billed to Lessee, should be made payable to Ruth Eckerd Hall, Inc. The Hall reserves the right to request payment by cashier's check.

SECTION 2
AREAS OF SPECIAL INTEREST

The following is a summation of Lessee expenses, both fixed and optional. Also included is a listing of where an explanation of each expense can be found in the contents of the Usage Policy or the Lease Agreement.

SECTION 3
BASIC PROVISIONS

1. LESSEE ACCEPTS AS IS:

The Hall or Center's agents have made no representation or promises with respect to the said building or leased premises except as herein expressly set forth. The utilization of the leased premises by Lessee shall be conclusive evidence, as against Lessee, the Lessee accepts same "as is" and that said premises and the building of which the same form a part were in good and satisfactory condition at the time such possession was so taken.

    A. HEAT, ETC.: As part of this Agreement, the Hall will provide heat and air conditioning in compliance with the Federal energy guidelines, electrical power, water, and normal pre-and post-event cleaning, except restoring & cleaning of stage, which shall be the responsibility of the Lessee.

    B. SUBLET/USE: Lessee may not sublet any rented space(s), or in any way assign the rented space(s) to any other person or organization. Lessee may not utilize the rented space(s) for any purpose or time period other than what is specified in the Agreement.

2. COMPLIANCE WITH LAWS AND LICENSING:

    A. COMPLIANCE WITH LAWS: No activities in violation of Federal, State, or Local laws or the Board of Health shall be permitted in Center premises, and it shall be the responsibility of the Lessee, while under the terms and Period of this Agreement, to enforce this provision.

    B. LICENSE/PERMITS/COPYRIGHTS: The Lessee shall obtain and pay the fee for all licenses and permits necessary to conduct operations specified by this Agreement. The Lessee will assume all costs arising from the use of patented, trademarked, franchised or copyrighted music, materials, devices processes or dramatic rights used on or incorporated in the event. Lessee agrees to indemnify, defend and hold harmless Ruth Eckerd Hall, Inc., and the City of Clearwater, from any claims or costs, including legal fees, which might arise from question of use of any such material described above. The Hall may require evidence of such licenses being in effect, such as ASCAP, BMI and SESAC, etc.

    C. FIRE/SAFETY CODES: All sets, costumes, props, flashpots, laser lighting equipment, and any other material used by the Lessee must conform to all existing fire and safety codes. The provisions of fire prevention code that prohibits smoking, flammable decorations, open flames, explosive or inflammable fluids, gases and compounds must be observed. The Hall requires written evidence that all such codes have been observed and that operators have the required license(s). When pyrotechnics are used, the Lessee must provide a "Clearwater Fire Department, Class A, Explosives Permit", along with a copy of the Federal license of the person responsible for

Appendix I (continued)

devising, supervising and discharging display. Payment of the "Fire Watch" with a minimum of two Fire Marshals will be the responsibility of the Lessee.

D. SMOKING: In compliance with Florida Clean Indoor Air Act, Section 386.201 of Florida Statutes, the Richard B. Baumgardner Center for the Performing Arts, including the Ruth Eckerd Hall, is a non-smoking facility. The Lessee will fully cooperate in enforcing the "No Smoking" law at all times.

E. NON-RESIDENT ALIENS: Should the artist(s) to be presented by the Lessee be a non-resident alien individual, partnership or corporation, the Lessee expressly agrees to perform all obligation and to assume all liabilities as the withholding agent pursuant to the requirement of Section 1441 and 1442 of the Internal Revenue Code and Federal Regulations promulgated thereunder.

3.. LESSEE MUST PROVIDE TO MANAGEMENT:

A. TAX EXEMPTION: Non-profit, tax exempt organizations shall submit to the Asst. Director of Operations such tax exemption certificates as shall pertain. Such certificates will be required upon signing of contract. Such certificates will be kept on file by the Hall, although the Asst. Director of Operations may require re-filing from time to time.

B. SIGNED CONTRACT FOR ACT: Lessee agrees to furnish Center, at the time of Lease Agreement signing, a copy of the signed contract between Lessee and the Act to be presented. Portions of this signed contract concerning financial arrangement with Lessee may be excised.

C. ROYALTY LICENSES: If Lessee holds any or all of the ASCAP, BMI, and SESAC licenses, a copy of these licenses must be provided; otherwise Royalty charges will be assessed on the Final Expense Report.

4. INSURANCE:

A. CERTIFICATES OF INSURANCE: Certificates of Insurance evidencing the insurance coverage specified below, by a company licensed to do business in the State of Florida, shall be furnished by the Lessee to the Hall at least 30 days prior to the event. Any deductibles listed on the Insurance Certificate must be paid by Lessee.

B. WORKERS' COMPENSATION: Coverage to apply for all Lessee's employees for Statutory Limits in compliance with applicable State and Federal laws. In addition, the policy must include Employer's Liability with a limit of $100,000 each accident.

C. COMPREHENSIVE GENERAL LIABILITY: Coverage must be afforded on a form no more restrictive than the latest edition of the Comprehensive General Liability Policy filed by the Insurance Services Office and must include:

1) Minimum limits of $1,000,000 per occurrence combined single limit for Bodily Injury Liability and Property Damage Liability.
2) Premises and/or Operations.
3) Independent Contractors.
4) Products and/or Completed Operations.
5) Liquor Liability, where applicable.
6) ADDITIONAL INSURED—THE CITY OF CLEARWATER AND RUTH ECKERD HALL, INC.

D. BUSINESS AUTO POLICY: Coverage must be afforded on a form no more restrictive than the latest edition of the Business Auto Policy filed by the Insurance Services Office and must include:

1) Minimum limits of $1,000,000 per occurrence combined single limit for Bodily Injury Liability and Property Damage Liability.
2) Owned Vehicles.
3) Hired and Non-Owned Vehicles.
4) Employers' Non-Ownership.

E. INDEMNITY: The Lessee shall indemnify and hold harmless Ruth Eckerd Hall, Inc. and the City of Clearwater against any and all liability, penalties, damages, expenses and judgments by reason of any injury or claim of injury to person or property, of any nature and howsoever caused, arising out of the use, occupation or possession of the leased premises, within the thirty-eight acre boundaries of the Hall property, or the streets, parking areas, and sidewalks adjacent thereto, by the Lessee at any time during the terms of the lease. The Lessee is hereby subrogated to any rights of the Hall against any parties whomsoever in connection therewith. The Hall shall promptly deliver to the Lessee the original or a true copy of any summons or other process, pleading or notice issued in any such suit or other proceeding to assert or enforce any such claim. The Lessee shall have the right to defend any such suit with attorneys of its own selection at Lessee's expense, the Hall shall have a right, if it sees fit, to participate in such defense at its own expense.

F. The Hall will not be responsible for any damage or loss to Lessee's Property, or that of the Lessee's agents, employees, contractors, or subcontractors.

5. PUBLIC SAFETY:

The Lessee shall neither encumber nor obstruct the sidewalk in front of premises (or entrance to halls, stairs, lobbies, and audience chambers), nor allow the same to be obstructed or encumbered in any manner. Lessee further agrees not to bring

Appendix I (continued)

onto the premises any material, substances, equipment, or object which is likely to endanger the life of, or cause bodily injury to any person on the premises, or which is likely to constitute a hazard to property thereon, without the prior approval of the Hall Director. The Hall shall have the right to refuse to allow any such material, substances, equipment or object be brought onto the premises and the further right to require its immediate removal therefrom if found thereon.

6. CANCELLATION:

In case of cancellation by the Lessee, notification must be given in writing to the Center at least 90 days prior to the date of scheduled event. The Center may require the contract rent, or full deposit made by Lessee, as liquidated damages, plus any additional expenses incurred, and the Lessee and the Center shall be relieved of any further obligations under this agreement. In addition, it shall be the responsibility of the Lessee to make a reasonable amount of public announcements, at Lessee's expense, concerning the cancellation, as soon as possible following the cancellation and including all daily newspapers, news departments at all commercial television stations, and at any radio stations on which paid or unpaid advertisements for the event were run.

7. INTERRUPTION OR TERMINATION OF EVENT:

The Hall shall retain the right to cause the interruption of any event in the interest of public safety, and to likewise cause the termination of such event when, in the sole judgment of Center, such act is necessary in the interest of public safety.

8. EVACUATION OF FACILITY:

Should it become necessary, in the judgment of the Hall staff, to evacuate the premises because of a bomb threat or for other reasons of public safety, the Lessee will retain possession of the premises for sufficient time to complete presentation of his activity without additional rental charge providing such time does not interfere with another event scheduled at the Hall. If, at the discretion of the Hall Management, it is not possible to complete presentation of the activity, rental shall be forfeited, prorated, or adjusted at the discretion of the Hall Management based on the situation, and the Lessee hereby waives any claim for damages or compensation from the Hall.

9. BONDING/ADDITIONAL SECURITY:

The Hall, at its discretion, may require such bonding as is deemed necessary and may require additional security guards to be charged to the Lessee.

10. DAMAGE/CLEAN-UP RESPONSIBILITY:

Lessee shall be responsible for any and all damages to the Hall premises caused by acts of Lessee or Lessee's agents, employees, contractors, subcontractors, patrons, guests and artists whether accidental or otherwise. Lessee further agrees to leave the Hall premises in the same condition as existed on the date Lessee took possession, ordinary wear and use excepted. Additional charges incurred because of an unusual amount of post-event clean-up will be borne by the Lessee. Restoring and cleaning of stage will be the responsibility of the Lessee.

SECTION 4
TECHNICAL

1. STAGE MANAGER:

Lessee agrees to furnish a qualified Stage Manager to run the event backstage or to accept the employment of a Stage Manager from the Hall.

2. PERSONNEL:

Compensation will be at the prevailing stagehand rate and will include overtime, all insurance fees and taxes. The Hall is a Union Hall, and all stagehands are arranged through I.A.T.S.E. local. The Hall recognized the Union as the sole representative for all employees employed in carpentry, electrical, property, sound, projection, wardrobe, truck loading, rigging and other related or incidental work in support of all stage performances. All terms and conditions as required by the Union concerning minimum hours, breaks, meal penalties, and minimum staffing will be observed by the Lessee and enforced by the Hall. Rates for stagehand labor are subject to change at any time. Questions concerning the Union requirements should be directed to the Hall Technical Director at (727) 712-2711.

3. STAGEHAND CALLS:

A. It is Management's policy to require twenty-four (24) hours notice of cancellation of stagehand calls. If less than twenty-four (24) hours is given, the Lessee will be charged a minimum five (5) hour call at the prevailing rates for each stagehand. Additional information regarding technical specifications may be obtained by contacting the Hall Technical Director (727) 712-2711.

B. ONLY authorized professional personnel, as determined by Center management, are allowed to operate any theatre equipment.

Appendix I (continued)

4. DELIVERY OF GOODS:

   A. Sets, costumes, and other materials belonging to the Lessee delivered prior to contracted time will not be accepted by the Hall staff without written arrangements and additional charges to the Lessee. The Hall makes no guarantee that space would be available to receive materials arriving early.

   B. The Hall will not accept any goods shipped to the Hall for the Lessee, or for any person claiming to be acting for the Lessee, if any sum is to be paid the carrier upon his delivery thereof.

   C. The Hall is not responsible for lost, damaged or stolen items.

5. SOUND/LIGHTING CONSOLES:

   Clearwater Fire Department regulations strictly limit the installation and operation of sound and/or lighting control consoles in the audience chamber of the auditorium.

6. TIME:

   Time shall be of the essence of this Lease Agreement, and the time granted shall not be extended for the occupancy of use of the premises or for the installation or removal of equipment without the permission of the Hall, and all such additional time shall be paid for according to the schedule of fees fixed by the Hall, if such permission is granted.

7. TELEPHONE AND FAX CHARGES:

   Any expenses incurred by Center for telephone and fax charges made necessary to properly execute Lessee's event will be paid by the Lessee.

8. DRESSING ROOM KEYS:

   For each Dressing Room key required, Lessee agrees to pay a $500.00 deposit, which will be returned as keys are returned back to the Hall Technical Director.

SECTION 5
HOUSE/PERFORMANCE

1. LESSEE REPRESENTATIVE:

   Lessee will furnish to the Asst. Director of Operations the name, address and phone number of the Lessee's Representative. This Representative will be the sole person authorized to make decisions or to negotiate with staff of the Hall.

This Representative, who must be present at each performance, will be the sole person authorized to resolve problems and conflicts or to negotiate any alterations in performance procedure with the staff of the Hall.

2. ACTS & INTERMISSION:

Lessee agrees that for all programs lasting one (1) hour or more, excepting religious services or other engagements specifically excluded, an intermission of not less than 15 minutes be held, subject to modification by Ruth Eckerd Hall, Incorporated when necessary to meet unusual conditions. The length of acts and intermissions must be made known to the Asst. Director of Operations two weeks prior to the performance.

3. DEPOSITS AND DATE CONFIRMATIONS:

A deposit of approximately 50% of total estimated costs and a signed contract will confirm rental dates. Until a completely executed contract and deposit are received by the Center, the proposed date of the event is subject to change. The Center reserves the right to hold ticketing monies to cover event operational expenses in the event the balance due is not received within 15 days following the event.

4. MAINTENANCE AND DEPRECIATION SURCHARGE:

Lessee will be charged a fee per ticket sold or per person in attendance, or a percentage of ticket sales, whichever is greater, to offset the expense of the maintenance and depreciation of the Hall and its premises.

5. TRAFFIC CONTROL:

Center management will arrange for, at Lessee's expense, a traffic officer to control the traffic light at the intersection of McMullen-Booth Road and Ruth Eckerd Hall Drive. The fee will be at the prevailing rate. To maintain patron safety, Center reserves the right to make all traffic control arrangements deemed necessary. All traffic control arrangements made by the Hall will be billed to the Lessee.

6. PARKING GUARDS:

Parking guards direct traffic in the parking areas. Parking guard expense will be at the prevailing rate.

Appendix I (continued)

7.   SECURITY GUARD:

A security guard is required to be on duty for the duration of the Lessee's event. Security guard expense will be at the prevailing rate.

8.   USHERS:

The Hall reserves the right to supervise, through its Asst. Director of Operations and House Manager, the services of all ushers (their numbers, appearance, training, etc.).

9.   TIME:

House will be opened to audience one-half hour prior to scheduled performance time. The program will begin at the time printed on the tickets. If the program is one hour or longer, there shall be an intermission of at least 15 minutes. Specific arrangements to the contrary can be made with the Asst. Director of Operations.

10.   VIDEO/AUDIO:

Non-production related activities (NPRA) include activities such as photographing, audio recording and video recording during rehearsals and/or performance at the Hall. Unless prior arrangements are made, no less than 7 days in advance, and approved by Ruth Eckerd Hall, Inc., these activities are prohibited. The NPRA rate is an element of rent based on the Rental Schedule. This fee is applicable when such activities are performed by the Lessee or Lessee's agents, employees, patrons, guests, artists or, at the request of the Lessee, by Center personnel. Rates may be obtained by contacting the Event Services Manager.

11.   BROADCAST RIGHTS:

Center reserves all rights and privileges for outgoing radio and television broadcasts originating from the Hall during the term of this Agreement. Should Center grant to Lessee such privilege, Center has the right to require advance payment of any estimated related costs to Center. Center may also require payment seven days in advance for said privilege, in addition to rental fee. Such permission must be obtained in writing in advance of broadcast date. Center must receive credit for all broadcasts/cablecasts of the taped event. The broadcast requirements may be obtained from the Hall's Asst. Director of Operations.

12.   SECURITY:

All security arrangements deemed necessary by the Hall will be made by the Hall and will be billed to the Lessee. Firearms of any kind may not be carried, displayed, or used by any person, other than security personnel authorized by the Hall.

13. **LIST OF PERFORMERS:**

Lessee shall provide a list of names of performers to be left with the security guard at the Artists' Entrance. Only those persons on the list will be admitted on that afternoon or evening of the performance.

14. **PUBLIC AREAS:**

Lessee agrees to abide by the discretion of the Asst. Director of Operations concerning activities, dress, etc., of those persons acting on behalf of Lessee in public areas.

15. **CONCURRENT USE:**

The Hall reserves the right to rent other parts of the Hall at the same time as the Lessee's rental of said premises, and the use of the lobby, vestibules, hallways, Ticket Office, lounges and other public rooms and facilities, at the discretion of the Hall shall be concurrent with the use of such others as the Hall may determine (provided that such renting to others shall not unreasonably interfere with the use of said premises by the Lessee).

The Lessee understands and acknowledges that the Lessee has no rights whatsoever to enter or use the areas in the said building compromising the administrative offices of the Hall, the mechanical rooms or any other areas except such as are designated in this Agreement or otherwise specified by the Hall in writing.

16. **STAFF RIGHT TO ENTRY:**

Lessee will afford Center staff personnel the right to enter any part of the Center at any time if they are performing an official function of the Center.

17. **FUTURE ATTRACTIONS:**

The Hall reserves the right to distribute to the audience, announcements and literature concerning future attractions to be held in the Hall whether such attractions are under the auspices of the Lessee or not.

18. **OPEN REHEARSALS:**

Any rehearsal attended by more than twenty-five (25) non-production personnel will be considered a performance and the Asst. Director of Operations must be advised thirty (30) days in advance in order to provide adequate staffing.

Appendix I (continued)

19. SEATING ON STAGE:

The Lessee will not permit or cause to permit seating on the stage, stage wings or in the aisles. The sole exception to this restriction is when the audience is a planned and integral part of the action.

20. FOOD/BEVERAGES:

A. FOR CAST: The Lessee agrees that when food and beverages are required on premises for cast and/or crew, the Food and Beverage Department will be contacted in reference to provision and location of these food and beverage items. Food or beverage service will not be provided in any area of the building without approval of the Food and Beverage Department. Under no circumstances are food and beverages permitted in the auditorium or on stage. All alcoholic beverages must be administered through Ruth Eckerd Hall, Inc. as required by the state liquor license.

B. BAR SERVICE: Bar service will be provided when requested by the Lessee. Requests to have bar service must be made through the Food and Beverage Manager at least two weeks prior to the contracted event date. If revenue generated from bar sales is less than $350.00 per bartender, a service fee of $50.00 per bartender will be charged. Please contact the Food and Beverage Manager at (727) 712-2705 for further details.

C. CATERING: Ruth Eckerd Hall's Food and Beverage Department will handle food and beverage service as required by the contract rider if the Lessee so desires. Arrangements to have the Food and Beverage Department professionally handle this area, as well as the fees involved, can be made through the Food and Beverage Department at (727) 712-2705.

21. LODGING FORBIDDEN:

The Lessee, or any person or persons claiming to be acting for the Lessee, is prohibited from using the Hall as a sleeping or lodging accommodation.

22. ANIMALS:

Lessee will not allow animals to be kept in the Hall. Upon written permission of the Hall Director, animals used in performance may be brought in to the Hall only during actual rehearsal or performance.

23. COLLECTIONS:

No collections, donations or solicitations of money or goods of any kind, whether for charity or otherwise, shall be made or attempted on the Hall premises, including parking areas, without first obtaining written permission of the Hall Director no later than one week in advance.

24. MERCHANDISE (Concessions):

The Hall reserves and retains to itself the right to operate, license and/or permit others to operate, any and all concessions at or in all the facilities on the site of the Hall, during the period of this Agreement.

A. The Hall reserves the right to use such areas as are, in its opinion, necessary for such concessions and WHERE these concessions will be made available.

B. The Hall will determine which concessions will be in Operation during the period of the Agreement.

C. When written permission is granted to Lessee to operate a concession of any kind, the Hall will receive twenty-five (25) percent of all net sales of any object or document. If the Hall is required to provide a seller for said concessions, the Hall will receive thirty (30) percent of all net sales.

D. No free samples of food, beverage or any product may be given away or otherwise distributed without prior written approval of the Hall one week in advance.

E. At no time will concession sales be permitted in the auditorium.

SECTION 6
PUBLICITY/PROMOTION

1. PROMOTION/PUBLICITY:

Lessee agrees to withhold all publicity and promotion of Lessee's event until a date is established and a contract executed, for initiation of ticket sales and all publicity and promotion can indicate such date. Failure to designate the specific date that tickets are to go on sale may result in additional charges for Center's Ticket Office services.

2. ADVERTISING:

In all advertising, Lessee has the authority to use the Hall Ticket Office number only when, in the judgment of Center management, Lessee has made available for advance sale a sufficient number of tickets, in all price categories, so that the Hall Ticket Office can properly accommodate and satisfy the demands of the ticket-buying public. THE HALL MANAGEMENT MUST REVIEW AND APPROVE ALL ADVERTISING AND ANNOUNCEMENT COPY THAT RELATES TO THE USE OF THE HALL TICKET OFFICE TELEPHONE NUMBER.

3. CORRECT ADVERTISING COPY:

The Lessee agrees that all advertising—newspaper, radio, television, posters, heralds, flyers, brochures, etc.—will contain the following information:

Appendix I (continued)

A. The true and correct name of the presenting agency or organization: i.e. "Country Music Stars, Inc., presents . . ." (Abbreviations are not acceptable)

B. The specific and correct name of the audience chamber in which the event will take place: i.e. Ruth Eckerd Hall, or Margarete Heye Great Room

C. The correct institutional name of the theater complex: i.e. Ruth Eckerd Hall at the Richard B. Baumgardner Center for the Performing Arts information and tickets: Ruth Eckerd Hall Ticket Office, (727) 791-7400.

4. POSTERS, SIGNAGE, ETC.:

Lessee will display no posters, photographs, models, etc., without written permission of the Hall's Asst. Director of Operations, and then only in such areas as specified and such material as are APPROVED IN ADVANCE BY THE HALL DIRECTOR OF MARKETING AND COMMUNICATIONS. Further, the Lessee is prohibited from driving any tack, nail or screw into the ceilings, walls or floors of the Hall so as to mar, deface or injure Center property. The Lessee is prohibited from displaying any signs, models, etc. on the Hall's premises including parking areas, entrance and adjacent roadway without the written permission of the Hall's Director.

5. OBJECTIONABLE MATERIAL:

Should the show contain any materials that may be viewed by any segment of the community as being morally objectionable, the management reserves the right to require of the Lessee the inclusion in all advertising of a phrase, acceptable to Center management that alerts the potential ticket-buyer to the maturity of the theme or actions.

6. MAIL PROCEDURE FOR LESSEE:

A. All mailing for Lessees using Ruth Eckerd Hall's list MUST be approved by Ruth Eckerd Hall Management. Not all lists are available for use. Ruth Eckerd Hall's lists are not available for purchase.

B. All mailings done for Lessees will be mailed by and paid for by the Lessee. Ruth Eckerd Hall's bulk permit is not available for renters use by law. Lessee may pick up mailing at Ruth Eckerd Hall at the time and place designated by the Marketing Department.

C. ALL MATERIALS MAILED by Ruth Eckerd Hall using Ruth Eckerd Hall's lists MUST BE APPROVED BY THE DIRECTOR OF MARKETING AND COMMUNICATIONS BEFORE THEY ARE PRINTED. Ruth Eckerd Hall reserves the right to refuse mailing material which is incorrect or was not approved prior to printing.

D. Ruth Eckerd Hall charges a fee for this mailing service which is set by the Director of Marketing and Communications with the approval of the President and CEO of Ruth Eckerd Hall, Inc.

E. No copy of Ruth Eckerd Hall's mailing list will be supplied to the Lessee.

SECTION 7
TICKET AND TICKET OFFICE

1. TICKET OFFICE SERVICES:

   Full ticket office services are available at an additional charge. Ticket sales on Ruth Eckerd Hall premises are handled by Ruth Eckerd Hall Ticket Office staff only. No pre-printed tickets will be sold. Base charge includes initial and ongoing consultation between Lessee and Director of Ticketing/Information Services on program, price, configurations, capacities, audit, ticket ordering and administration. Contact the Asst. Director of Operations for prevailing rates.

2. THIRD PARTY TICKET AGENCIES:

   Should Lessee opt to utilize an outside ticket agency, Director of Ticketing/Information Services must be consulted regarding wheelchair, companion, house, director and Center sales.

   Lessee will provide a list of satellite locations to the Ticket Office by the first day of public sale. This information will be available to the public.

   When Ruth Eckerd Hall sells in conjunction with outside agencies, the Director of Ticketing/Information Services will coordinate allotments. Any ticket agency fees incurred through the sale of tickets at outlets other than the Ruth Eckerd Hall Ticket Office will be borne entirely by the Lessee.

3. CONSIGNMENT:

   There is no charge for the initial consignment of tickets. ALL UNSOLD TICKETS WILL BE RETURNED TO THE TICKET OFFICE 72 HOURS PRIOR TO PERFORMANCE. LESSEE WILL BE CHARGED FOR ALL CONSIGNED TICKETS NOT RETURNED WITHIN 72 HOURS OF THE PERFORMANCE. DISCOUNTED OR COMPLIMENTARY TICKETS MUST BE CONSIGNED AS SUCH OR WILL BE CONSIDERED SOLD AT FACE VALUE.

4. TICKET ORDERING:

   Lessee must provide the Director of Ticketing/Information Services with the name, address and phone number of one (1) authorized person as a contact for the Ticket Office. Lesee's Representative will then be the sole person to deal with the Director of Ticketing/Information Services.

   All communications between contact person and Director of Ticketing/ Information Services must be written whenever possible. No verbal messages are

Appendix I (continued)

to be given to the Ticket Office cashiers. No requests for audit reports on show are to be made at the window. CASHIERS ARE NOT AUTHORIZED TO GIVE OUT SUCH INFORMATION. Audit information, number of tickets sold, and any pre-performance information should be through a Ticket Office Supervisor or Director of Ticketing/Information Services only. Lessee will indicate prior to public sale any special seating needs for individual shows, i.e. blocked seats, group seats, company seats, etc.

Lessee will provide a description of the performance to the Director of Ticketing/Information Services, through the use of the PUBLICITY/CALENDAR OF EVENTS AND TICKET OFFICE SERVICES form, to enable Ticket Office staff to better inform the public about Lessee's event. TICKET OFFICE SERVICES CANNOT BE INITIATED UNTIL THE PUBLICITY/CALENDAR OF EVENTS AND TICKET OFFICE SERVICES FORM IS COMPLETED.

5. REFUND OF TICKET REVENUE:

In keeping with the Ruth Eckerd Hall policy of retaining public faith, Ruth Eckerd Hall, Inc. retains the right to make determination of ticket refunds for cause. Reasons can include, but are not limited to, seats blocked by equipment when exchange for comparable location is not possible, failure of projection equipment, or failure of act to show or to go on stage within reasonable time of schedule provided by Lessee.

Ruth Eckerd Hall, Incorporated will exert every caution against bad checks from customers and will make every effort to collect such, but ultimate responsibility is that of the Lessee.

6. TICKET DISTRIBUTION:

Any tickets that leave the Ticket Office must be (1) paid for, (2) complimentary, or (3) consignment. (Lessee understands that he/she is fully responsible for any tickets consigned.)

A. COMPLIMENTARY
The Hall reserves the right to monitor the use, number and distribution of complimentary tickets by the Lessee. Complimentary ticket requests must be in writing to the Ticket Office Manager not less than one week before the performance.
Complimentary tickets, Center seats and House seats not used by the Hall will be returned for sale. The Hall will use extreme discretion in distributing complimentary tickets and/or sale of the House seats, and Center seats, and will discount to Lessee for their use.
B. DISCOUNTS:
Lessee must advise Director of Ticketing/Information Services, in writing, when initial ticket information is given, of its intention to sell tickets at a

discount. Such information must include the precise amount of discount, number of tickets, restrictions, and the scale categories and seat numbers involved.

C. GROUP DISCOUNTS:

Lessee must identify the group discount and the restrictions that apply, i.e. minimum numbers, locations, cancellations, and fees in writing to the Ticket Office.

D. TICKET GIVEAWAYS:

Arrangements for ALL ticket giveaways must be made through the Box Office three weeks in advance.

E. DIRECTOR'S SEATS:

The Hall reserves the right to hold six (6) Director's seats for performances.

F. DISABILITY LOCATIONS:

The Hall reserves the right to control the distribution of wheelchair and companion seating in the Hall's Ticket Office.

G. CENTER SEATS:

The Hall reserves the right to hold and distribute up to one (1) percent of the total seats of House capacity for its use.

7. TICKET OFFICE ACCESS AND SUPERVISION:

Access is restricted to authorized personnel of Ruth Eckerd Hall, Inc. only. Supervision of sales is under the sole discretion of Ticket Office management.

8. TICKET OFFICE RECEIPTS:

Performance audit will be taken at closing of Ticket Office. A preliminary audit on "run of show" will be presented by Center to Lessee within 48 hours after the final performance and will include a recapitulation of each performance. Sales tax on ticket revenue will be withheld and submitted by the Hall (where applicable).

All receipts will be immediately deposited in Center account. A check will be presented to the Lessee with final audit in accordance with terms of this agreement.

9. FINAL SETTLEMENT:

A Final Revenue/Expense Report will be issued within 10 working days of the Lessee's date of performance. Revenue due to Lessee will be paid within 30 days of final settlement, and final payment of Lessee's expenses will be paid within the same time period. Day of show final settlement may be arranged by contacting the Asst. Director of Operations at (727) 712-2776, no later than 30 days before the day of show.

APPENDIX J: Sample Technical Rider

SAMPLE TECHNICAL RIDER

DATE OF ENGAGEMENT:

VENUE:

**LOADING AREA**: It is imperative that loading areas and backstage areas be cleared of all vehicles and equipment prior to load-in and load-out. During inclement weather, it is essential for snow removal equipment and sand or salt to be available in order to clear the loading area for load-in and load-out. This area must be clear before trucks arrive. In the event of rainy weather, it is imperative for the **PURCHASER**[1] to have a covered area for **ARTIST** to walk into building. In the event that a covered area is not available, several large umbrellas must be available to cover the **ARTIST**.

**MINIMUM MANPOWER REQUIREMENTS:** PLEASE NOTE THAT ALL TIMES ARE SUBJECT TO ADJUSTMENT AND THAT **PURCHASER'S** PRODUCTION MANAGER IS EXPECTED TO BE ON SITE AT THE FIRST CREW CALL. **PURCHASER** AGREES TO PROVIDE THE FOLLOWING PERSONNEL ACCORDING TO THE FOLLOWING CALL SCHEDULE. ALL CALLS ARE TO BE VERIFIED AND/OR AMENDED BY **ARTIST'S** PRODUCTION MANAGER PRIOR TO SHOW DATE. TIMES ARE VENUE SENSITIVE. PURCHASER FURTHER AGREES TO ARRANGE FOR AND EFFECT ALL UNION OBLIGATIONS PRIOR TO DATE OF PERFORMANCE WITH THE APPROPRIATE UNION SHOP STEWARDS. IT IS THE SOLE RESPONSIBILITY OF **PURCHASER** TO NEGOTIATE WITH ANY LEGALLY CONTRACTED UNION REPRESENTATIVES HOLDING CONTRACT JURISDICTION ON THE VENUE, TO DETERMINE EXACT PERSONNEL REQUIREMENTS.

Rigging Call/ Load-In:

(4)	Truck Loaders
(10)	Working Stagehands
(2)	Riggers
(1)	House Electrician

Show Call: 1/2 hour before show time:

(2)	Truss Spot Operators
(2)	Flyman
(1)	House Electrician

Load-out:

(4)	Truck Loaders
(12)	Working Stagehands
(2)	Riggers
(1)	House Electrician

PURCHASER must provide **2** runners available exclusively for **ARTIST'S** use. These persons shall be separate from the stagehands, have a valid driver's license, and have a vehicle in clean and good working condition, with insurance. **ARTIST** will not be responsible for any costs associated with runners' vehicles, including fuel. Runners should have a working knowledge of the areas musical instrument, hardware, and electronic stores. They should report to **ARTIST'S** Stage Manager and to be available from load-in until released by **ARTIST'S** Stage Manager.

STAGING: ARTIST requires the stage performance size to be minimum of **40'** wide, **32'** deep and **4'** high. There must be a stage to ceiling clearance of **32'**.

A **stage left wing** area should be a minimum of **8'** wide, **12'** deep and **2'** high (unless otherwise stated).

A **stage right wing** area should be a minimum of **8'** wide, **12'** deep and **2'** high (unless otherwise stated). Both the stage left and the stage right wings should not be built until instructed by **ARTIST'S** Stage Manager on the day of load-in.

Stage Construction Requirements:
All temporary stages must be able to support **500** Pounds per square foot. Care and attention must be used in the construction. The surface of the stage must have a smooth finish (no deep grooves, protrusions, or crevices) and frictionless. All areas must be completely level, wobble-free and stable. The stage area must be complete prior to the beginning of load-in. The set-up time for the production will not be penalized due to incomplete or improper construction of the stage.

Stairs are required at the upstage right and upstage left corners of the stage. These stairs should have handrails on both sides and be illuminated during performance.

Additional stairs without handrails may be required to allow access to the audience during the performance from the downstage edge of the stage.

Performance area should be completely clear and free of all non-show and performance related equipment. All house equipment, including lighting, sound and staging not required for the performance must be struck or flown out from the stage and wing areas.

HOUSE MIX POSITION: **PURCHASER** must provide the following area:

An area measuring **16'** wide by **8'** deep at a distance of **75'** to **100'** from the lip of the stage in the center of the house should be available.

IN VENUES WITH FIXED SEATING:
x rows, **x** seats in a row must be provided for the mix position.

IN VENUES WITH PORTABLE SEATING:
The **SOUND & LIGHTING MIX** position requires a riser measuring **16'** feet wide by **8'** deep. This position is placed center of the house.

IN VENUES WITH A BALCONY OR OVERHANG:
UNDER NO CIRCUMSTANCES CAN THE CONSOLE AREAS BE PLACED DIRECTLY UNDER THE FRONT LIP OF THE BALCONY DUE TO THE DANGER OF DRINKS AND FOREIGN OBJECTS FALLING ON THE EQUIPMENT.

PURCHASER agrees that a representative of **ARTIST** shall have sole and absolute authority in mixing, and controlling all sound and lighting while **ARTIST** is performing.

All seat kills must be done prior to the tickets going on sale.

Appendix J (continued)

STAGE POWER REQUIREMENTS: **PURCHASER** must provide the following minimum power requirements:

LIGHTING: 400 amps per leg,[2] **3** phase, **5** wire **120** volts/ **60 Hz** with separate neutral and proper earth ground. Must be within **x** of USR[3] corner of the stage

SOUND: **200** amps per leg, **3** phase, **5** wire **120** volts/ **60 Hz**[4] with separate neutral and proper earth ground. Must be within **x** of USL[5] corner of the stage. SOUND SERVICE GROUND MUST BE TOTALLY SEPARATE FROM LIGHTING GROUND, AND THE NEUTRAL MUST BE BONDED TO THIS GROUND.

RIGGING and UTILITY: **60** per leg, **3** phase, **5** wire **120** volts/ **60 Hz** with separate neutral and proper earth ground.

All **5** wire disconnects to be within **100** feet of upstage center, with lugs[6] supplied to accept **4/0** cable tails, adequately fused with spare fuses available, and be accessible to **ARTIST'S** technicians at all times.

All power must be without fluctuation or deviation of more than **x** percent in voltage or **x** in frequency. Delta power is not acceptable.

In the event house power is not adequate to provide the correct power for any part of the production, then **PURCHASER** must supply, at its sole expense, generators to supply the requested power.

SPOTLIGHTS: **PURCHASER** agrees to provide front of house spotlights. In some cases, it may be necessary to remove seats, so that the temporary follow spot platforms and spotlights can be installed. This should be done prior to the stage call (building schedule permitting). Each spotlight must have a separately fused **x** -amp circuit.

The above follow spots must be in good working condition, with good working irises and dousers, and be cleaned and tested prior to the performance.

PURCHASER agrees to provide **x** experienced operators. Operators must be available thirty (30) minutes prior to show time for the pre-show briefings. **PURCHASER** will insure that operators are at their positions not less than twenty (20) minutes prior to commencement of the **ARTIST'S** performance. Any overtime incurred due to spotlight operator's tardiness will be the direct responsibility of the **PURCHASER** and will not be a deductible show expense.

LIGHTS DURING THE SHOW: The **PURCHASER** will make arrangements for all lights not specifically required by local safety ordinances to be turned off or covered during the performance. This is especially applies to clocks, scoreboards, advertising billboards, and concessions in the venue. All doorways to lighted hallways must be curtained. Scoreboards and signs in the performance area must be turned off fifteen (15) minutes prior to the performance.

SOUND CHECK: THIS IS A CLOSED SOUND CHECK AND **PURCHASER** WILL INSURE THE VENUE IS CLEAR OF EVERYONE EXCEPT THOSE DIRECTLY INVOLVED IN THE SOUND CHECK. **PURCHASER** shall insure that **ARTIST** will be able to have a sound check for a minimum of **x** hours prior to the opening of the venue to the public. **PURCHASER** agrees not to open the venue to the audience until approval is given by **ARTIST'S** Production Manager

BARRICADE: In the event **ARTIST'S** Production Manager deems necessary **PURCHASER** will provide a freestanding barricade for performance.

DRESSING ROOMS: **PURCHASER** shall arrange for clean, sanitized, well-lit lockable dressing rooms with keys provided to **ARTIST'S** Stage Manager upon request. All rooms shall contain 110-volt/20 amp power with plenty of power outlets or quad boxes, hot and cold running water, toilet facilities. All dressing rooms shall have proper heating/ventilation or **ARTIST** can control air conditioning, temperatures of which. When private toilets are not available in suite, then there should be private toilet facilities adjacent to the dressing rooms. Toilet facilities shall be clean and stocked with all necessary items.   In the event dressing room facilities have no floor covering, carpeting or suitable floor covering must be provided and discussed with **ARTIST'S** Production Manager in advance.

PRODUCTION OFFICE: One (1) Large Room for the sole use of **ARTIST'S** staff. Venue staff and **PURCHASER'S** staff should have alternate and separate facilities. This room is to contain the following: Minimum 20 amps/60hz at 110 volts AC Electrical Service with at least two outlets.

> Two (2) telephone lines with touch-tone telephones able to make and receive calls from load-in until two (2) hours after show, with no call waiting. The telephones should have modular plugs and unrestricted long distance access.
>
> One (1) fax / computer line with direct dial incoming and outgoing features and no call waiting.
>
> Two (2) six to eight foot (6'-8') banquet tables
>
> Chairs as required
>
> Local telephone book (yellow and white pages)

CLIMATE CONTROL: THE TEMPERATURE IN THE PERFORMANCE AREA MUST BE BETWEEN SEVENTY TO SEVENTY TWO DEGREES (70°-72°) FOUR (4) HOURS PRIOR TO THE PERFORMANCE.

VENUE ACCESS: **PURCHASER** shall cause the venue to be available for rehearsal, sound check, and technical set-up for period of at least twelve (12) hours prior to the opening of the venue to the audience. Non-essential persons will be prohibited backstage and in the performance area during rehearsals, sound check and set-up.

DRAPES: **PURCHASER** shall provide drapes to mask the backstage area from the audience. Placement of these drapes will be at the direction of **ARTIST'S** Production Manager. If this is a partial arena date, curtains should extend the entire width of the arena at the partition line, from the floor to a line eight feet (8') higher than the highest seat.

FLOOR COVERING: **PURCHASER** shall provide sufficient rubber matting, carpeting, etc., needed to cover any cable snakes in the audience and backstage areas.

Appendix J (continued)

Notes

[1] The authors wish to thank Andrey Shenin for creating this sample technical rider, and special thanks to David Kissel for providing technical definitions. A technical rider is issued by the promoter on behalf of the artist. The purchaser is the venue.

[2] Electricity, in the United States is generated in three phases, or three lines from the power plant. Each phase is commonly called a leg.

[3] Upstage right.

[4] Alternating current actually shifts direction; the number of times it shifts per second is labeled in hertz.

[5] Upstage left.

[6] A lug is the fastening device found in a power disconnect box for attaching wire to the incoming power. It is sized by the wire size, which is determined by the amperage of the required use. In this rider, they are asking for lugs that will accept 4/0 wire (pronounced 4ought)

APPENDIX K: Portland Center for the Performing Arts Settlement

PORTLAND CENTER FOR THE PERFORMING ARTS
PO Box 2746, Portland, OR 97208

NIGHT OF SETTLEMENT
INVOICE

Attendance		Address		
Drop Count:	2,447		Promoter:	**Concert Promoter**
Paid Count:	2,569		Event:	**ABC Rock Band**
Comps:	78		Contract #:	**5443**
BO Total:	2,647		Facility:	**ASCH**
Capacity:	2,808		Date of Event:	**11/08/05**
Kills:				
Seats Available:	2,808		MERC Invoice #:	**5443**
% BO Total:	94.3%		Date of Invoice:	**11/08/05**
Souvenirs:	tbd			

TRANSACTION	AMOUNT	BALANCE
RECEIPTS:		
PCPA Ticket Sales	4,215.00	
Outlet & Agency Sales	101,975.00	
Promoter Sales	7,245.00	
Total Gross Sales	113,435.00	
Less: User Fee	6,420.85	
GROSS SALES WITHOUT USER'S FEE		$ 107,014.15
RENT:		
Base Rent		
-or % of adjusted gross (whichever is higher)-		
8 % of Adjusted Gross	8,561.13	
Less Advance Deposit		
Total Rent Due		**8,561.13**
ADDITIONAL CHARGES:		
User Fee	6,420.85	
Agency Ticket Commission (TM or TW)		
Box Office Labor Ticketing Charges	169.50	
Box Office Credit Card Ticketing Charges	125.48	
Events Services - Admissions Labor	2,004.45	
Event Services - Additional Labor		
Operations - Extra Charges	1,148.00	
Ops - Stagedoor Security	361.84	
Ops - Stagehand Labor	3,579.28	
Ops - Additional Labor		
I.A.T.S.E. Local 28 Labor	7,593.08	
Piano Tuning (Steve Davis)	-	
Peer Security (Coast to Coast)	1,665.98	
Catering Clean up Fee	-	
Linen Rental		
Security/Medical	102.00	
Insurance (Gales Creek)		
Misc. Charges for Pass Through Expenses		
Utility Charges - Electrical		
Utility Charges - Telephone (Line/Long Distance)	-	
Utility Charges - Internet Access		
Other Misc. Charges		
Total Additional Charges		**23,170.46**
TOTAL PCPA CHARGES		$ 31,731.59
SETTLEMENT:		
Gross Sales With User's Fee	113,435.00	
Less: Promoter Sales	7,245.00	
Less: Wire Transfers to Promoter		
Less: Cash Advances		
Less: PCPA Charges	31,731.59	
DUE LICENSEE		$ 74,458.41

I certify the above to be a true and correct itemization of the receipts and charges for the above event, and understand
it is subject to final review by MERC Accounting Department. Interest will be assessed at one and one-half percent
(1.5%) thirty (30) days from the invoice date. Please remit payment to PCPA, PO Box 2746, Portland, OR 97208

MERC: _____   DATE: _____

Promoter: _____   DATE: _____

APPENDIX L: Westside Theatre Settlement

The Sample Westside Show Co., LLC
c/o The General Manager s Office
xxx West 44th Street, Suite xxx
New York, New York 10036

"SAMPLE SHOW"
SETTLEMENT: WEEK/ENDING 11-13-05

BOX OFFICE GROSS	w/e 11-13-05		**$50,000.00**
Basic License Fee	w/e 11-20-05		(7,000.00)
Percentage License Fee	w/e 11-13-05 (Five Percent of GWBOR)		(2,500.00)
SERVICE:			
Box Office Staff	w/e 11-13-05	($1,175.00)	
House Manager	w/e 11-13-05	(550.00)	
Asst House Manager	w/e 11-13-05	(400.00)	
			(2,125.00)
Payroll Taxes (17%)			(361.25)
Vacation (4%)			(85.00)
Sick Pay (3.125%)			(66.41)
Health ($75.00/person/wk)			(300.00)
Administration			(600.00)
Porter w/e 11-13-05			(375.00)
Ushers w/e 11-13-05 (10 @ $17.50/perf, 6 @ $15.00/perf)			(265.00)
Payroll Taxes for Ushers (17%)			(45.05)

"SAMPLE SHOW"
SETTLEMENT w/e 11-13-05

Electricity		(600.00)
Air Conditioning, w/e 11-13-05		(480.00)
Carting		(75.00)
Sanitary Supplies		(75.00)
Backstage Payphone		(17.00)
Box Office Telephones		(75.00)
Box Office Expenses		(75.00)
AT&T Long Distance Charges		0.00
Money and Securities Insurance		(6.50)
Company Bills		0.00
Admissions Insurance Admissions, w/e 11-13-05 ($.30/per capita)	1397	(419.10)
Advance against post-closing expenses		(200.00)

NET DUE THE SAMPLE WESTSIDE SHOW CO., LLC: $ 34,254.69

DATE _____ CHECK # _____

FOR RENO PRODUCTIONS, INC.

FOR THE SAMPLE WST SHOW CO., LLC

BIBLIOGRAPHY

Baugus, R.V. "Making for Great Theater." *Facility Manager*, February/March 2005. *www.iaam.org/Facility_manager/Pages/2005_Feb_Mar/Feature_1.htm*.

Brown, E. Victor. "The Hills of Ann Arbor." *Stage Directions*, February 2005, 26-31.

Carter, Alice. "The Odd Facts." *Stage Directions*, July 2005, 58–61.

Conner, William. "Burning Issues in Fire Safety Curtain Regulation." *Facility Manager*, July/August 2003. *www.iaam.org/Facility_manager/Pages/2003_Jul_Aug/Perf_Arts.htm*.

DesPlaines, Joe. "A Crisis Response Doesn't End with Evacuation." *Facility Manager*, February/March 2005. *www.iaam.org/Facility_manager/Pages/2005_Feb_Mar/BusinessFinance.htm*.

Edgers, Geoff. "Filling the Seats: With So Many New Stages, It's an Exciting Time for Local Theater. But Can Attendance Keep Pace?" *Boston Globe*, 14 November 2004.

Elder, Eldon. *Will It Make a Theatre?: Find, Renovate, and Finance the Non-Traditional Performance Space.* Washington, D.C.: Americans for the Arts, 1993.

Fingerman, Bob. "Renting Versus Presenting: The Best of Both Worlds." *Facility Manager*, July/August 2003. *www.iaam.org/Facility_manager/Pages/2003_Jul_Aug/Feature_3.htm*.

Forgey, Benjamin. "On D St. NW, a Theater that Wins Applause." *Washington Post*, 14 May 2005.

Freedman, Robert. "Facility Management." Interview by Tobie Stein. E-mails to author, 27 November 2005, 19 April 2006, 20 April 2006, and 28 February 2007.

Gerchak, Keith. "Westport Renaissance." *Stage Directions*, July 2005, 50–53.

Giovannini, Joseph. "Time of the Signs." *New York Magazine*, 26 June 2000–3 July 2000.

Graham, Peter, and Ray Ward. *Public Assembly Facility Management: Principles and Practices.* Coppell, Tex.: International Association of Assembly Managers, 2004.

Grippo, Charles. *Business and Legal Forms for Theater.* New York: Allworth Press, 2004.

Grossberg, Richard. "Facility Management." Interview by Tobie Stein. E-mail to author, 1 September 2006.

Harding James. "Question Regarding Codes for Theaters." E-mails to Tobie Stein and Cristin Kelly, 6 February 2007 and 17 February 2005.

Henly, Lawrence. "Resident Companies: Friend or Foe?" *Facility Manager*, February/March 2005. *www.iaam.org/Facility_manager/Pages/2005_Feb_Mar/University.htm*.

Herbst, Judith. "Of Ticketing, Toilets and Towels." *Facility Manager*, July/August 2003. *www.iaam.org/Facility_manager/Pages/2003_Jul_Aug/Feature_2.htm*.

International Association of Assembly Managers, Inc., *www.iaam.org*.

——. "Facility Manager." *www.iaam.org/Facility_manager/Pages/Facility_Issues.htm*.

Jepson, Barbara. "Where Stagehands Clean Up in More Ways than One: Practice May Get You to Carnegie Hall, But Unions Ensure You'll Pay for It." *Wall Street Journal*, 16 November 2004, Editorial section.

Kotkin, Joel. "Suburban Culture." *Wall Street Journal*, 19 January 2005, Editorial section.

Manhattan Theatre Club. "Biltmore Theatre Organization Chart." New York, 2006. Photocopy.

——. "Biltmore Theatre Incident Report." New York, 2006. Photocopy.

——. "Post Orders." New York, 2006. Photocopy.

McKinley, Jesse. "Bookings Greet 42nd Street Studios." *New York Times*, 14 June 2000.

Mettes, Mark. "Was That a Crashing Sound I Just Heard?" *Facility Manager*, February/March 2005. *www.iaam.org/Facility_manager/Pages/2005_Feb_Mar/Perf_Arts.htm*.

Mulcahy, Lisa. "Rigging the Odds." *Stage Directions*, February 2005, 51–53.

Nance, Kevin. "Secrets Uncovered at Former Shubert." *Chicago Sun-Times*, 8 February 2006.

Peithman, Stephen. "Thinking Outside the Box." *Stage Directions*, July 2005, 46-49.

Pogrebin, Robin. "An Intermission for Renovation Begins at Alice Tully Hall." *New York Times*, 30 April 2007.

——. "Theater Troupe to Get a $38 Million Brooklyn Home." *New York Times*, 4 February 2005.

Portland Center for the Performing Arts. "Building Maintenance Supervisor Job Description," Portland, Oreg., 2002. Photocopy.

——. "Event Critique." Portland, Oreg., 2005. Photocopy.

——. "Operations Manager Job Description." Portland, Oreg., 2002.

——. "Portland Center for the Performing Arts Organizational Chart." Portland, Oreg., 2006. Photocopy.

——. "Portland Center for the Performing Arts Settlement," 8 November 2005. Photocopy.

Rothschild, Phillip. "Incentives for Motivating Event Staff: Perceptions of Effectiveness Among Venue Professionals." *Facility Manager*, February/March 2005. *www.iaam.org/Facility_manager/Pages/2005_Feb_Mar/SalesMarket.htm*.

Ruggieri, Melissa. "Preservation, Renovation Go Hand in Hand Here." *Amusement Business*, September 2004, 21.

Ruth Eckerd Hall. "Director of Operations Job Description." Clearwater, Fla., 2003.

——. "House Management Report." Clearwater, Fla., 2005. Photocopy.

——. "Space Request Form." Clearwater, Fla., 2006. Photocopy.

——. "Theater Usage Policy." Clearwater, Fla., 2006. Photocopy.

Schiffman, Jean. "The Pride of Silicon Valley." *Stage Directions*, July 2005, 40–44.

Scioscia, Leon. "A Hard Day's Journey into Light." *Facility Manager*, May/June 2003. *www.iaam.org/Facility_manager/Pages/2003_May_Jun/Perf_Arts.htm*.

Shenin, Andrey. "Box Office Statement." 2006. Photocopy.

——. "Event Timeline." 2006. Photocopy.

——. "Facility Management." Interview by Tobie Stein. E-mails to author, 12 December 2005 and 27 April 2006.

——. "Sample Technical Rider." 2006. Photocopy.

Simmons, Valerie. "Facility Management." Interview by Tobie Stein. E-mails to author, 7 March 2006 and 22 August 2006.

——. "Proposed Job Description: Theater Manager." Manhattan Theatre Club, Biltmore Theatre, New York, 2005. Photocopy.

Thinnes, Walter. "Facility Management." Interview by Tobie Stein. E-mail to author, 13 September 2006.

Vernaci, Gina. *Organizational Structures and Managerial Positions.* Interview by Tobie Stein. E-mails to author, 1 November 2005, 16 February 2006, and 20 February 2006.

Webb, Duncan M. *Running Theaters: Best Practices for Leaders and Managers.* New York: Allworth Press, 2004.

Webber, Rebecca. "Theater Underground." *Stage Directions,* October 2004, 36–41.

Westside Theatre. "House Manager's Report." New York, 2005. Photocopy.

———. "The Sample Westside Show Company, LLC. Settlement." New York, 2005. Photocopy.

———. "Westside Theatre Policies." New York, February 2007. Photocopy.

Williams, Robyn. "Facility Management." Interview by Tobie Stein. E-mails to author, 21 November 2005 and 20 April 2006.

Wolf, Thomas. "Appendix H: Technical Production Guide." In *Presenting Performances: A Basic Handbook for the Twentieth Century.* Washington, D.C.: Association of Performing Arts Presenters, 2000. Adapted from M.K. Barrell, *Technical Production Handbook* (Denver, Colo.: Western States Arts Federation, 1991).

CHAPTER TWELVE

Career Development Strategies: The Role of the Internship

In this chapter we will explore the role of the internship from two significant points of view: the employer's and the student's. Graduate students in the Brooklyn College performing arts management program were asked to conduct interviews with managers in the performing arts management field about utilizing the internship as a career development strategy, finding the right internship, and structuring a successful internship; these interviews also addressed creating and maintaining the status and value of the internship through ongoing recognition, training, evaluation, and mentorship.

Although the following pages detail the experiences of graduate students and the managers who supervise them, many of the managers we interviewed utilize undergraduate interns as well. Therefore, the authors feel that the information provided will also be valuable for undergraduate students.

THE ROLE OF THE INTERNSHIP

Performing arts managers require and utilize interns on an ongoing basis. Interns are primarily graduate and undergraduate college students interested in gaining valuable hands-on work experience before they enter the workforce and earn a living wage. They are, in essence, "professionals in the making."[1] The finest internships offer students the opportunity to be mentored and supervised by a seasoned manager; expose the students to the behaviors and attitudes of the managers within organizations; teach the students various skill sets that support their classroom education; and allow the students to practice the behaviors and skills learned by performing a specific project with proper guidelines and evaluation. In addition, managers who supply the best internships indicate that students are valued by providing performance feedback on an ongoing basis; including the interns in meetings and special projects; paying a stipend; allowing the students to network and gain visibility with all members of the organization; and giving references for future internships and employment.

Managers of both commercial and nonprofit organizations also see the value in hiring interns to supplement their workforce and productivity levels. Since economic and personnel resources are often limited, many performing arts organizations use interns in positions ordinarily reserved for entry-level and middle-level employees. Performing arts managers also view interns as potential staff members and believe internships "are the key to developing a high-quality workforce."[2] Since internships are often ten to fifteen weeks in duration, performing arts managers have the opportunity to develop relationships with their interns; most managers take this time to train interns, advise them on the correct procedures and processes, and assess whether or not the interns will "fit" into the organization.

JOB PREPARATION: UTILIZING THE INTERNSHIP AS A CAREER DEVELOPMENT STRATEGY

Internships serve as a career development strategy, preparing students for future employment. Jerry,[3] now a leading manager in a performing arts organization, summarizes the benefits of his internship:

The best thing I received from my internship was a broader sense of how theater communities work with each other and how they talk to each other. I learned what it is like to be in an office environment, and how to behave in one. If you are lucky enough to find a mentor within the office, you can learn to emulate how she works and carries herself. You can start to find your voice by mirroring what you see or by learning from others' mistakes. You get the practical side of what you are learning in school. It's one thing to talk and write about how things work, but when you are able to apply these theories, or you see others applying them, they take a tangible shape. You can determine if this is really what you want to do, or if you want to do something else, before you leave school.

Managers and students alike believe that the internship prepares the student for entering the workforce. Students learn the skills needed to find and land a job. Many students see internships as résumé and confidence builders; as ways in which to discover what they like and don't like to do; as a safe and comfortable environment for learning the right and wrong ways to act and behave; and as a place to network with potential employers. Employers view interns as an applicant pool for full-time employees, because they have invested in the recruitment and training of their interns. An internship truly prepares students for entering the workforce if the managers are committed to teaching the students such functional skills as marketing, fundraising, and finance, as well as interpersonal skills that help them navigate their way through the culture of the organization.

To best take advantage of this career development tool, students must be savvy participants in their internships. They must initiate conversations with their supervisors, observe what to do and what not to do in their organizations, and make every interaction with every person affiliated with the organization count.

Learning Tangible Skills

Students are taught to "speak the language of the organization" through practice and observation. For example, in one large performing arts center, "the development intern is taught how to seat people for a special event, how to create mailing lists for a gala, and how to speak to patrons about buying tickets for the gala. The education intern is talking to teachers, setting up workshops, speaking to teaching artists, and sitting in on curriculum meetings." Students are prepared in this particular organization to learn and leave with "at least three skills other than filing, faxing, and copying." Another manager expects that her interns be able to "point back to a project and know what the measurable outcomes are. Tangible work is critical in moving on to the next phase of one's career."

Learning the Unspoken Rules

In addition to learning functional skills, students learn the unspoken rules or "the inside scoop" of the organization through observation. Stan believes that "an internship is very valuable for seeing how an organization actually works. Interns are able to see how different aspects of the organization interact, how different people interact with each other, and how different departments work with each other. Interns are able to step back, see how things work, and then fit in." Another student mentions, "I was able to observe how an organization functions for an entire year. I was privy to information about their successes and failures. I can use that new knowledge, as well as the knowledge from my past work experiences, to enter the workforce with a better understanding of how different organizations operate."

In her internship, Karen learned a lot about "the dynamics of a booking and producing office, as well as different methods and styles of communication, from everyone in the office. Watching my manager run a meeting was a lesson in professionalism and control. Observing and participating in the routing meetings demonstrated when and how to push an idea and when to hold back. Sometimes observing the wrong way was even more instructive than seeing the correct methods."

Emma reveals that "internships have allowed me to explore different work environments and observe various communication styles. In recent years, I have begun to see the difference between the cultures of large and small organizations. I have also found that the more connected I feel to the product an organization produces, the more motivated and productive I am. Another advantage is that I can safely make mistakes on the job. These, of course, aren't deliberate mistakes, but rather mistakes that come from inexperience."

Testing the Waters

The internship allows the student to "test his dreams."[4] The student learns what types of jobs interest her, and what jobs do not. An internship supervisor confesses that "in the long run, the most successful internships were ones that I hated, because I discovered that I didn't want to do marketing, and I don't like asking people for money. The managers steered me away from development and marketing." David views the internship as a method of "sampling many areas within the performing arts." This sampling "gives the student the opportunity to try many new things and choose the areas that interest him most." Celeste agrees that "the whole point of an internship is to 'test the waters.' You have nothing to lose, so go in and try it and make sure that this is the career you want. If it is, you have found your niche and should go for it. If not, at least you are not stuck at some job that you hate for two years. You might even find something that you do like when you didn't think that you would."

Ed believes that internships allow both the student and the employer to see if the "marriage" will work. He states:

An internship is an opportunity for an individual to further clarify what her interests are. Following the internship, the student may decide that perhaps our business, or a portion of our business, is not what drives her. For example, I've observed that a student who is 'born to be a producer' probably won't be happy in an office environment. If that student is not inside the house or in the back of the house, then she won't be happy. An internship in an office will help her discover that fact. On the management side, I would rather take a chance on hiring an intern than making the investment in a full-time employee, who might tell me, "You know what, this really isn't the environment for me," after six months. It is a test drive on both sides.

Networking
In addition to learning new skills, students are able to network with student peers, fellow employees, and outside professionals, such as corporate and foundation donors, board members, press agents, and members of the press.

Student interns learn a great deal from each other. One intern states, "The education intern spoke to me about the different school districts and the problems she faced while interacting with these schools. The programming intern taught me the things she must deal with backstage and about artist hospitality. I also learned about grant writing from the development intern."

Some performing arts organizations organize weekly seminars for the interns so they can meet and network with managers and other employees in the organization. One manager explains, "In our weekly intern seminars, every department manager will come and speak to the interns, and that's how we 'break the ice.' It is my hope that after every seminar, everyone will feel comfortable speaking with each other."

Networking with industry professionals is another vital part of this career development strategy. Students meet professionals with whom they will be able to work down the road. Barbara, an education manager, provides examples in her organization: "The marketing intern can communicate with public relations agents and members of the press. The development intern networks and communicates with board members, government officials, and individual patrons. Programming interns interact on a daily basis with artists, agents, and backstage crew, so all of them are exposed to different people and have opportunities to network."

In many cases these industry contacts lead the student to finding a full-time job. One manager boasted that 30 percent of his staff is former interns. Why are organizations likely to hire their interns? Another manager explains:

We are much more likely to hire somebody who has been an intern for us than not. If a position opens up, the first place we look is our internship pool, especially for entry-level positions. An internship can be almost like an extended job interview. You get a sense of an intern's job skills, and you get a chance to train him within the culture of the organization. So, if the intern is interested, and he would be good in the position, we would be silly not to take advantage of that. A vast majority of people in our office have come from our internship pool. And that's true of just about every department. At some point or another, they all started as interns and became staff.

Another manager states, "I would be more likely to hire someone with internship experience. The students perform the same skills during the internship that they will perform in a full-time job. We hired two of our former interns, our managers of education and development."

Jennifer, a manager with a nonprofit presenting organization, reinforces the notion that organizations are more likely to hire the interns whom they have trained:

We often hire people from our intern positions. It's probably the best way to get a job here, if you are entering the institution as an entry-level worker. I believe that if the intern has been willing to work in an internship, he has proven himself in some way. You know the intern, you've worked with him, and you know he will show up—you know something about that person.

Managers view their interns as "insiders," as people whom they have groomed, who are motivated to work, and who have the qualities of a successful employee.

Taking Initiative

Learning skills, as well as the behaviors and attitudes needed to enter the workforce, depend not only on the manager's ability to teach and provide opportunities for the student, but on the student's own initiative and motivation. Richard attests, "If the intern takes advantage of every opportunity that arises, whether it be working on a project or simply observing, the experience can provide an awareness of the industry that no textbook can. For example, most of the managers I work with are open and willing to talk with me, but I typically begin these conversations." Craig emphasizes, "An ambitious intern can take advantage of networking opportunities. Some of the networking opportunities include staff and professional meetings; social events; and interactions with clients, vendors, artists, and agents." Taking initiative is seen as a professional value in many organizations and is what sets interns apart when being considered for a full-time position.

Prepared for Full-time Employment

At the end of their internships, students are often pleased with the results of their experiences. They feel comfortable working in a professional environment and have the confidence that they have learned the skills necessary to find employment. Donna feels "a lot more comfortable about entering the workforce after working in an office environment, and I will feel even more comfortable after my next internship." Karen boasts, "Following this internship, I feel that I could enter any booking and touring office in the industry and feel comfortable with contracts or booking. Prior to this internship, I was not qualified to hold these types of positions." Sally agrees: "My internship taught me all about contracts and made me realize that I have what it takes to get a job in general management. I don't believe that an organization would hire me as a general management associate without having the experience that I gained during my internship."

CLASSROOM DISCUSSION

When preparing for full-time employment, why is it important to have internship experience?

What will an internship teach you?

What types of tangible skills can you learn?

What are "unspoken rules" in an organization? How do you go about learning them?

Talk about the networking process. Why is it important? With whom should you network, and why?

Why is it important to take initiative in your internship? Role-play in class: Create a situation where a student has to take initiative in an organization.

FINDING THE RIGHT INTERNSHIP

Simply put, one size does not fit all when it comes to internships. Students come to internships with varying degrees of experience. Some students may have had some previous internship or work experience; others are changing careers and are looking to break into another industry; and others may not have any internship experience at all. It's also crucial that managers understand the degree of work experience the intern will need for the job and the extent to which the managers within the organization are willing to spend time teaching the intern "the ropes." Therefore, a successful internship is about managing expectations.

If the student has a great deal of work experience, but the supervisor is unwilling to give the student advanced assignments, both the student and the organization's manager will be unhappy. If the student walks in with little or no work experience and is afraid to ask for guidance, and the organization's staff members have no experience working with this type of student, the experience won't be pleasant for either party. It's imperative for both the student and the performing arts manager to be clear about the type of internship offered. In the following section, students and managers discuss the structuring of a successful internship, paying special attention to the recruitment, interview, and orientation processes.

STRUCTURING THE SUCCESSFUL INTERNSHIP

Managers of performing arts organizations have the chance to express the degree to which they value their interns in their online and printed recruitment materials; their communication with the college intern placement administrators; the interviews and follow-up conducted with the students; and their orientation processes.

The Job Advertisement

To recruit interns, managers create job advertisements that appear in printed media and online. The job advertisement is often an abbreviated version of the detailed job description. In creating the job advertisement language, performing arts managers must keep in mind that students are seeking not only to learn and master a set of skills in order to be competitive in the marketplace, but, in many cases, they are also given college credit for the internship.

The performing arts manager must understand that the audience for an online or printed internship advertisement is twofold: the student and the person directing the internship program. Professors directing internship programs and college intern administrators are looking to place their students in internships that will correspond to their courses of study, as well as give the students the chance to articulate both verbally and in writing the interpersonal skills, analytical skills, and practical competencies they have mastered. The college internship advisors will want to make sure that their students are being observed, coached, and mentored by performing arts managers. (Mentors within an organization guide their protégées and teach them the spoken and unspoken rules of the organization. The student's supervisor, as well as other managers in the organization who don't necessarily supervise the student, can practice mentoring.)

When managers recruit interns, they must convey within the job description that the student will be properly supervised, be given a project that utilizes specific skill sets, be paid a stipend, and be evaluated. When the student and his college advisor are reading the job description, they should feel that the student will be respected as a young professional; the advertisement should communicate that, in addition to being given the mundane tasks of filing, copying, and data entry, the intern will be able to participate in and contribute to the day-to-day operations of a particular department in the organization, as well as have the opportunity to learn and practice the skill sets and behaviors necessary to obtain a job in the field.

The following job descriptions, displayed in figs. 12.1 and 12.2, were written to recruit both undergraduate and graduate students.

Fig. 12.1. Sample Internship Job Description

FINANCIAL MANAGEMENT: Responsible for processing all invoices and bills, artist payments, and artist per diems for the season; inputting data; and managing financial database. Will be responsible for generating updated expense printouts on a regular basis. Intern is the liaison with the accounting department. Works with long-lead planning with staff, including creating event reports, ticket templates, and other materials. Proficient knowledge of Microsoft Access is mandatory. Position requires data entry into the financial management database. Dates of internship: January 30 through September 1.

COMPANY MANAGEMENT/ARTIST SERVICES: Responsible for coordinating all the local transportation needs for the visiting artists; assisting with the coordination of artist and backstage hospitality, including parties, hotel rooming lists, and travel arrangements; coordinating meeting and greeting artists at the airport, and hotel check-ins and check-outs; and producing backstage lists, ID cards, artist guides, and welcome packages. Knowledge of Microsoft Access is preferred. Position requires data entry into company management database. Intern will work with company manager.

REQUIREMENTS
- Excellent communication, organizational, and office skills are a must
- Computer knowledge essential
- Theater, Dance, Music, Arts Administration, or Production majors preferred
- Must be detailed-oriented, capable of working under pressure, and able to work on multiple jobs simultaneously
- Must have initiative, sense of humor, and enthusiasm
- Must be able to work long hours and weekends
- Candidates must be enrolled in school at the time of the internship
- Undergraduate and graduate students are welcome to apply

STIPEND: $250 per week

APPLICATION REQUIREMENTS
Please send résumé, cover letter, and brief statement explaining which position you are applying for and your reasons for applying for this internship.

Fig. 12.2. Sample Internship Job Description[5]

EXECUTIVE DIRECTOR INTERN JOB DESCRIPTION

Spring 20xx

The Executive Director Intern will work with the Executive Director and his assistant, both independently and as part of this small team, on special projects and ongoing management tasks.

Special Projects, in addition to others as assigned, are anticipated to include the following:
- Serving as primary staff contact for board committee for long-range planning process, including providing comparative analysis, meeting coordination, and plan drafting and editing.
- Serving as a coordinator for the creation of a master plan, budget, and contracts for the Theater's two-year relocation of the theaters, shops, offices, and rehearsal spaces.
- Researching, evaluating, and planning earned income initiatives, including national and international touring opportunities.
- Participating in Capital Campaign research and design of donor solicitation strategies.
- Conducting historical research: *American Theatre* Magazine, *Theatre Almanac*.

The ongoing activities of the Executive Director's office will include but not be limited to:
- Coordinating and providing staff support to select Board of Trustee committees, including but not limited to the Nominating Committee and Long-Range Planning Committee.
- Serving as part of the team that monitors Trustee activity, including tracking the involvement of new Trustees and coordinating other special Board functions as necessary.
- Preparing statistical and comparative analysis of national and regional theaters.
- Assisting the Executive Director and Director of Finance and Administration in the annual budgeting process.
- Providing the Executive Director with donor prospect research where necessary.
- Assisting with and writing at least one grant proposal to a corporate or private foundation.
- Conducting general office and administrative support as required.

Position requires the following:
- Excellent writing, organization, communication, and computer literacy skills.
- Ability to work with corporate executives and political and business leaders, as well as staff and artists.
- Ability to manage multiple projects with tight deadlines.

CLASSROOM DISCUSSION

What is your impression concerning the content of these job descriptions?

To what degrees do they clearly state the employer's expectations of the student, both in terms of required skills and the tasks to be performed on the job?

To what degree will the students be supervised, and by whom?

Will the student be exposed to other members of the staff, as well as contacts outside the organization?

What new skills will the student learn?

What type of student should apply for these jobs?

Why do you think the first organization is asking for a written statement? (See Fig. 12.1.)

To what extent do the managers of these organizations value their interns, and how can you determine whether or not the students will be valued?

Creating Impressions During and After the Interview

If the organization is interested in hiring the student as an intern, it will request an interview. When the student interviews with the manager in an organization, impressions are made on both sides of the manager's desk. Managers of organizations are impressed with candidates who present themselves in an appropriate manner. The student doesn't have to wear a suit, but should be dressed in a professional manner. (As part of a professional presentation, students should remember to turn off their cell phones.)

The student must be prepared to talk about the position; he must read the job description (or at least the job advertisement) before coming to the interview. The student should also "know the history of the organization, its mission, and its upcoming season." One manager reinforces this: "One question I always ask is, 'Why us?' I always ask the student if she has taken a look at our Web site. If the student doesn't know the kind of work we do, if she doesn't know our mission, I don't hire that student. There's no point in having someone who doesn't want to be here."

Some managers also indicate that they want relevant experience. For example, retail experience that encompasses both customer service and sales is relevant to the skills required for development professionals. Basic computer skills, as well as writing and verbal skills, are crucial as well. Maggie, a marketing manager, believes that students should bring their résumés with them, as well as letters of recommendation. The résumé should be well written and neat. An example of a résumé one student used while interviewing for an internship is shown on page 512.

Please note that résumés should not be more than one page. The listing for each job held should list two or three bullet-pointed responsibilities or achievements for each position. The student's educational background should also be included.

In addition to having a suitable appearance, knowledge, and relevant experience, managers are looking for the right attitude. For some managers, the right attitude is demonstrating concrete knowledge "about the organization or a function within the organization, such as public relations." For other managers, having the right attitude is about possessing leadership skills, such as the ability to inspire or transform, as this manager notes:

When I am interviewing someone, qualifications (in terms of specific skill sets) are not very important to me, because I can teach anybody what she needs to do. I can teach anybody to use the ticketing software here and how to work with it. I can teach anyone how to use our graphics software and produce an ad. What is important to me is atti-

tude. I very much believe that when you go into an interview, you shouldn't try to "wow" someone with where you went to school. It's important that you inspire, that you connect with someone on a higher ground. I want to have a conversation regarding how the organization can be transformed.

How does a student communicate that she has this ability? This manager explains, "It has to do with how the candidate projects herself. Does she seem confident? Is she comfortable? Would I want this person representing my organization and me? Is she looking me in the eye? Is she answering my questions? Do I feel that this person would be a good fit, knowing that I'd be spending a lot of time around her?"

Having the "right attitude" is also defined as having the "right personality." But what does this mean? For one manager, it means "having the ability to handle a high-stress environment, and not taking things personally. I don't have time to have an intern around [with] whom I have to walk on eggshells. Our office is very small, and it's very stressful, high-paced, and tension-filled. We don't have the space in our office for someone who is going to get on everyone's nerves."

Students must be careful not to convey the wrong attitude or impression during an interview. When asked what impresses a manager least during an interview, this manager admits, "The immediate questioning of the amount of overtime the intern will have to put in, negative remarks about past employers or supervisors, and asking how important his responsibilities will be."

For many students, developing the right attitude or organizational personality comes with experience. However, Robert, a general manager, explains why he hired an intern who had been in the workforce for only one year. "He knew how to dress, knew how to talk on the phone, and knew how to ask questions. He also knew that when he didn't know something, he could come to us. He had no fear about saying, 'Let me just double-check this before I send this out,' or, 'I am really confused—can you explain this again?' He also understood when it was time to be serious, and when it was okay to have fun."

Though the majority of managers hiring interns do not require a significant amount of organizational experience, it is imperative that the student's and the manager's expectations about previous professional experience be discussed prior to hiring the intern. Though job descriptions can be amended to meet the skill level of the student, the organization's

Fig. 12.3. Sample Résumé

NANCY SMITH
30 E. 26th Street, Apt. 23
Brooklyn, NY 11205
444-444-4444
nsmith@aol.com

Experience

July 2003–Present   *Education Department Intern*
Sample Performing Arts Center, New York, NY
- Assist in coordination of participating dance company staff on study guides, school outreach efforts, scheduling, choice of pieces, and program content
- Assist in development and coordination of professional development workshops for NYC public school teachers and administrators

August 2002–May 2003   *Program Associate Intern*
Sample Opera Company, New York, NY
- Designed and facilitated artist-in-residency programs for New York City public schools
- Responsible for proposal and budget creation, artist coordination, and workshop management

May 2001–August 2002   *Assistant Editor*
Sample Publication, New York, NY
- Edited and proofread articles and columns for six outdoor-oriented magazines
- Nurtured relationships with manufacturers to ensure continued corporate cooperation and factual accuracy
- Compiled detailed listings of over 1,400 products for publications
- Wrote monthly "New Products" column describing improved or newly available products of interest to our consumers

May 2000–May 2002   *Development Intern*
Sample Theater, New York, NY
- Independently compiled a working database of relevant foundation materials using the resources available at the Foundation Center Library
- Researched individuals as potential fundraising prospects using Internet, playbills, and other resources
- Developed relationships with staff in all departments to further effectiveness of development team
- Interviewed prospective interns for all departments of the theater

Education
- MFA candidate, Performing Arts Management, Brooklyn College, The City University of New York. Expected graduation: June 2003
- BA, Arts Administration, Theater Concentration, Baruch College, The City University of New York: June 2001

Relevant Skills
- Microsoft Office, Photoshop, strong writer

managers may not have the time or patience to train a student without some prior experience.

However, a student should not accept an internship with no promise of learning new and advanced skills. The manager must give the student the impression that he will gain real work experience that will be useful in finding a job. Celia tries to ascertain, within the interview itself, how much she thinks she will be able to learn in a potential internship. She reveals:

I always go into an interview situation feeling that I am interviewing the prospective employer as much as she is interviewing me. It's important for students to realize that we have the right to ask questions, because internships serve as the foundation for our future careers. During the interview, I try to make note of what type of conversation we are having. Is there mutual dialogue, or is the interviewer just dictating? Is the interviewer asking questions about my interests, or only listing his needs? If the interviewer has an interest in what my expectations are for the internship, I assume that this interest will continue if we work together.

During the interview, I also try to deduce whether my learning will occur in a hands-on fashion, or by observing. I know that I am someone who learns best by doing the task and working for someone who trusts me to try something new. The final criteria I employ to measure an internship's value is the range of experiences I will gather. In my current internship, I was able to branch out and learn from the education, marketing, development, and programming departments. Having a host of experiences makes it easier to focus on where I want my career to go from here.

Keith, a graduate student with prior management experience, enters his internship interview with questions concerning: the type and size of the organization and department; the time commitment; the various projects and tasks; opportunities to learn; opportunities for growth, promotion, and full-time employment; the reporting relationship; and the overall working environment.

Face-to-face interviews with students are an opportunity for the manager to make the student feel that his contribution to the organization will matter. The manager conducting the interview should ask the person responsible for supervising the student to be available to meet and interview the student. The manager should also make arrangements for the student to meet other managers with whom the student will be interacting within the organization. Sarah, a public relations manager, tells potential interns "how the department is structured, how the department interacts with other departments, and that they will learn through trial and error." In addition, the manager and/or the supervisor should go over the job description, making sure the student understands what will be expected of her.

For example, Carrie goes over the job description with the student to make sure the student has a "clear understanding of the roles and responsibilities of the internship." Martha creates job descriptions that "are rather generic. The job description describes the role of the intern, which is basically to support our staff and X, Y, and Z projects. It just states the time commitment and the stipend. Because of this, I tend to be really clear in the interview about the times we need covered. I work really hard to find someone who will stay for that time frame." Michael also believes that going over the job description with the prospective intern during the interview is crucial. "I would hope that during the interview/get-to-know-you process, before the intern is brought on, [. . .] each department head or intern supervisor would discuss current and future projects; explain to the intern what his duties [and] day-to-day experience would be; and ask the intern what his interests are in order to try to incorporate the intern into potential projects."

Another manager states, "The job descriptions are discussed during the interview process to make sure that the student is interested in the job. The descriptions are refined as the internship continues and as needs arise; the internships are really tailored to the intern's interests." Barbara discusses the intern's role and responsibilities with the intern during the interview process so that "there are no false expectations set up. You don't want the intern thinking that he will come in and run the office. So we tell the interns their duties; some of it is grunt work, and some of it will be more interesting."

After the interview, the manager should let the student know when a decision regarding the hiring of the intern will be made. The manager should call the student when the decision is made. E-mail should never be substituted for a personal call; a personal call from the manager or the supervisor indicates that the student's presence in the organization is appreciated and crucial. If the student doesn't receive the internship, the organization's management should let the student know the reason for that decision. The explanation will help the student recognize whether he could have done something differently, the degree to which the process was competitive, and whether the student should consider reapplying in the future. Again, this type of communication on the part of the employer shows the student the degree to which interns are valued.

If the student receives the internship, the manager should make sure that the student understands the internship schedule (e.g., the time and date to report for the first day of work, the weekly time schedule), the dress code, the name and location of the internship supervisor, and any other pertinent information the student will need to know before arriving on his first scheduled day of work.

CLASSROOM DISCUSSION

In choosing an internship, what are the things that matter most to you?

When preparing for your interview, what should you know about the organization?

How will you answer the question, "Why us?"

What types of questions should you ask the interviewer?

What does "having the right attitude" mean to you?

What are the relevant skills that you can bring to the internship?

Create a résumé with a job objective.

Orientation: Setting the Tone for Good Communication

On the first day of work, the student's supervisor should be there to greet the student, show the student where she will be sitting, where her computer and phone will be, where the employees have lunch and break for coffee, where the restrooms are located, etc. Additionally, the student should be introduced to the staff and given a staff directory of phone numbers and e-mail addresses. In addition to providing an orientation of the physical building, the orientation should include a detailed discussion concerning the responsibilities of the position, the ways in which the intern will be trained, and methods for communicating expectations. Managers should assure the student that she will be part of an environment where she feels comfortable learning and asking questions. Finally, managers should explain the process by which the student will be evaluated and the ways in which she will receive feedback on her performance.

Cindy, a development manager, feels that orientation should take place on the same day for all of her interns. "We have a manual that we hand out that gives them the history of the organization and a description of who's who. Our managing director welcomes the interns, gives them a tour, and introduces members of the organization. We show the interns where the files are located and encourage them to explore and read our files. We view our interns as employees, so everything is open to them." Another manager encourages the students to read the files and everything else available to them, including the "Web site, scripts of current, past, and future seasons, donor proposals and packets, donor databases, and press files."

Nancy, the managing director of a dance company, agrees:

> During orientation, our interns receive the same information as full-time employees: rules and regulations of the company, information about issues relating to confidentiality, and policies and procedures related to their work. Once they have gone through the process of learning how to use the phone, we take them around and introduce them as our interns. Prior to the interns' arrival, we reach out to our management offices to find out what their needs will be, and we try to match the interns with the management offices in a mutually beneficial way.

When interns enter this large performing arts organization for the first time, they are given a structured orientation:

> When interns arrive, they get their own desks, computers with their own personal drives, and e-mail addresses for professional reasons. They learn the computer system and our phone system. We teach them how we want them to answer the phone. We give them a tour of the building, and they meet many of the eighty people who work here.

Some organizations have formal human resources departments that orient students in the proper use of e-mail and phone calls to avoid their overuse and abuse. Others instruct the students on proper attire, as well as the appropriate way to speak to a journalist or a donor.

Jason, who works for a small theater, also has a structured orientation process for his interns:

We begin by introducing the intern around the office. During the first day, we ask the intern to look through a number of background materials: brochures, board lists, lists of major gifts from the previous year, and so forth. Then I give the intern his first project, one that he probably despises me for—filing. It's not so much the process of filing that I'm trying to teach, but the need to familiarize oneself with the correspondence and how our relationship with each funder has evolved.

Students recognize the importance of structured orientation processes, and the degree to which these processes can make a difference in establishing a comfort level. Karen's experience was a positive one: "I was taken through the office and introduced to everyone who was available. There are several department offices on the floor, so I was told where the different departments are located. I was also told which department each employee worked in and with whom I should speak regarding certain matters."

Some organizations utilize their own interns to orient new interns because "it has been my experience that interns learn best from other interns. The older interns not only help the new interns learn their jobs, but the new interns also get the inside track on personalities within the organization."

Not every student is given a formal orientation. Susan reveals, "I was not told anyone's title, much less primary duties. Luckily, it was a small office, so I was able to learn my way around relatively quickly." Cathy had a similar experience: "I was not given a personal orientation. I was not given an organization chart, and I was not made aware of the job titles and departments of the organization. Anything I learned, I discovered on my own. I had ample opportunities to explore the files, but I wasn't particularly encouraged to interact with others, and my physical location made it difficult to casually interact with others." In the absence of a formal orientation, students are forced to "sink or swim."

Job Responsibilities

In addition to orienting the student to her surroundings, the supervisor should sit with the intern and discuss her job responsibilities and the projects she will be assigned, as well as her day-to-day tasks. Linda was "given clear direction as to what my specific tasks and responsibilities would be. I would be assisting the director with tour management for several artists on our roster. I would be helping to coordinate travel, local hospitality, schedule, and residency activities." Fred "was given an in-depth explanation of each task, including its background, method of completion, and several alternate options should one method be unsuccessful." He was then "left to perform the task on my own, and as a result was able to devise the way I felt best accomplished the task."

Sam, an employer, "actually spends the first week having the intern work side by side with [him], going through the everyday functions of the department and preparing the intern for things that aren't everyday functions, e.g., how a 'show week' is different from a week in the office." He states, "I always try to make sure that the intern has a 'side-by-side experience,' whether it's a performance or a meeting for grant money." Martha agrees with this method of training. "My intern doesn't do anything by herself for the first three weeks or so. We work hand in hand on every single thing. But after that, the training wheels are taken off."

Again, not every student has a formal job description or is given clear direction. In the absence of clear direction, a student must be determined to make the most out of the experience. David discusses how he was able to create a good experience from a challenging situation:

Upon my arrival, my direct supervisor was no longer with the organization. The managing director introduced me to the staff and told me their roles and responsibilities. Overall, the orientation was informative, but finding someone who could properly explain my exact responsibilities was difficult. The person who would have been my supervisor tried to make herself available on the phone, but was never available for on-site training. Even though I understood the idea of my position, my day-to-day tasks were never explained, putting me in a rather stressful situation. In essence, I was teaching myself more than I believe an intern should, since this is a work/education experience. My position became one with much more responsibility than I anticipated, but ultimately, I felt the experience enhanced my desire to explore and learn. Even though there was no one to guide me in the traditional way, making the beginning process a slow and demanding one, I realized that there was a great deal of opportunity at the organization to grow professionally. In time, the managing director and I developed a task list and discussed how to prioritize all the tasks to be done and what approach I should take to [complete] them.

It's evident from this example that the managing director eventually took responsibility for making sure that David had what he needed to do his job. Supervisors need to give their interns a clear understanding of what the tasks are and how to accomplish them.

Communicating Expectations

Within the orientation, supervisors should also review the methods and processes for communicating that day-to-day goals have been achieved. Some supervisors prefer that their interns communicate by e-mail; others prefer face-to-face meetings scheduled daily or on a weekly basis. The supervisor should express her expectations to the student concerning the preferred method of communication and what needs to be communicated.

For example, Meg is expected to send her supervisor a "state of the intern" e-mail every morning, listing her daily tasks and asking if any additions, omissions, or priority changes to be made.

Keith knows that his supervisor will observe his work during a performance, workshop, community outreach effort, or verbal proposal, and will then speak to him in a one-on-one meeting about his performance and areas that need improvement. During a collaborative process, such as a marketing project or a development proposal, Keith is evaluated in writing by members of the organization; he is expected to incorporate the advice and continue to work until the project is complete.

During the one- to two-week training period, one manager tells his intern that she will meet with her supervisor on a daily basis. During the meeting, the intern will get "a to-do list, talk about what was accomplished in previous days, and talk about an anticipated to-do list for the upcoming days." The intern "will give me her opinions, ideas, and suggestions, and then I will critique her work. Interns really need to know that they are accountable for the work that they are doing, and that they are not just here to sit and fill a requirement. They are essential employees of the organization. I want to make sure that they know they can talk to me if they aren't being challenged, or if I am giving them too much."

Amy sets a weekly meeting with her intern so that the intern knows that "we're going to talk about the project, his progress, and what needs improvement. I think that this meeting opens the door for asking questions. It's important to establish a schedule for talking openly."

Learning the proper channels for communication is of great consequence. For example, one supervisor insists, "We can't be testing things publicly. There is an understanding from the beginning that everything in this office goes through me." However, another supervisor believes that interns "shouldn't have to go through me for everything. Instead of coming to me, I tell them whom to contact and give them the go-ahead to interact."

Some managers offer a more laid-back approach and actually place the burden to communicate on the intern. One manager says, "I usually try to check in every couple of weeks to see how things are going. I ask the interns to keep me in the loop in terms of what they are doing and how they are feeling. It's the intern's job to tell us how we are doing. If the intern is unhappy, he needs to step up and say, 'I want to be exposed to this. I'm not happy with this responsibility.' Interact with us." Another manager reinforces this message: "At the end of the day, the internship is the student's responsibility. It is not the absolute responsibility of the supervisor to ensure that the intern is having a rewarding experience. Ultimately, that is on the intern's plate, and that is a difficult thing for some interns to grasp."

The lesson here is that students must assume, or at least share, responsibility for communicating expectations with their supervisors. One student reinforces this attitude: "I had to realize that I shouldn't settle because I'm an intern. I am also a staff member, and I have the authority to ask to be challenged as a staff member. I need to confront my superiors and ask for what I want."

Learning in a Comfortable Environment

Since interns are not only new members of the organization, but often newcomers to the workforce in general, it's essential for the supervisor to create a comfortable environment where the student feels she can ask the questions needed to fulfill her assignments and to build her skill sets. "Not all students know how to ask the best questions or frame their questions properly," according to Carol, the facility manager of a performing arts center. Carol tries to "teach the students how to get to the answers they need by approaching the right people, and by not being afraid to approach the right people."

To facilitate learning, Sam has his interns "study the list of people who call on a weekly basis, so that they understand who these people are, what [companies] they are from, and what they need." He feels it's necessary to understand who is calling and not just take a message. On the other side, former intern Kate recognized that since she had no experience writing grant proposals and gathering marketing materials, she needed to be coached by her supervisors. "They supported me through each step of the process. They were open to my ideas and approaches to these projects and allowed me to bring my own style to the work. Their presence provided a comfort until I was able to work on my own, and they never pressured me or made me feel intimidated to ask any questions whatsoever. The managing director accompanied me to off-site meetings and never hesitated to assist me by explaining things I did not understand."

In some cases, the student needs to learn the "appropriate times to discuss her responsibilities. There were certain times where I knew it was inappropriate to interrupt my supervisor because she was working on an important task." Managers need to instruct students in knowing when to push an idea and when to hold back. Ken recommends that interns "need to pull back, sit back, observe, learn, and then think about how they can participate." Andy briefs his intern on "who we will be meeting, and also how much talking should or shouldn't be done." He coaches her "in getting her point across without necessarily badgering anyone." Michael is able to teach his intern these things by taking her to meetings, where she can observe his interactions and learn how he deals with people.

Not all students feel comfortable speaking to their supervisors about the learning process. Supervisors observe this lack of comfort when "mistakes are made that could have been easily avoided by asking a question." Neal says, "If I feel like they are uncomfortable approaching me, I will watch them more often, spend more time with them, and help them work through their problems. People are often afraid to ask questions that they think will make them look stupid, and they have to be taught to get past that." Steve believes that if the intern is having trouble, it is the supervisor's responsibility to monitor and control the situation. He states, "The interns aren't being evaluated on the problems that occur. It's about their ability to do the job, and the understanding that there will be obstacles that will be out of the intern's control. That's when I need to become involved."

Mary contends that the source of feeling uncomfortable often comes from the "intern feeling like he doesn't have enough to do." She says, "I try to check in and inspire the interns to come to me with these types of concerns. It's a challenge to make sure that our department heads are monitoring each intern's experience. I need to make sure that both the department and the intern are getting what they need out of the experience."

Despite the fact that managers try to deal with communication problems that arise, some students still feel uncomfortable approaching their supervisors. Ted remarks, "I think my supervisor and I have two different styles and personalities, and in the three months I was there, we never really clicked. I'd say that about 75 percent of the dialogues we had were initiated by me; the only time my supervisor initiated dialogue was to give me new assignments. From my first days in the organization, I always got the impression I was interrupting when I asked for help. This certainly put a strain on our relationship."

Evaluation

In addition, the supervisor should let the student know during the orientation that he will be critiquing the student's work on an as-needed basis, so that the student understands where she stands on a given assignment—whether she has succeeded or needs to improve. Evaluation of the intern is a necessary part of the internship, and the student must understand early on in the internship that she will be evaluated both on her execution of day-to-day activities and on her overall performance. Max, a marketing manager, discusses his need to evaluate the intern's performance on a regular basis during the interview: "An intern who isn't going to be comfortable with constructive criticism won't be comfortable here. There are so many fine points in this business and to this job, and there are so many things that change on a week-to-week basis, that no one could ever know everything. I'm going to evaluate the intern's performance when I need to, because it helps me get my job done."

CLASSROOM DISCUSSION

Do some role-playing: It's the first day of your internship. You arrive on time, and you are very excited about starting and learning a whole new set of skills. You sit in the reception area and wait for your supervisor to arrive. She is late. Finally, after twenty minutes, she arrives. She tells you that she was "in a meeting." She brings you into the main office and shows you where you will be sitting. The desk is cluttered with paper. There is no computer or phone for you to use, even though you know that you will need them to do your job. She leaves you there and disappears into her office. How do you respond?

What are the principal components of an orientation process?

What is "side-by-side" training, and why is it important to be trained this way?

Why is it necessary for your supervisor to tell you the best way to communicate your needs and expectations, or to "check in"?

How do you communicate with your supervisor: e-mail, face-to-face, or both? What are the pros and cons of each method of communication?

In your organization, what are the proper channels for getting something approved?

How do you know when it's the best time to interrupt your boss? How do you figure that out?

Do you feel that your organization has provided a comfortable learning environment? Why or why not?

During your orientation, what did your supervisor tell you about the evaluation process?

CREATING INTERNSHIP STATUS AND VALUE

In order for the internship to be considered successful, both the manager and the student must feel that all members of the organization recognize the importance of the intern. If the organizational leadership considers the intern as an essential position, all members of the organization will value or acknowledge the intern as a necessary part of the organization. Students know right away when the organization holds them in high esteem and the degree to which they will be valued within the organization. When students feel like part of a team; are recognized for their participation and accomplishments; learn new skills; are properly evaluated; and are mentored by their supervisors and other members of the organization, they are obviously going to feel respected and appreciated. However, when students are ignored, treated poorly, and not made to feel part of the organization, both the organization and the students lose valuable time and opportunities.

In the following section, both students and employers talk about establishing value through recognition.

Interns are Part of the Team

Martha interns for an organization that "places significant value on its interns." She states, "Multiple departments have one or more undergraduate or graduate students as interns. They are paid a stipend of $150 per week, [are] given meaty tasks according to their professional levels, and are respected and appreciated. I personally felt valued and appreciated at my internship because both my supervisors made a point to include me in their everyday work, and when doing so, they treated me as a professional subordinate, not a lowly intern.

"There was one specific moment when my boss asked that I run and get coffee for the artistic director. This situation was much more comical than insulting because when I returned, everyone apologized profusely and said, 'He needed coffee right that second, and you were the only one free to do it!' I laughed and replied, 'It doesn't bother me.'"

Not surprisingly, supervisors of performing arts organizations recognize that interns serve a central purpose in supplementing regular staff. Since many nonprofit organizations are facing government funding cutbacks, "assistant-level employees have been let go." One manager admits, "The interns are not only doing special project work; they are doing the work we need to get done every day."

Another internship supervisor states that the "interns are included in everything. In this office, we don't separate them from the activity. We don't have a staff meeting or an office meeting without them. Interns are folded into everything we do. Sometimes they get more opportunities than our staff. The interns, for example, get invited to opening-night parties. We really think of them as staff members that are called interns."

Andrew has an internship with an organization that never refers him as an intern. "At no point was I ever referred to as 'the intern.' In fact, my supervisor, who is also the owner of the company, was so appalled that my first e-mail was assigned as 'reception' (instead of as my name) that he contacted our office manager to make sure that I was issued an e-mail address with my name."

Bonnie had a similar experience at her internship. She says that she often "feels like less of an intern and more of a staff member." She is proud to say that she "just got her business card printed the other day." Rebecca concurs and reveals, "I am given meaningful projects, am invited to staff meetings, and was given a personal box so that I can receive mail. In addition, I was given a first-day orientation that made me feel like an employee."

Sam spent a semester interning for a small commercial theatrical company that later hired him full-time. He states that "interns at my company were treated like equals; we were seen as an essential part of the team and involved in all office activities. Everyone shared in the mundane filing and copying tasks; these tasks, often given to an intern, were kept to a minimum. I felt that my time and intelligence were valued, as my supervisor allowed me to take on the more important tasks in the organization. I know that this isn't always the case in other internships." Sam's supervisor stated that "interns are an integral part of our marketing team, and a valuable asset to the overall operation of the company. Since we have a relatively small staff, we rely on the interns to support our team and to provide access to other performing arts companies that may later serve as our clients. Being part of this process is very important to us."

Recognition and Acknowledgement

Acknowledgement of the interns can take many forms, such as: invitations to participate in special lunches and seminars; asking students' opinions in meetings and one-on-one lunches; free tickets to performances; and, especially, paying a small stipend.

Special Lunches and Seminars

Many of the organizations surveyed for this chapter have special seminars and lunches for their interns that allow the interns to network with each other and the organization's employees, as well as provide a comfortable learning environment in which to ask questions. In one organization, the director of development shares her program: "This year, we asked one of our nationally recognized artists to have lunch with our interns. We also have a lunch program where the director of each department in our company gives an overview of her job: what she does, how she operates, and how the intern fits into that department."

Another organization provides an internal education initiative for all staff members, which the interns are encouraged to attend. The program's "first class is about business writing. Representatives from grants, publicity, and publications departments conduct a one- [to] two-hour workshop. It's a way to engage staff members to use internal resources. We also plan on giving a tutorial on our database system and a research workshop." This manager hosts "weekly seminars and get-togethers. If nothing is planned for the week, I host a breakfast, so everyone can get together and talk. I also do a year-end wrap-up meeting. I organize outings and give the interns tickets to performances. It gives the students a chance to bond and work together as a group." Many organizations include their interns in staff meetings, dress rehearsals, opening nights, and play readings. One organization has softball and bowling leagues, where interns can mingle with staff after work.

Inviting Participation

Some organizations demonstrate their commitment to their interns by asking them to play a substantial role in the organization. One intern explains:

I was involved in every aspect of the department and was given the opportunity to play a large part in the organization as a whole, because I was making decisions for a department that brings in 10 percent of our budget. My opinion was asked on anything that pertained to education, and I made presentations to the organization every two weeks at the staff meeting. The presentation would be an overview of everything going on in my department. I was also asked to speak at board meetings.

Marla says her intern is also treated like a staff member and is expected to contribute in the following manner:

My intern serves to manage my program and is expected to run the department on a day-to-day basis. She facilitates the marketing strategy that we both put together. She handles all of the data in terms of anything that we might need for development. She advances all of the dates with the artists, and deals with all of the production, while I oversee her. She helps me negotiate the contracts. She really has her hands in everything. If there's a week that I have to be out of the office, she will run the office.

The Importance of Paying a Stipend

It goes without saying that managers of organizations must make every effort to pay their interns a weekly stipend. One manager explains: "We pay a weekly stipend. Getting some type of monetary compensation is important. I've worked in offices where we didn't pay our interns anything, and I think that receiving a stipend makes them feel like a more valued part of the organization."

Another manager remembers what it was like to be an intern and feels that students really need the money:

When I was an internship manager, the organization I worked for cut the stipend, so it was less than it was when I was an intern. This was shocking to me, and it really upset me, because it was a small item in the budget; the organization acted like it was a cost-saving measure. I feel like I never could have taken an internship unless I was paid. I had no parents supporting me. I don't want someone of lesser means to not be able to take my internship. It's important that interns be able to support themselves.

This student agrees:

Unfortunately, there is always the factor of money. There are several internships that I would like to do, but cannot because they do not offer any compensation. Financial stability was a large factor in determining my fall semester internship. Without the added support of a stipend, I would not be able to live and study in New York.

Finally, this student discusses her justification for being paid a stipend:

I think it's very important to earn a stipend. In many cases, students have given up full-time jobs to go back to school and take internships. We need to take out loans to pay for school, as well as to pay our bills and live. The stipend allows us to at least pay for transportation to and from the internship, as well as some meals. Interns do a great deal of work and are assets to the organizations for which they work. I believe that we should be compensated for our time, work, and professionalism.

"We Don't Get to Sit at the Big Kids' Table"

In each of the cases presented above, the organization's senior management has established value and status for its interns by creating a work environment where interns are a vital part of the day-to-day operations. While feeling like a crucial part of the team may occur for some interns, others complain that they aren't part of the team, and

essentially aren't being recognized for their efforts. (In fact, internship supervisors readily admit that interns are not always given proper credit.) Some of the primary indicators of student dissatisfaction are expressed below.

Lack of Respect and Money

Exclusion from everyday life in an organization, being treated differently from full-fledged staff members, and lack of monetary compensation discourage students. Ben remarks, "When the executive director meets with my supervisor, I am never included in the meetings. When managers of other theaters visit our offices, I am never introduced to these people, and I am never invited to sit in on these meetings." While students understand that "some of the work we are assigned to do is mindless, it doesn't give us hope or satisfaction when full-time staff members joke about the work interns are given."

Some students are made to feel that the title "intern" is as demeaning as the type of work assigned. For example, at one organization's orientation, the executive director told Joe and the other interns that they should not ever refer to themselves as interns, but as assistants or associates, because these titles are professional. However, when Joe and his supervisor attended a meeting together, his supervisor introduced him as her intern. Joe felt that he was not being introduced as a professional.

Another student has mixed feelings about the way in which interns are treated. She says, "In my organization, interns were used primarily as slave labor. They ran errands, made copies, sent faxes, prepared mailings, got coffee, etc. Within my department, on the other hand, I felt truly valued because I was given responsibility. They also provided me with a higher stipend than they paid the other interns. While this made me feel as though they valued my time and energy, it also told me that they did not value the others."

Another student voices a different complaint: "The downfall of interning at my organization is that the interns don't receive a stipend. Interns play an important role within the organization, and I feel that the organization should show its appreciation by offering more than travel money to cover getting to and from the organization." Lack of monetary compensation is certainly an issue. Many students take on low-paying internships in lieu of a higher-paying job. Robert admits, "The disadvantages of being an intern who is treated like a staff member involve money. If I feel as though I have too much on my plate, and I'm getting stressed out, I think about the fact that I am essentially paying for this stress. I think about how much I would be getting paid if I were doing the same job in the real world."

Respect Comes from the Top

Professionals admit that performing arts organizations need to improve the degree to which interns are valued. One manager confesses, "Our organization doesn't place enough emphasis on how important interns are. I've heard that the interns don't feel as valued as they should, which is something that starts with the top of the organization." Another manager recognizes that there is an undercurrent of frustration among interns:

"There is the knowledge [among staff members] that the interns don't get a living wage, they don't get benefits, there isn't comp time, and there aren't really sick days. So, I think there is not resentment, but a sort of underlying discomfort and unhappiness about that."

CLASSROOM DISCUSSION

What are the various ways organizations can
    recognize the accomplishments of the interns?
Why is it vital for interns to receive recognition?
Do you think all organizations should pay their
    interns a stipend? Why or why not?

Ongoing Training and Evaluation

During the course of the internship, the supervisor should provide the intern with ongoing recognition, training, and evaluation. Assessing the degree to which a student is learning is a necessary part of the internship experience. Students should also be evaluated on the degree to which they have successfully completed the tasks assigned. In addition, they should be able to assess the degree to which they are learning a given set of tasks, as well as evaluating the quality of the tasks assigned. When the internship is considered to be an extraordinary experience, the student feels that he is learning new skills, is recognized for learning these skills and achieving his goals, and is evaluated fairly based on mutually agreed-upon expectations between him and his supervisor.

In the best-case scenario, the expectations are met on both sides. Terry learned a whole new set of skills, and her supervisor took the time to assess her progress by asking her a series of questions. Here is what Terry had to say about this process:

The general manager exposed me to specific events that I would not have been able to participate in otherwise. These events included a negotiation meeting with Actors' Equity to renegotiate the standard contract, as well as an arbitration settlement between the organization and the stagehands. She also invited me to review past contracts, budgets, co-production settlements, joint-venture agreements, and so forth. She would then meet with me to discuss my understanding of these documents, allowing me to ask extensive questions.

Betty is a development professional who also takes the time to train her interns. She says, "I tend to give my interns more analytical projects, especially if they are graduate students. Basically, everything in development is an algebra problem. For example, I ask my interns: If this is our goal for the year, what are the price breakdowns we would need to achieve this goal, and how many tickets do we need to sell at these different price points?"

Sometimes, students feel that they aren't communicating well with their supervisors. One manager we interviewed admits, "We forget, not being teachers, that we should actually be training the interns. We really don't have anything set up officially where we can give the interns feedback. We tend to throw them in and see if they [will] sink or swim." When students find this type of attitude to be prevalent or the norm in the organization, it's crucial for them to ask their professor or college intern administrator for guidance. Timing and diplomacy are critical elements in improving the relationship between the student intern and the supervisor. Professors who direct internship programs, as well as college intern administrators, can help navigate the situations with the students, helping them improve their communication with their supervisors.

While the manager has the ability and the responsibility to support the development and training of the intern, the intern can also help with his own training, with suitable guidance from his supervisor, organizational mentor, career counselor, college advisor, or a combination thereof.

Correct guidance from a supervisor, or the person responsible for making sure that the student understands her job responsibilities, is necessary to ensure that the student learns the expectations of her role at the organization. In the absence of clear direction, the student will have three choices:

Make an assumption and do what she thinks her supervisor wants; do nothing; or ask the supervisor for clarification and for a demonstration of what is required. Sometimes the student may feel uncomfortable asking the supervisor for guidance, especially when the student is new to an organization and is not yet acquainted with the correct protocol. In this case, the supervisor should be sensitive to this particular situation and ask the student if she understands what the task is and how to perform it. The supervisor should also make it clear that the student is free to openly ask questions of the supervisor or anyone else in the organization.

If the supervisor doesn't make it clear that the student is permitted to ask for guidance under any circumstances, it may be necessary for the student to arrange a meeting with the supervisor to discuss an alternate method of communication. For example, perhaps the supervisor hasn't explained his expectations regarding the process of calling a donor to see if that donor will be attending the upcoming fundraiser. In the absence of clear direction, the student feels she can't complete this assignment. The supervisor assumes that the student has made the call and asks the student to report on the conversation. The student, however, never made the call because she didn't know where to find information on the donor, detailing the donor's relationship with the organization. The student understands from her class on fundraising that before a donor is called, it's essential to access the donor file and study the donor's history of support for the organization. The student was never shown where the donor files are or told what information these files contain, what the relationship is between her supervisor and the donor, or what other information might be relevant to this task. As the supervisor didn't communicate this particular information to the student, the student decided not to complete the assignment.

When the student asks for a meeting with the supervisor, she must be prepared to discuss her rationale for not completing her task, as well as to suggest ways in which she can better serve her supervisor in the future. The student should never blame the supervisor for not giving her proper guidance, but rather should ask her supervisor to explain his process for completing the task. Within this face-to-face meeting between the student and the supervisor, the supervisor will learn that it may be necessary to do a better job of teaching the student the proper way to approach a donor; the student will learn both the processes of approaching a donor and the need to speak to her supervisor when she doesn't understand what his expectations are.

Evaluation Methods

We have discussed the importance of giving students immediate and ongoing feedback on performance. This verbal evaluation method should be combined with written self-evaluation questionnaires and essays, conducted by the student, as well as a formal in-person exit interview, where both the student and the organization's management can have a better understanding of what went well and what needs to be improved.

Questions directed to students and employers should explore the extent to which students have the ability to relate their classroom theories to their work experience, and have been given projects that build skill sets, as well as the degree to which students have been properly trained, evaluated, and recognized for their contributions. Additional questions for the student and employer should solicit information about the student's confidence in his career path and his qualifications for finding a job, as well as his capacity for interacting with fellow employees in the workplace. Additionally, when a student is evaluated by the organization, he is often graded based on subjective criteria, including his attitude, motivation, and value to the organization. Jerry confesses that he evaluates an intern based on "how much of a go-getter he is, whether he takes initiative, how well he takes criticism and accepts that a mistake has been made, and how willing he is to adapt and make changes once new information is given." Gary evaluates his intern "based not on [. . .] how well she did something, but on how hard she tried, and how engaged she was with the project." He says, "If I give an intern a project and she really has no idea what to do, but she spends a couple of hours trying, and I can really tell that she has hit the wall, my evaluation will be positive."

Self-Evaluation and Exit Interviews

Figure 12.4 shows an example of an evaluation form that Brooklyn College uses, both as a self-evaluation form for students and as an exit interview tool for supervisors.[6] Professors and administrators directing internship programs may use this form to discuss the student's performance with the supervisor, as well as with the student.

Fig. 12.4. Internship Evaluation Form

BROOKLYN COLLEGE MFA PERFORMING ARTS MANAGEMENT PROGRAM
INTERNSHIP EVALUATION FORM

STUDENT'S NAME _____   YEAR _____
INTERNSHIP ORGANIZATION _____   SEMESTER _____
IMMEDIATE SUPERVISOR _____   Final Grade _____
SUPERVISOR'S TITLE _____
SUPERVISOR'S PHONE # _____

Please complete the following form and return it by May 1.
Approximate number of weeks you will have spent as an intern at this organization by the end
of the semester _____

Approximate total number of hours you will have spent as an intern this semester _____

Average number of days per week you spend on the job _____

How do you grade the quality of your assignments? A B C D F

How do you grade the quality of your work supervision? A B C D F

How do you grade the quality of your job satisfaction? A B C D F

How do you grade the internship as an overall learning experience? A B C D F

Please write a two-page essay discussing your responsibilities, skills you acquired, and how you
implemented them on the job; also discuss the most important things you learned and evaluate the
strengths and weaknesses of the organization in terms of training, evaluation, and recognition.

May Professor Stein share the above information with your internship supervisor? Yes _____ No _____

Professor Stein will complete the following in consultation with your supervisor.
Promptness and loyalty to agreed-upon work schedule A B C D F
Basic office skills (i.e., computers, writing, phones) A B C D F
Basic attitude toward work A B C D F
Ability to work with fellow workers and outsiders A B C D F
Degree of self-motivation A B C D F
Ability to follow instructions A B C D F
Overall value to the organization A B C D F

CLASSROOM DISCUSSION

To what degree do you receive ongoing training
and feedback in your internship? If you do,
how does your supervisor continue to teach
you new things?

How does your supervisor let you know you need
to improve? Give an example.

What is the purpose of a self-evaluation, and how
will it help you and the organization?

Are you asked to do a self-evaluation? What kinds
of questions are you asked to answer?

Have you ever had an exit interview? What kind
of questions were you asked? How will this
feedback help you and the organization?

The Role of the Mentor

Some of the most rewarding internships are developed because one or more individuals in the

organization "go that extra mile" in making sure that the student is treated with respect and receives the proper training and guidance to flourish within the organization and beyond. A mentor can play this crucial role. In the final section of this chapter, both students and supervisors describe their definitions of this special role.

They Understand, Listen, and Are Perceptive

Since many managers in the performing arts management field began as interns, paid their dues, and worked their way up the career ladder, they understand "what it's like to come into an office, work twenty hours a week, go to school four nights a week, have homework at night, and still have to figure out how you're going to pay rent, feed, and clothe yourself."

Greg believes that a mentor can do two really crucial things: listen and be perceptive. "If the intern has a concern, I will make the time to listen. You have to also be perceptive, because *listening comes from asking the question*. You have to know that it's important when someone looks tired or sad. It's important to understand why someone is half an hour late when he is never late. Interns go through a lot of stuff when they aren't here, and sometimes they just need to go home for a few hours. You have to be perceptive and look at the person, not just the worker." Another supervisor agrees: "Being a mentor does not only mean teaching them everything they need to know about their jobs. It's about asking them: How are you doing? How's your family? What is going on in your life? Is something too difficult for you to handle?"

Teacher and Friend

"A mentor is a cross between teacher and friend. I do think that the intern has to feel comfortable with her mentor. The intern has to feel like she can lean on the mentor professionally. The best situation is for an intern to feel she has full reign over what she is doing, but that a strong guiding hand is there when she needs it. She has to feel that she can go to her mentor, and it's really the mentor's responsibility to instill that feeling." Amy recognizes that her mentor does "make it clear that she is welcome to contact him, and put his name down as a reference for another internship or job."

A mentor takes the time to explain not just what to do, but how to do it and why it should be done. A manager explains, "When you initiate the internship, you need to make sure the intern understands why she is here, what she is doing, where the company is headed, and what her role is. Also, she needs to know why she is doing the projects she is doing. We shouldn't just be assigning projects, but explaining what their larger purposes are. For example, if the intern is preparing for a meeting, she should know why the meeting is taking place."

Mentors want to "make sure that they are allowing their interns to learn and are not just giving them basic assignments." One mentor confides, "I will give her a job to accomplish and explain how to do it, and she will go off and do it on her own. Then I will come back to evaluate it. She is able to do her own work and then come to me, and I advise her and see if we are on the same path, going in the same direction."

Career Advice

Mentors have plenty of stories to tell about their own careers that can provide insight into their career paths. An intern should not be afraid to approach his supervisor or anyone else in the organization for this type of valuable insight. Since an internship is perceived by the industry as an "essential stepping stone to career success,"[7] it behooves the intern to be resourceful and proactive in making sure that she "interviews" the managers in her organization who inspire her. She should make a formal appointment, bring a list of questions, listen, thank the person, and ask for advice about her next internship or job interview. The list of questions should include an inquiry into the manager's background and expertise, and also should include a request for introductions to other members of the organization as well as to his contacts in the field.

Here is a sample list of questions that may be asked in an informational interview with a development professional:

- Tell me about your background. What positions did you hold before coming to this organization?
- You obviously recognize the value of internships. Please tell me the ways in which a student can make the most of her internship.
- What is the best approach for establishing a relationship with a mentor in an organization?
- What specifically drew you to fundraising? Why does fundraising interest you?
- What's your operating budget? How much do you raise? What percentage is raised from foundation and government sources?
- What is your relationship with your marketing department? How do you work together?

- Tell me about your relationship with your managing and artistic directors. How do they support what you do?
- How does the board support your fundraising efforts?
- Who else in the organization, as well in other organizations, would you recommend I speak with, and would you be willing to provide me an introduction to your colleagues?

CLASSROOM DISCUSSION

What distinguishes a mentor from a regular supervisor?

Why is it necessary to have a mentor?

If you don't have a mentor, how should you go about finding one?

What types of questions should you ask the mentor about her career path?

Develop a list of questions, interview a manager you respect in your organization, and discuss your findings in class with your professor and classmates.

NOTES

1. Roseanne White Geisel. "Interns on the Payroll," *HR Magazine* (December 2004), 89.
2. Ibid.
3. All names of individuals in this chapter have been changed.
4. Adele Scheele. "Internships as Direction Finders; Book Excerpt from *Jumpstart Your Career in College*," *Washingtonpost.com*, April 6, 2004.
5. The authors thank Arena Stage, Washington, D.C., for the use of the Executive Director Internship Job Description.
6. The authors thank the Brooklyn College MFA Program in Performing Arts Management for the use of this form.
7. Jennifer Lee, "Crucial Unpaid Internships Increasingly Separate the Haves from the Have-Nots," *New York Times*, August 10, 2004.

BIBLIOGRAPHY

Arena Stage. "Arena Stage Internship Job Description." Washington, D.C., 2005.

ARTSEARCH, *www.tcg.org/artsearch*.

Backstage. "Internships: More than Just an Unpaid Job." *Backstage.com* (4 September 2003).

Brim, Orville G., Jr. and Stanton Wheeler. *Socialization After Childhood*. New York: John Wiley and Sons, 1966.

Brooklyn College. "Internship Evaluation Form, 2007." Brooklyn College, Brooklyn, N.Y., 2007. Photocopy.

Cook, Sherry J., R. Stephen Parker, and Charles E. Pettijohn. "The Perceptions of Interns: A Longitudinal Case Study." *Journal of Education for Business*. 79 (January/February 2004): 179–85.

Geisel, Roseanne White. "Interns on the Payroll." *HR Magazine*, December 2004.

Goffman, Erving. *The Presentation of Self in Everyday Life*. New York: Doubleday, 1959.

Institute for the Management of Creative Enterprises. "Searchable Databases of Arts Resources." Carnegie Mellon University's Institute for the Management of Creative Enterprises. *www.artsnet.org/databases/ artsresources*.

Lee, Jennifer. "Crucial Unpaid Internships Increasingly Separate the Haves from the Have-Nots." *New York Times*, 10 August 2004, late edition.

Lewis, Diane E. "Internships are Key Resume Booster." *Boston Globe*, 13 April 2003, 3rd ed.

Lincoln Center Festival. "Lincoln Center Festival 2006 Internship Opportunities." New York, 2005.

Oldman, Mark. "Student Internships Are Key to Careers, CNNfn: Interview with Mark Oldman." By Ken Dolan and Daria Dolan. *Dolans Unscripted* (22 April 2004): Transcript #042203cb133.

Oldman, Mark and Samer Hamadeh, eds. *The Internship Bible*. New York: Princeton Review Publishing, 2004.

Performing Arts Managers [anonymous]. Interviews by Brooklyn College MFA Performing Arts Management students. Tape recordings, 1 February 2005–31 May 2005. Brooklyn College, Brooklyn, N.Y.

Performing Arts Managers [anonymous]. Interviews by Brooklyn College MFA Performing Arts Management students. Tape recordings, 1 September 2005–25 December 2005. Brooklyn College, Brooklyn, N.Y.

Rosow, Irving. *Socialization to Old Age*. Los Angeles: University of California Press, 1974.

Rothman, Michelle. "Firms Offer Interns 'Foot in the Door,'" *Washington Times*, 26 April 2004, final edition.

Scheele, Adele. "Internships as Direction Finders; Book Excerpt from *Jumpstart Your Career in College*," *Washingtonpost.com* (6 April 2004).

Slayter, Mary Ellen. "For a Working Transition from College, Try an Internship." *Washington Post*, final edition, 21 November 2004.

Stein, Tobie S. *Workforce Transitions from the Profit to the Nonprofit Sector*. New York: Kluwer Academic/Plenum Publishers, 2002.

Vault, Inc., *www.vault.com*.

Volz, Jim. *The Backstage Guide to Working in Regional Theater*. New York: Back Stage Books, 2007.

INDEX

acceptance (contract), 365

accountability. *See also* internal controls; Sarbanes-Oxley Act
  definition of, 151
  financial management, importance of, 151

accountant, commercial organization, role of, 43, 117. *See also* certified public accountant

accounting. *See also* accrual accounting; cash-based accounting
  basic equation for, 133
  cycle of, 135
  double-entry bookkeeping process of, 135
  FASB nonprofit organization standards for, 135–136
  Gemwood Dance Company, basic equation examples for, 133–135

accrual accounting, 135

acknowledgment letter
  corporate contributions department, example of, 201
  corporate contributions department, necessity of, 200
  direct mail appeal, example of, 185
  government funding, considerations for, 212
  Minnesota Opera's annual fundraising campaign and, 238

Actor's Equity Association (AEA), 104
  collective bargaining agreements, contracts of, 370
  contract types of, 370–371
  employment and, 371–372
  governance of, 369
  membership/benefits of, 369–370
  touring productions and, 399–401

ADA. *See* Americans with Disabilities Act

advance. *See* wrap and advance report

advertising
  budget creation, revenue estimation from, 139
  "call to action" of, 305
  example of, 333
  for internships, 508–509
  print, 305–306
  publicity compared to, 311
  radio/television/outdoor/web, 306
  rate of return for, 307

AEA. *See* Actor's Equity Association

affinity marketing, 308

AFL-CIO. *See* American Federation of Labor and Congress of Industrial Organizations

AFM. *See* American Federation of Musicians

AFTRA. *See* American Federation of Television and Radio Artists

AGMA. *See* American Guild of Music Artists

AGVA. *See* American Guild of Variety Artists

Alley Theatre, strategic planning of, 70–76
  artistic initiatives, 70
  audience initiatives, 71
  education program expansion, 71, 73–76
  infrastructure initiatives, 72

American Federation of Labor and Congress of Industrial Organizations (AFL-CIO), 369

American Federation of Musicians (AFM), 104
  Broadway production contracts and, 373
  collective bargaining agreements for, 372–373
  mission statement of, 372
  operations manager, contract negotiations with, 429–430

American Federation of Television and Radio Artists (AFTRA), 369

American Guild of Music Artists (AGMA), 369
  collective bargaining agreements of, 374
  governance of, 373

American Guild of Variety Artists (AGVA), 369

Americans with Disabilities Act (ADA), 445

amortized expenses, 140

anchor production, 412

ancillary income, 425
  definition of, 441
  operations manager and, 442–443

annual fundraising campaign
  capital campaign challenges during, 213
  Minnesota Opera acknowledgment letter for, 238
  purpose of, 167–168

annual operating budget
  definition of, 137
  example of, 162–163
  expense budget added to, 311
  nonprofit organizations' process for creating, 143

annuity plans. *See* defined contribution plan

annuity trusts, 192

APAP. *See* Association of Performing Arts Presenters

appending, 293

articles of incorporation, 84

artistic director
  dance companies, responsibilities of, 26
  marketing director working with, 280–281
  opera companies, role of, 26–27
  theater companies, role of, 26

artistic leadership. *see* leadership

arts integrated instruction
  of Kennedy Center, 348–349
  purpose of, 348

Arts Midwest, 406

Books from Allworth Press

Allworth Press is an imprint of Allworth Communications, Inc. Selected titles are listed below.

Running Theaters: Best Practices for Leaders and Managers
by Duncan M. Webb (6 × 9, 254 pages, paperback, $19.95)

Booking Performance Tours: Marketing and Acquiring Live Arts and Entertainment
by Tony Micocci (6 × 9, 304 pages, paperback, $24.95)

Great Producers: Visionaries of the American Theater
By Iris Dorbian (6 × 9, 224 pages, paperback, $24.95)

Building the Successful Theater Company
by Lisa Mulcahy (6 × 9, 240 pages, paperback, $19.95)

Branding for Nonprofits: Developing Identity with Integrity
by D.K. Holland (6 × 9, 208 pages, paperback, $19.95)

Booking and Tour Management for the Performing Arts, Third Edition
by Rena Shagan (6 × 9, 288 pages, paperback, $19.95)

The Art of Digital Branding
by Ian Cocoran (6¼ × 9¼, 272 pages, paperback, $24.95)

Careers in Technical Theater
by Mike Lawler (6 × 9, 256 pages, paperback, $19.95)

Technical Theater for Nontechnical People, Third Edition
by Drew Campbell (6 × 9, 288 pages, paperback, 40 b&w illustrations, $19.95)

The Perfect Stage Crew: The Complete Technical Guide for High School, College, and Community Theater
by John Kaluta (6 × 9, 256 pages, paperback, 45 b&w illustrations, $19.95)

Business and Legal Forms for Theater
by Charles Grippo (8½ × 11, 192 pages, paperback, CD-ROM, $29.95)

The Stage Producer's Business and Legal Guide
by Charles Grippo (6 × 9, 256 pages, paperback, $19.95)

The Business of Theatrical Design
by James L. Moody (6 × 9, 288 pages, paperback, $19.95)